# ENVIRONMENTAL PHILOSOPHY

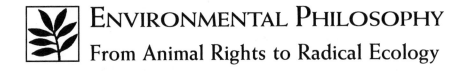

# Environmental Philosophy
## From Animal Rights to Radical Ecology

## THIRD EDITION

General Editor

**Michael E. Zimmerman**
*Tulane University*

Associate Editors

**J. Baird Callicott**
*University of North Texas*

**George Sessions**
*Sierra College*

**Karen J. Warren**
*Macalester College*

**John Clark**
*Loyola University, New Orleans*

Prentice Hall

Upper Saddle River, New Jersey 07458

*Library of Congress Cataloging-in-Publication Data*

Environmental philosophy : from animal rights to radical ecology / general editor
Michael E. Zimmerman ; associate editors J. Baird Callicott . . . [et al.].—3rd ed.
    p.  cm.
  Includes bibliographical references.
  ISBN 0-13-028913-2
  1. Human ecology—Philosophy.  2. Environmental ethics.  I. Zimmerman, Michael E.,
(date)–  II. Callicott, J. Baird

GF21.E56    2001
179′.1—dc21

                                        00-063713

Acquisition Editor: Ross Miller
Editorial Assistant: Carla Worner
Production Editor: Jean Lapidus
Prepress and Manufacturing Buyer: Sherry Lewis
Copy Editor: Stephen C. Hopkins
Cover Design: Joseph Sengotta
Cover Art: Jacqueline Bishop, "Imaginary Nest," 1995.
Oil on panel. Reprinted by permission of the artist.

This book was set in 10/12 New Baskerville by Publications Development Company of Texas
and was printed and bound by RR Donnelley & Sons Company.
The cover was printed by Phoenix Color Corporation.

© 2001, 1998, and 1993 by Prentice-Hall, Inc.
A Division of Pearson Education
Upper Saddle River, New Jersey 07458

Printed in the United States of America
10  9  8  7  6  5  4  3  2  1

ISBN 0-13-028913-2

PRENTICE-HALL INTERNATIONAL (UK) LIMITED, *London*
PRENTICE-HALL OF AUSTRALIA PTY. LIMITED, *Sydney*
PRENTICE-HALL CANADA INC., *Toronto*
PRENTICE-HALL HISPANOAMERICANA, S.A., *Mexico*
PRENTICE-HALL OF INDIA PRIVATE LIMITED, *New Delhi*
PRENTICE-HALL OF JAPAN, INC., *Tokyo*
PEARSON EDUCATION ASIA PTE. LTD., *Singapore*
EDITORA PRENTICE-HALL DO BRASIL, LTDA., *Rio de Janeiro*

# Contents

# Preface to the Third Edition

The editors of *Environmental Philosophy* are very pleased that this anthology has proven so successful that Prentice Hall encouraged us to bring out a Third Edition. When first published in 1993, this collection was unique in providing coverage of deep ecology, ecofeminism, and social ecology, as well as animal rights and environmental ethics. The value of including such a broad spectrum of positions in environmental philosophy in one anthology has been confirmed in part by the fact that competing anthologies now include such coverage. The environmental problems facing humankind in the twenty-first century are too complex either to be understood or to be resolved solely in terms of environmental ethics, despite the important contribution that ethical analysis can play in dealing with them. Deep ecology and ecofeminism, in particular, emphasize that environmental problems often arise in connection with cultural attitudes and social practices, some of which are so imbedded that they are virtually invisible to most people. By adding the section on political ecology in the Second Edition, and by improving it in the Third Edition, we seek to demonstrate that political institutions and economic practices not only generate environmental problems, but also help solve them. Specific improvements to the Third Edition are described at the end of the General Introduction.

In all the domains just mentioned—social, cultural, political, and economic—philosophy can and should play an important role. One of the important contributions that philosophers can make, as Socrates showed long ago, is to criticize and thus show the limits of their own cultures. Social theorists, cultural leaders, politicians, and economists play the role of philosopher when they contrast how things *are* with how things *ought* to be. They, and all of us, need to learn the art of careful reflection if we are to fulfill our role as philosopher–citizens in this crucial period of earth history. The editors, all of whom were trained as professional philosophers, hope that the Third Edition of this anthology will provide students of environmental philosophy with the conceptual and critical tools needed to help improve environmental conditions during the decades ahead.

Many thanks to my associate editors for their continuing efforts to improve our anthology. On behalf of my associates and myself, I would also like to thank Ross Miller, Jean Lapidus, and their colleagues at Prentice Hall for their assistance in bringing out the Third Edition of *Environmental Philosophy.*

**Michael E. Zimmerman**
New Orleans, Louisiana

# GENERAL INTRODUCTION

*Michael E. Zimmerman*

Michael E. Zimmerman is professor of philosophy at Tulane University. For seven years, he was co-director of Tulane's environmental studies program. Author of two books on the work of Martin Heidegger, and many academic articles, he has also published *Contesting Earth's Future: Radical Ecology and Postmodernity.* Zimmerman is on the executive committee of the International Association for Environmental Philosophy.

Thirty years ago, most Anglo-American philosophers were studying epistemology, linguistic usage, and meta-ethics, while Americans studying continental philosophy were focused on phenomenology and existentialism. Postwar American philosophers, unlike the public-minded philosophers of the pre–World War II era, usually did not conduct research or teach about major cultural, social, or political issues. In the 1960s and 1970s, however, the countercultural revolution—including the antiwar movement, the civil rights movement, the women's movement, the animal rights movement, and the environmental movement—introduced a host of issues that were so compelling and politically polarizing that they could not be ignored by philosophers, who were teaching on the same campuses where many of these movements arose. A new generation of American philosophers, influenced by one or another of these movements, began seeking ways to introduce consideration of them into classrooms and professional journals.

Philosophers concerned about environmental issues raised basic questions about humanity's relationship with nature. Are humans the only inherently valuable beings in the known universe, or does the natural world—plants, animals, bioregions—have its own worth, independent of the use to which it can be put by human beings? Do humans have moral obligations only to other humans, or do we also have moral obligations to animals, to plants, and even to whole ecosystems? To what extent do ecological problems arise from anthropocentrism and from humanity-nature dualism? Do humans have any obligations to future generations? Is it morally wrong to exterminate a species

1

of plant or animal? When we are told that industrial technology furthers man's progress, what is meant by "man"? Is it merely an illusion that wealthy groups seem to gain the most from technological innovation, often at the expense of poor or dispossessed people? To what extent do technological innovations free people, and to what extent do those innovations generate serious social and ecological problems? Is human freedom compatible with the disappearance of everything wild and free in nature? How do we know that history has any direction at all, much less a "progressive" one? If there is a progressive trend in history, on what basis do we assume that it requires in almost every instance that humans dominate nonhumans?

Some of these questions had already been raised by previous American theologians, philosophers, and naturalists, including Jonathan Edwards, Ralph Waldo Emerson, Henry David Thoreau, John Muir, John Burroughs, and Aldo Leopold. Their celebration of the beauty of the natural world and their concern about its fate at the hands of a rapidly expanding and industrious American population, however, were heeded only irregularly, especially when the North American continent seemed too vast ever to be overrun or substantially harmed by human settlements and activity. Although it has been a century since Frederick Jackson Turner proclaimed the end of the American frontier era, the better part of the twentieth century saw Americans "developing" the continent with reckless abandon. During the Great Depression, World War II, and the postwar industrial boom, a number of Americans counseled their fellow citizens to conserve natural resources and to respect the land, but the time was not yet ripe for a dramatic reevaluation of accepted attitudes toward the nonhuman realm.

Many commentators point to Rachel Carson's best-selling book *Silent Spring* (1962) as the catalyst for the environmental movement, which took the nation by storm within a decade after the book's publication. Maintaining that widespread use of the pesticide DDT had killed millions of America's beloved songbirds by weakening their eggs (hence, the "silent spring"), Carson urged her fellow citizens to examine critically their taken-for-granted attitudes toward living nature. Her cautionary tale not only demonstrated that birds were dying from misguided human practices but also implied that people might be next. Today, public opinion polls clearly demonstrate that the great majority of Americans take seriously the possibility that a combination of industrialization, on the one hand, and the growing human population, on the other, could lead to problems so serious that they might undermine the future well-being of humankind. Moreover, a great many Americans believe that the natural world is valuable in and of itself, not simply because of its utility for humans.

To understand how dramatic are the changes that have taken place in public and academic attitudes toward environmental issues, the reader need only contemplate the fact that a college anthology like this one—now in its third edition—would have been completely unthinkable a little over a generation ago. At that time, few philosophers, no matter what their conceptual orientation and intellectual interests, would have regarded the idea of environmental philosophy as anything other than absurd. Although some philosophers may still look askance at this idea, its success can be measured by the substantial number of college-level courses now offered in environmental ethics and environmental philosophy. Moreover, numerous academic departments offer courses and concentrations in environmentally related topics, and interdisciplinary environmental studies programs are a common feature of American colleges and universities.

Environmental philosophy is often regarded as identical to environmental ethics, that is, as an effort to examine critically the notion that nature has inherent worth and to inquire into the possibility that humans have moral duties to animals, plants, and ecosystems. As the questions posed earlier indicate, however, the scope of environmental philosophy reaches beyond ethical issues and includes diverse metaphysical, epistemological, cultural, and political issues as well. In the mid-1980s, I had become frustrated by the lack of anthologies dealing with the particular issues that I wanted to address in my own course, Humanity's Place in Nature, which I first offered at Tulane University in 1981. It was not until 1990, however, that I decided to devise an anthology that would be suitable for advanced undergraduates and graduate students and that would provide coverage of areas that were, in my view, particularly important for understanding environmental philosophy. To provide the best possible coverage of areas in which I had an interest but had not necessarily mastered, I decided to assemble a team of experts, each of whom would edit his or her own section of the anthology. Four deservedly well-known environmental philosophers—J. Baird Callicott (environmental ethics as such), George Sessions (deep ecology), Karen J. Warren (ecofeminism), and John Clark (political ecology)—graciously agreed to my proposal to compose the anthology now before you. Because these philosophers have provided excellent introductions to their own sections, I will not duplicate their efforts here. I would, however, like to offer the following general observations, the aim of which is both to provide a brief overview of my own understanding of the current state of affairs in environmental philosophy and to explain the reason for the changes that have been made in this third edition.

In the first edition, I maintained that environmental philosophy may be roughly divided into three major fields. The first field, environmental ethics, asserts that progress could be made in ending the ecological crisis by challenging anthropocentric ethical norms and extending moral considerability to nonhuman beings. Like other experts confronted with a new problem that they have not been trained to solve, some ethicists seek to use their own available tools—that is, modern moral theories—to address the environmental crisis. Many environmental ethicists envision the following possibility: Just as today one is morally and legally obligated to refrain from abusing or killing humans, so tomorrow one may be morally and legally obligated to refrain from abusing or killing many kinds of living beings—except, of course, for nontrivial reasons. Unfortunately, however, because moral theory focuses primarily on individuals, because human individuals differ in important respects from nonhuman beings, and because many ecologists are more concerned with species and ecosystems than with individual plants and animals, moral extensionism has run into some difficulties.

Some environmental ethicists are sharply critical of Western anthropocentrism and humanity–nature dualism, but others adhere to a less radical position, sometimes known as "weak" anthropocentrism. According to this position, humans are intrinsically more valuable than nonhumans, but at least *some* nonhuman beings have a worth of their own and thus ought not to be treated merely as means for human ends. A weak anthropocentrist would justify protecting wild habitats from development or defending an endangered species, not simply because doing so might benefit some group of humans, but also because the habitat and species are somehow good in themselves, or inherently valuable. Just what this "good" might be and just what groups of entities (animals? plants? ecosystems?) are deserving of moral considerability have been the subjects of extensive debate among environmental ethicists.

The second field of environmental philosophy, radical ecology, often associated with the countercultural movement, includes deep ecology, ecofeminism, and social ecology, among others. Radical ecophilosophers consider themselves radical for at least two reasons. First, they claim that their analyses disclose the conceptual, attitudinal, social, political, and cultural origins of the ecological crisis. Second, they argue that only a revolution or a cultural paradigm shift can save the planet from ecological devastation. Although acknowledging that reforming current practices (e.g., requiring tighter controls on industrial pollution or encouraging recycling) may help matters in the short run, radical ecologists generally believe that such reforms will be insufficient in the long run because they address only the symptoms, not the roots, of the ecological crisis.

Despite agreeing in many respects about the limitations of environmental reformism, radical ecophilosophers have different views about what constitutes the roots of the ecological crisis. A number of deep ecologists think that one of its roots is anthropocentrism: the view that humans alone are the origin and measure of all value. Presumably, such a view breeds an arrogance that leads people to treat nonhuman beings as nothing but raw material for satisfying human needs and desires. Many ecofeminists think that the major root of the ecological crisis is patriarchy: an oppressive social structure that justifies the exploitation of women and nature because it regards both as somehow inferior to men. In some cases, ecofeminists maintain that oppressive hierarchies in general are responsible for exploitative behavior, whether such behavior is directed at women, lower-class people, animals, or ecosystems. Similarly, many social ecologists assert that the principal root of the ecological crisis is the social hierarchy. Authoritarian social structures allow some people to dominate others and also to waste, despoil, and needlessly harm nonhuman beings. One reason that I decided to develop this anthology was that no anthology available in the 1980s provided decent coverage of radical ecology, although I myself regarded it as very important.

The third field in environmental philosophy, anthropocentric reformism, argues that the root of our environmental problems is not anthropocentric and patriarchal attitudes, not the institutions and practices that embody them, and not the moral obtuseness that prevents people from discerning the moral considerability or inherent value of nonhuman beings. Rather, air and water pollution, the wasteful use of natural resources, and other environmentally harmful practices stem from ignorance, greed, illegal behavior, and shortsightedness. Such imprudent and morally blameworthy practices may be curbed by enacting legislation, changing public policy, increasing education, altering tax laws, returning public lands to private ownership, emphasizing moral obligations to future generations, promoting wise stewardship of nature, and otherwise encouraging more prudent use of natural resources. According to anthropocentric reformers, though nature has value only as an instrument for human ends, those ends are complex and numerous, ranging from the food provided by plants and animals to the aesthetic pleasure evoked by a wild landscape. Anthropocentric reformers, then, see no need either for revolutionary cultural and political changes or for alterations in human-centered moral theory.

When contemplating the possible fields to be covered in the first edition of this anthology and when taking into account the amount of space available, I concluded that the first two fields—environmental ethics and radical ecology—deserved extensive coverage but that the third—anthropocentric reformism—could be omitted because it was already sufficiently well known and understood. Moreover, I concluded that by limiting radical ecology to deep ecology, ecofeminism, and social ecology, I would have provided sufficient coverage of this topic. In choosing editors who would focus on these three branches of radical ecology, I had hoped to encourage constructive conversations among deep ecologists, ecofeminists, and social ecologists because some representatives from each of these branches were engaging in what I regarded as fruitless and often intemperate debates.

Responses from readers and reviewers encouraged me to reevaluate these two conclusions about the content of the first edition of this anthology. For the second edition, some readers wanted coverage of anthropocentric reformism, for example, free-market and government regulatory (liberal) approaches to environmental problems. Warning that young people feel despair not only in the face of the grim future envisioned by some radical ecologists but also in the face of the unlikely prospects of the revolutionary changes purportedly needed to avert such a future, reformists maintain that significant improvements to current and future environmental conditions can take place if, for example, appropriate market mechanisms are brought into play. Other readers pointed out that there are kinds of radical ecology—including ecosocialism and bioregionalism—that received no coverage in the first edition.

Still others complained that the first edition had defined "social ecology" too narrowly. The second edition accommodated such concerns when John Clark changed the "Social Ecology" section to "Political Ecology" and completely altered its contents.

For the *third* edition, we again listened to our readers and reviewers. In the "Environmental Ethics" section, J. Baird Callicott has reintroduced an excellent essay that appeared in the first edition as a bridge between the individualist and holistic approaches to environmental ethics: "Animal Liberation, Environmental Ethics: Bad Marriage, Quick Divorce," by Mark Sagoff. Callicott concludes his section with a related essay of his own, "Animal Rights and Environmental Ethics: Back Together Again." In addition, Callicott has included an important essay on a concern sometimes raised in regard to holistic environmental ethics: ecofascism, which may be defined as the (sometimes forcible) subordination of individual human interests to collective interests, which include those of a nonhuman nature.

In addition to completely rewriting her introduction to the "Ecofeminism" section, Karen J. Warren has added two new essays by authors particularly concerned about women and the environment in countries in the so-called developing world. Vandana Shiva, an internationally known ecofeminist and environmental activist, has contributed an insightful essay on how environmental degradation particularly affects women and children. Deane Curtin's essay, "Recognizing Women's Environmental Expertise," argues that a form of systemic violence follows from the fact that women's environmental expertise is ignored, especially in the developing world.

For the "Political Ecology" section, John Clark has provided a new introduction, as well as a new essay, "The Matter of Freedom: Ecofeminist Lessons in Social Ecology." This essay helps to connect up themes in Professor Warren's section with important aspects of social and political ecology. Furthermore, Clark has included a new essay by Charles Bliese, "Traditionalist Conservatism and Environmental Ethics." Finally, in addition to including a revised version of Jim O'Connor's essay, "Socialism and Ecology," Clark has reintroduced "What Is Social Ecology?", an important essay that Murray Bookchin composed specifically for the first edition of this anthology.

I would like to offer deep appreciation to my associate editors, who have worked hard to continue improving this anthology, the aim of which is to inform students about various approaches to environmental philosophy, so that those students may help to improve the conditions needed for life to continue flourishing on the blue-green planet.

# PART 1
# Environmental Ethics

# INTRODUCTION

*J. Baird Callicott*

J. Baird Callicott is professor of philosophy and religion studies at the University of North Texas. He is the author of *In Defense of the Land Ethic: Essays in Environmental Philosophy, Beyond the Land Ethic: More Essays in Environmental Philosophy,* and *Earth's Insights: A Multicultual Survey of Ecological Ethics from the Mediterranean Basin to the Australian Outback,* and more than a hundred book chapters, journal articles, and book reviews in environmental philosophy.

In 1973, with the publication of three seminal papers, environmental ethics made its formal debut on the staid and conservative stage of professional philosophy. That spring, the young Australian philosopher Peter Singer published "Animal Liberation" in *The New York Review of Books.* That summer, "The Shallow and the Deep, Long Range Ecology Movement: A Summary" by the distinguished Norwegian philosopher and mountaineer Arne Naess appeared in the international philosophy journal *Inquiry.* That fall, another young Australian philosopher, Richard Sylvan (then Routley), addressed his colleagues at the Fifteenth World Congress of Philosophy in Varna, Bulgaria, with a question: "Is There a Need for a New, an Environmental, Ethic?"

Over the next several years, a few more papers in this novel and exciting area of research appeared in such professional journals as *Ethics* and the *Journal of Philosophy.* Then, in 1979, Eugene C. Hargrove established a new quarterly, *Environmental Ethics,* and the floodgates opened. Articles in environmental ethics poured forth. College courses began to be offered in the subject. By the middle of the next decade a number of book-length discussions had appeared. Thus a whole new field of philosophy has come into being.

The three seminal papers of 1973 stand at the fountainhead not of one but of three increasingly divergent streams of thought. Deep ecology, flowing from the paper by Naess, has now solidified into an eight-point "platform," which has been adopted by members of the radical green movement, including its covert operatives, the "ecowarriors" of Earth First! Moreover, deep ecology has become a "practice" aimed at directly *experiencing* connectedness with

7

nature. Deep ecology seems, accordingly, vaguely antiintellectual and overtly hostile to the impersonal (as the deep ecologists think of it) "ethical reduction" of what they believe should be a more intimate relationship to the natural world than that typical of morality. The ethical theory of animal liberation and animal rights has become the philosophical wing of an even more visible and increasingly militant movement. The goals of that movement, however, have been not only different from but also often in conflict with the goals of the environmental movement. And as moral philosophies, animal liberation/rights and environmental ethics are now recognized as separate fields of study, each with its own agenda.

Accordingly, in this anthology, deep ecology has its own section, while this first part is divided into two distinct groups of essays: individualistic approaches and holistic approaches. Since the conflict between animal liberation/rights and environmental ethics has been more profound or at least longer standing than the internecine disputes among ecofeminism, deep ecology, and social ecology, one might suppose that essays in animal welfare ethics might be excluded from this anthology. But there are good reasons for including some of those essays here.

Historically, animal liberation/rights and environmental ethics were conflated. Even today, although the schism between the two occurred in the early 1980s, most philosophers, let alone laypeople, regard them as being pretty much the same thing. Because we are large vertebrates ourselves, thoughts of other large vertebrates understandably come to mind when we consider the natural environment. Wild animals *are* a significant part of the natural environment, but domestic animals—who get the lion's share of attention from animal welfare ethicists—are not. And the natural environment comprises much, much more than just our furry friends.

Practically, animal liberation/rights and environmental ethics often overlap and, as just noted, often conflict. For example, domestic cattle and sheep, feral rabbits, goats, pigs, and the like often threaten to destroy delicate ecosystems and to extinguish endangered plant species. The ethics of most environmentalists would require preserving ecosystems and certainly plant species at all costs, even if that should mean assassinating the commonplace herbivorous mammals, while the ethics of animal liberationists and animal rights activists would favor the mammals, even if that should mean further ecological degradation and the erosion of biodiversity.

Methodologically, however, animal liberation/rights and environmental ethicists are united by a resolute commitment to the methods of traditional Western philosophy. Both spin their theories out of the strands of thought found in the history of European and Euro-American thought. Both develop moral philosophies that ground ethical theories, which in turn imply practical precepts. Both believe in the power of reason to persuade and to engender consensus. And both believe in the power of ideas to direct individual action, to change social values, and to forge new cultural ideals.

Theoretically, and most important for our purposes here, animal liberation/rights broke new ground in moral philosophy by taking a step beyond the species barrier. The very able and persuasive articulation of animal liberation by Singer and animal rights by Tom Regan—both decidedly nonanthropocentic (nonhuman centered) moral philosophies—blazed a path followed by a second wave of philosophers with wider concerns. Thus while animal liberation/rights is an end point in support of the agenda of the very popular animal welfare movement, it can be regarded, as it is here, as only the first step toward a more encompassing environmental ethic oriented to all living things severally or individually.

We begin Part One of this anthology with Sylvan's summons to the global community of philosophers to focus philosophy's formidable powers of conceptual analysis and cognitive creativity on the environmental problematique. In 1973, an adequate, nonanthropocentric environmental ethic simply did not exist in Western intellectual traditions, Sylvan argues, although one had been prophetically envisioned by the great American conservationist Aldo Leopold at midcentury. So he urged contemporary philosophers to take up Leopold's mantle and make it their business to provide one.

The principal deficiency, as Sylvan's arresting "last people" and "last man" ethical thought experiments at the heart of his paper are intended to drive home, is that the "base class" of traditional Western ethics is coextensive with the class of human beings. Adapting a term from liberal feminism (ecofeminism by then had not emerged as such), traditional Western ethical theory has been guilty of "human [as well as male] chauvinism." Hence, the principal theoretical problem that Sylvan sets out for the philosophers who would respond to his challenge is how to enlarge the ethical base class so that it will include nonhuman, as well as human, beings.

Notice that Sylvan mentions, among the large class of ethically disenfranchised beings, that an eventual environmental ethic might embrace, both individual plants (trees) and animals (dingoes), on the one hand, and environmental collectives or wholes such as species (*the* blue whale) and ecosystems, on the other. As he is simply sketching the problem, not attempting to solve it, he is rather casual about what nonhuman beings ought and ought not to be included in the moral base class of an adequate environmental ethic or how theoretically to go about expanding the base class.

We may regard Peter Singer's paper, "All Animals Are Equal," as an attempt to address the philosophical problem as Sylvan has set it out, though Singer was, of course, not deliberately responding to Sylvan's plea. In traditional Western moral philosophy, human chauvinism, or what Singer and Richard Ryder (also drawing on the rhetoric of contemporaneous feminism) call "speciesism" (an analogy with sexism), is not simply asserted without defense. Moral philosophers from Plato to Rawls have spent considerable energy explaining what makes human beings so special and what makes us and us alone worthy of moral treatment. Singer exploits this ubiquitous feature of classic Western moral philosophy and poses the following dilemma for any human chauvinist ethics.

If what entitles a human being to be a member of the moral base class (call it the philosopher's preferred "criterion for moral standing") is pitched high enough to exclude other animals, then it will also exclude the human "marginal cases"—human infants, the severely retarded, and abjectly senile people. If we are serious about the possession of a certain capacity—say the capacity to reason or to speak—demarcating the difference between those who do deserve moral consideration and those who don't, and if we are self-consistent, then we should permit treating the marginal cases just as we treat other morally disenfranchised beings: without qualms, researchers might perform painful medical experiments and test products on unwanted babies, state fish and game departments might open a hunting season on the retarded, and Purina might make dog food out of the senile.

Outrageous, to be sure. That's just the point. But to bring the marginal cases into the moral base class, we shall have to lower the entry requirement. To what level? Singer turns for an answer to the criterion proposed by Jeremy Bentham: sentience, the capacity to experience pleasure and pain. Sentience is arguably a more relevant criterion for moral treatment than some more exclusive alternative since the minimum consideration one asks of others is not to be harmed by them. And one may suppose that to be harmed, in the last analysis, means to be hurt, to be caused to suffer. Where exactly the "insuperable line," as Bentham calls it, falls between those animals who are and those who are not sentient is far from clear, but it *is* entirely clear that at the very least all vertebrates ought to be included in the moral base class as so delineated.

The enormous appeal of Singer's animal liberation ethic stems, ironically, from the fact that he has really put forth nothing new. Rather, he has simply demanded that the value theory—pleasure is good and pain is evil—of classical utilitarianism be consistently applied. Classical utilitarianism insisted on the *impartial* accounting of pleasures and pains but arbitrarily limited it to the pleasures and pains of human beings. Remove this ad hoc limitation and *voilà*, one has animal liberation.

That, however, exposed Singer's animal liberation ethic to all the problems that classical utilitarianism's ingenious critics had worked out over two centuries. Singer is an advocate of vegetarianism for purely moral reasons, but even this basic practical implication of the ethical enfranchisement of animals is suspect on purely utilitarian grounds. We might raise animals in comfort, slaughter them painlessly, and still enjoy our steaks, chops, and bacon and eggs.

Such considerations as these led Tom Regan to counter Singer's animal liberation ethic with the equally familiar and classical antidote—rights (animal rights in this case). According to Regan, those animals who are subjects of a life, which from their own point of view may be better or worse, have "inherent value" and therefore rights, which "trump" the "principle of utility" that roughly directs us to do whatever would produce a greater balance on average of pleasure over pain among all the sentient creatures whom one's actions affect.

For Singer and Regan, the ethical entitlement of "animals" is a philosophical goal in and of itself. If, however, our goal is to develop the more inclusive environmental ethic originally envisioned by Sylvan, animal liberation and animal rights are at best a way station.

Obviously, plants are left totally out of account by animal liberation/rights, to say nothing of the nonliving parts of ecosystems about which we environmentalists are concerned, such as the soil, water, and air. Moreover, despite his title, "All Animals Are Equal," for Singer not even *all* animals are included in his charmed circle of moral patients since many kinds of animals may not be sentient. The animals to which Regan's theory would extend rights are even more narrowly restricted—indeed, much more so.

In a 1978 paper, "On Being Morally Considerable," Kenneth E. Goodpaster tentatively took moral philosophy beyond animal liberation/rights into environmental ethics proper. He agreed with Bentham and Singer that withholding ethical entitlement from entities that fail to meet the more restrictive of historically proposed criteria (such as being rational) for "moral considerability" was neither intellectually honest nor ultimately warranted. But he disagreed with them that the insuperable line should be drawn by the sentience criterion. From a biological point of view sentience is a means, not an end—a means to life. Hence, not sentience but "being alive" should be the criterion for moral considerability. Furthermore, such a criterion is arguably more relevant to the benefit for which it selects since nonsentient living things may also intelligibly be said to have interests, and if so, they may be directly benefited or harmed—even though harming them may not hurt them, may not cause them consciously to suffer. But Goodpaster's reasoning clearly follows the form classically established by Bentham and recently elaborated by Singer.

Goodpaster's "life-principle" ethic is minimalistic. He expressly avoids the issue of how much weight we ought to give the interests of plants and other barely living beings. And he even admits that while technically they may be morally considerable, practically they may fall well below the human "threshold" of moral sensitivity. Thus we may forever be unable actually to take the interests of all the living things that our actions affect into account as we make our day-to-day practical decisions.

Three years later, the distinguished American philosopher Paul W. Taylor proffered a much stronger version of biocentrism (literally, a "life-centered" ethical theory). According to Taylor, all living things are "teleological centers of life." An organism's *telos* (Greek for "end, goal") is to reach a state of maturity and to reproduce. Our actions can interdict the fulfillment of an organism's *telos*, and to do just that is to harm it. Taylor agrees with Goodpaster that all living things have interests and thus a good of their own, quite regardless of the uses to which we might put them and quite independently of whether they are sentient or care. While Taylor withholds rights from nonhuman natural entities, he argues that *all* wild organisms have *equal* inherent worth. (Taylor's limitation of moral considerability to *wild* teleological centers of life appears to be theoretically unjustified, however.)

The idea that all wild organisms (from fruit flies to sperm whales) are of equal moral worth runs counter to our considered ethical intuitions according to which long-lived, conscious beings are intrinsically more valuable than ephemeral, insentient beings. However, even if we were persuaded by Taylor's bioegalitarianism, the resulting environmental ethic would be beside the point, not to mention diabolically difficult to practice. The welfare of grubs, bugs, and shrubs is simply not the focus of environmental concern. As Sylvan's programmatic paper suggests, environmental concern focuses less on individual living things (though their well-being is not ignored entirely) than on species and other "holistic" entities, on biotic communities, ecosystems, wilderness, and the planetary biosphere as a whole.

In "Animal Liberation and Environmental Ethics: Bad Marriage, Quick Divorce," Mark Sagoff highlights many of the differences between the individualistic and holistic approaches to nonanthropocentric moral philosophy. His discussion is confined to the individualistic animal welfare ethics, but appropriately generalized, it applies with equal force to the exclusively individualistic life-principle or respect-for-life ethics. It's not just that the animal welfare ethics do not go far enough, rather they run in a different and often contrary direction to environmental concerns, Sagoff argues. In addition to conflicts between the welfare of domestic or feral sentient animals and endangered plant species or overall ecosystem health, there are also conflicts of interest between domestic and feral animals, on the one hand, and wild animals on the other. In "Animal Rights, Human Wrongs," Regan expresses a concern for both whales and gibbon apes. But most of the concern of animal liberation/rights has been lavished on animals like cattle (especially veal calves or "bobby calves," as Regan refers to them), chickens, and the like that are factory farmed. While factory farming is environmentally destructive because of the depletion of irrechargable aquifers, soil erosion, and chemical pollution of soils and waters, the well-being of domestic creatures themselves—plants included, certainly, as well as animals—is just not an environmental issue. Environmentally speaking, wild animal and plant *populations* are the important issue, and they are often severely affected adversely by competition from domestic and feral types.

In sum, as Sagoff forcefully points out, environmental concerns are predominantly holistic, not individualistic. Thus the exclusively individualistic approach to environmental ethics inadequately addresses these concerns. Environmental concerns and exclusively individualistic environmental ethics pass one another by, like the proverbial ships in the night, without meeting or making contact.

Well, what to do? Perhaps we can get a clue by diagnosing the problem. Singer, Regan, Goodpaster, and Taylor all provide variations on a common theoretical theme that could be called the standard paradigm of traditional moral philosophy. The standard paradigm identifies and justifies a property or characteristic that entitles the possessor to moral considerability. The principal difference between the theories of Singer, Regan, Goodpaster, and

Taylor and those of their anthropocentric predecessors lies in the choice of the ethically enfranchising property or characteristic. Most traditional exponents of the standard paradigm carefully select a property or characteristic that they believe only human beings possess. Singer, Regan, Goodpaster, and Taylor have deliberately chosen theirs to include not only all human beings but also a wide range of nonhuman beings. All vertebrates possess Singer's, all mammals possess Regan's, and all living things possess Goodpaster's and Taylor's.

Attempts have been made to attribute unconscious interests—similar to those attributed to plants and insentient animals by Goodpaster and Taylor—to environmental wholes, such as species and ecosystems. And attempts have been made to argue that mere existence is a property warranting moral consideration. But such attempts have not been taken seriously. Biocentrism thus represents the end point of this simple line of argument. It stretches this familiar pattern of moral reasoning to its limit. Like a rubber band asked to encircle too big a bundle, attempts to stretch it further have snapped its credibility.

The holistic approach to environmental ethics would seem, therefore, to require either a different theoretical paradigm or some theoretical means of cogently augmenting biocentrism. Basing his theory on hints and suggestions offered by Aldo Leopold, J. Baird Callicott has pursued the former alternative, while Holmes Rolston III has pursued the latter. Leopold claims that "a land ethic changes the role of *Homo sapiens* from conqueror of the land community to plain member and citizen of it. It implies respect for his fellow-members and also respect for the *community as such.*" Indeed, as "The Land Ethic" progresses, "fellow-members" recede farther and farther from the author's attention and concern for the "community as such" looms ever larger in importance. When Leopold finally comes to write the summary moral maxim or golden rule of the land ethic, he seems to have forgotten about individual plants and animals altogether, and only the ecosystem as a whole remains as the object of moral considerability: "A thing is right when it tends to preserve the integrity, stability, and beauty of the biotic community. It is wrong when it tends otherwise."

Because of the perfect fit of the land ethic with their holistic concerns, contemporary environmentalists have made it their ethic of choice. But Leopold was a forester by training and wildlife ecologist by profession, not a philosopher. Hence his brief but suggestive foray into ethics is not theoretically well formed or fully argued; and it is deeply problematic. In "Holistic Environmental Ethics and the Problem of Ecofascism," J. Baird Callicott attempts explicitly to construct the theoretical superstructure that occasionally shows through the informal texture of Leopold's prose, and to address one of its most vexing problems with the land ethic that its critics have identified: the problem of "ecofascism."

The standard paradigm requires us to grant moral considerability to whatever the philosopher's preferred (and justified) criterion of moral considerability identifies as morally considerable—no matter how we may *feel* about such beings. Callicott argues that Leopold's land ethic belongs to the tradition of moral philosophy classically articulated in the eighteenth century by David Hume and Adam Smith, in which ethics are rooted precisely in altruistic feelings like benevolence, sympathy, and loyalty. According to Callicott, Charles Darwin suggested that such feelings were naturally selected in many species, including our prehuman ancestors, because without them individuals could not bond together into mutually beneficial societies and communities. Rudimentary ethics emerged as human beings evolved to the point where they could articulate codes of conduct conforming to their social sentiments. As human societies grew in scope and complexity, so did our ethics. By now, we have reached the point where the enlightened among us regard all human persons as members of one world community, the "global village," subject to a common ethics of humanity, the "human rights" ethic.

Leopold envisions the land ethic to be the next stage of human moral evolution, for presently ecology portrays terrestrial nature to be a biotic community composed of plants and animals, soils and waters. A universal ecological literacy would trigger sympathy and fellow-feeling for *fellow members* of the biotic community *and* feelings of loyalty and patriotic regard for the *community as a whole*, Callicott suggests. How to balance human interests against those of nonhuman natural entities and nature as a whole is as big a problem for the feeling-based land ethic as for any other environmental ethic. Callicott defends the land ethic against the charge that it amounts to "environmental fascism," which some of its exclusively individualistic critics have, in retaliation for his very generous critique of their views, leveled against it.

First, he points out that the land ethic is not intended to replace all the community-related ethics that preceded it. Just because we now understand that we are members of a biotic community that engenders a land ethic, it does not follow that we are not also members of various human communities; nor does the emergence of the land ethic imply that we are relieved of all the duties and obligations engendered by such multiple community memberships. But how to prioritize these duties and obligations when they conflict? That is the question. Callicott suggests we employ two second-order principles to resolve conflicts between the first-order duties and obligations generated by our multiple community memberships. The first, SOP-1, states that duties and obligations generated by membership in nearer and dearer communities take precedence over those generated by membership in more remote and impersonal communities. For example, one feels a greater obligation to contribute to the care of one's own aged mother, a duty generated by the most venerable and intimate of all communities, the family, than to contribute to the care of someone else's mother half way around the world, who is, with oneself, a member of a more remote and impersonal community, the global village. The second, SOP-2, states that greater interests prevail over lesser interests. For example, one feels a greater obligation to prevent a murder, if one is in a position to do so, than to prevent shoplifting; in the former case, the victim's vital interest in life is at stake, in the latter, the victim's lesser interest in a small amount of money is at stake. The two second-order principles are designed to be employed sequentially, such that the second either reinforces or countermands the indication of the first. Thus, in the famous case of the endangered spotted owl and its old-growth-forest habitat versus the individual loggers, mill workers, and timber company owners in the Pacific Northwest, we reason as follows. Applying SOP-1, we should give preference to the interests of the latter, because they are our fellow human beings and, for those of us who are citizens of the United States, our fellow Americans. But SOP-2 countermands SOP-1—because the species in question faces irreversible extinction and its habitat wholesale destruction, while the nonvital interests of the individual human beings in a certain kind of work and a certain kind of lifestyle can be compensated and substituted for. Through local, state, and federal governments, we can and should compensate people who lose jobs because of our collective efforts to conserve endangered species, and provide them with training for other kinds of employment.

Nevertheless, if the biocentrism of Goodpaster and Taylor errs in being exclusively individualistic, the ecocentrism (short for ecosystem-centered ethic) of Leopold and Callicott may err in being excessively—though by no means exclusively—holistic. Rolston has attempted a different synthesis of individualism and holism. At the foundation of his theory lies the core claim of biocentrism—that any and every living thing is intrinsically valuable and thus morally considerable. But for his approach to be more plausible than that of Goodpaster and Taylor, he must somehow reconcile the moral considerability of individual plants (from the lowliest shrub to the most magnificent sequoia) and animals (from gnats to mountain gorillas) with common sense, and he must also somehow make his theory reach environmental wholes. Rolston has been working at this project since the publication of his 1975 essay, "Is There an Ecological Ethic?", which was as seminal as the slightly earlier paper by Sylvan reprinted here. His "Challenges in Environmental Ethics" summarizes the fruits of a quarter century of inquiry.

To the equal baseline intrinsic value of living things, each with a good of its own, Rolston adds a value premium, so to speak, for sentience and an additional value premium for self-consciousness. Thus sentient animals possess more intrinsic value than plants and insentient animals; and we self-conscious rational animals possess the most intrinsic value of all individual natural entities. Therefore, in cases of conflict, human interests take precedence over those of individual animals and plants, as most sensible people believe; and, by the same token, the interests of sentient animals take precedence over those of insentient animals and plants. Rolston then awards a value dividend, as it were, to species, the perpetuation of which is the reproductive end of specimens, and to ecosystems as the matrix in which baseline intrinsically valuable living things evolved and on which they remain dependent for their flourishing. In Rolston's essentially biocentric system, like the moon that shines by a borrowed light, natural wholes, such as species and ecosystems, possess an intrinsic value derived from the baseline intrinsic value of living organisms and thus enjoy only derivative moral considerability. Furthermore, it is not clear how applying Rolston's system might adjudicate conflicts of interest between wholes and individuals. That problem, however, is endemic to all ethics that go beyond traditional anthropocentrism, and so it would be unfair to suggest that Rolston's environmental ethic is any less decisive, in respect to such practical conundrums, than are any of its competitors.

The concluding essay, "Animal Liberation and Environmental Ethics: Back Together Again," attempts to reunite moral concern for both animals and the environment, after Sagoff has put them asunder, thus bringing Part One full circle. The author, J. Baird Callicott, proposes to accomplish that task of reconciliation by means of a communitarian moral philosophy. We are, he points out, members of multiple communities, each of which generates a special set of duties and obligations—both to the members of that community and to the community as a whole. We have obligations to family members that are not only stronger than but different from those we have to our fellow citizens. Our obligations to the communities as a whole of which we are members also differ. To our nation-states, we each have patriotic duties, which are different from the duties we have to humanity as a whole. Upon such considerations as these, Callicott argues that the duties and obligations generated by the biotic community, both to its members severally and to the community as a whole, are different from those generated by all our other community memberships—indeed radically different because the biotic community is so different from all the other communities to which we belong.

Mary Midgley, however, has pointed out that between the various human communities to which we belong and the biotic community lies a whole "'nother" set of duty-generating communities to which we also belong, which she calls the "mixed community," and which includes domestic animals. Some domestic animals are our pets, which we might think of as surrogate family members. Because of this quasi-family status, we believe that pet-owners (a term that has become controversial of late, for the reasons that Callicott indirectly illuminates) have a positive obligation to feed, shelter, and provide veterinary care for their pets; while to the wild squirrels that live in nearly as close proximity, no such duties exist. Other domestic animals, draft animals (horses, oxen, Asian elephants) were, historically, members of other sorts of mixed communities—work teams, perhaps we could call them. The human and animal members of such teams had mutual, though asymmetrical, obligations to one another, that are not the same as those among pets and their owners. Still other domestic animals (cows, pigs, chickens) were, historically, members of still other sorts of mixed communities—barnyard communities, perhaps we could call them. And the human members of those communities had obligations to the animal members that differ from their obligations to their pets and draft animals. Callicott does not try to work out the details of the duties and obligations engendered by mixed communities, rather his point is to show that we can articulate a wide spectrum of reasonable, mutually comparable ethics—human-to-human, human-to-animal, human-to-nature— in terms of a common ethical theory and moral philosophy.

# IS THERE A NEED FOR A NEW,
# AN ENVIRONMENTAL, ETHIC?

*Richard Sylvan (Routley)*

Richard Sylvan (formerly Routley) was a fellow with the Research School of Social Sciences at the Australian National University in Canberra. With Don Mannison and Michael McRobbie, he edited *Environmental Philosophy*.

## 1

It is increasingly said that civilization, Western civilization at least, stands in need of a new ethic (and derivatively of a new economics) setting out people's relations to the natural environment, in Leopold's words "an ethic dealing with man's relation to land and to the animals and plants which grow upon it."[1] It is not of course that old and prevailing ethics do not deal with man's relation to nature; they do, and on the prevailing view man is free to deal with nature as he pleases, i.e., his relations with nature, insofar at least as they do not affect others, are not subject to moral censure. Thus assertions such as "Crusoe ought not to be mutilating those trees" are significant and morally determinate but, inasmuch at least as Crusoe's actions do not interfere with others, they are false or do not hold—and trees are not, in a good sense, moral objects.[2] It is to this, to the values and evaluations of the prevailing ethics, that Leopold and others in fact take exception. Leopold regards as subject to moral criticism, as wrong, behavior that on prevailing views is morally permissible. But it is not, as Leopold seems to think, that such behavior is beyond the scope of the prevailing ethics and that an *extension* of traditional morality is required to cover such cases, to fill a moral void. If Leopold is right in his criticism of prevailing conduct what is required is a *change* in the ethics, in attitudes, values, and evaluations. For as matters stand, as he himself explains,

This essay was originally published in *Proceedings of the XV World Congress of Philosophy*, No. 1. Varna, Bulgaria, 1973, pp. 205–210. Reprinted with permission of author.

men do not feel morally ashamed if they interfere with a wilderness, if they maltreat the land, extract from it whatever it will yield, and then move on; and such conduct is not taken to interfere with and does not rouse the moral indignation of others. "A farmer who clears the woods off a 75 percent slope, turns his cows into the clearing, and dumps its rainfall, rocks, and soil into the community creek, is still (if otherwise decent) a respected member of society."[3] Under what we shall call *an environmental ethic* such traditionally permissible conduct would be accounted morally wrong, and the farmer subject to proper moral criticism.

Let us grant such evaluations for the purpose of the argument. What is not so clear is that a *new* ethic is required even for such radical judgments. For one thing it is none too clear what is going to count as a new ethic, much as it is often unclear whether a new development in physics counts as a new physics or just as a modification or extension of the old. For, notoriously, ethics are not clearly articulated or at all well worked out, so that the application of identity criteria for ethics may remain obscure.[4] Furthermore we tend to cluster a family of ethical systems which do not differ on core or fundamental principles together as one ethic; e.g., the Christian ethic, which is an umbrella notion covering a cluster of differing and even competing systems. In fact then, there are two other possibilities, apart from a new environmental ethic, which might cater for the evaluations, namely that of an extension or modification of the prevailing ethics or that of the development of principles that are already encompassed or latent within the prevailing ethic. The second possibility, that environmental evaluations can be incorporated within (and ecological problems solved within) the framework of prevailing Western ethics, is open because there isn't a single ethical system uniquely assumed in Western civilization: on many issues, and especially on controversial issues such as infanticide, women's rights, and drugs, there are competing sets of principles. Talk of a new ethic and prevailing ethics tends to suggest a sort of monolithic structure, a uniformity, that prevailing ethics, and even a single ethic, need not have.

Indeed Passmore has mapped out three important traditions in Western ethical views concerning man's relation to nature; a dominant tradition, the despotic position, with man as despot (or tyrant), and two lesser traditions, the stewardship position, with man as custodian, and the co-operative position with man as perfecter.[5] Nor are these the only traditions; primitivism is another, and both romanticism and mysticism have influenced Western views.

The dominant Western view is simply inconsistent with an environmental ethic; for according to it nature is the dominion of man and he is free to deal with it as he pleases (since—at least on the mainstream Stoic-Augustine view—it exists only for his sake), whereas on an environmental ethic man is not so free to do as he pleases. But it is not quite so obvious that an environmental ethic cannot be coupled with one of the lesser traditions. Part of the problem is that the lesser traditions are by no means adequately characterized anywhere, especially when the religious backdrop is removed, e.g., *who* is man steward for and responsible to? However both traditions are inconsistent with an environmental ethic because they imply policies of complete interference, whereas on an environmental ethic some worthwhile parts of the earth's surface should be preserved from substantial human interference, whether of the "improving" sort or not. Both traditions would in fact prefer to see the earth's land surfaces reshaped along the lines of the tame and comfortable north-European small farm and village landscape. According to the co-operative position man's proper role is to develop, cultivate, and perfect nature—all nature eventually—by bringing out its potentialities, the test of perfection being primarily usefulness for human purposes; while on the stewardship view man's role, like that of a farm manager, is to make nature productive by his efforts though not by means that will deliberately degrade its resources. Although these positions both depart from the dominant position in a way which enables the incorporation of some evaluations of an environmental ethic, e.g., some of those concerning the irresponsible farmer, they do not go far enough: for in the present situation of expanding populations confined to finite natural areas, they will lead to, and enjoin, the perfecting, farming and utilizing of all natural areas. Indeed these lesser traditions lead to, what a thoroughgoing environmental ethic would reject, a principle of total use, implying that every natural area should be cultivated or otherwise used for human ends, "humanized."[6]

As the important Western traditions exclude an environmental ethic, it would appear that such an ethic, not primitive, mystical or romantic, would be new all right. The matter is not so straightforward; for the dominant ethic has been substantially qualified by the rider that one is not always entitled to do as one pleases where this physically interferes with others. Maybe some such proviso was implicit all along (despite evidence to the contrary), and it was simply assumed that doing what one pleased with natural items would not affect others (the noninterference assumption). Be this as it may, the *modified* dominant position appears, at least for many thinkers, to have supplanted the dominant position; and the modified position can undoubtedly go much further towards an environmental ethic. For example, the farmer's polluting of a community stream may be ruled immoral on the grounds that it physically interferes with others who use or would use the streams. Likewise business enterprises which destroy the natural environment for no satisfactory returns or which cause pollution deleterious to the health of future humans, can be criticized on the sort of welfare basis (e.g., that of Barkley and Seckler) that blends with the modified position; and so on.[7] The position may even serve to restrict the sort of family size one is entitled to have since in a finite situation excessive population levels will interfere with future people. Nonetheless neither the modified dominant position nor its Western variants, obtained by combining it with the lesser traditions, is adequate as an environmental ethic, as I shall try to show. A new ethic *is* wanted.

## 2

As we noticed (an) *ethic* is ambiguous, as between a specific ethical system, a *specific* ethic, and a more generic notion, a super ethic, under which specific ethics cluster.[8] An ethical system S is, near enough, a propositional system (i.e., a structured set of propositions) or theory which includes (like individuals of a theory) a set of values and (like postulates of a theory) a set of general evaluative judgments concerning conduct, typically of what is obligatory, permissible, and wrong, of what are rights, what is valued, and so forth. A general or lawlike proposition of a system is a principle; and certainly if systems $S_1$ and $S_2$ contain different principles, then they are different systems. It follows that any environmental ethic differs from the important traditional ethics outlined. Moreover if environmental ethics differ from Western ethical systems on some *core* principle embedded in Western systems, then these systems differ from the Western super ethic (assuming, what seems to be so, that it can be uniquely characterized)—in which case if an environmental ethic *is* needed then a new ethic is wanted. It suffices then to locate a core principle and to provide environmental counter examples to it.

It is commonly assumed that there are what amount to core principles of Western ethical systems, principles that will accordingly belong to the super ethic. The fairness principle inscribed in the Golden Rule provides one example. Directly relevant here, as a good stab at a core principle, is the commonly formulated liberal principle of the modified dominance position. A recent formulation runs as follows:

"The liberal philosophy of the Western world holds that one should be able to do what he wishes, providing (1) that he does not harm others and (2) that he is not likely to harm himself irreparably."[9]

Let us call this principle *basic (human) chauvinism*—because under it humans, or people, come first and everything else a bad last—though sometimes the principle is hailed as a *freedom* principle because it gives permission to perform a wide range of actions (including actions which mess up the environment and natural things) providing they do not harm others. In fact it tends to cunningly shift the onus of proof to others. It is worth remarking that *harming others* in the restriction is narrower than a restriction to the (usual) interests of others; it is not enough that it is in my interests, because I detest you, that you stop breathing; you are free to breathe, for the time being anyway, because it does not harm me. There remains a problem however as to exactly what counts as harm or interference. Moreover the width of the principle is so far obscure because "other" may be filled out in significantly different ways: it makes a difference to the extent, and privilege, of the chauvinism whether "other" expands to "other human"—which is too restrictive—or to "other person" or to "other sentient being"; and it makes a difference to the adequacy of the principle, and inversely to its economic applicability, to which class of others it is intended to apply, whether to future as well as to present others, whether to remote future others or only to nondiscountable future others and whether to possible others. The latter would make the principle completely unworkable, and it is generally assumed that it applies at most to present and future others.

It is taken for granted in designing counter examples to basic chauvinist principles, that a semantic analysis of permissibility and obligation statements stretches out over ideal situations (which may be incomplete or even inconsistent), so that what is permissible holds in some ideal situation, what is obligatory in every ideal situation, and what is wrong is excluded in every ideal situation. But the main point to grasp for the counter examples that follow, is that ethical principles if correct are universal and are assessed over the class of ideal situations.

(i) The *last man* example. The last man (or person) surviving the collapse of the world system lays about him, eliminating, as far as he can, every living thing, animal, or plant (but painlessly if you like, as at the best abattoirs). What he does is quite permissible according to basic chauvinism, but on environmental grounds what he does is wrong. Moreover one does not have to be committed to esoteric values to regard Mr. Last Man as behaving badly (the reason being perhaps that radical thinking and values have shifted in an environmental direction in advance of corresponding shifts in the formulation of fundamental evaluative principles).

(ii) The *last people* example. The last man example can be broadened to the last people example. We can assume that they know they are the last people, e.g., because they are aware that radiation effects have blocked any chance of reproduction. One considers the last people in order to rule out the possibility that what these people do harms or somehow physically interferes with later people. Otherwise one could as well consider science fiction cases where people arrive at a new planet and destroy its ecosystems, whether with good intentions such as perfecting the planet for their ends and making it more fruitful or, forgetting the lesser traditions, just for the hell of it.

Let us assume that the last people are very numerous. They humanely exterminate every wild animal and they eliminate the fish of the seas, they put all arable land under intensive cultivation, and all remaining forests disappear in favor of quarries or plantations, and so on. They may give various familiar reasons for this, e.g., they believe it is the way to salvation or to perfection, or they are simply satisfying reasonable needs, or even that it is needed to keep the last people employed or occupied so that they do not worry too much about their impending extinction. On an environmental ethic the last people have behaved badly; they have simplified and largely destroyed all the natural ecosystems, and with their demise the world will soon be an ugly and largely wrecked place. But this conduct may conform with the basic chauvinist principle, and as well with the principles enjoined by the lesser traditions. Indeed the main point of elaborating this example is because, as the last man example reveals, basic chauvinism may conflict with stewardship or co-operation principles. The conflict may be removed it seems by conjoining a further proviso to the basic principle, the effect (3) that he does not willfully destroy natural resources. But as the last people do not destroy resources willfully, but perhaps "for the best of reasons," the variant is still environmentally inadequate.

(iii) The *great entrepreneur* example. The last man example can be adjusted so as to not fall foul of clause (3). The last man is an industrialist; he runs a giant complex of automated factories and farms which he proceeds to extend. He produces automobiles among other things, from renewable and recyclable resources of course, only he dumps and recycles these shortly after manufacture and sale to a dummy buyer instead of putting them on the road for a short time as we do. Of course he has the best of reasons for his activity, e.g., he is increasing gross world product, or he is improving output to fulfill some plan, and he will be increasing his own and general welfare since he much prefers increased output and productivity. The entrepreneur's behavior is on the Western ethic quite permissible; indeed his conduct is commonly thought to be quite fine and may even meet Pareto optimality requirements given prevailing notions of being "better off."

Just as we can extend the last man example to a class of last people, so we can extend this example to the *industrial society* example: the society looks rather like ours.

(iv) The *vanishing species* example. Consider the blue whale, a mixed good on the economic picture. The blue whale is on the verge of extinction because of his qualities as a private good, as a source of valuable oil and meat. The catching and marketing of blue whales does not harm the whalers; it does not harm or physically interfere with others in any good sense, though it may upset them and they may be prepared to compensate the whalers if they desist; nor need whale hunting be willful destruction. (Slightly different examples which eliminate the hunting aspect of the blue whale example are provided by cases where a species is eliminated or threatened through destruction of its habitat by man's activity or the activities of animals he has introduced, e.g., many plains-dwelling Australian marsupials and the Arabian oryx.) The behavior of the whalers in eliminating this magnificent species of whale is accordingly quite permissible—at least according to basic chauvinism. But on an environmental ethic it is not. However, the free-market mechanism will not cease allocating whales to commercial uses, as a satisfactory environmental economics would; instead the market model will grind inexorably along the private demand curve until the blue whale population is no longer viable—if that point has not already been passed.[10]

In sum, the class of permissible actions that rebound on the environment is more narrowly circumscribed on an environmental ethic than it is in the Western super ethic. But aren't environmentalists going too far in claiming that these people, those of the examples and respected industrialists, fishermen and farmers are behaving, when engaging in environmentally degrading activities of the sort described, in a morally impermissible way? No, what these people do is to a greater or lesser extent evil, and hence in serious cases morally impermissible. For example, insofar as the killing or forced displacement of primitive peoples who stand in the way of an industrial development is morally indefensible and impermissible, so also is the slaughter of the last remaining blue whales for private profit. But how to reformulate basic chauvinism as a satisfactory freedom principle is a more difficult matter. A tentative, but none too adequate beginning might be made by extending (2) to include harm to or interference with others who would be so affected by the action in question were they placed in the environment and (3) to exclude speciecide. It may be preferable, in view of the way the freedom principle sets the onus of proof, simply to scrap it altogether, and instead to specify classes of rights and permissible conduct, as in a bill of rights.

3

A radical change in a theory sometimes forces changes in the meta-theory; e.g., a logic which rejects the Reference Theory in a thoroughgoing way requires a modification of the usual meta-theory which also accepts the Reference Theory and indeed which is tailored to cater only for logics which do conform. A somewhat similar phenomenon seems to occur in the case of a meta-ethic adequate for an environmental ethic. Quite apart from introducing several environmentally important notions, such as *conservation, pollution, growth,* and *preservation,* for meta-ethical analysis, an environmental ethic compels reexamination and modified analyses of such characteristic actions as *natural right, ground* of right, and of the relations of obligation and permissibility to rights; it may well require reassessment of traditional analyses of such notions as *value* and *right,* especially where these are based on chauvinist assumptions; and it forces the rejection of many of the more prominent meta-ethical positions. These points are illustrated by a very brief examination of accounts of *natural right* and then by a sketch of the species bias of some major positions.[11]

Hart accepts, subject to defeating conditions which are here irrelevant, the classical doctrine of natural rights according to which, among other things, "any adult human . . . capable of choice is at liberty to do (i.e., is under no obligation to abstain from) any action which is not one coercing or restraining or designed to injure other persons."[12] But this sufficient condition for a human natural right depends on accepting the very human chauvinist principle an environmental ethic rejects, since if a person has a natural right he has a right; so too the *definition* of a natural right adopted by classical theorists and accepted with minor qualifications by Hart presupposes the same defective principle. Accordingly an environmental ethic would have to amend the classical notion of a natural right, a far from straightforward matter now that human rights with respect to animals and the natural environment are, like those with respect to slaves not all that long ago, undergoing major reevaluation.

An environmental ethic does not commit one to the view that natural objects such as trees have rights (though such a view is occasionally held, e.g., by pantheists. But pantheism is false since artefacts are not alive). For moral prohibitions forbidding certain actions with respect to an object do not award that object a correlative right. That it would be wrong to mutilate a given tree or piece of property does not entail that the tree or piece of property has a correlative right not to be mutilated (without seriously stretching the notion of a right). Environmental views can stick with mainstream theses according to which rights are coupled with corresponding responsibilities and so with bearing obligations, and with corresponding interests and concern; i.e., at least, whatever has a right also has responsibilities and therefore obligations, and whatever has a right has interests. Thus although any person may have a right by no means every living thing can (significantly) have rights, and arguably most sentient objects other than persons cannot have rights. But persons can relate morally, through obligations, prohibitions and so forth, to practically anything at all.

The species bias of certain ethical and economic positions which aim to make principles of conduct or reasonable economic behavior calculable is easily brought out. These positions typically employ a single criterion $p$, such as preference or happiness, as a *summum bonum;* characteristically each individual of some *base* class, almost always humans, but perhaps including future humans, is supposed to have an ordinal $p$ ranking of the states in question (e.g., of affairs, of the economy); then some principle is supplied to determine a collective $p$ ranking of these states in terms of individual $p$ rankings, and what is best or ought to be done is determined either directly, as in act-utilitarianism under the Greatest Happiness principle, or indirectly, as in rule-utilitarianism, in terms of some optimization principle applied to the collective ranking. The species bias is transparent from the selection of the base class. And even if the base class is extended to embrace persons, or even some animals (at the cost, like that of including remotely future humans, of losing testability), the positions are open to familiar criticism, namely that the whole of the base class may be prejudiced in a way which leads to unjust principles. For example if every member of the base class detests dingoes, on the basis of mistaken data as to dingoes' behavior, then by the Pareto ranking test the collective ranking will rank states where dingoes are exterminated very highly, from which it will generally be concluded that dingoes ought to be exterminated (the evaluation of most Australian farmers anyway). Likewise it would just be a happy accident, it seems, if collective demand (horizontally summed from individual demand) for a state of the economy with blue whales as a mixed good, were to succeed in outweighing private whaling demands; for if no one in the base class happened to know that blue whales exist or cared a jot that they do then "rational" economic decision-making would do nothing to prevent their extinction. Whether the blue whale survives should not have to depend on what humans know or what they see on television. Human interests and preferences are far too parochial to provide a satisfactory basis for deciding on what is environmentally desirable.

These ethical and economic theories are not alone in their species chauvinism; much the same applies to most going meta-ethical theories which, unlike intuitionistic theories, try to offer some rationale for their basic principles. For instance, on social contract positions obligations are a matter of mutual agreements between individuals of the base class; on a social justice picture rights and obligations spring from the application of symmetrical fairness principles to members of the base class, usually a rather special class of persons, while on a Kantian position which has some vague obligations somehow arise from respect for members of the base class persons. In each case if members of the base class happen to be ill disposed to items outside the base class then that is too bad for them: that is (rough) justice.

## NOTES

1. Aldo Leopold. *A Sand Country Almanac with Essays on Conservation from Round River* (New York: Ballantine Books, 1966), p. 238.
2. A view occasionally tempered by the idea that trees house spirits.
3. Leopold. *Sand County*, p. 245.
4. To the consternation no doubt of Quineans. But the fact is that we can talk perfectly well about inchoate and fragmentary systems the identity of which may be indeterminate.
5. John Passmore. *Man's Responsibility for Nature: Ecological Problems and Western Traditions* (New York: Scribner's, 1974).
6. If "use" is extended, somewhat illicitly, to include use for preservation, this total use principle is rendered innocuous at least as regards its actual effects. Note that the total use principle is tied to the resource view of nature.
7. P. W. Barkley and D. W. Seckler. *Economic Growth and Environmental Decay: The Solution Becomes the Problem* (New York: Harcourt, Brace, Jovanovich, 1972).
8. A *meta-ethic* is, as usual, a theory about ethics, super ethics, their features and fundamental notions.
9. Barkley and Seckler. *Economic Growth and Environmental Decay*, p. 58. A related principle is that (modified) free enterprise can operate within similar limits.
10. The tragedy of the commons type reasons are well explained in Barkley and Seckler, *Economic Growth and Environmental Decay*.
11. Some of these points are developed by those protesting about human maltreatment of animals; see especially the essays collected in S. and R. Godlovitch and J. Harris, eds., *Animals, Men and Morals: An Enquiry into the Maltreatment of Non-humans* (New York: Grove Press, 1971).
12. H. L. A. Hart. "Are There Any Natural Rights?" reprinted in A. Quinton, ed., *Political Philosophy* (London: Oxford University Press, 1967).

# ALL ANIMALS ARE EQUAL[1]

*Peter Singer*

Peter Singer is the Ira W. DeCamp professor of bioethics in the Center for Human Values at Princeton University. He is the author of *Animal Liberation: A New Ethics for Our Treatment of Animals*, *Practical Ethics*, and *The Expanding Circle: Ethics and Sociobiology*.

In recent years a number of oppressed groups have campaigned vigorously for equality. The classic instance is the Black Liberation movement, which demands an end to the prejudice and discrimination that has made blacks second-class citizens. The immediate appeal of the black liberation movement and its initial, if limited success made it a model for other oppressed groups to follow. We became familiar with liberation movements for Spanish-Americans, gay people, and a variety of other minorities. When a majority group—women—began their campaign, some thought we had come to the end of the road. Discrimination on the basis of sex, it has been said, is the last universally accepted form of discrimination, practiced without secrecy or pretense even in those liberal circles that have long prided themselves on their freedom from prejudice against racial minorities.

One should always be wary of talking of "the last remaining form of discrimination." If we have learnt anything from the liberation movements, we should have learnt how difficult it is to be aware of latent prejudice in our attitudes to particular groups until this prejudice is forcefully pointed out.

A liberation movement demands an expansion of our moral horizons and an extension or reinterpretation of the basic moral principle of equality. Practices that were previously regarded as natural and inevitable come to be seen as the result of an unjustifiable prejudice. Who can say with confidence that all his or her attitudes and practices are beyond criticism? If we wish to avoid being numbered amongst the oppressors, we must be prepared to rethink even our most fundamental attitudes. We need to consider them from

This essay originally appeared in *Philosophic Exchange*, Vol. 1, No. 5 (Summer, 1974), 243–257. Reprinted with permission.

the point of view of those most disadvantaged by our attitudes, and the practices that follow from these attitudes. If we can make this unaccustomed mental switch we may discover a pattern in our attitudes and practices that consistently operates so as to benefit one group—usually the one to which we ourselves belong—at the expense of another. In this way we may come to see that there is a case for a new liberation movement. My aim is to advocate that we make this mental switch in respect of our attitudes and practices towards a very large group of beings: members of species other than our own—or, as we popularly though misleadingly call them, animals. In other words, I am urging that we extend to other species the basic principle of equality that most of us recognise should be extended to all members of our own species.

All this may sound a little far-fetched, more like a parody of other liberation movements than a serious objective. In fact, in the past the idea of "The Rights of Animals" really has been used to parody the case for women's rights. When Mary Wollstonecroft, a forerunner of later feminists, published her *Vindication of the Rights of Women* in 1792, her ideas were widely regarded as absurd, and they were satirized in an anonymous publication entitled *A Vindication of the Rights of Brutes*. The author of this satire (actually Thomas Taylor, a distinguished Cambridge philosopher) tried to refute Wollstonecroft's reasonings by showing that they could be carried one stage further. If sound when applied to women, why should the arguments not be applied to dogs, cats, and horses? They seemed to hold equally well for these "brutes"; yet to hold that brutes had rights was manifestly absurd; therefore the reasoning by which this conclusion had been reached must be unsound, and if unsound when applied to brutes, it must also be unsound when applied to women, since the very same arguments had been used in each case.

One way in which we might reply to this argument is by saying that the case for equality between men and women cannot validly extended to nonhuman animals. Women have a right to vote, for instance, because they are just as capable of making rational decisions as men are; dogs, on the other hand, are incapable of understanding the significance of voting, so they cannot have the right to vote. There are many other obvious ways in which men and women resemble each other closely, while humans and other animals differ greatly. So, it might be said, men and women are similar beings, and should have equal rights, while humans and nonhumans are different and should not have equal rights.

The thought behind this reply to Taylor's analogy is correct up to a point, but it does not go far enough. There *are* important differences between humans and other animals, and these differences must give rise to *some* differences in the rights that each have. Recognizing this obvious fact, however, is no barrier to the case for extending the basic principle of equality to nonhuman animals. The differences that exist between men and women are equally undeniable, and the supporters of Women's Liberation are aware that these differences may give rise to different rights. Many feminists hold that women have the right to an abortion on request. It does not follow that since these same people are campaigning for equality between men and women they must support the right of men to have abortions too. Since a man cannot have an abortion, it is meaningless to talk of his right to have one. Since a pig can't vote, it is meaningless to talk of its right to vote. There is no reason why either Women's Liberation or Animal Liberation should get involved in such nonsense. The extension of the basic principle of equality from one group to another does not imply that we must treat both groups in exactly the same way, or grant exactly the same rights to both groups. Whether we should do so will depend on the nature of the members of the two groups. The basic principle of equality, I shall argue, is equality of consideration; and equal consideration for different beings may lead to different treatment and different rights.

So there is a different way of replying to Taylor's attempt to parody Wollstonecroft's arguments, a way which does not deny the differences between humans and nonhumans, but goes more deeply into the question of equality, and concludes by finding nothing absurd in the idea that the basic principle of equality applies to so-called "brutes." I believe that we reach this conclusion if we examine the basis on which our opposition to discrimination on grounds of race or sex ultimately rests. We will then see that we would be on shaky ground if we were to demand equality for blacks, women, and other groups of oppressed humans while denying equal consideration to nonhumans.

When we say that all human beings, whatever their race, creed or sex, are equal, what is it that we are asserting? Those who wish to defend a hierarchical, inegalitarian society have often pointed out that by whatever test we choose, it simply is not true that all humans are equal. Like it or not, we must face the fact that humans come in different shapes and sizes; they come with differing moral capacities, differing intellectual abilities, differing amounts of benevolent feeling and sensitivity to the needs of others, differing abilities to communicate effectively, and differing capacities to experience pleasure and pain. In short, if the demand for equality were based on the actual equality of all human beings, we would have to stop demanding equality. It would be an unjustifiable demand.

Still, one might cling to the view that the demand for equality among human beings is based on the actual equality of the different races and sexes. Although humans differ as individuals in various ways, there are no differences between the races and sexes *as such.* From the mere fact that a person is black, or a woman, we cannot infer anything else about that person. This, it may be said, is what is wrong with racism and sexism. The white racist claims that whites are superior to blacks, but this is false—although there are differences between individuals, some blacks are superior to some whites in all of the capacities and abilities that could conceivably be relevant. The opponent of sexism would say the same: a person's sex is no guide to his or her abilities, and this is why it is unjustifiable to discriminate on the basis of sex.

This is a possible line of objection to racial and sexual discrimination. It is not, however, the way that someone really concerned about equality would choose, because taking this line could, in some circumstances, force one to accept a most inegalitarian society. The fact that humans differ as individuals, rather than as races or sexes, is a valid reply to someone who defends a hierarchical society like, say, South Africa, in which all whites are superior in status to all blacks. The existence of individual variations that cut across the lines of race or sex, however, provides us with no defence at all against a more sophisticated opponent of equality, one who proposes that, say, the interests of those with I.Q. ratings above 100 be preferred to the interests of those I.Q.s below 100. Would a hierarchical society of this sort really be so much better than one based on race or sex? I think not. But if we tie the moral principle of equality to the factual equality of the different races or sexes, taken as a whole, our opposition to racism and sexism does not provide us with any basis for objecting to this kind of inegalitarianism.

There is a second important reason why we ought not to base our opposition to racism and sexism on any kind of factual equality, even the limited kind which asserts that variations in capacities and abilities are spread evenly between the different races and sexes: we can have no absolute guarantee that these abilities and capacities really are distributed evenly, without regard to race or sex, among human beings. So far as actual abilities are concerned, there do seem to be certain measurable differences between both races and sexes. These differences do not, of course, appear in each case, but only when averages are taken. More important still, we do not yet know how much of these differences is really due to the different genetic endowments of the various races and sexes, and how much is due to environmental differences that are the result of past and continuing discrimination. Perhaps all of the important differences will eventually prove to be environmental rather than genetic. Anyone opposed to racism and sexism will certainly hope that this will be so, for it will make the task of ending discrimination a lot easier; nevertheless it would be dangerous to rest the case against racism and sexism on the belief that all significant differences are environmental in origin. The opponent of, say, racism who takes this line will be unable to avoid conceding that if differences in ability did after all prove to have some genetic connection with race, racism would in some way be defensible.

It would be folly for the opponent of racism to stake his whole case on a dogmatic commitment to one particular outcome of a difficult scientific issue which is still a long way from being settled. While attempts to prove that differences in certain selected abilities between races and sexes are primarily genetic in origin have certainly not been conclusive, the same must be said of attempts to prove that these differences are largely the result of environment. At this stage of the investigation we cannot be certain which view is correct, however much we may hope it is the latter.

Fortunately, there is no need to pin the case for equality to one particular outcome of this scientific investigation. The appropriate response to those who claim to have found evidence of genetically based differences in ability between the races or sexes is not to stick to the belief that the genetic explanation must be wrong, whatever evidence to the contrary may turn up: instead we should make it quite clear that the claim to equality does not depend on intelligence, moral capacity, physical strength, or similar matters of fact. Equality is a moral ideal, not a simple assertion of fact. There is no logically compelling reason for assuming that a factual difference in ability between two people justifies any difference in the amount of consideration we give to satisfying their needs and interests. The principle of the equality of human beings is not a description of an alleged actual equality among humans: it is a prescription of how we should treat humans.

Jeremy Bentham incorporated the essential basis of moral equality into his utilitarian system of ethics in the formula: "Each to count for one and none for more than one." In other words, the interests of every being affected by an action are to be taken into account and given the same weight as the like interests of any other being. A later utilitarian, Henry Sidgwick, put the point in this way: "The good of any one individual is of no more importance, from the point of view (if I may say so) of the Universe, than the good of any other."[2] More recently, the leading figures in contemporary moral philosophy have shown a great deal of agreement in specifying as a fundamental presupposition of their moral theories some similar requirement which operates so as to give everyone's interests equal consideration—although they cannot agree on how this requirement is best formulated.[3]

It is an implication of this principle of equality that our concern for others ought not to depend on what they are like, or what abilities they possess—although precisely what this concern requires us to do may vary according to the characteristics of those affected by what we do. It is on this basis that the case against racism and the case against sexism must both ultimately rest; and it is in accordance with this principle that speciesism is also to be condemned. If possessing a higher degree of intelligence does not entitle one human to use another for his own ends, how can it entitle humans to exploit nonhumans?

Many philosophers have proposed the principle of equal consideration of interests, in some form or other, as a basic moral principle; but, as we shall see in more detail shortly, not many of them have recognised that this principle applies to members of other species as well as to our own. Bentham was one of the few who did realize this. In a forward-looking passage, written at a time when black slaves in the British dominions were still being treated much as we now treat nonhuman animals, Bentham wrote:

> The day *may* come when the rest of the animal creation may acquire those rights which never could have been witholden from them but by the hand of tyranny. The French have already discovered that the blackness of the skin is no reason why a human being should be abandoned without redress to the caprice of a tormentor. It may one day come to be recognised that the number of the legs, the villosity of the skin, or the termination of the *os sacrum*, are reasons equally insufficient for abandoning a sensitive being to the same fate. What else is it that should trace the insuperable line? Is it the faculty of reason, or perhaps the faculty of discourse? But a full-grown horse or dog is beyond comparison a more rational, as well as a more conversable animal, than an infant of a day, or a week, or even a month, old. But suppose they were otherwise, what would it avail? The question is not, Can they reason? nor Can they *talk*? but, *Can they suffer*?[4]

In this passage Bentham points to the capacity for suffering as the vital characteristic that gives a being the right to equal consideration. The capacity for suffering—or more strictly, for suffering and/or enjoyment or happiness—is not just another characteristic like the capacity for language, or for higher mathematics. Bentham is not saying that those who try to mark "the insuperable line" that determines whether the interests of a being should be considered happen to have selected the wrong characteristic. The capacity for suffering and enjoying things is a prerequisite for having interests at all, a condition that must be satisfied before we can speak of interests in any meaningful way. It would be nonsense to say that it was not in the interests of a stone to be kicked along the road by a schoolboy. A stone does not have interests because it cannot suffer. Nothing that we can do to it could possibly make any difference to its welfare. A mouse, on the other hand, does have an interest in not being tormented, because it will suffer if it is.

If a being suffers, there can be no moral justification for refusing to take that suffering into consideration. No matter what the nature of the being, the principle of equality requires that its suffering be counted equally with the like suffering—in so far as rough comparisons can be made—of any other being. If a being is not capable of suffering, or of experiencing enjoyment or happiness, there is nothing to be taken into account. This is why the limit of sentience (using the term as a convenient, if not strictly accurate, shorthand for the capacity to suffer or experience enjoyment or happiness) is the only defensible boundary of concern for the interests of others. To mark this boundary by some characteristic like intelligence or rationality would be to mark it in an arbitrary way. Why not choose some other characteristic, like skin color?

The racist violates the principle of equality by giving greater weight to the interests of members of his own race, when there is a clash between their interests and the interests of those of another race. Similarly the speciesist allows the interests of his own species to override the greater interests of members of other species.[5] The pattern is the same in each case. Most human beings are speciesists. I shall now very briefly describe some of the practices that show this.

For the great majority of human beings, especially in urban, industrialized societies, the most direct form of contact with members of other species is at meal-times: we eat them. In doing so we treat them purely as means to our ends. We regard their life and well-being as subordinate to our taste for a particular kind of dish. I say "taste" deliberately—this is purely a matter of pleasing our palate. There can be no defense of eating flesh in terms of satisfying nutritional needs, since it has been established beyond doubt that we could satisfy our need for protein and other essential nutrients far more efficiently with a diet that replaced animal flesh by soy beans, or products derived from soy beans, and other high-protein vegetable products.[6]

It is not merely the act of killing that indicates what we are ready to do to other species in order to gratify our tastes. The suffering we inflict on the animals while they are alive is perhaps an even clearer indication of our speciesism than the fact that we are prepared to kill them.[7] In order to have meat on the table at a price that people can afford, our society tolerates methods of meat production that confine sentient animals in cramped, unsuitable conditions for the entire durations of their lives. Animals are treated like machines that convert fodder into flesh, and any innovation that results in a higher "conversion ratio" is liable to be adopted. As one authority on the subject has said, "cruelty is acknowledged only when profitability ceases."[8] So hens are crowded four or five to a cage with a floor area of twenty inches by eighteen inches, or around the size of a single page of the *New York Times*. The cages have wire floors, since this reduces cleaning costs, though wire is unsuitable for the hens' feet; the floors slope, since this makes the eggs roll down for easy collection, although this makes it difficult for the hens to rest comfortably. In these conditions all the birds' natural instincts are thwarted: they cannot stretch their wings fully, walk freely, dust-bathe, scratch the ground, or build a nest. Although they have never known other conditions, observers have noticed that the birds vainly try to perform these actions. Frustrated at their inability to do so, they often develop what farmers call "vices," and peck each other to death. To prevent this, the beaks of young birds are often cut off.

This kind of treatment is not limited to poultry. Pigs are now also being reared in cages inside sheds. These animals are comparable to dogs in intelligence, and need a varied, stimulating environment if they are not to suffer from stress and boredom. Anyone who kept a dog in the way in which pigs are frequently kept would be liable to prosecution, in England at least, but because our interest in exploiting pigs is greater than our interest in exploiting dogs, we object to cruelty to dogs while consuming the produce of cruelty to pigs. Of the other animals, the condition of veal calves is perhaps worst of all, since these animals are so closely confined that they cannot even turn around or get up and lie down freely. In this way they do not develop unpalatable muscle. They are also made anaemic and kept short of roughage, to keep their flesh pale, since white veal fetches a higher price; as a result they develop a craving for iron and roughage, and have been observed to gnaw wood off the sides of their stalls, and lick greedily at any rusty hinge that is within reach.

Since, as I have said, none of these practices cater for anything more than our pleasures of taste, our practice of rearing and killing other animals in order to eat them is a clear instance of the sacrifice of the most important interests of other beings in order to satisfy trivial interests of our own. To avoid speciesism we must stop this practice, and each of us has a moral obligation to cease supporting the practice. Our custom is all the support that the meat-industry needs. The decision to cease giving it that support may be difficult, but it is no more difficult than it would have been for a white Southerner to go against the traditions of his society and free his slaves; if we do not change our dietary habits, how can we censure those slaveholders who would not change their own way of living?

The same form of discrimination may be observed in the widespread practice of experimenting on other species in order to see if certain substances are safe for human beings, or to test some psychological theory about the effect of severe punishment on learning, or to try out various new compounds just in case something turns up. People sometimes think that all this experimentation is for vital medical purposes, and so will reduce suffering overall. This comfortable belief is very wide of the mark. Drug companies test new shampoos and cosmetics that they are intending to put on the market by dropping them into the eyes of rabbits, held open by metal clips, in order to observe what damage results. Food additives, like artificial colorings and preservatives, are tested by what is known as the "$LD_{50}$"—a test designed to find the level of consumption at which 50 percent of a group of animals will die. In the process, nearly all of the animals are made very sick before some finally die, and others pull through. If the substance is relatively harmless, as it often is, huge doses have to be force-fed to the animals, until in some cases sheer volume or concentration of the substance causes death.

Much of this pointless cruelty goes on in the universities. In many areas of science, nonhuman animals are regarded as an item of laboratory equipment, to be used and expended as desired. In psychology laboratories experimenters devise endless variations and repetitions of experiments that were of little value in the first place. To quote just one example, from the experimenter's own account in a psychology journal: at the University of Pennsylvania, Perrin S. Cohen hung six dogs in hammocks with electrodes taped to their hind feet. Electric shock of varying intensity was then administered through the electrodes. If the dog learnt to press its head against a panel on the left, the shock was turned off, but otherwise it remained on indefinitely. Three of the dogs, however, were required to wait periods varying from 2 to 7 seconds while being shocked before making the response that turned off the current. If they failed to wait, they received further shocks. Each dog was given from 26 to 46 "sessions" in the hammock, each session consisting of 80 "trials" or shocks, administered at intervals of one minute. The experimenter reported that the dogs, who were unable to move in the hammock, barked or bobbed their heads when the current was applied. The reported findings of the experiment were that there was a delay in the dogs' responses that increased proportionately to the time the dogs were required to endure the shock, but a gradual increase in the intensity of the shock had no systematic effect in the timing of the response. The experiment was funded by the National Institutes of Health, and the United States Public Health Service.[9]

In this example, and countless cases like it, the possible benefits to mankind are either nonexistent or fantastically remote; while the certain losses to members of other species are very real. This is, again, a clear indication of speciesism.

In the past, argument about vivisection has often missed this point, because it has been put in absolutist terms: would the abolitionist be prepared to let thousands die if they could be saved by experimenting on a single animal? The way to reply to this purely hypothetical question is to pose another: would the experimenter be prepared to perform his experiment on an orphaned human infant, if that were the only way to save many lives? (I say "orphan" to avoid the complication of parental feelings, although in doing so I am being overfair to the experimenter, since the nonhuman subjects of experiments are not orphans.) If the experimenter is not prepared to use an orphaned human infant, then his readiness to use nonhumans is simple discrimination, since adult apes, cats, mice and other mammals are more aware of what is happening to them, more self-directing and, so far as we can tell, at least as sensitive to pain, as any human infant. There seems to be no relevant characteristic that human infants possess that adult mammals do not have to the same or higher degree. (Someone might try to argue that what makes it wrong to experiment on a human infant is that the infant will, in time and if left alone, develop into more than the nonhuman, but one would then, to be consistent, have to oppose abortion, since the fetus has the same potential as the infant— indeed, even contraception and abstinence might be wrong on this ground, since the egg and sperm, considered jointly, also have the same potential. In any case, this argument still gives us no reason for selecting a non-human, rather than a human with severe and irreversible brain damage, as the subject for our experiments.)

The experimenter, then, shows a bias in favor of his own species whenever he carries out an experiment on a nonhuman for a purpose that he would not think justified him in using a human being at an equal or lower level of sentience, awareness, ability to be self-directing, etc. No one familiar with the kind of results yielded by most experiments on animals can have the slightest doubt that if this bias were eliminated the number of experiments performed would be a minute fraction of the number performed today.

Experimenting on animals, and eating their flesh, are perhaps the two major forms of speciesism in our society. By comparison, the third and last form of speciesism is so minor as to be insignificant, but it is perhaps of some special interest to those for whom this paper was written. I am referring to speciesism in contemporary philosophy.

Philosophy ought to question the basic assumptions of the age. Thinking through, critically and carefully, what most people take for granted is, I believe, the chief task of philosophy, and it is this task that makes philosophy a worthwhile activity. Regrettably, philosophy does not always live up to its historic role. Philosophers are human beings and they are subject to all the preconceptions of the society to which they belong. Sometimes they succeed in breaking free of the prevailing ideology: more often they become its most sophisticated defenders. So, in this case, philosophy as practiced in the universities today does not challenge anyone's preconceptions about our relations with other species. By their writings, those philosophers who tackle problems that touch upon the issue reveal that they make the same unquestioned assumptions as most other humans, and what they say tends to confirm the reader in his or her comfortable speciesist habits.

I could illustrate this claim by referring to the writings of philosophers in various fields—for instance, the attempts that have been made by those interested in rights to draw the boundary of the sphere of rights so that it runs parallel to the biological boundaries of the species *homo sapiens*, including infants and even mental defectives, but excluding those other beings of equal or greater capacity who are so useful to us at mealtimes and in our laboratories. I think it would be a more appropriate conclusion to this paper, however, if I concentrated on the problem with which we have been centrally concerned, the problem of equality.

It is significant that the problem of equality, in moral and political philosophy, is invariably formulated in terms of human equality. The effect of this is that the question of the equality of other animals does not confront the philosopher, or student, as an issue in itself—and this is already an indication of the failure of philosophy to challenge accepted beliefs. Still, philosophers have found it difficult to discuss the issue of human equality without raising, in a paragraph or two, the question of the status of other animals. The reason for this, which should be apparent from what I have said already, is that if humans are to be regarded as equal to one another, we need some sense of "equal" that does not require any actual, descriptive equality of capacities, talents or other qualities. If equality is to be related to any actual characteristics of humans, these characteristics must be some lowest common denominator, pitched so low that no human lacks them—but then the philosopher comes up against the catch that any such set of characteristics which covers *all* humans will not be possessed *only by humans*. In other words, it turns out that in the only sense in which we can truly say, as an assertion of fact, that all humans are equal, at least some members of other species are also equal—equal, that is, to each other and to humans. If, on the other hand, we regard the statement "All humans are equal" in some non-factual way, perhaps as a prescription, then, as I have already argued, it is even more difficult to exclude non-humans from the sphere of equality.

This result is not what the egalitarian philosopher originally intended to assert. Instead of accepting the radical outcome to which their own reasonings naturally point, however, most philosophers try to reconcile their beliefs in human equality and animal inequality by arguments that can only be described as devious.

As a first example, I take William Frankena's well-known article "The Concept of Social Justice."[10] Frankena opposes the idea of basing justice on merit, because he sees that this could lead to highly inegalitarian results. Instead he proposes the principle that:

> . . . all men are to be treated as equals, not because they are equal, in any respect but simply because they are human. They are human because they have emotions and desires, and are able to think, and hence are capable of enjoying a good life in a sense in which other animals are not.

But what is this capacity to enjoy the good life which all humans have, but no other animals? Other animals have emotions and desires, and appear to be capable of enjoying a good life. We may doubt that they can think—although the behavior of some apes, dolphins and even dogs suggest that some of them can—but what is the relevance of thinking? Frankena goes on to admit that by "the good life" he means "not so much the morally good life as the happy or satisfactory life," so thought would appear to be unnecessary for enjoying the good life; in fact to emphasise the need for thought would make difficulties for the egalitarian since only some people are capable of leading intellectually satisfying lives, or morally good lives. This makes it difficult to see what Frankena's principle of equality has to do with simply being *human*. Surely every sentient being is capable of leading a life that is happier or less miserable than some alternative life, and hence has a claim to be taken into account. In this respect the distinction between humans and nonhumans is not a sharp division, but rather a continuum along which we move gradually, and with overlaps between the species, from simple capacities for enjoyment and satisfaction, or pain and suffering, to more complex ones.

Faced with a situation in which they see a need for some basis for the moral gulf that is commonly thought to separate humans and animals, but can find no concrete difference that will do the job without undermining the equality of humans, philosophers tend to waffle. They resort to high-sounding phrases like "the intrinsic dignity of the human individual."[11] They talk of the "intrinsic worth of all men" as if men (humans?) had some worth that other beings did not,[12] or they say that humans, and only humans, are "ends in themselves" while "everything other than a person can only have value for a person."[13]

This idea of a distinctive human dignity and worth has a long history; it can be traced back directly to the Renaissance humanists, for instance to Pico della Mirandola's *Oration on the Dignity of Man*. Pico and other humanists based their estimate of human dignity on the idea that man possessed the central, pivotal position in the "Great Chain of Being" that led from the lowliest forms of matter to God himself; this view of the universe, in turn, goes back to both classical and Judeo-Christian doctrines. Contemporary philosophers have cast off these metaphysical and religious shackles and freely invoke the dignity of mankind without needing to justify the idea at all. Why should we not attribute "intrinsic dignity" or "intrinsic worth" to ourselves? Fellow-humans are unlikely to reject the accolades we so generously bestow on them, and those to whom we deny the honor are unable to object. Indeed, when one thinks only of humans, it can be very liberal, very progressive, to talk of the dignity of all human beings. In so doing, we implicitly condemn slavery, racism, and other violations of human rights. We admit that we ourselves are in some fundamental sense on a par with the poorest, most ignorant members of our own species. It is only when we think of humans as no more than a small subgroup of all the beings that inhabit our planet that we may realize that in elevating our own species we are at the same time lowering the relative status of all other species.

The truth is that the appeal to the intrinsic dignity of human beings appears to solve the egalitarian's problems only as long as it goes unchallenged. Once we ask *why* it should be that all humans—including infants, mental defectives, psychopaths, Hitler, Stalin, and the rest—have some kind of dignity or worth that no elephant, pig, or chimpanzee can ever achieve, we see that this question is as difficult to answer as our original request for some relevant fact that justifies the inequality of humans and other animals. In fact, these two questions are really one: talk of intrinsic dignity or moral worth only takes the problem back one step, because any satisfactory defence of the claim that all and only humans have intrinsic dignity would need to refer to some relevant capacities or characteristics that all and only humans possess. Philosophers frequently introduce ideas of dignity, respect and worth at the point at which other reasons appear to be lacking, but this is hardly good enough. Fine phrases are the last resource of those who have run out of arguments.

In case there are those who still think it may be possible to find some relevant characteristic that distinguishes all humans from all members of other species, I shall refer again, before I conclude, to the existence of some humans who quite clearly are below the level of awareness, self-consciousness, intelligence, and sentience, of many nonhumans. I am thinking of humans with severe and irreparable brain damage, and also of infant humans. To avoid the complication of the relevance of a being's potential, however, I shall henceforth concentrate on permanently retarded humans.

Philosophers who set out to find a characteristic that will distinguish humans from other animals rarely take the course of abandoning these groups of humans by lumping them in with the other animals. It is easy to see why they do not. To take this line without rethinking our attitudes to other animals would entail that we have the right to perform painful experiments on retarded humans for trivial reasons; similarly it would follow that we had the right to rear and kill these humans for food. To most philosophers these consequences are as unacceptable as the view that we should stop treating nonhumans in this way.

Of course, when discussing the problem of equality it is possible to ignore the problem of mental defectives, or brush it aside as if somehow insignificant.[14] This is the easiest way out. What else remains? My final example of speciesism in contemporary philosophy has been selected to show what happens when a writer is prepared to face the question of human equality and animal inequality without ignoring the existence of mental defectives, and without resorting to obscurantist mumbo jumbo. Stanley Benn's clear and honest article "Egalitarianism and Equal Consideration of Interests"[15] fits this description.

Benn, after noting the usual "evident human inequalities" argues, correctly I think, for equality of consideration as the only possible basis for egalitarianism. Yet Benn, like other writers, is thinking only of "equal consideration of human interests." Benn is quite open in his defence of this restriction of equal consideration:

> . . . not to possess human shape *is* a disqualifying condition. However faithful or intelligent a dog may be, it would be a monstrous sentimentality to attribute to him interests that could be weighed in an equal balance with those of human

beings . . . if, for instance, one had to decide between feeding a hungry baby or a hungry dog, anyone who chose the dog would generally be reckoned morally defective, unable to recognize a fundamental inequality of claims.

This is what distinguishes our attitude to animals from our attitude to imbeciles. It would be odd to say that we ought to respect equally the dignity or personality of the imbecile and of the rational man . . . but there is nothing odd about saying that we should respect their interests equally, that is, that we should give to the interests of each the same serious consideration as claims to considerations necessary for some standard of well-being that we can recognize and endorse.

Benn's statement of the basis of the consideration we should have for imbeciles seems to me correct, but why should there be any fundamental inequality of claims between a dog and a human imbecile? Benn sees that if equal consideration depended on rationality, no reason could be given against using imbeciles for research purposes, as we now use dogs and guinea pigs. This will not do: "But of course we do distinguish imbeciles from animals in this regard," he says. That the common distinction is justifiable is something Benn does not question; his problem is how it is to be justified. The answer he gives is this:

. . . we respect the interests of men and give them priority over dogs not *insofar* as they are rational, but because rationality is the human norm. We say it is *unfair* to exploit the deficiencies of the imbecile who falls short of the norm, just as it would be unfair, and not just ordinarily dishonest, to steal from a blind man. If we do not think in this way about dogs, it is because we do not see the irrationality of the dog as a deficiency or a handicap, but as normal for the species. The characteristics, therefore, that distinguish the normal man from the normal dog make it intelligible for us to talk of other men having interests and capacities, and therefore claims, of precisely the same kind as we make on our own behalf. But although these characteristics may provide the point of the distinction between men and other species, they are not in fact the qualifying conditions for membership, or the distinguishing criteria of the class of morally considerable persons; and this is precisely because a man does not become a member of a different species, with its own standards of normality, by reason of not possessing these characteristics.

The final sentence of this passage gives the argument away. An imbecile, Benn concedes, may have no characteristics superior to those of a dog; nevertheless this does not make the imbecile a member of "a different species" as the dog is. *Therefore* it would be "unfair" to use the imbecile for medical research as we use the dog. But why? That the imbecile is not rational is just the way things have worked out, and the same is true of the dog—neither is any more responsible for their mental level. If it is unfair to take advantage of an isolated defect, why is it fair to take advantage of a more general limitation? I find it hard to see anything in this argument except a defence of preferring the interests of members of our own species because they are members of our own species. To those who think there might be more to it, I suggest the following mental exercise.

Assume that it has been proven that there is a difference in the average, or normal, intelligence quotient for two different races, say whites and blacks. Then substitute the term "white" for every occurrence of "men" and "black" for every occurrence of "dog" in the passage quoted; and substitute "high I.Q." for "rationality" and when Benn talks of "imbeciles" replace this term by "dumb whites"—that is, whites who fall well below the normal white I.Q. score. Finally, change "species" to "race." Now re-read the passage. It has become a defence of a rigid, no-exceptions division between whites and blacks, based on I.Q. scores, *not withstanding an admitted overlap* between whites and blacks in this respect. The revised passage is, of course, outrageous, and this is not only because we have made fictitious assumptions in our substitutions. The point is that in the original passage Benn was defending a rigid division in the amount of consideration due to members of different species, despite admitted cases of overlap. If the original did not, at first reading, strike us as being as outrageous as the revised version does, this is largely because although we are not racists ourselves, most of us are speciesists. Like the other articles, Benn's stands as a warning of the ease with which the best minds can fall victim to a prevailing ideology.

## NOTES

1. Passages of this article appeared in a review of *Animals, Men and Morals*, edited by S. and R. Godlovitch and J. Harris (Gollancz and Taplinger, London 1972) in *The New York Review of Books*, April 5, 1973. The whole direction of my thinking on this subject I owe to talks with a number of friends in Oxford in 1970–71, especially Richard Keshen, Stanley Godlovitch, and, above all, Roslind Godlovitch.
2. *The Methods of Ethics* (7th Ed.) p. 382.
3. For example, R. M. Hare, *Freedom and Reason* (Oxford, 1963) and J. Rawls, *A Theory of Justice* (Harvard, 1972); for a brief account of the essential agreement on this issue between these and other positions, see R. M. Hare, "Rules of War and Moral Reasoning," *Philosophy and Public Affairs*, vol. 1, no. 2 (1972).
4. *Introduction to the Principles of Morals and Legislation*, ch. XVII.
5. I owe the term "speciesism" to Dr. Richard Ryder.
6. In order to produce 1 lb. of protein in the form of beef or veal, we must feed 21 lbs. of protein to the animal. Other forms of livestock are slightly less inefficient, but the average ratio in the U.S. is still 1:8. It has been estimated that the amount of protein lost to humans in this way is equivalent to 90 percent of the annual world protein deficit. For a brief account, see Frances Moore Lappe, *Diet for a Small Planet* (Friends of The Earth/Ballantine, New York 1971), pp. 4–11.
7. Although one might think that killing a being is obviously the ultimate wrong one can do to it, I think that the infliction of suffering is a clearer indication of speciesism because it might be argued that at least part of what is wrong with killing a human is that most humans are conscious of their existence over time, and have desires and purposes that extend into the future—see, for instance, M. Tooley, "Abortion and Infanticide," *Philosophy and Public Affairs*, vol. 2, no. 1 (1972). Of course, if one took this view one would have to hold—as Tooley does—that killing a human infant or mental defective is not in itself wrong, and is less serious than killing certain higher mammals that probably do have a sense of their own existence over time.
8. Ruth Harrison, *Animal Machines* (Stuart, London, 1964). This book provides an eye-opening account of intensive farming methods for those unfamiliar with the subject.

9. *Journal of the Experimental Analysis of Behavior*, vol. 13, no. 1 (1970). Any recent volume of this journal, or of other journals in the field, like the *Journal of Comparative and Physiological Psychology*, will contain reports of equally cruel and trivial experiments. For a fuller account, see Richard Ryder, "Experiments on Animals" in *Animals, Men and Morals*.

10. In R. Brandt (ed.) *Social Justice* (Prentice Hall, Englewood Cliffs, 1962); the passage quoted appears on p. 19.

11. Frankena, *op. cit.* p. 23.

12. H. A. Bedau, "Egalitarianism and the Idea of Equality" in *Nomos IX: Equality*, ed. J. R. Pennock and J. W. Chapman, New York 1967.

13. G. Vlastos, "Justice and Equality" in Brandt, *Social Justice*, p. 48.

14. E. G. Bernard Williams, "The Idea of Equality," in *Philosophy, Politics and Society* (second series) ed. P. Laslett and W. Runciman (Blackwell, Oxford, 1962), p. 118; J. Rawls, *A Theory of Justice*, pp. 509–10.

15. *Nomos IX: Equality*; the passages quoted are on pp. 62ff.

# ANIMAL RIGHTS, HUMAN WRONGS

*Tom Regan*

Tom Regan is professor of philosophy and university alumni distinguished professor at North Carolina State University. He is the author of *The Case for Animal Rights,* and with Peter Singer, he edited *Animal Rights and Human Obligations.*

## THE KANTIAN ACCOUNT

It is a commonplace to say that morality places some limits on how animals may be treated. We are not to kick dogs, set fire to cats' tails, torment hamsters or parakeets. Philosophically, the issue is not so much *whether* but *why* these acts are wrong.

An answer favored by many philosophers, including Thomas Aquinas and Immanuel Kant, is that people who treat animals in these ways develop a habit which, in time, inclines them to treat humans similarly.[1] People who torment animals will, or are likely to, torment people. It is this spillover effect that makes mistreating animals wrong. We are not concerned directly with the ill-treatment that the animals themselves receive. Rather, our concern is that this bodes ill for humankind. So, on this Kantian account, the moral principle runs something like this: don't treat animals in ways that will lead you to mistreat human beings.

One need have no quarrel with this principle itself. The real quarrel lies with the grounds on which this principle is allegedly based. Peter Singer argues that there is a close parallel between this view and those of the racist and sexist, a view which, following Richard Ryder, he denominates speciesism.[2] The racist believes that the interests of others matter only if they happen to be members of his own race. The speciesist believes that the interests of others matter only if they happen to be members of his own species. Racism has been unmasked for the prejudice that it is. The color of one's skin cannot be used to

This essay originally appeared in *Environmental Ethics*, Vol. 2, No. 2 (Summer 1980), 99–120. Reprinted with permission.

determine the relevance of an individual's interests. Singer and Ryder both argue that neither can the number of one's legs, whether one walks upright or on all fours, lives in the trees, the sea or the suburbs. Here they recall Bentham.[3] There is, they argue forcefully, no rational, unprejudiced way to exclude the interests of nonhuman animals just because they are not the interests of human beings. Because the Kantian account would have us think otherwise, we are right to reject it.

## THE CRUELTY ACCOUNT

A second view about constraints on how animals may be treated involves the idea of cruelty. The reason we are not to kick dogs is that we are not to be cruel to animals and kicking dogs is cruel. It is the prohibition against cruelty which covers and conveniently sums up our negative duties to animals, duties concerning how animals are *not* to be treated.

The prohibition against cruelty can be given a distinctively Kantian twist. This happens when the grounds given are that cruelty to animals leads people to be cruel to other people. John Locke suggests, but does not clearly endorse, this view:

> One thing I have frequently observed in Children, that when they have got possession of any poor Creature, they are apt to use it ill: They often *torment*, and treat very roughly, young Birds, Butterflies, and such other poor Animals, which fall into their Hands, and that with a seeming kind of Pleasure. This I think should be watched in them, and if they incline to any such *Cruelty*, they should be taught the contrary Usage, For the Custom of Tormenting and Killing of Beasts, will, by Degrees, harden their Minds even towards Men; and they who delight in the Suffering and Destruction of Inferior Creatures, will not be apt to be very compassionate, or benign to those of their own kind.[4]

Locke's position suggests the speciesism which characterizes the Kantian account and will not do for the same reasons. However, Locke's understanding of what cruelty is—tormenting a sentient creature or causing it to suffer, "with a seeming kind of Pleasure"—seems correct and has important implications. Many thinkers, including many persons active in the humane movement, champion the prohibition against cruelty to animals because it is wrong to be cruel to the animals themselves. This way of grounding the prohibition against cruelty, which I call "the cruelty account," deserves our critical attention.

It is difficult to overestimate the importance the idea of preventing cruelty has played, and continues to play, in the movement to secure better treatment for animals. Entire societies are devoted to this cause, the Society for the Prevention of Cruelty to Animals (SPCA) in the United States and the Royal Society for the Prevention of Cruelty to Animals (RSPCA) in Great Britain being perhaps the best known examples. I do not wish to deny the importance of preventing cruelty nor to deprecate the crusading work done by these organizations, but I must conclude that to stake so much on the prevention of cruelty both clouds the fundamental moral issues and runs a serious risk of being counterproductive.

*Cruel* is a term of moral appraisal used to refer either to the character of a person or to an individual action. Persons are cruel who are inclined to delight in or, in Locke's phrase, to take "a seeming kind of Pleasure" in causing pain. An individual action is cruel if one takes pleasure in making another suffer. It is clear that someone's being cruel is distinct from someone's causing pain. Surgeons cause pain. Dentists cause pain. Wrestlers, boxers, football players cause pain. But it does not follow that they are cruel people or that their individual actions are cruel. To establish cruelty we need to know more than that someone caused pain; we also need to know the state of mind of the agent, whether he/she took "a seeming kind of Pleasure" in the pain inflicted. It is faulty to reason in this way:

> Those who cause pain are cruel. Surgeons (football players, etc.) cause pain. Therefore, surgeons (football players, etc.) are cruel.

But just as clearly, it is faulty to reason in the following way:

> Those who cause pain are cruel. Those who experiment on animals (or kill whales, or raise veal calves in isolation, etc.) cause pain. Therefore those who treat animals in these ways are cruel.

Those who are inclined to march under the banner of anti-cruelty must soon recognize the speciousness of this line of reasoning, if their thought, however well intentioned, is not to cloud the issues.

Once cruelty is understood in the way Locke saw that it should be, we can understand why more is needed. Take the case of the use of animals in the Draize test. Increasingly people want to object morally to this, to say it is wrong. However, if this required establishing cruelty, the weight of the evidence would be on the side of the experimenters and against the objectors, for there is no adequate evidence for believing that people who administer the Draize test are cruel people or that they are cruel when they administer this test. Do they take "a seeming kind of Pleasure" in causing the animals pain? That they cause *pain* to the animals is certain. But causing pain does not establish cruelty. Except for a few sadists in the scientific community, there is good reason to believe that researchers are no more cruel than are most persons.

Does this mean that using animals in the Draize test is right? Precisely not. Rather, to ask whether this is right is logically distinct from, and should not be confused with, asking whether someone is cruel. Cruelty has to do with a person's state of mind. The moral rightness or wrongness of a person's actions is different. Persons can do what is right or wrong whatever their state of mind. Researchers using the Draize test can be doing what is wrong, whether or not they enjoy causing animals to suffer. If they do enjoy this, we shall certainly think less of them as persons. But even if they enjoy the pain it will not follow that the pain is unjustified, any more than it will follow that the pain is justified if they feel sorry for the animals or feel nothing all. The more we are able to keep in view how the morality of what a person does is distinct from his/her state of mind, distinct from the presence or absence of taking pleasure in pain, the better the chances will be for significant dialogue between vivisectors and anti-vivisectionists.

To charge vivisectors with cruelty *can* only serve to call forth all their defenses, because the charge will be taken as a denunciation of *what they are* (evil people) rather than of *what they do*. It will also give them an easy way out. After all, *they* are in privileged position to know their own mental states; *they* can take a sober moment and see whether in fact they do take a "seeming kind of Pleasure" in causing pain. If, as will usually be the case, they find that they honestly do not, then they can reply that they are not cruel (evil) people. So we see now where the well-intentioned efforts of those defending animals can be and often are counterproductive. If it's cruelty they are charged with, and they are not cruel, then they can come away with a feeling that their hands are clean. They win, and the litany of accusations about cruelty is so much water off their backs. It is no good trying to improve the lot of animals by trying to convince persons who are not cruel that they are.

Some will complain that my argument is "too picky." They might say that cruelty has been interpreted too narrowly: what is meant is treating animals badly in ways they don't deserve, harming or wronging them. In practice this is what anti-cruelty charges often come to. But then this is the way the charges should be made, lest they be misunderstood or be counterproductive. To ask for more care in the charges leveled is not to strain at gnats. It is to begin to make the charges more difficult to answer. Perhaps a name like "The Society for the Prevention of Maltreatment of Animals" is not as euphonious as "The Anti-Cruelty Society," but a lack of euphony is a price those laboring for animal welfare should gladly pay.

## THE UTILITARIAN ACCOUNT

Utilitarians give a different account of the constraints regarding how animals ought to be treated. The utilitarian account, or one version of it, involves two principles.[5] The first is a principle of equality. This principle declares that the desires, needs, hopes, etc. of different individuals, when these are of equal importance *to* these individuals, *are* of equal importance or value no matter who the individuals are, prince or pauper, genius or moron, white or black, male or female, *human or animal*. This equality of interests principle seems to provide a philosophical basis for avoiding the grossest forms of prejudice, including racism, sexism and, following Ryder and Singer, speciesism. Whether it succeeds is an issue which we shall take up below.

The second principle is that of utility itself. Roughly speaking, according to this principle, we are to act so as to bring about the greatest possible balance of good over evil, for example, the greatest possible balance of satisfaction over dissatisfaction, taking the interests of everyone affected into account *and* counting equal interests equally. Now, since animals have interests, *their* interests must be taken into account, and because their interests are frequently as important to them as comparable interests are to human beings, *their* interests must be given the same weight as comparable human interests. It is because kicking dogs and setting fire to cats' tails run counter to the principles of equality and utility that, on this utilitarian account, they are wrong.

Granted, this is a very rough sketch; nonetheless, it enables us to understand the main features of the utilitarian account, and also to find points of resemblance and contrast between it and the other accounts so far described. Like the Kantian account, but unlike the cruelty account, the utilitarian account emphasizes results or consequences, but unlike the Kantian account, and resembling the cruelty account, the utilitarian account recognizes the moral status of animals in their own right. We are not to measure morality by the speciesist yardstick of human interest alone. Finally, unlike the cruelty account, but in concert with the Kantian, the utilitarian does not conflate the morality of an act with the mental state of the agent. The utilitarian can be as opposed to cruelty as anyone else, but within the utilitarian theory right and wrong are determined by consequences, not feelings and intentions: the ordinary moral constraints placed on how we may treat animals are accounted for because they are necessary if we are not to violate the equality of interests principle *or* if we are to succeed in bringing about the greatest possible balance of good over bad.

The utilitarian account has much to recommend it. How far can it take us in challenging the way in which animals are routinely treated, for example, as subjects in scientific research? Peter Singer, a utilitarian whose work has well deserved influence, holds that utilitarianism leads to far-reaching consequences here. Singer argues that we become vegetarians *and* that we oppose much (even if not quite all) research involving animal subjects. Singer's main argument is that the intensive rearing of animals as well as their routine use in experimentation violates the equality of interests principle. The animals involved, we have reason to believe, have an interest in not being made to suffer, and this interest, we have further reason to believe, is as important to them as is the comparable interest in the case of human beings. This being so, Singer contends, it is wrong to do to animals what we would not do to humans. It cannot be right to raise animals intensively or use them in research if we would morally oppose doing these things to human beings. We do condemn cannibalism and the coerced use of humans in research and we must, Singer argues, morally condemn the comparable treatment of animals. We have a moral obligation to become vegetarians and oppose much, if not quite all, vivisection.

As clear and powerful as this argument is, I do not believe that Singer succeeds in making a fully convincing case. He shows that animals are treated differently than human beings, but not that this differential treatment violates either the equality of interests principle or the principle of utility. Consider the equality of interests principle first. We can count equal interests equally, no matter whose interests they are, and still treat individuals quite differently. For example, I might correctly regard my son's and my neighbor's son's interests in receiving a medical education as being equal and yet help only my son. I treat them differently but I do *not* necessarily count their equal interests differently, and neither do I thereby do anything that is in any obvious sense morally reprehensible. I have duties to my son which I do not have to the children of others.

The general point is this: the differential treatment of individuals with equal interests does not by itself violate the equality of interests principle. Singer has to give an *argument* which shows *more* than that they are treated differently. What argument does he give and how adequate is it? Singer proceeds by asking whether we would do to humans what we allow to be done to animals.[6] For example, would a researcher use an orphaned, profoundly retarded human baby in the sort of painful experiment in which he is willing to use a more intellectually and emotionally developed animal? If the researcher says no, Singer charges him with speciesism, with violating the equality of interests principle. The animal's interest in avoiding pain is just as important to it as is the infant's interest to him/her.

This argument begs the question. It assumes that by treating the involved individuals differently, we count their equal interests differently. As I have explained, however, this is not always true. Whether it is true in any particular case, therefore, is something which must be established, not simply assumed on the basis of differential treatment. Singer, I believe, assumes just this, and thus begs the question.

Singer's argument has a further deficiency, which involves the principle of utility. First, Singer does not show that the differential treatment of animals runs counter to the utilitarian objective of bringing about the greatest possible balance of good over evil. To show this Singer would have to give an elaborate, detailed description, not only of how animals are treated, a part of the task which he does complete with great skill, but an analysis of what, all considered, are the consequences for everyone involved. He would have to inquire how the world's economy depends on present levels of productivity in the animal industry, how many people's lives are directly and indirectly involved with the maintenance or growth of this industry, etc. Even more, he would have to show in detail what would probably be the consequences of a collapse or slowdown of the animal industry's productivity.

Secondly, Singer needs to make a compelling case for the view that *not* raising animals intensively or *not* using them routinely in research leads to better consequences, all considered, than those which now result from treating animals in these ways. Singer is required to show that better consequences *would* result, or at least that it is *very probable* that they would. Showing that it is possible or conceivable that they might is insufficient. It comes as a disappointment, therefore, that we do not find anything approaching this kind of required empirical data. What we find, instead, are passages where he bemoans (rightly, I believe) the fact that animals are fed protein-rich grains which could be fed to malnourished human beings.[7] The point, however, is not whether these grains *could* be fed to the malnourished; it is whether we have solid empirical grounds for believing that they *would* be made available to and eaten by these people, if they were not fed to animals, *and* that the consequences resulting from this shift would be better, all considered. I hope I am not unfair to Singer in observing that these calculations are missing, not only here, but, to my knowledge, throughout the body of his published writings.

This, then, is the first thing to note regarding Singer and the principle of utility: *he fails to show, with reference to this principle, that it is wrong* to treat animals as they are now being treated in modern farming and scientific research. The second thing to note is that, for all we know and so long as we rely on the principle of utility, the present treatment of animals might actually be justified. The grounds for thinking so are as follows.

On the face of it, utilitarianism seems to be the fairest, least prejudicial view available. Everyone's interests count, and no one's counts for more or less than the equal interests of anyone else. The trouble is, as we have seen, that there is no necessary connection, no preestablished harmony between respect for the equality of interests principle *and* promoting the utilitarian objective of maximizing the balance of good over bad. On the contrary, the principle of utility might be used to justify the most radical kinds of differential treatment between individuals or groups of individuals, and thus it might justify forms of racism and sexism, for these prejudices can take different forms and find expression in different ways. One form consists in not even taking the interests of a given race or sex into account at all; another takes these interests into account but does not count them equally with those of the equal interests of the favored group. Another does take their interests into account equally, but adopts laws and policies, engages in practices and customs which give greater opportunities to the members of the favored group, because doing so promotes the greatest balance of good over evil, all considered.

Thus, forms of racism or sexism, which seem to be eliminated by the utilitarian principle of equality of interests, could well be resurrected and justified by the principle of utility. If a utilitarian here replies that denying certain humans an equal opportunity to satisfy or promote their equal interests on racial or sexual grounds must violate the equality of interests principle and so, on his position, is wrong, we must remind him that differential treatment is not the same as, and does not entail, violating the equality of interests principle. It is quite possible, for example, to count the equal interests of blacks and whites the same (and thus to honor the equality principle) and still discriminate between races when it comes to what members of each race are permitted to do to pursue those interests, on the grounds that such discrimination promotes the utilitarian objective. So, utilitarianism, despite initial appearances, does not provide us with solid grounds on which to exclude all forms of racism or sexism.

Similarly with speciesism. The same kind of argument can show a possible utilitarian justification of an analogous speciesism. We count the equal interests of animals and humans equally; it just so happens that the consequences of treating animals in ways that humans are not treated, such as intensively raising animals, but not humans, are better, all considered, than are other arrangements. Thus, utilitarianism might provide a basis for speciesist practices. Whether it *actually* does depends on whether the consequences are better, all considered, if animals continue to be treated as they are. Since Singer fails to provide us with empirical data showing that the consequences would be better if we changed, it follows that, for all we know, the present speciesist way of treating animals might actually be justified, given his version of utilitarianism.

## ANIMAL RIGHTS

Our results to this point are mainly negative. I have thus far argued (1) that the moral principles we seek cannot refer to the agent's state of mind, to whether the agent takes a "seeming kind of Pleasure" in causing animal suffering. (2) These principles cannot refer only to consequences that harm or benefit human beings, since this prejudicially leaves out of account the harms and benefits to the animals themselves. (3) These principles cannot refer only to the utilitarian objective of maximizing the balance of good over evil, even if animal harms and benefits are taken into account. What is wanted, then, is an account which avoids each of these shortcomings. This account is to be found, I believe, by postulating the existence of animal rights. Indeed, I believe that only if we postulate human rights can we provide a theory which adequately guards humans against the abuses which utilitarianism might permit.

Various analyses of the concept of a right have been proposed. We will bypass the nooks and crannies of these competing analyses so as to focus attention on the role that moral rights play in our thinking about the status of the individual, relative to the interests of the group. Here the truth seems to lie where Ronald Dworkin sees it: the rights of the individual trump the goals of the group.[8]

What does this mean? It means that the moral rights of the individual place a justifiable limit on what the group can do to the individual. Suppose a group of people stand to gain enjoyment by arranging for others to be harmed. Imagine, for example, the Romans enjoying how the Christians go up against lions. Such a group does wrong because they allow their interests to override the individual's moral rights. This does not mean that there are no circumstances in which an individual's rights must give way to the collective interest. Imagine that Bert has inadvertently swallowed the microfilmed code which we must have in order to prevent a massive nuclear explosion in New Zealand. Bert sits safely in Tucson, Arizona. We explain the situation but Bert refuses to consent to our request that we operate, retrieve the code, and prevent the explosion. He cites his right to determine what is to be done to his body. In such a case it is not implausible to say that Bert's right must give way to the collective interests of others.

Individual rights then normally, but not always, trump collective interests. To give a precise statement of the conditions which determine which ought to prevail is very difficult indeed, but the following conditions, which deal only with the right not to be harmed, at least seem to incorporate necessary conditions for overriding this right.[9]

An individual's right not to be harmed can justifiably be overridden only if—

  **a.** we have very good reason to believe that overriding the individual's right by itself will prevent, and is the only realistic way to prevent, vastly greater harm to other innocent individuals; or
  **b.** we have very good reason to believe that allowing the individual to be harmed is a necessary link in a chain of events which collectively will prevent vastly greater harm to innocent individuals, *and* we have very good reason to believe that this chain of events is the only realistic way to prevent this vastly greater harm; or
  **c.** we have very good reason to believe that it is only if we override the individual's right that we can have a reasonable hope of preventing vastly greater harm to other innocent individuals.

There is much that is vague in these conditions, e.g., "vastly greater harm," "innocent individuals," "reasonable hope." At present, however, we will have to make do with them as they stand. Even so we can see that these conditions attempt to do justice to the complexity of conflicts of interest. In particular, they attempt to explain how, in a principled way, we might justify overriding an individual's right not to be harmed even though *just* doing this will not guarantee the prevention of vastly greater harm. Condition (b) brings this out—harming an individual is only one part of a more complex series of events which we have very good reason to believe will prevent vastly greater harm, or because—as (c) brings out—we simply do not know how things will turn out, but do have very good reason to believe that we have no reasonable hope of preventing some catastrophe unless we allow an individual to be harmed. Possibly some will find these conditions too liberal. Condition (c) in particular might seem too lenient. Even (b) might go too far. I am not certain what to say here and beg to leave this issue unresolved, except to say that the case for not harming animals is proportionately greater the more one is inclined to restrict the above set just to condition (a). For reasons that will become clearer, however, even the more liberal view, that harm can not be justified unless one of the three conditions is met, is sufficient to make a strong case against our routine abuse of animals.

These conditions share an extremely important feature. Each specifies what we must know or have good reason to believe if we are justified in overriding an individual's right not to be harmed. Each requires anyone who would harm an individual to show that this does not involve violating the individual's right. Part of the importance of the question, whether animals have rights, specifically, the right not to be harmed, now comes into clear focus. *If* they have this right, then it will be violated whenever animals are harmed and condition (a), (b), or (c) is not satisfied. Moreover, the onus of justification is always on those who harm animals to explain how they are not violating the right of animals not to be harmed, if animals have this right. So, the question continues to press itself upon us. Do animals have the right not to be harmed?

This is not an easy question to answer. One is reminded of Bentham's observation that the idea of moral rights is "nonsense on stilts." Bentham meant this in the case of *human* moral rights. One can only speculate regarding what he might have thought concerning the moral rights of *animals*! So, how is one to procede? The circuitous path we must cautiously travel, I think, is in broad outline as follows.[10]

We begin by asking about our reasons for thinking that human beings have the moral right not to be harmed; then we go on to ask whether, given these reasons, a case can be made for saying that animals have this right as well. Let us go back to the idea that individual human beings have this right and that, except in extreme cases, this right trumps collective interest. Why? What is there about being a human being to which we can point and say, "*That's* why you must not harm the individual even if the group benefits"?

The heart of the answer lies, I believe, in thinking that human beings have a certain kind of value, inherent value. By this I mean that each human being has value logically independently of whether he/she is valued by anyone else (or, what perhaps comes to the same thing, whether he/she is the object of anyone else's interest).[11] The view that human beings have inherent value implies that the kind of value properly attributable to them is not exclusively instrumental. Humans have value not just because, and not just so long as, they are good for something. They have value distinct from their utility and skill.

If this is true, we can explain, in general terms reminiscent of Kant, what is involved in mistreating human beings. Humans are mistreated if they are treated as valuable only if they forward the interests of other beings. To treat a human being thus is to show a lack of proper respect for the sort of value humans have. In Kant's terms, what has value in itself must always be treated as an end, never merely as a means. However, this is precisely what we are doing if we harm an individual so that others might gain pleasure or profit; we are treating the individual merely as a means, as valuable only to the extent he/she contributes to the collective interest.

Now, *if* we accept the postulate that human beings have inherent value, we can press on and ask how rights enter the picture. They enter in being grounded in inherent value. In other words, it is individuals who have inherent value who have moral rights, and it is *because* they have value of this kind that they have a moral right not to be treated in ways that deny their having this kind of value. Rather than rights being connected with the *value of consequences* which affect individuals for good or ill, rather than rights being justified by the utility of recognizing them, rights are based on *the value of individuals*. In the case of the right not to be harmed, then, what we can say is that individuals who have inherent value have the right not to be harmed, which precludes treating them merely as a means. This would fail to treat these individuals with that respect to which, because of the kind of value they have, they are entitled.

Now, certainly the foregoing is not a definitive account of the view that individuals having inherent value have basic moral rights, in particular the right not to be harmed. One omission is especially conspicuous. What is there about being a human being that underlies this inherent value? Any answer is controversial, and a sustained defense of the answer proposed here is not possible.[12] But here is the answer I would give: human beings not only are alive; *they have a life*.[13] What is more, we are the subjects of a life that is better or worse for us, logically independently of anyone else's valuing us or finding us useful.

I do not mean that others cannot contribute to or detract from the value of our lives. On the contrary, the great goods of life (love, friendship, and, in general, fellow feeling) and its great evils (hatred, enmity, loneliness, alienation) all involve our relationships with other persons. What I mean, rather, is that our being *the subject* of a life that is better or worse for us does not depend logically on what others do or do not do. This fact, I believe, provides the illumination we seek. Humans have inherent value because we are ourselves the subjects of a life that is more or less valuable to us. In sum:

> Human beings have inherent value because, logically independently of the interest of others, each individual is the subject of a life that is better or worse for that individual. Because of the type of value that human beings have, it is wrong (a sign of disrespect and a violation of rights) to treat humans as if they had value merely as a means (e.g., to use humans merely to advance the pleasures of the group). In particular, to harm human beings for the sake of the profit or pleasure of any group is to violate their right not to be harmed.

The question now arises whether this same line of argument can be developed in the case of animals. It can, at least in the case of those animals who are the subjects of a life that is better or worse for them, logically independently of whether they are valued by anyone else. And there can be no rational doubt that there *are* numerous species of animals of which this is true.... They too have a distinctive kind of value in their own right, if we do; therefore, they too have a right not to be treated in ways that fail to respect this value, if we do. And, like humans, this right of theirs will be overridden unjustifiably if they are harmed merely to advance the profits or pleasures of others.

## CONCLUSION

Two final philosophical points are in order, before I bring the results of my argument to bear on how animals are treated in the world at large. First, it is important to realize that I have not *proven* that animals have rights, or even that *human* beings have rights. Rather, I have argued that if humans have rights, so do many animals. More particularly, I have argued for what appears to be the most promising line of argument for explaining human rights, the view that we have inherent value, and that this can rationally be extended to animals of some kinds. So, while I admit that I have not proven that animals (or humans) have rights, I hope at least to have made clear the direction in which future argument ought to proceed. Erecting pointers, to be sure, is not the same as constructing proofs, but pointers are the best I can do here.

Second, the history of moral philosophy teaches us that utilitarianism dies hard. Just when one thinks it has been forced off the stage for good, one finds it loitering in the wings, awaiting yet another curtain call. The utilitarian can be counted on to say that there is nothing introduced by the idea of rights for which he cannot account.[14] One has only to see that the utilitarian objective is promoted if we recognize a strict obligation not to harm individuals except in extreme cases, *and* that, furthermore, utility is promoted by saying that individuals have the right not to be harmed, this invocation of a right functioning as an especially forceful way of conveying the idea that we ought not to harm individuals.

I am not convinced by this attempt to resurrect utilitarianism, and here I raise my final and most fundamental objection to it. The utilitarian is in no position to say that he knows that the utilitarian objective is promoted by talk of individuals having rights. But even if it is true that talk of rights helps promote the utilitarian objective, and for this reason such talk ought to be encouraged and honored, there can only be a *contingent* connection between any right, such as the right not to be harmed, and the fact that respecting this right forwards the utilitarian objective. The most that the utilitarian can say is that recognizing the right not to be harmed *as a matter of fact* fits in with forwarding his goal of maximizing the balance of good over evil.[15] The utilitarian must also accept that things could have been (and could become) otherwise. He must accept the possibility that it could have been or might become all right to harm individuals if this ever happened to forward the utilitarian objective. But neither the wrongness of harming individuals nor the right not to be harmed can change in the ways utilitarian theory implies they can. They are not contingent upon *utility*. Neither depends on the value of consequences. Instead, each depends on *the value of individuals*.

Let us put this in perspective before applying it.... Making an informed judgment about the morality of whaling or the use of the Draize test we must know both facts and moral principles. Otherwise, we cannot know which facts are morally relevant; and without this preliminary knowledge, we do not know what moral judgments to make. To determine what these principles are ... is one of the distinctive tasks of moral philosophy. Three positions were examined and found wanting: the Kantian account, the cruelty account, and the utilitarian account. We then considered an account ascribing rights to animals, a position which meets the objections which were fatal to the views examined earlier. Unlike the Kantian account, the rights account insists upon the moral status of animals in their own right; unlike the cruelty account, the rights account does not confuse the morality of acts with the mental states of agents; and unlike utilitarianism, this account closes the door to the justification of prejudices which merely happen to bring about the best consequences. This emphasis on the value of individuals becomes prominent now as we turn at last to the task of applying the rights account to the whale, the veal calf, and the others.

It would be grotesque to suggest that the whale, the rabbit, the gibbon, the bobbie calf, the millions of animals brought so much pain and death at the hands of humans are not harmed, for harm is not restricted to human beings. They are harmed, harmed in a literal, not a metaphorical sense. They are made to endure what is detrimental to their welfare, even death. Those who would harm them, therefore, must justify doing so. Thus, members of the whaling industry, the cosmetics industry, the farming industry, the network of hunters-exporters-importers must justify the harm they bring animals in a way that is consistent with recognizing the animals' right not to be harmed. To produce such a justification it is not enough to argue that people profit, satisfy their curiosity, or derive pleasure from allowing animals to be treated in these ways. These facts are not the morally relevant ones. Rather, what must be shown is that overriding the right of animals not to be harmed is justified because of further facts. For example, because we have very good reason to believe that overriding the individual's right prevents, and is the only realistic way to prevent, vastly greater harm to other innocent individuals.

Let us ask the whaling industry whether they have so justified their trade. Have they made their case in terms of the morally relevant facts? Our answer must be: No! And the cosmetic industry? No! The farmers who raise veal calves? No! The retailer of exotic animals? No! A thousand times we must say: no! I do not say that they cannot possibly justify what they do. The individual's right not to be harmed, we have argued, almost always trumps the interests of the group, but it is possible that such a right must sometimes give way. Possibly the rights of animals must sometimes give way to human interests. It would be a mistake to rule this possibility out. Nevertheless, the onus of justification must be borne by those who cause the harm to show that they do not violate the rights of the individuals involved.

We allow then that it is *possible* that harming animals might be justified; but we also maintain that those harming animals typically fail to show that the harm caused is *actually* justified. A further question we must ask ourselves is what, morally speaking, we ought to do in such a situation? Reflection on comparable situations involving human beings will help make the answer clear.

Consider racism and sexism. Imagine that slavery is an institution of the day and that it is built on racist or sexist lines. Blacks or women are assigned the rank of slave. Suppose we are told that in extreme circumstances even slavery might conceivably be justified, and that we ought not to object to it or try to bring it down, even though no one has shown that it is actually justified in the present case. Well, I do not believe for a moment that we would accept such an attempt to dissuade us from toppling the institution of slavery. Not for a moment would we accept the general principle involved here, that an institution actually is justified because it might conceivably be justified. We would accept the quite different principle that we are morally obligated to oppose any practice which appears to violate rights unless we are shown that it really does not do so. To be satisfied with anything less is to cheapen the value attributable to the victims of the practice.

Exactly the same line of reasoning applies in the case where animals are regarded as so many dispensable commodities, models, subjects, etc. We ought not to back away from bringing these industries and related practices to a halt just because it is *possible* that the harm caused to the animals *might* be justified. If we do, we fail to mean it when we say that animals are not mere things, that they are the subjects of a life that is better or worse for them, that they have inherent value. As in the comparable case involving harm to human beings, our duty is to act, to do all that we can to put an end to the harm animals are made to endure. The fact that the animals themselves cannot speak out on their own behalf, the fact that they cannot organize, petition, march, exert political pressure, or raise our level of consciousness—all this does not weaken our obligation to act on their behalf. If anything, their impotence makes our obligation the greater.[16] . . .

## NOTES

1.  Relevant selections from both St. Thomas and Kant are included in Regan and Singer, *Animal Rights and Human Obligations.* What I call the Kantian account is critized further in my "Exploring the Idea of Animal Rights" in D. Paterson and R. Ryder, eds., *Animal Rights: A Symposium* (London: Centaur Press, 1979). Kant's views are criticized at length by Elizabeth Pybus and Alexander Broadie, "Kant's Treatment of Animals," *Philosophy* 49 (1974): 375–83. I defend Kant against their objections in my "Broadie and Pybus on Kant," *Philosophy* 51 (1976): 471–72. Broadie and Pybus reply in their "Kant on the Maltreatment of Animals," *Philosophy* 53 (1978): 560–61. At present I am persuaded that Broadie and Pybus are correct in arguing that Kant cannot account for the idea that animals themselves can be maltreated.
2.  Singer, *Animal Liberation,* and Ryder, *Victims of Science.*
3.  The famous passage from Bentham reads as follows (from *The Principles of Morals and Legislation* (1789), chap. 17, sect. 1, reprinted in Regan and Singer, *Animal Rights and Human Obligations*): "The day has been, I grieve to say in many places it is not yet past, in which the greater part of the species, under the denomination of slaves, have been treated by the law exactly upon the same footing as, in England for example, the inferior races of animals are still. The day may come, when the rest of the animal creation may acquire those rights which never could have been withholden from them but by the hand of tyranny. The French have already discovered that the blackness of the skin is no reason why a human being should be abandoned without redress to the caprice of a tormentor.

It may come one day to be recognized, that the number of the legs, the villosity of the skin, or the termination of the os sacrum, are reasons equally insufficient for abandoning a sensitive being to the same fate. What else is it that should trace the insuperable line? Is it the faculty of reason, or, perhaps, the faculty of discourse? But a full-grown horse or dog is beyond comparison a more rational, as well as a more conversable animal, than an infant of a day, or a week, or even a month, old. But suppose the case were otherwise, what would it avail? The question is not, Can they reason? nor, Can they talk? but, Can they suffer?"

4. John Locke, *Some Thoughts Concerning Education*, 5th ed. (London, 1905). See also James Axtell, ed., *The Educational Writings of John Locke* (Cambridge: Cambridge University Press, 1968), sec. 116, pp. 225–26.

5. The utilitarian position I consider is the one associated with Bentham and forcefully presented by Peter Singer. That Singer is a utilitarian is made unmistakably clear in his "The Fable of the Fox and the Unliberated Animals" *Ethics* 88 (1978): 119–25.

6. See Singer, *Animal Liberation*, especially pp. 78–83.

7. Ibid., chap. 4.

8. Ronald Dworkin, *Taking Rights Seriously* (Cambridge: Harvard University Press, 1977).

9. The present statement of these conditions deviates somewhat from my earlier effort in "The Moral Basis of Vegetarianism," *Canadian Journal of Philosophy* 5 (1975): 181–214. I believe the inclusion of conditions (b) and (c) marks an improvement over the earlier formulation. However, a fuller statement has to include more than simply the idea of *preventing* vastly greater harm; for example, *reducing* already existing harm also has a place.

10. See my "An Examination and Defense of One Argument Concerning Animal Rights," *Inquiry* 22 (1979): 189–219.

11. Whether sense can be made of including irreversibly comatose human beings in the class of beings having inherent value is a troublesome question indeed.

12. I do not believe it is absurd to think of natural objects which lack consciousness, or collections of such objects, as having inherent value, in the sense in which I use this expression. An *X* has inherent value if it has value logically independently of anyone's valuing *X*. I do not say this is easy to clarify or to defend, and it may be wrongheaded. At present, however, I believe it is a view that must be held, if we are to develop an environmental ethic, as distinct from an ethic for the use of theenvironment.

13. The distinction between being alive and having a life is one James Rachels frequently makes. See, for example, his "Euthanasia" in Tom Regan, ed., *Matters of Life and Death* (New York: Random House, 1980). Rachels does not, so far as I am aware, relate this distinction to the idea of inherent value.

14. It is possible that Mill meant to give rights a utilitarian basis. On this see David Lyons, "Human Rights and the General Welfare," *Philosophy and Public Affairs* 6 (1977): 113–29, reprinted in David Lyons, ed., *Rights* (Belmont, Calif.: Wadsworth, 1979). The principal objection to this enterprise is the third objection I raise against utilitarianism here.

15. I do not believe utilitarianism is alone in implying that the duty not to harm an individual (or the individual's right not to be harmed) are *contingent* moral truths, which *might* have been otherwise (or *might* become otherwise). Certain aspects of Kant's theory as well as ethical egoism arguably imply this as well. This is absolutely fatal to these theories, a point I argue in my "Utilitarianism, Vegetarianism, and Animal Rights," in *Philosophy and Public Affairs*.

16. For a more complete list of recent philosophical work relating to the topics discussed in the present essay, see Charles Magel and Tom Regan, "Animal Rights and Human Obligations: A Select Bibliography," *Inquiry* 22 (1979): 243–47.

# ON BEING MORALLY CONSIDERABLE

*Kenneth E. Goodpaster*

Kenneth E. Goodpaster holds the David and Barbara Koch Chair in business ethics at the University of St. Thomas, St. Paul, Minnesota. With Kenneth M. Sayre, he edited *Ethics and Problems of the 21st Century*.

> A thing is right when it tends to preserve the integrity, stability, and beauty of the biotic community. It is wrong when it tends otherwise.
>
> —*Aldo Leopold*

What follows is a preliminary inquiry into a question which needs more elaborate treatment than an essay can provide. The question can be and has been addressed in different rhetorical formats, but perhaps G. J. Warnock's formulation of it[1] is the best to start with:

> Let us consider the question to whom principles of morality apply from, so to speak, the other end—from the standpoint not of the agent, but of the "patient." What, we may ask here, is the condition of moral *relevance*? What is the condition of having a claim to be *considered*, by rational agents to whom moral principles apply? (148)

In the terminology of R. M. Hare (or even Kant), the same question might be put thus: In universalizing our putative moral maxims, what is the scope of the variable over which universalization is to range? A more legalistic idiom, employed recently by Christopher D. Stone,[2] might ask: What are the requirements for "having standing" in the moral sphere? However the question gets formulated, the thrust is in the direction of necessary and sufficient conditions on *X* in

This essay originally appeared in *The Journal of Philosophy*, LXXV, 6 (June 1978), 308–25. Reprinted with permission.

(1) For all *A*, *X* deserves moral consideration from *A*, where *A* ranges over rational moral agents and moral 'consideration' is construed broadly to include the most basic forms of practical respect (and so is not restricted to "possession of rights" by *X*).

## I

The motivation for addressing such a question stems from several sources. The last decade has seen a significant increase in the concern felt by most persons about "the environment." This new awareness manifests itself in many ways. One is a quest for methods of "technology assessment," for criteria for social choice that capture the relevant costs and benefits (be they quantifiable or not). On another front, heated controversies have arisen over endangered species and our treatment of animals generally (both as sources of food and as sources of experimental knowledge). The morality of abortion and, in general, the proper uses of medical technology have also tried our ethical sensitivities about the scope and nature of moral considerability.

These developments emphasize the importance of clarity about the *framework* of moral consideration as much as about the *application* of that framework. We need to understand better, for example, the scope of moral respect, the sorts of entities that can and should receive moral attention, and the nature of the "good" which morality (since it at least *includes* beneficence) is supposed to promote. In addition, we need principles for weighing or adjudicating conflicting claims to moral consideration.

The question focused on here is therefore only a first step toward the larger task. It is a framework question more than an application question—though its practical relevance is not so remote as to be purely a matter of logical speculation. My convictions about the proper answer to the question are sketched in another place,[3] but they can be summarized more explicitly as follows.

Modern moral philosophy has taken ethical egoism as its principal foil for developing what can fairly be called a *humanistic* perspective on value and obligation. That is, both Kantian and Humean approaches to ethics tend to view the philosophical challenge as that of providing an epistemological and motivational generalization of an agent's natural self-interested concern. Because of this preoccupation with moral "takeoff," however, too little critical thought has been devoted to the flight and its destination. One result might be a certain feeling of impotence in the minds of many moral philosophers when faced with the sorts of issues mentioned earlier, issues that question the breadth of the moral enterprise more than its departure point. To be sure, questions of conservation, preservation of the environment, and technology assessment *can* be approached simply as application questions, e.g., "How shall we evaluate the alternatives available to us instrumentally in relation to humanistic satisfactions?" But there is something distressingly uncritical in this way of framing such issues—distressingly uncritical in the way that deciding foreign policy solely in terms of "the national interest" is uncritical. Or at least, so I think.

It seems to me that we should not only wonder about, but actually follow "the road not taken into the wood." Neither rationality nor the capacity to experience pleasure and pain seem to me necessary (even though they may be sufficient) conditions on moral considerability. And only our hedonistic and concentric forms of ethical reflection keep us from acknowledging this fact. Nothing short of the condition of *being alive* seems to me to be a plausible and nonarbitrary criterion. What is more, this criterion, if taken seriously, could admit of application to entities and systems of entities heretofore unimagined as claimants on our moral attention (such as the biosystem itself). Some may be inclined to take such implications as a *reductio* of the move "beyond humanism." I am beginning to be persuaded, however, that such implications may provide both a meaningful ethical vision and the hope of a more adequate action guide for the long-term future. Paradigms are crucial components in knowledge—but they can conceal as much as they reveal. Our paradigms of moral considerability are individual persons and their joys and sorrows. I want to venture the belief that the universe of moral consideration is more complex than these paradigms allow.

## II

My strategy, now that my cards are on the table, will be to spell out a few rules of the game (in this section) and then to examine the "hands" of several respected philosophers whose arguments seem to count against casting the moral net as widely as I am inclined to (sections III, IV, and V). In the concluding section (VI), I will discuss several objections and touch on further questions needing attention.

The first (of four) distinctions that must be kept clear in addressing our question has already been alluded to. It is that between moral *rights* and moral *considerability*. My inclination is to construe the notion of rights as more specific than that of considerability, largely to avoid what seem to be unnecessary complications over the requirements for something's being an appropriate "bearer of rights." The concept of rights is used in wider and narrower senses, of course. Some authors (indeed, one whom we shall consider later in this paper) use it as roughly synonymous with Warnock's notion of "moral relevance." Others believe that being a bearer of rights involves the satisfaction of much more demanding requirements. The sentiments of John Passmore[4] are probably typical of this narrower view:

> The idea of "rights" is simply not applicable to what is non-human . . . It is one thing to say that it is wrong to treat animals cruelly, quite another to say that animals have rights. (116/7)

I doubt whether it is so clear that the class of rights-bearers is or ought to be restricted to human beings, but I propose to suspend this question entirely by framing the discussion in terms of the notion of moral considerability (following Warnock), except in contexts where there is reason to think the widest sense of 'rights' is at work. Whether beings who deserve moral consideration in themselves, not simply by reason of their utility to human beings, also possess moral *rights* in some narrow sense is a question which will, therefore, remain open here—and it is a question the answer to which need not be determined in advance.

A second distinction is that between what might be called a *criterion of moral considerability* and a *criterion of moral significance*. The former represents the central quarry here, while the latter, which might easily get confused with the former, aims at governing *comparative* judgments of moral "weight" in cases of conflict. Whether a tree, say, deserves any moral consideration is a question that must be kept separate from the question of whether trees deserve more or less consideration than dogs, or dogs than human persons. We should not expect that the criterion for having "moral standing" at all will be the same as the criterion for adjudicating competing claims to priority among beings that merit that standing. In fact, it may well be an insufficient appreciation of this distinction which leads some to a preoccupation with rights in dealing with morality. I suspect that the real force of attributions of "rights" derives from comparative contexts, contexts in which moral considerability is presupposed and the issue of strength is crucial. Eventually, of course, the priority issues have to be dealt with for an operational ethical account—this much I have already acknowledged—but in the interests of clarity, I set them aside for now.

Another important distinction, the third, turns on the difference between questions of intelligibility and questions of normative substance. An adequate treatment of this difficult and complicated division would take us far afield,[5] but a few remarks are in order. It is tempting to assume, with Joel Feinberg,[6] that we can neatly separate such questions as

**(2)** What sorts of being can (logically) be said to deserve moral consideration?

from questions like

**(3)** What sorts of beings do, as a matter of "ethical fact" deserve moral consideration?

But our confidence in the separation here wanes (perhaps more quickly than in other philosophical contexts where the conceptual/substantive distinction arises) when we reflect upon the apparent *flexibility* of our metamoral beliefs. One might argue plausibly, for example, that there were times and societies in which the moral standing of blacks was, as a matter of *conceptual analysis*, deniable. Examples could be multiplied to include women, children, fetuses, and various other instances of what might be called "metamoral disenfranchisement." I suspect that the lesson to be learned here is that, as William Frankena has pointed out,[7] metaethics is, and has always been, a partially normative discipline. Whether we are to take this to mean that it is really impossible ever to engage in morally neutral conceptual analysis in ethics is, of course, another question. In any case, it appears that, with respect to the issue at hand, keeping (2) and (3) apart will be difficult. At the very least, I think, we must be wary of arguments that purport to answer (3) *solely* on the basis of "ordinary language"–style answers to (2).

Though the focus of the present inquiry is more normative than conceptual [hence aimed more at (3) than at (2)], it remains what I called a "framework" inquiry nonetheless, since it prescinds from the question of relative weights (moral significance) of moral considerability claims.

Moreover—and this brings us to the fourth and last distinction—there is another respect in which the present inquiry involves framework questions rather than questions of application. There is clearly a sense in which we are subject to *thresholds* of moral sensitivity just as we are subject to thresholds of cognitive or perceptual sensitivity. Beyond such thresholds we are "morally blind" or suffer disintegrative consequences analogous to "information overload" in a computer. In the face of our conative limitations, we often will distinguish between moral demands that are relative to those limitations and moral demands that are not. The latter demands represent claims on our consideration or respect which we acknowledge as in some sense ideally determinative if not practically determinative. We might mark this distinction by borrowing Ross's categories of "prima facie vs. actual duty" except that (A) these categories tend to map more naturally onto the distinction mentioned earlier between considerability and significance, and (B) these categories tend to evoke conditionality and lack thereof of a sort which is rooted more in a plurality of "external" moral pressures than in an agent's "internal" capacities for practical response. Let us, then, say that the moral considerability of *X* is *operative* for an agent *A* if and only if the thorough acknowledgement of *X* by *A* is psychologically (and in general, causally) possible for *A*. If the moral considerability of *X* is defensible on all grounds independent of operativity, we shall say that it is *regulative*. An agent may, for example, have an obligation to grant regulative considerability to all living things, but be able psychologically and in terms of his own nutrition to grant operative consideration to a much smaller class of things (though note that capacities in this regard differ among persons and change over time).

Using all these distinctions, and the rough and ready terminology that they yield, we can now state the issue in (1) as a concern for a relatively substantive (vs. purely logical) criterion of moral considerability (vs. moral significance) of a regulative (vs. operative) sort. As far as I can see, *X*'s being a living thing is both necessary and sufficient for moral considerability so understood, whatever may be the case for the moral *rights* that rational agents should acknowledge.

## III

Let us begin with Warnock's own answer to the question, now that the question has been clarified somewhat. In setting out his answer, Warnock argues (in my view, persuasively) against two more restrictive candidates. The first, what might be called the *Kantian principle*, amounts to little more than a reflection of the requirements of moral *agency* onto those of moral considerability:

(4) For $X$ to deserve moral consideration from $A$, $X$ must be a rational human person.

Observing that such a criterion of considerability eliminates children and mentally handicapped adults, among others, Warnock dismisses it as intolerably narrow.

The second candidate, actually a more generous variant of the first, sets the limits of moral considerability by disjoining "potentiality":

(5) For all $A$, $X$ deserves moral consideration from $A$ if and only if $X$ is a rational human person or is a potential rational human person.

Warnock's reply to this suggestion is also persuasive. Infants and imbeciles are no doubt potentially rational, but this does not appear to be the reason why we should not maltreat them. And we would not say that an imbecile reasonably judged to be incurable would thereby reasonably be taken to have no moral claims (151). In short, it seems arbitrary to draw the boundary of moral *considerability* around rational human beings (actual or potential), however plausible it might be to draw the boundary of moral *responsibility* there.[8]

Warnock then settles upon his own solution. The basis of moral claims, he says, may be put as follows:

> . . . just as liability to be judged as a moral agent follows from one's general capability of alleviating, by moral action, the ills of the predicament, and is for that reason confined to rational beings, so the condition of being a proper "beneficiary" of moral action is the capability of *suffering* the ills of the predicament—and for that reason is not confined to rational beings, nor even to potential members of that class. (151)

The criterion of moral considerability then, is located in the *capacity to suffer.*

(6) For all $A$, $X$ deserves moral consideration from $A$ if and only if $X$ is capable of suffering pain (or experiencing enjoyment).

And the defense involves appeal to what Warnock considers to be (analytically) the *object* of the moral enterprise: Amelioration of "the predicament."

Now two issues arise immediately in the wake of this sort of appeal. The first has to do with Warnock's own over-all strategy in the context of the quoted passage. Earlier on in his book, he insists that the appropriate analysis of the concept of morality will lead us to an "object" whose pursuit provides the framework for ethics. But the "object" seems to be more restrictive:

> . . . the general object of moral evaluation must be to contribute in some respects, by way of the actions of rational beings, to the amelioration of the human predicament—that is, of the conditions in which *these* rational beings, humans, actually find themselves (16; emphasis in the original).

It appears that, by the time moral considerability comes up later in the book, Warnock has changed his mind about the object of morality by enlarging the "predicament" to include nonhumans.

The second issue turns on the question of analysis itself. As I suggested earlier, it is difficult to keep conceptual and substantive questions apart in the present context. We can, of course, stipulatively *define* 'morality' as both having an object and having the object of mitigating suffering. But, in the absence of more argument, such definition is itself in need of a warrant. Twentieth-century preoccupation with the naturalistic or definist fallacy should have taught us at least this much.

Neither of these two observations shows that Warnock's suggested criterion is wrong, of course. But they do, I think, put us in a rather more demanding mood. And the mood is aggravated when we look to two other writers on the subject who appear to hold similar views.

W. K. Frankena, in a recent paper,[9] joins forces:

> Like Warnock, I believe that there are right and wrong ways to treat infants, animals, imbeciles, and idiots even if or even though (as the case may be) they are not persons or human beings—just because they are capable of pleasure and suffering, and not just because their lives happen to have some value to or for those who clearly are persons or human beings.

And Peter Singer[10] writes:

> If a being is not capable of suffering, or of experiencing enjoyment or happiness, there is nothing to be taken into account. This is why the limit of sentience (using the term as a convenient, if not strictly accurate, shorthand for the capacity to suffer or experience enjoyment or happiness) is the only defensible boundary of concern for the interests of others (154).

I say that the mood is aggravated because, although I acknowledge and even applaud the conviction expressed by these philosophers that the capacity to suffer (or perhaps better, *sentience*) is sufficient for moral considerability, I fail to understand their reasons for thinking such a criterion necessary. To be sure, there are hints at reasons in each case. Warnock implies that nonsentient beings could not be proper "beneficiaries" of moral action. Singer seems to think that beyond sentience "there is nothing to take into account." And

Frankena suggests that nonsentient beings simply do not provide us with moral reasons for respecting them unless it be potentially for sentience.[11] Yet it is so clear that there *is* something to take into account, something that is not merely "potential sentience" and which surely does qualify beings as beneficiaries and capable of harm—namely, *life*—that the hints provided seem to me to fall short of good reasons.

Biologically, it appears that sentience is an adaptive characteristic of living organisms that provides them with a better capacity to anticipate, and so avoid, threats to life. This at least suggests, though of course it does not prove, that the capacities to suffer and to enjoy are ancillary to something more important rather than tickets to considerability in their own right. In the words of one perceptive scientific observer:

> If we view pleasure as rooted in our sensory physiology, it is not difficult to see that our neurophysiological equipment must have evolved via variation and selective retention in such a way as to record a positive signal to adaptationally satisfactory conditions and a negative signal to adaptationally unsatisfactory conditions. . . . The pleasure signal is only an evolutionarily derived indicator, not the goal itself. It is the applause which signals a job well done, but not the actual completion of the job.[12]

Nor is it absurd to imagine that evolution might have resulted (indeed might still result?) in beings whose capacities to maintain, protect, and advance their lives did not depend upon mechanisms of pain and pleasure at all.

So far, then, we can see that the search for a criterion of moral considerability takes one quickly and plausibly beyond humanism. But there is a tendency, exhibited in the remarks of Warnock, Frankena, and Singer, to draw up the wagons around the notion of sentience. I have suggested that there is reason to go further and not very much in the way of argument not to. But perhaps there is a stronger and more explicit case that can be made for sentience. I think there is, in a way, and I propose to discuss it in detail in the section that follows.

## IV

Joel Feinberg offers (51) what may be the clearest and most explicit case for a restrictive criterion on moral considerability (restrictive with respect to life). I should mention at the outset, however, that the context for his remarks is

(I) the concept of "rights," which, we have seen, is sometimes taken to be narrower than the concept of "considerability"; and

(II) the *intelligibility* of rights-attributions, which, we have seen, is problematically related to the more substantive issue of what beings deserve moral consideration.

These two features of Feinberg's discussion might be thought sufficient to in-
validate my use of that discussion here. But the context of his remarks is
clearly such that 'rights' is taken very broadly, much closer to what I am calling moral considerability than to what Passmore calls "rights." And the thrust
of the arguments, since they are directed against the *intelligibility* of certain
rights attributions, is *a fortiori* relevant to the more substantive issue set out in
(1). So I propose to treat Feinberg's arguments as if they were addressed to
the considerability issue in its more substantive form, whether or not they
were or would be intended to have such general application. I do so with
due notice to the possible need for scare-quotes around Feinberg's name, but
with the conviction that it is really in Feinberg's discussion that we discover
that the clearest line of argument in favor of something like sentience, an argument which was only hinted at in the remarks of Warnock, Frankena, and
Singer.

The central thesis defended by Feinberg is that a being cannot intelligibly be said to possess moral rights (read: deserve moral consideration) unless
that being satisfies the "interest principle," and that only the subclass of humans and higher animals among living beings satisfies this principle:

> . . . the sorts of beings who can have rights are precisely those who have (or can
> have) interests. I have come to this tentative conclusion for two reasons: (1) be-
> cause a right holder must be capable of being represented and it is impossible
> to represent a being that has no interests, and (2) because a right holder must
> be capable of being a beneficiary in his own person, and a being without inter-
> ests is a being that is incapable of being harmed or benefited, having no good
> or "sake" of its own (51).

Implicit in this passage are the following two arguments, interpreted in terms
of moral considerability:

**(A1)** Only beings who can be represented can deserve moral consideration.
Only beings who have (or can have) interests can be represented.
Therefore, only beings who have (or can have) interests can deserve moral
consideration.
**(A2)** Only beings capable of being beneficiaries can deserve moral consideration.
Only beings who have (or can have) interests are capable of being beneficiaries.
Therefore, only beings who have (or can have) interests can deserve moral
consideration.

I suspect that these two arguments are at work between the lines in Warnock,
Frankena, and Singer, though of course one can never be sure. In any case, I
propose to consider them as the best defense of the sentience criterion in recent literature.

I am prepared to grant, with some reservations, the first premises in
each of these obviously valid arguments. The second premises, though, are
*both* importantly equivocal. To claim that only beings who have (or can have)

interests can be represented might mean that "mere things" cannot be represented because they have nothing to represent, no "interests" as opposed to
"usefulness" to defend or protect. Similarly, to claim that only beings who
have (or can have) interests are capable of being beneficiaries might mean
that "mere things" are incapable of being benefited or harmed—they have no
"well-being" to be sought or acknowledged by rational moral agents. So construed, Feinberg seems to be right; but he also seems to be committed to allowing any *living* thing the status of moral considerability. For as he himself
admits, even plants

> . . . are not "mere things"; they are vital objects with inherited biological
> propensities determining their natural growth. Moreover we do say that certain
> conditions are "good" or "bad" for plants, thereby suggesting that plants, unlike
> rocks, are capable of having a "good." (51)

But Feinberg pretty clearly wants to draw the nets tighter than this—and he
does so by interpreting the notion of "interests" in the two second premises
more narrowly. The contrast term he favors is not 'mere things' but 'mindless
creatures.' And he makes this move by insisting that "interests" logically presuppose *desires* or "wants" or "aims," the equipment for which is not possessed
by plants (nor, we might add, by many animals or even some humans?).

But why should we accept this shift in strength of the criterion? In doing
so, we clearly abandon one sense in which living organisms like plants do have
interests that can be represented. There is no absurdity in imagining the representation of the needs of a tree for sun and water in the face of a proposal to
cut it down or pave its immediate radius for a parking lot. We might of course,
on reflection, decide to go ahead and cut it down or do the paving, but there
is hardly an intelligibility problem about representing the tree's interest in
our deciding not to. In the face of their obvious tendencies to maintain and
heal themselves, it is very difficult to reject the idea of interests on the part of
trees (and plants generally) in remaining alive.[13]

Nor will it do to suggest, as Feinberg does, that the needs (interests) of
living things like trees are not really their own but implicitly *ours*: "Plants may
need things in order to discharge their functions, but their functions are assigned by human interests, not their own" (54). As if it were human interests
that assigned to trees the tasks of growth or maintenance! The interests at
stake are clearly those of the living things themselves, not simply those of the
owners or users or other human persons involved. Indeed, there is a suggestion in this passage that, to be capable of being represented, an organism
must *matter* to human beings somehow—a suggestion whose implications for
human rights (disenfranchisement) let alone the rights of animals (inconsis-
tently for Feinberg, I think)—are grim.

The truth seems to be that the "interests" that nonsentient beings share
with sentient beings (over and against "mere things") are far more plausible
as criteria of *considerability* than the "interests" that sentient beings share

(over and against "mindless creatures"). This is not to say that interests construed in the latter way are morally irrelevant—for they may play a role as criteria of moral *significance*—but it is to say that psychological or hedonic capacities seem unnecessarily sophisticated when it comes to locating the minimal conditions for something's deserving to be valued for its own sake. Surprisingly, Feinberg's own reflections on "mere things" appear to support this very point:

> . . . mere things have no conative life: no conscious wishes, desires, and hopes; or urges and impulses; or unconscious drives, aims, and goals; or latent tendencies, direction of growth, and natural fulfillments. Interests must be compounded somehow out of conations; hence mere things have no interests. (49)

Together with the acknowledgment, quoted earlier, that plants, for example, are not "mere things," such observations seem to undermine the interest principle in its more restrictive form. I conclude, with appropriate caution, that the interest principle either grows to fit what we might call a "life principle" or requires an arbitrary stipulation of psychological capacities (for desires, wants, etc.) which are neither warranted by (A1) and (A2) nor independently plausible.

## V

Thus far, I have examined the views of four philosophers on the necessity of sentience or interests (narrowly conceived) as a condition on moral considerability. I have maintained that these views are not plausibly supported, when they are supported at all, because of a reluctance to acknowledge in nonsentient living beings the presence of independent needs, capacities for benefit and harm, etc. I should like, briefly, to reflect on a more general level about the roots of this reluctance before proceeding to a consideration of objections against the "life" criterion which I have been defending. In the course of this reflection, we might gain some insight into the sources of our collective hesitation in viewing environmental ethics in a "nonchauvinistic" way.[14]

When we consider the reluctance to go beyond sentience in the context of moral consideration—and look for both explanations and justifications—two thoughts come to mind. The first is that, given the connection between beneficence (or nonmaleficence) and morality, it is natural that limits on moral considerability will come directly from limits on the range of beneficiaries (or "maleficiaries"). This is implicit in Warnock and explicit in Feinberg. The second thought is that, if one's conception of the good is *hedonistic* in character, one's conception of a beneficiary will quite naturally be restricted to beings who are capable of pleasure and pain. If pleasure or satisfaction is the only ultimate gift we have to give, morally, then it is to be expected that only those equipped to receive such a gift will enter into our moral deliberation. And if pain or dissatisfaction is the only ultimate harm we can cause, then it is to be expected that only those equipped for it will deserve our consideration. There seems, therefore, to be a noncontingent connection between a hedonistic or quasi-hedonistic[15] theory of value and a response to the moral-considerability question which favors sentience of interest possession (narrowly conceived).

One must, of course, avoid drawing too strong a conclusion about this connection. It does not follow from the fact that hedonism leads naturally to the sentience criterion either that it entails that criterion or that one who holds that criterion must be a hedonist in his theory of value. For one might be a hedonist with respect to the good and yet think that moral consideration was, on other grounds, restricted to a subclass of the beings capable of enjoyment or pain. And one might hold to the sentience criterion for considerability while denying that pleasure, for example, was the only intrinsically good thing in the life of a human (or nonhuman) being. So hedonism about value and the sentience criterion of moral considerability are not logically equivalent. Nor does either entail the other. But there is some sense, I think, in which they mutually support each other—both in terms of "rendering plausible" and in terms of "helping to explain." As Derek Parfit is fond of putting it, "there are not entailments, but then there seldom are in moral reasoning."[16]

Let me hazard the hypothesis, then, that there is a nonaccidental affinity between a person's or a society's conception of value and its conception of moral considerability. More specifically, there is an affinity between hedonism or some variation on hedonism and a predilection for the sentience criterion of considerability or some variation on it. The implications one might draw from this are many. In the context of a quest for a richer moral framework to deal with a new awareness of the environment, one might be led to expect significant resistance from a hedonistic society unless one forced one's imperatives into an instrumental form. One might also be led to an appreciation of how technology aimed at largely hedonistic goals could gradually "harden the hearts" of a civilization to the biotic community in which it lives—at least until crisis or upheaval raised some questions.[17]

# VI

Let us now turn to several objections that might be thought to render a "life principle" of moral considerability untenable quite independently of the adequacy or inadequacy of the sentience or interest principle.

(O1) A principle of moral respect or consideration for life in all its forms is mere Schweitzerian romanticism, even if it does not involve, as it probably does, the projection of mental or psychological categories beyond their responsible boundaries into the realms of plants, insects, and microbes.

(R1) This objection misses the central thrust of my discussion, which is *not* that the sentience criterion is necessary, but applicable to all life forms—rather the point is that the possession of sentience is not necessary for moral considerability. Schweitzer himself may have held the former view—and so have been "romantic"—but this is beside the point.

**(O2)** To suggest seriously that moral considerability is coextensive with life is to suggest that conscious, feeling beings have no more central role in the moral life than vegetables, which is downright absurd—if not perverse.

**(R2)** This objection misses the central thrust of my discussion as well, for a different reason. It is consistent with acknowledging the moral considerability of all life forms to go on to point out differences of moral significance among these life forms. And as far as perversion is concerned, history will perhaps be a better judge of our civilization's treatment of animals and the living environment on that score.

**(O3)** Consideration of life can serve as a criterion only to the degree that life itself can be given a precise definition; and it can't.

**(R3)** I fail to see why a criterion of moral considerability must be strictly decidable in order to be tenable. Surely rationality, potential rationality, sentience, and the capacity for or possession of interests fare no better here. Moreover, there do seem to be empirically respectable accounts of the nature of living beings available which are not intolerably vague or open-textured:

> The typifying mark of a living system ... appears to be its persistent state of low entropy, sustained by metabolic processes for accumulating energy, and maintained in equilibrium with its environment by homeostatic feedback processes.[18]

Granting the need for certain further qualifications, a definition such as this strikes me as not only plausible in its own right, but ethically illuminating, since it suggests that the core of moral concern lies in respect for self-sustaining organization and integration in the face of pressures toward high entropy.

**(O4)** If life, as understood in the previous response, is really taken as the key to moral considerability, then it is possible that larger systems besides our ordinarily understood "linear" extrapolations from human beings (e.g., animals, plants, etc.) might satisfy the conditions, such as the biosystem as a whole. This surely would be a *reductio* of the life principle.

**(R4)** At best, it would be a *reductio* of the life principle in this form or without qualification. But it seems to me that such (perhaps surprising) implications, if true, should be taken seriously. There is some evidence that the biosystem as a whole exhibits behavior approximating to the definition sketched above,[19] and I see no reason to deny it moral considerability on that account. Why should the universe of moral considerability map neatly onto our medium-sized framework of organisms?

**(O5)** There are severe epistemological problems about imputing interests, benefits, harms, etc. to nonsentient beings. What is it for a tree to have needs?

**(R5)** I am not convinced that the epistemological problems are more severe in this context than they would be in numerous others which the objector would probably not find problematic. Christopher Stone has put this point nicely:

> I am sure I can judge with more certainty and meaningfulness whether and when my lawn wants (needs) water than the Attorney General can judge whether and when the United States wants (needs) to take an appeal from an adverse judgment by a lower court. The lawn tells me that it wants water by a certain dryness of the blades and soil—immediately obvious to the touch—the appearance of bald spots, yellowing, and a lack of springiness after being walked on; how does "the United States" communicate to the Attorney General? (24).

We make decisions in the interests of others or on behalf of others every day—"others" whose wants are far less verifiable than those of most living creatures.

**(O6)** Whatever the force of the previous objections, the clearest and most decisive refutation of the principle of respect for life is that one cannot *live* according to it, nor is there any indication in nature that we were intended to. We must eat, experiment to gain knowledge, protect ourselves from predation (macroscopic and microscopic), and in general deal with the overwhelming complexities of the moral life while remaining psychologically intact. To take seriously the criterion of considerability being defended, all these things must be seen as somehow morally wrong.

**(R6)** This objection, if it is not met by implication in (R2), can be met, I think, by recalling the distinction made earlier between regulative and operative moral consideration. It seems to me that there clearly are limits to the operational character of respect for living things. We must eat, and usually this involves killing (though not always). We must have knowledge, and sometimes this involves experimentation with living things and killing (though not always). We must protect ourselves from predation and disease, and sometimes this involves killing (though not always). The regulative character of the moral consideration due to all living things asks, as far as I can see, for sensitivity and awareness, not for suicide (psychic or otherwise). But it is not vacuous, in that it does provide a *ceteris paribus* encouragement in the direction of nutritional, scientific, and medical practices of a genuinely life-respecting sort.

As for the implicit claim, in the objection, that since nature doesn't respect life, we needn't, there are two rejoinders. The first is that the premise is not so clearly true. Gratuitous killing in nature is rare indeed. The second, and more important, response is that the issue at hand has to do with the appropriate moral demands to be made on rational moral agents, not on beings who are not rational moral agents. Besides, this objection would tell equally against *any* criterion of moral considerability so far as I can see, if the suggestion is that nature is a moral.

I have been discussing the necessary and sufficient conditions that should regulate moral consideration. As indicated earlier, however, numerous other questions are waiting in the wings. Central among them are questions dealing with how to balance competing claims to consideration in a world in which such competing claims seem pervasive. Related to these questions would be problems about the relevance of developing or declining status in life (the very young and the very old) and the relevance of the part-whole relation (leaves to a tree; species to an ecosystem). And there are many others.

Perhaps enough has been said, however, to clarify an important project for contemporary ethics, if not to defend a full-blown account of moral considerability and moral significance. Leopold's ethical vision and its implications for modern society in the form of an environmental ethic are important—so we should proceed with care in assessing it.

## NOTES

1. *The Object of Morality* (New York: Methuen, 1971); parenthetical page references to Warnock will be to this book.
2. *Should Trees Have Standing?* (Los Altos, Calif.: William Kaufmann, 1974); parenthetical page references to Stone will be to this book.

3. "From Egoism to Environmentalism," in Goodpaster and K. M. Sayre, eds., *Ethics and Problems of the 21st Century* (Notre Dame, Ind.: University Press, 1978).

4. *Man's Responsibility for Nature* (New York: Scribner's, 1974).

5. Cf. R. M. Hare, "The Argument from Received Opinion," in *Essays on Philosophical Method* (New York: Macmillan, 1971), p. 117.

6. "The Rights of Animals and Unborn Generations," in Blackstone, *Philosophy and Environmental Crisis* (University of Georgia, 1974), p. 43; parenthetical page references to Feinberg will be to this paper.

7. "On Saying the Ethical Thing," in Goodpaster, ed., *Perspectives on Morality* (Notre Dame, Ind.: University Press, 1976), pp. 107–124.

8. Actually, it seems to me that we ought not to draw the boundary of moral responsibility just here. See my "Morality and Organizations," in *Proceedings of the Second National Conference on Business Ethics* (Waltham, Mass.: Bentley College, 1978).

9. "Ethics and the Environment," in Goodpaster and Sayre, *op. cit.*

10. "All Animals Are Equal," in Tom Regan and Peter Singer, *Animal Rights and Human Obligations* (Englewood Cliffs, N.J.: Prentice-Hall, 1976). See p. 316.

11. "I can see no reason, from the moral point of view, why we should respect something that is alive but has no conscious sentiency and so can experience no pleasure or pain, joy or suffering, unless perhaps it is potentially a consciously sentient being, as in the case of a fetus. Why, if leaves and trees have no capacity to feel pleasure or to suffer, should I tear no leaf from a tree? Why should I respect its location any more than that of a stone in my driveway, if no benefit or harm comes to any person or sentient being by my moving it?" ("Ethics and the Environment").

12. Mark W. Lipsey, "Value Science and Developing Society," paper delivered to the Society for Religion in Higher Education, Institute on Society, Technology and Values (July 15–Aug. 4, 1973), p. 11.

13. See Albert Szent-Gyorgyi, *The Living State* (New York; Academic Press, 1972), esp. ch. VI, "Vegetable Defense Systems."

14. Cf. R. and V. Routley, "Not for Humans Only," in Goodpaster and Sayre, note 3. R. Routley is, I think, the originator of the phrase "human chauvinism."

15. Frankena uses the phrase "quasi-hedonist" in *Ethics* (Englewood Cliffs, N.J.: Prentice-Hall, 1973), p. 90.

16. "Later Selves and Moral Principles," in A. Montefiori, ed., *Philosophy and Personal Relations* (Boston: Routledge & Kegan Paul, 1973), p. 147.

17. There is more, but much depends, I think, on defending claims about the value theory at work in our society and about the need for noninstrumental approaches to value change. Value theory, like scientific theory, tends to evolve by trying to accommodate to the conventional pattern any new suggestions about what is good or should be respected. I suspect that the analogy holds true for the explanations to be given of ethical revolutions—a new and simpler way of dealing with our moral sense emerges to take the place of the old contrivances—be they egoistic, utilitarian, or in the present case hedonistic (if not humanistic). Such topics are, of course, not the topics of this essay. Perhaps I can be excused for raising them here by the contention that a line of argument in ethics (indeed, in philosophy generally) needs not only to be criticized—it needs to be *understood*.

18. K. M. Sayre, *Cybernetics and the Philosophy of Mind* (New York: Humanities, 1976), p. 91.

19. See J. Lovelock and S. Epton, "The Quest for Gaia," *The New Scientist*, LXV, 935 (Feb. 6, 1975): 304–309.

# THE ETHICS OF RESPECT
# FOR NATURE

*Paul W. Taylor*

Paul W. Taylor is professor emeritus of philosophy at Brooklyn College, City University of New York. He is the author of *Respect for Nature: A Theory of Environmental Ethics.*

## HUMAN-CENTERED AND LIFE-CENTERED SYSTEMS OF ENVIRONMENTAL ETHICS

When the basic characteristics of the attitude of respect for nature are made clear, it will be seen that a life-centered system of environmental ethics need not be holistic or organicist in its conception of the kinds of entities that are deemed the appropriate objects of moral concern and consideration. Nor does such a system require that the concepts of ecological homeostasis, equilibrium, and integrity provide us with normative principles from which could be derived (with the addition of factual knowledge) our obligations with regard to natural ecosystems. The "balance of nature" is not itself a moral norm, however important may be the role it plays in our general outlook on the natural world that underlies the attitude of respect for nature. I argue that finally it is the good (well-being, welfare) of individual organisms, considered as entities having inherent worth, that determines our moral relations with the Earth's wild communities of life.

In designating the theory to be set forth as life-centered, I intend to contrast it with all anthropocentric views. According to the latter, human actions affecting the natural environment and its nonhuman inhabitants are right (or wrong) by either of two criteria: they have consequences which are favorable (or unfavorable) to human well-being, or they are consistent (or inconsistent) with the system of norms that protect and implement human rights. From this

This essay originally appeared in *Environmental Ethics*, Vol. 3, No. 3 (Fall 1981), pp. 197–218. Reprinted with permission.

human-centered standpoint it is to humans and only to humans that all duties are ultimately owed. We may have responsibilities *with regard to* the natural ecosystems and biotic communities of our planet, but these responsibilities are in every case based on the contingent fact that our treatment of those ecosystems and communities of life can further the realization of human values and/or human rights. We have no obligation to promote or protect the good of nonhuman living things, independently of this contingent fact.

A life-centered system of environmental ethics is opposed to human-centered ones precisely on this point. From the perspective of a life-centered theory, we have prima facie moral obligations that are owed to wild plants and animals themselves as members of the Earth's biotic community. We are morally bound (other things being equal) to protect or promote their good for *their* sake. Our duties to respect the integrity of natural ecosystems, to preserve endangered species, and to avoid environmental pollution stem from the fact that these are ways in which we can help make it possible for wild species populations to achieve and maintain a healthy existence in a natural state. Such obligations are due those living things out of recognition of their inherent worth. They are entirely additional to and independent of the obligations we owe to our fellow humans. Although many of the actions that fulfill one set of obligations will also fulfill the other, two different grounds of obligation are involved. Their well-being, as well as human well-being, is something to be realized *as an end in itself.*

If we were to accept a life-centered theory of environmental ethics, a profound reordering of our moral universe would take place. We would begin to look at the whole of the Earth's biosphere in a new light. Our duties with respect to the "world" of nature would be seen as making prima facie claims upon us to be balanced against our duties with respect to the "world" of human civilization. We could no longer simply take the human point of view and consider the effects of our actions exclusively from the perspective of our own good. . . .

We can think of the good of an individual nonhuman organism as consisting in the full development of its biological powers. Its good is realized to the extent that it is strong and healthy. It possesses whatever capacities it needs for successfully coping with its environment and so preserving its existence throughout the various stages of the normal life cycle of its species. The good of a population or community of such individuals consists in the population or community maintaining itself from generation to generation as a coherent system of genetically and ecologically related organisms whose average good is at an optimum level for the given environment. (Here *average good* means that the degree of realization of the good of *individual organisms* in the population or community is, on average, greater than would be the case under any other ecologically functioning order of interrelations among those species populations in the given ecosystem.)

The idea of a being having a good of its own, as I understand it, does not entail that the being must . . . take an interest in what affects its life for better or for worse. We can act in a being's interest or contrary to its interest without its being interested in what we are doing to it in the sense of wanting or not wanting us to do it. It may, indeed, be wholly unaware that favorable and unfavorable events are taking place in its life. I take it that trees, for example, have no knowledge or desires or feelings. Yet is is undoubtedly the case that trees can be harmed or benefited by our actions. We can crush their roots by running a bulldozer too close to them. We can see to it that they get adequate nourishment and moisture by fertilizing and watering the soil around them. Thus we can help or hinder them in the realization of their good. It is the good of trees themselves that is thereby affected. . . .

When construed in this way, the concept of a being's good is not coextensive with sentience or the capacity for feeling pain. William Frankena has argued for a general theory of environmental ethics in which the ground of a creature's being worthy of moral consideration is its sentience. I have offered some criticisms of this view elsewhere, but the full refutation of such a position, it seems to me, finally depends on the positive reasons for accepting a life-centered theory of the kind I am defending in this essay. . . .[1]

Since I am concerned only with human treatment of wild organisms, species populations, and communities of life as they occur in our planet's natural ecosystems, it is to those entities alone that the concept "having a good of its own" will here be applied. I am not denying that other living things, whose genetic origin and environmental conditions have been produced, controlled, and manipulated by humans for human ends, do have a good of their own in the same sense as do wild plants and animals. It is not my purpose in this essay, however, to set out or defend the principles that should guide our conduct with regard to their good. It is only insofar as their production and use by humans have good or ill effects upon natural ecosystems and their wild inhabitants that the ethics of respect for nature comes into play. . . .

## THE BIOCENTRIC OUTLOOK ON NATURE

[The] belief system underlying the attitude of respect for nature I call (for want of a better name) "the biocentric outlook on nature." Since it is not wholly analyzable into empirically confirmable assertions, it should not be thought of as simply a compendium of the biological sciences concerning our planet's ecosystems. It might best be described as a philosophical world view, to distinguish it from a scientific theory or explanatory system. However, one of its major tenets is the great lesson we have learned from the science of ecology: the interdependence of all living things in an organically unified order whose balance and stability are necessary conditions for the realization of the good of its constituent biotic communities.

Before turning to an account of the main components of the biocentric outlook, it is convenient here to set forth the overall structure of my theory of environmental ethics as it has now emerged. The ethics of respect for nature is made up of three basic elements: a belief system, an ultimate moral attitude, and a set of rules of duty and standards of character. These elements are connected with each other in the following manner. The belief system provides a certain outlook on nature which supports and makes intelligible an autonomous agent's adopting, as an ultimate moral attitude, the attitude of respect for nature. It supports and makes intelligible the attitude in the sense that, when an autonomous agent understands its moral relations to the natural world in terms of this outlook, it recognizes the attitude of respect to be the only *suitable* or *fitting* attitude to take toward all wild forms of life in the Earth's biosphere. Living things are now viewed as *the appropriate objects of the attitude of respect* and are accordingly regarded as entities possessing inherent worth. One then places intrinsic value on the promotion and protection of their good. As a consequence of this, one makes a moral commitment to abide by a set of rules of duty and to fulfill (as far as one can by one's own efforts) certain standards of good character. Given one's adoption of the attitude of respect, one makes that moral commitment because one considers those rules and standards to be validly binding on all moral agents. They are seen as embodying forms of conduct and character structures in which the attitude of respect for nature is manifested.

This three-part complex which internally orders the ethics of respect for nature is symmetrical with a theory of human ethics grounded on respect for persons. Such a theory includes, first, a conception of oneself and others as persons, that is, as centers of autonomous choice. Second, there is the attitude of respect for persons as persons. When this is adopted as an ultimate moral attitude it involves the disposition to treat every person as having inherent worth or "human dignity." Every human being, just in virtue of her or his humanity, is understood to be worthy of moral consideration, and intrinsic value is placed on the autonomy and well-being of each. This is what Kant meant by conceiving of persons as ends in themselves. Third, there is an ethical system of duties which are acknowledged to be owed by everyone to everyone. These duties are forms of conduct in which public recognition is given to each individual's inherent worth as a person.

This structural framework for a theory of human ethics is meant to leave open the issue of consequentialism (utilitarianism) versus nonconsequentialism (deontology). That issue concerns the particular kind of system of rules defining the duties of moral agents toward persons. Similarly, I am leaving open in this paper the question of what particular kind of system of rules defines our duties with respect to the natural world.

The biocentric outlook on nature has four main components. (1) Humans are thought of as members of the Earth's community of life, holding that membership on the same terms as apply to all the nonhuman members. (2) The Earth's natural ecosystems as a totality are seen as a complex web of interconnected elements, with the sound biological functioning of each being dependent on the sound biological functioning of the others. (This is the component referred to above as the great lesson that the science of ecology has taught us.) (3) Each individual organism is conceived of as a teleological center of life, pursuing its own good in its own way. (4) Whether we are concerned with standards of merit or with the concept of inherent worth, the claim that humans by their very nature are superior to other species is a groundless claim and, in the light of elements (1), (2), and (3) above, must be rejected as nothing more than an irrational bias in our own favor.

The conjunction of these four ideas constitutes the biocentric outlook on nature. In the remainder of this paper I give a brief account of the first three components, followed by a more detailed analysis of the fourth. I then conclude by indicating how this outlook provides a way of justifying the attitude of respect for nature.

## HUMANS AS MEMBERS OF THE EARTH'S COMMUNITY OF LIFE

We share with other species a common relationship to the Earth. In accepting the biocentric outlook we take the fact of our being an animal species to be a fundamental feature of our existence. We consider it an essential aspect of "the human condition." We do not deny the differences between ourselves and other species, but we keep in the forefront of our consciousness the fact that in relation to our planet's natural ecosystems we are but one species population among many. Thus we acknowledge our origin in the very same evolutionary process that gave rise to all other species and we recognize ourselves to be confronted with similar environmental challenges to those that confront them. The laws of genetics, of natural selection, and of adaptation apply equally to all of us as biological creatures. In this light we consider ourselves as one with them, not set apart from them. We, as well as they, must face certain basic conditions of existence that impose requirements on us for our survival and well-being. Each animal and plant is like us in having a good of its own. Although our human good (what is of true value in human life, including the exercise of individual autonomy in choosing our own particular value systems) is not like the good of a nonhuman animal or plant, it can no more be realized than their good can without the biological necessities for survival and physical health.

When we look at ourselves from the evolutionary point of view, we see that not only are we very recent arrivals on Earth, but that our emergence as a new species on the planet was originally an event of no particular importance to the entire scheme of things. The Earth was teeming with life long before we appeared. Putting the point metaphorically, we are relative newcomers, entering a home that has been the residence of others for hundreds of millions of years, a home that must now be shared by all of us together.

The comparative brevity of human life on Earth may be vividly depicted by imagining the geological time scale in spatial terms. Suppose we start with algae, which have been around for at least 600 million years. (The earliest protozoa actually predated this by several *billion* years.) If the time that algae have been here were represented by the length of a football field (300 feet), then the period during which sharks have been swimming in the world's oceans and spiders have been spinning their webs would occupy three quarters of the length of the field; reptiles would show up at about the center of the field; mammals would cover the last third of the field; hominids (mammals of the family *Hominidae*) the last two feet; and the species *Homo sapiens* the last six inches.

Whether this newcomer is able to survive as long as other species remains to be seen. But there is surely something presumptuous about the way humans look down on the "lower" animals, especially those that have become extinct. We consider the dinosaurs, for example, to be biological failures, though they existed on our planet for 65 million years. One writer has made the point with beautiful simplicity:

> We sometimes speak of the dinosaurs as failures; there will be time enough for that judgment when we have lasted even for one tenth as long. . . .[2]

The possibility of the extinction of the human species, a possibility which starkly confronts us in the contemporary world, makes us aware of another respect in which we should not consider ourselves privileged beings in relation to other species. This is the fact that the well-being of humans is dependent upon the ecological soundness and health of many plant and animal communities, while their soundness and health does not in the least depend upon human well-being. Indeed, from their standpoint the very existence of humans is quite unnecessary. Every last man, woman, and child could disappear from the face of the Earth without any significant detrimental consequence for the good of wild animals and plants. On the contrary, many of them would be greatly benefited. The destruction of their habitats by human "developments" would cease. The poisoning and polluting of their environment would come to an end. The Earth's land, air, and water would no longer be subject to the degradation they are now undergoing as the result of large-scale technology and uncontrolled population growth. Life communities in natural ecosystems would gradually return to their former healthy state. Tropical forests, for example, would again be able to make their full contribution to a life-sustaining atmosphere for the whole planet. The rivers, lakes, and oceans of the world would (perhaps) eventually become clean again. Spilled oil, plastic trash, and even radioactive waste might finally, after many centuries, cease doing their terrible work. Ecosystems would return to their proper balance, suffering only the disruptions of natural events such as volcanic eruptions and glaciation. From these the community of life could recover, as it has so often done in the past. But the ecological disasters now perpetrated on it by humans—disasters from which it might never recover—these it would no longer have to endure.

If, then, the total, final, absolute extermination of our species (by our own hands?) should take place and if we should not carry all the others with us into oblivion, not only would the Earth's community of life continue to exist, but in all probability its well-being would be enhanced. Our presence, in short, is not needed. If we were to take the standpoint of the community and give voice to its true interest, the ending of our six-inch epoch would most likely be greeted with a hearty "Good riddance!"

## THE NATURAL WORLD AS AN ORGANIC SYSTEM

To accept the biocentric outlook and regard ourselves and our place in the world from its perspective is to see the whole natural order of the Earth's biosphere as a complex but unified web of interconnected organisms, objects, and events. The ecological relationships between any community of living things and their environment form an organic whole of functionally interdependent parts. Each ecosystem is a small universe itself in which the interactions of its various species populations comprise an intricately woven network of cause-effect relations. Such dynamic but at the same time relatively stable structures as food chains, predator-prey relations, and plant succession in a forest are self-regulating, energy-recycling mechanisms that preserve the equilibrium of the whole.

As far as the well-being of wild animals and plants is concerned, this ecological equilibrium must not be destroyed. The same holds true of the well-being of humans. When one views the realm of nature from the perspective of the biocentric outlook, one never forgets that in the long run the integrity of the entire biosphere of our planet is essential to the realization of the good of its constituent communities of life, both human and nonhuman.

Although the importance of this idea cannot be overemphasized, it is by now so familiar and so widely acknowledged that I shall not further elaborate on it here. However, I do wish to point out that this "holistic" view of the Earth's ecological systems does not itself constitute a moral norm. It is a factual aspect of biological reality, to be understood as a set of causal connections in ordinary empirical terms. Its significance for humans is the same as its significance for nonhumans, namely, in setting basic conditions for the realization of the good of living things. Its ethical implications for our treatment of the natural environment lie entirely in the fact that our *knowledge* of these causal connections is an essential *means* to fulfilling the aims we set for ourselves in adopting the attitude of respect for nature. In addition, its theoretical implications for the ethics of respect for nature lie in the fact that it (along with the other elements of the biocentric outlook) makes the adopting of that attitude a rational and intelligible thing to do.

## INDIVIDUAL ORGANISMS AS TELEOLOGICAL CENTERS OF LIFE

As our knowledge of living things increases, as we come to a deeper understanding of their life cycles, their interactions with other organisms, and the manifold ways in which they adjust to the environment, we become more fully aware of how each of them is carrying out its biological functions according to the laws of its species-specific nature. But besides this, our increasing knowledge and understanding also develop in us a sharpened awareness of the uniqueness of each individual organism. Scientists who have made careful studies of particular plants and animals, whether in the field or in laboratories, have often acquired a knowledge of their subjects as identifiable individuals. Close observation over extended periods of time has led them to an appreciation of the unique "personalities" of their subjects. Sometimes a scientist may come to take a special interest in a particular animal or plant, all the while remaining strictly objective in the gathering and recording of data. Nonscientists may likewise experience this development of interest when, as amateur naturalists, they make accurate observations over sustained periods of close acquaintance with an individual organism. As one becomes more and more familiar with the organism and its behavior, one becomes fully sensitive to the particular way it is living out its life cycle. One may become fascinated by it and even experience some involvement with its good and bad fortunes (that is, with the occurrence of environmental conditions favorable or unfavorable to the realization of its good). The organism comes to mean something to one as a unique, irreplaceable individual. The final culmination of this process is the achievement of a genuine understanding of its point of view and, with that understanding, an ability to "take" that point of view. *Conceiving of it as a center of life, one is able to look at the world from its perspective.*

This development from objective knowledge to the recognition of individuality, and from the recognition of individuality to full awareness of an organism's standpoint, is a process of heightening our consciousness of what it means to be an individual living thing. We grasp the particularity of the organism as a teleological center of life, striving to preserve itself and to realize its own good in its own unique way.

It is to be noted that we need not be falsely anthropomorphizing when we conceive of individual plants and animals in this manner. Understanding them as teleological centers of life does not necessitate "reading into" them human characteristics. We need not, for example, consider them to have consciousness. Some of them may be aware of the world around them and others may not. Nor need we deny that different kinds and levels of awareness are exemplified when consciousness in some form is present. But conscious or not, all are equally teleological centers of life in the sense that each is a unified system of goal-oriented activities directed toward their preservation and well-being.

When considered from an ethical point of view, a teleological center of life is an entity whose "world" can be viewed from the perspective of *its* life. In looking at the world from that perspective we recognize objects and events occurring in its life as being beneficent, maleficent, or indifferent. The first are occurrences which increase its powers to preserve its existence and realize its good. The second decrease or destroy those powers. The third have neither of these effects on the entity. With regard to our human role as moral agents, we can conceive of a teleological center of life as a being whose standpoint we can take in making judgments about what events in the world are good or evil, desirable or undesirable. In making those judgments it is what promotes or protects the being's own good, not what benefits moral agents themselves, that sets the standard of evaluation. Such judgments can be made about anything that happens to the entity which is favorable or unfavorable in relation to its good. As was pointed out earlier, the entity itself need not have any (conscious) *interest* in what is happening to it for such judgments to be meaningful and true.

It is precisely judgments of this sort that we are disposed to make when we take the attitude of respect for nature. In adopting that attitude those judgments are given weight as reasons for action in our practical deliberation. They become morally relevant facts in the guidance of our conduct.

## THE DENIAL OF HUMAN SUPERIORITY

This fourth component of the biocentric outlook on nature is the single most important idea in establishing the justifiability of the attitude of respect for nature. Its central role is due to the special relationship it bears to the first three components of the outlook. This relationship will be brought out after the concept of human superiority is examined and analyzed.[3]

In what sense are humans alleged to be superior to other animals? We are different from them in having certain capacities that they lack. But why should these capacities be a mark of superiority? From what point of view are they judged to be signs of superiority and what sense of superiority is meant? After all, various nonhuman species have capacities that humans lack. There is the speed of a cheetah, the vision of an eagle, the agility of a monkey. Why should not these be taken as signs of *their* superiority over humans?

One answer that comes immediately to mind is that these capacities are not as *valuable* as the human capacities that are claimed to make us superior. Such uniquely human characteristics as rational thought, aesthetic creativity, autonomy and self-determination, and moral freedom, it might be held, have a higher value than the capacities found in other species. Yet we must ask: valuable to whom, and on what grounds?

The human characteristics mentioned are all valuable to humans. They are essential to the preservation and enrichment of our civilization and culture. Clearly it is from the human standpoint that they are being judged to be desirable and good. It is not difficult here to recognize a begging of the question. Humans are claiming human superiority from a strictly human point of view, that is, from a point of view in which the good of humans is taken as the standard of judgment. All we need to do is to look at the capacities of nonhuman animals (or plants, for that matter) from the standpoint of *their* good to find a contrary judgment of superiority. The speed of the cheetah, for example, is a sign of its superiority to humans when considered from the standpoint of the good of its species. If it were as slow a runner as a human, it would not be able to survive. And so for all the other abilities of nonhumans which further their good but which are lacking in humans. In each case the claim to human superiority would be rejected from a nonhuman standpoint.

When superiority assertions are interpreted in this way, they are based on judgments of *merit*. To judge the merits of a person or an organism one must apply grading or ranking standards to it. (As I show below, this distinguishes judgments of merit from judgments of inherent worth.) Empirical investigation then determines whether it has the "good-making properties" (merits) in virtue of which it fulfills the standards being applied. In the case of humans, merits may be either moral or nonmoral. We can judge one person to be better than (superior to) another from the moral point of view by applying certain standards to their character and conduct. Similarly, we can appeal to nonmoral criteria in judging someone to be an excellent piano player, a fair cook, a poor tennis player, and so on. Different social purposes and roles are implicit in the making of such judgments, providing the frame of reference for the choice of standards by which the nonmoral merits of people are determined. Ultimately such purposes and roles stem from a society's way of life as a whole. Now a society's way of life may be thought of as the cultural form given to the realization of human values. Whether moral or nonmoral standards are being applied, then, all judgments of people's merits finally depend on human values. All are made from an exclusively human standpoint.

The question that naturally arises at this juncture is: why should standards that are based on human values be assumed to be the only valid criteria of merit and hence the only true signs of superiority? This question is especially pressing when humans are being judged superior in merit to nonhumans. It is true that a human being may be a better mathematician than a monkey, but the monkey may be a better tree climber than a human being. If we humans value mathematics more than tree climbing, that is because our conception of civilized life makes the development of mathematical ability more desirable than the ability to climb trees. But is it not unreasonable to judge nonhumans by the values of human civilization, rather than by values connected with what it is for a member of *that* species to live a good life? If all living things have a good of their own, it at least makes sense to judge the merits of nonhumans by standards derived from *their* good. To use only standards based on human values is already to commit oneself to holding that humans are superior to nonhumans, which is the point in question.

A further logical flaw arises in connection with the widely held conviction that humans are *morally* superior beings because they possess, while others lack, the capacities of a moral agent (free will, accountability, deliberation, judgment, practical reason). This view rests on a conceptual confusion. As far as moral standards are concerned, only beings that have the capacities of a moral agent can properly be judged to be *either* moral (morally good) *or* immoral (morally deficient). Moral standards are simply not applicable to beings that lack such capacities. Animals and plants cannot therefore be said to be morally inferior in merit to humans. Since the only beings that can have moral merits *or be deficient in such merits* are moral agents, it is conceptually incoherent to judge humans as superior to nonhumans on the ground that humans have moral capacities while nonhumans don't.

Up to this point I have been interpreting the claim that humans are superior to other living things as a grading or ranking judgment regarding their comparative merits. There is, however, another way of understanding the idea of human superiority. According to this interpretation, humans are superior to nonhumans not as regards their merits but as regards their inherent worth. Thus the claim of human superiority is to be understood as asserting that all humans, simply in virtue of their humanity, have *a greater inherent worth* than other living things.

The inherent worth of an entity does not depend on its merits.[4] To consider something as possessing inherent worth, we have seen, is to place intrinsic value on the realization of its good. This is done regardless of whatever particular merits it might have or might lack, as judged by a set of grading or ranking standards. In human affairs, we are all familiar with the principle that one's worth as a person does not vary with one's merits or lack of merits. The same can hold true of animals and plants. To regard such entities as possessing inherent worth entails disregarding their merits and deficiencies, whether they are being judged from a human standpoint or from the standpoint of their own species.

The idea of one entity having more merit than another, and so being superior to it in merit, makes perfectly good sense. Merit is a grading or ranking concept, and judgments of comparative merit are based on the different degrees to which things satisfy a given standard. But what can it mean to talk about one thing being superior to another in inherent worth? In order to get at what is being asserted in such a claim it is helpful first to look at the social origin of the concept of degrees of inherent worth.

The idea that humans can possess different degrees of inherent worth originated in societies having rigid class structures. Before the rise of modern democracies with their egalitarian outlook, one's membership in a hereditary class determined one's social status. People in the upper classes were looked up to, while those in the lower classes were looked down upon. In such a society one's social superiors and social inferiors were clearly defined and easily recognized.

Two aspects of these class-structured societies are especially relevant to the idea of degrees of inherent worth. First, those born into the upper classes were deemed more worthy of respect than those born into the lower orders. Second, the superior worth of upper class people had nothing to do with their merits nor did the inferior worth of those in the lower classes rest on their lack of merits. One's superiority or inferiority entirely derived from a social position one was born into. The modern concept of a meritocracy simply did not apply. One could not advance into a higher class by any sort of moral or nonmoral achievement. Similarly, an aristocrat held his title and all the privileges that went with it just because he was the eldest son of a titled nobleman. Unlike the bestowing of knighthood in contemporary Great Britain, one did not earn membership in the nobility by meritorious conduct.

We who live in modern democracies no longer believe in such hereditary social distinctions. Indeed, we would wholeheartedly condemn them on moral grounds as being fundamentally unjust. We have come to think of class systems as a paradigm of social injustice, it being a central principle of the democratic way of life that among humans there are no superiors and no inferiors. Thus we have rejected the whole conceptual framework in which people are judged to have different degrees of inherent worth. That idea is incompatible with our notion of human equality based on the doctrine that all humans, simply in virtue of their humanity, have the same inherent worth. (The belief in universal human rights is one form that this egalitarianism takes.)

The vast majority of people in modern democracies, however, do not maintain an egalitarian outlook when it comes to comparing human beings with other living things. Most people consider our own species to be superior to all other species and this superiority is understood to be a matter of inherent worth, not merit. There may exist thoroughly vicious and depraved humans who lack all merit. Yet because they are human they are thought to belong to a higher class of entities than any plant or animal. That one is born into the species *Homo sapiens* entitles one to have lordship over those who are one's inferiors, namely, those born into other species. The parallel with hereditary social classes is very close. Implicit in this view is a hierarchical conception of nature according to which an organism has a position of superiority or inferiority in the Earth's community of life simply on the basis of its genetic background. The "lower" orders of life are looked down upon and it is considered perfectly proper that they serve the interests of those belonging to the highest order, namely humans. The intrinsic value we place on the well-being of our fellow humans reflects our recognition of their rightful position as our equals. No such intrinsic value is to be placed on the good of other animals, unless we choose to do so out of fondness or affection for them. But their well-being imposes no moral requirement on us. In this respect there is an absolute difference in moral status between ourselves and them.

This is the structure of concepts and beliefs that people are committed to insofar as they regard humans to be superior in inherent worth to all other species. I now wish to argue that this structure of concepts and beliefs is completely groundless. If we accept the first three components of the biocentric outlook and from that perspective look at the major philosophical traditions which have supported that structure, we find it to be at bottom nothing more than the expression of an irrational bias in our own favor. The philosophical traditions themselves rest on very questionable assumptions or else simply beg the question. I briefly consider three of the main traditions to substantiate the point. These are classical Greek humanism, Cartesian dualism, and the Judeo-Christian concept of the Great Chain of Being.

The inherent superiority of humans over other species was implicit in the Greek definition of man as a rational animal. Our animal nature was identified with "brute" desires that need the order and restraint of reason to rule them (just as reason is the special virtue of those who rule in the ideal state). Rationality was then seen to be the key to our superiority over animals. It enables us to live on a higher plane and endows us with a nobility and worth that other creatures lack. This familiar way of comparing humans with other species is deeply ingrained in our Western philosophical outlook. The point to consider here is that this view does not actually provide an argument *for* human superiority but rather makes explicit the framework of thought that is implicitly used by those who think of humans as inherently superior to nonhumans. The Greeks who held that humans, in virtue of their rational capacities, have a kind of worth greater than that of any nonrational being, never looked at rationality as but one capacity of living things among many others. But when we consider rationality from the standpoint of the first three elements of the ecological outlook, we see that its value lies in its importance for *human* life. Other creatures achieve their species-specific good without the need of rationality, although they often make use of capacities that humans lack. So the humanistic outlook of classical Greek thought does not give us a neutral (non-question-begging) ground on which to construct a scale of degrees of inherent worth possessed by different species of living things.

The second tradition, centering on the Cartesian dualism of soul and body, also fails to justify the claim to human superiority. That superiority is supposed to derive from the fact that we have souls while animals do not. Animals are mere automata and lack the divine element that makes us spiritual beings. I won't go into the now familiar criticisms of this two-substance view. I only add the point that, even if humans are composed of an immaterial, unextended soul and a material, extended body, this in itself is not a reason to deem them of greater worth than entities that are only bodies. Why is a soul substance a thing that adds value to its possessor? Unless some theological reasoning is offered here (which many, including myself, would find unacceptable on epistemological grounds), no logical connection is evident. An immaterial something which thinks is better than a material something which does not think only if thinking itself has value, either intrinsically or instrumentally. Now it is intrinsically valuable to humans alone, who value it as an end in itself, and it is instrumentally valuable to those who benefit from it, namely humans.

For animals that neither enjoy thinking for its own sake nor need it for living the kind of life for which they are best adapted, it has no value. Even if "thinking" is broadened to include all forms of consciousness, there are still many living things that can do without it and yet live what is for their species a good life. The anthropocentricity underlying the claim to human superiority runs throughout Cartesian dualism.

A third major source of the idea of human superiority is the Judeo-Christian concept of the Great Chain of Being. Humans are superior to animals and plants because their Creator has given them a higher place on the chain. It begins with God at the top, and then moves to the angels, who are lower than God but higher than humans, then to humans, positioned between the angels and the beasts (partaking of the nature of both), and then on down to the lower levels occupied by nonhuman animals, plants, and finally inanimate objects. Humans, being "made in God's image," are inherently superior to animals and plants by virtue of their being closer (in their essential nature) to God.

The metaphysical and epistemological difficulties with this conception of a hierarchy of entities are, in my mind, insuperable. Without entering into this matter here, I only point out that if we are unwilling to accept the metaphysics of traditional Judaism and Christianity, we are again left without good reasons for holding to the claim of inherent human superiority.

The foregoing considerations (and others like them) leave us with but one ground for the assertion that a human being, regardless of merit, is a higher kind of entity than any other living thing. This is the mere fact of the genetic makeup of the species *Homo sapiens.* But this is surely irrational and arbitrary. Why should the arrangement of genes of a certain type be a mark of superior value, especially when this fact about an organism is taken by itself, unrelated to any other aspect of its life? We might just as well refer to any other genetic makeup as a ground of superior value. Clearly we are confronted here with a wholly arbitrary claim that can only be explained as an irrational bias in our own favor.

That the claim is nothing more than a deep-seated prejudice is brought home to us when we look at our relation to other species in the light of the first three elements of the biocentric outlook. Those elements taken conjointly give us a certain overall view of the natural world and of the place of humans in it. When we take this view we come to understand other living things, their environmental conditions, and their ecological relationships in such a way as to awake in us a deep sense of our kinship with them as fellow members of the Earth's community of life. Humans and nonhumans alike are viewed together as integral parts of one unified whole in which all living things are functionally interrelated. Finally, when our awareness focuses on the individual lives of plants and animals, each is seen to share with us the characteristic of being a teleological center of life striving to realize its own good in its own good in its own unique way.

As this entire belief system becomes part of the conceptual framework through which we understand and perceive the world, we come to see ourselves as bearing a certain moral relation to nonhuman forms of life. Our ethical role in nature takes on a new significance. We begin to look at other species as we look at ourselves, seeing them as beings which have a good they are striving to realize just as we have a good we are striving to realize. We accordingly develop the disposition to view the world from the standpoint of their good as well as from the standpoint of our own good. Now if the groundlessness of the claim that humans are inherently superior to other species were brought clearly before our minds, we would not remain intellectually neutral toward that claim but would reject it as being fundamentally at variance with our total world outlook. In the absence of any good reasons for holding it, the assertion of human superiority would then appear simply as the expression of an irrational and self-serving prejudice that favors one particular species over several million others.

Rejecting the notion of human superiority entails its positive counterpart: the doctrine of species impartiality. One who accepts that doctrine regards all living things as possessing inherent worth—the *same* inherent worth, since no one species has been shown to be either "higher" or "lower" than any other. Now we saw earlier that, insofar as one thinks of a living thing as possessing inherent worth, one considers it to be the appropriate object of the attitude of respect and believes that attitude to be the only fitting or suitable one for all moral agents to take toward it.

Here, then, is the key to understanding how the attitude of respect is rooted in the biocentric outlook on nature. The basic connection is made through the denial of human superiority. Once we reject the claim that humans are superior either in merit or in worth to other living things, we are ready to adopt the attitude of respect. The denial of human superiority is itself the result of taking the perspective on nature built into the first three elements of the biocentric outlook.

Now the first three elements of the biocentric outlook, it seems clear, would be found acceptable to any rational and scientifically informed thinker who is fully "open" to the reality of the lives of nonhuman organisms. Without denying our distinctively human characteristics, such a thinker can acknowledge the fundamental respects in which we are members of the Earth's community of life and in which the biological conditions necessary for the realization of our human values are inextricably linked with the whole system of nature. In addition, the conception of individual living things as teleological centers of life simply articulates how a scientifically informed thinker comes to understand them as the result of increasingly careful and detailed observations. Thus, the biocentric outlook recommends itself as an acceptable system of concepts and beliefs to anyone who is clear-minded, unbiased, and factually enlightened, and who has a developed capacity of reality awareness with regard to the lives of individual organisms. This, I submit, is as good a reason for making the moral commitment involved in adopting the attitude of respect for nature as any theory of environmental ethics could possibly have.

## MORAL RIGHTS AND THE MATTER OF COMPETING CLAIMS

I have not asserted anywhere in the foregoing account that animals or plants have moral rights. This omission was deliberate. I do not think that the reference class of the concept, bearer of moral rights, should be extended to include nonhuman living things. My reasons for taking this position, however, go beyond the scope of this paper. I believe I have been able to accomplish many of the same ends which those who ascribe rights to animals or plants wish to accomplish. There is no reason, moreover, why plants and animals, including whole species populations and life communities, cannot be accorded *legal* rights under my theory. To grant them legal protection could be interpreted as giving them legal entitlement to be protected, and this, in fact, would be a means by which a society that subscribed to the ethics of respect for nature could give public recognition to their inherent worth.

There remains the problem of competing claims, even when wild plants and animals are not thought of as bearers of moral rights. If we accept the biocentric outlook and accordingly adopt the attitude of respect for nature as our ultimate moral attitude, how do we resolve conflicts that arise from our respect for persons in the domain of human ethics and our respect for nature in the domain of environmental ethics? This is a question that cannot adequately be dealt with here. My main purpose in this paper has been to try to establish a base point from which we can start working toward a solution to the problem. I have shown why we cannot just begin with an initial presumption in favor of the interests of our own species. It is after all within our power as moral beings to place limits on human population and technology with the deliberate intention of sharing the Earth's bounty with other species. That such sharing is an ideal difficult to realize even in an approximate way does not take away it's claim to our deepest moral commitment.

## NOTES

1. See W. K. Frankena, "Ethics and the Environment," in K. E. Goodpaster and K. M. Sayre, eds., *Ethics and Problems of the 21st Century* (Notre Dame, University of Notre Dame Press, 1979), pp. 3–20. I critically examine Frankena's views in "Frankena on Environmental Ethics," *Monist*, Vol. 64, No. 3 (July 1981), pp. 313–24.
2. Stephen R. L. Clark, *The Moral Status of Animals* (Oxford: Clarendon Press, 1977), p. 112.
3. My criticisms of the dogma of human superiority gain independent support from a carefully reasoned essay by R. and V. Routley showing the many logical weaknesses in arguments for human-centered theories of environmental ethics. R. and V. Routley, "Against the Inevitability of Human Chauvinism," in K. E. Goodpaster and K. M. Sayre, eds., *Ethics and Problems of the 21st Century* (Notre Dame: University of Notre Dame Press, 1979), pp. 36–59.
4. For this way of distinguishing between merit and inherent worth, I am indebted to Gregory Vlastos, "Justice and Equality," in R. Brandt, ed., *Social Justice* (Englewood Cliffs, N.J.: Prentice-Hall, 1962), pp. 31–72.

# ANIMAL LIBERATION AND ENVIRONMENTAL ETHICS: BAD MARRIAGE, QUICK DIVORCE

*Mark Sagoff*

Mark Sagoff is director and senior research scholar at the Institute for Philosophy and Public Policy at the University of Maryland. He is the author of *The Economy of the Earth: Philosophy, Law, and the Environment.*

## I

"The land ethic," Aldo Leopold wrote in *A Sand County Almanac,* "simply enlarges the boundaries of the community to include soils, waters, plants, and animals, or collectively, the land."[1] What kind of community does Leopold refer to? He might mean a *moral* community, for example, a group of individuals who respect each other's right to treatment as equals or who regard one another's interests with equal respect and concern. He may also mean an *ecological* community, that is, a community tied together by biological relationships in interdependent webs or systems of life.[2]

Let us suppose, for a moment, that Leopold has a *moral* community in mind; he would expand our *moral* boundaries to include not only human beings, but also soils, waters, plants and animals. Leopold's view, then, might not differ in principle from that of Christopher Stone, who has suggested that animals and even trees be given legal standing, so that their interests may be represented in court.[3] Stone sees the expansion of our moral consciousness in this way as part of a historical progress by which societies have recognized the equality of groups of oppressed people, notably blacks, women and children.[4] Laurence Tribe eloquently makes the same point:

This essay originally appeared in *Law Journal*, Vol. 22, No. 2, 297–307. Reprinted by permission.

What is crucial to recognize is that the human capacity for empathy and identi-fication is not static; the very process of recognizing rights in those higher ver-tebrates with whom we can already empathize could well pave the way for still further extensions as we move upward along the spiral of moral evolution. It is not only the human liberation movements—involving first blacks, then women, and now children—that advance in waves of increased consciousness.[5]

Peter Singer, perhaps more than any other writer, has emphasized the analogy between human liberation movements (for example, abolitionism and suffragism) and "animal liberation" or the "expansion of our moral hori-zons" to include members of other species in the "basic principle of equality."[6] Singer differs from Stone and Tribe, however, in two respects. First, he argues that the capacity of animals to suffer pain or to enjoy pleasure or happiness places people under a moral obligation which does not need to be enhanced by a doctrine about rights. Second, while Stone is willing to speak of the in-terests of his lawn in being watered,[7] Singer argues that "only a being with subjective experiences, such as the experience of pleasure or the experience of pain, can have interests in the full sense of the term."[8] A tree, as Singer ex-plains, may be said to have an "interest" in being watered, but all this means is that it needs water to grow properly as an automobile needs oil to function properly.[9] Thus, Singer would not include rocks, trees, lakes, rivers, or moun-tains in the moral community or the community of morally equal beings.

Singer's thesis, then, is not necessarily that animals have rights which we are to respect. Instead, he argues that they have utilities that ought to be treated on an equal basis with those of human beings. Whether Tribe and Stone argue a weaker or a different thesis depends upon the rights they be-lieve animals and other natural things to have. They may believe that all ani-mals have a right to be treated as equals, in effect, they may agree with Singer that the interests of *all* animals should receive equal respect and concern. On the other hand, Tribe, Stone or both may believe that animals have a right only to life or only to those very minimal and basic rights without which they could not conceivably enjoy any other right.[10] I will, for the moment, assume that Tribe and Stone agree that animals have basic rights, for example, a right to live or a right not to be killed for their meat. I will consider later the possi-bility that environmental law might protect the rights of animals without nec-essarily improving their welfare or protecting their lives.

Moral obligations to animals, to their well-being or to their rights, may arise in either of two ways. First, duties to nonhuman animals may be based on the principle that cruelty to animals is obnoxious, a principle nobody denies. Muckraking journalists (thank God for them) who depict the horrors which all too often occur in laboratories and on farms, appeal quite properly to the conviction and intuition that people should never inflict needless pain on an-imals and especially not for the sake of profit. When television documentaries or newspaper articles report the horrid ways in which domestic animals are often treated, the response is, as it should be, moral revulsion. This anger is directed at human responsibility for the callous, wanton and needless cruelty human beings inflict on domestic animals. It is not simply the pain but the way it is caused which justified moral outrage.

Moral obligations, however, might rest instead on a stronger contention, which is that human beings are obliged to prevent and to relieve animal suffering however it is caused. Now, insofar as the animal equality or animal liberation movement makes a philosophically interesting claim, it insists on the stronger thesis, that there is an obligation to serve the interests, or at least to protect the lives, of *all* animals who suffer or are killed, whether on the farm or in the wild. Singer, for example, does not stop with the stultifying platitude that human beings ought not to be cruel to animals. No; he argues the controversial thesis that society has an obligation to prevent the killing of animals and even to relieve their suffering wherever, however, and as much as it is able, to a reasonable cost to itself.

## II

I began by supposing that Aldo Leopold viewed the community of nature as a *moral* community—one in which human beings, as members, have obligations to all other animals, presumably to minimize their pain. I suggested that Leopold, like Singer, may be committed to the idea that the natural environment should be preserved and protected only insofar as, and because, its protection satisfies the needs or promotes the welfare of individual animals and perhaps other living things. I believe, however, that this is plainly not Leopold's view. The principle of natural selection is not obviously a humanitarian principle; the predator–prey relation does not depend on moral empathy. Nature ruthlessly limits animal populations by doing violence to virtually every individual before it reaches maturity; these conditions respect animal equality only in the darkest sense. Yet these are precisely the ecological relationships which Leopold admires; they are the conditions which he would not interfere with, but protect. Apparently, Leopold does not think that an ecological system has to be an egalitarian moral system in order to deserve love and admiration. An ecological system has a beauty and an authenticity that demands respect—but plainly not on humanitarian grounds.

In a persuasive essay, J. Baird Callicott describes a number of differences between the ideas of Leopold and those of Singer—differences which suggest that Leopold's environmental ethic and Singer's humane utilitarianism lead in opposite directions. First, while Singer and other animal liberationists deplore the suffering of domestic animals, "Leopold manifests an attitude that can only be described as indifference."[11] Second, while Leopold expresses an urgent concern about the disappearance of species, Singer, consistently with his premises, is concerned with the welfare of individual animals, without special regard to their status as endangered species. Third, the preservation of wilderness, according to Leopold, provides "a means of perpetuating, in sport form, the more virile and primitive skills. . . ."[12] He had hunting in mind. Leopold recognized that since top predators are gone, hunters may serve an important ecological function. Leopold was himself an enthusiastic hunter and wrote unabashedly about his exploits pursuing game. The term "game" as applied to animals, Callicott wryly comments, "appears to be morally equivalent to referring to a sexually appealing young woman as a "piece" or to a strong, young black man as a "buck"—if animal rights, that is, are to be considered on par with women's rights and the rights of formerly enslaved races."[13]

Singer expresses disdain and chagrin at what he calls "'environmentalist'" organizations such as the Sierra Club and the Wildlife Fund, which actively support or refuse to oppose hunting. I can appreciate Singer's aversion to hunting, but why does he place the word "environmentalist" in shudder quotes when he refers to organizations like the Sierra Club? Environmentalist and conservationist organizations traditionally have been concerned with ecological, not humanitarian issues. They make no pretense of acting for the sake of individual animals; rather, they attempt to maintain the diversity, integrity, beauty and authenticity of the natural environment. These goals are ecological, not eleemosynary. Their goals are entirely consistent, then, with licensing hunters to shoot animals whose populations exceed the carrying capacity of their habitats. Perhaps hunting is immoral; if so, environmentalism is consistent with an immoral practice, but it is environmentalism without quotes nonetheless. The policies environmentalists recommend are informed by the concepts of population biology, not the concepts of animal equality. The SPCA does not set the agenda for the Sierra Club.

I do not in any way mean to support the practice of hunting; nor am I advocating environmentalism at this time. I merely want to point out that groups like the Sierra Club, the Wilderness Society, and the World Wildlife Fund do not fail in their mission insofar as they devote themselves to causes other than the happiness or welfare of individual creatures; that never was their mission. These organizations, which promote a love and respect for the functioning of natural ecosystems, differ ideologically from organizations that make the suffering of animals their primary concern—groups like the Fund for Animals, the Animal Protection Institute, Friends of Animals, the American Humane Association, and various single issue groups such as Friends of the Sea Otter, Beaver Defenders, Friends of the Earthworm, and Worldwide Fair Play for Frogs.[14]

D. G. Ritchie, writing in 1916, posed a difficulty for those who argue that animals have rights or that we have obligations to them created simply by their capacity to suffer. If the suffering of animals creates a human obligation to mitigate it, is there not as much an obligation to prevent a cat from killing a mouse as to prevent a hunter from killing a deer? "Are we not to vindicate the rights of the persecuted prey of the stronger?" Ritchie asks. "Or is

our declaration of the rights of every creeping thing to remain a mere hypocritical formula to gratify pug-loving sentimentalists?"[15]

If the animal liberation or animal equality movement is not to deterio-
rate into "a hypocritical formula to gratify pug-loving sentimentalists," it must
insist, as Singer does, that moral obligations to animals are justified, in the
first place, by their distress, and, in the second place, by human ability to relieve that distress. The liberationist must morally require society to relieve animal suffering wherever it can and at a lesser cost to itself, whether in the
chicken coop or in the wild. Otherwise, the animal liberationist thesis becomes interchangeable with the platitude one learns along with how to tie
shoestrings: people ought not to be cruel to animals. I do not deny that human
beings are cruel to animals, that they ought not to be, that this cruelty should
be stopped and that sermons to this effect are entirely appropriate and necessary. I deny only that these sermons have anything to do with environmentalism or provide a basis for an environmental ethic.

# III

In discussing the rights of human beings, Henry Shue describes two that are
basic in the sense that "the enjoyment of them is essential to the enjoyment of
all other rights."[16] These are the right to physical security and the right to
minimum subsistence. These are positive, not merely negative rights. In other
words, these rights require governments to provide security and subsistence,
not merely to refrain from invading security and denying subsistence. These
basic rights require society, where possible, to rescue individuals from starvation; this is more than the merely negative obligation not to cause starvation.
No; if people have basic rights—and I have no doubt they do—then society has
a positive obligation to satisfy those rights. It is not enough for society simply
to refrain from violating them.

This, surely, is true of the basic rights of animals as well, if we are to give
the conception of "right" the same meaning for both people and animals. For
example, to allow animals to be killed for food or to permit them to die of disease or starvation when it is within human power to prevent it, does not seem
to balance fairly the interests of animals with those of human beings. To speak
of the rights of animals, of treating them as equals, of liberating them, and at
the same time to let nearly all of them perish unnecessarily in the most brutal
and horrible ways is not to display humanity but hypocrisy in the extreme.

Where should society concentrate its efforts to provide for the basic
welfare—the security and subsistence—of animals? Plainly, where animals
most lack this security, when their basic rights, needs, or interests are most
thwarted and where their suffering is most intense. Alas, this is in nature. Ever
since Darwin, we have been aware that few organisms survive to reach sexual
maturity; most are quickly annihilated in the struggle for existence. Consider
as a rough but reasonable statement of the facts the following:

All species reproduce in excess, way past the carrying capacity of their niche. In her lifetime a lioness might have 20 cubs; a pigeon, 150 chicks; a mouse, 1,000 kits; a trout, 20,000 fry, a tuna or cod, a million fry or more; an elm tree, several million seeds; and an oyster, perhaps a hundred million spat. If one assumes that the population of each of these species is, from generation to generation, roughly equal, then on the average only one offspring will survive to replace each parent. All the other thousands and millions will die, one way or another.[17]

The ways in which creatures in nature die are typically violent: predation, starvation, disease, parasitism, cold. The dying animal in the wild does not understand the vast ocean of misery into which it and billions of other animals are born only to drown. If the wild animal understood the conditions into which it is born, what would it think? It might reasonably prefer to be raised on a farm, where the chances of survival for a year or more would be good, and to escape from the wild, where they are negligible. Either way, the animal will be eaten: few die of old age. The path from birth to slaughter, however, is often longer and less painful in the barnyard than in the woods. Comparisons, sad as they are, must be made to recognize where a great opportunity lies to prevent or mitigate suffering. The misery of animals in nature—which humans can do much to relieve—makes every other form of suffering pale in comparison. Mother Nature is so cruel to her children she makes Frank Perdue look like a saint.

What is the practical course society should take once it climbs the spiral of moral evolution high enough to recognize its obligation to value the basic rights of animals equally with that of human beings? I do not know how animal liberationists, such as Singer, propose to relieve animal suffering in nature (where most of it occurs), but there are many ways to do so at little cost. Singer has suggested, with respect to pest control, that animals might be fed contraceptive chemicals rather than poisons.[18] It may not be beyond the reach of science to attempt a broad program of contraceptive care for animals in nature so that fewer will fall victim to an early and horrible death. The government is spending hundreds of millions of dollars to store millions of tons of grain. Why not lay out this food, laced with contraceptives, for wild creatures to feed upon? Farms which so overproduce for human needs might then satisfy the needs of animals. The day may come when entitlement programs which now extend only to human beings are offered to animals as well.

One may modestly propose the conversion of national wilderness areas, especially national parks, into farms in order to replace violent wild areas with more humane and managed environments. Starving deer in the woods might be adopted as pets. They might be fed in kennels; animals that once wandered the wilds in misery might get fat in feedlots instead. Birds that now kill earthworms may repair instead to birdhouses stocked with food, including textured soybean protein that looks and smells like worms. And to protect the brutes from cold, their dens could be heated, or shelters provided for the all too many who will otherwise freeze. The list of obligations is long, but for that reason it is more, not less, compelling. The welfare of all animals is in human hands. Society must attend not solely to the needs of domestic animals, for they are in a privileged class, but to the needs of all animals, especially those which, without help, would die miserably in the wild.

Now, whether you believe that this harangue is a *reductio* of Singer's position, and thus that it agrees in principle with Ritchie, or whether you think it should be taken seriously as an ideal is of no concern to me. I merely wish to point out that an environmentalist must take what I have said as a *reductio*, whereas an animal liberationist must regard it as stating a serious position, at least if the liberationist shares Singer's commitment to utilitarianism. Environmentalists cannot be animal liberationists. Animal liberationists cannot be environmentalists. The environmentalist would sacrifice the lives of individual creatures to preserve the authenticity, integrity, and complexity of ecological systems. The liberationist—if the reduction of animal misery is taken seriously as a goal—must be willing, in principle, to sacrifice the authenticity, integrity and complexity of ecosystems to protect the rights, or guard the lives, of animals.

# IV

A defender of the rights of animals may answer that my argument applies only to someone like Singer who is strongly committed to a utilitarian ethic. Those who emphasize the rights of animals, however, need not argue that society should enter the interests of animals equitably into the felicific calculus on which policy is based. For example, Laurence Tribe appeals to the rights of animals not to broaden the class of wants to be included in a Benthamite calculus but to "move beyond wants" and thus to affirm duties "ultimately independent of a desire-satisfying conception."[19] Tribe writes:

> To speak of "rights" rather than "wants," after all, is to acknowledge the possibility that want-maximizing or utility-maximizing actions will be ruled out in particular cases as inconsistent with a structure of agreed-upon obligations. It is Kant, not Bentham, whose thought suggests the first step toward making us "different persons from the manipulators and subjugators we are in danger of becoming."[20]

It is difficult to see how an appeal to rights helps society to "move beyond wants" or to affirm duties "ultimately independent of a desire-satisfying conception." Most writers in the Kantian tradition analyze rights as claims to something in which the claimant has an interest.[21] Thus, rights-theorists oppose utilitarianism not to go beyond wants but because they believe that some wants or interests are moral "trumps" over other wants and interests.[22] To say innocent people have a right not to be hanged for crimes they have not committed, even when hanging them would serve the general welfare, is to say that the interest of innocent people not to be hanged should outweigh the general interest in deterring crime. To take rights seriously, then, is simply to take some interests, or the general interest, more seriously than other interests for moral reasons. The appeal to rights simply is a variation on utilitarianism, in that it accepts the general framework of interests, but presupposes that there are certain interests that should not be traded off against others.[23]

A second problem with Tribe's reply is more damaging than the first. Only *individuals* may have rights, but environmentalists think in terms of protecting *collections, systems* and *communities.* Consider Aldo Leopold's oft-quoted remark: "A thing is right when it tends to preserve the integrity, stability, and beauty of the biotic community. It is wrong when it tends to do otherwise."[24] The obligation to preserve the "integrity, stability, and beauty of the biotic community," whatever those words mean, implies no duties whatever to individual animals in the community, except in the rare instance in which an individual is important to functioning of that community. For the most part, individual animals are completely expendable. An environmentalist is concerned only with maintaining a population. Accordingly, the moral obligation Leopold describes cannot be grounded in or derived from the rights of individuals. Therefore, it has no basis in rights at all.[25]

Consider another example: the protection of endangered species.[26] An individual whale may be said to have rights, but the species cannot; a whale does not suddenly have rights when its kind becomes endangered.[27] No; the moral obligation to preserve species is not an obligation to individual creatures. It cannot, then, be an obligation that rests on rights. This is not to say that there is no moral obligation with regard to endangered species, animals or the environment. It is only to say that moral obligations to nature cannot be enlightened or explained—one cannot even take the first step—by appealing to the rights of animals and other natural things.

# V

Garrett Hardin, in his "Foreword" to *Should Trees Have Standing?*, suggests that Stone's essay answers Leopold's call for a "new ethic to protect land and other natural amenities. . . ."[28] But as one reviewer has pointed out,

> Stone himself never refers to Leopold, and with good reason: he comes from a different place, and his proposal to grant rights to natural objects has emerged not from an ecological sensibility but as an extension of the philosophy of the humane movement.[29]

A humanitarian ethic—an appreciation not of nature, but of the welfare of animals—will not help us to understand or to justify an environmental ethic. It will not provide necessary or valid foundations for environmental law.

# NOTES

1. Leopold, *A Sand County Almanac* (1949) at 204.
2. For discussion, see Heffernan, "The Land Ethic: A Critical Appraisal" (1982), 4 *Envt'l Ethics* 235. Heffernan notes that "when Leopold talks of preserving the 'integrity, stability and beauty of the biotic community' he is referring to preserving the characteristic structure of an ecosystem and its capacity to withstand change or stress." *Id.* at 237.
3. Stone, *Should Trees Having Standing?* (1974).
4. *Id.* at 44.
5. Tribe, *Ways Not to Think About Plastic Trees: New Foundations in Environmental Law* (1973), 83 *Yale L. J.* 1315 at 1345.
6. Singer, "All Animals Are Equal" (1974), 1 *Phil. Exchange* 103.
7. Stone, *supra* note 3, at 24.
8. Singer, "Not For Humans Only: The Place of Nonhumans in Environmental Issues," in Goodpaster and Sayre, eds., *Ethics and the Problems of the Twenty-first Century* (1979) at 194.
9. *Id.* at 195.
10. For a discussion of basic rights, see Shue, *Basic Rights* (1980).
11. Callicott, "Animal Liberation: A Triangular Affair" (1980), 2 *Envt'l Ethics* 311 at 315.
12. Leopold, *supra* note 1, at 269.
13. Callicott, *supra* note 11, at 314–15.
14. Singer, *supra* note 8, at 201.
15. Ritchie, *Natural Rights* (3rd ed., 1916) at 107. For an excellent discussion of this passage, see Clark, "The Rights of Wild Things" (1979), 22 *Inquiry* 171.
16. Shue, *supra* note 10, at 18–29.
17. Hapgood, *Why Males Exist* (1979) at 34.
18. Singer, *supra* note 8, at 198.
19. Tribe, "From Environmental Foundations to Constitutional Structures: Learning From Nature's Future" (1974), 84 *Yale L. J.* 545 at 551, 552.
20. *Id.* at 552.
21. For discussion, see Feinberg, "Duties, Rights, and Claims" (1966), 3 *Amer. Phil. Q.* 137.
22. See Dworkin, "Liberalism," in Hampshire, ed., *Public and Private Morality* (1978) at 113–43. Rights "function as trump cards held by individuals." *Id.* at 136.
23. Barry observes:

> On the surface, rights theories stand in opposition to utilitarianism, for rights, whatever their foundation (or lack thereof), are supposed to trump claims that might be made on behalf of the general welfare. The point here is, however, that the whole notion of rights is simply a variation on utilitarianism in that it accepts the definition of the ethical problem as conterminous with the problem of conflicting interests, and replaces the felicific calculus (in which the interests are simply added) with one which does not permit certain interests to be traded off against others.

Barry, "Self-government Revisited," in Miller and Siedentop, eds., *The Nature of Political Theory* (1983) at 125; see generally 121–54.
24. Leopold, *supra* note 1, at 262.
25. For discussion of this point, see Katz, "Is There a Place For Animals in the Moral Consideration of Nature" (1983), 4 *Ethics and Animals* 74; Norton, "Environmental Ethics and Nonhuman Rights" (1982), 4 *Envt'l Ethics* 17; Rodman, "The Liberation of Nature?" (1977), 20 *Inquiry* 83; Goodpaster, "On Being Morally Considerable" (1978), 75 *J. Phil.* 308. Tom Regan discusses this issue in "The Case for Animal Liberation" (1983):

> Because paradigmatic rights-holders are individuals, and because the dominant thrust of contemporary environmental efforts (e.g., wilderness preservation) is to focus on the whole rather than on the part (i.e., the individual), there is an understandable reluctance on the part of environmentalists to "take rights seriously," or at least a reluctance to take them as seriously as the rights view contends we should. . . . A rights-based environmental ethic . . . ought not to be dismissed out of hand by environmentalists as being in principle antagonistic to

the goals for which they work. It isn't. Were we to show proper respect for the rights of individuals who make up the biotic community, would not the *community* be preserved?

(*Id.* at 362.) I believe this is an empirical question, the answer to which is "no." The environmentalist is concerned about preserving evolutionary processes; whether these processes, e.g., natural selection, have deep enough respect for the rights of individuals to be preserved on those grounds, is a question that might best left be addressed by an evolutionary biologist.

26.  *The Endangered Species Act of 1973,* 16 U.S.C. § 1531 (1976 & Supp. I 1977 & Supp. II 1978 & Supp. III 1979).

27.  Feinberg, "The Rights of Animals and Unborn Generations," in Blackstone, ed., *Philosophy and the Environmental Crisis* (1974) 43 at 55–56.

28.  Hardin, "Foreward," in Stone, *supra* note 3, at xii.

29.  Rodman, *supra* note 25, at 110.

# THE LAND ETHIC

*Aldo Leopold*

Aldo Leopold (1887–1949) was professor of wildlife management at the University of Wisconsin from 1933 until his death. He is the author of *A Sand County Almanac*, often called the bible of the contemporary environmental movement.

When god-like Odysseus returned from the wars in Troy, he hanged all on one rope a dozen slave-girls of his household whom he suspected of misbehavior during his absence.

This hanging involved no question of propriety. The girls were property. The disposal of property was then, as now, a matter of expediency, not of right and wrong.

Concepts of right and wrong were not lacking from Odysseus' Greece: witness the fidelity of his wife through the long years before at last his black-prowed galleys clove the wine-dark seas for home. The ethical structure of that day covered wives, but had not yet been extended to human chattels. During the three thousand years which have since elapsed, ethical criteria have been extended to many fields of conduct, with corresponding shrinkages in those judged by expediency only.

## THE ETHICAL SEQUENCE

This extension of ethics, so far studied only by philosophers, is actually a process in ecological evolution. Its sequences may be described in ecological as well as in philosophical terms. An ethic, ecologically, is a limitation on freedom of action in the struggle for existence. An ethic, philosophically, is a differentiation of social from anti-social conduct. These are two definitions of one thing. The thing has its origin in the tendency of interdependent individuals or groups to evolve modes of co-operation. The ecologist calls these symbioses. Politics and economics are advanced symbioses in which the original free-for-all competition has been replaced, in part, by co-operative mechanisms with an ethical content.

The complexity of co-operative mechanisms has increased with population density, and with the efficiency of tools. It was simpler, for example, to define the anti-social uses of sticks and stones in the days of the mastodons than of bullets and billboards in the age of motors.

The first ethics dealt with the relation between individuals; the Mosaic Decalogue is an example. Later accretions dealt with the relation between the individual and society. The Golden Rule tries to integrate the individual to society; democracy to integrate social organization to the individual.

There is as yet no ethic dealing with man's relation to land and to the animals and plants which grow upon it. Land, like Odysseus' slave-girls, is still property. The land-relation is still strictly economic, entailing privileges but not obligations.

The extension of ethics to this third element in human environment is, if I read the evidence correctly, an evolutionary possibility and an ecological necessity. It is the third step in a sequence. The first two have already been taken. Individual thinkers since the days of Ezekiel and Isaiah have asserted that the despoliation of land is not only inexpedient but wrong. Society, however, has not yet affirmed their belief. I regard the present conservation movement as the embryo of such an affirmation.

An ethic may be regarded as a mode of guidance for meeting ecological situations so new or intricate, or involving such deferred reactions, that the path of social expediency is not discernible to the average individual. Animal instincts are modes of guidance for the individual in meeting such situations. Ethics are possibly a kind of community instinct in-the-making.

## THE COMMUNITY CONCEPT

All ethics so far evolved rest upon a single premise: that the individual is a member of a community of interdependant parts. His instincts prompt him to compete for his place in that community, but his ethics prompt him also to co-operate (perhaps in order that there may be a place to compete for).

The land ethic simply enlarges the boundaries of the community to include soils, waters, plants, and animals, or collectively: the land.

This sounds simple: do we not already sing our love for and obligation to the land of the free and the home of the brave? Yes, but just what and whom do we love? Certainly not the soil, which we are sending helter-skelter downriver. Certainly not the waters, which we assume have no function except to turn turbines, float barges, and carry off sewage. Certainly not the plants, of which we exterminate whole communities without batting an eye. Certainly not the animals, of which we have already extirpated many of the largest and most beautiful species. A land ethic of course cannot prevent the alteration, management, and use of these "resources," but it does affirm their right to continued existence, and, at least in spots, their continued existence in a natural state.

In short, a land ethic changes the role of *Homo sapiens* from conqueror of the land-community to plain member and citizen of it. It implies respect for his fellow-members, and also respect for the community as such.

In human history, we have learned (I hope) that the conqueror role is eventually self-defeating. Why? Because it is implicit in such a role that the conqueror knows, *ex cathedra*, just what makes the community clock tick, and just what and who is valuable, and what and who is worthless, in community life. It always turns out that he knows neither, and this is why his conquests eventually defeat themselves.

In the biotic community, a parallel situation exists. Abraham knew exactly what the land was for: it was to drip milk and honey into Abraham's mouth. At the present moment, the assurance with which we regard this assumption is inverse to the degree of our education.

The ordinary citizen today assumes that science knows what makes the community clock tick; the scientist is equally sure that he does not. He knows that the biotic mechanism is so complex that its workings may never be fully understood.

That man is, in fact, only a member of a biotic team is shown by an ecological interpretation of history. Many historical events, hitherto explained solely in terms of human enterprise, were actually biotic interactions between people and land. The characteristics of the land determined the facts quite as potently as the characteristics of the men who lived on it.

Consider, for example, the settlement of the Mississippi valley. In the years following the Revolution, three groups were contending for its control: the native Indian, the French and English traders, and the American settlers. Historians wonder what would have happened if the English at Detroit had thrown a little more weight into the Indian side of those tipsy scales which decided the outcome of the colonial migration into the cane-lands of Kentucky. It is time now to ponder the fact that the cane-lands, when subjected to the particular mixture of forces represented by the cow, plow, fire, and axe of the pioneer, became bluegrass. What if the plant succession inherent in this dark and bloody ground had, under the impact of these forces, given us some worthless sedge, shrub, or weed? Would Boone and Kenton have held out? Would there have been any overflow into Ohio, Indiana, Illinois, and Missouri? Any Louisiana Purchase? Any transcontinental union of new states? Any Civil War?

Kentucky was one sentence in the drama of history. We are commonly told what the human actors in this drama tried to do, but we are seldom told that their success, or the lack of it, hung in large degree on the reaction of particular soils to the impact of the particular forces exerted by their occupancy. In the case of Kentucky, we do not even know where the bluegrass came from—whether it is a native species, or a stowaway from Europe.

Contrast the cane-lands with what hindsight tells us about the Southwest, where the pioneers were equally brave, resourceful, and persevering. The impact of occupancy here brought no bluegrass, or other plant fitted to withstand the bumps and buffetings of hard use. This region, when grazed by livestock, reverted through a series of more and more worthless grasses, shrubs, and weeds to a condition of unstable equilibrium. Each recession of plant types bred erosion; each increment to erosion bred a further recession of plants. The result today is a progressive and mutual deterioration, not only of plants and soils, but of the animal community subsisting thereon. The early settlers did not expect this: on the ciénegas of New Mexico some even cut ditches to hasten it. So subtle has been its progress that few residents of the region are aware of it. It is quite invisible to the tourist who finds this wrecked landscape colorful and charming (as indeed it is, but it bears scant resemblance to what it was in 1848).

This same landscape was "developed" once before, but with quite different results. The Pueblo Indians settled the Southwest in pre-Columbian times, but they happened *not* to be equipped with range livestock. Their civilization expired, but not because their land expired.

In India, regions devoid of any sod-forming grass have been settled, apparently without wrecking the land, by the simple expedient of carrying the grass to the cow, rather than vice versa. (Was this the result of some deep wisdom, or was it just good luck? I do not know.)

In short, the plant succession steered the course of history; the pioneer simply demonstrated, for good or ill, what successions inhered in the land. Is history taught in this spirit? It will be, once the concept of land as a community really penetrates our intellectual life.

# THE ECOLOGICAL CONSCIENCE

Conservation is a state of harmony between men and land. Despite nearly a century of propaganda, conservation still proceeds at a snail's pace; progress still consists largely of letterhead pieties and convention oratory. On the back forty we still slip two steps backward for each forward stride.

The usual answer to this dilemma is "more conservation education." No one will debate this, but is it certain that only the *volume* of education needs stepping up? Is something lacking in the *content* as well?

It is difficult to give a fair summary of its content in brief form, but, as I understand it, the content is substantially this: obey the law, vote right, join some organizations, and practice what conservation is profitable on your own land; the government will do the rest.

Is not this formula too easy to accomplish anything worth-while? It defines no right or wrong, assigns no obligation, calls for no sacrifice, implies no change in the current philosophy of values. In respect of land-use, it urges only enlightened self-interest. Just how far will such education take us? An example will perhaps yield a partial answer.

By 1930 it had become clear to all except the ecologically blind that southwestern Wisconsin's topsoil was slipping seaward. In 1933 the farmers were told that if they would adopt certain remedial practices for five years, the public would donate CCC labor to install them, plus the necessary machinery and materials. The offer was widely accepted, but the practices were widely forgotten when the five-year contract period was up. The farmers continued only those practices that yielded an immediate and visible economic gain for themselves.

This led to the idea that maybe farmers would learn more quickly if they themselves wrote the rules. Accordingly the Wisconsin Legislature in 1937 passed the Soil Conservation District Law. This said to farmers, in effect: *We, the public, will furnish you free technical service and loan you specialized machinery, if you will write your own rules for land-use. Each county may write its own rules, and these will have the force of law.* Nearly all the counties promptly organized to accept the proffered help, but after a decade of operation, *no county has yet written a single rule.* There has been visible progress in such practices as strip-cropping, pasture renovation, and soil liming, but none in fencing woodlots against grazing, and none in excluding plow and cow from steep slopes. The farmers, in short, have selected those remedial practices which were profitable anyhow, and ignored those which were profitable to the community, but not clearly profitable to themselves.

When one asks why no rules have been written, one is told that the community is not yet ready to support them; education must precede rules. But the education actually in progress makes no mention of obligations to land over and above those dictated by self-interest. The net result is that we have more education but less soil, fewer healthy woods, and as many floods as in 1937.

The puzzling aspect of such situations is that the existence of obligations over and above self-interest is taken for granted in such rural community enterprises as the betterment of roads, schools, churches, and baseball teams. Their existence is not taken for granted, nor as yet seriously discussed, in bettering the behavior of the water that falls on the land, or in the preserving of the beauty or diversity of the farm landscape. Land-use ethics are still governed wholly by economic self-interest, just as social ethics were a century ago.

To sum up: we asked the farmer to do what he conveniently could to save his soil, and he has done just that, and only that. The farmer who clears the woods off a 75 percent slope, turns his cows into the clearing, and dumps its rainfall, rocks, and soil into the community creek, is still (if otherwise decent) a respected member of society. If he puts lime on his fields and plants his crops on contour, he is still entitled to all the privileges and emoluments of his Soil Conservation District. The District is a beautiful piece of social machinery, but it is coughing along on two cylinders because we have been too timid, and too anxious for quick success, to tell the farmer the true magnitude of his obligations. Obligations have no meaning without conscience, and the problem we face is the extension of the social conscience from people to land.

No important change in ethics was ever accomplished without an internal change in our intellectual emphasis, loyalties, affections, and convictions. The proof that conservation has not yet touched these foundations of conduct lies in the fact that philosophy and religion have not yet heard of it. In our attempt to make conservation easy, we have made it trivial.

## SUBSTITUTES FOR A LAND ETHIC

When the logic of history hungers for bread and we hand out a stone, we are at pains to explain how much the stone resembles bread. I now describe some of the stones which serve in lieu of a land ethic.

One basic weakness in a conservation system based wholly on economic motives is that most members of the land community have no economic value. Wildflowers and songbirds are examples. Of the 22,000 higher plants and animals native to Wisconsin, it is doubtful whether more than 5 percent can be sold, fed, eaten, or otherwise put to economic use. Yet these creatures are members of the biotic community, and if (as I believe) its stability depends on its integrity, they are entitled to continuance.

When one of these non-economic categories is threatened, and if we happen to love it, we invent subterfuges to give it economic importance. At the beginning of the century songbirds were supposed to be disappearing. Ornithologists jumped to the rescue with some distinctly shaky evidence to the effect that insects would eat us up if birds failed to control them. The evidence had to be economic in order to be valid.

It is painful to read these circumlocutions today. We have no land ethic yet, but we have at least drawn nearer the point of admitting that birds should continue as a matter of biotic right, regardless of the presence or absence of economic advantage to us.

A parallel situation exists in respect of predatory mammals, raptorial birds, and fish-eating birds. Time was when biologists somewhat over-worked the evidence that these creatures preserve the health of game by killing weaklings, or that they control rodents for the farmer, or that they prey only on 'worthless' species. Here again, the evidence had to be economic in order to be valid. It is only in recent years that we hear the more honest argument that predators are members of the community, and that no special interest has the right to exterminate them for the sake of a benefit, real or fancied, to itself. Unfortunately this enlightened view is still in the talk stage. In the field the extermination of predators goes merrily on: witness the impending erasure of the timber wolf by fiat of Congress, the Conservation Bureaus, and many state legislatures.

Some species of trees have been 'read out of the party' by economics-minded foresters because they grow too slowly, or have too low a sale value to pay as timber crops: white cedar, tamarack, cypress, beech, and hemlock are examples. In Europe, where forestry is ecologically more advanced, the non-commercial tree species are recognized as members of the native forest community, to be preserved as such, within reason. Moreover some (like beech) have been found to have a valuable function in building up soil fertility. The interdependence of the forest and its constituent tree species, ground flora, and fauna is taken for granted.

Lack of economic value is sometimes a character not only of species or groups, but of entire biotic communities: marshes, bogs, dunes, and 'deserts' are examples. Our formula in such cases is to relegate their conservation to government as refuges, monuments, or parks. The difficulty is that these communities are usually interspersed with more valuable private lands; the government cannot possibly own or control such scattered parcels. The net effect is that we have relegated some of them to ultimate extinction over large areas. If the private owner were ecologically minded, he would be proud to be the custodian of a reasonable proportion of such areas, which add diversity and beauty to his farm and to his community.

In some instances, the assumed lack of profit in these 'waste' areas has proved to be wrong, but only after most of them had been done away with. The present scramble to reflood muskrat marshes is a case in point.

There is a clear tendency in American conservation to relegate to government all necessary jobs that private landowners fail to perform. Government ownership, operation, subsidy, or regulation is now widely prevalent in forestry, range management, soil and watershed management, park and wilderness conservation, fisheries management, and migratory bird management, with more to come. Most of this growth in governmental conservation is proper and logical, some of it is inevitable. That I imply no disapproval of it is implicit in the fact that I have spent most of my life working for it. Nevertheless the question arises: What is the ultimate magnitude of the enterprise? Will the tax base carry its eventual ramifications? At what point will governmental conservation, like the mastodon, become handicapped by its own dimensions? The answer, if there is any, seems to be in a land ethic, or some other force which assigns more obligation to the private landowner.

Industrial landowners and users, especially lumbermen and stockmen, are inclined to wail long and loudly about the extension of government ownership and regulation to land, but (with notable exceptions) they show little disposition to develop the only visible alternative: the voluntary practice of conservation on their own lands.

When the private landowner is asked to perform some unprofitable act for the good of the community, he today assents only with outstretched palm. If the act costs him cash this is fair and proper, but when it costs only forethought, open-mindedness, or time, the issue is at least debatable. The overwhelming growth of land-use subsidises in recent years must be ascribed, in large part, to the government's own agencies for conservation education: the land bureaus, the agricultural colleges, and the extension services. As far as I can detect, no ethical obligation toward land is taught in these institutions.

To sum up: a system of conservation based solely on economic self-interest is hopelessly lopsided. It tends to ignore, and thus eventually to eliminate, many elements in the land community that lack commercial value, but that are (as far as we know) essential to its healthy functioning. It assumes, falsely, I think, that the economic parts of the biotic clock will function without the uneconomic parts. It tends to relegate to government many functions eventually too large, too complex, or too widely dispersed to be performed by government.

An ethical obligation on the part of the private owner is the only visible remedy for these situations.

## THE LAND PYRAMID

An ethic to supplement and guide the economic relation to land presupposes the existence of some mental image of land as a biotic mechanism. We can be ethical only in relation to something we can see, feel, understand, love, or otherwise have faith in.

The image commonly employed in conservation education is 'the balance of nature.' For reasons too lengthy to detail here, this figure of speech fails to describe accurately what little we know about the land mechanism. A much truer image is the one employed in ecology: the biotic pyramid. I shall first sketch the pyramid as a symbol of land, and later develop some of its implications in terms of land-use.

Plants absorb energy from the sun. This energy flows through a circuit called the biota, which may be represented by a pyramid consisting of layers. The bottom layer is the soil. A plant layer rests on the soil, an insect layer on the plants, a bird and rodent layer on the insects, and so on up through various animal groups to the apex layer, which consists of the larger carnivores.

The species of a layer are alike not in where they came from, or in what they look like, but rather in what they eat. Each successive layer depends on those below it for food and often for other services, and each in turn furnishes food and services to those above. Proceeding upward, each successive layer decreases in numerical abundance. Thus, for every carnivore there are hundreds of his prey, thousands of their prey, millions of insects, uncountable plants. The pyramidal form of the system reflects this numerical progression from apex to base. Man shares an intermediate layer with the bears, raccoons, and squirrels which eat both meat and vegetables.

The lines of dependency for food and other services are called food chains. Thus soil-oak-deer-Indian is a chain that has now been largely converted to soil-corn-cow-farmer. Each species, including ourselves, is a link in many chains. The deer eats a hundred plants other than oak, and the cow a hundred plants other than corn. Both, then, are links in a hundred chains. The pyramid is a tangle of chains so complex as to seem disorderly, yet the stability of the system proves it to be a highly organized structure. Its functioning depends on the co-operation and competition of its diverse parts.

In the beginning, the pyramid of life was low and squat; the food chains short and simple. Evolution has added layer after layer, link after link. Man is one of thousands of accretions to the height and complexity of the pyramid. Science has given us many doubts, but it has given us at least one certainty: the trend of evolution is to elaborate and diversify the biota.

Land, then, is not merely soil; it is a fountain of energy flowing through a circuit of soils, plants, and animals. Food chains are the living channels which conduct energy upward; death and decay return it to the soil. The circuit is not closed; some energy is dissipated in decay, some is added by absorption from the air, some is stored in soils, peats, and long-lived forests; but it is a sustained circuit, like a slowly augmented revolving fund of life. There is always a net loss by downhill wash, but this is normally small and offset by the decay of rocks. It is deposited in the ocean and, in the course of geological time, raised to form new lands and new pyramids.

The velocity and character of the upward flow of energy depend on the complex structure of the plant and animal community, much as the upward flow of sap in a tree depends on its complex cellular organization. Without this complexity, normal circulation would presumably not occur. Structure means the characteristic numbers, as well as the characteristic kinds and functions, of the component species. This interdependence between the complex structure of the land and its smooth functioning as an energy unit is one of its basic attributes.

When a change occurs in one part of the circuit, many other parts must adjust themselves to it. Change does not necessarily obstruct or divert the flow of energy; evolution is a long series of self-induced changes, the net result of which has been to elaborate the flow mechanism and to lengthen the circuit. Evolutionary changes, however, are usually slow and local. Man's invention of tools has enabled him to make changes of unprecedented violence, rapidity, and scope.

One change is in the composition of floras and faunas. The larger predators are lopped off the apex of the pyramid; food chains, for the first time in history, become shorter rather than longer. Domesticated species from other lands are substituted for wild ones, and wild ones are moved to new habitats. In this world-wide pooling of faunas and floras, some species get out of bounds as pests and diseases, others are extinguished. Such effects are seldom intended or foreseen; they represent unpredicted and often untraceable readjustments in the structure. Agricultural science is largely a race between the emergence of new pests and the emergence of new techniques for their control.

Another change touches the flow of energy through plants and animals and its return to the soil. Fertility is the ability of soil to receive, store, and release energy. Agriculture, by overdrafts on the soil, or by too radical a substitution of domestic for native species in the superstructure, may derange the channels of flow or deplete storage. Soils depleted of their storage, or of the organic matter which anchors it, wash away faster than they form. This is erosion.

Waters, like soil, are part of the energy circuit. Industry, by polluting waters or obstructing them with dams, may exclude the plants and animals necessary to keep energy in circulation.

Transportation brings about another basic change: the plants or animals grown in one region are now consumed and returned to the soil in another. Transportation taps the energy stored in rocks, and in the air, and uses it elsewhere; thus we fertilize the garden with nitrogen gleaned by the guano birds from the fishes of seas on the other side of the Equator. Thus the formerly localized and self-contained circuits are pooled on a world-wide scale.

The process of altering the pyramid for human occupation releases stored energy, and this often gives rise, during the pioneering period, to a deceptive exuberance of plant and animal life, both wild and tame. These releases of biotic capital tend to becloud or postpone the penalties of violence.

This thumbnail sketch of land as an energy circuit conveys three basic ideas:

(1) That land is not merely soil.
(2) That the native plants and animals kept the energy circuit open; others may or may not.
(3) That man-made changes are of a different order than evolutionary changes, and have effects more comprehensive than is intended or foreseen.

These ideas, collectively, raise two basic issues: Can the land adjust itself to the new order? Can the desired alterations be accomplished with less violence?

Biotas seem to differ in their capacity to sustain violent conversion. Western Europe, for example, carries a far different pyramid than Caesar found there. Some large animals are lost; swampy forests have become meadows or plow-land; many new plants and animals are introduced, some of which escape as pests; the remaining natives are greatly changed in distribution and abundance. Yet the soil is still there and, with the help of imported nutrients, still fertile; the waters flow normally; the new structure seems to function and to persist. There is no visible stoppage or derangement of the circuit.

Western Europe, then, has a resistant biota. Its inner processes are tough, elastic, resistant to strain. No matter how violent the alterations, the pyramid, so far, has developed some new *modus vivendi* which preserves its habitability for man, and for most of the other natives.

Japan seems to present another instance of radical conversion without disorganization.

Most other civilized regions, and some as yet barely touched by civilization, display various stages of disorganization, varying from initial symptoms to advanced wastage. In Asia Minor and North Africa diagnosis is confused by climatic changes, which may have been either the cause or the effect of advanced wastage. In the United States the degree of disorganization varies locally; it is worst in the Southwest, the Ozarks, and parts of the South, and least in New England and the Northwest. Better land-uses may still arrest it in the less advanced regions. In parts of Mexico, South America, South Africa, and Australia a violent and accelerating wastage is in progress, but I cannot assess the prospects.

This almost world-wide display of disorganization in the land seems to be similar to disease in an animal, except that it never culminates in complete disorganization or death. The land recovers, but at some reduced level of complexity, and with a reduced carrying capacity for people, plants, and animals. Many biotas currently regarded as 'lands of opportunity' are in fact already subsisting on exploitative agriculture, i.e., they have already exceeded their sustained carrying capacity. Most of South America is overpopulated in this sense.

In arid regions we attempt to offset the process of wastage by reclamation, but it is only too evident that the prospective longevity of reclamation projects is often short. In our own West, the best of them may not last a century.

The combined evidence of history and ecology seems to support one general deduction: the less violent the man-made changes, the greater the probability of successful readjustment in the pyramid. Violence, in turn, varies with human population density; a dense population requires a more violent conversion. In this respect, North America has a better chance for permanence than Europe, if she can contrive to limit her density.

This deduction runs counter to our current philosophy which assumes that because a small increase in density enriched human life, that an indefinite increase will enrich it indefinitely. Ecology knows of no density relationship that holds for indefinitely wide limits. All gains from density are subject to a law of diminishing returns.

Whatever may be the equation for men and land, it is improbable that we as yet know all its terms. Recent discoveries in mineral and vitamin nutrition reveal unsuspected dependencies in the up-circuit: incredibly minute quantities of certain substances determine the value of soils to plants, of plants to animals. What of the down-circuit? What of the vanishing species, the preservation of which we now regard as an esthetic luxury? They helped build the soil; in what unsuspected ways may they be essential to its maintenance? Professor Weaver proposes that we use prairie flowers to reflocculate the wasting soils of the dust bowl; who knows for what purpose cranes and condors, otters and grizzlies may some day be used?

## LAND HEALTH AND THE A-B CLEAVAGE

A land ethic, then, reflects the existence of an ecological conscience, and this in turn reflects a conviction of individual responsibility for the health of the land. Health is the capacity of the land for self-renewal. Conservation is our effort to understand and preserve this capacity.

Conservationists are notorious for their dissensions. Superficially these seem to add up to mere confusion, but a more careful scrutiny reveals a single plane of cleavage common to many specialized fields. In each field one group (A) regards the land as soil, and its function as commodity-production; another group (B) regards the land as a biota, and its function as something broader. How much broader is admittedly in a state of doubt and confusion.

In my own field, forestry, group A is quite content to grow trees like cabbages, with cellulose as the basic forest commodity. It feels no inhibition against violence; its ideology is agronomic. Group B, on the other hand, sees forestry as fundamentally different from agronomy because it employs natural species, and manages a natural environment rather than creating an artificial one. Group B prefers natural reproduction on principle. It worries on biotic as well as economic grounds about the loss of species like chestnut, and the threatened loss of the white pines. It worries about a whole series of secondary forest functions: wildlife, recreation, watersheds, wilderness areas. To my mind, group B feels the stirrings of an ecological conscience.

In the wildlife field, a parallel cleavage exists. For Group A the basic commodities are sport and meat; the yardsticks of production are ciphers of take in pheasants and trout. Artificial propagation is acceptable as a permanent as well as a temporary recourse—if its unit costs permit. Group B, on the other hand, worries about a whole series of biotic side-issues. What is the cost in predators of producing a game crop? Should we have further recourse to exotics? How can management restore the shrinking species, like prairie grouse, already hopeless as shootable game? How can management restore the threatened rarities, like trumpeter swan and whooping crane? Can management principles be extended to wildflowers? Here again it is clear to me that we have the same A–B cleavage as in forestry.

In the larger field of agriculture I am less competent to speak, but there seem to be somewhat parallel cleavages. Scientific agriculture was actively developing before ecology was born, hence a slower penetration of ecological concepts might be expected. Moreover the farmer, by the very nature of his techniques, must modify the biota more radically than the forester or the wildlife manager. Nevertheless, there are many discontents in agriculture which seem to add up to a new vision of 'biotic farming.'

Perhaps the most important of these is the new evidence that poundage or tonnage is no measure of the food-value of farm crops; the products of fertile soil may be qualitatively as well as quantitatively superior. We can bolster poundage from depleted soils by pouring on imported fertility, but we are not necessarily bolstering food-value. The possible ultimate ramifications of this idea are so immense that I must leave their exposition to abler pens.

The discontent that labels itself 'organic farming,' while bearing some of the earmarks of a cult, is nevertheless biotic in its direction, particularly in its insistence on the importance of soil flora and fauna.

The ecological fundamentals of agriculture are just as poorly known to the public as in other fields of land-use. For example, few educated people realize that the marvelous advances in technique made during recent decades are improvements in the pump, rather than the well. Acre for acre, they have barely sufficed to offset the sinking level of fertility.

In all of these cleavages, we see repeated the same basic paradoxes: man the conqueror *versus* man the biotic citizen; science the sharpener of his sword *versus* science the search-light on his universe; land the slave and servant *versus* land the collective organism. Robinson's injunction to Tristram may well be applied, at this juncture, to *Homo sapiens* as a species in geological time:

> Whether you will or not
> You are a King, Tristram, for you are one
> Of the time-tested few that leave the world,
> When they are gone, not the same place it was.
> Mark what you leave.

## THE OUTLOOK

It is inconceivable to me that an ethical relation to land can exist without love, respect, and admiration for land, and a high regard for its value. By value, I of course mean something far broader than mere economic value; I mean value in the philosophical sense.

Perhaps the most serious obstacle impeding the evolution of a land ethic is the fact that our educational and economic system is headed away from, rather than toward, an intense consciousness of land. Your true modern is separated from the land by many middlemen, and by innumerable physical gadgets. He had no vital relation to it; to him it is the space between cities on which crops grow. Turn him loose for a day on the land, and if the spot does not happen to be a golf links or a 'scenic' area, he is bored stiff. If crops could be raised by hydroponics instead of farming, it would suit him very well. Synthetic substitutes for wood, leather, wool, and other natural land products suit him better than the originals. In short, land is something he has 'outgrown.'

Almost equally serious as an obstacle to a land ethic is the attitude of the farmer for whom the land is still an adversary, or a taskmaster that keeps him in slavery. Theoretically, the mechanization of farming ought to cut the farmer's chains, but whether it really does is debatable.

One of the requisites for an ecological comprehension of land is an understanding of ecology, and this is by no means co-extensive with 'education'; in fact, much higher education seems deliberately to avoid ecological concepts. An understanding of ecology does not necessarily originate in courses bearing ecological labels; it is quite as likely to be labeled geography, botany, agronomy, history, or economics. This is as it should be, but whatever the label, ecological training is scarce.

The case for a land ethic would appear hopeless but for the minority which is in obvious revolt against these 'modern' trends.

The 'key-log' which must be moved to release the evolutionary process for an ethic is simply this: quit thinking about decent land-use as solely an economic problem. Examine each question in terms of what is ethically and esthetically right, as well as what is economically expedient. A thing is right when it tends to preserve the integrity, stability, and beauty of the biotic community. It is wrong when it tends otherwise.

It of course goes without saying that economic feasibility limits the tether of what can or cannot be done for land. It always has and it always will. The fallacy the economic determinists have tied around our collective neck, and which we now need to cast off, is the belief that economics determines *all* land-use. This is simply not true. An innumerable host of actions and attitudes, comprising perhaps the bulk of all land relations, is determined by the land-users' tastes and predilections, rather than by his purse. The bulk of all land relations hinges on investments of time, forethought, skill, and faith rather than on investments of cash. As a land-user thinketh, so is he.

I have purposely presented the land ethic as a product of social evolution because nothing so important as an ethic is ever 'written.' Only the most superficial student of history supposes that Moses 'wrote' the Decalogue; it evolved in the minds of a thinking community, and Moses wrote a tentative summary of it for a 'seminar.' I say tentative because evolution never stops.

The evolution of a land ethic is an intellectual as well as emotional process. Conservation is paved with good intentions which prove to be futile, or even dangerous, because they are devoid of critical understanding either of the land, or of economic land-use. I think it is a truism that as the ethical frontier advances from the individual to the community, its intellectual content increases.

The mechanism of operation is the same for any ethic: social approbation for right actions: social disapproval for wrong actions.

By and large, our present problem is one of attitudes and implements. We are remodeling the Alhambra with a steamshovel, and we are proud of our yardage. We shall hardly relinquish the shovel, which after all has many good points, but we are in need of gentler and more objective criteria for its successful use.

# HOLISTIC ENVIRONMENTAL ETHICS AND THE PROBLEM OF ECOFASCISM

*J. Baird Callicott*

J. Baird Callicott is professor of philosophy and religion studies at the University of North Texas. He is editor of *Companion to a Sand County Almanac: Interpretive and Critical Essays,* co-editor with Susan L. Flader of *The River of the Mother of God and Other Essays by Aldo Leopold,* and co-editor with Eric T. Freyfogle of *For the Health of the Land: Previously Unpublished and Other Writings by Aldo Leopold.*

## THE DARWINIAN ROOTS OF THE LAND ETHIC

Of all the environmental ethics so far devised, the land ethic, first sketched by Aldo Leopold, is most popular among professional conservationists and least popular among professional philosophers. Conservationists are preoccupied with such things as the anthropogenic pollution of air and water by industrial and municipal wastes, the anthropogenic reduction in numbers of species populations, the outright anthropogenic extinction of species, and the invasive anthropogenic introduction of other species into places not their places of evolutionary origin. Conservationists as such are not concerned about the injury, pain, or death of nonhuman specimens—that is, of individual animals and plants—except in those rare cases in which a species' populations are so reduced in number that the conservation of every specimen is vital to the conservation of the species. On the other hand, professional philosophers, most of them schooled in and intellectually committed to the Modern classical theories of ethics, are ill prepared to comprehend morally such "holistic" concerns. Professional philosophers are inclined to dismiss holistic concerns as nonmoral or to reduce them to concerns about either human welfare or the welfare of nonhuman organisms severally. And they are mystified by the land ethic, unable to grasp its philosophical foundations and pedigree.

Without a grasp of its philosophical foundations and pedigree, however, it is difficult to know how the land ethic might be related to the more familiar moral concerns that loom large in the Modern era (roughly the seventeenth through the twentieth centuries)—such as human happiness, human dignity, and human rights—and how it might be applied to and illuminate cases other than those Leopold himself considers in his brief sketch of it in *A Sand County Almanac*. In this essay, I outline the philosophical foundations and pedigree of the land ethic and indicate how it might be related to more familiar Modern moral concerns and how it might be applied to those contemporary environmental concerns that Leopold himself could not have considered. In particular, I address the most serious and disturbing theoretical and practical challenge to the land ethic raised by professional philosophers—the problem of ecofascism.

To discover its philosophical foundations and pedigree, we may begin by looking for clues in the text of "The Land Ethic." Leopold provides the most important clue in the second section of the essay, entitled 'The Ethical Sequence.' Having observed that ethics have grown considerably in scope and complexity during the three thousand years of recorded history in Western civilization, Leopold (1949, 202) writes,

> This extension of ethics, so far studied only by philosophers [and, Leopold's insinuation is clear, therefore not very revealingly studied] is actually a process in ecological evolution. An ethic, ecologically, is a limitation on freedom of action in the struggle for existence. An ethic, philosophically, is a differentiation of social from anti-social conduct. These are two definitions of one thing. The thing has its origin in the tendency of interdependent individuals or groups to evolve modes of cooperation.

Leopold, I should hasten to point out, was no better a student of philosophy, than most professional philosophers are of conservation and its concerns. Hence his characterization of an ethic, "philosophically," is, put most charitably, incomplete. In any case, what he hints at, rather insistently and unmistakably, is some sort of evolutionary interpretation of ethics. Leopold's use here of such words and phrases as "evolution," "struggle for existence," "origin," "evolve," "social and anti-social conduct" evokes not only a general evolutionary context in which to locate an understanding ethics, it alludes, more particularly, to the classical evolutionary account of ethics in Charles Darwin's *The Descent of Man,* the third chapter of which is devoted to "the moral sense." Doubtless, therefore, Darwin's account of the origin and development of "the thing" is what mainly informed Leopold's thinking about ethics.

## THE EVOLUTIONARY ORIGIN OF ETHICS

The existence of ethics presents a problem for Darwin's attempt to show how all things human can be understood as gradually evolved by natural (and sexual) selection, from traits possessed by closely related species, his project in *The Descent of Man.* Ethics demands that moral agents selflessly consider other interests in addition to their own. The theory of evolution would seem to predict, however, that the selfish would outcompete the selfless in the "struggle for existence," and thus survive and reproduce in greater numbers. Therefore greater and greater selfishness, not selflessness, would seem to be selected for in any population of organisms, including those ancestral to Homo sapiens. But history indicates the opposite: that our remote human ancestors were more callous, brutal, and ruthless than are we. At least so it seemed to a refined English gentleman who, while serving as naturalist on the round-the-world voyage of the *H. M. S. Beagle,* had observed first hand what he and his contemporaries regarded as states of savagery and barbarism similar to those from which European and Asian civilizations were believed to have emerged. Absent a convincing evolutionary explanation of its existence and progressive development, Darwin's pious opponents might point to ethics among human beings as a clear signature by the hand of Providence on the human soul.

To the conundrum presented him by the existence and putatively progressive development of ethics, Darwin's resolution is straightforward and elegant. For many kinds of animals, and especially for Homo sapiens, life's struggle is more efficiently prosecuted collectively and cooperatively than singly and competitively. Poorly armed by nature, as solitaries hominids would fall easy prey to their natural enemies or starve for lack of the wherewithal to obtain food. Together our primate ancestors might stand some chance of fending off predators and attacking prey larger than themselves. Like many other similarly situated species, evolving human beings thus formed primitive societies; or, stated more precisely, those hominids that formed primitive societies evolved. But without some rudimentary ethics, human societies cannot stay integrated. As Darwin (1871, 93) puts it, "No tribe could hold together if murder, robbery, treachery, &c., were common; consequently such crimes within the limits of the same tribe 'are branded with everlasting infamy'; but excite no such sentiment beyond these limits."

Darwin's speculative reconstruction of the evolutionary pathway to ethics begins with altruistic "parental and filial affections" which motivate parents (perhaps only the female parent in many species) to care for their offspring and their offspring to desire the company of their parents. Such affectionally bonded nuclear families are small and often ephemeral societies, lasting, as in the case of bears, only until the next reproductive cycle. But the survival advantage to the young of being reared in such social units is obvious. Should the parental and filial affections chance to spill beyond the parental-filial relationship to that between siblings, cousins, and other close kin, such plurally bonded animals might stick together in more stable and permanent groups and defend themselves and forage communally and cooperatively. In which case there might also accrue additional advantages to the members of such groups in the struggle for life. Thus do mammalian societies originate in Darwin's account.

By themselves, the social impulses and sentiments are not ethics. An ethic is a set of behavioral rules, or a set of principles or precepts for governing behavior. The moral sentiments are, rather, the foundations of ethics, as David Hume and Adam Smith argued a century or so before Darwin considered the matter. In addition to the social sentiments and instincts, Homo sapiens evolved a high degree of intelligence and imagination and uniquely possesses a symbolic language. Hence, we human beings are capable of generally representing those kinds of behavior that are destructive of society ("murder, robbery, treachery, &c.") and articulating prohibitions of them in emotionally colored formulae—commandments—which today we call moral rules.

## THE ALTERNATIVE MODERNIST ACCOUNT OF THE ORIGIN OF ETHICS

Darwin's account of the origin of ethics is quite different from the account of the origin of ethics inherited by most professional philosophers. That account was originally advanced by thinkers contemporary with Socrates in the fifth century B.C.F., and was reasserted in the early Modern period by Thomas Hobbes in the seventeenth century. The social contract theory, as it is called, treats human society as discontinuous with animal societies—or, rather, animal societies are not acknowledged to exist at all—and to be something that was deliberately created by its members. In the "state of nature," with which the social contract theory begins, fully human human beings are imagined to roam the world as solitary individuals engaged in a war of each against all. In this circumstance of universal war, the life of each person is, in the famous characterization of Hobbes, not only "solitary, [but] poor, nasty, brutish, and short." Further, in such a circumstance neither agriculture nor industry is possible, because no enforceable property rights exist; no one would bother to sow, tend, and harvest crops or laboriously produce anything else that others might appropriate at will. Observing that such a rude condition of human life is untoward, at some point in time people are imagined, by social contract theorists, to decide to declare a truce, hold a convention, and hammer out some rules of behavior (moral codes and laws), and settle on some means to enforce them (a sovereign), thus hoping to make their lives more pleasant and predictable, less hazardous and capricious. Ethics thus were founded upon selfish rationality, not selfless sentimentality. Society, moreover, is an artifice, a deliberate *human* contrivance, not something rather common in nature that naturally evolved.

Because the social contract theory reduces morality to enlightened self-interest, one might argue that it is not a theory of *ethics* at all. A proper ethic, one might insist, requires moral agents to respect others or give due regard to the interests of others. In the utilitarian school, founded by Jeremy Bentham in the eighteenth century, happiness, defined in terms of pleasure and pain, is the summum bonum and a moral agent is required to act in such a way as to maximize happiness (pleasure) and minimize misery (pain), no mater whose happiness or misery is at stake, the agent's own or someone else's. In the deontological school, founded by Immanuel Kant also in the eighteenth century, a moral agent should never use another moral agent as a means only, but should treat other moral agents as intrinsically valuable ends in themselves. But to the hard question, Why should a moral agent give due regard to others or their interests?, both schools end by generalizing egoism. I demand that others consider my happiness (if I am inclined to be a utilitarian) or my intrinsic value as a morally autonomous being (if I am inclined to be a deontologist) in choosing a course of action that might affect me; therefore, to be logically self-consistent, I must consider either the happiness or intrinsic value of others in choosing courses of action that might affect them. Though both utilitarianism and deontology, by far the two most pervasive and influential Modern schools of ethics, are putatively other-oriented, at the end of the day, they prove to be no less founded on rational self-regard than the nakedly egoistical social contract theory of ethics.

The social contract theory and its subtler and more palatable descendants, utilitarianism and deontology, were not useful to Darwin because they ground ethics in reason, the most advanced and delicate of animal capacities. From an evolutionary point of view, however, reason could only have emerged in an intensely social environment, complete with a fully articulate language. But the emergence, persistence, and development of such a social environment depends, in turn, on the existence of ethics—"no tribe could hold together . . . &c."—as already noted. Therefore, from an evolutionary point of view, the social contract theory and its variants put the cart before the horse. Indeed, from an evolutionary point of view, the hypothesized state of nature—the supposition that rational human beings ever actually lived as solitaries in a condition of universal war—is absurd and preposterous. Darwin, therefore, turned to the now nearly forgotten sentiment-based moral philosophies of the Scottish Enlightenment, citing Hume's *Enquiry Concerning the Principles of Morals* and Smith's *Theory of Moral Sentiments* in *The Descent of Man*.

## THE DEVELOPMENT OF ETHICS CORRELATIVE TO THE DEVELOPMENT OF SOCIETY

So much, then, for the origin of ethics; Darwin goes on to account for the development of ethics. As human social groups competed with one another for resources, the larger and better organized outcompeted the smaller and less well organized. Hence, clans, firstly, merged into tribes; tribes, next, into nations; and nations, eventually, into republics. The emergence of each of these levels of social organization was attended by a corresponding extension of ethics. Darwin (1871, 100–101) sums up this parallel growth of ethics and society as follows: "As man advances in civilisation, and small tribes are united into larger communities, the simplest reason would tell each individual that he ought to extend his social instincts and sympathies to all the members of the same nation, though personally unknown to him. This point being once reached there is only an artificial barrier to prevent his sympathies extending to the men of all nations and races."

Quite remarkably, the influence of Hume, who lived long before evolutionary thinking was habitual, can be found even in Darwin's speculations about the development of ethics correlative to that of society. Compare the passage quoted from Darwin in the previous paragraph with this one from Hume ([1751] 1957, 23):

> But suppose the conjunction of the sexes to be established in nature, a family immediately arises; and particular rules being found requisite for its subsistence, these are immediately embraced; though without comprehending the rest of mankind within their prescriptions. Suppose that several families unite together into one society, which is totally disjoined from all others, the rules which preserve peace and order, enlarge themselves to the utmost extent of that society. . . . But again suppose that several distinct societies maintain a kind of intercourse for mutual convenience and advantage, the boundaries of justice still grow larger in proportion to the largeness of men's views and the force of their mutual connexions. History, experience, reason sufficiently instruct us in this natural progress of human sentiments, and in the gradual enlargement of [them].

Further, with the emergence of each new level in the social hierarchy—the clan, the tribe, the nation, the republic, the global village—the content of the moral code changed or was supplemented to reflect and facilitate the novel structure of each newly emerged level. At the tribal level of society, "when the question is put . . . , is it worse to kill a girl of a foreign tribe, or to marry a girl of one's own, an answer just opposite to ours would be given," Darwin (1871, 91) observes. Since Darwin's day, matrimonial ethics have developed further still. In contemporary post-patriarchal society, we would still answer that it is certainly wrong to *kill* a girl of any ethnic group, but we would add that neither is it right to marry a *girl* of one's own ethnic group or, for that matter, any other. Among ourselves, mature men are allowed to marry only women some four to six years beyond menarche—otherwise they would be guilty of "statutory rape"—and it is, though lawful, "inappropriate" for men to marry or sexually consort with women much younger than themselves.

## THE LAND ETHIC AS THE NEXT STEP IN THE DARWINIAN SOCIETY—ETHICS PAS DE DEUX

During Darwin's lifetime, as during Hume's, a universal ethic of human rights was only dimly visible on the horizon. By the mid-twentieth century, when Leopold was gestating the land ethic, a universal human rights ethic may have seemed more nearly attainable. In any case, Leopold, often called a prophet, looked farther ahead than did Darwin himself, indeed farther ahead than Darwin could have looked in the absence of a well-developed ecological world-view. Leopold (1949, 203) summarizes Darwin's natural history of ethics with characteristic compression: "All ethics so far evolved rest upon a single prem-ise: that the individual is a member of a community of interdependent parts." Then he adds an ecological element, the community model of the biota es-poused most notably by Charles Elton (1927): Ecology "simply enlarges the boundaries of the community to include soils, waters, plants, and animals, or collectively: the land" (Leopold 1949, 204). When we all learn to "see land as a community to which we belong," not as "a commodity belonging to us" (Leopold 1949, viii), that same "simplest reason," of which Darwin speaks, might kick in. And, when it does, what results will be a land ethic that "changes the role of *Homo sapiens* from conqueror of the land community to plain member and citizen of it" (Leopold 1949, 204).

So, now the philosophical foundations and pedigree of the land ethic should be manifest. Basically, what Leopold did to cook up the land ethic was to take over Darwin's recipe for the origin and development of ethics, and add an ecological ingredient, the Eltonian "community concept." Darwin in turn had taken over a sentiment-based theory of ethics from Hume and Smith. Leopold may never have studied Hume's or Smith's moral philosophies; cer-tainly he never cites them; indeed he may have known of Hume only as a his-torian and Smith only as an economist. But because he surely did read Darwin and allude in "The Land Ethic" to Darwin's account of the origin and devel-opment of ethics, the philosophical foundations and pedigree of his land ethic are traceable through Darwin to the sentiment-based ethical theories of Hume and Smith.

## THE HOLISM OF THE LAND ETHIC AND ITS ANTECEDENTS

According to Leopold (1949, 204, emphasis added), "a land ethic implies re-spect for . . . fellow-members *and also for the community as such*." The land ethic, in other words, has a holistic dimension to it that is completely foreign to the mainstream Modern moral theories going back to Hobbes. The holistic dimen-sion of the land ethic—respect for the community as such, in addition to re-spect for its members severally—is, however, not in the least foreign to the Darwinian and Humean theories of ethics upon which it is built. Darwin (1871, 96–97) could hardly be more specific or emphatic on this point: "Ac-tions are regarded by savages and were probably so regarded by primeval man, as good or bad, solely as they obviously affect the welfare of the tribe,—not that of the species, nor that of an individual member of the tribe. This conclu-sion agrees well with the belief that the so-called moral sense is aboriginally derived from the social instincts, for both relate at first exclusively to the com-munity." Gary Varner (1991, 179) states flatly that "concern for communities as such has no historical antecedent in David Hume." But it does. Demonstrably. Hume ([1751] 1957, 47) insists, evidently against Hobbes and other social contract theorists, that "we must renounce the theory which accounts for every moral sentiment by the principle of self-love. We must adopt a more publick affection, and allow that the interests of society are not, even on their own account, entirely indifferent to us." Nor is this an isolated remark. Over and over we read in Hume's ethical works such statements as this: "It appears that a tendency to publick good, and to the promoting of peace, harmony, and order in society, does always by affecting the benevolent principles of our frame engage us on the side of the social virtues" (Hume [1751] 1957, 56). And this: "Everything that promotes the interests of society must communicate pleasure, and what is pernicious, give uneasiness" (Hume [1751] 1957, 58).

That is not to say that in Hume, certainly, and even in Darwin there is no theoretical provision for a lively concern for the individual members of society, as well as for society per se. The sentiment of sympathy being so central to it, I should expressly acknowledge that in the moral philosophy of Adam Smith, one finds little ethical holism. *Sympathy* means "with feeling." And that "all-important emotion of sympathy," as Darwin (1871, 81) styles it, can hardly extend to a transorganismic entity, such as society per se, which has no feelings per se. Hume and Darwin, however, recognized other moral sentiments than sympathy, some of which—patriotism, for example—relate as exclusively and specifically to society as sympathy does to sentient individuals.

In the Leopold land ethic, at any rate, the holistic aspect eventually eclipses the individualistic aspect. Toward the beginning of "The Land Ethic," Leopold, as noted, declares that a land ethic "implies respect for fellow-members" of the biotic community, as well as "for the community as such." Toward the middle of "The Land Ethic," Leopold (1949, 210) speaks of a "biotic right" to "continue" but such a right accrues, as the context indicates, to species, not to specimens. Toward the end of the essay, Leopold (1949, 224–25) writes a summary moral maxim, a golden rule, for the land ethic: "A thing is right when it tends to preserve the integrity, stability, and beauty of the biotic community. It is wrong when it tends otherwise." In it there is no reference at all to "fellow members." They have gradually dropped out of account as the "The Land Ethic" proceeds to its climax.

Why? One reason has already been noted. Conservationists, among whom Leopold counted himself, are professionally concerned about biological and ecological wholes—populations, species, communities, ecosystems—not their individual constituents. And the land ethic is tailored to suit conservation concerns, which are often confounded by concerns for individual specimens. For example, the conservation of endangered plant species is often most directly and efficiently effected by the deliberate eradication of the feral animals that threaten them. Preserving the integrity of a biotic community often requires reducing the populations of some component species, be they native or non-native, wild or feral. Certainly animal liberation and animal rights—advocated by Peter Singer and Tom Regan, respectively—would prohibit such convenient but draconian solutions to conservation problems. So would a more inclusive individualistic environmental ethic, such as that proffered by Paul Taylor (1986). Another reason is that ecology is about metaorganismic entities—biotic communities and ecosystems—not individuals, and the land ethic is expressly informed by ecology and reflects an ecological worldview. Its holism is precisely what makes the land ethic the environmental ethic of choice among conservationists and ecologists. In short, its holism is the land ethic's principal asset.

Whether by the end of the essay he forgets it or not, Leopold does say in "The Land Ethic" that "fellow-members" of the "land community" deserve "respect." How can we pretend to respect them if, in the interest of the integrity, stability, and beauty of the biotic community, we chop some down, gun others down, set fire to still others, and so on. Such brutalities are often involved in what conservationists call "wildlife management." Here again, to resolve this conundrum, we may consult Darwin, who indicates that ethics originated among Homo sapiens in the first place to serve the welfare of the community. Certainly, among the things that threaten to dissolve a human community are "murder, robbery, treachery, &c." However, as ethics evolve correlatively to social evolution, not only do they widen their scope, they change in content, such that what is wrong correlative to one stage of social development, may not be wrong correlative to the next. In a tribal society, as Darwin observes, exogamy is a cardinal precept. It is not in a republic. Nevertheless, in all human communities—from the savage clan to the family of man—the "infamy" of murder, robbery, treachery, &c. remains "everlasting." But the multispecies *biotic* community is so different from all our human communities that we cannot assume that what is wrong for one human being to do to another, even at every level of *social* organization, is wrong for one fellow member of the *biotic* community to do to another.

The currency of the economy of nature, we must remember, is energy. And it passes from one member to another, not from hand to hand like money in the human economy, but from stomach to stomach. As Leopold (1949, 107) observes of the biotic community, "The only truth is that its members must suck hard, live fast, and die often." In the biotic community there are producers and consumers; predators and prey. One might say that the integrity and stability of the biotic community depends upon death as well as life; indeed, one might say further, that the life of one member is premised squarely on the death of another. So one could hardly argue that our killing of fellow members of the biotic community is, prima facie, land ethically wrong. It depends on who is killed, for what reasons, under what circumstances, and how. The filling in of these blanks would provide, in each case, an answer to the question about respect. Models of respectful, but often violent and lethal, use of fellow members of the biotic community are provided by traditional American Indian peoples (Callicott and Overholt 1993).

# THE PROBLEM OF ECOFASCISM

Its holism is the land ethic's principal strength, but also its principal liability. Remember that according to Leopold, evolutionary and ecological biology reveal that "land [is] a community to which we belong" not "a commodity belonging to us" and that from the point of view of a land ethic, we are but "plain members and citizens of the biotic community." Then it would seem that the summary moral maxim of the land ethic applies to Homo sapiens no less than to the other members and citizens of the biotic community, plain or otherwise. A human population of more than six billion individuals is a dire threat to the integrity, stability, and beauty of the biotic community. Thus the existence of such a large human population is land ethically wrong. To right that wrong should we not do what we do when a population of white-tailed deer or some other species irrupts and threatens the integrity, stability, and beauty of the biotic community? We immediately and summarily reduce it, by whatever means necessary, usually by randomly and indiscriminately shooting the members of such a population to death—respectfully, of course—until its numbers are optimized. It did not take the land ethic's critics long to draw out the vitiating—but, as I shall go on to argue directly, only apparent—implication of the land ethic. According to William Aiken (1984, 269), from the point of view of the land ethic, "massive human diebacks would be good. It is our duty to cause them. It is our species' duty, relative to the whole, to eliminate 90 percent of our numbers." Its requirement that individual organisms, apparently also including individual *human* organisms, be sacrificed for the good of the whole, makes the land ethic, according to Tom Regan (1983, 262), a kind of "environmental fascism." Frederick Ferré (1996a, 18) echoes and amplifies Aiken's and Regan's indictment of the land ethic: "Anything we could do to exterminate excess people . . . would be morally 'right'! To refrain from such extermination would be 'wrong'! . . . Taken as a guide for human culture, the land ethic—despite the best intentions of its supporters—would lead toward classical fascism, the submergence of the individual person in the glorification of the collectivity, race, tribe, or nation." Finally, Kristin Shrader-Frechette adds her voice to those expressing moral outrage at the land "ethic": "In subordinating the welfare of all creatures to the integrity, stability, and beauty of the biotic community, then one subordinates individual human welfare, in all cases, to the welfare of the biotic community" (Shrader-Frechette 1996, 63).

Michael Zimmerman (1995) had defended the land ethic against the charge of ecofascism, pointing out that in addition to subordinating the welfare of the individual to that of the community, fascism involves other characterizing features, salient among them nationalism and militarism. And there is no hint of nationalism and militarism in the land ethic. But however one labels it, if the land ethic implies what Aiken, Regan, Ferré, and Shrader-Frechette allege that it does, it must be rejected as monstrous. Happily, it does not. To think that it does, one must assume that Leopold proffered the land ethic as a substitute for, not an addition to, our venerable and familiar human ethics. But he did not. Leopold refers to the various stages of ethical development—from tribal mores to universal human rights and, finally, to the land ethic—as "accretions." Accretion means an "increase by external addition or accumulation." The land ethic is an accretion—that is, an addition—to our several accumulated social ethics, not something that is supposed to replace them. If, as I here explain, Leopold is building the land ethic on theoretical foundations that he finds in Darwin, then it is obvious that with the advent of each new stage in the accreting development of ethics, the old stages are not erased or replaced, but added to. I, for example, am a citizen of a republic, but I also remain a member of an extended family, and a resident of a municipality. And it is quite evident to us all, from our own moral experience, that the duties attendant on citizenship in a republic (to pay taxes, to serve in the armed forces or in the Peace Corps, for example) do not cancel or replace the duties attendant on membership in a family (to honor parents, to love and educate children, for example) or residence in a municipality (to support public schools, to attend town meetings). Similarly, it is equally evident—at least to Leopold and his exponents, if not to his critics—that the duties attendant upon citizenship in the biotic community (to preserve its integrity, stability, and beauty) do not cancel or replace the duties attendant on membership in the human global village (to respect human rights).

## PRIORITIZING THE DUTIES GENERATED BY MEMBERSHIP IN MULTIPLE COMMUNITIES

This consideration has led Varner (1991) to argue that any proponent of the land ethic, Leopold presumably included, must be a moral pluralist. True enough, if by moral pluralist one means only that one tries simultaneously to adhere to multiple moral maxims (Honor thy Father and thy Mother; Love thy Country; Respect the Rights of All Human Beings Irrespective of Race, Creed, Color, or National Origin; Preserve the Integrity, Stability, and Beauty of the Biotic Community, for example). But if being a moral pluralist means espousing multiple moral philosophies and associated ethical theories, as it does in Christopher Stone's celebrated and influential *The Case for Moral Pluralism* (1987), then proponents of the land ethic are not necessarily committed to pluralism. On the contrary, the univocal theoretical foundations of the land ethic naturally generate multiple sets of moral duties—and correlative maxims, principles, and precepts—each related to a particular social scale (family, republic, global village, biotic community, for parallel example) all within a single moral philosophy. That moral philosophy is the one sketched here, beginning with the Humean social instincts and affections that evolve into ethics proper and grow more expansive and complicated apace with the Darwinian scenario of social evolution.

The land ethic involves a limited pluralism (multiple moral maxims, multiple sets of duties, or multiple principles and precepts) not a thoroughgoing pluralism of moral philosophies *sensu* Stone (1987)—Aristotelian ethics for this quandary, Kantian ethics for that, utilitarianism here, social-contract theory there (chapters 8 and 9). Thus, as Shrader-Frechette (1996, 63) points out, the land ethic must provide "second-order ethical principles and a priority ranking system that specifies the respective conditions under which [first-order] holistic and individualistic ethical principles ought to be recognized." Leopold provides no such second-order principles for prioritizing among first-order principles, but they can be easily derived from the communitarian foundations of the land ethic. By combining two second-order principles we can achieve a priority ranking among first-order principles, when, in a given quandary, they conflict. The first second-order principle (SOP-1) is that obligations generated by membership in more venerable and intimate communities take precedence over those generated in more recently emerged and impersonal communities. I think that most of us, for example, feel that our family duties (to care for aged parents, say, to educate minor children) take precedence over our civic duties (to contribute to United Way charities, say, to vote for higher municipal taxes to better support more indigent persons on the dole), when, because of limited means, we are unable to perform both family and civic duties. The second second-order principle (SOP-2) is that stronger interests (for lack of a better word) generate duties that take precedence over duties generated by weaker interests. For example, while duties to one's own children, all things being equal, properly take precedence over duties toward unrelated children in one's municipality, one would be ethically remiss to shower one's own children with luxuries while unrelated children in one's municipality lacked the bare necessities (food, shelter, clothing, education) for a decent life. Having the bare necessities for a decent life is a stronger interest than is the enjoyment of luxuries, and our duties to help supply proximate unrelated children with the former take precedence over our duties to supply our own children with the latter.

These second-order principles apply as well in quandaries in which duties to individuals conflict with duties to communities per se. In a case made famous by Jean-Paul Sartre in *L'existentialisme est un Humanisme,* a young man is caught in the dilemma of going off to join the French Free Forces in England during the Nazi occupation of France in World War II or staying home with his mother. Sartre, of course, is interested in the existential choice that this forces on the young man and in pursuing the thesis that his decision in some way makes a moral principle, not that it should be algorithmically determined by the application of various moral principles. But the second-order principles here set out apply to the young man's dilemma quite directly and, one might argue, decisively—existential freedom notwithstanding. SOP-1 requires the young man to give priority to the first-order principle, Honor Thy Father and Thy Mother, over the other first-order principle at play, Serve Thy

Country. But SOP-2 reverses the priority dictated by SOP-1. The very existence of France as a transorganismic entity is threatened. The young man's mother has a weaker interest at stake, for, as Sartre reports, his going off—and maybe getting killed—would plunge her into "despair." His mother being plunged into despair would be terrible, but not nearly as terrible as the destruction of France would be if not enough young men fought on her behalf. So the resolution of this young man's dilemma is clear; he should give priority to the first-order principle, Serve Thy Country. Had the young man been an American and had the time been the early 1970s and had the dilemma been stay home with his mother or join the Peace Corps and go to Africa, then he should give priority to the first-order principle Honor Thy Father and Thy Mother and stay home. Had the young man been the same person as Sartre constructs, but had his mother been a Jew whom the Nazis would have sent to a horrible death in a concentration camp if her son did not stay home and help her hide, then again, he should give priority to the first-order principle, Honor Thy Father and Thy Mother, and stay home.

## THE PRIORITY PRINCIPLES APPLIED TO THE OLD-GROWTH FOREST QUANDARY

Let me consider now those kinds of quandaries in which our duties to human beings conflict with our duties to *biotic* communities as such. Varner (1991, 176) supplies a case in point:

> Suppose that an environmentalist enamored with the Leopold land ethic is considering how to vote on a national referendum to preserve the spotted owl by restricting logging in Northwest forests. . . . He or she would be required to vote, not according to the land ethic, but according to whatever ethic governs closer ties to a human family and/or larger human community. Therefore, if a relative is one of 10,000 loggers who will lose jobs if the referendum passes, the environmentalist is obligated to vote against it. Even if none of the loggers is a family member, the voter is still obligated to vote against the referendum.

The flaw in Varner's reasoning is that he applies only SOP-1—that obligations generated by membership in more venerable and intimate communities take precedence over those generated in more recently emerged and impersonal communities. If that were the only second-order communitarian principle then he would be right. But SOP-2—that stronger interests generate duties that take precedence over duties generated by weaker interests—reverses the priority determined by applying SOP-1 in this case. The spotted owl is threatened with preventable anthropogenic extinction—threatened with biocide, in a word—and the old-growth forest biotic communities of the Pacific Northwest are threatened with destruction. These threats are the environmental-ethical equivalent of genocide and holocaust. The loggers, on the other hand, are threatened with economic losses, for which they can be compensated dollar for dollar. More important to the loggers, I am told, their lifestyle is threatened. But livelihood and lifestyle, for both of which adequate substitutes can be found, is a lesser interest than life itself. If we faced the choice of cutting down millions of four-hundred-year-old trees or cutting down thousands of forty-year-old loggers, our duties to the loggers would take precedence by SOP-1, nor would SOP-1 be countermanded by SOP-2. But that is not the choice we face. The choice is between cutting down four-hundred-year-old trees, rendering the spotted own extinct, and destroying the old-growth forest biotic community, on the one hand, and displacing forest workers in an economy that is already displacing them through automation and raw-log exports to Japan and other foreign markets. And the old-growth logging lifestyle is doomed, in any case, to self-destruct, for it will come to an end with the "final solution" to the old-growth forest question, if the jack-booted timber barons (who disingenuously blame the spotted owl for the economic insecurity of loggers and other workers in the timber industry) continue to have their way. With SOP-2 supplementing SOP-1, the indication of the land ethic is crystal clear in the exemplary quandary posed by Varner, and it is opposite to the one Varner, applying only SOP-1, claims it indicates.

# CONCLUSION

The holistic Leopold land ethic is not a case of ecofascism. The land ethic is intended to supplement, not replace, the more venerable community-based social ethics, in relation to which it is an accretion or addition. Neither is the land ethic a "paper tiger," an environmental ethic with no teeth (Nelson 1996). Choice among which community-related principle should govern a moral agent's conduct in a given moral quandary may be determined by the application of two second-order principles. The first, SOP-1, requires an agent to give priority to the first-order principles generated by the more venerable and more intimate community memberships. Thus, when holistic environment-oriented duties are in direct conflict with individualistic human-oriented duties, the human-oriented duties take priority. The land ethic is, therefore, not a case of ecofascism. However, the second second-order principle, SOP-2, requires an agent to give priority to the stronger interests at issue. When the indication determined by the application of SOP-1 is reinforced by the application of SOP-2, an agent's choice is clear. When the indication determined by the application of SOP-1 is contradicted by the application of SOP-2, an agent's choice is equally clear: SOP-2 countermands SOP-1. Thus, when holistic environment-oriented duties are in conflict with individualistic human-oriented duties, and the holistic environmental interests at issue are significantly stronger than the individualistic human interests at issue, the former take priority.

# BIBLIOGRAPHY

AIKEN, W. 1984. "Ethical Issues in Agriculture." In *Earthbound: New Introductory Essays in Environmental Ethics,* edited by T. Regan, 247–288. New York: Random House.

CALLICOTT, J. B., and T. W. OVERHOLT. 1993. "American Indian Attitudes Toward Nature." In *Philosophy from Africa to Zen: An Invitation to World Philosophy,* edited by R. C. Solomon and K. M. Higgins, 55–80. Lanham, Md.: Rowman and Littlefield.

DARWIN, C. R. 1987. *The Descent of Man and Selection in Relation to Sex.* London: J. Murray.

ELTON, C. 1927. *Animal Ecology.* London: Sidgwick and Jackson.

FERRÉ, F. 1996a. "Persons in Nature: Toward an Applicable and Unified Environmental Ethics." *Ethics and the Environment* 1:15–25.

HUME, D. [1751] 1957. *An Enquiry Concerning the Principles of Morals.* Reprint, New York: Library of the Liberal Arts.

LEOPOLD, A. 1949. *A Sand County Almanac and Sketches from Here and There.* New York: Oxford University Press.

NELSON, M. 1996. "Holism and Fascists and Paper Tigers . . . Oh My!" *Ethics and the Environment* 2:103–107.

REGAN, T. 1983. *The Case for Animal Rights.* Berkeley: University of California Press.

SCHRADER-FRECHETTE, K. S. 1996. "Individualism, Holism, and Environmental Ethics." *Ethics and the Environment* 1:55–69.

STONE, C. D. 1987. *Earth and Other Ethics: The Case for Moral Pluralism.* New York: Harper & Row.

TAYLOR, P. 1986. *Respect for Nature: A Theory of Environmental Ethics.* Princeton, NJ: Princeton University Press.

VARNER, G. E. 1991. "No Holism without Pluralism." *Environmental Ethics* 19:175–179.

ZIMMERMAN, MICHAEL E. 1995. "The Threat of Ecofascism." *Social Theory and Practice* 21:207–238.

# CHALLENGES IN ENVIRONMENTAL ETHICS

*Holmes Rolston III*

Holmes Rolston III is professor of philosophy at Colorado State University. He is author of *Philosophy Gone Wild: Essays in Environmental Ethics* and *Environmental Ethics: Duties to and Values in the Natural World.* His 1997–1998 Gifford Lectures have been published as *Genes, Genesis and God: Values and Their Origins in Natural and Human History.*

Ethicists had settled on at least one conclusion as ethics became modern in Darwin's century: that the moral has nothing to do with the natural. To argue otherwise commits the naturalistic fallacy, moving without justification from what *is* in nature *ought to be* in culture. Science describes natural history, natural law; ethics prescribes human conduct, moral law; and to confuse the two makes a category mistake. Nature simply *is*, without objective value; the preferences of human subjects establish value; and these human values, appropriately considered, generate human duties. Only humans are ethical subjects and only humans are ethical objects. Nature is amoral; the moral community is interhuman.

In the last third of this century, unsettled as we enter the next millennium, there is foreboding revolution. Only the human species contains moral agents, but perhaps conscience on such an earth ought not be used to exempt every other form of life from consideration, with the resulting paradox that the sole moral species acts only in its collective self-interest toward all the rest. There is something overspecialized about an ethic, held by the dominant class of *Homo sapiens*, that regards the welfare of only one of several million species as an object and beneficiary of duty. We need an interspecific ethics.

This essay was originally prepared for an American Philosophical Association symposium on Rolston's book *Environmental Ethics*. A revised version appears in *Ecology, Economics, Ethics: The Broken Circle* (Yale University Press, New Haven, London, 1991).

Whatever ought to be in culture, this biological world that *is* also *ought to be*; we must argue from the natural to the moral.

If this requires a paradigm change about the sorts of things to which duty can attach, so much the worse for those humanistic ethics no longer functioning in, nor suited to, their changing environment. The anthropocentrism associated with them was fiction anyway. There is something Newtonian, not yet Einsteinian, besides something morally naive, about living in a reference frame where one species takes itself as absolute and values everything else relative to its utility. If true to their specific epithet, ought not *Homo sapiens* value this host of life as something with a claim to care in its own right? Man may be the only measurer of things, but is man the only measure of things? The challenge of environmental ethics is a principled attempt to redefine the boundaries of ethical obligation.

Still there is the sense of anomaly that forebodes paradigm overthrow. An ecological conscience? Sometimes this seems to be a category mistake, joining a scientific adjective with an ethical noun, rather like Christian biochemistry mismatches a religious adjective and a scientific noun. With analysis, we suspect that the relation is three-place. Person A has a duty to person B concerning the environment C, and no one has ever denied that natural things have instrumental value to humans. Humans are helped or hurt by the condition of their environment, and we have duties to humans that concern their valuable environment, an environment they are able to value. So conservatives may shrink back into the persistent refusal of philosophers to think biologically, to naturalize ethics in the deep sense. They will fear that it is logically incoherent to suppose there is a nonanthropogenic value, or that this is too metaphysically speculative ever to be operational and that it does not make any pragmatic difference anyway, claiming that an adequate environmental ethic can be anthropogenic, even anthropocentric.

When we face up to the crisis, however, we undergo a more direct moral encounter. Environmental ethics is not a muddle; it is an invitation to moral development. All ethics seeks an appropriate respect for life, but respect for human life is only a subset of respect for all life. What ethics is about, in the end, is seeing outside your own sector of self-interest, of class interest. A comprehensive ethic will find values in and duties to the natural world. The vitality of ethics depends on our knowing what is really vital, and there will be found the intersection of value and duty. An ecological conscience requires an unprecedented mix of science and conscience, of biology and ethics.

## 1. HIGHER ANIMALS

We have direct encounters with life that has eyes, at least where our gaze is returned by something that itself has a concerned outlook. The relation is two-place: I-thou, subject to subject. Compared with concern about soil and water, which are instrumentally vital but blind, when we meet the higher animals there is somebody there behind the fur and feathers. "The environment" is external to us all, but where there is inwardness in this environment, perhaps we ought to be conscious of other consciousness. Whatever matters to animals, matters morally.

Wild animals defend their own lives, because they have a good of their own. Animals hunt and howl, seek shelter, build nests and sing, care for their young, flee from threats, grow hungry, thirsty, hot, tired, excited, sleepy, seek out their habitats and mates. They suffer injury and lick their wounds. They can know security and fear, endurance and fatigue, comfort and pain. When they figure out their helps and hurts in the environment, they do not make man the measure of things at all; more, man is not the only measurer of things.

Still, man is the only moral measurer of things, and how should he count these wild, nonmoral things? One might expect classical ethics to have sifted well an ethics for animals. Our ancestors did not think about endangered species, ecosystems, acid rain, or the ozone layer, but they lived in closer association with wild and domestic animals than do we. Nevertheless, until recently, the scientific, humanistic centuries since the so-called Enlightenment have not been sensitive ones for animals. Animals were mindless, living matter; biology was mechanistic. Even psychology, rather than defending animal experience, was behaviorist. Philosophy, as we have already said, thought man the measure of things. Across several centuries of hard science and humanist ethics there has been little compassion for animals. We eat millions of them every year and we use many millions more in industry and research, as though little matters unless it matters to humans.

So far as we got ethically, we rather oddly said that we should be humane toward nonhuman animals. "The question is not," said Bentham, "Can they reason, nor Can they talk? but, Can they suffer?" These nonhumans do not share with humans the capacity to reason or talk, but they do share the capacity to suffer, and human ethics can be extended so far forth to our animal cousins. We may be unsure about insects and fish, but at least we will need an avian and a mammal ethics.

The progress of recent science itself has increasingly smeared the human–nonhuman boundary line. Animal anatomy, biochemistry, perception, cognition, experience, behavior, and evolutionary history are kin to our own. Animals have no immortal souls, but then persons may not either, or beings with souls may not be the only kind that count morally. Ethical progress further smeared the boundary. Sensual pleasures are a good thing, ethics should be egalitarian nonarbitrary, nondiscriminatory. There are ample scientific grounds that animals enjoy pleasures and suffer pains; and ethically no grounds to value these in humans and not in animals. The *is* in nature and the *ought* in ethics are not so far apart after all. We should treat animals humanely, that is, treat animals equally with ourselves where they have equal interests.

Recently, then, there has been a vigorous reassessment of human duties to sentient life. More has been written on this subject in the past fifteen years than in the previous fifteen centuries. The world cheered in the fall of 1988 when humans rescued two whales from the winter ice. A sign in Rocky Mountain National Park enjoins humans not to harass bighorn sheep: "Respect their right to life." We have passed animal welfare legislation and set up animal care committees in our universities. We have made a vital breakthrough past humans, and the first lesson in environmental ethics has been learned.

But the risk of ethical inadequacy here lies in a moral extension that expands rights as far as mammals and not much further, a psychologically based ethic that counts only felt experience. We respect life in our nonhuman but near-human animal cousins, a semi-anthropic and still quite subjective ethics. Justice remains a concern for just-us subjects. Extending our human ethics, we say that the sheep, too, have rights and that we should be humane to the whales. There has, in fact, not been much theoretical breakthrough, no paradigm shift. We do not yet have a biologically based ethics.

We certainly need an ethic for animals, but that is only one level of concern in a comprehensive environmental ethics. When we try to use culturally extended rights and psychologically based utilities to protect the flora or even the insentient fauna, to protect endangered species or ecosystems, we can only stammer. Indeed, we get lost trying to protect bighorns, because in the wild the cougar is not respecting the rights or utilities of the sheep she slays. There are no rights in the wild, and nature is indifferent to the welfare of particular animals. Further, in culture, humans slay sheep and eat them regularly, while humans have every right not to be eaten by either humans or cougars.

A bison fell through the ice into a river in Yellowstone Park; the environmental ethic there, letting nature take its course, forbade would-be rescuers from either saving or mercy killing the suffering animal. A drowning human would have been saved at once. It was as vital to the struggling bison as to any human to get out; the poor thing froze to death that night. Was the Yellowstone ethic callous to life, inhumane? Or had it other vitalities to consider? This ethic seems rather to have concluded that a moral extension is too nondiscriminating; we are unable to separate an ethics for humans from an ethics for wildlife. To treat wild animals with compassion learned in culture does not appreciate their wildness.

Man, said Socrates, is the political animal; humans maximally are what they are in culture, where the natural selection pressures (impressively productive in ecosystems) are relaxed without detriment to the species *Homo sapiens*, and indeed with great benefit to its member persons. Wild and even domestic animals cannot enter culture; they do not have that capacity. They cannot acquire language at sufficient levels to take part in culture; they cannot make their clothing, or build fires, much less read books or receive an education.

Worse, cultural protection can work to their detriment; with too much human or humane care their wildness is made over into a human artifact. A cow does not have the integrity of a deer, a poodle that of a wolf. Culture is a good thing for humans, often a bad thing for animals. Culture does make a relevant ethical difference, and environmental ethics has different criteria from interhuman ethics.

Can they talk? and, Can they reason?, indicating cultural capacities, are relevant questions, not just, Can they suffer? Compassionate respect for life in its suffering is only part of the analysis. Sometimes in an environmental ethic we do need to follow nature, and not so much to treat animals humanely, like we do humans, as to treat animals naturally, for what they are by themselves. Even when we treat them humanely within culture, part of the ethic may also involve treating them naturally.

"Equality" is a positive word in ethics, "discriminatory" a pejorative one. On the other hand, simplistic reduction is a failing in the philosophy of science and epistemology; to be "discriminating" is desirable in logic and value theory. Something about treating humans as equals with bighorns and cougars seems to "reduce" humans to merely animal levels of value, a "no more" counterpart in ethics of the "nothing but" fallacy often met in science. Humans are "nothing but" naked apes. Something about treating sheep and cougars as the equals of humans seems to elevate them unnaturally, unable to value them for what they are. There is something insufficiently discriminating in such judgments—species blind in a bad sense, blind to the real differences between species, valuational differences that do count morally. To the contrary, a discriminating ethicist will insist on preserving the differing richness of valuational complexity, wherever found.

Two tests of discrimination are pain and diet. It might be thought that pain is a bad thing, whether in nature or culture. Perhaps when dealing with humans in culture, additional levels of value and utility must be protected by conferring rights that do not exist in the wild, but meanwhile at least we should minimize animal suffering. That is indeed a worthy imperative in culture where animals are removed from nature and bred, but it may be misguided where animals remain in ecosystems. When the bighorn sheep of Yellowstone caught pinkeye—blinded, injured, and starving in result—300 bighorns, over half the herd, perished. Wildlife veterinarians wanted to treat the disease, as they would have in any domestic herd, and as they did with Colorado bighorns infected with an introduced lungworm, but the Yellowstone ethicists left them to suffer, seemingly not respecting their life. Had they no mercy? Was this again inhumane?

They knew rather that, while intrinsic pain is a bad thing whether in humans or in sheep, pain in ecosystems is instrumental pain, through which the sheep are naturally selected for a more satisfactory adaptive fit. Pain in a medically skilled culture is pointless, once the alarm to health is sounded, but pain operates functionally in bighorns in their niche, even after it becomes no longer in the interests of the pained individuals. To have interfered in the interests of the blinded sheep would have weakened the species. The question, Can they suffer? is not as simple as Bentham thought. What we *ought* to do depends on what *is*. The *is* of nature differs significantly from the *is* of culture, even when similar suffering is present in both.

Some ethicists will insist that at least in culture we can minimize animal pain, and that will constrain our diet. There is predation in nature; humans evolved as omnivores. But humans, the only moral animals, should refuse to participate in the meat-eating phase of their ecology, just as they refuse to live merely by the rules of natural selection. Humans do not look to the behavior of wild animals as an ethical guide in other matters (marriage, truth telling, promise keeping, justice, charity). There they do not follow nature. Why should they justify their dietary habits by watching what animals do?

But the difference is that these other matters are affairs of culture; these are person-to-person events, not events at all in spontaneous nature. By contrast, eating is omnipresent in wild nature; humans eat because they are in nature, not because they are in culture. Eating animals is not an event between persons, but is a human-to-animal event; and the rules for this come from the ecosystems in which humans evolved and which they have no duty to remake. We must eat to live; nature absolutely requires that. We evolved to eat as omnivores; that animal nature underruns over human nature. Even in culture meat eating is still relatively natural; there is nothing immoral about fitting into one's ecology. We follow nature, treat animals naturally, capture nutritional values, and learn our place in the scheme of life and death. This respects life, profoundly so. Humans, then, can model their dietary habits from their ecosystems, though they cannot and should not so model their interpersonal justice or charity. When eating they ought to minimize animal suffering, and they also may gladly affirm their ecology. The boundary between animals and humans has not been rubbed out after all; only what was a boundary line has been smeared into a boundary zone. We have discovered that animals count morally, though we are only beginning to solve the challenge of how to count them.

## 2. ORGANISMS

In college zoology I did an experiment on nutrition in rats, to see how they grew with and without vitamins. When the experiment was completed, I was told to take the rats out and drown them. I felt squeamish but did it. In college botany I did an experiment on seedlings to test how they grew with this or that fertilizer. The experiment over, I threw out the seedlings without a second thought. While there can be ethics about sentient animals, after that perhaps ethics is over. Respect for life ends somewhere in zoology; it is not part of botany. No consciousness, no conscience. Without sentience, ethics is nonsense.

Or do we want an ethic that is more objective about life? In Yosemite National Park for almost a century humans entertained themselves by driving through a tunnel cut in a giant sequoia. Two decades ago the Wawona tree, weakened by the cut, blew down in a storm. People said: Cut us another drive-through sequoia. The Yosemite environmental ethic, deepening over the years, said no! You ought not to mutilate majestic sequoias for amusement. Respect their life! Indeed, some ethicists count the value of redwoods so highly that they will spike redwoods, lest they be cut. In the Rawah Wilderness in alpine Colorado, old signs read, "Please leave the flowers for others to enjoy." When they rotted out, the new signs urged a less humanist ethic: "Let the flowers live!"

But trees and flowers cannot care, so why should we? We are not considering animals that are close kin, nor can they suffer or experience anything. There are no humane societies for plants. Plants are not valuers with preferences that can be satisfied or frustrated. It seems odd to claim that plants need our sympathy, odd to ask that we should consider their point of view. They have no subjective life, only objective life.

Fishermen in Atlantic coastal estuaries and bays toss beer bottles overboard, a convenient way to dispose of trash. On the bottom, small crabs, attracted by the residual beer, make their way inside the bottles and become trapped, unable to get enough foothold on the slick glass neck to work their way out. They starve slowly. Then one dead crab becomes bait for the next victim, an indefinitely resetting trap! Are those bottle traps of ethical concern, after fishermen have been warned about this effect? Or is the whole thing out of sight, out of mind, with crabs too mindless to care about? Should sensitive fishermen pack their bottle trash back to shore—whether or not crabs have much, or any, felt experience?

Flowers and sequoias live; they ought to live. Crabs have value out of sight, out of mind. Afraid of the naturalistic fallacy, conservative ethicists will say that people should enjoy letting flowers live or that it is silly to cut drive-through sequoias, aesthetically more excellent for humans to appreciate both for what they are. The crabs are out of sight, but not really out of mind; humans value them at a distance. But these ethically conservative reasons really do not understand what biological conservation is in the deepest sense. Nothing matters to a tree, but much is *vital.*

An organism is a spontaneous, self-maintaining system, sustaining and reproducing itself, executing its program, making a way through the world, checking against performance by means of responsive capacities with which to measure success. It can reckon with vicissitudes, opportunities, and adversities that the world presents. Something more than physical causes, even when less than sentience, is operating within every organism. There is *information* superintending the causes; without it the organism would collapse into a sand heap. This information is a modern equivalent of what Aristotle called formal and final causes; it gives the organism a *telos,* "end," a kind of (nonfelt) goal. Organisms have ends, although not always ends-in-view.

All this cargo is carried by the DNA, essentially a *linguistic* molecule. By a serial "reading" of the DNA, a polypeptide chain is synthesized, such that its sequential structure determines the bioform into which it will fold. Ever-lengthening chains (like ever-longer sentences), are organized into genes (like paragraphs and chapters). Diverse proteins, lipids, carbohydrates, enzymes—all the life structures are "written into" the genetic library. The DNA is thus a *logical set,* not less than a biological set, informed as well as formed. Organisms use a sort of symbolic logic, use these molecular shapes as symbols of life. The novel resourcefulness lies in the epistemic content conserved, developed, and thrown forward to make biological resources out of the physicochemical sources. This executive steering core is cybernetic—partly a special kind of cause and effect system, and partly something more: partly a historical information system discovering and evaluating ends so as to map and make a way through the world, partly a system of significances attached to operations, pursuits, resources. In this sense, the genome is a set of *conservation* molecules.

The genetic set is really a *propositional* set—to choose a provocative term—recalling how the Latin *propositum* is an assertion, a set task, a theme, a plan, a proposal, a project, as well as a cognitive statement. From this it is also a motivational set, unlike human books, since these life motifs are set to drive the movement from genotypic potential to phenotypic expression. Given a chance, these molecules seek organic self-expression. They thus proclaim a life way, and with this an organism, unlike an inert rock, claims the environment as source and sink, from which to abstract energy and materials and into which to excrete them. It "takes advantage" of its environment. Life thus arises out of earthen sources (as do rocks), but life turns back on its sources to make resources out of them (unlike rocks). An acorn becomes an oak; the oak stands on its own.

So far we have only description. We begin to pass to value when we recognize that the genetic set is a *normative set*; it distinguishes between what *is* and what *ought to be*. This does not mean that the organism is a moral system, for there are no moral agents in nature; but the organism is an axiological, evaluative system. So the oak grows, reproduces, repairs its wounds, and resists death. The physical state that the organism seeks, idealized in its programmatic form, is a valued state. *Value* is present in this achievement. *Vital* seems a better word for it than *biological*. We are not dealing simply with an individual defending its solitary life but with an individual having situated fitness in an ecosystem. Still, we want to affirm that the living individual, taken as a "point experience" in the web of interconnected life, is *per se* an intrinsic value.

A life is defended for what it is in itself, without necessary further contributory reference, although, given the structure of all ecosystems, such lives necessarily do have further reference. The organism has something it is conserving, something for which it is standing: its life. Organisms have their own standards, fit into their niche though they must. They promote their own realization, at the same time that they track an environment. They have a technique, a know-how. Every organism has a *good-of-its-kind*; it defends its own kind as a *good kind*. In that sense, as soon as one knows what a giant sequoia tree is, one knows the biological identity that is sought and conserved. Man is neither the measurer nor the measure of things; value is not anthropogenic, it is biogenic.

There seems no reason why such own-standing normative organisms are not morally significant. A moral agent deciding his or her behavior, ought to take account of the consequences for other evaluative systems. This does not follow nature, if we mean by that to imitate ethical agents there, for nature is amoral. But it does follow nature, if we mean by that we respect these amoral organic norms as we shape our conduct. Such an ethic will be teleological, I suppose, since it values the *telos* in organisms, but it seems equally deontological, since it owes (Gk: *deont-*) respect for life in itself, intrinsically, and not just instrumentally, consequentially. (Frankly, the classical teleological/deontological distinction seems as troublesome as helpful in moral analysis here.)

Within the community of moral agents one has not merely to ask whether *x* is a normative system, but, since the norms are a personal option, to judge the norm and the consequences. But within the biotic community organisms are amoral normative systems, and there are no cases where an organism seeks a good of its own that is morally reprehensible. The distinction between having a good of its kind and being a good kind vanishes, so far as any faulting of the organism is concerned. To this extent, everything with a good of its kind is a good kind and thereby has intrinsic value.

One might say that an organism is a bad organism if, during the course of pressing its normative expression, it upsets the ecosystem or causes widespread disease, bad consequences. Remember though, that an organism cannot be a good kind without situated environmental fitness. By natural selection the kind of goods to which it is genetically programmed must mesh with its ecosystemic role. Despite the ecosystem as a perpetual contest of goods in dialectic and exchange, it is difficult to say that any organism is a bad kind in this instrumental sense either. The misfits are extinct, or soon will be. In spontaneous nature any species that preys upon, parasitizes, competes with, or crowds another will be a bad kind from the narrow perspective of its victim or competitor.

But if we enlarge that perspective it typically becomes difficult to say that any species is a bad kind overall in the ecosystem. An "enemy" may even be good for the "victimized" species, though harmful to individual members of it, as when predation keeps the deer herd healthy. Beyond this, the "bad kinds" typically play useful roles in population control, in symbiotic relationships, or in providing opportunities for other species. The *Chlamydia* microbe is a bad kind from the perspective of the bighorns, but when one thing dies, something else lives. After the pinkeye outbreak, the golden eagle population in Yellowstone flourished, preying on the bighorn carcasses. For them *Chlamydia* is a good kind instrumentally.

Some biologist-philosophers will say that, even though an organism evolves to have a situated environmental fitness, not all such situations are good arrangements; some can be clumsy or bad. True, the vicissitudes of historical evolution do sometimes result in ecological webs that are suboptimal solutions, within the biologically limited possibilities and powers of interacting organisms. Still, such systems have been selected over millennia for functional stability; and at least the burden of proof is on a human evaluator to say why any natural kind is a bad kind and ought not to call forth admiring respect. Something may be a good kind intrinsically but a bad kind instrumentally in the system; these will be anomalous cases, however, with selection pressures against them. These claims about good kinds do not say that things are perfect kinds, or that there can be no better ones, only that natural kinds are good kinds until proven otherwise.

What is almost invariably meant by a "bad" kind is that an organism is instrumentally bad when judged from the viewpoint of human interests, of humane interests. "Bad" so used is an anthropocentric word; there is nothing at all biological or ecological about it, and so it has no force evaluating objective nature, however much humanist force it may sometimes have.

A really *vital* ethic respects all life, not just animal pains and pleasures, much less just human preferences. In the Rawahs, the old signs, "Leave the flowers for others to enjoy," were application signs using an old, ethically conservative, humanistic ethic. The new ones invite a change of reference frame—a wilder, more logical because more biological ethic, a radical ethic that goes down to the roots of life, that really is conservative because it understands biological conservation at depths. What the injunction, "Let the flowers live!" means is: "Daisies, marsh-marigolds, geraniums, larkspurs are evaluative systems that conserve goods of their kind, and, in the absence of evidence to the contrary, are good kinds. There are trails here by which you may enjoy these flowers. Is there any reason why your human interests should not also conserve these good kinds?" A drive-through sequoia causes no suffering; it is not cruel. but it is callous and insensitive to the wonder of life. The ethically conservative will complain that we have committed the naturalistic fallacy; rather, we invite a radical commitment to respect all life.

## 3. SPECIES

Certain rare species of butterflies occur in hummocks (slightly elevated forested ground) on the African grasslands. It was formerly the practice of unscrupulous collectors to go in, collect a few hundred specimens, and then burn out the hummock with the intention of destroying the species, thereby driving up the price of their collections. I find myself persuaded that they morally ought not do this. Nor will the reason resolve into the evil of greed, but it remains the needless destruction of a butterfly species.

This conviction remains even when the human goods are more worthy. Coloradans are considering whether to build the Two Forks Dam to supply urban Denver with water. This would require destroying a canyon and altering the Platte River flow, with many negative environmental consequences, including endangering a butterfly, the Pawnee montane skipper, *Hesperia leonardus montana*, as well as endangering the whooping crane downstream. I doubt whether the good of humans who wish more water for development, both for industry and for bluegrass lawns, warrants endangering species of butterflies and cranes.

Sometimes the stakes are alleged to rise even higher. The Bay checkerspot, *Euphydryas editha bayensis*, proposed to be listed as an endangered species, inhabits peripheral tracts of a large facility on which United Technologies Corporation, a missile contractor, builds and tests Minuteman and Tomahawk propulsion systems. The giant defense contractor has challenged the proposed listing and thinks it airy and frivolous that a butterfly should slow the delivery of warhead missile propulsion systems, and so went ahead and dug a water pipeline through a butterfly patch. They operated out of the classical ethics that says that butterflies do not count but that the defense of humans does.

But a more radical, environmental ethics demurs. The good of humans might override the good of butterfly species but the case must be argued. Lest this seem the foolishness of a maverick philosopher, I point out that such conviction has been written into national law. The Endangered Species Act requires that the case must be argued before a high level "God" committee.

A species exists; a species ought to exist. Environmental ethics must make both claims and move from biology to ethics with care. Species exist only instantiated in individuals, yet are as real as individual plants or animals. The claim that there are specific forms of life historically maintained in their environments over time seems as certain as anything else we believe about the empirical world. At times biologists revise the theories and taxa with which they map these forms, but species are not so much like lines of latitude and longitude as like mountains and rivers, phenomena objectively there to be mapped. The edges of these natural kinds will sometimes be fuzzy, to some extent discretionary. One species will slide into another over evolutionary time. But it does not follow from the fact that speciation is sometimes in progress that species are merely made up, not found as evolutionary lines with identity in time as well as space.

A consideration of species is revealing and challenging because it offers a biologically based counterexample to the focus on individuals—typically sentient and usually persons—so characteristic in classical ethics. In an evolutionary ecosystem, it is not mere individuality that counts, but the species is also significant because it is a dynamic life form maintained over time. The individual represents (re-presents) a species in each new generation. It is a token of a type, and the type is more important than the token.

A species lacks moral agency, reflective self-awareness, sentience, or organic individuality. The older, conservative ethic will be tempted to say that specific-level processes cannot count morally. Duties must attach to singular lives, most evidently those with a psychological self, or some analogue to this. In an individual organism, the organs report to a center; the good of a whole is defended. The members of a species report to no center. A species has no self. It is not a bounded singular. There is no analogue to the nervous hookups or circulatory flows that characterize the organism.

But singularity, centeredness, selfhood, individuality, are not the only processes to which duty attaches. A more radically conservative ethic knows that having a biological identity reasserted genetically over time is as true of the species as of the individual. Identity need not attach solely to the centered organism; it can persist as a discrete pattern over time. Thinking this way, the life that the individual has is something passing through the individual as much as something it intrinsically possesses. The individual is subordinate to the species, not the other way around. The genetic set, in which is coded the *telos*, is as evidently the property of the species as of the individual through which it passes. A consideration of species strains any ethic fixed on individual organisms, much less on sentience or persons. But the result can be biologically sounder, though it revises what was formerly thought logically permissible or ethically binding. This is a higher teleological ethic, finding now the specific *telos*, and concerned about consequences at that level; again, it is deontological, duty bound to the dynamic form of life for what it is in itself.

The species line is the *vital* living system, the whole, of which individual organisms are the essential parts. The species too has its integrity, its individuality, its "right to life" (if we must use the rhetoric of rights); and it is more important to protect this vitality than to protect individual integrity. The right to life, biologically speaking, is an adaptive fit that is right for life, that survives over millennia, and this generates at least a presumption that species in niche are good right where they are, and therefore that it is right for humans to let them be, to let them evolve.

Processes of value that we earlier found in an organic individual reappear at the specific level: defending a particular form of life, pursuing a pathway through the world, resisting death (extinction), regeneration maintaining a normative identity over time, creative resilience discovering survival skills. It is as logical to say that the individual is the species' way of propagating itself as to say that the embryo or egg is the individual's way of propagating itself. The dignity resides in the dynamic form; the individual inherits this, exemplifies it, and passes it on. If, at the specific level, these processes are just as evident, or even more so, what prevents duties arising at that level? The appropriate survival unit is the appropriate level of moral concern. This would be following nature specifically.

Sensitivity to this level, however, can sometimes make an environmental ethicist seem callous. On San Clemente Island, the U.S. Fish and Wildlife Service and the California Department of Fish and Game planned to shoot 2,000 feral goats to save three endangered plant species, *Malacothamnus clementinus, Castilleja grisea, Delphinium kinkiense*, of which the surviving individuals numbered only a few dozens. After a protest, some goats were trapped and relocated. But trapping all was impossible and many hundreds were killed. Is it inhumane to count plant species more than mammal lives, a few plants more than a thousand goats?

Those who wish to restore rare species of big cats to the wilds have asked about killing genetically inbred, inferior cats, presently held in zoos, in order to make space available for the cats needed to reconstruct and maintain a population genetically more likely to survive upon release. All the Siberian tigers in zoos in North America are descendants of seven animals; if these were replaced by others nearer to the wild type and with more genetic variability, the species could be saved in the wild. When we move to the level of species, we may kill individuals for the good of their kind.

Or we may now refuse to let nature take its course. The Yellowstone ethicists let the bison drown, callous to its suffering; they let the blinded bighorns die. But in the spring of 1984 a sow grizzly and her three cubs walked across the ice of Yellowstone Lake to Frank Island, two miles from shore. They stayed several days to feast on two elk carcasses, when the ice bridge melted. Soon afterward, they were starving on an island too small to support them. This time the Yellowstone ethicists promptly rescued the grizzlies and released them on the mainland, in order to protect an endangered species. They were not rescuing individual bears so much as saving the species. They thought that humans had already and elsewhere imperiled the grizzly, and that they ought to save this form of life.

Humans have more understanding than ever of the natural world they inhabit, of the speciating processes, more predictive power to foresee the intended and unintended results of their actions, and more power to reverse the undesirable consequences. The duties that such power and vision generate no longer attach simply to individuals or persons but are emerging duties to specific forms of life. The wrong that humans are doing, or allowing to happen through carelessness, is stopping the historical vitality of life, the flow of natural kinds.

Every extinction is an incremental decay in this stopping life, no small thing. Every extinction is a kind of superkilling. It kills forms (*species*), beyond individuals. It kills "essences" beyond "existences," the "soul" as well as the "body." It kills collectively, not just distributively. It kills birth as well as death. Afterward nothing of that kind either lives or dies. A shutdown of the life stream is the most destructive event possible. Never before has this level of question—superkilling by a superkiller—been deliberately faced. What is ethically callous is the maelstrom of killing and insensitivity to forms of life and the sources producing them. What is required is principled responsibility to the biospheric earth.

Several billion years' worth of creative toil, several million species of teeming life, have been handed over to the care of this late-coming species in which mind has flowered and morals have emerged. Life on earth is a many splendored thing; extinction dims its luster. If, in this world of uncertain moral convictions, it makes any sense to claim that one ought not to kill individuals, without justification, it makes more sense to claim that one ought not to superkill the species, without superjustification. That moves from what *is* to what *ought to be*; and the fallacy is not committed by naturalists who so argue but by humanists who cannot draw these conclusions.

# 4. ECOSYSTEMS

"A thing is right," urged Aldo Leopold, concluding his land ethic, "when it tends to preserve the integrity, stability, and beauty of the biotic community; it is wrong when it tends otherwise." Again, we have two parts to the ethic: first that ecosystems exist, both in the wild and in support of culture; secondly that ecosystems ought to exist, both for what they are in themselves and as modified by culture. Again, we must move with care from the biological claims to the ethical claims.

Classical, humanistic ethics finds ecosystems unfamiliar territory. It is difficult to get the biology right, and, superimposed on the biology, to get the ethics right. Fortunately, it is often evident that human welfare depends on ecosystemic support, and in this sense all our legislation about clean air, clean water, soil conservation, national and state forest policy, pollution controls, oil spills, renewable resources, and so forth is concerned about ecosystem level processes. Further, humans find much of value for themselves in preserving wild ecosystems and our wilderness and park system is accordingly ecosystem oriented.

Still, a comprehensive environmental ethics needs the best, naturalistic reasons, as well as the good, humanistic ones, for respecting ecosystems. The ecosystem is the community of life; in it the fauna and flora, the species have entwined destinies. Ecosystems generate and support life, keep selection pressures high, enrich situated fitness, evolve congruent kinds in their places with sufficient containment. The ecologist finds that ecosystems are objectively satisfactory communities in the sense that organismic needs are sufficiently met for species long to survive, and the critical ethicist finds (in a subjective judgment matching the objective process) that such ecosystems are satisfactory communities to which to attach duty. Our concern must be for the fundamental unit of survival.

Giant forest fires raged over Yellowstone National Park in the summer of 1988, consuming nearly a million acres, despite the efforts of a thousand firefighters. By far the largest fires ever known in the park, the fires seemed a disaster. But the Yellowstone land ethic enjoins: Let nature take its course. Let it burn! So the fires were not fought at first, but in midsummer national authorities overrode that policy and ordered the fires put out. Even then, weeks later, fires continued to burn, partly because they were too big to control, but partly, too, because Yellowstone personnel did not altogether want the fires put out. Despite the evident destruction of trees, shrubs, and wildlife, they believe that fires are a good thing. Fires reset succession, release nutrients, recycle materials, renew the biotic community. (Nearby, in the Teton wilderness, a storm blew down 15,000 acres of trees, and some proposed that the area be declassified as wilderness for commercial salvage of the timber. But a similar environmental ethics said: No, let it rot.)

Aspen are important in the Yellowstone ecosystem. While some aspen stands are climax and self-renewing, many are seral and give way to conifers.

Aspen groves support many birds and much wildlife, especially the beavers, whose activities maintain the riparian zones. Aspen are rejuvenated after fires, and the Yellowstone land ethic wants the aspen for its critical role in the biotic community. Elk browse the young aspen stems. To a degree this is a good thing, since it gives elk critical nitrogen, but in excess it is a bad thing. The elk have no predators, since the wolves are gone, and as a result they overpopulate. Excess elk also destroy the willows and this in turn destroys the beavers. Rejuvenating the aspen might require managers to cull hundreds of elk—all for the sake of a healthy ecosystem.

The Yellowstone ethic wishes to restore wolves to the greater Yellowstone ecosystem. At the level of species, this is partly for what the wolf is in itself, but it is partly because the greater Yellowstone ecosystem does not have its full integrity, stability, and beauty without this majestic animal at the top of the trophic pyramid. Restoring the wolf as a top predator would mean suffering and death for many elk, but that would be a good thing for the aspen and willows, for the beavers and riparian habitat, with mixed benefits for the bighorns and mule deer, whose food the overpopulating elk consume, but who would also be consumed by the wolves. The Yellowstone ethic demands wolves, as it does fires, in appropriate respect for life in its ecosystem.

Letting nature take its ecosystemic course is why the Yellowstone ethic forbade rescuing the drowning bison, but rescued the sow grizzly with her cubs, the latter to insure that the big predators remain. After the bison drowned, coyotes and magpies, foxes and ravens fed on the carcass. Later, even a grizzly bear fed on it. All this is a good thing because the system cycles on. On that account rescuing the whales trapped in the winter ice seems less of a good thing, when we note that rescuers had to drive away polar bears that attempted to eat the dying whales.

An ecosystem, the conservative ethicist will say, is too low a level of organization to be respected intrinsically. Ecosystems can seem little more than random, statistical processes. A forest can seem a loose collection of externally related parts, the collection of fauna and flora a jumble, hardly a community. The plants and animals within an ecosystem have needs, but their interplay can seem simply a matter of distribution and abundance, birth rates and death rates, population densities, parasitism and predation, dispersion, checks and balances, stochastic process. Much is not organic at all (rain, groundwater, rocks, soil particles, air), while some organic material is dead and decaying debris (fallen trees, scat, humus). These things have no organized needs. There is only catch-as-catch-can scrimmage for nutrients and energy, a game played with loaded dice, not really enough integrated process to call the whole a community.

Unlike higher animals, ecosystems have no experiences; they do not and cannot care. Unlike plants, an ecosystem has no organized center, no genome. It does not defend itself against injury or death. Unlike a species, there is no ongoing *telos*, no biological identity reinstantiated over time. The organismic parts are more complex than the community whole. More troublesome still, an ecosystem can seem a jungle where the fittest survive, a place of contest and conflict, beside which the organism is a model of cooperation. In animals, the heart, liver, muscles and brain are tightly integrated, as are the leaves, cambium, and roots in plants. But the ecosystem community is pushing and shoving between rivals, each aggrandizing itself, or else indifference and haphazard juxtaposition, nothing to call forth our admiration.

Environmental ethics must break through the boundary posted by disoriented ontological conservatives, who hold that only organisms are "real," actually existing as entities, whereas ecosystems are nominal—just interacting individuals. Oak trees are real but forests are nothing but collections of trees. But any level is real if it shapes behavior on the level below it. Thus the cell is real because that pattern shapes the behavior of amino acids; the organism because that pattern coordinates the behavior of hearts and lungs. The biotic community is real because the niche shapes the morphology of the oak trees within it. Being real at the level of community only requires an organization that shapes the behavior of its members.

The challenge is to find a clear model of community and to discover an ethics for it—better biology for better ethics. Even before the rise of ecology, biologists began to conclude that the combative survival of the fittest distorts the truth. The more perceptive model is coaction in adapted fit. Predator and prey, parasite and host, grazer and grazed are contending forces in dynamic process where the well-being of each is bound up with the other—coordinated (orders that couple together) as much as heart and liver are coordinated organically. The ecosystem supplies the coordinates through which each organism moves, outside which the species cannot really be located. A species is what it is where it is.

The community connections are looser than the organism's internal interconnections—but not less significant. Admiring organic unity in organisms and stumbling over environmental looseness is like valuing mountains and despising valleys. The matrix the organism requires in order to survive is the open, pluralistic ecology. Internal complexity—heart, liver, muscles, brain— arises as a way of dealing with a complex, tricky environment. The skin-out processes are not just the support, they are the subtle source of the skin-in processes. In the complete picture, the outside is as *vital* as the inside. Had there been either simplicity or lock-step concentrated unity in the environment, no organismic unity could have evolved. Nor would it remain. There would be less elegance in life.

To look at one level for what is appropriate at another makes a categorical mistake. One should not look for a single center or program in ecosystems, much less for subjective experiences. Instead, one should look for a matrix, for interconnections between centers (individual plants and animals, dynamic lines of speciation), for creative stimulus and open-ended potential. Everything will be connected to many other things, sometimes by obligate associations, more often by partial and pliable dependencies and, among other things, there will be no significant interactions. There will be functions in a communal sense: shunts and criss-crossing pathways, cybernetic subsystems, and feedback loops. An order arises spontaneously and systematically when many self-concerned units jostle and seek their own programs, each doing their own thing and forced into informed interaction.

An ecosystem is a productive, projective system. Organisms defend only their selves, with individuals defending their continuing survival and species increasing the numbers of kinds. But the evolutionary ecosystem spins a bigger story, limiting each kind, locking it into the welfare of others, promoting new arrivals, bringing forth kinds and the integration of kinds. Species *increase their kind;* but ecosystems *increase kinds,* superimposing the latter increase onto the former. *Ecosystems are selective systems, as surely as organisms are selective systems.* The natural selection comes out of the system and is imposed on the individual. The individual is programmed to make more of its kind, but more is going on systemically than that; the system is making more kinds.

This extends natural selection theory beyond the merely tautological formulation that the system selects the best adapted to survive. Ecosystems select for those features that appear over the long ranges, for individuality, for diversification, for sufficient containment, for quality supervening on quantity of life. They do this, appropriately to the community level, by employing conflict, decenteredness, probability, succession, spontaneous generation of order, and historicity. Communal processes—the competition between organisms, more or less probable events, plant and animal successions, speciation over historical time—generate an ever-richer community.

Hence the evolutionary toil, elaborating and diversifying the biota, that once began with no species and results today in five million species, increasing over time the quality of lives in the upper rungs of the tropic pyramids. One-celled organisms evolved into many-celled, highly integrated organisms. Photosynthesis evolved and came to support locomotion—swimming, walking, running, flight. Stimulus-response mechanisms became complex instinctive acts. Warm-blooded animals followed cold-blooded ones. Complex nervous systems, conditioned behavior and learning emerged. Sentience appeared—sight, hearing, smell, tastes, pleasure, pain. Brains coupled with hands. Consciousness and self-consciousness arose. Culture was superimposed on nature.

These developments do not take place in all ecosystems or at every level. Microbes, plants, and lower animals remain, good of their kinds, and serving continuing roles, good for other kinds. The understories remain occupied. As a result, the quantity of life and its diverse qualities continue—from protozoans to primates to people. There is a push-up, lock-up, ratchet effect that conserves the upstrokes and the outreaches. The later we go in time the more accelerated are the forms at the top of the tropic pyramids, the more elaborated are the multiple tropic pyramids of earth. There are upward arrows over evolutionary time.

The system is a game with loaded dice, but the loading is a prolife tendency, not mere stochastic process. Though there is no *nature* in the singular, the system has a nature, a loading that pluralizes, putting *natures* into diverse kinds, nature$_1$, nature$_2$, nature$_3$ . . . nature$_n$. It does so using random elements (in both organisms and communities), but this is a secret of its fertility, producing steadily intensified interdependencies and options. An ecosystem has no head, but it has a "heading" for species diversification, support, and richness. Though not a superorganism, it is a kind of vital field.

*Instrumental value* uses something as a means to an end; *intrinsic value* is worthwhile in itself. No warbler eats insects to become food for a falcon; the warbler defends its own life as an end in itself and makes more warblers as it can. A life is defended intrinsically, without further contributory reference. But neither of these traditional terms is satisfactory at the level of the ecosystem. Though it has value *in* itself, the system does not have any value *for* itself. Though a value producer, it is not a value owner. We are no longer confronting instrumental value, as though the system were of value instrumentally as a fountain of life. Nor is the question one of intrinsic value, as though the system defended some unified form of life for itself. We have reached something for which we need a third term: *systemic value*. Duties arise in an encounter with the system that projects and protects these member components in biotic community. If you like, that is an ethic that is teleological again, but since we are respecting both processes and products, perhaps a better word for it now is communitarian. We follow nature, this time ecologically.

Ethical conservatives, in the humanist sense, will say that ecosystems are of value only because they contribute to human experiences. But that mistakes the last chapter for the whole story, one fruit for the whole plant. Humans count enough to have the right to flourish there, but not so much that they have the right to degrade or shut down ecosystems, not at least without a burden of proof that there is an overriding cultural gain. Earlier, environmental ethics will say that ecosystems are of value because they contribute to animal experiences or to organismic life. Later, the deeper, more conservative and more radical view sees that the stability, integrity, and beauty of biotic communities are what are most fundamentally to be conserved.

## 5. VALUE THEORY

In practice the ultimate challenge of environmental ethics is the conservation of life on earth. In principle the ultimate challenge is a value theory profound enough to support that ethic. We need an account of how nature carries value, and an ethics that appropriately respects those values. For subjectivists both the theory and the ethics will be nothing but human constructs; but objectivists in environmental ethics will use such theory to discover facts, how nature carries values, and from this sometimes there will follow what humans ought to do. The values that nature carries belong as much to the biology of natural history as to the psychology of human experience. Some of the values that nature carries are up to us, our assignment. But fundamentally there are powers in nature that move to us and through us. The splendors of earth do not simply lie in their roles as human resources, supports of culture, or stimulators of experience.

There is no value without an evaluator. So runs a well-entrenched dogma. Humans clearly evaluate their world; sentient animals may also. But plants cannot evaluate their environment; they have no options and make no choices. *A fortiori*, species and ecosystems, earth and nature cannot be bona fide evaluators. Value, like a tickle or remorse, must be felt to be there. Its *esse* is *percipi*. Nonsensed value is nonsense. There are no thoughts without a thinker, no percepts without a perceiver, no deeds without a doer, no targets without an aimer. Valuing is felt preferring; value is the product of this process.

If value arrives only with consciousness, experiences where humans find value there have to be dealt with as appearances of various sorts. The value has to be relocated in the valuing subject's creativity as a person meets a valueless world, or even a valuable one—one *able* to be *valued*—but which before the human bringing of value ability contains only possibility and not any actual value. Value can only be extrinsic to nature, never intrinsic to it. Nature offers but the standing possibility of valuation; value is not generated until humans appear with their valuing ability.

But the valuing subject in an otherwise valueless world is an insufficient premise for the experienced conclusions of those who respect all life. Conversion to a biological view seems truer to world experience and more logically compelling. Here the order of knowing reverses—and also enhances—the order of being. This, too, is a perspective, but ecologically better informed. Science has been steadily showing how the consequents (life, mind) are built on their precedents (energy, matter), however much they overlap them. Life and mind appear where they did not before exist, and with this levels of value emerge that did not before exist. But that gives no reason to say that all value is an irreducible emergent at the human (or upper animal) level. Nature does, of course, offer possibilities for human valuation, but the vitality of the system is not something that goes on in the human mind, nor is its value. The possibility of valuation is carried to us by evolutionary and ecological natural history, and such nature is already valuable before humans arrive to evaluate what is taking place.

How do we humans come to be charged up with values, if there was and is nothing in nature charging us up so? Some value is anthropogenic, generated by humans, but some is biogenic, in the natural genesis. A comprehensive environmental ethics reallocates value across the whole continuum. Value increases in the emergent climax, but is continuously present in the composing precedents. The system is *value-able, able* to produce *value*. Human evaluators are among its products. But when we value we must not forget our communal bonds. Sometimes we need to evaluate (appraise the worth of) what we ourselves may not value (personally prefer). Against the standard view that all value requires a beholder, some value requires only a holder, and some value is held within the historic system that carries value to and through individuals.

Here we do not want a subjective morality but an objective one, even though we find that subjectivity is the most valuable output of the objective system. Is there any reason for ethical subjects to discount the vital systemic processes unless and until accompanied by sentience? Perhaps to evaluate the entire biological world on the basis of sentience is as much a categorical mistake as to judge it according to whether justice and charity are found there. The one mistake judges biological places by extension from psychology, the other from culture. What is "right" about the biological world is not just the production of pleasures and positive experiences. What is "right" includes ecosystemic patterns, organisms in their generating, sustaining environments.

Some value depends on subjectivity, yet all value is generated within the geosystemic and ecosystemic community. Systemically, value fades from subjective to objective value, but also fans out from the individual to its role and matrix. Things do not have their separate natures merely in and for themselves, but they face outward and co-fit into broader natures. Value-in-itself is smeared out to become value-in-togetherness. Value seeps out into the system, and we lose our capacity to identify the individual as the sole locus of value.

Intrinsic value, that of an individual "for what it is in itself," becomes problematic in a holistic web. True, the system produces such values more and more with its evolution of individuality and freedom. Yet to decouple this from the biotic, communal system is to make value too internal and elementary; this forgets relatedness and externality. Every intrinsic value has leading and trailing *ands* pointing to value from which it comes and toward which it moves. Adapted fitness makes individualistic value too system independent. Intrinsic value is a part in a whole, not to be fragmented by valuing it in isolation. An isolated *telos* is biologically impossible; the ethic cannot be teleological in that sense, nor can we term it deontological either, if this requires respect for an intrinsic value regardless of ecosystemic consequences. (The classical distinction fails again.)

Everything is good in a role, in a whole, although we can speak of objective intrinsic goodness wherever a good kind defends itself. We can speak of subjective intrinsic goodness when such an event registers as a point experience, at which point humans pronounce both their experience and what it is of good without need to enlarge their focus. The system is a value transformer where form and being, process and reality, fact and value are inseparably joined. Intrinsic and instrumental values shuttle back and forth, parts-in-wholes and wholes-in-parts, local details of value embedded in global structures, gems in their settings, and their setting-situation a corporation where value cannot stand alone. Every good is in community.

This is what is radically wrong with anthropocentric or merely anthropogenic value. It arrogates to humans what permeates the community. Subjective self-satisfactions are, and ought to be, sufficiently contained within the objectively satisfactory system. The system creates life, selects for adaptive fit, constructs increasingly richer life in quantity and quality, supports myriads of species, escalates individually, autonomy, and even subjectivity, within the limits of decentralized community. When persons appraise this natural history, if such land is not a valuable, satisfactory biotic community, why not? Does earth and its community of life not claim their concern and care?

In environmental ethics one's beliefs about nature, which are based upon but exceed science, have everything to do with beliefs about duty. The way the world *is* informs the way it *ought* to be. We always shape our values in significant measure in accord with our notion of the kind of universe that we live in, and this drives our sense of duty. Our model of reality implies a model of conduct. Perhaps we can leave open what metaphysics ultimately underlies our cosmos, but for an environmental ethics at least we will need an earthbound metaphysics, a metaecology. Differing models sometimes imply similar conduct, but often they do not. A model in which nature has no value apart from human preferences will imply different conduct from one where natures projects fundamental values, some objective and others that further require human subjectivity superposed on objective nature.

This evaluation is not scientific description; hence not ecology per se, but we do move to metaecology. No amount of research can verify that, environmentally, the right is the optimum biotic community. Yet ecological description generates this valuing of nature, endorsing the systemic rightness. The transition from *is* to *good* and thence to *ought* occurs here; we leave science to enter the domain of evaluation, from which an ethic follows.

What is ethically puzzling and exciting is that an *ought* is not so much *derived* from an *is* as discovered simultaneously with it. As we progress from descriptions of fauna and flora, of cycles and pyramids, of autotrophs coordinated with heterotrophs, of stability and dynamism, on to intricacy, planetary opulence and interdependence, to unity and harmony with oppositions in counterpoint and synthesis, organisms evolved within and satisfactorily fitting their communities, arriving at length of beauty and goodness, it is difficult to say where the natural facts leave off and where the natural values appear. For some at least, the sharp *is/ought* dichotomy is gone; the values seem to be there as soon as the facts are fully in, and both alike properties of the system. This conviction, and the conscience that follows from it, can yield our best adaptive fit on earth.

# ANIMAL LIBERATION AND ENVIRONMENTAL ETHICS: BACK TOGETHER AGAIN

*J. Baird Callicott*

J. Baird Callicott is professor of philosophy and religion studies at the University of North Texas. He is co-editor with Roger T. Ames of *Nature in Asian Traditions of Thought: Essays in Environmental Philosophy*, with Fernando J.R. da Rocha of *Earth Summit Ethics: Toward a Reconstructive Postmodern Philosophy of Environmental Education*, and with Michael P. Nelson of *The Great New Wilderness Debate*.

Probably more than any other one thing, my article "Animal Liberation: A Triangular Affair" had led to an increasingly acrimonious estrangement between advocates of individualistic animal welfare ethics and advocates of holistic ecocentric ethics.[1] I think this estrangement is regrettable because it is divisive. Animal welfare ethicists and environmental ethicists have overlapping concerns. From a practical point of view, it would be far wiser to make common cause against a common enemy—the destructive forces at work ravaging the nonhuman world—than to continue squabbling among ourselves.

Not long after the schism emerged, that is, not long after the appearance of "Triangular Affair," Mary Anne Warren took a positive step toward reconciliation. She insisted that ecocentric environmental ethics and animal welfare ethics were "complementary," not contradictory.[2]

Warren's approach is thoroughly pluralistic. She argues that animals, like human beings, have rights. But she also argues that animals do not enjoy the *same* rights as human beings and that the rights of animals are not *equal* to human rights. And she argues, further, that animal rights and human rights are grounded in different psychological capacities. A holistic environmental ethic, Warren suggests, rests upon still other foundations—the instrumental value of "natural resources" to us and to future generations and the "intrinsic value" we (or at least some of us) intuitively find in plants, species, "mountains, oceans, and the like."[3]

Warren recommends, in short, a wholly reasonable ethical eclecticism. Human beings have strong rights because we are autonomous; animals have weaker rights because they are sentient; the environment should be used with respect—even though it may not have rights—because it is a whole and unified thing which we value in a variety of ways. Conflicts will certainly arise among all the foci of the human/animal/environment triangle—an example cited by Warren concerns introduced feral goats which threaten native plant species on New Zealand—but well-meaning people can muddle through the moral wilderness, balancing and compromising the competing interests and incommensurable values. In general, Warren concludes, "Only by *combining* the environmentalist and animal rights perspectives can we take account of the full range of moral considerations which ought to guide our interactions with the nonhuman world."[4]

However reasonable, there is something philosophically unsatisfying in Warren's ethical eclecticism. Moral philosophy historically has striven for theoretical unity and closure—often at considerable sacrifice of moral common sense. Consider, for example, Kant's deontological dismissal of the moral value of actions tainted with "inclination," even when the inclination in question is wholly altruistic. Or consider the morally outrageous consequences that some utilitarians have been led to accept in order faithfully to adhere to the theoretical foundations of utilitarianism.

In striving for theoretical unity and consistency, moral philosophy is not unlike natural philosophy. When a variety of apparently disparate phenomena (e.g., falling bodies, planetary motions, and tides) can be embraced by a single idea (gravity), the natural philosopher feels that a deep (though perhaps not ultimate) truth about nature has been struck. Similarly in moral philosophy, we strive to explain the commonly held welter of practical precepts and moral intuitions by appeal to one (or at most a very few theoretically related) imperative(s), principle(s), summary maxim(s), or Golden Rule(s). And if we succeed we feel that we have discovered something true and deep about morality.

The moral philosopher's love for theoretical unity, coherency, and self-consistency may represent more than a matter of mere intellectual taste. There is a practical reason to prefer theoretical unity in moral philosophy just as there is in natural philosophy. Probably more than anything else, the failure of the Ptolemaic system of astronomy—with its hodgepodge of ad hoc devices—accurately to predict the positions of the planets led Copernicus to unify the celestial phenomena by introducing a single radical assumption: that the sun, not the earth, is at the center of it all. In moral philosophy, when competing moral claims cannot be articulated in the same terms, they cannot be decisively compared and resolved. Ethical eclecticism leads, it would seem inevitably, to moral incommensurability in hard cases. So we are compelled to go back to the theoretical drawing board.

To achieve something more than a mere coalition of convenience—to achieve, rather, a lasting alliance—between animal welfare ethics and ecocentric environmental ethics will require the development of a moral theory that embraces both programs *and* that provides a framework for the adjudication of the very real conflicts between human welfare, animal welfare, and ecological integrity. It is the purpose of this essay to suggest such a theory on terms, shall we say, favorable to ecocentric environmental ethics, just as Tom Regan has suggested such a theory on terms favorable to animal welfare ethics.

Regan proposes a "rights-based environmental ethic" consistent with and, indeed, launched from his "rights view" version of animal welfare ethics. He himself has not worked out the grounds for the rights of individual trees and other non-"subjects-of-a-life," but he urges environmental ethicists seriously to take up the challenge. Writes Regan,

> The implications of the successful development of a rights-based environmental ethic, one that made the case that individual inanimate objects (e.g., *this* redwood) have inherent value and a basic moral right to treatment respectful of that value, should be welcomed by environmentalists. . . . A rights-based environmental ethic remains a live option, one that, though far from being established, merits continued exploration. . . . Were we to show proper respect for the rights of individuals who make up the biotic community, would not the *community* be preserved?[5]

To this (actually rhetorical) question Mark Sagoff replied, "I believe [that] this is an empirical question, the answer to which is 'no.' The environmentalist is concerned about preserving evolutionary processes, e.g., natural selection, whether these processes have deep enough respect for the rights of individuals . . ." or not.[6] Nature, as Sagoff points out, is not fair; it does not respect the rights of individuals. To attempt to safeguard the rights of each and every individual member of an ecosystem would, correspondingly, be to attempt to stop practically all trophic processes beyond photosynthesis—and even then we would somehow have to deal ethically with the individual life-threatening and hence rights-violating competition among plants for sunlight. An ethic for the preservation of nature, therefore, could hardly get off on the right foot if, at the start, it condemns as unjust and immoral the trophic asymmetries lying at the heart of evolutionary and ecological processes. An environmental ethic cannot be generated, as it were by an invisible hand, from a further extension of rights (on the basis of some yet-to-be-worked-out-theory) to "individual inanimate objects."

I have another, and I think better, proposal which was suggested to me by the work of Mary Midgley.

Midgley, in her book *Animals and Why They Matter,* grounds the mattering—that is, in more familiar contemporary philosophical terminology, the moral considerability—of animals in what she calls "the mixed community":

> All human communities have involved animals. The animals . . . became tame,
> not just through fear of violence, but because they were able to form individual
> bonds with those who tamed them by coming to understand the social signals
> addressed to them. . . . They were able to do this, not only because the people
> taming them were social beings, but because they themselves were so as well.[7]

Midgley goes on to draw out a number of consequences from this pregnant and profound observation. Since we and the animals who belong to our
mixed human-animal community are coevolved social beings participating in
a single society, we and they share certain feelings that attend upon and enable sociability—sympathy, compassion, trust, love, and so on. Her main point
is to show that it is preposterous to believe, with those whom she identifies as
"Behaviourists," that animals members of our mixed community are mere automata, devoid of a rich subjective life. And her subordinate point is to show
that the species-barrier to human-animal social interaction is both artificial
and unhistorical. We have enjoyed, and there is no good philosophical reason
why we should not continue to enjoy, interspecies social relationships and intimacy. Says Midgley, "the problem here is not about anthropomorphism, but
about Behaviourism, and it arises already on the human scene. The barrier
[between subjects] does not fall between us and the dog. It falls between you
and me. . . . Natural sympathy, as Hume rightly said, has a basis in common
humanity. Does it therefore follow that it stops at the species-barrier?"[8]

Midgley, curiously, does not go on to elaborate a positive moral theory
which incorporates to the best advantage the very thorough and convincing
case she has made for the existence of a wide variety of animal consciousness—from that of dogs to that of work elephants—each with its species' pe-
culiarities, but each broadly based in, shall we say, a common bio-sociality.
Midgley certainly does not go on to argue, à la Peter Singer, that the "sentiency" ambient among animal members of the mixed community, which she
has so fully and forcefully defended, should constitute a *criterion* for equal
moral consideration; nor does she argue, à la Tom Regan, that having a rich
subjective life entitles domestic animals to equal moral *rights*. Her approving
mention of Hume, however, and her emphasis on social affections and sympathy suggest to me that, if pressed, Midgley would sketch a Humean ethical
theory to make moral hay of her defense of the subjectivity of animals and the
possibility of intersubjective interaction between species.

David Hume's moral theory is distinguished from the prevailing modern alternatives—utilitarianism and deontology—primarily by two features:
(1) Morality is grounded in feelings, not reason; although reason has its
role to play in ethics, it is part of the supporting cast. And (2) altruism is as
primitive as egoism; it is not reducible either to enlightened self-interest or
to duty.

A pertinent contrast to Hume's understanding of ethics is afforded by
Peter Singer. In *Animal Liberation* he heaped scorn on "sentimental appeals
for sympathy" toward animals and avowed that his animal welfare ethic was

grounded exclusively in "basic moral principles which we all accept; and the application of these principles to victims . . . is demanded by reason, not emotion."[9] Singer follows the usual theoretical approach of normal modern moral philosophy—elegantly described by Kenneth Goodpaster—which has been to generalize egoism.[10] Baldly stated, it comes to this: I insist upon moral consideration from others or moral rights for myself. My entitlement to moral standing or moral rights may be plausibly defended by appeal to a psychological characteristic or capacity possessed by me which is arguably relevant to ethical treatment. But then "others" are entitled to equal moral consideration to the extent that they possess, in equal measure, the same psychological characteristic. I may not love others (in this connection, Singer wants us to know that he keeps no pets) or sympathize with them; indeed I may be entirely indifferent to their concerns or even actively dislike them. Still, I am compelled by the logic of my own moral claim upon others to grudgingly grant their similar claims upon me.

Hume took a different course. He argued that both our moral judgments and our actions are rooted in altruistic feelings or sentiments that are very often opposed to "self-love." Writes Hume, "So far from thinking that men have no affection for anything beyond themselves, I am of opinion that tho' it be rare to meet with one, who loves any single person better than himself; yet 'tis rare to meet with one, in whom all the kind affections, taken together, do not overbalance all the selfish."[11] According to Hume, these kind affections are the soil in which our morals are rooted and from which they take their nourishment.

Aldo Leopold, in "The Land Ethic" of *A Sand County Almanac*, evidently patterned his own concept of an "ethical sequence" on Charles Darwin's discussion of the evolution of ethics in *The Descent of Man*, and Darwin cites both Hume's *Treatise* and Adam Smith's *Theory of the Moral Sentiments* as the philosophical antecedents of his own "natural history" of ethics. I have argued in a variety of venues and in considerable detail that, therefore, Hume's moral theory is the historical ancestor of Aldo Leopold's land ethic, the modern ethic of choice of the environmental movement and of many contemporary environmental philosophers. What's more, the moral fulcrum of the Leopold land ethic is the ecological concept of the "biotic community."

Mary Midgley's suggested animal welfare ethic and Aldo Leopold's seminal environmental ethic thus share a common, fundamentally Humean understanding of ethics as grounded in altruistic feelings. And they share a common ethical bridge between the human and nonhuman domains in the concept of community—Midgley's "mixed community" and Leopold's "biotic community." Combining these two conceptions as a metahuman moral community we have the basis of a unified animal-environmental ethical theory.

Hume regarded the social feelings upon which the edifice of ethics is erected to be a brute fact of human nature. Darwin explained how we came to have such feelings, as he explained so many other curious natural facts, by appeal to the evolutionary principle of natural selection.

Darwin's biosocial reduction of Hume's moral theory is particularly ingenious since, at first glance, altruism seems, from an evolutionary point of view, anomalous and paradoxical. Given the ceaseless struggle for the limited means to life lying at the heart of Darwin's conception of nature, concern for others and deferential behavior would appear to be maladaptive tendencies quickly eliminated from a gene pool, should they ever chance to emerge. Or so it would seem—until we consider the survival-reproductive advantages of social membership. Concern for others and self-restraint are necessary for social amalgamation and integration, Darwin argued. "Ethical" behavior is, in effect, the dues an individual pays to join a social group; and the survival advantages of group membership to individuals more than compensate them for the personal sacrifices required by morality. Since most animals, including most human beings, are not sufficiently intelligent to make a benefit-cost analysis of their social actions, we are outfitted, Darwin theorized, with "social instincts" impelling us toward socially conducive moral behavior.

What is right and what is wrong, Darwin suggests, reflects, more or less, the specific organizational structure of society—since ethics have evolved to facilitate social cohesion. The "ethics" of a hierarchically structured pack of wolves, for example, require celibacy of most its members. The ethics of apolitical and egalitarian human tribal societies require members periodically to redistribute their wealth. Who is and who is not an appropriate beneficiary of one's moral sympathies, similarly, reflects the *perceived* boundaries of social membership. In our dealings with those whom we regard as members, the rules apply; in our dealings with those whom we regard as outsiders, we do as we please.

Midgley's marvelous insight is that, however exclusive of other human beings the perceived boundaries of historical human societies may have been, they all, nevertheless, have included some animals—aboriginally man's hunting partner, the dog; and, after the Neolithic Revolution, a variety of herd, farm, and work animals: everything from the cow and pig to the Asian elephant and water buffalo. Consonant with my analysis in "A Triangular Affair," Midgley suggests therefore that a big part of the immorality of the treatment of animals in the current industrial phase of human civilization is that we have broken trust with erstwhile fellow members of our traditionally mixed communities. Animals have been depersonalized and mechanized and that goes a long way toward explaining the moral revulsion we all feel toward the factory farm and animal research laboratory.

How we ought and ought not treat one another (including animals) is determined, according to the logic of biosocial moral theory, by the nature and organization of communities. Even to those deeply sympathetic to the plight of animals there is something deeply amiss in the concept of *equal* moral consideration or *equal* moral rights for animals, required by the logic of extending the prevailing modern moral paradigms, just as there is something deeply amiss in the idea of requiring equal consideration for all human beings regardless of social relationship.

Peter Singer, once again, provides a revealing example of the latter as well as of the former. He argues that he has failed in his duty because he does not donate the greatest portion of his modest income to help alleviate the suffering of starving people living halfway around the world, *even though* to do so would impoverish not only himself, but his own children.[12] Suffering is suffering, no matter whose it may be, and it is the duty of a moral agent to be impartial in weighing the suffering of one against the suffering of another. Since the starving suffer more from his withholding money from them than his children would suffer were he to impoverish them short of starvation, Singer concludes that therefore he should give the greater portion of his income to the starving.

From Midgley's biosocial point of view, we are members of nested communities each of which has a different structure and therefore different moral requirements. At the center is the immediate family. I have a duty not only to feed, clothe, and shelter my own children, I also have a duty to bestow affection on them. But to bestow a similar affection on the neighbor's kids is not only not my duty, it would be considered anything from odd to criminal were I to behave so. Similarly, I have obligations to my neighbors which I do not have to my less proximate fellow citizens—to watch their houses while they are on vacation, for example, or to go to the grocery for them when they are sick or disabled. I have obligations to my fellow citizens which I do not have toward human beings in general *and* I have obligations to human beings in general which I do not have toward animals in general.

These subtly shaded social-moral relationships are complex and overlapping. Pets, for example, are—properly so, Midgley argues—surrogate family members and merit treatment not owed either to less intimately related animals, for example to barnyard animals, *or*, for that matter, to less intimately related human beings.

Barnyard animals, over hundreds of generations, have been genetically engineered (by the old-fashioned method of selective breeding) to play certain roles in the mixed community. To condemn the morality of these roles—as we rightly condemn human slavery and penury—is to condemn the very being of these creatures. The animal welfare ethic of the mixed community, thus, would not censure using draft animals for work or even slaughtering meat animals for food so long as the keeping and using of such animals was not in violation—as factory farming clearly is—of a kind of evolved and unspoken social contract between man and beast.

But it is not my intention here to attempt to detail our duties to the various classes of the animal members of mixed communities. Rather, I wish to argue that whatever our various duties to various kinds of domestic animals may, from this point of view, turn out to be, they differ in a general and profound way from our duties toward the wild animal members of the biotic community.

One of the principal frustrations with the familiar utilitarian and deontological approaches to animal liberation that I have experienced, as an environmental ethicist, is the absence of a well-grounded distinction between our proper ethical relations with, on the one hand, domestic and, on the other, wild animals. According to the conventional approach, cattle and antelope, pigs and porcupines, bears and battery hens are entitled to equal moral consideration and/or equal rights.

The Midgley-Leopold biosocial moral theory, by contrast, clearly provides the missing distinction. Domestic animals are members of the mixed community and ought to enjoy, therefore, all the rights and privileges, whatever they may turn out to be, attendant upon that membership. Wild animals are, by definition, not members of the mixed community and therefore should not lie on the same spectrum of graded moral standing as family members, neighbors, fellow citizens, fellow human beings, pets, and other domestic animals.

Wild animals, rather, are members of the biotic community. The structure of the biotic community is described by ecology. The duties and obligations of a biotic community ethic or "land ethic," as Leopold called it, may, accordingly, be derived from an ecological description of nature—just as our duties and obligations to members of the mixed community can be derived from a description of the mixed community.

Most generally and abstractly described, the ecosystem is, to quote Leopold, "a fountain of energy flowing through a circuit of soils, plants, and animals."[13] The currency, in other words, of the economy of nature is solar energy captured upon incidence by green plants and thereafter transferred from animal organism to animal organism—not from hand to hand, like coined money, but, so to speak, from stomach to stomach. The most fundamental fact of life in the biotic community is eating . . . *and being eaten.* Each species is adapted to a trophic niche; each is a link in a food chain, and a knot in a food web. Whatever moral entitlements a being may have as a member of the biotic community, *not* among them is the right to life. Rather, each being should be respected and left alone to pursue its modus vivendi—even if its way of life causes harm to other beings, including other sentient beings. The integrity, stability, and beauty of the biotic community depends upon *all* members, in their appropriate numbers, functioning in their co-evolved life ways.

Among the most disturbing implications drawn from conventional indiscriminate animal liberation/rights theory is that, were it possible for us to do so, we ought to protect innocent vegetarian animals from their carnivorous predators. Nothing could be more contrary to the ethics of the biotic community than this suggestion. Not only would the (humane) eradication of predators destroy the community, it would destroy the species which are the intended beneficiaries of this misplaced morality. Many prey species depend upon predators to optimize their populations. And, at a deeper level, we must remember that the alertness, speed, grace, and all the other qualities we most admire in herbivorous animals—all the qualities, indeed, which make them subjects-of-a-life and thus worthy of moral consideration and/or rights—were evolved in direct response to their carnivorous symbionts.[14]

The Humean biosocial moral theory differently applied to larger-than-human communities by Midgley and Leopold has, unlike the more familiar approach to generalizing egoism, historically provided for a holistic as well as an individualistic moral orientation. We care, in other words, for our communities per se, over and above their individual members—for our families per se, for our country, and for mankind. As Midgley might say, *they* "matter" to us as well. Hence, according to Hume, "we must renounce the theory which accounts for every moral sentiment by the principle of self-love. We must adopt a more *publick affection* and allow that the interests of society are not, *even on their own account,* entirely indifferent to us."[15]

Darwin's holism is even more pronounced:

> We have now seen that actions are regarded by savages, and were probably so regarded by primeval man, as good or bad, solely as they obviously affect the welfare of the tribe—not that of the species, nor that of the individual member of the tribe. This conclusion agrees well with the belief that the so-called moral sense is aboriginally derived from social instincts, for both relate exclusively to the community.[16]

And the holistic dimension of Aldo Leopold's land ethic all but overwhelms the individualistic. Leopold provides only "respect" for individual members of the biotic community, but "biotic rights" for species and, in the last analysis, "the integrity, beauty, and stability of the biotic community" is the measure of right and wrong actions affecting the environment.

The hyperholism of the land ethic is also itself a function of an ecological description of the biotic community. But since the biosocial moral paradigm provides for various coexisting, cooperating, and competing ethics—each corresponding to our nested overlapping community entanglements—our holistic environmental obligations are not preemptive. We are still subject to all the other more particular and individually oriented duties to the members of our various more circumscribed and intimate communities. And since they are closer to home, they come first. In general, obligations to family come before obligations to more remotely related fellow humans. For example, *pace* Singer, one should not impoverish one's own children just short of starvation in order to aid actually starving people on another continent. But neither should one promote or even acquiesce in human starvation, no matter how distant, to achieve environmental goals—as some overzealous environmental activists have actually urged. Similarly, one should not allow a wild predator to help herself to one's free-range chickens, members of one's immediate mixed community. But neither should one interfere, other things being equal, in the interaction of the wild members of the biotic community.

So the acknowledgment of a holistic environmental ethic does not entail that we abrogate our familiar moral obligations to family members, to fellow citizens, to all mankind, *nor* to fellow members, individually, of the mixed community, that is, to domesticate animals. On the other hand, the outer orbits of our various moral spheres exert a gravitational tug on the inner ones.

One may well deprive one's children of a trip to Disneyland or give them fewer toys at Christmas in order to aid starving people on another continent. Similarly, one may well make certain sacrifices oneself or impose certain restrictions on the animal members of one's mixed community for the sake of ecological integrity. Dairy cattle, for example, can be very destructive of certain plant communities and should be fenced out of them when other pasture or fodder is available—despite their own preferences and the economic interests of dairy farmers.

Animal liberation and environmental ethics may thus be united under a common theoretical umbrella—even though, as with all the laminated layers of our social-ethical accretions, they may occasionally come into conflict. But since they may be embraced by a common theoretical structure, we are provided a means, in principle, to assign priorities and relative weights and thus to resolve such conflicts in a systematic way.

## NOTES

1. J. Baird Callicott, "Animal Liberation: A Triangular Affair," *Environmental Ethics* 2 (1980): 311–328.
2. Mary Anne Warren, "The Rights of the Nonhuman World" in Robert Elliot and Arran Gare, *Environmental Philosophy: A Collection of Readings* (University Park: The Pennsylvania State University Press, 1983), pp. 109–131.
3. Ibid., pp. 130–131.
4. Ibid., p. 131.
5. Tom Regan, *The Case for Animal Rights* (Berkeley: University of California Press, 1983), pp. 362–363.
6. Mark Sagoff, "Animal Liberation and Environmental Ethics: Bad Marriage, Quick Divorce," *Osgoode Hall Law Journal* 22 (1984): 306.
7. Mary Midgley, *Animals and Why They Matter* (Athens: University of Georgia Press, 1983), p. 112.
8. Ibid., pp. 130, 131.
9. Peter Singer, *Animal Liberation: A New Ethics for Our Treatment of Animals* (New York: Avon Books, 1977), pp. xi–xiii.
10. Kenneth Goodpaster, "From Egoism to Environmentalism" in K. Goodpaster and K. Sayre, eds., *Ethics and Problems of the 21st Century* (Notre Dame: Notre Dame University Press, 1979), 21–35.
11. David Hume, *A Treatise of Human Nature* (Oxford: The Clarendon Press, 1969), p. 487.
12. Peter Singer, *The Expanding Circle: Ethics and Sociobiology* (New York: Farrar, Straus, and Giroux, 1982).
13. Aldo Leopold, *A Sand County Almanac* (New York: Oxford University Press, 1949), p. 216.
14. See Holmes Rolson III, "Beauty and the Beast: Aesthetic Experience of Wildlife" in D. J. Decker and G. R. Goff, eds., *Valuing Wildlife: Economic and Social Perspectives* (Boulder: Westview Press, 1987), pp. 187–196.
15. David Hume, *An Enquiry Concerning the Principles of Morals* (Oxford: The Clarendon Press, 1777), p. 219, emphasis added.
16. Charles Darwin, *The Descent of Man and Selection in Relation to Sex* (New York: J. A. Hill and Company, 1904), p. 120.

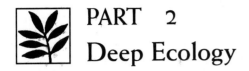

# PART 2
# Deep Ecology

# INTRODUCTION

*George Sessions*

George Sessions is emeritus professor of philosophy at Sierra College in Rocklin, California. Author of numerous essays about ecophilosophy and deep ecology, and coauthor (with Bill Devall) of *Deep Ecology*, Sessions recently published the anthology *Deep Ecology for the 21st Century*.

## I. THE ECOLOGICAL REVOLUTION OF THE 1960s AND THE RISE OF THE DEEP ECOLOGY MOVEMENT

The decade of the 1960s produced a major ecological revolution—a revolution in consciousness concerning our outlook toward other species and the need to protect the integrity of wild ecosystems, wild evolutionary processes, and what is left of the wild world. Philosophically, the ecological revolution of the 1960s, and the rise of the long-range deep ecology movement, was characterized, at its deepest level, by a move from anthropocentrism to ecocentrism. An ecological critique of anthropocentrism as being at the root of the ecological crisis was pervasive among conservationists and ecologists throughout the 1960s, deriving its impetus from the writings of Henry David Thoreau, John Muir, Robinson Jeffers, Aldo Leopold, and Aldous Huxley and the infusion of Zen Buddhism into conservationist and counterculturalist thinking.

The ecological critique of anthropocentrism received its most explicit and influential statement during the 1960s in the widely reprinted 1966 paper "Historical Roots of Our Ecologic Crisis," written by U.C.L.A. historian, Lynn White, Jr. White argued that Christianity had desacralized nature, encouraged its exploitation, and promoted an anthropocentric worldview in which humans are portrayed as superior to, and in charge of, the rest of nature.

Modern science and technology, he claimed, are "permeated with Christian arrogance towards nature." He argued that Marxism and other so-called "post-Christian" ideologies in the West are Judeo-Christian heresies that promote the same exploitive attitudes toward nature. In an effort to reform Christianity ecologically, White proposed a return to the views of Saint Francis, who preached "the equality of all creatures."[1]

The ecocentric change in consciousness of the 1960s also involved a corresponding awareness that the direction of megatechnological, progress-oriented industrial growth societies had to be drastically changed. For example, Stanford ecologist Paul Ehrlich referred to Lynn White's paper and the Zen Buddhism of the 1960s counterculture in his enormously influential *The Population Bomb* in 1968; he claimed that "we've got to change from a growth-oriented exploitive system to one focused on stability and conservation. Our entire system of orienting to nature must undergo a revolution."[2]

## II. THOREAU AND THE PRESERVATION OF HUMAN AND NONHUMAN WILDNESS

Thoreau's statements in 1851 that "in wildness was the preservation of the world" and that "all good things are wild and free" were totally revolutionary. It is of crucial importance to realize that Thoreau was referring to both human and nonhuman wildness.[3] During the 1960s, biologists, conservationists, ecotheologians, and ecophilosophers were beginning to realize that the dominant anthropocentric ideology of Western civilization that promotes the technological domination, management, and control of Earth—the domestication, urbanization, and humanization of Earth—in the name of progress was producing a human and ecological disaster. Wildness, autonomy, and freedom (in both humans and nonhumans) were rapidly disappearing. These themes had been dramatically explored earlier in Zamyatin's *We*, Huxley's *Brave New World*, and Orwell's *1984*. Inspired by Thoreau, Muir, and Leopold, conservation leaders such as David Brower (executive director of the Sierra Club, throughout the 1950s and 1960s) began to realize that the protection of wildness was the *key* philosophical and ecological issue. From 1960 through 1964, Brower published highly influential Sierra Club Exhibit Format books publicizing the ecocentric philosophies of Thoreau, Muir, and Jeffers. The 1962 Thoreau book was entitled *In Wildness Is the Preservation of the World*.[4]

In 1972, the environmental textbook writer G. Tyler Miller provided a concise and dramatic overview of the ecological analysis and worldview in the 1960s, claiming that "the ecological . . . revolution will be the most all-encompassing revolution in the history of mankind. It involves questioning and altering almost all of our ethical, political, economic, sociological, psychological, and technological rules or systems."[5]

# III. THE 1980s ANTHROPOCENTRIC-ECONOMIC REACTION AND THE RISE OF SUSTAINABLE DEVELOPMENT

The radical and comprehensive thrust of the 1960s ecocentric ecological revolution could not be sustained, however, against the powerful, vested multinational corporate interests and the entrenched Western paradigm of "progress" (and among the left, the achievement of social justice) through unending economic growth and development. Radical environmentalists and ecologists such as Paul Ehrlich have been looked on as "doomsayers" who want to interfere with private property rights and with unlimited corporate expansion and profit making. For growth-oriented economists, modern humanity has created a "second nature" reality of urbanism and stock markets that transcends and replaces the reality of the biological world. Spokespersons for the corporate establishment, such as the economist Julian Simon, argue that there is no human overpopulation problem and that the resources of the Earth, and the limits to human activity, are not determined by the carrying capacity of the Earth's ecological systems but only by the unlimited technological ingenuity and creativity of the human mind and by the free play of market forces.[6] The contemporary vision of the multinational corporations tends toward the development of a deconstructionist, artificial world of "simulacra" and "hyperreality" as they rapidly turn the world (including the last of the wild ecosystems) into an artificial, megatechnological Disneyland theme park and shopper's paradise and as they attempt to create an economic "new world order" through the "globalization of corporate power."[7]

The politically conservative "Reagan reaction" against environmentalism in the United States coincided, during the 1980s, with a change in philosophy toward nature among world leaders in the United Nations. In 1982, the General Assembly had adopted the ecocentric World Charter for Nature, which asserted that the intrinsic value of every form of life is to be recognized: "Nature shall be respected and its essential processes shall not be disrupted." However, by 1987 the U.N. Brundtland Report was based on the increasingly popular but essentially unecological concept of "sustainable development." Ignoring the increasingly frantic warnings of the world's scientists about the ecological state of the world, the Brundtland Report called, instead, for "a new era" of economic growth and development. The concept of sustainable development also became the conceptual basis for the 1992 U.N. Rio environmental conference. As Wolfgang Sachs points out, "The UN Conference in Rio inaugurated environmentalism as the highest state of developmentalism." The Rio conference (and the Brundtland Report) reverted to an anthropocentric, utilitarian "shallow environmentalism" by viewing nature essentially as a "resource base" for unending economic growth and development. For example, in the convention on biodiversity protection, the flora and fauna of the world were treated essentially as genetic raw material for exploitation by biotechnology and pharmaceutical corporations.[8]

The global ecological-overpopulation crisis, warned about with such insistence by Paul Ehrlich and other ecologists in the 1960s, has now reached such proportions that 58 of the National Academies of Sciences throughout the world have issued dire warnings. In 1992, 1,575 of the world's leading scientists released the World's Scientists' Warning to Humanity, claiming that "human beings and the natural world are on a collision course." Anne and Paul Ehrlich now claim that the only realistic solution to the ecological crisis is to "reduce the scale of the human enterprise." The Brundtland Report and Rio conference also fly in the face of recent studies, which show that the majority of Americans (and possibly citizens in other Western industrial countries) already hold the rudiments of a spiritual-ecocentric worldview.[9]

# IV. THE ROOTS OF THE 1960s ECOLOGICAL REVOLUTION IN DAVID BROWER AND THE SIERRA CLUB WILDERNESS CONFERENCES

While many historians believe that the ecological revolution began with the publication of Rachel Carson's *Silent Spring* in 1962 (which also critiqued anthropocentrism) and culminated in the major demonstrations of Earthday I in 1970, the roots of post–World War II ecocentric, ecological consciousness extend back much further. Two key books (William Vogt's *The Road to Survival* and Fairfield Osborn's *Our Plundered Planet*, both published in 1948) led to a major debate over issues of human overpopulation, diminishing forests and wildlife, and the ability of technology to solve these problems.[10] Aldo Leopold's *Sand County Almanac* (1949) provided, with its ecocentric "land ethic," a philosophical perspective for these issues. According to Anne and Paul Ehrlich, "The works of Leopold, Vogt and Osborn . . . greatly influenced our own thinking and that of many other ecologists of our generation."[11]

The Sierra Club Wilderness Conferences, beginning in 1949, soon led to discussions of wilderness philosophy, with club leaders such as David Brower and various ecologists coming down on the side of ecocentrism. In so doing, they believed they were following the philosophies of Muir and Leopold. During the 1950s, professional ecologists convinced club leaders at these conferences that wilderness areas should be viewed primarily as wild species habitats and that without stabilization and reduction of the human population the protection of wilderness and the wild would be a lost cause.[12]

Members of the Sierra Club under Brower, and biologists in general, became increasingly radical as the decade of the 1960s progressed. The 1967 annual issue of the *Sierra Club Bulletin* carried an article by Brower calling for an Earth International Park to protect the Earth's remaining wild areas and wild species. Brower claimed, "I believe in wilderness for itself alone. I believe in the rights of creatures other than man." In January 1969, he ran a full-page advertisement promoting the Earth International Park idea in the *New York Times*. A paper by botanist Hugh Iltus, pleading for protection of what was left of the wild world, appeared in the same 1967 issue of the *Bulletin*. Iltus claimed,

> Life's diversity is threatened with imminent destruction . . . it will be all but over in 20 or 30 years for this exuberant biotic wealth. . . . Surely [the graying heads of the National Academy of Sciences] in their wisdom, must see that the living world is falling apart at the seams. . . . One more generation of ecological idiots is one too many.

Iltus also argued that humans have a genetic need for wild environments, a claim that, along with E. O. Wilson's "biophilia hypothesis" and the genetic theories of Paul Shepard, has become the basis of the burgeoning new field of ecopsychology.[13]

While Rachel Carson dramatically focused widespread public attention on environmental problems in 1962, Michael McCloskey (Brower's successor as the Sierra Club's executive director in 1969) has pointed out, correctly in my estimation, that the wilderness movement of the 1950s marks the beginning of the modern environmental-ecological movement. The post–World War II ecological revolution and the clarification of its ecocentric philosophy, according to McCloskey, began with the 1950s Wilderness Conferences and continued with the crusading activism of the Sierra Club during the 1950s and 1960s under Brower's leadership.[14]

The environmental historian Donald Worster summarizes the radical nature of the environmental philosophizing and activism of the ecological revolution:

> [For the most thoughtful environmentalists and ecologists of the 1960s and 1970s] the goal was to save the living world around us, millions of species of plants and animals, including humans, from destruction from our technology, population, and appetites. The only way to do that . . . was to think the radical thought that there must be limits to growth in three areas—limits to population, limits to technology, and limits to appetite and greed.[15]

# V. THE ECOLOGICAL REVOLUTION, URBAN-INDUSTRIAL POLLUTION, ENVIRONMENTALISM, AND SOCIAL JUSTICE

Worster suggests, by implication, that there were less thoughtful environmentalists during the decade of the 1960s who didn't see the need for an ecological "revolution" and a philosophical shift to ecocentrism. As urban-industrial pollution developed into a major problem after World War II, "newer man-centered leaders" arose in the environmental ranks during the

1960s, according to environmental historian Stephen Fox, such as the Marxist biologist Barry Commoner and Ralph Nader. These leaders saw industrial pollution as the essence of the environmental problem, while viewing as unimportant the issues of human overpopulation and the necessity for a radical restructuring of the industrial growth paradigm. Further, as Fox points out, they viewed concern for the protection of wilderness and wild species with disdain.[16] Commoner became known as the "pollution man" and appeared on the cover of *Time* magazine in 1970 as "the Paul Revere of ecology." By Earthday 1970, the environmental movement had split essentially into an anthropocentric urban-pollution wing, led by Commoner, Nader, and Murray Bookchin, and an ecocentric wing, centered around Brower, Ehrlich, and most professional ecologists.

In his influential book *The Closing Circle* (1971), Commoner rejected the analyses of Paul Ehrlich and Lynn White concerning the roots of the ecological crisis, thereby refusing to acknowledge the deeper philosophical, religious, and social causes. He claimed instead that the environmental crisis was caused mainly by the replacement of natural fibers and products with synthetic chemicals after World War II. Environmental problems could be solved simply by changing to environmentally benign technologies. Ehrlich countered with his I = PAT formula (that environmental impact is a function of population size, times the level of affluence or consumption, times the nature of the technology employed). Based on this formula, the United States was the world's biggest environmental disaster because of its per capita high-consumption lifestyles and the high levels of industrial chemicals and gases it was spewing into the atmosphere. According to Chris Lewis, in Commoner's more recent book (*Making Peace with the Planet*, 1990), Commoner claims that

> if humanity must give up progress, economic growth, and development—give up the modern world—to end its war against nature and make peace with the planet, it would be a tragic defeat. Commoner refuses to accept calls for controlling population growth, ending economic growth and development, and transforming the modern world. He argues that because humanity lives in two worlds, the natural world or the ecosphere and a social world of its own creation—the techno-sphere—the environmental crisis is not an ecological problem but a social and political problem.[17]

Chemical pollution and toxic wastes, a very visible and dramatic aspect of the environmental crisis in industrial countries during the 1950s and 1960s, resulted in major air and water pollution and carcinogenic chemicals in foods—all of which posed a significant hazard to human health. It was the pervasive and obvious effects of industrial-chemical pollution on human health that made the environmental crisis a major issue for the public in the 1960s. These problems were close to the daily lives of urban people, and so it was natural for them to identify the environmental crisis with urban pollution and with "cleaning up the environment." The accelerating loss of wildlife habitat, biodiversity, and the Earth's wildness was a far more subtle issue, further removed from their urban lives and difficult to comprehend from their anthropocentric perspective. Carson's *Silent Spring*—which, more than any other single event awakened people to the environmental crisis—was focused on chemical pesticide poisoning. Carson drew a parallel between the atomic radiation being carried by the jetstream from above-ground Russian nuclear testing over the North Pole to the North American continent and the DDT that was similarly being carried into food chains all over the globe. And just as Eskimo children in villages in the Arctic circle had the highest radiation counts in their bones from the fallout, it was discovered that there was DDT in the fatty tissue of penguins in the Antarctic. But as an ecocentric marine biologist, Carson was not interested solely in the issue of human health: she confided to her editor that while her intention in writing the book was to emphasize the menace to human health, nevertheless she was convinced that the dangers pesticides posed to "the basic ecology of all living things . . . outweighs by far . . . any other aspect of the problem."

Beginning in the 1980s, following Bookchin's lead, there has been an explicit attempt to couple anthropocentric social justice with the urban-pollution wing, promoted primarily by social ecologists, eco-Marxists, ecosocialists, postmodern deconstructionists, and others with a leftist anthropocentric political background. For example, ecosocialist David Pepper (in his book, *Eco-socialism: From Deep Ecology to Social Justice*, 1993) claims that "social justice . . . or the increasing global lack of it, is the most pressing of all environmental problems."[18]

In the 1980s, humanity was shocked to learn that industrial-chemical pollution had reached such proportions that the ozone layer was being depleted and that the onset of the greenhouse effect would drastically alter the global climate of the Earth. Designated wild areas and species habitat do not stand apart from such effects as acid rain in the streams and lakes. The greenhouse effect will drastically alter wild ecosystems; ozone depletion causes animals to go blind and could be the cause of the rapid loss of amphibians worldwide. Chemical pesticides could be causing genetic mutations in frogs across the United States. Industrial-chemical pollution and protection of what's left of the wild world can no longer be separated at this point in history. The issue of world overpopulation cannot be separated from levels of consumption, industrial pollution, and continued economic growth and development, as well as from issues concerning the protection of wildlife habitat, biodiversity, and the Earth's wildness. However, as Anne and Paul Ehrlich have recently pointed out, "The ravaging of biodiversity . . . is the most serious single environmental peril facing civilization."[19] But anthropocentric urban-pollution and social justice concerns cannot be allowed to take precedence over the issue of dealing realistically with the urgency of the global ecological crisis. It comes down to a question of priorities and of developing a realistic ecological worldview.

# VI. ARNE NAESS AND THE ARTICULATION OF THE DEEP ECOLOGY MOVEMENT

It was the major philosophical split between the anthropocentric industrial-pollution wing and the ecocentric wing in environmentalism during the 1960s that prompted Norwegian ecophilosopher Arne Naess to present his short paper "The Shallow and the Deep, Long-Range Ecology Movements" (in which he coined the term "deep ecology") to a Third World Futures conference in Bucharest in 1972. The shallow movement, Naess claimed, was anthropocentric and was concerned mainly with pollution and resource depletion and "the health and affluence of people in the developed countries." The deep ecology movement had arisen from the experiences of field ecologists such as Rachel Carson and was engaged in deep questioning about the goals and viability of industrial-growth societies. In his paper, Naess was attempting to articulate the philosophical and scientific conclusions and intuitions of the 1960s ecocentric ecological revolution, which, Naess claimed, were similiar all over the world. These included the internal interrelatedness of ecosystems, ecological egalitarianism, appreciation of diversity and symbiosis, ecological complexity, a "deep-seated respect, or even veneration" for wild nature, anti-class posture, and local autonomy and decentralization. The "fight against pollution and resource depletion" was included as one aspect of the overall deep ecology position.[20]

Naess had begun to write and lecture on philosophy and ecology at the University of Oslo in 1968. This early work developed into his book *Okologi, Samfunn og Livsstil* in 1973 (the first ecophilosophy book written by a professional philosopher). It has continued to undergo revisions and, in 1989, it was revised and translated into English as *Ecology, Community and Lifestyle*. The poet Gary Snyder also worked out a unique deep ecology position beginning in the 1960s. Together with fellow Californians Peter Berg and the ecologist Raymond Dasmann, Snyder has developed the foundations for ecocentric bioregionalism. Naess and Snyder are the two most influential international spokespersons for the deep ecology movement.[21]

During the late 1960s, Naess also began to work out his own personal ecological philosophy based on the philosophies of Spinoza and Gandhi, which he calls Ecosophy T (for Tvergastein, his high mountain hut located between Oslo and Bergen). Ecosophy T is based on one ultimate norm, "Self-Realization!"—which refers to the whole of nature (the Tao), and all the human and nonhuman individuals that it comprises, realizing itself. Deep ecology is both a philosophical and social-political activist movement. In 1984, Naess developed the eight-point deep ecology platform, which begins with the basic ecocentric philosophical norms of the deep ecology movement and leads to general policy statements about activism and social change. (Naess's personal Ecosophy T "total view" and the eight-point platform are discussed in detail in Naess's paper, "The Deep Ecology Movement," in this section.)

That there are *three* distinct positions—(1) the 1972 shallow-deep ecology Bucharest paper, (2) Naess's personal Ecosophy T "total view," and (3) the 1984 eight-point platform—has produced considerable confusion over what the deep ecology movement actually stands for. This confusion was further compounded in 1990 when the Australian ecophilosopher Warwick Fox published his book, *Toward a Transpersonal Ecology*, which attempted to identify deep ecology with the concept of "self-realization," which is also essentially Fox's "transpersonal ecology" version of ecopsychology.[22]

Naess intended for the 1984 eight-point platform to replace the 1972 Bucharest paper as a contemporary characterization of the deep ecology movement. Andrew McLaughlin has argued that the eight-point platform is "the heart of Deep Ecology." Some critics of the deep ecology movement have taken exception to remarks made by Earth First! activists, while others have criticized the concept of "self-realization." Most critics, McLaughlin argues, miss the unique logic of the deep ecology position. To criticize this position in a relevant manner, one must criticize some aspect of the eight-point platform. Self-realization is central to Naess' personal Ecosophy T total view, and to Fox's transpersonal ecology, but it is not part of the eight-point platform; therefore it is not representative of the position of the deep ecology movement. Our "urgent task," McLaughlin says, is not needless philosophical quibbling but environmental activism and "social change," designed to bring about what Naess calls *wide* ecological sustainability—by which he means "the protection of the full richness and diversity of life forms on the Earth."[23]

Most deep ecology movement theorists now identify the movement with the deep questioning process, the eight-point platform, and the need for humans to identify with nonhumans and the wild world. Naess has suggested that the movement is also characterized by "spiritual activism": that is, acting from the basis of a fundamental philosophic-religious ecosophy (or "total view") and acting nonviolently.

## VII. COMMENTARY ON THE PAPERS

I have included "The Viable Human" by the leading Catholic ecotheologian, Thomas Berry, because it provides a wonderfully concise and comprehensive overview of the contemporary environmental situation. Berry asserts that a spiritual, ecocentric paradigm shift is necessary to come to grips with the global ecological crisis. His ecocentrism is expressed in the claim that "the community of all living species is the greater reality and the greater value."

Industrial entrepreneurs bear a great deal of responsibility for the crisis by promoting an economic-technological-consumerist "wonderworld," whereas in actuality they are creating a "wasteworld." Echoing Orwell's analysis of "Newspeak," Berry claims that contemporary language has been degraded to support the entrepreneur's vision, which includes "the most extravagant modes of commercial advertising to create the illusory world in which the human community is now living." Education has also been warped to the point where it now basically serves as a handmaiden to the entrepreneur's vision. Educational and religious professionals, Berry claims, are failing to adequately address the ecological crisis. Elsewhere, Berry has stated that population stabilization and eventual reduction are ecologically necessary.

Arne Naess's "The Deep Ecological Movement," written in 1986, is the best short, contemporary statement of the position of the deep ecology movement, together with a short description and diagram of Naess's own personal Ecosophy T "total view" (for a more detailed discussion, see Naess, *Ecology, Community, and Lifestyle*). Naess provides illuminating contrasts between shallow and deep ecology on a number of key environmental issues. The essay includes a statement of the 1984 eight-point deep ecology platform, together with what Naess calls the "Apron Diagram," which helps explain what Andrew McLaughlin calls the "unique logic" of the deep ecology position. At Level 1 of the diagram, there is a wide diversity of philosophical and religious positions, such as Christianity, Buddhism, Spinozism, Whiteheadianism, and so forth. Diversity at Level 1 is encouraged to ensure individual and cultural diversity and pluralism. Naess's "Self-Realization!" norm from his personal Ecosophy T position (and Warwick Fox's "transpersonal ecology" position) fit at Level 1 of the Apron Diagram. This diversity of religious and philosophical "fundamentals" or "ultimate norms" *can* (or, it is hoped, *would*) nevertheless converge, at Level 2 of the diagram, to logically support the ecocentric eight-point platform. It is at Level 2 (the platform level) that one looks for ecocentric agreement among philosophical and religious traditions around the world. Level 3 consists of hypotheses and factual statements about the ecological state of the world, such as ozone layer depletion, the rates of species extinction, and so forth. At Level 4, specific environmental actions to be taken would exhibit differences while remaining consistent with and following logically from Levels 2 and 3 of the diagram. At Level 4, the kinds of societies existing around the world that would be consistent with the eight-point platform at Level 2 would reflect considerable cultural diversity, mirroring and paralleling the kind of diversity found at Level 1 (the level of religious-philosophical "fundamentals" or "ultimate premises").

Naess also describes, and provides a logical diagram of, his own personal philosophical "total view," which he calls Ecosophy T. Ecosophy T is logically developed from his single Level 1 norm, "self-realization," and extends down through the various levels of the Apron Diagram.

One environmental ethics textbook author points out that "it sometimes seems that Deep Ecology acts as a lightning rod for environmental criticism and backlash. Because Deep Ecology does critique the dominant worldview, we should not be surprised to find significant critical reaction."[24] In his paper "Demystifying the Critiques of Deep Ecology," the leading deep ecology theorist Harold Glasser goes a long way toward clarifying many of the misconceptions. Glasser distinguishes what he calls "Naess's deep ecology approach to ecophilosophy" (DEA) from the deep ecology movement and from Naess's

Ecosophy T. First, Glasser points to four general weaknesses that are common to discussions and critiques of the deep ecology position. Next, he attempts to clarify Naess's approach to the DEA:

> The DEA should be viewed as a *Gestalt*. . . . In my view the DEA consists of at least six coupled elements: (1) the unifying notion of total views, (2) the DEA as a normative-derivational system, the reasoning techniques, (3) "deep questioning" and (4) "loose derivation," (5) the adoption of ultimate premises that incorporate "wide-identification," and (6) the Eight Points of the deep ecology platform.

In "The Deep Ecology–Ecofeminism Debate and Its Parallels," Warwick Fox examines the charges raised against deep ecology by ecofeminists and social ecologists, who have been vociferous critics of deep ecology. This began with the critique by the Australian sociologist and ecofeminist Ariel Salleh in 1984. Social ecologist Murray Bookchin attacked the deep ecology movement at the first meeting of the U.S. Greens in 1987. Much of Bookchin's critique centered around statements made by Dave Foreman and other activists in the Earth First! movement: statements that were not representative of the deep ecology position.[25]

Fox points out that ecocentrism logically and necessarily involves an egalitarian attitude toward all beings; thus it subsumes under its theoretical framework the egalitarian concerns of the various social justice movements, including ecofeminism and social ecology. Ecofeminist criticism is usually directed at deep ecology's analysis of the environmental crisis as rooted in anthropocentrism. But why, Fox asks, should we focus on androcentrism (male-centeredness) as *the* root cause rather than, say, race, Westernization, or social hierarchy? For it is possible to imagine a society that has realized social, racial, and gender equality but is still ecologically exploitive. This holds as well for Bookchin's social hierarchy analysis.

Fox makes the very important point that both ecofeminists and social ecologists tend to remain anthropocentric in practice as well: they continue to focus on their respective social-political agendas while the practical strategies and activism needed to deal with the global ecological crisis itself receive a low priority or are ignored entirely. For example, ecofeminists and social ecologists have displayed very little interest in the crucial Thoreau-Muir dialogue about protecting wildness. They seem to be preoccupied with their respective forms of social justice, often ignoring the larger issues of the contemporary corporate-megatechnological enslavement of humans and the wild in general. Some ecofeminists even extoll the virtues of megatechnology and ever expanding industrial cities. Donna Haraway, for example, encourages women to reject their organic origins and become "cyborgs": a merging of humans with machines and megatechnology that is remarkably like the New Age, artificial worlds vision of Teilhard de Chardin.

Fox also discusses how ecofeminists and social ecologists misinterpret deep ecology's critique of anthropocentrism to mean that *humans in general* are the cause of the environmental crisis, often equating this view with misanthropy. As Fox points out, deep ecology's critique of anthropocentrism is directed at human-centeredness (a legitimating ideology), not at humans per se—a logical mistake that he refers to as "the fallacy of misplaced misanthropy."

Arne Naess has not been very impressed with the tenor of this "debate" (instigated by the ecofeminists and Murray Bookchin) from the very beginning. He has said, "Away with all single-cause explanations of the ecological crisis!" And, of course, the critique of anthropocentrism is not a part of the eight-point deep ecology platform—the main distinguishing characteristic of the deep ecology movement (along with other distinguishing characteristics identified by Glasser and others). And so, in a strict sense, this "debate" has been largely irrelevant.

A very influential and widely reprinted paper by the Indian social ecologist Ramachandra Guha argues that the deep ecology movement, with its emphasis on the protection of biodiversity and the Earth's wild ecosystems, is not relevant to Third World concerns.[26] The deep ecology movement, he claims, is not relevant to what he sees as "the two fundamental ecological problems facing the globe: (i) overconsumption by the industrialized world and urban elites in the Third World and (ii) growing militarization. . . ." Guha's analysis is incredible in that it ignores what the 1992 World's Scientists' Warning to Humanity, and most ecologists, identify as the major global ecological problems: human overpopulation, ozone layer depletion, greenhouse effect, and biodiversity destruction. Guha sees the wildlife preserves for protecting tigers and other endangered species in India as a form of "elite ecological imperialism" and "a direct transfer of resources from the poor to the rich." Third World environmentalism, Guha claims, should place primary emphasis on human issues of "equality and social justice." The deep ecology movement, he erroneously asserts, has little or no interest in the issues of restructuring society to achieve ecological sustainability and social justice, steady-state economics, and a "radical shift in consumption and production patterns." Guha goes so far as to claim that the deep ecology movement is not relevant even to First World environmentalism: "A truly radical ecology in the American context," he claims, "ought to work toward a synthesis of the appropriate technology, alternate lifestyle, and peace movements." Guha's analysis is an excellent example of how social ecologists and others who put social justice concerns first are ignorant of—and blinded by anthropocentric ideologies to—the realities of the global ecological crisis.

Arne Naess has responded to Guha's paper, arguing basically that biodiversity concerns are very relevant to the Third World and that many people in the Third World are concerned about the multiple aspects of the ecological crisis, including the protection of biodiversity and the wild. Naess claims that Third World people must progress economically, while rich countries must curtail their excessive consumption. The severe overpopulation in the Third World will require that most of the poor live in urban areas in the near future; they cannot continue to destroy tropical forests. Naess refers to Gary

Snyder's point that, throughout history, humans have lived in wilderness in moderate numbers without appreciably reducing biological richness and diversity. But this is now not possible in First World countries, where high-consumption lifestyles and other highly destructive practices require the establishment of large designated wilderness areas to protect wildlife habitat and biodiversity.[27]

Guha's paper gave Naess the opportunity to rethink the relationship among ecology, social justice, and "militarization." As a way of heading off the leftist social justice takeover of the environmental-ecology movement, and helping to ensure that these movements cooperate constructively with each other, Naess proposes that the international green movement for social change be thought of as basically comprising three movements: (1) the peace movement, (2) the social justice movement, and (3) the ecology movement. It promotes only confusion, he claims, to identify the entire green movement (and the social justice and peace movements) with the ecology movement. The deep ecology movement strongly supports sustainability for all societies, but sustainability in the ecologically "wide" sense of protecting "the full richness and diversity of life forms on the planet": it is beneath human dignity, Naess claims, to aspire to less. While Naess argues that societies will not have reached full sustainability until significant progress has been made toward attaining all the goals of the green movement, nevertheless a very high priority must be placed on ecological issues: "Considering the accelerating rate of irreversible ecological destruction worldwide, I find it acceptable to continue fighting ecological unsustainability whatever the state of affairs may be concerning the other two goals of Green societies." Supporters of the deep ecology movement, he claims, "should concentrate on specific issues relating to the *ecological* crisis (including its social and political consequences)."[28]

A great deal of current deep ecological literature is concerned with practical biological and political strategies for implementing the ecocentric perspective, bioregionalism, and protection of biodiversity and what remains of the Earth's wildness. In "Ecocentrism, Wilderness, and Global Ecosystem Protection," I discuss recent research by conservation biologists that demonstrates that existing designated wilderness areas and wildlife preserves are ecologically inadequate to protect wild species and allow for continued speciation. It is claimed that the concepts of "ecological restoration" and "mitigation" are often misused by environmental professionals to justify further ecosystem destruction and habitat fragmentation.

Important recent refinements to ecosystem zoning proposals include Arne Naess's concept of "free nature" and Paul Taylor's concept of the "bioculture." Naess claims that an acceptable ecological ideal for the Earth would consist of one-third wilderness, one-third "free nature," and one-third bioculture. Dave Foreman discusses the Wildland Project strategy for protecting biodiversity (endorsed by E. O. Wilson, Paul Ehrlich, and other leading conservation biologists), which consists of greatly expanded wilderness areas and wildlife refuges with interconnecting wildlife corridors.

# SELECTED BIBLIOGRAPHY

BARNET, RICHARD, and JOHN CAVANAUGH. *Global Dreams: Imperial Corporations and the New World Order.* New York: Simon and Schuster, 1994.

COHEN, MICHAEL. *The Pathless Way: John Muir and American Wilderness.* Madison: University of Wisconsin Press, 1984. Excellent discussion of the development of Muir's ecocentrism.
_____. *The History of the Sierra Club: 1892–1970.* San Francisco: Sierra Club Books, 1988.

DALY, HERMAN. *Steady State Economics,* 2nd ed. Washington, DC: Island Press, 1991.

DRENGSON, ALAN, and YUICHI INOUE (eds.). *The Deep Ecology Movement.* Berkeley, CA: North Atlantic Books, 1995. Good introductory collection of deep ecology essays.

ECKERSLEY, ROBYN. *Environmentalism and Political Theory: Toward an Ecocentric Approach.* Albany: State University of New York Press, 1992. Outstanding political analysis of ecocentrism.

EHRENFELD, DAVID. *The Arrogance of Humanism.* Oxford: Oxford University Press, 1978. An excellent critique of the technocratic managerial mind-set and a defense of ecocentrism by a professional ecologist.

EHRLICH, PAUL, and ANNE EHRLICH. *The Population Explosion.* New York: Simon & Schuster, 1990.
_____. *Healing the Planet: Strategies for Resolving the Environmental Crisis.* Reading, MA: Addison-Wesley, 1991.
_____. *Betrayal of Science and Reason: How Anti-environmental Rhetoric Threatens Our Future.* Washington, DC: Island Press, 1996. The Ehrlichs summarize the worldwide consensus among the scientific community on the magnitude and seriousness of the ecological crisis. An appendix includes the warnings by the world's National Academies of Sciences in the 1990s and the 1992 World's Scientists' Warning to Humanity.

FOREMAN, DAVE. *Confessions of an Ecowarrior.* New York: Harmony Books, 1991.

FOX, STEPHEN. *John Muir and His Legacy: The American Conservation Movement.* Boston: Little, Brown, 1981. Outstanding history of the Muir-inspired American conservation movement.

FOX, WARWICK. *Toward a Transpersonal Ecology.* Boston: Shambhala Publications, 1990. Good history and bibliography of the deep ecology movement and exposition of Fox's transpersonal psychology position.

GLASSER, HAROLD. "Deep Ecology." *International Encyclopedia of Social and Behavioral Sciences,* ed. J. H. Smelser and P. B. Bates. Oxford: Pergamon Press, 2001.

KELLERT, STEPHEN, and E. O. WILSON (eds.). *The Biophilia Hypothesis.* Washington, DC: Island Press, 1993. A scholarly examination of Wilson's hypothesis that humans have a genetic need for wild environments.

LACHAPELLE, DOLORES. *Sacred Land Sacred Sex: Rapture of the Deep.* Durango, CO: Kivaki Press, 1988.

MANDER, JERRY. *In the Absence of the Sacred: The Failure of Technology and the Survival of the Indian Nations.* San Francisco: Sierra Club Books, 1991. A devastating critique of contemporary corporate-consumer-megatechnology visions.
_____. (ed.). *The Case Against the Global Economy.* San Francisco: Sierra Club Books, 1996. Mander, Ralph Nader, and others take on GATT, NAFTA, and the multinational corporate vision of the global economic "new world order."

MCLAUGHLIN, ANDREW. *Regarding Nature: Industrialism and Deep Ecology.* Albany: State University of New York Press, 1993.

NAESS, ARNE. *Ecology, Community, and Lifestyle: Outline of an Ecosophy.* Cambridge: Cambridge University Press, 1989. Naess's main treatise on deep ecology.

NASH, RODERICK. *The Rights of Nature: A History of Environmental Ethics.* Madison: University of Wisconsin Press, 1989.

NOSS, REED, and ALLEN COOPERRIDER. *Saving Nature's Legacy: Protecting and Restoring Biodiversity.* Washington, DC: Island Press, 1994. Conservation biologists outline the Wildlands Project for protecting wild species and ecosystems.

OELSCHLAEGER, MAX. *The Idea of Wilderness: From Prehistory to the Age of Ecology.* New Haven, CT: Yale University Press, 1991. Excellent account of the ecocentrism of Thoreau, Muir, and Snyder.

_____ (ed.). *The Company of Others: Essays in Celebration of Paul Shepard.* Durango, CO: Kivaki Press, 1995. A tribute to Paul Shepard's genius, published just before his recent death.

SALE, KIRKPATRICK. *The Green Revolution: The American Environmental Movement 1962–1992.* New York: Hill and Wang, 1993. Good, short history of environmentalism.

_____. *Rebels Against the Future.* Reading, MA: Addison-Wesley, 1995. A history of Luddism and discussion of the neo-Luddite movement.

SESSIONS, GEORGE (ed.). *Deep Ecology for the 21st Century.* Boston: Shambhala Publications, 1995. An attempt at a comprehensive and contemporary statement of the deep ecology position. Extensive bibliography.

_____. "Postmoderism and Environmental Justice: The Demise of the Ecology Movement?" *The Trumpeter* 12, 3 (1995): 150–54. This article and the next two provide critiques of postmodern deconstructionism and the attempt by some in the social justice movement to coopt the environmental-ecological movement.

_____. "Political Correctness, Ecological Realities, and the Future of the Ecology Movement." *The Trumpeter* 12, 4 (1995): 191–96.

_____. "Reinventing Nature, The End of Wilderness? A Response to William Cronon's *Uncommon Ground.*" *The Trumpeter* 13, 1 (1996): 33–38.

_____. "Critical Notice of Martha Lee, *Earth First!: Environmental Apocalypse.*" *The Trumpeter* 13, 4 (1996): 197–200.

_____. "Comments on Jack Turner's *The Abstract Wild.*" *Wild Duck Review* 3, 1 (February 1997).

SHEPARD, PAUL. *Nature and Madness.* San Francisco: Sierra Club Books, 1982. A classic in the field of ecopsychology.

_____. *The Others: How Animals Made Us Human.* Washington, DC: Island Press, 1995.

_____. *The Only World We've Got.* San Francisco: Sierra Club Books, 1996.

_____. *Traces of an Omnivore.* Washington, DC: Island Press, 1996.

SNYDER, GARY. *The Practice of the Wild.* San Francisco: North Point Press, 1990. Snyder's seminal statement on wildness. Snyder and Paul Shepard argue for the human genetic need for the wild and for the move to bioregionalism.

_____. *Mountains and Rivers Without End.* Washington, DC: Counterpoint Press, 1996.

SOULE, MICHAEL, and GARY LEASE. *Reinventing Nature? A Response to Postmodern Deconstructionism.* Washington, DC. Island Press, 1995. Conservation biologists and others respond to William Cronon and other postmodernists who promote Disneyland-type, urban, hyperreal environments over reinhabitation, bioregionalism, and protection and restoration of the wild.

TURNER, JACK. *The Abstract Wild.* Tucson: University of Arizona Press, 1996. A brilliant, uncompromising defense of the wild and critique of the economic paradigm and shallow managerial environmentalism.

WITOSZEK, NINA (ed.). *Rethinking Deep Ecology.* University of Oslo: Centre for Development and the Environment, 1996.

WITOSZEK, NINA, and ANDREW BRENNAN, eds. *Philosophical Dialogues: Arne Naess and the Progress of Ecophilosophy.* University of Oslo: Centre for Development and Environment, 1997.

ZAKIN, SUSAN. *Coyotes and Town Dogs: Earth First! and the Environmental Movement.* New York, Viking Press, 1993. The best account of the Earth First! movement.

ZIMMERMAN, MICHAEL E. *Contesting Earth's Future: Radical Ecology and Postmodernity.* Berkeley and Los Angeles: University of California Press, 1993.

## NOTES

1. Lynn White, Jr., "Historical Roots of Our Ecologic Crisis," *Science* 155 (1967): 1203–7. For discussions of the impact of White's paper, see Stephen Fox, *John Muir and His Legacy: The American Conservation Movement* (Boston: Little, Brown, 1981), pp. 358–74; Roderick Nash, *The Rights of Nature: A History of Environmental Ethics* (Madison: University of Wisconsin Press, 1989), pp. 87–120.

2. Paul Ehrlich, *The Population Bomb* (New York: Ballantine Books, 1968), pp. 169–72.

3. For discussions of Thoreau's concern for protecting wildness in both humans and nonhumans, see Jack Turner, "In Wildness Is the Preservation of the World," and Thomas Birch, "The Incarceration of Wildness," both reprinted in George Sessions (ed.), *Deep Ecology for the 21st Century* (Boston: Shambhala Publications, 1995), pp. 331–55.

4. For a discussion of Brower's Exhibit Format books, see Michael P. Cohen, *A History of the Sierra Club: 1892–1970* (San Francisco: Sierra Club Books, 1988), pp. 254–64, 291–99, 345–52.

5. G. Tyler Miller, Jr., *Replenish the Earth: A Primer in Human Ecology* (Belmont, CA: Wadsworth, 1972), p. 152. Miller's book presents an excellent summary of the ecological-environmental crisis as it was understood by biologists and other scientists at the beginning of the 1970s. See also G. Tyler Miller, Jr., *Living in the Environment: An Introduction to Environmental Science*, 9th ed. (Belmont, CA: Wadsworth, 1996).

6. A vivid presentation of the clash between Ehrlich and Simon and between Ehrlich and Barry Commoner is provided in the excellent Public Broadcasting System (PBS) video "Paul Ehrlich and the Population Bomb," aired in April 1996.

7. On the globalization of corporate power, see Jerry Mander (ed.), *The Case Against the Global Economy* (San Francisco: Sierra Club Books, 1996). For the corporate vision of the world as a megatechnological-consumerist-Disneyland theme park, see Jerry Mander, *In the Absence of the Sacred* (San Francisco: Sierra Club Books, 1991); Paul Shepard, "Virtually Hunting Reality in the Forests of Simulacra," in Michael Soulé and Gary Lease (eds.), *Reinventing Nature? Responses to Postmodern Deconstruction* (Washington, DC: Island Press, 1995), pp. 17–29.

8. For a discussion of the "Reagan reaction," see Kirkpatrick Sale, *The Green Revolution: The American Environmental Movement 1962–1992* (New York: Hill and Wang, 1993); for critiques of sustainable development, the Bruntland Report, and the 1992 Rio conference, see Donald Worster, "The Shaky Ground of Sustainability," and Wolfgang Sachs, "Global Ecology and the Shadow of 'Development,'" in Sessions, *Deep Ecology*, pp. 417–44.

9. For a statement of the warnings of the National Academies of Sciences and the World's Scientists' Warning to Humanity, see Paul and Anne Ehrlich, *Betrayal of Science and Reason: How Anti-environmental Rhetoric Threatens Our Future* (Washington, DC: Island Books, 1966), pp. 233–50; Anne and Paul Ehrlich, *Healing the Planet: Strategies for Resolving the Environmental Crisis* (Reading MA: Addison-Wesley, 1991), pp. 35–37. For a discussion of the 1995 M.I.T. study of the current attitudes of Americans toward wild nature, see Tom Hayden, *The Lost Gospel of the Earth* (San Francisco: Sierra Club Books, 1996), pp. 232–34.

10. The influence of the Vogt and Osborn books is discussed in Robert Gottlieb, *Forcing the Spring: The Transformation of the American Environmental Movement* (Washington, DC: Island Press, 1993), pp. 36–41, although Gottlieb disparagingly refers to them as "neo-Malthusian" in tone. Both the books by Gottlieb and Mark Dowie, *Losing Ground: American Environmentalism at the Close of the Twentieth Century* (Cambridge MA: M.I.T. Press, 1995) are leftist in orientation; they propose that the environmental movement shift its

priorities away from the protection of the Earth's biodiversity, wild ecosystems, and ecological integrity (the position taken by most contemporary ecologists and world scientists' organizations) to an urban pollution and social justice agenda (referred to now as the movement for environmental justice). Those who put social justice issues first or attempt to redirect environmentalism toward an environmental justice agenda remain anthropocentric and apparently fail to fully comprehend the nature and severity of the global ecological crisis.

11. Anne and Paul Ehrlich, *Earth* (New York: Franklin Watts, 1987), pp. 167–68.

12. For a discussion of the Sierra Club Wilderness Conferences and Brower's conversion to ecocentrism, see Cohen, *History of the Sierra Club*, pp. 116–17, 124–34, 214–17, 232–33, 369, 414, 436–37.

13. David Brower, "Toward an Earth International Park," and Hugh H. Iltus, "Whose Fight Is the Fight for Nature?" *Sierra Club Bulletin* 52, 9 (October 1967): 20, 34–39. This issue of the *Bulletin* also published the paper by White, "Historical Roots of Our Ecologic Crisis," pp. 123–27. For a discussion of the *New York Times* ad, see Cohen, *History of the Sierra Club*, pp. 424–26.

14. Cohen, *History of the Sister Club*, pp. 133–34.

15. Donald Worster, "The Shaky Ground of Sustainability," in Sessions, *Deep Ecology*, pp. 417–18.

16. Stephen Fox, *John Muir and His Legacy: The American Conservation Movement* (Boston: Little, Brown, 1981). Chapter 9 of Fox's book is an excellent summary of the conflicting trends in the development of environmentalism throughout the 1960s and early 1970s. For a revealing account of the anthropocentric, social justice–oriented new left approach to environmental issues during this period, see Gottlieb, *Forcing the Spring*, chap. 3. It is illuminating to contrast the environmental concerns of the new left with the little manifesto, "Four Changes," written by the Zen Buddhist counterculturalist and deep ecologist Gary Snyder in 1969 (reprinted in Sessions, *Deep Ecology*, pp. 141–50).

17. Chris Lewis, "Telling Stories About the Future: Environmental History and Apocalyptic Science," *Environmental History Review* 17, 3 (1993): 42–60.

18. For critiques of the attempt by leftists to redirect the environmental movement away from the major problems of the global ecological crisis and toward an urban-pollution–social justice agenda, see George Sessions, "Postmodernism and Environmental Justice: The Demise of the Ecology Movement?" *The Trumpeter* 12, 3 (1995): 150–54; George Sessions, "Political Correctness, Ecological Realities, and the Future of the Ecology Movement," *The Trumpeter* 12, 4 (1995): 191–96; George Sessions, "Reinventing Nature, The End of Wilderness?: A Response to William Cronon's *Uncommon Ground*," *The Trumpeter* 13, 1 (1996): 33–38.

19. Ehrlich, *Healing the Planet*, pp. 35–37.

20. A summary of the talk was published as Arne Naess, "The Shallow and the Deep, Long-Range Ecology Movements: A Summary," *Inquiry* (Oslo) 16 (1973); reprinted in Sessions, *Deep Ecology*, pp. 151–55.

21. Arne Naess, *Ecology, Community, and Lifestyle: Outline of an Ecosophy*, David Rothenberg (trans.) (Cambridge: Cambridge University Press, 1989); Snyder, "Four Changes"; Gary Snyder, "Re-inhabitation," in *The Old Ways* (San Francisco: City Lights Books, 1977); Raymond Dasmann, *The Destruction of California* (New York: Macmillan, 1965); Peter Berg and Raymond Dasmann, "Reinhabiting California," in Peter Berg (ed.), *Reinhabiting a Separate Country* (San Francisco: Planet Drum Foundation, 1978); Gary Snyder, *The Practice of the Wild* (San Francisco: North Point Press, 1990).

22. Warwick Fox, *Toward a Transpersonal Ecology* (Boston: Shambhala Publications, 1990). For a critique of Fox's attempt to replace deep ecology with "transpersonal ecology," see Harold Glasser, "On Warwick Fox's Assessment of Deep Ecology," *Environmental Ethics* 19, 1 (1997): 69–85; Harold Glasser, "Naess's Deep Ecology Approach and Environmental Policy," *Inquiry* (Oslo) 39, 2 (1996): 157–87.

23. See Andrew McLaughlin, "The Heart of Deep Ecology" and Arne Naess, "Politics and the Ecological Crisis," in Sessions, *Deep Ecology*, pp. 85–93 and 445–53, respectively.

24. Joseph R. DesJardins, *Environmental Ethics: An Introduction to Environmental Philosophy*, 2nd ed. (Belmont, CA: Wadsworth, 1997), p. 215. In his section on deep ecology, unfortunately, DesJardins repeats many of the misconceptions he decries.

25. Ariel Salleh, "Deeper Than Deep Ecology: The Ecofeminist Connection," *Environmental Ethics* 6, 4 (1984): 339–45; Murray Bookchin, "Social Ecology Versus Deep Ecology: A Challenge for the Ecology Movement," *Socialist Review* 88, 3 (1988): 11–29; reprinted in D. VanDeVeer and C. Pierce (eds.), *Environmental Ethics and Policy Book* (Belmont, CA: Wadsworth, 1994), pp. 228–38. See also Steve Chase (ed.), *Defending the Earth: A Dialogue between Murray Bookchin and Dave Foreman* (Boston: South End Press, 1991); George Sessions, "Critical Notice of Martha Lee, *Earth First! Environmental Apocalypse*," *The Trumpeter* 13, 4 (1996): 197–200.

26. Ramachandra Guha, "Radical American Environmentalism and Wilderness Preservation: A Third World Critique," *Environmental Ethics* 11, 1 (1989): 71–83; reprinted in VanDeVeer and Pierce, *Environmental Ethics and Policy Book*, pp. 548–56.

27. Arne Naess, "The Third World, Wilderness, and Deep Ecology," in Sessions, *Deep Ecology*, pp. 397–407; see also David Johns, "The Relevance of Deep Ecology to the Third World," *Environmental Ethics* 12, 3 (1990): 233–52; Eric Katz and Lauren Oelchsli, "Moving Beyond Anthropocentrism: Environmental Ethics, Development, and the Amazon," *Environmental Ethics* 15, 1 (1993): 49–59.

28. See Arne Naess, "The Third World, Wilderness, and Deep Ecology," "Politics and the Ecological Crisis," and "Deep Ecology for the Twenty-Second Century," in Sessions, *Deep Ecology*, pp. 397–407, 445–53, and 463–67, respectively; see also Arne Naess, "The Three Great Movements, *The Trumpeter* 9, 2 (1992).

# THE VIABLE HUMAN

*Thomas Berry*

Thomas Berry is director of the Riverdale Center for Religious Research in New York and is widely regarded as one of the world's leading ecotheologians. He is the author of *The Dream of the Earth* (1988) and many papers in ecotheology.

To be viable, the human community must move from its present anthropocentric norm to a geocentric norm of reality and value. Within the solar system, the earth is the immediate context of human existence. And we recognize the sun as the primary source of earth's energies. Beyond the sun, however, is our own galaxy, and beyond that is the universal galactic system that emerged some 15 billion years ago through some ineffable mystery.

To establish this comprehensive context is important; it is the only satisfactory referent in our quest for a viable presence of the human within the larger dynamics of the universe. We suppose that the universe itself is *the* enduring reality and *the* enduring value even while it finds expression in a continuing sequence of transformations. In creating the planet Earth, its living forms, and its human intelligence, the universe has found, so far as we know, the most elaborate manifestation of its deepest mystery. Here, in its human form, the universe is able to reflect on and celebrate itself in a unique mode of conscious self-awareness.

Our earliest human documents reveal a special sensitivity in human intellectual, emotional, and aesthetic responses to the natural world. These responses reveal cosmic and biologic realms of thought as well as anthropocentric life attitudes. These realms were all centered in each other, the later dependent on the earlier for survival, the earlier dependent on the later for their manifestation.

Originally published in *Revision*, Vol. 9, No. 2 (Winter/Spring 1987). Reprinted with permission of the Helen Dwight Reid Education Foundation. Published by Heldref Publications, 1319 Eighteenth St., N.W., Washington, D.C. 20036-1802.

Instinctively, humans have always perceived themselves as a mode of being *of* the universe as well as distinctive beings *in* the universe. This was the beginning. The emergence of the human was a transformative moment for the earth as well as for the human. As with every species, the human being needed to establish its niche, a sustainable position in the larger community of life, to fulfill its need for food, shelter, and clothing, for security, for family and community. The need for community was special because of the unique human capacity for thought and speech, aesthetic appreciation, emotional sensitivities, and moral judgment. The fulfilling of these needs resulted in a cultural shaping that established the specific identifying qualities of the human being.

Whatever the cultural elaboration of the human, its basic physical as well as psychic nourishment and support came from the surrounding natural environment. In its beginnings, human society was integrated with the larger life society and the larger earth community composed of all the geological as well as biological and human elements. Just how long this primordial harmony endured we do not know beyond the last hundred thousand years of the Paleolithic period. Some ten thousand years ago, the Neolithic and then the Classical civilizations came into being. It must suffice to say that with the classical and generally literate civilizations of the past five thousand years, the great cultural worlds of the human developed, along with vast and powerful social establishments whereby humans became oppressive and even destructive of other life forms. Alienation from the natural world increased, and new ideals of human well-being neglected the needs of other living species. Because of this human dysfunctional relation with the earth, some of these earlier human cultures became nonsustainable. We can observe this especially in the classical Mediterranean civilizations of Greece and Rome. Even so, the human species as a whole was not seriously endangered; these experiences were regional and limited in their consequences. In recent times, however, this has changed.

A deep cultural pathology has developed in Western society and has now spread throughout the planet. A savage plundering of the entire earth is taking place through industrial exploitation. Thousands of poisons unknown in former times are saturating the air, the water, and the soil. The habitat of a vast number of living species is being irreversibly damaged. In this universal disturbance of the biosphere by human agents, the human being now finds that the harm done to the natural world is returning to threaten the human species itself.

The question of the viability of the human species is intimately connected with the question of the viability of the earth. These questions ultimately arise because at the present time the human community has such an exaggerated, even pathological, fixation on its own comfort and convenience that it is willing to exhaust any and all of the earth's resources to satisfy its own cravings. The sense of reality and of value is strictly directed toward the indulgences of a consumer economy. This nonsustainable situation can be clearly seen in the damage done to major elements necessary for the continued well-being of the planet. When the soil, the air, and the water have been extensively poisoned, human needs cannot be fulfilled. Strangely, this situation is the consequence of a human-centered norm of reality and value.

Once we grant that a change from an anthropocentric to a biocentric sense of reality and value is needed, we must ask how this can be achieved and how it would work. We must begin by accepting the fact that the life community, the community of all living species, is the greater reality and the greater value, and that the primary concern of the human must be the preservation and enhancement of this larger community. The human does have its own distinctive reality and its own distinctive value, but this distinctiveness must be articulated within the more comprehensive context. The human ultimately must discover the larger dimensions of its own being within this community context. That the value of the human being is enhanced by diminishing the value of the larger community is an illusion, the great illusion of the present industrial age, which seeks to advance the human by plundering the planet's geological structure and all its biological species.

This plundering is being perpetrated mainly by the great industrial establishments that have dominated the entire planetary process for the past one hundred years, during the period when modern science and technology took control not only of our natural resources but also of human affairs. If the viability of the human species is now in question, it is a direct consequence of these massive ventures, which have gained extensive control not only of our economies but also of our whole cultural development, whether it be economics, politics, law, education, medicine, or moral values. Even our language is heavily nuanced in favor of the consumer values fostered by our commercial industrial establishment.

Opposed to the industrial establishment is the ecological movement which seeks to create a more viable context for the human within the framework of the larger community. There must, however, be a clear understanding that this question of viability is not an issue that can be resolved in any permanent manner. It will be a continuing issue for the indefinite future.

The planet that ruled itself directly for the past millennia is now determining its future through human decision. Such has been the responsibility assumed by humans when we ventured into the study of the empirical sciences and their associated technologies. In this process, whatever the benefits, we endangered ourselves and every living organism on this planet.

If we look back over the total course of planetary development, we find that there was a consistent fluorescence of the life process in the larger arc of its development over some billions of years. There were innumerable catastrophic events in both the geological and biological realms, but none of these had the distinguishing characteristics or could cause such foreboding as Earth experiences at present.

The total extinction of life is not imminent, though the elaborate forms of life expression in the earth's ecosystems may be shattered in an irreversible manner. What is absolutely threatened is the degradation of the planet's more brilliant and satisfying forms of life expression. This degradation involves extensive distortion and a pervasive weakening of the life system, its comprehensive integrity as well as its particular manifestations.

While there are pathologies that wipe out whole populations of life forms and must be considered pernicious to the life process on an extensive scale, the human species has, for some thousands of years, shown itself to be a pernicious presence in the world of the living on a unique and universal scale. Nowhere has this been more evident than in the Western phase of development of the human species. There is scarcely any geological or biological reality or function that has not experienced the deleterious influence of the human. The survival of hundreds of thousands of species is presently threatened. But since the human survives only within this larger complex of ecosystems, any damage done to other species, or to the other ecosystems, or to the planet itself, eventually affects the human not only in terms of physical well-being but also in every other phase of human intellectual understanding, aesthetic expression, and spiritual development.

Because such deterioration results from a rejection of the inherent limitation of earthly existence and from an effort to alter the natural functioning of the planet in favor of a humanly constructed wonderworld for its human occupants, the human resistance to this destructive process has turned its efforts toward an emphasis on living creatively within the functioning of the natural world. The earth as a bio-spiritual planet must become, for the human, the basic reference in identifying what is real and what is worthwhile.

Thus we have the ecologist standing against industrial enterprise in defense of a viable mode of human functioning within the context of a viable planetary process. This opposition between the industrial entrepreneur and the ecologist has been both the central human issue and the central earth issue of this late twentieth century. My position is that the efforts of the entrepreneur to create a wonderworld are, in fact, creating a wasteworld, a nonviable environment for the human species. The ecologist is offering a way of moving toward a new expression of the true wonderworld of nature as the context for a viable human situation. The current difficulty is that the industrial enterprise has such extensive control over the planet that we must certainly be anxious about the future.

But we are tempted to diminish our assessment of the danger lest we be overwhelmed with the difficulty, for indeed, we are caught in a profound cultural pathology. We might even say that, at present, our dominant institutions, professions, programs, and activities are counterproductive in their consequences, addictive to a consumer society; and we are paralyzed by our inability to respond effectively. Such a description is well merited if we consider the extent to which we have poisoned our environment, the air we breathe, the water we drink, and the soil that grows our food.

Having identified the magnitude of the difficulty before us, we need to establish a more specific analysis of the problems themselves. Then we need to provide specific programs leading toward a viable human situation on a viable planet.

The industrial entrepreneur is in possession of the natural resources of the planet, either directly, by corporate control, or indirectly, through governments subservient to the industrial enterprise. This possession is, of course, within limits. Fragmentary regions of the planet have been set aside as areas to be preserved in their natural state or to be exploited at a later time. These regions survive at the tolerance of the industrial establishment. Some controls now exist through governmental and private protection. These must be expanded.

Ecologists recognize that reducing the planet to a resource base for consumer use in an industrial society is already a spiritual and psychic degradation. Our main experience of the divine, the world of the sacred, has been diminished as money and utility values have taken precedence over spiritual, aesthetic, emotional, and religious values in our attitude toward the natural world. Any recovery of the natural world will require not only extensive financial funding but a conversion experience deep in the psychic structure of the human. Our present dilemma is the consequence of a disturbed psychic situation, a mental imbalance, an emotional insensitivity, none of which can be remedied by any quickly contrived adjustment. Nature has been severely, and in many cases irreversibly, damaged. Healing can occur and new life can sometimes be evoked, but only with the same intensity of concern and sustained vigor of action as that which brought about the damage in the first place. Yet, without this healing, the viability of the human is severely limited.

The basic orientation of the common law tradition is toward personal rights and toward the natural world as existing for human use. There is no provision for recognition of nonhuman beings as subjects having legal rights. To the ecologists, the entire question of possession and use of the earth, either by individuals or by establishments, needs to be profoundly reconsidered. The naive assumption that the natural world exists solely to be possessed and used by humans for their unlimited advantage cannot be accepted. The earth belongs to itself and to all the component members of the community. The entire earth is a gorgeous celebration of existence in all its forms. Each living thing participates in the celebration as the proper fulfillment of its powers of expression. The reduction of the earth to an object simply for human possession and use is unthinkable in most traditional cultures. To Peter Drucker, the entrepreneur creates resources and values. Before it is possessed and used, "every plant is a weed and every mineral is just another rock" (*Innovation and Entrepreneurship*, 1985, p. 30). To the industrial entrepreneur, human possession and use is what activates the true value of any natural object.

The Western legal tradition, with its insistence on personal rights and the freedom of the human to occupy and use the land and all its component forms, is the greatest support for the entrepreneur. There is no question of other natural beings having rights over the human. Human use is not limited by any legally recognized rights of other natural beings but only by human determination of the limits that humans are willing to accept.

To achieve a viable human-earth community, a new legal system must take as its primary task to articulate the conditions for the integral functioning of the earth process, with special reference to a mutually enhancing human-earth relationship. Within this context, each component of the earth would be a separate community and together they would constitute the integral expression of the great community of the planet Earth.

In this context, each individual being is also supported by every other being in the earth community. In turn, each contributes to the well-being of every other. Justice would consist in carrying out this sequence of creative relationships. Within the human community there would, of course, be a need for articulating patterns of social relationships, in which individual and group rights would be recognized and defended and the basic elements of personal security and personal property would be protected. The entire complex of political and social institutions would be needed. Economic organizations would also be needed. But these would be so integral with the larger earth economy that they would enhance rather than obstruct each other.

Another significant aspect of contemporary life, wherein the industrial entrepreneur has a dominant position, is language. Since we are enclosed in an industrial culture, the words we use have their significance and validation defined within this industrial framework. A central value word used by our society is "progress." This word has great significance for increasing our scientific understanding of the universe, our personal and social development, our better health and longer life. Through modern technology, we can manufacture great quantities of products with greater facility. Human technology also enables us to travel faster and with greater ease. So on and on, endlessly, we see our increasing human advantage over the natural world.

But then we see that human progress has been carried out by desolating the natural world. This degradation of the earth is the very condition of the "progress" presently being made by humans. It is a kind of sacrificial offering. Within the human community, however, there is little awareness of the misunderstanding of this word. The feeling that even the most trivial modes of human progress are preferable to the survival of the most sublime and even the most sacred aspects of the natural world is so pervasive that the ecologist is at a loss as to how to proceed. The language in which our values are expressed has been co-opted by the industrial establishments and is used with the most extravagant modes of commercial advertising to create the illusory world in which the human community is now living.

One of the most essential roles of the ecologist is to create the language in which a true sense of reality, of value, and of progress can be communicated to our society. This need for rectification of language was recognized very early by the Chinese as a first task for any acceptable guidance of the society. Just now, a rectification is needed for the term "progress." As presently used, this word might be understood more properly to mean "retardation" or "destruction." The meaning of the term "profit" also needs to be rectified. Profit according to what norms and for whom? The profit of the corporation is the deficit of the earth. The profit of the industrial enterprise can also be considered the deficit of the quality of life, even for human society.

Gender has wide implications for our conception of the universe, the earth, and the life process, as well as for the relation of human individuals toward each other and for identifying social roles. The industrial establishment is the extreme expression of a nonviable patriarchal tradition. Only with enormous psychic and social effort and revolutionary processes has this control been mitigated with regard to the rights of serfs, slaves, women and children, ethnic groups, and the impoverished classes of our society. The rights of the natural world of living beings other than humans is still at the mercy of the modern industrial corporation as the ultimate expression of patriarchal dominance over the entire planetary process. The four basic patriarchal oppressions are rulers over people, men over women, possessors over nonpossessors, and humans over nature.

For the ecologist, the great model of all existence is the natural ecosystem, which is self-ruled as a community wherein each component has its unique and comprehensive influence. The ecologist, with a greater understanding of the human as a nurturing presence within the larger community of the geological and biological modes of earth, is closer to the feminine than to the masculine modality of being and of activity.

The purpose of education, as presently envisaged, is to enable humans to be "productive" within the context of the industrial society. A person needs to become literate in order to fulfill some function within the system, whether in the acquisition or processing of raw materials, manufacturing, distributing the product in a commercially profitable manner, managing the process or the finances, or finally, spending the net earnings in acquisition and enjoyment of possessions. A total life process is envisaged within this industrial process. All professional careers now tend toward the industrial-commercial model, especially medicine, law, and the engineering sciences.

In a new context, the primary educator as well as the primary lawgiver and the primary healer would be the natural world itself. The integral earth community would be a self-educating community within the context of a self-educating universe. Education at the human level would be the conscious sensitizing of the human to those profound communications made by the universe about us, by the sun and moon and stars, the clouds and rain, the contours of the earth and all its living forms. All the music and poetry of the universe would flow into the student, the revelatory presence of the divine, as well as insight into the architectural structures of the continents and the engineering skills whereby the great hydrological cycle functions in moderating the temperature of the earth, in providing habitat for aquatic life, in nourishing the multitudes of living creatures. The earth would also be our primary teacher of sciences, especially the biological sciences, and of industry and economics. It would teach us a system in which we would create a minimum of entropy, a system in which there is no unusable or unfruitful junk. Only in such an integral system is the future viability of the human assured.

Much more could be said about the function of the natural world as educator, but this may be sufficient to suggest the context for an education that would be available to everyone from the beginning to the end of life, when the earth that brought us into being draws us back into itself to experience the deepest of all mysteries.

In this ecological context, we see that the problems of human illness are not only increasing but also are being considerably altered in their very nature by the industrial context of life. In prior centuries, human illness was experienced within the well-being of the natural world with its abundance of air and water and foods grown in a fertile soil. Even city dwellers in their deteriorated natural surroundings could depend on the purifying processes of the natural elements. The polluting materials themselves were subject to natural composition and reabsorption into the ever-renewing cycles of the life process.

But this is no longer true. The purifying processes have been overwhelmed by the volume, the composition, and the universal extent of the toxic or non-biodegradable materials. Beyond all this, the biorhythms of the natural world are suppressed by the imposition of mechanistic patterns on natural processes.

The profession of medicine must now consider its role, not only within the context of human society, but in the context of the earth process. A healing of the earth is now a prerequisite for the healing of the human. Adjustment of the human to the conditions and restraints of the natural world constitutes the primary medical prescription for human well-being. Nothing else will suffice.

Behind the long disruption of the earth process is the refusal of our Western industrial society to accept any restraints upon its quest for release—not simply from the normal ills to which we are subject but release from the human condition itself. There exists in our tradition a hidden rage against those inner as well as outer forces that create a challenge or impose a limitation on our activities.

Some ancient force in the Western psyche seems to perceive limitation as the demonic obstacle to be eliminated rather than as a discipline to evoke creativity. Acceptance of the shadow aspect of the natural world is a primary condition for creative intimacy with the natural world. Without this opaque or even threatening aspect of the universe we would lose our greatest source of creative energy. This opposing element is as necessary for us as is the weight of the atmosphere that surrounds us. This containing element, even the gravitation that binds us to the earth, should be experienced as liberating and energizing rather than confining.

Strangely enough, it is our efforts to establish a thoroughly sanitized world that have led to our toxic world. Our quest for wonderworld is making wasteworld. Our quest for energy is creating entropy on a scale never before witnessed in the historical process. We have invented a counterproductive society that is now caught in the loop that feeds back into itself in what can presently be considered a runaway situation. This includes all our present human activities, although it is most evident in the industrial-commercial aspects of contemporary life.

The communications media are particularly responsible for placing the entire life process of the human in an uncontrolled situation. Producer and consumer feed each other in an ever-accelerating process until we experience an enormous glut of basic products. But we see unmatched deprivation for the growing numbers of people living in the shantytowns of the world.

There are no prominent newspapers, magazines, and periodicals that have consistently designated space for commentary on the ecological situation. There are sections for politics, economics, sports, arts, science, education, food, entertainment, and a number of other areas of life, including religion; but only on rare occasions are there references to what is happening to the planet. Of course, these periodicals are supported by the great industrial establishment, and the ecological situation is considered threatening or limiting to the industrial enterprise. In reality, industrial control of the media is among the most devastating forces threatening the viability of the human.

Efforts are made to mitigate the evils consequent to this industrial-commercial process by modifying the manner in which these establishments function, reducing the amount of toxic waste produced as well as developing more efficient modes of storing or detoxifying waste. Yet all of this is trivial in relation to the magnitude of the problem. So, too, are the regulatory efforts of the government; these are microphase solutions for macrophase problems.

We also witness the pathos of present efforts to preserve habitats for wildlife in some areas while elsewhere the tropical rain forests of the earth are being destroyed. Other efforts to alter present destructive activities are made by confrontational groups such as Greenpeace, Earth First!, and People for the Ethical Treatment of Animals. These are daring ventures that dramatize the stark reality of the situation. That such tactics (to save the whales at sea, the wilderness life on the land, and the millions of animals being tortured in laboratories under the guise of scientific research) are needed to force humans to examine and question our behavior is itself evidence of how deep a change is needed in human consciousness.

Beyond the mitigating efforts and confrontational tactics is the clarification of more creative modes of functioning in all our institutions and professions, especially through movements associated with reinhabiting the various bioregions of the world such as the Regeneration Project of the Rodale Institute, The Land Institute in Salina, Kansas, and the two North American Bioregional Congresses. These new and mutually enhancing patterns of human-earth relationships are being developed on a functional as well as a critical-intellectual basis. Among these organizations, the Green movement may be one of the most creative and effective in its overall impact as the years pass. This movement is finding expression in politics, in economics, in education, in healing, and in spiritual reorientation. These recent movements, oriented toward a more benign human relationship with the environment, indicate a pervasive change in consciousness that is presently our best hope for developing a sustainable future.

We might also now recover our sense of the maternal aspect of the universe in the symbol of the Great Mother, especially the Earth as the maternal principle out of which we are born. Once this symbol is recovered, the dominion of the patriarchal system that has brought such aggressive attitudes into our activities will be eliminated. If this is achieved, our relationship with the natural world should undergo its most radical readjustment since the origins of our civilization in classical antiquity.

We might also recover our archetypal sense of the cosmic tree and the tree of life. The tree symbol gives expression to the organic unity of the universe but especially of the earth in its integral reality. Obviously, any damage done to the tree will be experienced through the entire organism. This could be one of our most effective ways of creating not simply conscious decisions against industrial devastation of the earth but a deep instinctive repulsion to any such activity. This instinct should be as immediate as the instinct for survival itself.

In the United States, the educational and religious professionals should be especially sensitive in discerning what is happening to the planet. These professions present themselves as guides for the establishment of our values and interpretors of the significance of our lives. The study of education and religion should awaken an awareness of the world in which we live, how it functions, how the human fits into the larger community of life, and the role that the human fulfills in the great story of the universe, the historical sequence of developments that have shaped our physical and cultural landscape. Along with an awareness of the past and present, education and religion should guide the future.

The pathos of these times, however, is precisely the impasse we witness in our educational and religious programs. Both are living in a past fundamentalist tradition or venturing into New Age programs that are often trivial in their consequences, unable to support or to guide the transformation that is needed in its proper order of magnitude. We must recognize that the only effective program available is the program offered by the earth itself as our primary guide toward a viable human mode of being.

Both education and religion need to ground themselves within the story of the universe as we now understand this story through empirical knowledge. Within this functional cosmology we can overcome our alienation and begin the renewal of life on a sustainable basis. This story is a numinous revelatory story that could evoke the vision and the energy required to bring not only ourselves but the entire planet into a new order of magnificence.

Meanwhile, in the obscure regions of the human unconsciousness, where the primordial archetypal symbols function as ultimate controlling factors in human thought, emotion, and in practical decision making, a profound reorientation toward this integral human-earth relationship is gradually taking place. This archetypal journey must be experienced as the journey of each individual, since the entire universe has been involved in shaping our psyche as well as our physical being from that first awesome moment when the universe began. In the creation of a viable human, the universe reflects on and celebrates itself in conscious self-awareness, and finds a unique fulfillment.

# THE DEEP ECOLOGICAL MOVEMENT: SOME PHILOSOPHICAL ASPECTS

*Arne Naess*

Arne Naess is professor emeritus at the University of Oslo, Norway, where he was chairman of the philosophy department for many years. Naess coined the term and developed the basic concepts of "deep ecology" in 1972. Widely regarded as one of the leading scholars in Europe, he is the author of *Ecology, Community and Lifestyle* (English trans. 1989) and many books and papers on empirical linguistics, Spinoza, Gandhi, and ecosophy.

## 1. DEEP ECOLOGY ON THE DEFENSIVE

Increasing pressures for continued growth and development have placed the vast majority of environmental professionals on the defensive. By way of illustration:

The field-ecologist Ivar Mysterud, who both professionally and vigorously advocated deep ecological principles in the late 1960s, encountered considerable resistance. Colleagues at his university said he should keep to his science and not meddle in philosophical and political matters. He should resist the temptation to become a prominent "popularizer" through mass media exposure. Nevertheless, he persisted and influenced thousands of people (including myself).

Mysterud became a well-known professional "expert" at assessing the damage done when bears killed or maimed sheep and other domestic animals in Norway. According to the law, their owners are paid damages. And licensed hunters receive permission to shoot bears if their misdeeds become considerable.[1] Continued growth and development required that the sheep industry consolidate,

This essay originally appeared in *Philosophical Inquiry* 8, 1–2 (1986). Reprinted with permission.

and sheepowners became fewer, richer, and tended to live in cities. As a result of wage increases, they could not afford to hire shepherds to watch the flocks, so the sheep were left on their own even more than before. Continued growth also required moving sheep to what was traditionally considered "bear territory." In spite of this invasion, bear populations grew and troubles multiplied.

How did Mysterud react to these new problems? Did he set limits to the amount of human/sheep encroachment on bear territory? Did he attempt a direct application of his deep ecological perspective to these issues? Quite the contrary. He adopted what appeared to be a shallow wildlife management perspective, and defended the sheepowners: more money to compensate for losses, quicker compensation, and the immediate hiring of hunters who killed mostly "juvenile delinquent" bears accused of killing many sheep.

Protectors of big carnivores noted with concern the change of Mysterud's public "image"; had he really abandoned his former value priorities? Privately he insisted that he hadn't. But in public he tended to remain silent.

The reason for M.'s unexpected actions was not difficult to find: the force of economic growth was so strong that the laws protecting bears would be changed in a highly unfavorable direction if the sheepowners were not soon pacified by accepting some of their not unreasonable demands. After all, it did cost a lot of money to hire and equip people to locate a flock of sheep which had been harassed by a bear and, further, to prove the bear's guilt. And the bureaucratic procedures involved were time-consuming. M. had not changed his basic value priorities at all. Rather, he had adopted a purely defensive compromise. He stopped promoting his deep ecology philosophy publicly in order to retain credibility and standing among opponents of his principles and to retain his friendships with sheepowners.

And what is true of Mysterud is also true of thousands of other professional ecologists and environmentalists. These people often hold responsible positions in society where they might strengthen responsible environmental policy, but, given the exponential forces of growth, their publications, if any, are limited to narrowly professional and specialized concerns. Their writings are surely competent, but lack a deeper and more comprehensive perspective (although I admit that there are some brilliant exceptions to this).

If professional ecologists persist in voicing their value priorities, their jobs are often in danger, or they tend to lose influence and status among those who are in charge of overall policies.[2] Privately, they admit the necessity for deep and far-ranging changes, but they no longer speak out in public. As a result, people deeply concerned about ecology and the environment feel abandoned and even betrayed by the "experts" who work within the "establishment."

In ecological debates, many participants know a lot about particular conservation policies in particular places, and many others have strong views concerning fundamental philosophical questions of environmental ethics, but only a few have both qualities. When these people are silent, the loss is formidable.

For example, the complicated question concerning how industrial societies can increase energy production with the least undesirable consequences is largely a waste of time if this increase is pointless in relation to ultimate human ends. Thousands of experts hired by the government and other big institutions devote their time to this complicated problem, yet it is difficult for the public to find out or realize that many of these same experts consider the problem to be pointless and irrelevant. What these experts consider relevant are the problems of how to stabilize and eventually decrease consumption without losing genuine quality of life for humans. But they continue to work on the irrelevant problems assigned to them while, at the same time, failing to speak out, because the ultimate power is not in their hands.

## 2. A CALL TO SPEAK OUT

What I am arguing for is this: even those who completely subsume ecological policies under the narrow ends of human health and well-being cannot attain their modest aims, at least not fully, without being joined by the supporters of deep ecology. They need what these people have to contribute, and this will work in their favor more often than it will work against them. Those in charge of environmental policies, even if they are resource-oriented (and growth tolerating?) decision makers, will increasingly welcome, if only for tactical and not fundamental reasons, what deep ecology supporters have to say. Even though the more radical ethic may seem nonsensical or untenable to them, they know that its advocates are, in practice, doing conservation work that sooner or later must be done. They concur with the practice even though they operate from diverging theories. The time is ripe for professional ecologists to break their silence and express their deepest concerns more freely. A bolder advocacy of deep ecological concerns by those working within the shallow, resource-oriented environmental sphere is the best strategy for regaining some of the strength of this movement among the general public, thereby contributing, however modestly, to a turning of the tide.

What do I mean by saying that even the more modest aims of shallow environmentalism have a need for deep ecology? We can see this by considering the World Conservation Strategy—prepared by the International Union for the Conservation of Nature and Natural Resources (IUCN) in cooperation with the United Nations Environmental Programme (UNEP) and the World Wildlife Fund (WWF). The argument in this important document is thoroughly anthropocentric in the sense that all its recommendations are justified exclusively in terms of their effects upon human health and basic well-being.[3]

A more ecocentric environmental ethic is also recommended apparently for tactical reasons: "A new ethic, embracing plants and animals as well as people, is required for human societies to live in harmony with the natural world on which they depend for survival and well-being." But such an ethic would surely be more effective if it were acted upon by people who believe in its validity, rather than merely its usefulness. This, I think, will come to be understood more and more by those in charge of educational policies. Quite simply, it is indecent for a teacher to proclaim an ethic for tactical reasons only.

Furthermore, this point applies to all aspects of a world conservation strategy. Conservation strategies are more eagerly implemented by people who love what they are conserving, and who are convinced that what they love is intrinsically lovable. Such lovers will not want to hide their attitudes and values, rather they will increasingly give voice to them in public. They possess a genuine ethics of conservation, not merely a tactically useful instrument for human survival.

In short, environmental education campaigns can fortunately combine human-centered arguments with a practical environmental ethic based on either a deeper and more fundamental philosophic or religious perspective, and on a set of norms resting on intrinsic values. But the inherent strength of this overall position will be lost if those who work professionally on environmental problems do not freely give testimony to fundamental norms.

The above is hortatory in the positive etymological sense of that word. I seek "to urge, incite, instigate, encourage, cheer" (Latin: *hortari*). This may seem unacademic but I consider it justifiable because of an intimate relationship between hortatory sentences and basic philosophical views which I formulate in section 8. To trace what follows from fundamental norms and hypotheses is eminently philosophical.

## 3. WHAT IS DEEP ECOLOGY?

The phrase "deep ecology movement" has been used up to this point without trying to define it. One should not expect too much from definitions of movements; think, for example, of terms like "conservatism," "liberalism," or the "feminist movement." And there is no reason why supporters of movements should adhere exactly to the same definition, or to any definition, for that matter. It is the same with characterizations, criteria, or a set of proposed necessary conditions for application of the term or phrase. In what follows, a platform or key terms and phrases, agreed upon by George Sessions and myself, are tentatively proposed as basic to deep ecology.[4] More accurately, the sentences have a double function. They are meant to express important points which the great majority of supporters accept, implicitly or explicitly, at a high level of generality. Furthermore, they express a proposal to the effect that those who solidly reject one or more of these points should not be viewed as supporters of deep ecology. This might result because they are supporters of a shallow (or reform) environmental movement or rather they may simply dislike one or more of the eight points for semantical or other reasons. But they may well accept a different set of points which, to me, has roughly the same meaning, in which case I shall call them supporters of the deep ecology movement, but add that they *think* they disagree (maybe Henryk Skolimowski is an example of the latter). The eight points are:

1. The well-being and flourishing of human and non-human life on Earth have value in themselves (synonyms: intrinsic value, inherent worth). These values are independent of the usefulness of the non-human world for human purposes.
2. Richness and diversity of life forms contribute to the realization of these values and are also values in themselves.
3. Humans have no right to reduce this richness and diversity except to satisfy vital needs.
4. The flourishing of human life and cultures is compatible with a substantially smaller human population. The flourishing of non-human life *requires* a smaller human population.
5. Present human interference with the non-human world is excessive, and the situation is rapidly worsening.
6. Policies must therefore be changed. These policies affect basic economic, technological, and ideological structures. The resulting state of affairs will be deeply different from the present.
7. The ideological change will be mainly that of appreciating life quality (dwelling in situations of inherent value) rather than adhering to an increasingly higher standard of living. There will be a profound awareness of the difference between bigness and greatness.
8. Those who subscribe to the foregoing points have an obligation directly or indirectly to try to implement the necessary changes.

## Comments on the Eight Points of the Platform

RE (1): This formulation refers to the biosphere, or more professionally, to the ecosphere as a whole (this is also referred to as "ecocentrism"). This includes individuals, species, populations, habitat, as well as human and non-human cultures. Given our current knowledge of all-pervasive intimate relationships, this implies a fundamental concern and respect.

The term "life" is used here in a more comprehensive non-technical way also to refer to what biologists classify as "non-living": rivers (watersheds), landscapes, ecosystems. For supporters of deep ecology, slogans such as "let the river live" illustrate this broader usage so common in many cultures.

Inherent value, as used in (1), is common in deep ecology literature (e.g., "The presence of inherent value in a natural object is independent of any awareness, interest, or appreciation of it by any conscious being").[5]

RE (2): The so-called simple, lower, or primitive species of plants and animals contribute essentially to the richness and diversity of life. They have value in themselves and are not merely steps toward the so-called higher or rational life forms. The second principle presupposes that life itself, as a process over evolutionary time, implies an increase of diversity and richness.

Complexity, as referred to here, is different from complication. For example, urban life may be more complicated than life in a natural setting without being more complex in the sense of multifaceted quality.

RE (3): The term "vital need" is deliberately left vague to allow for considerable latitude in judgment. Differences in climate and related factors, together with differences in the structures of societies as they now exist, need to be taken into consideration.

RE (4): People in the materially richest countries cannot be expected to reduce their excessive interference with the non-human world overnight. The stabilization and reduction of the human population will take time. Hundreds of years! Interim strategies need to be developed. But in no way does this excuse the present complacency. The extreme seriousness of our current situation must first be realized. And the longer we wait to make the necessary changes, the more drastic will be the measures needed. Until deep changes are made, substantial decreases in richness and diversity are liable to occur: the rate of extinction of species will be ten to one hundred or more times greater than in any other short period of earth history.

RE (5): This formulation is mild. For a realistic assessment, see the annual reports of the Worldwatch Institute in Washington, D.C.

The slogan of "non-interference" does not imply that humans should not modify some ecosystems, as do other species. Humans have modified the earth over their entire history and will probably continue to do so. At issue is the *nature and extent* of such interference. The per capita destruction of wild (ancient) forests and other wild ecosystems has been excessive in rich countries; it is essential that the poor do not imitate the rich in this regard.

The fight to preserve and extend areas of wilderness and near-wilderness ("free Nature") should continue. The rationale for such preservation should focus mainly on the ecological functions of these areas (one such function: large wilderness areas are required in the biosphere for the continued evolutionary speciation of plants and animals). Most of the present designated wilderness areas and game reserves are not large enough to allow for such speciation.

RE (6): Economic growth as it is conceived of and implemented today by the industrial states is incompatible with points (1) through (5). There is only a faint resemblance between ideal sustainable forms of economic growth and the present policies of industrial societies.

Present ideology tends to value things because they are scarce and because they have a commodity value. There is prestige in vast consumption and waste (to mention only several relevant factors).

Whereas "self-determination," "local community," and "think globally, act locally," will remain key terms in the ecology of human societies, nevertheless the implementation of deep changes requires increasingly global action: Action across borders.

Governments in Third World countries are mostly uninterested in deep ecological issues. When institutions in the industrial societies try to promote ecological measures through Third World governments, practically nothing is accomplished (e.g., with problems of desertification). Given this situation, support for global action through non-governmental international organizations becomes increasingly important. Many of these organizations are able to act globally "from grassroots to grassroots" thus avoiding negative governmental interference.

Cultural diversity today requires advanced technology, that is, techniques that advance the basic goals of each culture. So-called soft, intermediate, and alternative technologies are steps in this direction.

RE (7): Some economists criticize the term "quality of life" because it is supposedly vague. But, on closer inspection, what they consider to be vague is actually the nonquantifiable nature of the term. One cannot quantify adequately what is important for the quality of life as discussed here, and there is no need to do so.

RE (8): There is ample room for different opinions about priorities: what should be done first; what next? What is the most urgent? What is clearly necessary to be done, as opposed to what is highly desirable but not absolutely pressing? The frontier of the environmental crisis is long and varied, and there is a place for everyone.

The above formulations of the eight points may be useful to many supporters of the deep ecology movement. But some will certainly feel that they are imperfect, even misleading. If they need to formulate in a few words what is basic to deep ecology, then they will propose an alternative set of sentences. I shall of course be glad to refer to them as alternatives. There ought to be a measure of diversity in what is considered basic and common.

Why should we call the movement "the deep ecological movement"?[6] There are at least six other designations which cover most of the same issues: "Ecological Resistance," used by John Rodman in important discussions; "The New Natural Philosophy" coined by Joseph Meeker; "Eco-philosophy," used by Sigmund Kvaloy and others to emphasize (1) a highly critical assessment of the industrial growth societies from a general ecological point of view, and (2) the ecology of the human species; "Green Philosophy and Politics" (while the term "green" is often used in Europe, in the United States "green" has a misleading association with the rather "blue" Green agricultural revolution); "Sustainable Earth Ethics," as used by G. Tyler Miller; and "Ecosophy" (ecowisdom), which is my own favorite term. Others could be mentioned as well.

And so, why use the adjective "deep"? This question will be easier to answer after the contrast is made between shallow and deep ecological concerns. "Deep ecology" is not a philosophy in any proper academic sense, nor is it institutionalized as a religion or an ideology. Rather, what happens is that various persons come together in campaigns and direct actions. They form a circle of friends supporting the same kind of lifestyle which others may think to be "simple," but which they themselves see as rich and many-sided. They agree on a vast array of political issues, although they may otherwise support different political parties. As in all social movements, slogans and rhetoric are indispensable for in-group coherence. They react together against the same threats in a predominantly nonviolent way. Perhaps the most influential participants are artists and writers who do not articulate their insights in terms of professional philosophy, expressing themselves rather in art or poetry. For these reasons, I use the term "movement" rather than "philosophy." But it is essential that fundamental attitudes and beliefs are involved as part of the motivation for action.

## 4. DEEP VERSUS SHALLOW ECOLOGY

A number of key terms and slogans from the environmental debate will clarify the contrast between the shallow and the deep ecology movements.[7]

### A. Pollution

Shallow Approach: Technology seeks to purify the air and water and to spread pollution more evenly. Laws limit permissible pollution. Polluting industries are preferably exported to developing countries.

Deep Approach: Pollution is evaluated from a biospheric point of view, not focusing exclusively on its effects on human health, but rather on life as a whole, including the life conditions of every species and system. The shallow reaction to acid rain, for example, is to tend to avoid action by demanding more research, and the attempt to find species of trees which will tolerate high acidity, etc. The deep approach concentrates on what is going on in the total ecosystem and calls for a high priority fight against the economic conditions and the technology responsible for producing the acid rain. The long-range concerns are one hundred years, at least.

The priority is to fight the deep causes of pollution, not merely the superficial, short-range effects. The Third and Fourth World countries cannot afford to pay the total costs of the war against pollution in their regions; consequently they require the assistance of the First and Second World countries. Exporting pollution is not only a crime against humanity, it is a crime against life in general.

### B. Resources

Shallow Approach: The emphasis is upon resources for humans, especially for the present generation in affluent societies. In this view, the resources of the earth belong to those who have the technology to exploit them. There is confidence that resources will not be depleted because, as they get rarer, a high market price will conserve them, and substitutes will be found through technological progress. Further, plants, animals, and natural objects are valuable only as resources for humans. If no human use is known, or seems likely ever to be found, it does not matter if they are destroyed.

Deep Approach: The concern here is with resources and habitats for all life-forms for their own sake. No natural object is conceived of solely as a resource. This leads, then, to a critical evaluation of human modes of production and consumption. The question arises: to what extent does an increase in production and consumption foster ultimate human values? To what extent does it satisfy vital needs, locally or globally? How can economic, legal, and educational institutions be changed to counteract destructive increases? How can resource use serve the quality of life rather than the economic standard of living as generally promoted by consumerism? From a deep perspective, there is an emphasis upon an ecosystem approach rather than the consideration merely of isolated life-forms or local situations. There is a long-range maximal perspective of time and place.

## C. Population

Shallow Approach: The threat of (human) "overpopulation" is seen mainly as a problem for developing countries. One condones or even applauds population increases in one's own country for short-sighted economic, military, or other reasons; an increase in the number of humans is considered as valuable in itself or as economically profitable. The issue of an "optimum population" for humans is discussed without reference to the question of an "optimum population" for other life-forms. The destruction of wild habitats caused by increasing human population is accepted as in inevitable evil, and drastic decreases of wildlife forms tend to be accepted insofar as species are not driven to extinction. Further, the social relations of animals are ignored. A long-term substantial reduction of the global human population is not seen to be a desirable goal. In addition, the right is claimed to defend one's borders against "illegal aliens," regardless of what the population pressures are elsewhere.

Deep Approach: It is recognized that excessive pressures on planetary life stem from the human population explosion. The pressure stemming from the industrial societies is a major factor, and population reduction must have the highest priority in those societies.

## D. Cultural Diversity and Appropriate Technology

Shallow Approach: Industrialization of the Western industrial type is held to be the goal of developing countries. The universal adoption of Western technology is held to be compatible with cultural diversity, together with the conservation of the positive elements (from a Western perspective) of present non-industrial societies. There is a low estimate of deep cultural differences in non-industrial societies which deviate significantly from contemporary Western standards.

Deep Approach: Protection of non-industrial cultures from invasion by industrial societies. The goals of the former should not be seen as promoting lifestyles similar to those in the rich countries. Deep cultural diversity is an analogue on the human level to the biological richness and diversity of life-forms. A high priority should be given to cultural anthropology in general education programs in industrial societies.

There should be limits on the impact of Western technology upon present existing non-industrial countries and the Fourth World should be defended against foreign domination. Political and economic policies should favor subcultures within industrial societies. Local, soft technologies should allow for a basic cultural assessment of any technical innovations, together with freely expressed criticism of so-called advanced technology when this has the potential to be culturally destructive.

## E. Land and Sea Ethics

Shallow Approach: Landscapes, ecosystems, rivers, and other whole entities of nature are conceptually cut into fragments, thus disregarding larger units and comprehensive gestalts. These fragments are regarded as the properties and resources of individuals, organizations or states. Conservation is argued in terms of "multiple use" and "cost/benefit analysis." The social costs and long-term global ecological costs of resource extraction and use are usually not considered. Wildlife management is conceived of as conserving nature for "future generations of humans." Soil erosion or the deterioration of ground water quality, for example, is noted as a human loss, but a strong belief in future technological progress makes deep changes seem unnecessary.

Deep Approach: The earth does not belong to humans. For example, the Norwegian landscapes, rivers, flora and fauna, and the neighboring sea are not the property of Norwegians. Similarly, the oil under the North Sea or anywhere else does not belong to any state or to humanity. And the "free nature" surrounding a local community does not belong to the local community.

Humans only inhabit the lands, using resources to satisfy vital needs. And if their non-vital needs come in conflict with the vital needs of nonhumans, then humans should defer to the latter. The ecological destruction now going on will not be cured by a technological fix. Current arrogant notions in industrial (and other) societies must be resisted.

## F. Education and the Scientific Enterprise

Shallow Approach: The degradation of the environment and resource depletion requires the training of more and more "experts" who can provide advice concerning how to continue combining economic growth with maintaining a healthy environment. We are likely to need an increasingly more dominating and manipulative technology to "manage the planet" when global economic growth makes further environmental degradation inevitable. The scientific enterprise must continue giving priority to the "hard sciences" (physics and chemistry). High educational standards with intense competition in the relevant "tough" areas of learning will be required.

Deep Approach: If sane ecological policies are adopted, then education should concentrate on an increased sensitivity to non-consumptive goods, and on such consumables where there is enough for all. Education should therefore counteract the excessive emphasis upon things with a price tag. There should be a shift in concentration from the "hard" to the "soft" sciences which stress the importance of the local and global cultures. The educational objective of the World Conservation Strategy ("building support for conservation") should be given a high priority, but within the deeper framework of respect for the biosphere.

In the future, there will be no shallow environmental movement if deep policies are increasingly adopted by governments, and thus no need for a special deep ecological social movement.

# 5. BUT WHY A "DEEP" ECOLOGY?

The decisive difference between a shallow and a deep ecology, in practice, concerns the willingness to question, and an appreciation of the importance of questioning, every economic and political policy in public. This questioning is both "deep" and public. It asks "why" insistently and consistently, taking nothing for granted!

Deep ecology can readily admit to the practical effectiveness of homocentric arguments:

> It is essential for conservation to be seen as central to human interests and aspirations. At the same time, people—from heads of state to the members of rural communities—will most readily be brought to demand conservation if they themselves recognize the contribution of conservation to the achievement of their needs as perceived by them, and the solution of their problems, as perceived by them.[8]

There are several dangers in arguing solely from the point of view of narrow human interests. Some policies based upon successful homocentric arguments turn out to violate or unduly compromise the objectives of deeper argumentation. Further, homocentric arguments tend to weaken the motivation to fight for necessary social change, together with the willingness to serve a great cause. In addition, the complicated arguments in human-centered conservation documents such as the World Conservation Strategy go beyond the time and ability of many people to assimilate and understand. They also tend to provoke interminable technical disagreements among experts. Special interest groups with narrow short-term exploitive objectives, which run counter to saner ecological policies, often exploit these disagreements and thereby stall the debate and steps toward effective action.

When arguing from deep ecological premises, most of the complicated proposed technological fixes need not be discussed at all. The relative merits of alternative technological proposals are pointless if our vital needs have already been met. A focus on vital issues activates mental energy and strengthens motivation. On the other hand, the shallow environmental approach, by focusing almost exclusively on the technical aspects of environmental problems, tends to make the public more passive and disinterested in the more crucial non-technical, lifestyle-related, environmental issues.

Writers within the deep ecology movement try to articulate the fundamental presuppositions underlying the dominant economic approach in terms of value priorities, philosophy, and religion. In the shallow movement, questioning and argumentation comes to a halt long before this. The deep ecology movement is therefore "the ecology movement which questions deeper." A realization of the deep changes which are required, as outlined in the deep ecology eight point platform (discussed in #3 above) makes us realize the necessity of "questioning everything."

The terms "egalitarianism," "homocentrism," "anthropocentrism," and "human chauvinism" are often used to characterize points of view on the shallow-deep spectrum. But these terms usually function as slogans which are often open to misinterpretation. They can properly imply that man is in some respects only a "plain citizen" (Aldo Leopold) of the planet on a par with all other species, but they are sometimes interpreted as denying that humans have any "extraordinary" traits, or that, in situations involving vital interests, humans have no overriding obligations towards their own kind. But this would be a mistake: they have!

In any social movement, rhetoric has an essential function in keeping members fighting together under the same banner. Rhetorical formulations also serve to provoke interest among outsiders. Of the many excellent slogans, one might mention "nature knows best," "small is beautiful," and "all things hang together." But sometimes one may safely say that nature does not always know best, that small is sometimes dreadful, and that fortunately things hang together sometimes only loosely, or not at all.

Only a minority of deep ecology supporters are academic philosophers, such as myself. And while deep ecology cannot be a finished philosophical system, this does not mean that its philosophers should not try to be as clear as possible. So a discussion of deep ecology as a derivational system may be of value to clarify the many important premise/conclusion relations.

# 6. DEEP ECOLOGY ILLUSTRATED
# AS A DERIVATIONAL SYSTEM

Underlying the eight tenets or principles presented in section 3, there are even more basic positions and norms which reside in philosophical systems and in various world religions. Schematically we may represent the total views logically implied in the deep ecology movement by streams of derivations from the most fundamental norms and descriptive assumptions (level 1) to the particular deci-sions in actual life situations (level 4).

The pyramidal model has some features in common with hypothetico-deductive systems. The main difference, however, is that some sentences at the top (= deepest) level are normative, and preferably are expressed by imperatives. This makes it possible to arrive at imperatives at the lowest derivational level: the crucial level in terms of decisions. Thus, there are "oughts" in our premises as well as in our conclusions. We never move from an "is" to an "ought," or vice versa. From a logical standpoint, this is decisive!

The above premise/conclusion structure (or diagram) of a total view must not be taken too seriously. It is not meant in any restrictive way to characterize creative thinking within the deep ecology movement. Creative thinking moves freely in any direction. But many of us with a professional background in science and analytical philosophy find such a diagram helpful.

As we dig deeper into the premises of our thinking, we eventually stop. Those premises we stop at are our ultimates. When we philosophize, we all stop at different places. But we all use premises which, for us, are ultimate. They belong to level 1 in the diagram. Some will use a sentence like "Every life form has intrinsic value" as an ultimate premise, and therefore place it at level

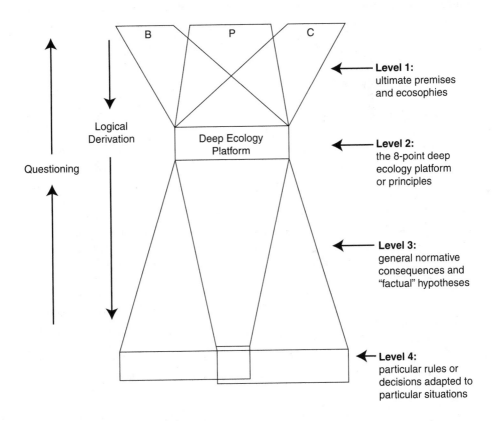

**Level 1:**
ultimate premises
and ecosophies

Logical
Derivation

Deep Ecology
Platform

**Level 2:**
the 8-point deep
ecology platform
or principles

Questioning

**Level 3:**
general normative
consequences and
"factual" hypotheses

**Level 4:**
particular rules or
decisions adapted to
particular situations

Examples of kinds of fundamental premises:

B = Buddhist
C = Christian
P = Philosophical (e.g., Spinozist or Whiteheadian)

1. Others try, as I do, to conceive of it as a conclusion based on a set of premises. For these people, this sentence does not belong to level 1. There will be different ecosophies corresponding to such differences.

Obviously, point 6 of the 8 point deep ecology tenets (see section 3) cannot belong to level 1 of the diagram. The statement "there must be new policies affecting basic economic structures" needs to be justified. If no logical justification is forthcoming, why not just assert instead that ecologically destructive "business as usual" economic policies should continue? In the diagram I have had ecosophies as ultimate premises in mind at level 1. None of the 8 points of the deep ecology principles belong at the ultimate level; they are derived as conclusions from premises at level 1.

Different supporters of the deep ecology movement may have different ultimates (level 1), but will nevertheless agree about level 2 (the 8 points). Level 4 will comprise concrete decisions in concrete situations which appear as conclusions from deliberations involving premises at levels 1 to 3. An important point: supporters of the deep ecology movement act from deep premises. They are motivated, in part, from a philosophical or religious position.

# 7. MULTIPLE ROOTS OF THE DEEP ECOLOGY PLATFORM

The deep ecology movement seriously questions the presuppositions of shallow argumentation. Even what counts as a rational decision is challenged, because what is "rational" is always defined in relation to specific aims and goals. If a decision is rational in relation to the lower level aims and goals of our pyramid, but not in relation to the highest level, then this decision should not be judged to be rational. This is an important point! If an environmentally oriented policy decision is not linked to intrinsic values or ultimates, then its rationality has yet to be determined. The deep ecology movement connects rationality with a set of philosophical or religious foundations. But one cannot expect the ultimate premises to constitute rational conclusions. There are no "deeper" premises available.

Deep ecological questioning thus reveals the fundamental normative orientations of differing positions. Shallow argumentation stops before reaching fundamentals, or it jumps from the ultimate to the particular; that is, from level 1 to level 4.

But it is not only normative claims that are at issue. Most (perhaps all) norms presuppose ideas about how the world functions. Typically the vast majority of assertions needed in normative systems are descriptive (or factual). This holds at all the levels.

As mentioned before, it does not follow that supporters of deep ecology must have identical beliefs about ultimate issues. They do have common attitudes about intrinsic values in nature, but these can, in turn (at a still deeper level), be derived from different, mutually incompatible sets of ultimate beliefs.

Thus, while a specific decision may be judged as rational from within the derivational system (if there is such) of shallow ecology, it might be judged as irrational from within the derivational system of deep ecology. Again, it should be emphasized that what is rational from within the deep ecology derivational pyramid does not require unanimity in ontology and fundamental ethics. Deep ecology as a conviction, with its subsequently derived practical recommendations, can follow from a number of more comprehensive world views, from differing ecosophies.

Those engaged in the deep ecology movement have so far revealed their philosophical or religious homes to be mainly in Christianity, Buddhism, Taoism, Baha'i, or in various philosophies. The top level of the derivational pyramid can, in such cases, be made up of normative and descriptive principles which belong to these religions and philosophies.

Since the late 1970s, numerous Christians in Europe and America, including some theologians, have actively taken part in the deep ecology movement. Their interpretations of the Bible, and their theological positions in general, have been reformed from what was, until recently, a crude dominating anthropocentric emphasis.

There is an intimate relationship between some forms of Buddhism and the deep ecology movement. The history of Buddhist thought and practice, especially the principles of non-violence, non-injury, and reverence for life, sometimes makes it easier for Buddhists to understand and appreciate deep ecology than it is for Christians, despite a (sometimes overlooked) blessedness which Jesus recommended in peace-making. I mention Taoism chiefly because there is some basis for calling John Muir a Taoist, for instance, and Baha'i because of Lawrence Arturo.

Ecosophies are not religions in the classical sense. They are better characterized as *general* philosophies, in the sense of total views, inspired in part by the science of ecology. At level 1, a traditional religion may enter the derivational pyramid through a set of normative and descriptive assumptions which would be characteristic of contemporary interpretations (hermeneutical efforts) of that religion.

Supporters of the deep ecology movement act in contemporary conflicts on the basis of their fundamental beliefs and attitudes. This gives them a particular strength and a joyful expectation or hope for a greener future. But, naturally, few of them are actively engaged in a systematic verbal articulation of where they stand.

# 8. ECOSOPHY T AS AN EXAMPLE OF A DEEP ECOLOGICAL DERIVATIONAL SYSTEM

I call the ecosophy I feel at home with "Ecosophy T." My main purpose in announcing that I feel at home with Ecosophy T is didactic and dialectic. I hope to get others to announce their philosophy. If they say they have none, I maintain that they have, but perhaps don't know their own views, or are too modest or inhibited to proclaim what they believe. Following Socrates, I want to provoke questioning until others know where they stand on basic matters of life and death. This is done using ecological issues, and also by using Ecosophy T as a foil. But Socrates pretended in debate that he knew nothing. My posture seems to be the opposite. I may seem to know everything and to derive it magically from a small set of hypotheses about the world. But both interpretations are misleading! Socrates did not consistently claim to know nothing, nor do I in my Ecosophy T pretend to have comprehensive knowledge. Socrates claimed to know, for instance, about the fallibility of human claims to have knowledge.

Ecosophy T has only one ultimate norm: "Self-realization!" I do not use this expression in any narrow, individualistic sense. I want to give it an expanded meaning based on the distinction between a large comprehensive Self and narrow egoistic self as conceived of in certain Eastern traditions of *atman*.[9] This large comprehensive Self (with a capital "S") embraces all the life forms on the planet (and elsewhere?) together with their individual selves (jivas). If I were to express this ultimate norm in a few words, I would say: "Maximize (long-range, universal) Self-realization!" Another more colloquial way to express this ultimate norm would be to say "Live and let live!" (referring to all of the life forms and natural processes on the planet). If I had to give up the term fearing its inevitable misunderstanding, I would use the term "universal symbiosis." "Maximize Self-realization!" could, of course, be misinterpreted in the direction of colossal ego trips. But "Maximize symbiosis!" could be misinterpreted in the opposite direction of eliminating individuality in favor of collectivity.

Viewed systematically, not individually, maximum Self-realization implies maximizing the manifestations of all life. So next I derive the second term, "Maximize (long-range, universal) diversity!" A corollary is that the higher the levels of Self-realization attained by any person, the more any further increase depends upon the Self-realization of others. Increased self-identity involves increased identification with others. "Altruism" is a natural consequence of this identification.

This leads to a hypothesis concerning an inescapable increase of identification with other beings when one's own self-realization increases. As a result, we increasingly see ourselves in other beings, and others see themselves in us. In this way, the self is extended and deepened as a natural process of the realization of its potentialities in others.

By universalizing the above, we can derive the norm, "Self-realization for every being!" From the norm, "Maximize diversity!" and a hypothesis that maximum diversity implies a maximum of symbiosis, we can derive the norm "Maximize symbiosis!" Further, we work for life conditions such that there is a minimum of coercion in the lives of others. And so on![10] The eight points of the deep ecology platform are derived in a fairly simple way.

A philosophy as a world view inevitably has implications for practical situations. Like other ecosophies, Ecosophy T therefore moves on, without apologies, to the concrete questions of lifestyles. These will obviously show great variation because of differences in hypotheses about the world in which each of us lives, and in the "factual" statements about the concrete situations in which we make decisions.

I shall limit myself to a discussion of a couple of areas in which my "style" of thinking and behaving seem somewhat strange to friends and others who know a little about my philosophy.

First, I have a somewhat extreme appreciation of diversity; a positive appreciation of the existence of styles and behavior which I personally detest

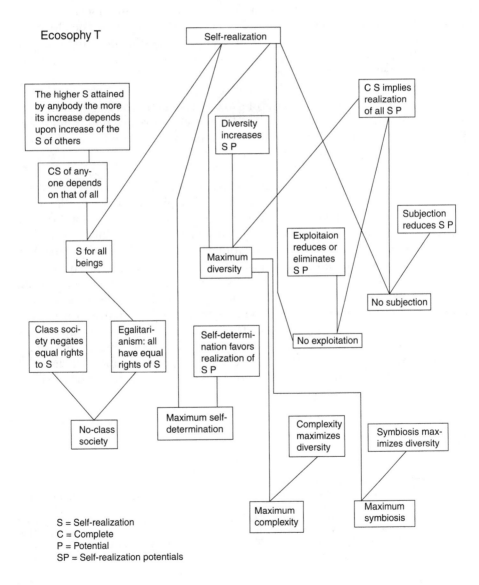

Ecosophy T

Self-realization

The higher S attained by anybody the more its increase depends upon increase of the S of others

C S implies realization of all S P

Diversity increases S P

CS of any-one depends on that of all

Subjection reduces S P

S for all beings

Maximum diversity

Exploitaion reduces or eliminates S P

No subjection

Class society negates equal rights to S

Egalitari-anism: all have equal rights of S

Self-determination favors realization of S P

No exploitation

No-class society

Maximum self-determination

Complexity maximizes diversity

Symbiosis maximizes diversity

Maximum complexity

Maximum symbiosis

S = Self-realization
C = Complete
P = Potential
SP = Self-realization potentials

or find nonsensical (but which are not clearly incompatible with symbiosis); an enthusiasm for the "mere" diversity of species, or varieties within a genus of plants or animals; I support, as the head of a philosophy department, doctrinal theses completely at odds with my own inclinations, with the requirement only that the authors are able to understand fairly adequately some basic features of the kind of philosophy I myself feel at home with; an appreciation of combinations of *seemingly* incompatible interests and behaviors, which makes for an increase of subcultures within industrial states and which might to some extent help future cultural diversity. So much for "diversity!"

Second, I have a somewhat extreme appreciation of what Kant calls "beautiful actions" (good actions based on inclination), in contrast with actions which are performed out of a sense of duty or obligation. The choice of the formulation "Self-realization!" is in part motivated by the belief that maturity in humans can be measured along a scale from selfishness to an increased realization of Self, that is, by broadening and deepening the self, rather than being measured by degrees of dutiful altruism. I see joyful sharing and caring as a natural process of growth in humans.

Third, I believe that multifaceted high-level Self-realization is more easily reached through a lifestyle which is "simple in means but rich in ends" rather than through the material standard of living of the average citizens of industrial states.

The simple formulations of the deep ecology platform and Ecosophy T are not meant primarily to be used among philosophers, but also in dialogues with the "experts." When I wrote to the "experts" and environmental professionals personally, asking whether they accept the eight points of the platform, many answered positively in relation to most or all of the points. And this includes top people in the ministries of oil and energy! Nearly all were willing to let their written answers be widely published. It is an open question, however, as to what extent they will try to influence their colleagues who use only shallow argumentation. But the main conclusion to be drawn is moderately encouraging: there are views of the human/nature relationship, widely accepted among established experts responsible for environmental decisions, which require a pervasive, substantial change of present policies in favor of our "living" planet, and these views are held not only on the basis of short-sighted human interests.

## NOTES

1. For more about interspecific community relationships, see Arne Naess, "Self-realization in Mixed Communities of Humans, Bears, Sheep, and Wolves," *Inquiry* 22 (1979): 321–41; Naess and Ivar Mysterud, "Philosophy of Wolf Policies I: General Principles and Preliminary Exploration of Selected Norms," *Conservation Biology* 1, 1 (1987): 22–34.

2. These problems are discussed further in Naess's keynote address to the second international Conference Conservation on Biology held at the University of Michigan in May 1985; published as "Intrinsic Value: Will the Defenders of Nature Please Rise?" *Conservation Biology* (1986): 504–15.

3. IUCN, *World Conservation Strategy: Living Resource Conservation for Sustainable Development* (Gland, Switzerland, 1980), section 13 ("Building Support for Conservation").

4. The deep ecology principles (or platform) were agreed upon during a camping trip in Death Valley, California (April, 1984) and first published in George Sessions (ed.), *Ecophilosophy VI* newsletter (May, 1984). They have subsequently appeared in a number of publications.

5. Tom Regan, "The Nature and Possibility of an Environmental Ethics," *Environmental Ethics* 3 (1981): 19–34, citation on p. 30.

6. I proposed the name "Deep, Long-Range Ecology Movement" in a lecture at the Third World Future Research conference in Bucharest in September 1972. A summary of that lecture ("The Shallow and the Deep, Long-Range Ecology Movement") was published in *Inquiry* 16 (1973): 95–100. Within the deep ecology movement it is fairly common to use the term "deep ecologist," whereas "shallow ecologist," I am glad to say, is rather uncommon. Both terms may be considered arrogant and slightly misleading. I prefer to use the awkward, but more egalitarian expression "supporter of the deep (or shallow) ecology movement," avoiding personification. Also, it is common to call deep ecology consistently anti-anthropocentric. This has led to misconceptions: see my "A Defense of the Deep Ecology Movement," *Environmental Ethics* 5 (1983).

7. The "shallow/deep" dichotomy is rough. Richard Sylvan has proposed a much more subtle classification; see his "A Critique of Deep Ecology," *Discussion Papers in Environmental Philosophy*, RSSS, Australian National University, No. 12 (1985).

8. *World Conservation Strategy*, section 13 (concluding paragraph).

9. The term *atman* is not taken in its absolutistic senses (not as a permanent indestructible "soul"). This makes it consistent with those Buddhist denials (the *avatman doctrine*) that the *atman* is to be taken in absolutist senses. Within the Christian tradition some theologians distinguish "ego" and "true self" in ways similar to these distinctions in Eastern religions. See the ecophilosophical interpretation of the gospel of Luke in Stephen Verney's *Onto the New Age* (Glasgow: Collins, 1976), pp. 33–41.

10. Many authors take some steps toward derivational structures, offering mild systematizations. The chapter "Environmental Ethics and Hope" (in G. Tyler Miller, *Living in the Environment*, 3rd ed. [Belmont, MA: Wadsworth, 1983]) is a valuable start, but the derivational relations are unclear. The logic and semantics of simple models of normative systems are briefly discussed in my "Notes on the Methodology of Normative Systems," *Methodology and Science* 10 (1977): 64–79. For a defense of the thesis that as soon as people assert anything at all, they assume a total view, implicitly involving an ontology, methodology, epistemology, and ethics, see my "Reflections about Total Views," *Philosophy and Phenomenological Research* 25 (1964–65): 16–29. The best and wittiest warning against taking systematizations too seriously is to be found in Søren Kierkegaard, *Concluding Unscientific Postscript.*

For criticism and defense of my fundamental norm ("Self-realization"), together with my answer, see *In Sceptical Wonder: Essays in Honor of Arne Naess* (Oslo: University Press, 1982). My main exposition of Ecosophy T was originally offered in the Norwegian work, *Okologi, samfunn og livsstil* (Oslo: University Press, 5th ed., 1976). Even there, the exposition is sketchy. (Editor's note: Naess's Norwegian book has been revised and reissued as Arne Naess (translated and edited by David Rothenberg), *Ecology, Community and Lifestyle* [Cambridge: Cambridge University Press, 1989].)

# DEMYSTIFYING THE CRITIQUES
# OF DEEP ECOLOGY

*Harold Glasser*

Harold Glasser is an assistant professor of environmental studies at Western Michigan University. He is general editor of the *Selected Works of Arne Naess,* an eleven volume collection to be published in 2001 and author of many articles on environmental values and policy.

## I. INTRODUCTION

Discussions of Naess's deep ecology approach to ecophilosophy (DEA), while widespread throughout the environmental philosophy literature, are often suffused with misconceptions and misunderstandings. Some of these are relatively trivial, but others, unfortunately, are quite serious. The more serious interpretation errors often result in misrepresentation and distortion of the DEA. When laden with these errors, the weight of even the most penetrating criticisms is diminished.

In this essay I offer an explication of the DEA, Naess's general, philosophical approach for promoting the development of ecologically responsible policies, lifestyles, and concrete decisions. The DEA must be distinguished from both the deep ecology movement and Naess's personal ecosophy (Ecosophy T). I will offer neither an analysis of the deep ecology movement, the loose group of individuals who endorse the deep ecology platform (but may not actually employ the DEA), nor an evaluation of Naess's personal ecosophy (Ecosophy T), formed by his particular implementation of the DEA. Although I regret adding yet another expression to this already confusing stew of terms,

An earlier version of this article appeared in Nina Witoszek (ed.), *Rethinking Deep Ecology* (Oslo: Center for Development and the Environment, University of Oslo, 1996), pp. 88–106. Although an extension and complete revision, this paper also draws liberally from Harold Glasser, "Deep Ecology Clarified: A Few Fallacies and Misconceptions," *The Trumpeter: Journal of Ecosophy* 12 (1995): 138–42.

I will use the expressions "deep ecology" and "DEA" as shorthand for my particular interpretation of Naess's deep ecology approach to ecophilosophy.

The purposes of this essay are threefold: first, to highlight several of the misconceptions, second, to suggest some possible reasons for their prevalence, and, third, to offer an alternative, hopefully clarifying, interpretation of the DEA. I am not suggesting that there are not valid explanations for the misconceptions and misunderstandings, quite the contrary. My primary purpose, however, is to show that while these errors of interpretation are unfortunate, they are frequently avoidable. By sincerely employing the *principle of charity* we can reap both a more insightful understanding of the DEA and a more profound understanding of its problems. And by seriously grappling with these issues, we spontaneously engage in the very process that Naess urges is essential to forging sound, mutually supportive, and pluralistic responses to the ecological crisis.

## II. MISCONCEPTIONS AND FALLACIES

People seem either to feel sympathy with the term "deep ecology" and what it conjures up (intrinsic value, a search for "root" causes, efforts to articulate one's total view, Naess and Sessions' "deep ecology platform," etc.) or they tend to feel antipathy towards the term.[1] A dynamic has emerged where supporters frequently neglect to give the DEA a critical eye, while foes often fail to offer it a receptive ear.

While some may argue about whether Naess should be considered as the "father" of deep ecology, he is undeniably the source for the interpretation of deep ecology I consider here. A host of expositions and criticisms of deep ecology (or elements of it) have been put forth.[2] Many of these contain careful and coherent analyses. Even some of these, however, are hindered by one or more forms of four weaknesses common to discussion of deep ecology.[3] My purpose in raising these "weaknesses" is not to criticize particular authors or engage in elaborate refutations, but rather to call attention to the dearth of accessible, thorough, and balanced treatments of Naess's DEA. This problem, regrettably, holds equally for its supporters and critics alike.

The first weakness consists of glossing over details when developing expository discussions. A common instance is the unfortunate use of the term "deep ecologists" for supporters or theoreticians of the deep ecology movement. While at first glance this seems like a relatively trivial use of shorthand, it has significant semantic implications, the most serious of which is that it implicitly suggests the existence of a counterpart to "deep ecologists," namely "shallow ecologists." This is an assertion Naess never intended to make and many times has counseled against. His use of the depth metaphor, following Kierkegaard, was directed at our level of problematizing.[4] Its purpose is to draw attention to the need for publicly questioning all of the practices, policies, values, and assumptions that propel the ecological crisis.

The term "deep" is not meant as a simple modifier to denote a particular branch of ecology. If we attempt to isolate "musical" from "chairs," the phrase "musical chairs" loses its meaning. Furthermore, the existence of a term "musical chairs" does not, by logical necessity, imply the existence of a similarly meaningful converse, "nonmusical chairs." Deep ecology is no more, or less, about *ecology* than economic science is about *science*. "Economic science," as a discipline and as commonly practiced, is not about making hypotheses regarding isolatable phenomena, developing controlled experiments to explain the phenomena, and confirming or refuting the original hypotheses through testing. Deep ecology is merely *informed* by our contemporary understanding of ecology as economic science is *informed* by our contemporary understanding of science. Just as it makes more sense to call a practitioner of economic science an "economist," it might, in many respects, be more apropos to refer to theoreticians or practitioners of the DEA as "deepists"; people who subscribe to, *inter alia*, a philosophy of publicly questioning all of the practices, policies, values, and assumptions that propel the ecological crisis. There is, however, no logical necessity that people subscribing to such a view of "deep questioning" will *necessarily* arrive at more ecologically sound policies, or personal practices, only a sincere *belief* that such reflection might help illuminate contradictions and conflicts. In any case, we cannot deny the obvious possibility of tainting those who do not subscribe to such a perspective with a derogatory sheen. While Naess, as an expert in semantics, cannot be absolved for the unfortunate semantic implications of his terminology, it behooves us to keep in mind his stated intention.

A second, quite common shortcoming results from drawing inferences from a scanty, selective, or dated reading of the literature or relying upon secondary or tertiary sources. The broad range, depth, volume, and evolutionary nature of Naess's philosophical writings demand a particularly labor intensive commitment to comprehensive analysis. Naess's publications on deep ecology[5] draw heavily from earlier work on empirical and applied semantics,[6] total views,[7] normative systems theory,[8] gestalt ontology,[9] scepticism,[10] democracy,[11] Spinoza,[12] Gandhi,[13] and the philosophy of science[14] as well as his lifelong love of the mountains.[15] The DEA represents a culmination and integration of Naess's life of philosophical inquiry fused with his political activism and love of nature. Naess's breadth, many unpublished papers, and tendency to revise, revise, and re-revise, however, make this weakness difficult to avoid even with a commitment to exhaustive analysis.

Examples of the "selective" reading weakness include assertions that deep ecology is inherently fascist, anti-humanist, or anti-feminist because the deep ecology platform and the vast majority of deep ecology writings fail to make explicit reference to denouncing fascism, oppression of women, and the general domination of some humans by other humans. To argue, however, that because Nazis were concerned with the welfare of animals and deep ecology theorists express concern for animals, then deep ecology has Fascist leanings, is simply guilt by association. Furthermore, the first statement of the deep ecology platform (DEP) makes explicit reference to the intrinsic value of *all* life, human and nonhuman alike and the second platform statement venerates the diversity of all life forms. While the particular means of achieving the goals of the DEP are left open, it seems fairly certain that any means which do not, at a minimum, honor and respect diversity, both human and non-human, will be in direct contradiction to these platform statements.

The deep ecology movement has as its primary focus the reversal of the ecological crisis. This focus, however, in no way precludes or undermines the overlapping concerns of the peace and social justice movements. Quite the contrary, it calls out for collaboration. The DEA is consistent with many possible interpretations of, and responses to, the roots and coevolutionary development of the ecological crisis.

The third, and perhaps most significant weakness, may result from a compounding of the two previous shortcomings, but is not necessarily derivative of them. It arises from incorporating critical misconceptions and methodological or logical fallacies. I will discuss five misconceptions and five methodological or logical fallacies.

The first misconception consists of equating ecocentrism with misanthropy. Ecocentrism refers to a valuation approach that characterizes ecosystems as wholes and defines value in terms of the well-being and flourishing of these ecosystems; it is an assertion of the intrinsic value of both whole ecosystems and every constituent. Misanthropy is literally the hatred of mankind. Clearly, the two terms are not equivalent. Furthermore, since humans are elements of ecosystems, it seems ludicrous to even suggest the conclusion that ecocentrism somehow implies misanthropy.

The second misconception consists of identifying "Self-realization!," the ultimate norm of Naess's personal Ecosophy T, or "biospherical egalitarianism in principle" as singular ultimate norms of deep ecology. Such conclusions, however, are precluded by Naess's repeated emphasis upon the existence of a wide plurality of ultimate norms that are consistent with the DEA.

The third misconception consists of attempting to isolate the DEP as the "heart" of deep ecology, treating the DEP *as* deep ecology, or dismissing the DEP as "non-distinctive." All three conclusions fail to acknowledge the gestalt nature of the DEA as a philosophical system, particularly its emphasis upon total views and its incorporation of normative systems theory.

The fourth misconception consists of pinpointing the genealogy of deep ecology in a stoic attempt to overcome the alienation resulting from the tragic loss of free nature. While this interpretation may be consistent with some supporters' views, it is inconsistent as *the* explanation, given the plurality of other viable explanations. For instance, Naess's repeated emphasis upon: the Pyrrhonian sceptics *ataraxia*,[16] the questioning of technological optimism, economic rationality, costs associated with biodiversity loss, etc., and the importance of learning how to live "rightly," with virtue and simplicity.

The fifth misconception consists of associating Naess's use of "depth" with a statement of an individual's character or the level of their willingness to reject anthropocentrism. While we cannot deny the unfortunate semantic implications of Naess's "depth metaphor," it is clear that his focus was directed at our willingness to raise and take seriously the search for fundamental causes and the consideration of radical responses.

The first methodological or logical fallacy consists of assuming that extension of care and concern to non-humans necessarily implies reducing care for humans. Do parents with nine children necessarily care less for each child than parents with two children?

The second methodological or logical fallacy consists of presuming that discussions of population reduction imply draconian measures. Why should one assume, however, that population cannot be reduced slowly, over centuries, and through democratic means?

The third methodological or logical fallacy consists of surmising that acceptance of "non-instrumental value" or "objective intrinsic value"[17] necessarily imply granting equal moral standing to all entities or the grading of intrinsic value. Naess uses the two terms, "inherent value" and "intrinsic value" interchangeably and in a non-technical sense that is ontological in origin. Efforts to preserve one species over another need not resort to moral arguments, as is often conjectured. Galvanized by an awareness of life's exigencies, these efforts do, however, necessitate accepting and evaluating a broad range of normative, sometimes conflicting criteria. Naess discusses walking in the mountains of Norway where he chooses to place his feet on the more common *Salix herbacea* rather than on the small, incredibly beautiful, and less common *Gentiana nivalis*.[18] His employment of *felt nearness* in no way implies a belief that either plant, or even Naess himself, has more right to live and blossom. Similarly, justification of this act does not necessitate any grading of intrinsic value.

The fourth methodological or logical fallacy consists of inferring that acceptance of intrinsic value necessitates acceptance of moral monism.[19] Again, I must emphasize that Naess's concept of "intrinsic" or "inherent" value is, however, ontological, not ethical or epistemological.[20] The DEA does not rest on a single moral principle, quite the contrary. It assumes both that there cannot exist perfect sets of principles to guide us through all moral dilemmas and that because each problem is context dependent and because a diverse array of viable alternatives usually exists, the existence of single "right" answers for every quandary is illusory.

The fifth methodological or logical fallacy consists of positing that because humans are a part of nature and because "nature knows best," then whatever humans do qualifies as natural, and hence morally unobjectionable. It is certainly true that humans are *a part* of nature and that this belief is consistent with the DEA. The assertion that "nature knows best," that it has an identifiable collective consciousness and some conception of "best" (utilitarian?, individualistic?, democratic?), however, is inconsistent with any theorizing on deep ecology I recognize. Furthermore, the DEP is quite specific about acknowledging that humans are also *apart* from nature, with unique obligations and special responsibilities for preserving the existing endowment of richness and diversity.

The final form of weakness is represented by the few disingenuous attempts at critical analyses that seek to set up deep ecology as a "straw man." These efforts, which often make use of the previously discussed examples, undertake to dismiss deep ecology and its contributions by demonstrating that it has fatal flaws. While some of the other weaknesses are more subtle, and thus insidious, these undertakings are usually "hatchet jobs" with transparent ulterior motives.

This brief review of the significant range of problems associated with the interpretation and exposition of deep ecology highlights the need for more accessible, thorough, and balanced treatments of Naess's DEA.[21] One possible explanation for the scarcity of such treatments rests in the difficulty of tracing Naess's own meanings. Following the zetetic sceptic tradition he eschews dogma by asserting that his own work is searching, "on the way"; it is necessarily fragmentary and ever amenable to improvements, modifications, and elaborations.[22] This evolutionary nature of the DEA along with Naess's tendency for liberal revisions, at times, however, make it truly difficult to pin down his interpretation of particular elements of the DEA.[23]

## III. ORIGINS OF THE MISUNDERSTANDINGS: SOME SPECULATION

Additional difficulty in tracing Naess's meanings may result from his philosophical commitment to vagueness as a device for encouraging widespread acceptance of the DEA.[24] "Methodological vagueness" is a sophisticated semantic device for facilitating the acceptance and agreement of statements and notions by emphasizing the positive aspect of ambiguity that is sometimes associated with a high level of generalization. Naess maintains that this device, by leaving open issues of an inconsequential nature, acts to facilitate communication and agreement on the consequential ones. One can readily appreciate the pragmatic merits of eliminating *irrelevant* and contentious details. However, one cannot help but also wonder if in the process of practical decision-making, *relevant* but contentious details might be glossed over. This may, unfortunately, lead some readers to mistake the benign motivation of Naess's methodological vagueness for simple rhetorical vagueness.

While Naess's sincerity, depth of intention, and intellectual integrity are beyond question, the propriety of emphasizing methodological vagueness raises some concern. Methodological vagueness has an antipodal side. As Naess himself has recognized, it can be employed to obfuscate conflicts, as with discussions that fail to point out the oxymoronic nature of the term "sustainable development."[25] As high level goals, sustainability and development (in the sense of access to health care, food, shelter, clean water, education, free nature, etc.) are admirable and certainly worthy of advocating, but coupled they tend to belie links to neoclassical welfare economics and the underlying conflicts between ecological sustainability and perpetual economic growth. Because the border separating issues of a consequential and an inconsequential nature is amorphous and subjective, as well as quite wide, the use of methodological vagueness can introduce a tension between parallel efforts orchestrated to isolate and clarify fundamental conflicts (deep questioning). There is a tradeoff between the benefits associated with positive expressions of ambiguity and the costs associated with its capacity for exploitation or potential for generating further confusion.

Failing to directly address "border" issues, like whether or not privileged ontological perceptions of nature exist, may only beg further speculation, confusion, and misconception. In order to fully reap the benefits of methodological vagueness, readers must be made aware that it has been employed both with deliberation and without attempt to obfuscate. The end result, otherwise, may be to turn away some possible supporters who eschew vagueness or, worse yet, wonder if the technique is being employed to avoid the asperities of deeper analyses.

Also central to the DEA is Naess's antidogmatism and insistence on radical pluralism. Naess, convinced that a successful response to the ecological crisis demands a diversity of perspectives, approaches, and lifestyles, imposes a minimum of external constraints while encouraging individuals to develop their own, critically thought out total views. By offering little guidance as to whether acceptance or rejection of particular norms or hypotheses is mandatory, this approach, however, also tends to stimulate further confusion over, and criticism of, the DEA. This leads some to believe that Naess makes it unnecessarily difficult for his readers to piece together a coherent picture of the DEA.

Questions arising from the use of methodological vagueness and the insistence upon radical pluralism are bound to generate frustration; they are an inevitable consequence of efforts to comprehend Naess's writings. Multiple readings of Naess's full range of work are necessary to absorb the depth and complexity of his contribution to environmental thought and policy. Readers will, however, be rewarded well for their journey.

## IV. THE DEEP ECOLOGY APPROACH: AN ATTEMPT AT CLARIFICATION

Presentations of the DEA as a systematic philosophical framework for supporting the development of ecologically inspired total views (as I attempt to do below) have been largely absent from other discussions of deep ecology.[26] The ontologically inspired DEA asks us to reconsider the notion of fundamental human/environment and spiritual/physical cleavages.[27] It weaves descriptive and prescriptive premises into a normative framework for melding a value system with a world view. A primary goal is to contribute towards arresting the ecological crisis by helping individuals to reason consistently from their ultimate beliefs.

The DEA should be viewed as a Gestalt where not only is the whole more than the sum of its parts, but the parts, as coevolving entities themselves, are more than *mere* parts. In my view the DEA consists of at least six coupled elements: (1) the unifying notion of total views, (2) the DEA as a normative-derivational system, the reasoning techniques, (3) "deep questioning" and (4) "loose derivation," (5) the adoption of ultimate premises that incorporate some form of "wide identification," and (6) the eight points of the deep ecology platform.

Naess argues that humans act as if we have systematic conceptual structures for relating to the world, *total views*, which integrate "our basic assumptions, our life philosophy, and our decisions in everyday life,"[28] whether or not we attempt to make such structures explicit. Contending that each individual's decisions regarding society and nature are guided by total views, Naess asserts that we should strive to clearly articulate them. While the process of articulating one's total view places significant demands upon the individual, Naess argues that we have no choice: "The essential idea is that, as humans, we are responsible in our actions as to motivations and premises relative to any question that can be asked of us."[29] The primary purpose of the DEA is to support individuals in carrying out this responsibility and thereby to facilitate democratic group decision-making.

Naess characterizes the DEA as a normative-derivational system. The systematization of the DEA is normative because it delimits the set of viable ultimate premises. The approach is derivational by virtue of being a logical systematization, where concrete consequences "follow" from premises and hypotheses. Naess's systematization is not derivational in the traditional hypothetico-deductive sense, but derivational only in his sense of being predicated upon an identifiable reasoning process.

The description of the DEA as a normative-derivational system is a pedagogical device for elucidating Naess's process of systematically reasoning from ultimate premises to concrete decisions or actions. The approach employs two reasoning techniques. "Loose derivation" is the synthetic process of building successively more particular norm-hypothesis chains by continually adding new, non-ultimate norms and hypotheses. It is "loose" in the sense that more precise norm and hypothesis statements do not follow *directly* from ultimate premises; they also depend upon the character of the additional, successively more precise norms and hypotheses. The inverse process, "deep questioning," allows norm conflicts to be examined and "deconstructed." It acts as a sort of touchstone to insure that derived consequences are consistent with each higher level norm and hypothesis. New information and insight may, at times, warrant the revision, or even the abandonment, of preceding norms and premises.

The DEA rests upon the assumption that certain, very basic premises are unproven or unprovable; the deep questioning process must eventually grind to a halt. Ultimate premises or ultimate norms are the unavoidable foundations upon which all theories or generalizations are built. Because of their generality, complexity, and inherent lack of preciseness, an almost infinite variety of ultimate norms exist. Naess argues that a wide variety of ultimate norms are consistent with the DEA.[30] As I understand Naess, the only restriction placed upon the set of ultimate norms to insure that they are deep ecological ultimate norms is that the DEP be derivable from them.[31] I use Naess's term, *wide identification,* to refer to this common element of deep ecological ultimate premises. It represents, at a minimum, an expansion of one's sphere of concern to include non-humans. It is often characterized by the perception that all life is interdependent; common goals bind all living beings to the life process. In its most expansive form, wide-identification is the perception that the interests of *all* entities in nature (both living and non-living, ecosystems and individuals) are our own. This is the notion of "Self-realization!" employed by Naess as the ultimate norm in Ecosophy T. While Naess may, in his own personal ecosophy, prefer this most expansive notion of identification, such a wide-reaching perspective is by no means necessary for acceptance of the DEP.

The DEP was worked out and agreed upon by Arne Naess and George Sessions in 1984.[32] It was intended to express "the most general and basic views" that supporters of the deep ecology movement (DEM) have in common.[33] Naess points out that the DEP was *not* supposed to indicate common views in concrete situations.[34] On the level of symbolizing a "call for ecological sustainability," the platform statements can be viewed as representing the general views held by supporters of the DEM. By outlining value priorities and calling for operational constraints on human behavior, the DEP acts as a filter, affecting the derivation process at all levels. On another level, however, the platform is, in some sense, a skeleton outline of a total view and thus represents *more* than basic and general views. For instance the DEP's first statement, representing a belief in the "intrinsic value" of all life, really constitutes an ultimate norm and should not be characterized as simply a "general and basic view."[35] It is relevant to point out that a less controversial first statement, simply advocating the importance of richness and diversity as non-use values, might facilitate a wider acceptance of the other seven platform statements.

Elements two through five of the DEA refer to the general process of reasoning from fundamentals to form total views. The DEP, as a synthetic product of this reasoning process, should be distinguished from it. Figure 1 outlines the *general process* of reasoning from fundamentals to arrive at concrete consequences, a primary element of the DEA. It explicitly leaves out the DEP because it represents a particular collection of norms and hypotheses obtained by engaging in the process. For a priori acceptance of the DEP violates the aim of the DEA; that is, it presupposes the existence of, and active engagement in, a similar process. What I am claiming is that the DEP should be distinguished from the reasoning process itself. In keeping with Naess's original suggestion, it must be put forth, and seen, as one possible precisation that helps to fill out the DEA by acting as a tentative set of guidelines for approaching the derivation of ecologically responsible concrete consequences.[36] Individuals should, however, scrutinize the DEP with the same deep questioning attitude that they would use to analyze any other collections of norms and premises. The goal of the DEA, after all, is to help individuals develop their own deep ecological total views.

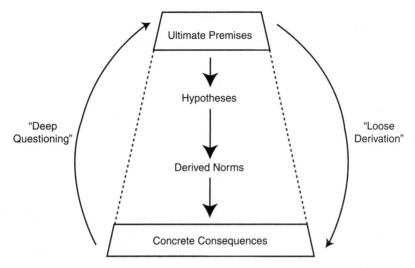

**Figure 1**  Process Diagram of the Normative Systems Aspects of the DEA.

I have deliberately not adhered to Naess's four-level systematization[37] in the process schema because the distinctions between levels 2 and 3, general principles and more or less general consequences derived from the DEP (i.e., lifestyles), are fuzzy. To reflect the vagaries of clearly distinguishing between and ordering these two categories, derived norms and hypotheses that fall under these headings are simply depicted between the dotted lines and the two clear boundaries, ultimate premises (our starting point) and concrete consequences (particular actions or decisions—our end point). My focus here is to draw attention to Naess's process for analyzing normative systems and to emphasize his strategy for helping us to construct our own total views. Naess enjoins us to make this effort to articulate our norms and hypotheses so that the entire decision-making process is readily discernible—to both ourselves and others.

The process figure also draws attention to two crucial techniques for developing a total view, *loose derivation* and *deep questioning*. Figure 1 is intended to show how the two techniques work in unison, enabling individuals to arrive at a variety of concrete rules and decisions that maintain consistency with ultimate premises. As has been mentioned before, a manifold of concrete consequences can follow from this built-in pluralism. The attraction of Naess's derivational structure is that it affords a substantial degree of flexibility. Such a perspective is compatible with a variety of, sometimes dissonant, ultimate norms, including those inspired by Christian stewardship, ecofeminism, creation myths, enlightened self-interest, Buddhism, Hinduism, scientific ecology, ecological integrity, social ecology, Taylor's "Respect for Nature,"[38] biospherical egalitarianism in principle, Wilson's Biophilia Hypothesis,[39] and Naess's "Self-realization!"[40] to name a few. It allows individuals to both maintain divergent fundamental premises and arrive at their own conclusions while still maintaining consistency with the goal of ecological harmony.

In closing, Naess reminds us that "we need to integrate life theory and life practice, clarify our value priorities, distinguish life quality from mere standard of life, and contribute in our own way to diminish unsustainability."[41] This quotation marries Naess's eudaemonic concern with his zetetic sceptic's response to the inherent vagueness of the sustainability notion. Here is where the logic of the DEA shines; society may never agree upon a satisfactory definition of "sustainability," but clear cases of unsustainability can be observed. These should be sought out and redressed while inquiry directed towards clarifying and elaborating the sustainability notion continues. The DEA is strongest on justification for a precautionary principle strategy that argues, in the face of ignorance and uncertainty, to preserve the existing heritage and thereby not foreclose options. It runs into some difficulty, however, in the areas of how to inculcate wide-identification, how to assess "vital needs," and how to inspire value priorities that insure environmental protection in the face of conflicting choices and opportunities.

The DEA's focus upon praxis (individual responsibility and action) separates it from more traditionally descriptive inquiries into ecophilosophy.[42] The significance of the DEA rests in its focus upon improving decision-making. The significance is not in the arguable *correctness* of the approach, but in its ability to help structure and focus our thinking about the environmental implications of individual and collective decisions. Naess's DEA has provided inspiration and one viable foundation for environmental protection, much work awaits us!

## NOTES

1. Nina Witoszek, the editor of the Center for Development and the Environment Occasional Papers Volume, argues that many people simply feel ambivalence towards deep ecology. While Witoszek may be correct, my experiences in lecturing on deep ecology and my awareness of the discussions in the literature, however, tend to strongly controvert this assertion.

2. The following discursive bibliographic entry attempts to highlight a few of the more salient expositions and criticisms of deep ecology.

   References focusing upon or highlighting exposition of deep ecology include: Jim Cheney, "Ecology, Community and Lifestyle: An Outline of an Ecosophy (a review of)," *Environmental Ethics* 13 (1991): 263–273; Bill Devall and George Sessions, *Deep Ecology: Living as if Nature Mattered* (Salt Lake City, Utah: Gibbs Smith Books, 1985); Arne Naess, *Ecology, Community, and Lifestyle: Outline of an Ecosophy,* translated and edited by David Rothenberg (Cambridge: Cambridge University Press, 1989a); Peter Reed, "Man Apart: An Alternative to the Self-Realization Approach," *Environmental Ethics* 11 (1989): 53–69; Peter Reed and David Rothenberg, ed., *Wisdom and the Open Air: The Norwegian Roots of Deep Ecology* (Minneapolis: University of Minnesota Press, 1993); David Rothenberg, "A Platform of Deep Ecology," *Environmentalist* 7 (1987): 185–190; David Rothenberg, *Is It Painful to Think: Conversations with Arne Naess* (Minneapolis: University of Minnesota Press, 1993); George Sessions, ed., *Deep Ecology for the Twenty-First Century* (Boston: Shambhala, 1995); Warwick Fox, *Toward a Transpersonal Ecology: Developing New Foundations for Environmentalism* (Boston and London: Shambhala, 1990).

   Books or articles where criticism or exposition of deep ecology figures centrally in the authors' arguments include: Robin Attfield, "Sylvan, Fox, and Deep Ecology: A View from the Continental Shelf," *Environmental Values* 2 (1993): 21–32; Steve Chase, ed., *Defending the Earth: A Dialog Between Murray Bookchin and Dave Foreman* (Boston: A Learning Alliance Book, 1991); Jim Cheney, "The Neo-Stoicism of Radical Environmentalism," *Environmental Ethics* 11 (1989): 293–325; Luc Ferry, *New Ecological Order* (Chicago: University of Chicago Press, 1995); William C. French, "Against Biospherical Egalitarianism," *Environmental Ethics* 17 (1995): 39–57; Harold Glasser, "Naess's Deep Ecology Approach and Environmental Policy," *Inquiry* 39 (1996): 157–187 [reprinted with a response by Arne Naess in *Philosophical Dialogues: Arne Naess and the Progress of Ecophilosophy,* ed. Nina Witoszek and Andrew Brennan (Lanham, Maryland: Rowman and Littlefield, 1999), 360–393]; Harold Glasser, "On Warwick Fox's Assessment of Deep Ecology," *Environmental Ethics* 19 (1997): 69–85; Al Gore, *Earth in the Balance: Ecology and the Human Spirit* (New York: Houghton Mifflin, 1992); Ramachandra Guha, "Radical Environmentalism and Wilderness Preservation: A Third World Critique," *Environmental Ethics* 11 (1989): 71–83; Martin W. Lewis, *Green Delusions: An Environmentalist Critique of Radical Environmentalism* (Durham: Duke University Press, 1992); Andrew McLaughlin, *Regarding Nature: Industrialism and Deep Ecology* (Albany: State University of New York, 1993); Freya Mathews, "Relating to Nature: Deep Ecology or Ecofeminism?" *The Trumpeter* 11 (1994): 159–166; Charles T. Rubin, *The Green Crusade: Rethinking the Roots of Environmentalism* (New York: Free Press, 1994); Richard A. Watson, "Misanthropy, Humanity, and the Eco-Warriors." *Environmental Ethics* 14 (1992): 95; Michael E. Zimmerman, "Rethinking the Heidegger–Deep Ecology Relationships," *Environmental Ethics* 15 (1993): 195–224; and Michael E. Zimmerman, *Contesting Earth's Future: Radical Ecology and Postmodernity* (Berkeley: University of California Press, 1994).

    Criticisms centered on deep ecology include: Murray Bookchin, "Social Ecology Versus 'Deep Ecology': A Challenge for the Ecology Movement," *Green Perspectives: Newsletter of the Green Program Project* (Summer 1987): 1–23; George Bradford, "How Deep Is Deep Ecology," *Fifth Estate* (Fall 1987): 5–30; William Grey, "A Critique of Deep Ecology," *Journal of Applied Philosophy* 3 (1986): 211–216; Ariel Salleh, "The Ecofeminism/Deep Ecology Debate," *Environmental Ethics* 14 (1992): 195–216; Ariel Salleh, "Class, Race, and Gender Discourse in the Ecofeminism/Deep Ecology Debate," *Environmental Ethics* 15 (1993): 225–244; Henryk Skolimowski, "Eco-Philosophy and Deep Ecology," *The Ecologist* 18 (1988): 124–127; Richard Sylvan (formerly Routley), "A Critique of Deep Ecology (Part I)," *Radical Philosophy* 40 (1985): 2–12; Richard Sylvan, "A Critique of Deep Ecology (Part II)," *Radical Philosophy* 41 (1985): 10–22; Richard Sylvan, "A Critique of (Wild) Western Deep Ecology: A Response to Warwick Fox's Response to an Earlier Critique," unpublished manuscript (1990): 57 pages; Richard A. Watson, "A Critique of Anti-Anthropocentric Biocentrism," *Environmental Ethics* 5 (1983): 245–256; Richard A. Watson, "Misanthropy, Humanity, and the Eco-Warriors," *Environmental Ethics* 14 (1992): 95. The most exhaustive compilation of criticisms of deep ecology that I am aware of appears in Fox, 1990, pp. 45–50.

3.   This explication of "weaknesses" common to discussions of deep ecology draws from the references cited in note 2.

4.   For a discussion of Naess's use of the "depth metaphor," see Harold Glasser, "The Deep Ecology Approach and Environmental Policy," *Inquiry* (1996).

5.   Naess has nearly 100 articles on deep ecology, in English alone (numerous Norwegian publications also exist). Close to one-half of the English articles are still unpublished.

6.   See Arne Naess, *Interpretation and Preciseness: A Contribution to the Theory of Communicative Action* (Oslo: Jacob Dybwad, 1953) and Arne Naess, *Communication and Argument: Elements of Applied Semantics,* translated by Alastair Hannay (Oslo: Universitetsforlaget, 1981). These books will be included as volumes II and VII, respectively, of the forthcoming *Selected Works of Arne Naess,* revised and edited by Harold Glasser (Dordrecht: Kluwer, 1998).

7.   See Arne Naess, "Reflections About Total Views," *Philosophy and Phenomenological Research* 25 (1964): 16–29.

8.   See Arne Naess, "Notes on the Methodology of Normative Systems," *Methodology and Science* 10 (1977): 64–79.

9.   See Arne Naess, "The World of Concrete Contents," *Inquiry* 28 (1985): 417–428, and Arne Naess, "Ecosophy and Gestalt Ontology," *The Trumpeter Journal of Ecosophy* 6 (1989b): 134–137, reprinted in Sessions, 1995, pp. 240–245.

10. See Arne Naess, *Scepticism* (London and New York: Humanities Press, 1968); to be included as volume III of the forthcoming *Selected Works of Arne Naess*, revised and edited by Harold Glasser (Dordrecht: Kluwer, 2001).

11. Arne Naess, "The Function of Ideological Convictions," in *Tensions That Cause Wars (Common statement and individual papers by a group of social scientists brought together by UNESCO)*, ed. H. Cantril, pp. 257–298 (Urbana: University of Illinois Press, 1950); Arne Naess, "Appendix I: The UNESCO Questionnaire on Ideological Conflicts Concerning Democracy," in *Democracy in a World of Tensions*, ed. Richard McKeon with the assistance of Stein Rokkan, pp. 513–521 (Chicago: University of Chicago Press, 1951); Arne Naess, Jens Christophersen, and Kjell Kvalø, *Democracy, Ideology, and Objectivity: Studies in the Semantics and Cognitive Analysis of Ideological Controversy* (Oslo: Universitetsforlaget, 1956); Arne Naess and Stein Rokkan, "Analytical Survey of Agreements and Disagreements," in *Democracy in a World of Tensions*, ed. Richard McKeon and with the assistance of Stein Rokkan, pp. 447–512 (Chicago: University of Chicago Press, 1951).

12. See Arne Naess, *Freedom Emotion and Self-Subsistence: The Structure of a Central Part of Spinoza's Ethics* (Oslo: Universitetsforlaget, 1975); to be included as volume VII of the forthcoming *Selected Works of Arne Naess*, revised and edited by Harold Glasser (Dordrecht: Kluwer, 1998); Arne Naess, "Spinoza and Ecology," *Philosophia* 7 (1977): 45–54; and Arne Naess, "Spinoza and Attitudes Towards Nature," unpublished manuscript (1990).

13. See Johan Galtung and Arne Naess, *Gandhis Politiske Etikk (Gandhi's Political Ethics)*, 2nd edition, 1968 (Oslo: Johan Grundt Tanum, 1955); Arne Naess, *Gandhi and the Nuclear Age*, translated by Alastair Hannay (Totowa, New Jersey: Rowman, 1965b); Arne Naess, "Can Violence Lead to Non-Violence: Gandhi's Point of View," in *Gandhi India and the World: An International Symposium*, ed. Sibnarayan Ray, pp. 287–299 (Philadelphia: Temple University Press, 1970d); Arne Naess, *Gandhi and Group Conflict: An Exploration of Satyagraha* (Oslo: Universitetsforlaget, 1974); to be included as volume VI of the forthcoming *Selected Works of Arne Naess*, revised and edited by Harold Glasser (Dordrecht: Kluwer, 1998); and Arne Naess, "Nonviolent Verbal Communication. The Gandhian Approach," unpublished manuscript (1993a): 9 pages.

14. See Arne Naess, *The Pluralist and Possibilist Aspect of the Scientific Enterprise* (Oslo: Universitetsforlaget, 1972); to be included as volume V of the forthcoming *Selected Works of Arne Naess*, revised and edited by Harold Glasser (Dordrecht: Kluwer, 1998). Two important earlier works, previously unavailable in translation, have been recently translated into English by Ingemund Gullvåg; see Naess, *Erkenntnis und Wissenschaftliches Verhalten (Science as Behavior)* (Oslo: Norwegian Academy of Sciences, Inaugural Dissertation, 1936), and Naess, *Hvilken Verde er den Virkelige? (Which World Is the Real One?)*, Vol. 37, Filosofiske Problemer (Oslo: Universitetsforlaget, 1969). These books will be included as volumes I and IV, respectively, of the forthcoming *Selected Works of Arne Naess*, revised and edited by Harold Glasser (Dordrecht: Kluwer, 1998).

15. See Arne Naess, "Modesty and the Conquest of Mountains," in *The Mountain Spirit*, ed. Michael C. Tobias and H. Drasdo (New York: The Overlook Press, 1979), pp. 13–16; Arne Naess, "Tvergastein: An Example of Place," unpublished manuscript (1992): 13 pages. In a "Letter to the King of Nepal," in *The Autobiography of a Shipping Man*, ed. Erling D. Naess (author), pp. 252–253 (Oslo: Seatrade Publications, 1971), Arne Naess requests that the King consecrate some of the Himalayan Mountains and make them off limits to climbing; and Arne Naess and Johan Brun (Bilder), *Det Gode Lange Livs Far: Hallingskarvet sett fra Tvergastein* (Oslo: N.W. Damm and Son, 1995).

    Additional references to Naess's literary activity on mountaineering are compiled in Arne Naess, "How My Philosophy Seemed to Develop," in *Philosophers on Their Own Work*, ed. Andre Mercier and Maja Svilar (Bern: Peter Lang, 1983), pp. 267–268.

16. *Ataraxia* is the absence of fanaticism concerning matters that cannot be proved and the tranquillity of mind that follows from such an acknowledgment.

17. For an instructive characterization of three different forms of "intrinsic value," see J. O'Neil, "The Varieties of Intrinsic Value," *The Monist* 75 (1992): 119–137. O'Neil makes an important distinction between the value that can be associated with objects that are ends in themselves (non-instrumental) and the value that an object itself possesses *independently* of the valuations of valuers (objective). He alerts us to the relative independence between meta-ethical commitments and ethical ones.

18. Naess discusses this point in "Intuition, Intrinsic Value and Deep Ecology: Arne Naess Replies," *The Ecologist* 14 (1984): 202.

19. This point is addressed in greater detail in Glasser, "Naess's Deep Ecology Approach and Environmental Policy."

20. I believe Naess views the concept of "valuing" as being dependent upon human consciousness, but would argue that some entities have instrumental value, that these entities may also have attributes independent from instrumental value, and that some of these attributes may even be independent from our ability to ascribe value.

21. It was only in 1995 that the first anthologies devoted to deep ecology theoreticians' and supporters' work appeared: George Sessions, ed., *Deep Ecology for the Twenty-First Century* (Boston: Shambhala, 1995), and Alan Drengson and Yuichi Inoue, ed., *The Deep Ecology Movement: An Introductory Anthology* (Berkeley, California: North Atlantic Books, 1995). Even these anthologies, regrettably, carry forth several of the aforementioned weaknesses.

22. Arne Naess, "How My Philosophy Seemed to Develop," in *Philosophers on Their Own Work*, ed. Andre Mercier and Maja Svilar, pp. 209–226 (Bern: Peter Lang, 1983).

23. Recent confusion over the most current and up-to-date version of the DEP and its elaborations testify to this matter.

24. Naess, 1989a, pp. 42–43.

25. See Arne Naess, "Sustainable Development and Deep Ecology," in *Ethics of Environment and Development: Global Challenge, International Response*, ed. R. J. Engel and J. G. Engel, pp. 87–96 (Tucson: University of Arizona Press, 1990a), and Arne Naess, "Sustainability! The Integral Approach," in *Conservation of Biodiversity for Sustainable Development*, ed. O. T. Sandlund, K. Hindar, and A. H. D. Brown, pp. 303–310 (Oslo: Scandinavian University Press, 1992a).

26. See the interpretations of deep ecology presented in: Sessions, 1995; Fox, 1990; Zimmerman, 1994; and Manes, 1990, pp. 139–150. See also Chase, 1991, for a chronicle of Bookchin and Foreman's debate over the meanings and distinctions between *deep ecology* and *social ecology*. Both Manes and Foreman fail to present a complete and coherent picture of the DEA. The misdirected criticism of the DEA, from Bookchin, Ferry, Gore, and many others, may originate, at least in part, from this absence of thoroughness and clarity.

27. Arne Naess, "From Ecology to Ecosophy, From Science to Wisdom," unpublished manuscript (1987): 2.

28. Arne Naess, "The Basics of Deep Ecology," *Resurgence* 126 (1988): 6.

29. Naess, 1989a, p. 38.

30. Arne Naess, "The Deep Ecology Movement: Some Philosophical Aspects," *Philosophical Inquiry* 8 (1986): 10–31.

31. This discussion was inspired, in part, by Naess's response to a question on the role of wide-identification in acceptance of the DEP (personal communication, 5/4/94).

32. Devall and Sessions, 1985, p. 69.

33. Naess, 1989a, p. 28.

34. Naess, 1989a, p. 28.

35. I made this point in an earlier, unpublished manuscript: Harold Glasser, "The Distinctiveness of the Deep Ecology Approach to Ecophilosophy" (1991): 29 pages.

36. Naess has continually emphasized (cf. Naess, 1989a, p. 28) that the DEP is only one of a variety of such formulations that are necessary to account for individual and cultural differences. It is interesting to ask if the DEP, as formulated, represents the most general of such possible formulations.

37. Naess, 1986, p. 23.

38. Paul W. Taylor, *Respect for Nature: A Theory of Environmental Ethics* (Princeton, New Jersey: Princeton University Press, 1986).

39. See E. O. Wilson, *Biophilia* (Cambridge, Massachusetts: Harvard University Press, 1984), and Stephen R. Kellert and E. O. Wilson, ed., *The Biophilia Hypothesis* (Washington, D.C.: Island Press, 1993).

40. See Arne Naess, "A Place of Joy in a World of Fact," *The North American Review* (Summer 1973b): 53–57, reprinted in Sessions, 1995, pp. 249–258; Naess, "Self-Realization: An Ecological Approach to Being in the World" (Keith Roby Memorial Lecture, March 12, 1986a), reprinted in Sessions, 1995, pp. 225–239; and Naess, 1989a.

41. Naess, 1992a, p. 303.

42. Naess, 1989a, pp. 36–38.

# THE DEEP ECOLOGY–ECOFEMINISM DEBATE AND ITS PARALLELS

*Warwick Fox*

Warwick Fox is senior lecturer in philosophy at the Centre for Professional Ethics, University of Central Lancashire. He is the author of *Toward a Transpersonal Ecology* (1995) and *The New Ethics* (forthcoming as this book goes to print), and the editor of *Ethics and the Built Environment* (2000).

## DEEP ECOLOGY'S ECOCENTRIC EGALITARIANISM

The question of the relative merits of deep ecology and ecofeminism has recently received considerable attention, primarily from an ecofeminist perspective. This question has an obvious significance to anyone concerned with ecophilosophy and ecopolitics since it contrasts two of the most philosophically and socially influential approaches that have developed in response to ecological concerns. For deep ecologists in particular, the ecofeminist critique of deep ecology is of interest for at least two reasons in addition to the direct challenge that it presents to deep ecological theorizing. First, as I argue throughout this paper, the same criticism that can be made of simplistic forms of ecofeminism can be applied with equal force to critiques of deep ecology that proceed from simplistic versions of a broad range of social and political perspectives—the "parallels" of my title. Second, addressing the ecofeminist critique of deep ecology provides an opportunity to further elucidate the nature of deep ecology's concern with anthropocentrism.

Before examining the ecofeminist critique of deep ecology, which centers on deep ecology's negative or critical focus on anthropocentrism, it is important to outline deep ecology's positive or constructive focus. Deep ecology is concerned with encouraging an egalitarian attitude on the part of humans

This essay originally appeared (in a somewhat longer version) in *Environmental Ethics* 11, 1 (Spring 1989): 5–25. Reprinted with permission.

not only toward all *members* of the ecosphere, but even toward all identifiable *entities* or *forms* in the ecosphere. Thus, this attitude is intended to extend, for example, to such entities (or forms) as rivers, landscapes, and even species and social systems considered in their own right. If deep ecologists sometimes write as if they consider these entities to be living entities, they do so on the basis of an extremely broad sense of the term *life*—a sense as broad as that implied in such expressions as "Let the river live!" It is ultimately of little consequence to deep ecologists, however, whether one wishes to consider the kind of egalitarianism they advocate as one that extends only toward living entities (in this extremely broad sense) or as one that extends toward both living and nonliving entities. Either way, the kind of egalitarian attitude they advocate is simply meant to indicate an attitude that, within obvious kinds of practical limits, allows all entities (including humans) *the freedom to unfold in their own way unhindered by the various forms of human domination.*

There are, of course, all sorts of problems involved in defining such things as how far these practical limits should extend or, in many cases, even where one entity ends and another begins. But, against this, it must be remembered that deep ecologists are not *intending* to advocate a specific set of guidelines for action; they are only intending to advocate a *general orientation.* Deep ecologists not only accept but welcome cultural diversity when it comes to effecting the specifics of this general orientation. After all, "the freedom to unfold in their own way unhindered by the various forms of human domination" applies to the unfolding of human cultures too. As Arne Naess puts it, where we draw the limit between justifiable and unjustifiable interference with respect to this general orientation "is a question that must be related to local, regional, and national particularities. Even then a certain area of disagreement must be taken as normal."[1] For deep ecologists, the only overriding consideration is that such limits should always be worked out *in the light of* the general orientation they advocate. Naess captures the sense of this general orientation while also conveying a sense of the cultural (and personal) diversity it allows for: "A rich variety of acceptable motives can be formulated for being *more reluctant* to injure or kill a living being of kind A than a being of kind B. The cultural setting is different for each being in each culture."[2] It is this general attitude of being reluctant, *prima facie*, to interfere with the unfolding of A *or* B—indeed, to desire that both should flourish—that characterizes the general orientation that is advocated by deep ecologists.

Deep ecologists have generally referred to this general orientation or attitude as one of "biospherical egalitarianism" or, more often (in order to suggest the intended comparison with an anthropo*centric* perspective more directly), "biocentric egalitarianism." However, because the prefix *bio-* refers, etymologically, to life or living organisms, it has sometimes been assumed that deep ecology's concerns *are* restricted to entities that are (in some sense) biologically alive. To correct this impression, Arne Naess and George Sessions have, in line with my preceding remarks, often pointed out that their sense of the term *life* is so broad, that it takes in "individuals, species, populations, habitat, as well as human and nonhuman cultures."[3] To avoid the possibility of confusion, however, I prefer to describe the kind of egalitarian attitude subscribed to by deep ecologists as *ecocentric* rather than *biocentric*. While there seems to be little reason for choosing between these terms on the basis of their ecological connotations, there are other grounds for preferring the term *ecocentric* to describe the kind of egalitarianism advocated by deep ecologists.[4] First, the term *ecocentric*, which etymologically means *oikos-*, home, or, by implication, Earth-centered, is more immediately informative than the term *biocentric*, which etymologically means life-centered and so requires an appended explanation of the broad sense in which the term *life* should be understood. Second, the term *ecocentric* seems closer to the spirit of deep ecology than the term *biocentric*, because, notwithstanding their broad usage of the term *life*, the motivation of deep ecologists depends more upon a profound sense that the Earth or ecosphere is *home* than it does upon a sense that the Earth or ecosphere is necessarily alive (you don't have to subscribe to some ecological form of *hylozoism* to be a supporter of deep ecology).

In accordance with this extremely broad, ecocentric egalitarianism, supporters of deep ecology hold that their concerns well and truly subsume the concerns of those movements that have restricted their focus to the attainment of a more egalitarian *human* society. Deep ecologists, in other words, consider their concerns to subsume the egalitarian concerns associated, for example, with feminism (as distinct from *eco*feminism), Marxism, anti-racism, and anti-imperialism.[5] In the eyes of deep ecologists, the emergence of a distinct *eco*feminism, a distinct "green" socialism, and so on, are—at least in their best forms—attempts by feminists, Marxists-cum-socialists, and so on, to redress the human-centeredness of their respective perspectives.[6] Needless to say, deep ecologists welcome these developments and they recognize that ecofeminism, green socialism, and so on have their own distinctive theoretical flavors and emphases because of the different theoretical histories that inform them. Nevertheless, they see no *essential* disagreement between deep ecology and these perspectives, *providing* that the latter are genuinely able to overcome their anthropocentric legacies.

## THE ECOFEMINIST CRITIQUE OF DEEP ECOLOGY

With respect to ecofeminism and deep ecology in particular, many observers agree that the two perspectives have much in common—notwithstanding their different theoretical histories.[7] However, some ecofeminist writers have begun to perceive a significant tension between their perspective and that of deep ecology. In an evenhanded examination of ecofeminist criticisms of deep ecology, Michael Zimmerman has presented what is probably the clearest formulation of what I take to be the essential ecofeminist charge against deep ecology: "Feminist critics of deep ecology assert that [deep ecology] speaks of a gender-neutral 'anthropocentrism' [i.e., human-centeredness] as the root of the domination of nature, when in fact *androcentrism* [i.e., male-centeredness] is the real root."[8] There seems to be wide support for the view that this represents the essential ecofeminist criticism of deep ecology. For example, one of the main criticisms made by Janet Biehl in her critique of deep ecology is that, "For ecofeminists the concept of anthropocentrism is profoundly, even "deeply" problematical. . . . By not excluding women from anthropocentrism, deep ecologists implicitly condemn women for being as anthropocentric as they condemn men for being—that is, for presuming to be above nature, for mastering it." Marti Kheel also notes at the outset of her critique of deep ecology that deep ecologists are concerned to "challenge the anthropocentric world view" whereas for ecofeminists "it is the androcentric world view that is the focal point of the needed shift." Likewise, the first difference in emphasis that Charlene Spretnak refers to in her comparison of deep ecology and ecofeminism is that of anthropocentrism versus androcentrism.[9]

Jim Cheney has claimed, nevertheless, in response to an earlier version of this paper, that it is wrong to regard Zimmerman's formulation as representing the essential ecofeminist charge against deep ecology. For Cheney, "The 'essential' [ecofeminist] charge is not that deep ecologists focus on *anthropo*centrism whereas the problem is really with *andro*centrism; rather, the central concern is . . . that deep ecology is *itself* in some sense androcentric."[10] In comparison to what I take to be the essential ecofeminist charge against deep ecology (as formulated concisely by Zimmerman), Cheney's formulation of the essential ecofeminist charge seems to represent a significant (if somewhat confusing) concession to deep ecology, since it suggests that ecofeminists are not overly concerned about deep ecologists' critical focus on anthropocentrism so long as deep ecologists do not formulate their critique of anthropocentrism in a way that is "itself in some sense androcentric." But whether Cheney's formulation represents a significant concession to deep ecology or not, my response to his charge is simple. The charge that I propose to address (as taken from Zimmerman's analysis) is clear-cut and serious—deep ecologists cannot deny that their *negative* focus is concerned, first and foremost, with anthropocentrism and ecofeminists cannot deny that their *negative* focus is concerned, first and foremost, with androcentrism. In contrast, the best that can be said about Cheney's claim that deep ecology is androcentric in its very formulation is that such a claim is entirely contentious.[11] Cheney's own recent attempt in *Environmental Ethics* to establish this claim is essentially based upon a misinterpretation of deep ecology as resting upon a "rights-based foundation."[12] Referring to a brief paper of my own, Cheney even acknowledges in his paper (albeit in a footnote) that if (as Fox claims) deep ecology does not rest upon "the language of intrinsic value and correlated concepts of rights . . . then deep ecology is not subject to some of the criticisms I have offered."[13]

More recently, Cheney has abandoned his previous view of deep ecology and accepted that deep ecologists are primarily concerned with the development of a state of being of wider *identification* and, hence, with the realization of a more expansive (sense of) Self.[14] This understanding of deep ecology appears to have much in common with Cheney's characterization of ecofeminism as being concerned with an ethics of love, care, and friendship as opposed to a theory of rights, justice, and obligation.[15] However, Cheney argues instead that the deep ecological emphasis on the realization of a more expansive (sense of) Self is a "totalizing view" that represents "the desperate endgame of masculine alienation from nature."[16] What Cheney means by his highly abstract and potentially obfuscating reference to a "totalizing view" is that deep ecologists identify "with particulars only in the derivative sense that the logos of the cosmos threads its way through the cosmos, binds it together as a totality, a cosmos. Identification, for the deep ecologist, does not involve seeing or hearing the other or seeing oneself in the other, but rather involves seeing the other *sub specie aeternitas*."[17]

What Cheney seems to object to in deep ecology, then, is not the emphasis on identification *per se* but rather the fact that deep ecologists emphasize identification within a cosmological context—that is, within the context of an awareness that all entities in the universe are part of a single, unfolding process. There is, however, a fundamental problem with arguing, as Cheney seems to want to, for a purely *personal* basis for identification (as opposed to a cosmological and, hence, *transpersonal* basis). Specifically, emphasizing a purely personal basis for identification—one that "leave[s] selves intact"[18]— necessarily implies an emphasis upon identification with entities with which one has considerable personal contact. In practice, this tends to mean that one identifies with *my* self first, *my* family next, *my* friends and more distant relations next, *my* ethnic grouping next, *my* species next, and so on—more or less what the sociobiologists say we are genetically predisposed to do. The problem with this is that, while extending love, care, and friendship to one's nearest and dearest is laudable in and of itself, the *other* side of the coin, emphasizing a purely personal basis for identification (*my*self first, *my* family next, and so on), looks more like the cause of possessiveness, war, and ecological destruction than the solution to these seemingly intractable problems. In contrast, to argue for a cosmological basis for identification is to attempt to convey a lived sense that all entities (including ourselves) are relatively autonomous modes of a single, unfolding process, that all entities are leaves on the tree of life. A lived sense of this understanding means that we strive, insofar as it is within our power to do so, not to identify ourselves exclusively with our leaf (our personal biographical self), our twig (our family), our minor subbranch (our community), our major subbranch (our race/gender), our branch (our species), and so on, but rather to identify ourselves with the tree. This necessarily leads, at the limit, to impartial identification with *all* particulars (all leaves on the tree).[19]

This distinction between personally based identification and cosmologically based identification certainly represents a difference in *theoretical* stance between Cheney's conception of ecofeminism on the one hand and deep ecology on the other. But whether this difference also reflects a basic difference between feminine and masculine modes of approaching the world (as Cheney wants to suggest) is a separate issue. On my reading of the literature, I do not see how anyone can—or why they would want to—deny that many women are *vitally* interested in cultivating a cosmological/transpersonal based sense of identification.[20] The cosmological/transpersonal voice *is* a "different voice" from the personal voice, but it does not seem to respect gender boundaries. Moreover, as the above discussion suggests, whatever one's view of the relationship or lack of relationship between these approaches and gender, a personally based approach to identification is vulnerable to criticism from an ecocentric perspective in a way in which a cosmological/transpersonal approach is not.

Because this brief examination of Cheney's critique of deep ecology suggests that there are major weaknesses with his claim that the essential ecofeminist charge against deep ecology is actually "that deep ecology is *itself*, in some sense androcentric," in what follows I, therefore, consider the essential ecofeminist charge against deep ecology to be the far more clear-cut and potentially far more serious charge (vis-à-vis Cheney's charge) that deep ecology "speaks of a gender-neutral 'anthropocentrism' as the root of the domination of nature, when in fact *androcentrism* is the real root."[21]

## PROBLEMS WITH THE ECOFEMINIST AND OTHER CRITIQUES

Having established the nature of the ecofeminist charge that I am concerned to address in what follows, it is important to note that this charge is *not* directed at deep ecology's positive or constructive task of encouraging an egalitarian attitude on the part of humans toward all entities in the ecosphere, but rather at deep ecology's negative or critical task of dismantling anthropocentrism. This distinction often seems to be overlooked by ecofeminist critics of deep ecology, who, presumably, are in general agreement with the constructive task of deep ecology.[22] But with respect to the critical task of these two perspectives, the fact remains that in the absence of a good answer to the ecofeminist charge, there is no reason—other than intellectual blindness or outright chauvinism in regard to issues concerning gender—why deep ecologists should not make androcentrism the focus of their critique rather than anthropocentrism. In addressing this challenge to the critical focus of deep ecology, I first make some general remarks about a certain style of social and political theorizing and then proceed to the essential deep ecological response to this ecofeminist charge.

To begin with, deep ecologists completely agree with ecofeminists that men have been far more implicated in the history of ecological destruction than women. However, deep ecologists also agree with similar charges derived from other social perspectives: for example, that capitalists, whites, and Westerners have been far more implicated in the history of ecological destruction than pre-capitalist peoples, blacks, and non-Westerners.[23] If ecofeminists also agree with these points, then the question arises as to why they do not also criticize deep

ecology for being neutral with respect to issues concerning such significant social variables as socioeconomic class, race, and Westernization. There appears
to be two reasons for this. First, to do so would detract from the priority that
ecofeminists wish to give to their own concern with androcentrism. Second,
and more significantly, these charges could also be applied with equal force to
the ecofeminist focus on androcentism itself.[24] How does one defend the
ecofeminist charge against deep ecology (i.e., that androcentrism is "the real
root" of ecological destruction) in the face of these charges?[25] For deep ecologists, it is simplistic on both empirical and logical grounds to think that one particular perspective on human society identifies *the* real root of ecological
destruction. Empirically, such thinking is simplistic (and thus descriptively
poor) because it fails to give due consideration to the multitude of interacting
factors at work in any given situation. (While on a *practical* level it can be perfectly reasonable to devote most of one's energy to one particular cause—if only
for straightforward reasons to do with time and energy—that, of course, is no
excuse for simplistic social *theorizing*.) Such thinking fails, in other words, to
adopt an ecological perspective with respect to the workings of human society
itself. Logically, such thinking is simplistic (and thus facile) because it implies
that the solution to our ecological problems is close at hand—all we have to do
is remove "the real root" of the problem—when it is actually perfectly possible
to conceive of a society that is nonandrocentric, socioeconomically egalitarian,
nonracist, and nonimperialistic with respect to other human societies, but
whose members nevertheless remain aggressively anthropocentric in collectively agreeing to exploit their environment for their collective benefit in ways
that nonanthropocentrists would find thoroughly objectionable. Indeed, the
"green" critique of socialism proceeds from *precisely* this recognition that a
socially egalitarian society does not necessarily imply an ecologically benign
society.

An interesting example of the failure to recognize this point is provided
by Murray Bookchin's anarcho-socialist inspired "social ecology" (I describe
this approach as "anarcho-socialist" in inspiration because it advocates decentralism and cooperativeness and stands opposed to all forms of hierarchy).
Bookchin is interesting in this context because, on the one hand, he correctly
observes in the course of a highly polemical attack upon deep ecology that it is
possible for a relatively ecologically benign human society also to be extremely
oppressive internally (he offers the example of ancient Egyptian society), and
yet, on the other hand, he fails to see that the reverse can also apply—that is,
that it is possible for a relatively egalitarian human society to be extremely exploitative ecologically.[26] For Bookchin, to accept this latter point would be to
argue against the basis of his own social ecology, since in his view a nonhierarchical, decentralist, and cooperative society is "a society that will live in harmony with nature *because* its members live in harmony with each other."[27]
Bookchin's presentation of social ecology thus conveys no real appreciation of
the fact that the relationships between the internal organization of human societies and their treatment of the nonhuman world can be as many and varied as

the outcomes of any other evolutionary process. One may certainly speak in terms of certain forms of human social organization being more *conducive* to certain kinds of relationships with the nonhuman world than others. Bookchin, however, insists far too much that there is a straightforward, necessary relationship between the internal organization of human societies and their treatment of the nonhuman world. To this extent, his social ecology is constructed upon a logically facile basis. Moreover, it serves to reinforce anthropocentrism, since the assumption that the internal organization of human societies determines their treatment of the nonhuman world carries with it the implication that we need only concentrate on *interhuman* egalitarian concerns for all to become ecologically well with the world—a point I take up again later.[28]

In doing violence to the complexities of social interaction, simplistic social and political analyses of ecological destruction are not merely descriptively poor and logically facile, they are also morally objectionable on two grounds, scapegoating and inauthenticity. Scapegoating can be thought of in terms of overinclusiveness. Simplistic analyses target all men, all capitalists, all whites, and all Westerners, for example, to an equal degree when in fact certain subclasses of these identified classes are far more responsible for ecological destruction than others. Not only that but significant minorities of these classes can be actively engaged in *opposing* the interests of both the dominant culture of their class and those members of their class most responsible for ecological destruction. Inauthenticity, on the other hand, can be thought of in terms of underinclusiveness. Simplistic analyses are inauthentic in that they lead to a complete denial of responsibility when at least partial responsibility for ecological destruction should be accepted. Such theorizing conveniently disguises the extent to which (at least a subset of) the simplistically identified oppressed group (e.g., women or the working class) also benefits from, and colludes with, those most responsible for ecological destruction (e.g., consider the case of animal destruction for furs and cosmetics consumed by Western and Westernized women, or the case of capitalists and unionists united in opposition to the antidevelopment stance of "greenies"). It can, of course, be argued in response that the hegemony of androcentrism or capitalism, for example, is such that women or unionists effectively have *no* power to choose in our society and so should not be burdened with *any* responsibility for ecological destruction. But this surely overplays the role of social determination and to that extent only serves to highlight the charge of inauthenticity. Moreover, attempting to escape the charge of inauthenticity in this way directly contradicts the view of feminists or Marxists, to continue with the same examples, that women or the working class *are* capable of self-conscious direction—of being a class *for* themselves, a revolutionary class.

Yet another kind of objection to simplistic analyses of the kind to which I have been referring is that while claiming to be "ecological" or "green," some of these critics in fact remain anthropocentric—albeit in the passive sense of serving to legitimize our continued preoccupation with interhuman affairs rather than in the aggressive sense of overtly discriminating against the nonhuman world. Advocates of these approaches say in essence: "Since the real root of our problems is androcentrism or capitalism, for example, we must *first* get our interactions between humans right (with respect to gender issues, with respect to the redistribution of wealth, and so on) and then everything else (including our ecological problems) will fall into place." Any form of direct concern with the question of the relationship between humans and the *nonhuman* world is thus trumped by concerns about the resolution of specific interhuman problems. The nonhuman world retains its traditional status as the background against which the significant action—human action—takes place.

Not surprisingly, deep ecologists find it particularly frustrating to witness representatives of simplistic social and political perspectives waving the banner of ecology while in fact continuing to promote, whether wittingly or unwittingly, the interhuman and, hence, human-centered agenda of their respective theoretical legacies. I have already commented on Bookchin's social ecology in regard to this point. Some ecofeminist writing is also relevant here. For example, the focus of Ariel Kay Salleh's critique of deep ecology is thoroughly interhuman. "To make a better world," she concludes, men have to be "brave enough to rediscover and to love the woman inside themselves," while women simply have to "be allowed to love what we are."[29] This conclusion follows from the fact that, in Salleh's version of feminism, women already "flow with the system of nature" by virtue of their essential nature.[30] Karen Warren and Michael Zimmerman have referred to this kind of approach to ecofeminism, according to which women are supposed to be "closer to nature" than men by virtue of their essential nature, as "radical feminism" (in contrast to liberal, traditional Marxist, and socialist feminism) and "essentialist feminism" respectively.[31] Warren correctly notes that "Radical feminists have had the most to say about eco-feminism," and both she and Zimmerman have made telling criticisms of this approach.[32] All I am drawing attention to here is the fact that this kind of "radical" approach simply serves to legitimize and, hence, to perpetuate our entirely *traditional* preoccupation with interhuman affairs. In accordance with the approach adopted by essentialist feminists, there is no need to give any serious consideration whatsoever to the possibility that women might, for example, discriminate against men, accumulate rather than distribute private wealth, be racist, support imperialism, or be ecologically destructive if the conditions of their historical subjugation were undone and the possibility of exercising genuine social and political power were available to them.[33] The upshot is that there is no need to worry about any form of human domination other than that of androcentrism. For deep ecologists, it's just another variation on the same old song—the song that reassures us that all will become ecologically well with the world if we just put this or that interhuman concern first.

I have objected to simplistic (and, hence, unecologically conceived) social and political analyses on the grounds that they are descriptively poor and logically facile, that they lend themselves to scapegoating on the one hand

and are inauthentic on the other, and that even in their ecological guises, they are passively anthropocentric. Many who align themselves with the perspectives to which I have referred might well personally agree with the points I have made so far and consider that in virtue of this agreement, these objections do not really apply to their perspective. Thus, this kind of reaction can be quite common in the face of the sorts of objections I have made: "How could anyone be so stupid as to think that we ecofeminists (for example) are not also concerned about issues concerning socioeconomic class, race, and imperialism?" The problem is, however, that there is often a large gap between the alleged and often genuine personal concerns of members of a social and political movement and the theoretical articulation of the perspective that informs their movement. The fact that individual members of a social and political movement agree with the points I have made provides no guarantee whatsoever that the theoretical articulation of the perspective that informs their movement does not itself fall foul of these objections—and it is with this theoretical articulation that I have been concerned. By way of qualification, however, I do not in any way wish to assert that any of the objections I have made are necessarily fatal to the theoretical prospects of the social and political perspectives to which I have referred, since it is possible, at least in principle, for each of these perspectives to be revised or, at a minimum, suitably qualified so as not to fall foul of these objections.[34] But, that said, one must nevertheless be careful not to underestimate the significance of these objections, since presentations of the social and political perspectives to which I have referred continue to fall foul of them on an all too regular basis.

Variations on some (but not all) of the objections I have outlined would apply just as much to deep ecology if it were the case that deep ecologists were simply saying that humans as a whole have been far more implicated in the history of ecological destruction than nonhumans. (The ecofeminist charge against deep ecology implies that deep ecologists are saying precisely this: it turns on the contention that deep ecologists have been overinclusive in criticizing humanity *in general* for the destruction of the nonhuman world when the target of their critical attack should properly be the class of men and, of course, masculine culture in general.) However, this is *not* the essential point that deep ecologists are making, and it is here that we enter into the essential response by deep ecologists to the essential criticism made of their perspective by ecofeminists.

## THE ESSENTIAL DEEP ECOLOGICAL RESPONSE TO THE ECOFEMINIST CRITIQUE

The target of the deep ecologists' critique is not humans *per se* (i.e., a general class of social actors) but rather human-*centeredness* (i.e., a legitimating ideology).[35] It is not just ecofeminist critics who miss this point. Some other critics also miss it in an even bigger way by attacking deep ecologists not simply on the grounds that they *criticize* humanity in general for its ecological destructiveness, but rather on the grounds that deep ecologists are actually *opposed* to humanity in general—that is, that they are essentially misanthropic. According to Murray Bookchin, for example, in deep ecology "'*Humanity*' is essentially seen as an ugly 'anthropocentric' thing—presumably, a malignant product of natural evolution."[36] Henryk Skolimowski also suggests (albeit rather indirectly) that deep ecologists are misanthropic. "I find it rather morbid," he writes in *The Trumpeter*, "when some human beings [and the context suggests that he means deep ecologists] think that the human lot is the bottom of the pit. There is something pathological in the contention that humans are a cancer among the species. This kind of thinking is not sane and it does not promote the sense of wholeness which we need nowadays." In line with my remarks here, Alan Drengson, *The Trumpeter*'s editor and a prominent deep ecology philosopher, intervenes immediately at this point by adding parenthetically: "And it is certainly not the thinking of deep ecologists. Ed."[37]

The extent to which people in general are ready to equate opposition to human-centeredness with opposition to humans per se can be viewed as a function of the dominance of the anthropocentric frame of reference in our society. Just as those who criticize capitalism, for example, are often labeled as "Communists" and, by implication, "the enemy," when, in reality, they may be concerned with such things as a more equitable distribution of wealth in society, so those who criticize anthropocentrism are liable to be labeled as *mis*anthropists when, in reality, they may be (and, in the context of environmentalism, generally are) concerned with encouraging a more egalitarian attitude on the part of humans toward all entities in the ecosphere. In failing to notice the fact that being opposed to human-*centeredness* (deep ecology's critical task) is logically distinct from being opposed to humans per se (or, in other words, that being opposed to anthropo*centrism* is logically distinct from being *mis*anthropic), and in equating the former with the latter, Bookchin and Skolimowski commit what I refer to as *the fallacy of misplaced misanthropy*.[38] Committing this fallacy in the context of criticizing deep ecology involves not just a crucial misreading of deep ecology's critical task, but also the oversight of two other considerations that contradict such a misreading. The first is that deep ecology's *constructive* task is to encourage an egalitarian attitude on the part of humans toward all entities in the ecosphere—including *humans*. The second is that deep ecologists are among the first to highlight and draw inspiration from the fact that not all humans have been human-centered either within the Western tradition or outside it. Far from being misanthropic, deep ecologists celebrate the existence of these human beings.

In making human-*centeredness* (rather than humans per se) the target of their critique, deep ecologists have contended that the assumption of human self-importance in the larger scheme of things has, to all intents and purposes, been the single deepest and most persistent assumption of (at least) all the *dominant* Western philosophical, social, and political traditions since the time of the classical Greeks—notwithstanding the fact that the dominant classes representing these traditions have typically adjudged themselves *more* human than others—and that, for a variety of reasons, this assumption is unwarranted and should be abandoned in favor of an ecocentric outlook.[39] Thus, what deep ecologists are drawing critical attention to is the fact that *whatever* class of social actors one identifies as having been most responsible for social domination and ecological destruction (e.g., men, capitalists, whites, Westerners), one tends at the most fundamental level to find a common kind of legitimation for the alleged superiority of these classes over others and, hence, for the assumed rightfulness of their domination of these others. Specifically, these classes of social actors have not sought to legitimate their position on the grounds that they are, for example, men, capitalists, white, or Western per se, but rather on the grounds that they have most exemplified whatever it is that has been taken to constitute the *essence of humanness* (e.g., being favored by God or possessing rationality). These classes of social actors have, in other words, habitually assumed themselves to be somehow *more fully human* than others, such as women ("the weaker vessel"), the "lower" classes, blacks, and non-Westerners ("savages," "primitives," "heathens"). The cultural spell of anthropocentrism has been considered sufficient to justify not only moral superiority (which, in itself, might be construed as carrying with it an obligation to help rather than dominate those who are less blessed), but also all kinds of domination within human society—let alone domination of the obviously nonhuman world.

That anthropocentrism has served as the most fundamental kind of legitimation employed by *whatever* powerful class of social actors one wishes to focus on can also be seen by considering the fundamental kind of legitimation that has habitually been employed with regard to large-scale or high-cost social enterprises such as war, scientific and technological development, or environmental exploitation. Such enterprises have habitually been undertaken not simply in the name of men, capitalists, whites, or Westerners, for example, but rather in the name of God (and thus our essential humanity—or our anthropocentric projection upon the cosmos, depending upon one's perspective) or simply in the name of humanity in general. (This applies notwithstanding the often sexist expression of these sentiments in terms of "man," "mankind," and so on, and notwithstanding the fact that certain classes of social actors benefit disproportionately from these enterprises.) Thus, to take some favorite examples, Francis Bacon and Descartes ushered in the development of modern science by promising, respectively, that it would lead to "enlarging the bounds of Human Empire" and that it would render humanity the "masters and possessors of nature."[40] Approximately three and a half centuries later, Neil Armstrong's moon walk—the culmination of a massive, politically directed, scientific and technological development effort—epitomized both the literal acting out of this vision of "enlarging the bounds of Human Empire" and the literal expression of its anthropocentric spirit: Armstrong's moon walk was, in his own words at the time, a "small step" for him, but a "giant leap for mankind." Here on Earth, not only do examples abound of environmental *exploitation* being undertaken in the name of humanity, but this also constitutes the fundamental kind of legitimation that is still most often employed for environmental *conservation and preservation*—it is implicit in every argument for the conservation or preservation of the nonhuman world on account of its use value to humans (e.g., its scientific, recreational, or aesthetic value) rather than for its own sake or its use value to *nonhuman* beings.

The cultural pervasiveness of anthropocentrism in general and anthropocentric legitimations in particular are further illustrated when one turns to consider those social movements that have *opposed* the dominant classes of social actors to which I have been referring. With respect to the pervasiveness of anthropocentrism in general, it can be seen that those countermovements that have been most concerned with exposing discriminatory assumptions and undoing their effects have typically confined their interests to the human realm (i.e., to such issues as imperialism, race, socioeconomic class, and gender). With respect to the pervasiveness of anthropocentric legitimations in particular, it can equally be seen that these countermovements have not sought to legitimate their own claims on the basis that they are, for example, women, workers, black, or non-Western per se, but rather on the grounds that they too have exemplified—at least equally with those to whom they have been opposed—either whatever it is that *has* been taken to constitute the essence of humanness or else some redefined essence of humanness. While it would, in any case, be contrary to the (human-centered) egalitarian concerns of these countermovements to seek to legitimate their own claims by the former kind of approach (i.e., on the basis that they are, for example, women, workers, black, or non-Western per se), the pity is (from a deep ecological perspective) that these countermovements have not been egalitarian enough. Rather than attempting to replace the ideology of anthropocentrism with some broader, ecocentrically inclined perspective, these countermovements have only served to reinforce it.

It should be clear from this brief survey that the history of anthropocentrism takes in not only the assumption of the centrality and superiority of humans *in general,* but also the various claims and counterclaims that various classes of humans have made with regard to the exemplification of whatever attributes have been considered to be quintessentially human. Deep ecologists recognize that the actual historical reasons for the domination of one class by another (and here I also refer to the domination that humans as a class now exert over the nonhuman world) cannot be identified in any simplistic manner; they can be as complex as any ecological web or the evolutionary path of any organism. However, deep ecologists also recognize that claims to some form of human exclusiveness have typically been employed to *legitimate* the bringing about and perpetuation of historical and evolutionary outcomes involving unwarranted domination. In consequence, deep ecologists have been attempting to get people to see that historical and evolutionary outcomes simply represent "the way things happen to have turned out"—nothing more—and that self-serving anthropocentric legitimations for these outcomes are just that.

What the ecofeminist criticism of deep ecology's focus on anthropocentrism overlooks, then, is the fact that deep ecologists are not primarily concerned with exposing the *classes of social actors* historically most responsible for social domination and ecological destruction, but rather with the task of sweeping the rug out from under the feet of these classes of social actors by exposing the most fundamental kind of *legitimation* that they have habitually employed in justifying their position. (This distinction between a concern with classes of social actors on the one hand and the most fundamental kind of legitimation they employ on the other hand should be apparent from the fact that deep ecology has been elaborated within a philosophical context rather than a sociological or political context—which is not to suggest that deep ecology does not have profound social and political implications.) Of course, ecofeminists, green socialists, and so on are also concerned with questions of legitimation, but they are generally concerned with these questions in a different sense than deep ecologists are concerned with them. The primary emphasis of ecofeminists, green socialists, and the other social and political analysts to whom I have referred is on the distribution of power in society and the ways in which that distribution is reinforced and reproduced. In this context, references to legitimation tend not to be to the "bottom line" rationale employed by these powerful classes (i.e., to legitimation in the fundamental or philosophical sense), but rather to the ways in which existing power structures utilize their sources of power to back up existing states of affairs (from overtly physical forms of power such as the police and the military to less tangible forms such as economic power and the manipulation of social status). To the extent that ecofeminists, green socialists, and so on *are* concerned to expose the fundamental, philosophical legitimation employed by the classes of social actors whose unwarranted degree of power is the focus of their critique, and to the extent that this concern extends out into a genuinely ecocentric perspective, it becomes difficult to see any significant difference between what they call ecofeminism, green socialism, and so on and what others call deep ecology (such differences as remain are simply differences of theoretical flavor and emphasis rather than differences of substance).

Deep ecologists want to unmask the ideology of anthropocentrism so that it can no longer be used as the "bottom line" legitimation for social domination and ecological destruction by *any* class of social actors (men, capitalists, whites, Westerners, humans generally—or even essentialist feminists!).[41] Thus, those who align themselves with certain perspectives on the distribution of power in human society (e.g., feminism, Marxism, anti-racism, or anti-imperialism) misunderstand the essential nature of deep ecology if they see it in terms of their perspective *versus* deep ecology (e.g., in the case of ecofeminism and deep ecology, androcentrism *versus* anthropocentrism)—or if they criticize deep ecology on the basis that it has "no analysis of power." Rather, just as deep ecologists have learned and incorporated much from, and should be open to, a range of perspectives on the distribution of power in human society, so those who align themselves with these social and political perspectives can learn and incorporate much from, and should be open to, the deep ecologists' critique of the most fundamental kind of legitimation that has habitually been employed by those most responsible for social domination and ecological destruction.

# NOTES

1. Arne Naess, "Sustainable Development and the Deep Long-Range Ecological Movement," unpublished manuscript.
2. Arne Naess, "Intuition, Intrinsic Value, and Deep Ecology," *The Ecologist* 14 (1984): 202 (emphasis added). Naess fully accepts that "any realistic praxis necessitates some killing, exploitation, and suppression" ("The Shallow and the Deep, Long-Range Ecology Movement: A Summary." *Inquiry* 16 [1973]: 95). For more on the relevance of tradition and culture, see Naess's paper "Self-realization in Mixed Communities of Humans, Bears, Sheep, and Wolves," *Inquiry* 22 (1979): 231–41.
3. See the eight point list of "basic principles" of deep ecology proposed by Arne Naess and George Sessions and published in numerous places including Bill Devall and George Sessions, *Deep Ecology: Living as if Nature Mattered* (Layton, Utah: Gibbs M. Smith, 1985), chap. 5; and Arne Naess, "The Deep Ecological Movement: Some Philosophical Aspects," *Philosophical Inquiry* 8 (1986): 10–31.
4. *Biocentric* and *ecocentric* are equally useful in connoting the biosphere and the ecosphere respectively and these latter terms are themselves generally used interchangeably. However, where a distinction *is* made between the terms *biosphere* and *ecosphere*, it is the latter term that is taken as the more inclusive.
5. I am, of course, speaking here of the full realization of deep ecology's concerns, i.e., of the breadth of deep ecology's concerns *in principle*. In practice, however, deep ecologists, like everyone else, can fail to realize the full implications of their own principles.
6. In referring to *green socialism* and to *socialists*. I am aware that the term *socialism*, considered in its own right, is today popularly construed as referring to virtually the whole range of (human) social egalitarian concerns and that the concerns of socialism and green socialism might therefore be considered as subsuming the concerns of feminism and ecofeminism respectively. But there are nevertheless significant differences between these approaches at the level of their theoretical flavors and emphases.
7. There is nothing to suggest that there is any incompatibility between deep ecology and an ecologically informed feminism in any of the works by the following authors, all of whom make explicit reference to both perspectives: Fritjof Capra, *The Turning Point: Science, Society, and the Rising Culture* (New York: Bantam Books, 1983), chap. 12; Don E. Marietta, Jr, "Environmentalism, Feminism, and the Future of American Society," *The Humanist*, May–June 1984, pp. 15–18 and 30; Bill Devall and George Sessions, *Deep Ecology*, chap. 6; Charlene Spretnak, "The Spiritual Dimension of Green Politics," appendix C in Charlene Spretnak and Fritjof Capra, *Green Politics: The Global Promise* (London: Paladin, Grafton Books, 1986); and Patsy Hallen, "Making Peace with Nature: Why Ecology Needs Feminism," *The Trumpeter* 4, No. 3 (1987): 3–14. Even those authors who do see a tension between these perspectives generally acknowledge that these perspectives at least bear a strong apparent similarity to each other. For example, Jim Cheney writes: "On the face of it, that *branch* of environmentalism called the 'deep ecology movement' seems to have answered the [ecofeminist] call for a nonhierarchical, nondomineering attitude toward nature" ("Eco-Feminism and Deep Ecology," *Environmental Ethics* 9 [1987]: 115–45).
8. Zimmerman, "Feminism, Deep Ecology, and Environmental Ethics," *Environmental Ethics* 9 (1987): 21–44.
9. Janet Biehl, "It's Deep, but Is It Broad? An Eco-feminist Looks at Deep Ecology," *Kick It Over*, Winter 1987, p. 2A; Marti Kheel, "Ecofeminism and Deep Ecology," and Charlene Spretnak, "Ecofeminism: Our Roots and Flowering." *The Elmwood Newsletter*, Winter 1988, p. 7.
10. Personal communication, 21 April 1988.
11. Zimmerman ("Feminism, Deep Ecology, and Environmental Ethics," pp. 38–42) provides a thoughtful consideration of the various problems associated with the kind of claim that Cheney makes.
12. Cheney, "Eco-Feminism and Deep Ecology," p. 129.
13. Ibid., p. 133. The brief paper of mine that Cheney refers to is "A Postscript on Deep Ecology and Intrinsic Value," *The Trumpeter* 2, no. 4 (1985): 20–23. For a far more extensive critique of the view that deep ecology rests upon what Cheney refers to as "the language of intrinsic value and correlated concepts of rights," see my monograph *Approaching Deep Ecology: A Response to Richard Sylvan's Critique of Deep Ecology*, Environmental

Studies Occasional Paper, no. 20 (Hobart: Centre for Environmental Studies, University of Tasmania, 1986).

14. Jim Cheney, "The Neo-Stoicism of Radical Environmentalism," unpublished early draft. This version of Cheney's critique of deep ecology follows his reading of my *Approaching Deep Ecology* and is, in large measure, a response to it.

15. See Cheney, "Eco-Feminism and Deep Ecology," p. 128.

16. Cheney, "Neo-Stoicism."

17. Ibid., p. 16.

18. Ibid., p. 15.

19. The fact that cosmologically based identification tends to be more *impartial* than personally based identification does not mean that it need be any less deeply felt. Consider Robinson Jeffers! For Jeffers, "This whole [the universe] is in *all its parts* so beautiful, and is felt by me to be so intensely in earnest, that I am *compelled* to love it" (quoted in Devall and Sessions, *Deep Ecology*, p. 101; emphasis added).

20. See, for example, Dolores LaChapelle, *Earth Wisdom* (Los Angeles: Guild of Tutors Press, 1978); Joanna Macy, "Deep Ecology and the Council of All Beings," and "Gaia Meditations (Adapted from John Seed)," *Awakening in the Nuclear Age*, Summer/Fall 1986, pp. 6–10 (both reprinted in *Revision*, Winter/Spring 1987, pp. 53–57); Freya Matthews, "Conservation and Self-Realization: A Deep Ecology Perspective," *Environmental Ethics* 10 (1988): 347–55; and Frances Vaughan, "Discovering Transpersonal Identity," *Journal of Humanistic Psychology* 25 (1985): 13–38.

21. Zimmerman, "Feminism, Deep Ecology, and Environmental Ethics," p. 37.

22. In a thoughtful analysis of the strengths and shortcomings of several varieties of feminism (liberal, traditional Marxist, radical, and socialist) for the development of a genuinely ecofeminist perspective, Karen J. Warren concurs that an ecologically informed feminism—"a transformative feminism"—would tie "the liberation of women to the elimination of all systems of oppression" ("Feminism and Ecology: Making Connections," *Environmental Ethics* 9 [1987]: 18). Unfortunately, however, many feminists who claim to be ecofeminists do not make their (presumed) commitment to an *ecocentric* egalitarianism particularly explicit, with the result that ecofeminist analyses can sometimes serve to reinforce anthropocentrism rather than overcome it. As for those ecofeminists, such as Warren, who are explicit about their commitment to an ecocentric egalitarianism, it becomes difficult to see any essential difference between their approach and that of deep ecology. As one ecofeminist-cum-deep ecologist said to me after reading Warren's article: "Why doesn't she just call it [i.e., Warren's vision of a transformative feminism] deep ecology? Why specifically attach the label *feminism* to it if she's advocating a genuinely nonprioritizing, biocentric egalitarianism?"

23. When I refer to any class of social actors, I expressly mean also to refer to the culture(s) associated with that class. However, I omit writing "men and their associated cultures," "non-Westerners and their associated cultures," and so on simply for ease of comprehension. In referring to capitalists and, hence, the culture of capitalism, I also mean to refer to "state capitalism" as found in the industrialized communist countries.

24. Indeed, even as I wrote this paper, a significant real-life example of such criticisms was being played out between the women of Greenham Common in the form of a "bitter dispute" over allegations of racism at the camp. Reports suggested that this dispute "threatens the world's most renowned peace camp after six years" (Deborah Smith, "Showdown at Greenham Common," *The Times on Sunday*, 25 October 1987, p. 27). Karen J. Warren similarly criticizes radical feminists—that group of feminists who "have had the most to say about ecofeminism"—for paying "little attention to the historical and material features of women's oppression (including the relevance of race, class, ethnic, and national background)" ("Feminism and Ecology," pp. 14–15).

25. Note that I am borrowing the phrase "the real root" from Michael Zimmerman's previously quoted formulation of what I consider to be the essential ecofeminist charge against deep ecology. I employ this phrase several times in the argument that follows.

26. Murray Bookchin, "Social Ecology Versus 'Deep Ecology,' " *Green Perspectives: Newsletter of the Green Program Project*, Summer 1987.

27. Ibid., p. 2 (emphasis added). This view is central to Bookchin's major statement of social ecology: *The Ecology of Freedom: The Emergence and Dissolution of Hierarchy* (Palo Alto: Cheshire Books, 1982).

28. This observation is in keeping with the anthropocentric flavor that many deep ecologists detect in Bookchin's work notwithstanding his avowed ecological orientation.

29. Salleh, "Deeper than Deep Ecology," p. 345. In another presentation of the ecofeminist sensibility, Don Davis also concludes by reiterating this conclusion of Salleh's ("Ecosophy: The Seduction of Sophia?" *Environmental Ethics* 8 [1986]: 151–62).

30. Salleh, "Deeper than Deep Ecology," p. 340.

31. Warren, "Feminism and Ecology," pp. 13–15, and Zimmerman, "Feminism, Deep Ecology," p. 40.

32. Warren, "Feminism and Ecology," p. 14. See also Alan E. Wittbecker, "Deep Anthropology: Ecology and Human Order," *Environmental Ethics* 8 (1986): 261–70, which provides a number of counterinstances to Salleh's essentialist feminist claim that the suppression of the feminine is "universal."

33. Stunningly obvious instances of these kinds of examples, such as the Prime Minister of England, Margaret Thatcher (the "Iron Lady"), sending warships to the Falklands, are typically explained in terms of the hegemony of androcentrism being such as to have overpowered the offending woman's essential nature. The implication is that if, as Salleh says, women could just "be allowed to love what we are," then it would no longer be possible to find such examples.

34. Where revised, such perspectives would no doubt continue to differ from deep ecology in terms of their theoretical flavors and emphases, but they would not differ from deep ecology in terms of their essential concerns. Whether these revised perspectives would be recognizable or acceptable to their earlier supporters is of course an interesting question.

35. Ecofeminists, green socialists, and so on are also concerned with questions of legitimation, but generally in a different sense than deep ecologists are.

36. Bookchin, "Social Ecology," p. 3 (emphasis added).

37. Henryk Skolimowski, "To Continue the Dialogue with Deep Ecology," *The Trumpeter* 4, no. 4 (1987): 31. Skolimowski has previously been taken to task for the anthropocentrism inherent in his own approach: see George Sessions' review of Skolimowski's *Eco-Philosophy* in *Environmental Ethics* 6 (1984): 167–74. Since then Skolimowski has become a regular critic of deep ecology: see his articles "The Dogma of Anti-Anthropocentrism and Ecophilosophy," *Environmental Ethics* 6 (1984): 283–88 (Skolimowski's response to Sessions' review); "In Defence of Ecophilosophy and of Intrinsic Value: A Call for Conceptual Clarity," *The Trumpeter* 3, no. 4 (1986): 9–12 (this issue of *The Trumpeter* also carried replies from Bill Devall, Arne Naess, and myself); "To Continue the Dialogue with Deep Ecology"; and "Eco-Philosophy and Deep Ecology," *The Ecologist* 18 (1988): 124–27. I defend Sessions' reading of Skolimowski in my "Further Notes in Response to Skolimowski," *The Trumpeter* 4, no. 4 (1987): 32–34.

38. Much of Bookchin's case for his (mistaken) contention that deep ecology is essentially a misanthropic enterprise rests on certain statements by one or two significant figures in Earth First!—especially Dave Foreman and his personal, unhistorical, and abhorrently simplistic views on population control. However, Bookchin overlooks the surely obvious fact that Foreman says elsewhere in the same interview (p. 42), "I am speaking for myself, not for Earth First!," and both he and Foreman overlook the equally obvious fact that such a view runs contrary to the deep-ecological principle of encouraging an egalitarian attitude on the part of humans toward all entities in the ecosphere. In contrast to Foreman, Arne Naess says in a recent paper: "Sustainable development today means development along the lines of each culture, not development along a common, centralized line. But faced with hungry children humanitarian action is a priority, whatever its relation to developmental plans and cultural invasion" ("Sustainable Development and the Deep-Long-Range Ecological Movement").

39. There are two significant qualifications to be noted in this statement. First, I say "to all intents and purposes" because where these traditions have supposedly been primarily theocentric rather than anthropocentric, it has of course still been humans who have, by divine decree, had "dominion . . . over all the earth [which they are enjoined to 'fill and subdue'] . . . and over every living thing that moves upon the earth" (Genesis 1:26 and 1:28). From a deep ecological perspective, personalistic theocentrisms, in which humans are made in the image of a god to whom they have a privileged personal relationship, are simply anthropocentric projections upon the cosmos. Second, I say "since the time of

the *classical* Greeks" (i.e., the Sophists, Socrates, Plato, and Aristotle) as distinct from the *early* Greeks, who initiated Western philosophy (i.e., the early and later Ionians, the Pythagoreans, the Eleatics, and the Atomists—often collectively referred to as the pre-Socratics), because, as Bertrand Russell has pointed out, "What is amiss, even in the best philosophy after Democritus [i.e., after the pre-Socratics], is an undue emphasis on man as compared with the universe" (Bertrand Russell, *History of Western Philosophy* [London: Unwin Paperbacks, 1979], p. 90). Russell's statement is meant to refer to humanity in general, although it also applies, of course, if its sexist expression is read as representing its intended meaning (i.e., if "man" is read as "men"). It should be noted in this regard, however, that the reason why Russell's statement is true in the gender specific sense is, as I argue below, precisely because men have seen themselves as essentially *more* human than women—an observation that returns us to Russell's intended meaning in a dialectical manner. For excellent discussions of the anthropocentric nature of Western philosophy since the time of the pre-Socratics, see George Sessions, "Anthropocentrism and the Environmental Crisis," *Humboldt Journal of Social Relations* 2 (1974): 71–81 and George Sessions, "Spinoza and Jeffers on Man in Nature," *Inquiry* 20 (1977): 481–528.

40.  Both quotes are from Brian Easlea's erudite and inspiring book *Liberation and the Aims of Science: An Essay on Obstacles to the Building of a Beautiful World* (London: Chatto and Windus, 1973), p. 253.

41.  I include a reference to essentialist feminists here because, as Michael Zimmerman points out ("Feminism, Deep Ecology," p. 40), "In recent years, a number of feminists have favoured . . . an essentialist view [that women are essentially more attuned to nature than men] and have concluded that woman is *better* than man" (my emphasis). Karen Warren criticizes this point of view sharply ("Feminism and Ecology," p. 15): "The truth is that women, like men, are both connected to nature and separate from it, natural and cultural beings . . . locating women either on the nature or on the culture side . . . mistakenly perpetuates the sort of oppositional, dualistic thinking for which patriarchal conceptual frameworks are criticized." But, even more fundamentally (since this is the end that such oppositional, dualistic thinks *serves*), essentialist feminism perpetuates the anthropocentric assumption that some humans are more equal than others by virtue of their essential nature.

# ECOCENTRISM, WILDERNESS, AND GLOBAL ECOSYSTEM PROTECTION

*George Sessions*

George Sessions is emeritus professor of philosophy at Sierra College in Rocklin, California. Author of numerous essays about ecophilosophy and deep ecology, and coauthor (with Bill Devall) of *Deep Ecology*, Sessions recently published the anthology *Deep Ecology for the 21st Century*.

## WILDERNESS: FROM MUIR TO PINCHOT TO MUIR

The ecophilosopher Holmes Rolston III has quoted disapprovingly from a 1978 U.S. Forest Service document on "wilderness management" that asserts: "Wilderness is for people. . . . The preservation goals established for such areas are designed to provide values and benefits to society. . . . Wilderness is not set aside for the sake of its flora or fauna, but for people."[1]

It is disappointing to find Forest Service theorists in the late 1970s still promoting narrowly human-centered views of the function and values of wilderness. In so doing, they follow in the footsteps of the U.S. Forest Service founder, Gifford Pinchot, who once claimed "there are just people and resources." As the ideological archrival of John Muir at the beginning of the twentieth century, Pinchot promoted the anthropocentrism and utilitarian resource management mentality that has pervaded conservationist and land-use agency policy since the turn of the century.

It is somewhat ironic that Forest Service theorists continue with this unecological anthropocentric approach when we consider that Aldo Leopold (the *founder* of the Forest Service wilderness concept in the 1920s) published

Originally published (in a longer version) in *The Wilderness Condition*, edited by Max Oelschlaeger (San Francisco: Sierra Club Books, 1992). Reprinted with permission.

his justly famous ecocentric "land ethic" over forty years ago, and when professional ecologists have been promoting the ecological functions of wilderness at the Sierra Club Wilderness Conferences since the late 1950s.

Unlike the Forest Service, the National Park Service began to implement an ecological approach to its wilderness and wildlife policies in the spring of 1963, following the suggestions of its Advisory Board on Wildlife Management (the so-called Leopold Report, named for its chairman, Starker Leopold, the son of Aldo Leopold and a zoologist at the University of California at Berkeley). The Leopold Report proposed that the wilderness parks, using Yellowstone as a model, be treated as "biotic wholes." Leopold's committee, according to Alston Chase, was proposing "a philosophy of management that could be applied universally" (for instance, to the African wildlife reserves).[2]

Alston Chase blames the wilderness ecosystem approach for the decline of wildlife and ecological deterioration of Yellowstone, and has proposed instead a heavily manipulative scientific wildlife management approach—one that would turn Yellowstone into what some have described as a "natural zoo." Ecologists claim that, like most parks when established, Yellowstone does not comprise a complete ecosystem. For the ecosystem approach to work, a "Greater Yellowstone Ecosystem" must be established and legally protected. In addition, predator/prey balances must be reestablished, as through the reintroduction of the wolf.[3]

When Congress passed the Forest Reserve Act in 1891 enabling President Benjamin Harrison to set aside 13 million acres in "forest reserves," Muir had reason to believe they would be protected as wilderness. But the "forest reserves" later became National Forests, and Pinchot and the Forest Service had other plans for them. Following Pinchot's advocacy of the Resource Conservation and Development position, the Forest Service (as a branch of the Department of Agriculture) sees its primary function as serving as a handmaiden for industrial "resource" exploitation. Ecologically destructive activities such as mining, domestic animal grazing, and sport hunting, are allowed even within National Forest designated wilderness areas. And just as the Pioneers cleared wild forests to make way for agriculture, the Forest Service has facilitated and promoted the destruction of the last unprotected old growth (ancient) forest ecosystems in America to make way for agriculture in the form of biologically sterile monocultural "tree farms"—where the trees consist of one or two commercially valuable species, are even-aged, and grow in nice neat rows like a field of corn.

For the Forest Service, the forests are a *commodity* to be managed, "enhanced," and exploited: either as an agricultural crop to be "harvested" or as designated areas where "the wilderness experience" serves as a human recreational commodity. Forest economists decide these issues by assigning an economic value to the various human "uses" of the forests and computing a cost-benefit analysis.

Further, the forests are to be "enhanced"—and *domesticated*—by replacing ancient forest biodiversity with genetically manipulated "superior" (more economically valuable) trees which grow straighter and faster. One wonders about the wisdom of this now that the genetically "enhanced" domestic grains of the agricultural Green Revolution have turned sour. At present, geneticists are scouring the world for the genetic variability of whatever little pockets of wild grains still remain that have not been genetically tampered with. On the other hand, John Muir has already responded to this genetic tampering with the forests when he claimed that "all wildness is finer than tameness." Similarly, for Thoreau: "In wildness is the preservation of the world."

As early as 1976, John Rodman pointed out:

> The charges frequently made in recent years by Preservationists and others—e.g., that the Forest Service is a captive (or willing) agent of corporate interests, that it allows ecologically-disruptive clear-cutting as well as cutting in excess of official quotas, while permitting grazing corporations to overgraze the land while paying fees far less than they would have to pay for the use of private land, etc.—represent less the latter-day capture of an agency by one or more of its constituents than a maturation of the basic principles of the founder [Pinchot]. The Forest Service is, in effect, a perennial government subsidy, in exchange for certain regulatory controls, to certain types of corporations.[4]

The massive clear-cutting of the last unprotected old-growth coniferous forests along the West Coast of North America (from California to Washington and into the Tongass National Forest in Southeast Alaska) is surpassed in unbridled destruction only by the unrestricted Canadian clear-cutting of British Columbia. At the present rate of clear-cutting along the British Columbia coast, this world's largest remaining temperate rain forest will be gone in fifteen years.[5] Surely, the loss of these last great ancient forest ecosystems in North America will go down as one of the great ecological crimes and blunders of this century, comparable to present rain forest destruction in the Amazon and the rest of Central and South America, Africa, Australia, and Southeast Asia. Japan's thirst for wood products for international markets has been primarily responsible for encouraging the destruction of 80 to 90 percent of the tropical forests in Sri Lanka and Southeast Asia over the last forty years. Japan is also a leading exploiter of the old-growth forests of Central and South America (including Brazil, Peru, and Chile) and the United States (including Southeast Alaska). Japanese corporations are now negotiating with Russia to clear cut the great pine forests of Siberia, the habitat of the Siberian tiger.

The destruction of the biodiversity of the last of the wild ancient forest ecosystems, and their replacement with unstable even-age tree plantations, is now occurring all over the world at an increasing rate.[6] Forestry critic Chris Maser points out that we are nowhere near attaining "sustainable forestry" even on those lands where tree cutting is appropriate, because we are training "plantation managers" instead of foresters. He writes: "We are liquidating our forests and replacing them with short-rotation plantations. Everything Nature does in designing forests adds to diversity, complexity, and stability through time. We decrease this by redesigning forests into plantations."[7] The destruction of ancient forests must cease, and a massive global effort should be made to try to *restore* diverse wild forest ecosystems. Fortunately, wide-scale public pressure is now being applied to modern forestry ideology to bring about major ecological reform. And even Pinchot-trained foresters are beginning to undergo a change of heart. As Canadian forester Bob Nixon recently remarked:

> As a forester, I learned to view forests as a source of industrial fibre. Now, I know that forests are much more than vertical assemblages of lumber, so very much more important than just a source of consumer products. . . . Natural forests, the new research tells us, are no longer something to move through, in the economic sense, in our quest for higher gains, but indeed a key element in the balanced functioning of planetary life.[8]

And how has wildness fared in Muir's National Parks under the anthropocentric orientation of twentieth-century America? The parks do not allow resource extraction within their boundaries, including their newly designated wilderness areas. But many of the parks have been damaged by NPS policies over the years that have catered to dominant American values and lifestyles, which see the parks as essentially natural "scenery" and recreational escapes for city-dwellers. This has encouraged a Disneyland atmosphere of excessive tourism and overdeveloped facilities, upgraded high-speed roads ("scenic drives"), mechanized recreation such as snowmobiling (which disturbs the tranquillity and the wildlife) and human overcrowding: what Edward Abbey called "industrial tourism."[9] In short, there has been a constant push from the commercially motivated to turn them into "theme parks" and international "roadside attractions."

## THE IMPLICATIONS OF CONSERVATION BIOLOGY FOR THE EARTH'S EVOLUTIONARY PROCESSES

The adequacy of currently designated wilderness areas and nature reserves throughout the world received a serious jolt in the 1980s from the findings of the new discipline of conservation biology.

In the 1960s, professional ecologists stepped outside their narrow areas of scientific expertise and began warning the public of the impending ecological disaster. They also proposed various public strategies to cope with these problems. The "intellectual activism" begun by these ecologists has been institutionalized into a new branch of ecology called "conservation biology." According to Mitch Friedman:

> Conservation biology considers the application of ecological theory and knowledge to conservation efforts. The development and utilization of this new discipline is a welcome advance in conservation, where ecological considerations tend to be overshadowed by political and economic forces, in part due to poor understanding of the effects of land-use decisions.[10]

Conservation biology has been spearheaded largely by Michael Soulé (an ecologist and a former student of Paul Ehrlich), who refers to conservation biology as a "crisis discipline" that has to apply its findings in the absence of certainty. This new field integrates ethical norms with the latest findings of ecological science.[11]

Soulé has provided scientific definitions for the terms "conservation" and "preservation." In his usage, "preservation" means "the maintenance of individuals or groups, but not for their evolutionary change." He proposes that "conservation" be taken to denote "policies and programs for the long-term retention of natural communities under conditions which provide for the potential for continuing evolution." Mitch Friedman carries this a step further by introducing the concept of "ecosystem conservation." This approach "involves the preservation of ecosystem wilderness: enough of the land area and functional components—the creatures *and* their habitat—to insure the continuation of processes which have co-evolved over immeasurable time."[12]

One can quibble over the choice of terms. "Conservation" has negative associations with Pinchot and the Resource Conservation and Development position. And "preservation" does not necessarily mean trying to maintain something in a static state, such as "preserving jam" or "deep-freezing" a wilderness. Perhaps "protection" would be a more neutral term. However, the term "ecosystem conservation" means protecting the ongoing dynamic continuum of evolutionary processes that constitutes the overall ecological health of the planet, in the sense described by Aldo Leopold.

It is thus clear that the *primary purpose* in setting aside and evaluating wilderness areas and wild nature preserves, from the standpoint of conservation biology and the ecological crisis, is the conservation and protection of wild plants, animals, and ecosystems (biotic diversity) and the continuation of wild evolutionary processes.

Based upon these objectives, we need to look at present global ecological realities. As Friedman points out:

> An element of panic is present within the literature of conservation biology, as well as among the conservation community at large. This panic originates predominately from the present rate of species extinction, and the forecasts for impending mass extinction. We presently have scarcely a clue of even the total number of species on the planet, with estimates ranging between three and thirty-seven million. Yet, some researchers are predicting that anthropogenic extinctions, at current rates (which do not consider military disasters or other unpredictable events), may eliminate as many as a third of the planet's species over the next several decades (Meyers, 1987). This is shocking to anyone who treasures the intrinsic values of Earth's natural diversity and fecundity, or who fears for the fate of humanity and the planet as a whole. While most of these extinctions are occurring as a result of tropical rainforest deforestation, the same processes are occurring in temperate areas, including the United States (Wilcove et al., 1986).[13]

A further crisis that conservation biology has brought to public attention, as the result of ecological research in the 1980s, is that existing nature reserves (namely, national park and forest wilderness areas) do not meet realistic ecological criteria: they are too small and disconnected to protect biodiversity and ecological/evolutionary processes. Friedman claims:

> It is not enough to preserve some habitat for each species if we want to conserve ecosystems; the habitat must remain in the conditions under which the resident species evolved. For this reason, national forests, under present "multiple use" management, may not be effective nature reserves for many species.

> Historically, national parks and other reserves have been established according to political, or other nonbiological considerations. . . . To conserve species diversity, the legal boundaries of nature reserves should be congruent with natural criteria (Newmark, 1985). For instance, a reserve may be large [e.g., Everglades National Park] while still not protecting the ecological integrity of the area.

> Newmark (1985) suggests that reserves contain not only entire watersheds, but at least the minimum area necessary to maintain viable populations of those species which have the largest home ranges. Others have stated that complete, intact ecosystems should be preserved (Terborgh and Winter, 1980; Noss, 1985).[14]

In the 1970s Michael Soulé examined twenty wildlife reserves in East Africa, including the massive Tsavo and Serengeti national parks. He and his fellow researchers projected that

> all of the reserves will suffer extinctions in the near future. Their study predicts that a typical reserve, if it becomes a habitat island, will lose almost half of its large mammal species over the next 500 years . . . when a habitat island, for instance a national park surrounded by national forest, is reduced in size (i.e., clearcutting along the park boundaries), the number of species in that island will decrease. The empirical evidence for the relaxation effect is alarming, and reflects the urgency with which we must re-evaluate our conservation strategies and remedy the situation.[15]

Edward Grumbine further points out that

> Newmark (1985) investigated eight parks and park assemblages and found that even the largest reserve was six times too small to support minimum viable populations of species such as grizzly bear, mountain lion, black bear, wolverine, and gray wolf. A recent study by Salwasser et al., (1987) looked beyond park boundaries and included adjacent public lands as part of conservation networks. The results were the same. Only the largest area (81,000 square km) was sufficient to protect large vertebrate species over the long term. . . . Virtually every study of this type has reached similar conclusions: No park in the coterminus U.S. is capable of supporting minimum viable populations of large mammals over the long term. And the situation is worsening.[16]

Frankel and Soulé claim that "an area on the order of 600,000 square km (approximately equal to all of Washington and Oregon) is necessary for speciation of birds and large mammals."[17]

Christopher Manes quotes Soulé as saying that "for the first time in hundreds of millions of years significant evolutionary change in most higher organisms is coming to a screeching halt. . . . Vertebrate evolution may be at an end." Manes claims that Soulé's remarks may be as significant as the findings of Copernicus or Darwin in that "only a hundred or so years after Darwin 'discovered' our fundamental relationship to nature in terms of evolution, we are, according to Soulé, putting an end to it."[18]

The inescapable conclusion is this: there needs to be widespread public recognition that current global wilderness and nature preserve protection policies are failing miserably. Past policies and strategies have been based on inadequate ecological understanding. Humans have effectivity clogged the evolutionary arteries of Mother Gaia.

Along with protecting the ozone layer, minimizing the severity of the greenhouse effect, and stabilizing (and then reducing) the growth and size of the human population, the most crucial ecological task facing humanity at this time is to devise and implement realistic nature reserve protection strategies.

## APPROACHES TO GLOBAL ECOSYSTEM PROTECTION ZONING

Even before conservation biologists were demonstrating the necessity for greatly expanded nature preserves throughout the world with interconnecting corridors, ecologists and environmentalists over twenty years ago had called for worldwide zoning to protect wild ecosystems and species. The first such proposal was made by David Brower in 1967. Declaring that less than 10 percent of the Earth had, at that time, escaped technological exploitation by humans, he proposed protecting the remaining wilderness and "granting other life forms the right to coexist" in what Jerry Mander called an Earth International Park.[19]

Another major zoning proposal was put forth in 1971 by the noted ecologist Eugene Odum. Odum proposed that:

> *The biosphere as a whole should be zoned*, in order to protect it from the human impact. We must strictly confine the Urban-Industrial Zone and the Production Zone (agriculture, grazing, fishing), enlarge the Compromise Zone, and drastically expand the Protection Zone, i.e., wilderness, wild rivers. Great expanses of seacoasts and estuaries must be included in the Protection Zone, along with forests, prairies and various habitat types. We must learn that the multiple-use Compromise Zone is no substitute, with its mining, lumbering, grazing, and recreation in the national forests, for the scientific, aesthetic, and genetic pool values of the Protection Zone. Such zoning, if carried out in time, may be the only way to limit the destructive impact of our technological–industrial–agri-business complex on earth.

In commenting upon Odum's proposal, John Phillips claimed that "to go so far as to zone the biosphere and set aside an adequate Protection Zone would be a supreme act of rationality by which the rational animal could protect the rest of life on earth, and himself, from his own irrational temptations."[20]

In 1973, Paul Shepard made a daring proposal for global ecosystem protection. In order to allow for the huge expanses of unmanaged wilderness needed "for ecological and evolutionary systems on a scale essential to their own requirements," he proposed that the interiors of continents and islands be allowed to return to the wild. Based on the now optimistic assumption that human population would stabilize by the year 2020 at 8 billion people, he proposed that humans live in cities strung in narrow ribbons along the edges of the continents. Hunting/gathering forays would range into the central wilderness, but there would be no permanent habitation.[21]

Based on his ecocentric orientation, Shepard foresaw the huge amounts of wilderness necessary for the healthy ecological and evolutionary functioning of the Earth. But his proposal has a number of practical and social/political problems, not the least of which would be (1) the physical problems involved in relocating humans to the edges of the continents, and (2) the pressures exerted by these concentrated human populations on the ocean shoreline ecosystems and estuaries. At this stage of history, it is probably more realistic to expand and interconnect ecosystem protection zones with the basically existing patterns of human settlement in mind.

Two other strategies that were developed to protect wild ecosystems are the Biosphere Reserve concept, as part of UNESCO's Man and the Biosphere Program, and the World Heritage Site system. According to Edward Grumbine:

> A model biosphere reserve consists of four integrated zones: a large protected core; a buffer zone; a restoration zone; and a stable cultural area where "indigenous people live in harmony with the environment." . . . the National Park Service has informally adopted the biosphere reserve model as a guide to regional land planning [and] after eighteen years, 41 biosphere reserves exist in the U.S. many of which occupy both national park and forest lands.[22]

Grumbine sees some possibilities with World Heritage Site designations, but he argues that there are serious problems with the Biosphere Reserve concept: the zones are not properly related and the "self-sustaining" core is not large enough to allow for speciation. He suggests that the biosphere reserve model be replaced by a national system of biological reserves.

## ECOLOGICAL RESTORATION, MITIGATION, AND STEWARDSHIP

Grumbine further argues that the establishment of biological reserves needs to be supplemented by a major program of *ecological restoration*:

> Restoration of damaged lands must be married to the goal of native diversity. This follows the wilderness recovery strategy of Noss (1986) and would include large scale restoration of natural fire cycles, recovery of threatened, endangered, and extirpated species, road closures and reforestation projects, stream rehabilitation to increase native anadromous fisheries, and much more (see

Berger, 1985). Once an area was restored, nature would take its course with minimal interference from managers. The amount of work to be done would likely offset the loss of jobs in exploitive industries.[23]

The concept of ecological restoration is a crucial one for all of the zones, but serious problems emerge when developers try to use it as a justification for "mitigation" procedures: claiming that we can continue to develop (that is, *destroy*) wild ecosystems, displace wildlife, and then compensate these losses by "restoring" an equivalent area elsewhere. This is a shortsighted foolhardy approach, part of the overall "Disneyland syndrome" and the mentality that "human ingenuity and technological know-how can solve all our problems." This neglects the difficult and expensive process of restoration, together with the probability that restoration projects will be only partially successful. In all likelihood, they cannot reproduce the incredibly complex and diverse wild ecosystems that were destroyed. Further, mitigation procedures and environmental impact reports (EIR's), as they now exist in environmental law and as taught in environmental management programs in colleges and universities, function basically to "grease the skids" of continued growth and development as wildlife habitat is fragmented and destroyed, and wild flora and fauna relentlessly continue to disappear.

The anthropocentric/ecocentric debate has resurfaced in the context of trying to clarify the concept of "ecological restoration." Some restoration theorists argue for a stewardship approach in which restoration areas are to be treated as agricultural farms to be continuously manipulated and "enhanced" by humans (which is similar to the ideology of the Forest Service and their genetically "enhanced" forests). For instance, restoration theorist John Harper proposes the manipulative, interventionist, Baconian/Cartesian model of science as appropriate for ecology and restoration ecology:

> The *raison d'être* for a science of ecology is presumably the development of an understanding of the workings of nature that would enable us to predict its behavior and to manage and control it to our liking. . . . [Thus] the importance of a more manipulative, experimental approach to ecological research such as that represented by restoration ecology.

There is a play on words here, a bit of Orwellian Newspeak, with Harper's concept of ecological restoration. If one is going to continuously manipulate, there is no *ecological* restoration. By proposing the human-dominant managerial stewardship model for restoration ecology (the "participatory happy gardener" image of René Dubos) Harper seems totally unconcerned with the continual extension of human domesticity and the elimination of more wildness while, at the same time he assumes that humans are competent to manage Nature. Professional ecologists such as Frank Egler have countered that "Nature is not only more complex than we think, it is more complex that we *can* think!"[24]

Critics claim that proponents of nature preserves (which are largely free of human intervention and manipulation) view Nature as "static." But from Thoreau and Muir to modern conservation biologists, the protection of wildness in nature (or wilderness) preserves has been seen as the protection of wild evolutionary change: in Soulé's words, as the conservation of "natural communities under conditions which provide for the potential for continuing evolution." Ecological restoration should be followed, as Grumbine suggests, by allowing nature to take its course "with minimal interference from managers." Stewardship concepts of restoration should be confined to the bioculture.

## FREE NATURE, BIOCULTURE, AND BIOREGIONALISM

Arne Naess has added an important refinement to zoning proposals and ecosystem protection strategies by distinguishing between *wilderness* protection zones (where people do not live and resource extraction is prohibited) and what he calls *free nature*. "Free nature" consists of areas of relatively sparse human habitation (for example, the foothills of the Sierra, parts of northern Europe, and much of the Third World) where wild natural processes are still essentially intact and dominant. These areas should be zoned to protect natural processes and wildlife while encouraging nonexploitive bioregional living. The remaining Fourth World tribal peoples who are still following traditional ways with minimal impact on wild ecosystems, can be thought of as living in free nature areas.[25]

One of the central features of thinking about ecological sustainable societies is the move toward decentralization and bioregional ways of life, which involves reinhabiting and restoring damaged ecosystems. But Roderick Nash, a major theorist and proponent of wilderness protection, has worried that a total movement toward bioregional reinhabitation of the Earth at this point (what he calls the "garden scenario") would be ecologically disastrous: "The problem, of course, is numbers. There are simply too many people on the planet to decentralize into garden environments and still have significant amounts of wilderness."[26] Elsewhere, Nash characterizes bioregionalism as "the contemporary attempt to 'reinhabit' wilderness areas."[27]

Nash is entirely justified in calling attention to the limitations of an overly ambitious bioregional program at this point in history. It is not clear, however, that the intent of contemporary bioregionalists is to reinhabit wilderness areas. Leading bioregional theorists such as Peter Berg, Gary Snyder, Raymond Dasmann, Thomas Berry, and Kirkpatrick Sale are fully aware of the importance of establishing greatly expanded wilderness/protection zones. Bioregional ways of life are appropriate for "free nature" and for ecologically restructured cities as suggested in such projects as Peter Berg's "green cities."[28] Redesigned ecological cities would contain wild and semi-wild areas interspersed with human inhabited areas, either by protecting and expanding upon wild or near-wild areas that now exist near cities, or by restoring such areas.

Roderick Nash points out that "in 1982 [Edward] Abbey expressed his basic belief that humans had no right to use more than a portion of the planet and they had already passed that limit. Wild places must be left wild." In 1985, Stanford ecologist Paul Ehrlich claimed that "in a country like the United States, there is not the slightest excuse for developing one more square inch of undisturbed land." In their 1987 survey of world environmental problems, Anne and Paul Ehrlich proposed that, as a general policy "the prime step [is] *to permit no development of any more virgin lands . . .* whatever remaining relatively undisturbed land exists that supports a biotic community of any significance should be set aside and fiercely defended against encroachment."[29] As the Ehrlichs point out, the 6 billion humans now on Earth have already destroyed or appropriated approximately 40 percent of biomass productivity on the land.[30]

Environmental ethicist Paul Taylor also promotes the idea of the protection of wilderness as species habitat. He claims that we must

> constantly place constraints on ourselves so as to cause the least possible interference in natural ecosystems and their biota. . . . If [humans] have a sufficient concern for the natural world, they can control their own population growth, change their habits of consumption, and regulate their technology so as to save at least part of the Earth's surface as habitat for wild animals and plants.[31]

Taylor finds it necessary to distinguish between the basic needs of humans versus their nonbasic wants. To allow for sufficient amounts of species habitat, humans must reduce their nonbasic wants and consumption habits when these come into conflict with the basic needs of other species for survival and well-being. Taylor's analysis coincides with Naess's distinction between vital and nonvital needs and wants, which is incorporated into the Deep Ecology platform.[32]

Paul Taylor makes another important contribution to the discussion of ecosystem protection zoning with his concept of the *bioculture.* He defines bioculture as "that aspect of any human culture in which humans create and regulate the environment of living things and systemically exploit them for human benefit."[33] Large-scale agriculture, pets, domestic animal and plant breeding, and "tree plantations" all belong to the human bioculture. Wilderness protection zoning, in effect, separates the world of the wild from the exploitive human activities of the bioculture. "Free nature" can be conceived of as a sort of hybrid buffer zone (where wild ecological processes predominate) situated between protection zones and biocultural zones.

Taylor's concept of the bioculture is a useful one. For instance, it helps us see that many movements are primarily involved with an ecological reform of the bioculture. The organic farm movement (inspired by Wendell Berry and Wes Jackson) is one example of this. The animal rights movement, in its concern with the "rights" of *all* animals, has, at least theoretically, failed to distinguish between the conditions of domestic animals in the bioculture and the very different situation of wild animals in wild ecosystems, sometimes with alarmingly anti-ecological results.

The present unecological goals and practices of the Forest Service (and similar practices worldwide) in clear-cutting wild forest ecosystems and replacing them with "tree plantations" can now be seen as an attempt to extend the bioculture at the expense of the wild. Taylor points out that the ethics of the bioculture differs fundamentally from the basically "noninterference" ethics appropriate to wilderness/protection zones. Perhaps some ecologically enlightened version of the "stewardship" model is appropriate for the bioculture, but not for wilderness/protection areas. Different kinds of problems arise when domestic animals gone ferral (and exotics) intrude in wild ecosystems, when wild animals stray from the protection zones into biocultural zones, and when there are mixed communities of wild and domestic as in "free nature."[34]

## WILDERNESS PROTECTION IN THE FIRST WORLD

The question still remains concerning how much of the Earth should be protected in wilderness and other ecosystem protection zones. The basic answer to this question has essentially been given by the recent research of the conservation biologists: enough habitat to protect the diversity and abundance of wild species, and the ongoing ecological health of the Earth, which involves, among other things, continued speciation and wild evolutionary change. Along these lines, Arne Naess has provided a future ecological vision toward which we can progress:

> I am not saying that we should have preserved the primordial forest as a whole, but looking back we can imagine a development such that, let us say, one third was preserved as wilderness, one third as free nature with mixed communities, which leaves one third for cities, paved roads, etc. [bioculture]. This would probably be enough, and I guess most people with influence in matters of the environment would agree. But of course, it is a wild fantasy, which is, incidentally, an important kind of wilderness![35]

To realize how ecologically out of balance we are in the United States, based upon Naess's suggestion, we have to consider Thomas Fleischner's point that "over 95 percent of the contiguous United States has been altered from its original state. Only 2 percent is legally protected from exploitive uses."[36] And even that 2 percent lacks adequate ecological protection. For example, Forest Service legally designated wilderness areas continue to allow mining, sport hunting, and domestic animal grazing within their boundaries. Legislative efforts are now being made to revise existing mining laws that have been the cause of much public land abuse. Some have claimed that, apart from ancient forest destruction, the greatest cause of ecological destruction on public lands (both wilderness and nonwilderness areas) is cattle and sheep grazing.

Domestic animal grazing destroys the natural plant and grass communities, causes erosion, damages streams and other water supplies, competes with wildlife, results in federal programs to kill large numbers of large predators (including the poisoning and trapping of huge numbers of "nontarget" wildlife), and should be phased out.[37]

To begin to achieve an ecological land-use balance, once the ecologically destructive uses of now-existing Forest Service wilderness have been eliminated, the remaining 3 percent of *de facto* (nondesignated) wilderness should be placed in protection zones. This would bring the contiguous United States to a total to 5 percent protected habitat. That still leaves the contiguous United States approximately 30 percent short of a ratio of one-third wilderness, one-third free nature, and one-third bioculture (disregarding, for the present, the zoning of free nature).

Under the provisions of the Wilderness Act of 1964, the congressional battles over legal classification of wilderness in the National Parks and National Forests have already been fought, and mainline reform environmentalists have compromised severely in both cases, particularly the latter. Now the battle to zone land as wilderness is occurring over the 250 million acres administered by the Bureau of Land Management (BLM). The BLM is studying only 10 percent of its land (25 million acres) for possible wilderness designation (most BLM land is contracted out to private corporations and individuals for mining and domestic animal grazing). The projections are that, after the political wrangling and compromises are concluded, only 10 to 15 million acres will be legally protected. It must be remembered that the lands being discussed here (Park Service, Forest Service, and BLM) are *public* lands!

The Wilderness Act of 1964, while framed and successfully lobbied by dedicated conservationists, is nevertheless a pre-ecological document and, accordingly, its stated purposes and provisions do not reflect the huge tracts of wilderness protection zones (and the degree of protection) required for species and wild ecosystem protection, especially for large mammal speciation. A recent news magazine article discussing the Wilderness Act and the upcoming BLM wilderness fight still couches the issues largely in terms of anthropocentric special-interest compromise politics: of wilderness recreation versus "motorized-recreation and commercial interests." The ecological issues are all but ignored.[38]

In order to boost the wilderness protection zone percentages toward the 30 percent figure, it would probably be necessary to place most Forest Service and BLM lands in protection zones and to restore them to wildlife habitat. A recent proposal by Deborah and Frank Popper of Rutgers University to return the Great Plains to buffalo habitat would also greatly increase ecosystem protection areas.

These strategies for protecting wildness and biodiversity have recently been refined and sophisticated. For instance, the Wildlands Project has been working closely with conservation biologists to develop a North American Wilderness Recovery Strategy. According to Dave Foreman:

Going far beyond current National Park, Wildlife Refuge, and Wilderness Area systems, where individual reserves are discrete islands of wildness in a sea of human-modified landscapes, [conservation biologists] call for large Wilderness cores, buffer zones, and biological corridors. . . . Biological corridors would provide secure travelways between core reserves for the dispersal of wide-ranging species, for genetic exchange between populations, and for migration of organisms in response to climate change. Surrounding the core reserves would be buffer zones where increasing levels of compatible human activity would be allowed away from the cores. . . . Conservation biologists propose to begin with existing National Parks, Wilderness Areas, and other protected or unprotected natural areas [and enlarge and connect them]. . . . The key concept in this new Wilderness Area model is *connectivity*.[39]

Foreman has recently discussed the history of the bioregional/reinhabitation movement beginning with the writings of Gary Snyder, Peter Berg, and Raymond Dasmann. He claims that:

The centerpiece of every bioregional group's platform should be a great core wilderness preserve where all the indigenous creatures are present and the natural flow is intact. Other wilderness preserves, both large and small, should be established and protected throughout the bioregion, and natural corridors established to allow for the free flow of genetic material between them and to such preserves in other bioregion. . . . These core wilderness preserves should be sacred shrines to us as reinhabitory people, but they transcend even their sacredness to us in simply being what they are—reserves of native diversity.[40]

## AN INTERNATIONAL PERSPECTIVE

Increasingly, our environmental problems are being recognized as global in scope and, as such, require effective international cooperation. Noel Brown, director of the United Nations Environmental Program, indicated that an Ecological Council (comparable to the Security Council) could soon be a reality.[41] With the human population predicted to soar to 10 to 15 billion people, if unchecked, by the middle of the next century (population biologists argue that 1 to 2 billion people worldwide, living comfortably at a basic-needs consumption level, would be maximum for what Naess calls "wide" ecological sustainability), the United Nations needs to reorganize its population control agencies and ecological protection programs to reflect a streamlined, effective, integrated biosphere approach to environmental problems. The United Nations General Assembly has already officially adopted an ecocentric orientation when it approved the World Charter for Nature in 1982. The charter asserts: "Every form of life is unique, warranting respect regardless of its worth to man, and, to accord other organisms such recognition, man must be guided by a moral code of action. . . Nature shall be respected and its essential processes shall not be disrupted."[42] The severity of the ecological crisis must be fully appreciated, and the Charter for Nature needs to be reaffirmed and effectively implemented. Humanity has now entered an era of what some ecologists are calling *biological meltdown*!

The urgency of the ecological crisis suggests that the United Nations should give the highest priority to stabilizing the human population in the shortest time possible while ensuring that human dignity and the ideals of justice are protected. Birth control programs, including making contraceptives freely available to all who want them, have *quite recently* proven to be highly effective in dramatically reducing birthrates in certain Third World countries. It is just as important that population be stabilized, and then reduced, in First World countries. The massive funding and implementation of such programs is needed immediately throughout the world. The United Nations should continue to help feed the hungry and improve basic living conditions in Third World countries, and discourage consumerism and further industrialization throughout the world as part of an overall program of ecological and economic sustainability. Major educational programs should be instituted to "ecologize" the peoples of the world.

Unlike First World countries, which are now overdeveloped, overpopulated, and ecologically unsustainable, Third World countries need to improve their overall material standards of living, although along ecologically sustainable paths. It is unrealistic and unjust to expect Third World countries to turn to the protection of their wild ecosystems *at the expense* of the vital needs of their human populations. But the magnitude and severity of the global ecological crisis must be fully appreciated. Third World countries should be encouraged to adopt as high a priority as possible on the establishment of ecosystem protection zones, and the protection of large areas of free nature.

## NOTES

1. John Hendee, George Stankey, and Robert Lucas, *Wilderness Management* (Washington, D.C.: USDA Forest Service Misc. Publication No. 1365, 1978), pp. 140–41; quoted in Holmes Rolston III, "Values Gone Wild," in Rolston, *Philosophy Gone Wild: Essays in Environmental Ethics* (Buffalo: Prometheus Books, 1986), p. 119.
2. Alston Chase, *Playing God in Yellowstone* (Boston: Atlantic Monthly Press, 1986), p. 33.
3. For a critique of Chase's views, see Dave Foreman, Doug Peacock, and George Sessions, "Who's 'Playing God in Yellowstone'?" *Earth First! Journal* 7, 11 (1986): 18–21.
4. John Rodman, "Resource Conservation—Economics and After," unpublished manuscript, Pitzer College, Claremont, Calif., 1976; see also Bill Devall and George Sessions, "The Development of Natural Resources and the Integrity of Nature," *Environmental Ethics* 6, 4 (1984): 293–322.
5. Joel Connelly, "British Columbia's Big Cut: Who Owns the Ancient Forests?" *Sierra* 76, no. 3 (1991): 42–53; see also Gary Snyder, *The Practice of the Wild* (San Francisco: North Point Press, 1990), pp. 116–43.
6. See Bill Devall (ed.), *Clearcut: The Tragedy of Industrial Forestry* (San Francisco: Sierra Club Books, 1994).
7. Chris Maser, *The Redesigned Forest* (San Pedro, Calif.: R&E Miles Publisher, 1988).
8. Bob Nixon, "Focus on Forests and Forestry," *The Trumpeter* 6, 2 (1989): 38.
9. Edward Abbey, *Desert Solitaire: A Season in the Wilderness* (New York: McGraw-Hill, 1968); see also Joseph Sax, *Mountains without Handrails* (Ann Arbor: University of Michigan Press, 1980).
10. Mitch Friedman, "How Much Is Enough?: Lessons from Conservation Biology," in Mitch Friedman (ed.), *Forever Wild: Conserving the Greater North Cascades Ecosystem* (Mountain Hemlock Press [P.O. Box 2962, Bellingham, WA 98227], 1988), p. 34. I have drawn much

of the following material on conservation biology from the excellent summaries in this book by Friedman and by Edward Grumbine, "Ecosystem Management for Native Diversity." For further discussions of the importance of conservation biology for environmentalism in the '90s, see James R. Udall, "Launching the Natural Ark," *Sierra* 76, 5 (1991): 80–89; Edward Grumbine, *Ghost Bears: Exploring the Biodiversity Crisis* (Washington, D.C.: Island Press, 1992).

11. Michael Soulé, "What Is Conservation Biology?" *Bioscience* 35 (1985): 727–34; quoted in Friedman, ibid.

12. Friedman, *Forever Wild*, pp. 1–2; see also O. H. Frankel and Michael Soulé, *Conservation and Evolution* (Cambridge: Cambridge University Press, 1981); Michael Soulé and D. Simberloff, "What Do Genetics and Ecology Tell Us about the Design of Nature Reserves?" *Biological Conservation* 35 (1986): 19–40.

13. Friedman, "How Much Is Enough?" p. 39; Norman Myers, "The Extinction Spasm Impending: Synergisms at Work," *Conservation Biology* I (1987): 14–21; A. P. Dobson, C. H. McLellan, and D. S. Wilcove, "Habitat Fragmentation in the Temperate Zone," in M. Soulé (ed.), *Conservation Biology: The Science of Scarcity and Diversity* (Sunderland, Mass.: Sinauer, 1986), pp. 237–56.

14. Friedman, ibid.; A. Runte, *National Parks: The American Experience* (Lincoln: University of Nebraska Press, 1987); W. D. Newmark, "Legal and Biotic Boundaries of Western North American National Parks: A Problem of Congruence," *Biological Conservation* 33 (1985): 197–208; W. D. Newmark, "A Land-Bridge Island Perspective on Mammalian Extinctions in Western North American Parks," *Nature* 325 (1987): 430–32; R. M. May and D. S. Wilcove, "National Park Boundaries and Ecological Realities," *Nature* 324 (1986): 206–7; J. Terborgh and B. Winter, "Some Causes of Extinction," in B. A. Wilcox and Michael Soulé, *Conservation Biology: An Evolutionary-Ecological Perspective* (Sunderland, Mass.: Sinauer, 1980), pp. 19–133; R. F. Noss, "Wilderness Recovery and Ecological Restoration," *Earth First!* 5, no. 8 (1985): 18–19; R. F. Noss, "Recipe for Wilderness Recovery," *Earth First!* 6 (1986): 22, 25.

15. Friedman, "How Much Is Enough?" p. 37; C. Holtby, B. A. Wilcox, and Michael Soulé, "Benign Neglect: A Model of Faunal Collapse in the Game Reserves of East Africa," *Biological Conservation* 15 (1979): 259–70.

16. Grumbine, "Ecosystem Management," p. 46; W. D. Newmark, "Legal and Biotic Boundaries."

17. Friedman, "How Much Is Enough?" p. 43; Frankel and Soulé, *Conservation and Evolution*.

18. Michael Soulé, "Conservation Biology: Its Scope and Challenge," in M. Soulé and B. Wilcox (eds.), *Conservation Biology*, p. 166; quoted in Christopher Manes, *Green Rage: Radical Environmentalism and the Unmaking of Civilization* (Boston: Little, Brown, 1990), pp. 34–35.

19. David Brower, "Toward an Earth International Park," *Sierra Club Bulletin* 52, 9 (1967): 20.

20. Eugene P. Odum, *Fundamentals of Ecology* (Philadelphia: W. B. Saunders, 1971), p. 269; John Phillips, a philosopher/ecologist at St. Cloud State University in Minnesota, developed Odum's proposal in 1974 and presented it in "On Environmental Ethics," read at American Philosophical Association, San Francisco, 1978.

21. Paul Shepard, *The Tender Carnivore and the Sacred Game* (New York: Scribner's, 1973), pp. 260–73.

22. Edward Grumbine, "Ecosystem Management for Native Diversity," pp. 48, 52–53.

23. Grumbine, ibid.; R. F. Noss, "Recipe for Wilderness Recovery"; J. J. Berger, *Restoring the Earth: How Americans Are Working to Renew Damaged Environments* (New York: Knopf, 1985).

24. John Harper, "The Heuristic Value of Ecological Restoration," in William Jordan (ed.), *Restoration Ecology* (Cambridge: Cambridge University Press, 1987), pp. 35–36; C. Mark Cowell, "Ecological Restoration and Environmental Ethics," *Environmental Ethics* 15, no. 1 (1993): 19–32; for critiques of stewardship models of ecological restoration, see Eric Katz, "The Big Lie: Human Restoration of Nature," *Technology and the Environment* (New York: JAI Press, 1992), pp. 231–41; Jamie Sayan, "Notes toward a Restoration Ethic," *Restoration and Management Notes* 7, 2 (1989): 57–59; see also Andrew McLaughlin, *Regarding Nature* (New York: State University of New York Press, 1993), pp. 214–17.

25. Arne Naess, "Ecosophy, Population, and Free Nature," *The Trumpeter* 5, 3 (1988).

26. Roderick Nash, *Wilderness and the American Mind*, 3rd ed. (New Haven: Yale University Press, 1982), pp. 380–84.

27. Roderick Nash, *The Rights of Nature*, pp. 270–71, n. 28.

28. See Peter Berg, Beryl Magilavy, Seth Zuckerman, *A Green City Program* (San Francisco: Planet Drum Books, 1989); Peter Berg (ed.), *Reinhabiting a Separate Country: A Bioregional Anthology of Northern California* (San Francisco: Planet Drum Foundation, 1978); Gary Snyder, "Re-inhabitation," in Snyder, *The Old Ways* (San Francisco: City Lights Books, 1977), pp. 57–66; Thomas Berry, "Bioregions: The Context for Reinhabiting the Earth," in Berry, *The Dream of the Earth*, pp. 163–70; Kirkpatrick Sale, *Dwellers in the Land: The Bioregional Vision* (San Francisco: Sierra Club Books, 1985).

29. Roderick Nash, *The Rights of Nature*, pp. 168–69; Paul Ehrlich, "Comments," *Defenders of Wildlife*, Nov./Dec. 1985; Anne and Paul Ehrlich, *Earth* (New York: Franklin Watts, 1987), p. 242.

30. Ehrlich and Ehrlich, ibid., p. 153.

31. Paul Taylor, *Respect for Nature: A Theory of Environmental Ethics* (Princeton: Princeton University Press, 1986), pp. 288, 310.

32. Ibid., pp. 269–77.

33. Ibid., pp. 53–58.

34. For a critique of the stewardship model as applied to agriculture, see Sara Ebenreck, "A Partnership Farmland Ethic," *Environmental Ethics* 5, 1 (1983): 33–45; Arne Naess, "Self-Realization in Mixed Communities of Humans, Bears, Sheep and Wolves," *Inquiry* 22 (1979): 231–42; Arne Naess and Ivar Mysterud, "Philosophy of Wolf Policies I," *Conservation Biology* 1, 1 (1987): 22–34.

35. Arne Naess, "Ecosophy, Population, and Free Nature," p. 118.

36. Thomas Fleischner, "Keeping It Wild: Toward a Deeper Wilderness Management," in Friedman, *Forever Wild*, p. 79.

37. For proposals to eliminate domestic grazing on public lands, see Denzel and Nancy Ferguson, *Sacred Cows at the Public Trough* (Bend, Ore.: Maverick Publications, 1983).

38. "The Battle for the Wilderness," *U.S. News and World Report* 107, 1 (July 1989): 16–21, 24–25.

39. See Dave Foreman and Howie Wolke, *The Big Outside* (New York: Harmony/Crown Books, 1992); John Davis (ed.), "The Wildlands Project: Plotting a Wilderness Recovery Strategy," *Wild Earth* (1993), special issue; Dave Foreman, "The Northern Rockies Ecosystem Protection Act and the Evolving Wilderness Area Model," *Wild Earth* 3, 4 (1993): 57–62.

40. Dave Foreman, "Who Speaks for Wolf?" in D. Foreman, *Confessions of an Ecowarrior* (New York: Harmony Books, 1991), pp. 37–50; for a bioregional ecologist's plan to save California's ecosystems and wildlife by limiting human population, see Raymond F. Dasmann, *The Destruction of California* (New York: Macmillan, 1965).

41. See W. R. Prescott, "The Rights of Earth: An Interview with Dr. Noel J. Brown," *In Context* 22 (1989): 29–34.

42. *World Charter for Nature. United Nations General Assembly* (New York: United Nations, A/RES/37/7, Nov. 9, 1982); see also Harold W. Wood, Jr., "The United Nations World Charter for Nature," *Ecology Law Quarterly* 12 (1985): 977–96.

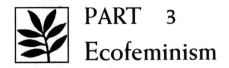

# PART 3
# Ecofeminism

# INTRODUCTION

*Karen J. Warren*

Karen J. Warren is professor of philosophy at Macalester College in St. Paul, Minnesota. Her scholarly interest in environmental ethics began in the early 1970s, when she completed a doctoral dissertation on the legal status of non-human natural objects (e.g., trees, rivers, ecosystems). Warren has edited or co-edited five books on ecofeminist philosophy, environmental ethics, and peace studies, and recently completed *Ecofeminist Philosophy: A Western Perspective on What It Is and Why It Matters*. She has published over fifty articles on issues in ethics, feminism (particularly ecological feminism), and critical thinking. Warren has given keynote addresses on ecofeminist philosophy throughout the United States, as well as in Argentina, Australia, Brazil, Costa Rica, Finland, Norway, Russia, and Sweden, and has taught philosophy and critical thinking about environmental issues for elementary and secondary school students and teachers.

The past few decades have witnessed an enormous interest in both the women's movement and the environmental movement. Many feminists have argued that the goals of these two movements are interconnected and mutually reinforcing. Ultimately, they involve the development of worldviews and practices that are free from male-biased models of domination. As Rosemary Radford Ruether wrote in 1975 in her book *New Woman/New Earth:*

> Women must see that there can be no liberation for them and so solution to the ecological crisis within a society whose fundamental model of relationships continues to be one of domination. They must unite the demands of the women's movement with those of the ecological movement to envision a radical reshaping of the basic socioeconomic relations and the underlying values of this [modern industrial] society. (204)

Since the early 1970s, many feminists, especially ecological feminists ("ecofeminists"), have defended Reuther's basic point: The environment is a feminist issue.

Just what makes the environment a feminist issue? In this essay I suggest possible answers to that question by discussing the scholarly literature of ecofeminism. Beginning with a characterization of ecofeminism, I identify ten types of "women–other human Others–nature interconnections." These are interconnections among how one treats humans and human groups who are oppressed, marginalized, exploited, or "Other," on the one hand, and how one treats nonhuman animals, plants, and nature, on the other hand. Discussion of these interconnections provides both an overview of key issues in ecofeminism and the reasons ecofeminists offer for the centrality of ecofeminist insights into feminism, environmentalism, and environmental philosophy. It also helps to situate the four essays included in Part Three (essays by Merchant, Shiva, Curtin, and Warren) within the range of scholarly positions on ecofeminism. I conclude by suggesting that the philosophical significance of ecofeminism is that it challenges feminism to take environmental issues seriously and it encourages environmental philosophy to take ecofeminism seriously.

# A CHARACTERIZATION OF ECOFEMINISM

Just as there is not one feminism, there is not one ecofeminism. *Ecological feminism (ecofeminism)* is an umbrella term for a variety of positions that have roots in different, sometimes competing, feminist practices and theories. Different ecofeminist perspectives reflect different feminist perspectives (e.g., liberal, Marxist, radical, socialist, black, and anticolonial feminisms). They also reflect different understandings of the nature of, and solutions to, contemporary environmental problems. So, it is an open question how many, which, and on what grounds any of the various positions in environmental philosophy that claim to be feminist are properly identified as ecofeminist. Stated differently, what one takes to be an ecofeminist position will depend largely on how one conceptualizes feminism, ecofeminism, and environmental philosophy.

What, then, can one say about ecofeminism? Despite important differences among ecofeminists, I think ecofeminists agree about three basic claims: First, there are significant interconnections among the unjustified dominations of women, other human Others (that is, other marginalized, exploited, or dominated humans), and nonhuman animals, plants, and nature. Second, it is important to feminism, environmentalism, and environmental philosophy to understand the variety of women–other human Others–nature interconnections. Third, a central project of ecofeminism is to replace unjustified structures of domination with genuinely just structures and practices. At the heart of ecofeminism is a movement to make visible women–other human Others–nature interconnections and, where harmful, dismantle them.

# WOMEN, OTHER HUMAN OTHERS, NATURE: INTERCONNECTIONS

There are at least ten interconnections among the unjustified dominations of women, other marginalized humans, and nonhuman nature that surface in the scholarly literature of ecofeminism. These interconnections provide sometimes complementary, sometimes competing, analyses of interlocking systems of domination. A casual, albeit philosophically uncritical, perusal of these ten interconnections helps to identify why ecofeminists claim that the environment (ecology) is a feminist issue.

## Historical (Typically Causal) Interconnections

The pervasiveness of the dominations of women and nature has led some ecofeminists to offer historical and causal explanations of their interconnections. Some ecofeminists trace these interconnections to prototypical patterns of domination that began with the invasion of Indo-European societies by nomadic tribes from Eurasia between the sixth and third millennia B.C. For example, in her book *The Chalice and the Blade,* Riane Eisler describes the time before these invasions by pastoral patriarchs as a peaceful agrarian era, as a partnership society ruled by "the chalice, not the blade." The chalice symbolizes a cooperative, peaceful, egalitarian, partnership society characterized by nurturing relationships among humans and with nonhuman nature. The blade, on the other hand, symbolizes an aggressive, violent, war-prone, male-dominated society characterized by unequal power relationships and militaristic domination. Eisler claims that "the root of the problem lies in a social system in which the power of the Blade is idealized" (Eisler 1988, xviii).

Other ecofeminists locate the historical-causal explanations of the interconnected dominations of women and nature in cultural and scientific changes that occurred more recently. For example, Carolyn Merchant argues in *The Death of Nature* that between 1500–1700 an older, organic worldview of nature, characterized as a kindly beneficent female "who provided for the needs of mankind in an ordered, planned universe," was replaced by a reductionist, mechanistic worldview of modern science, which also characterized nature as female but as disorderly, wild, uncontrollable female capable of rendering general chaos (Merchant 1980, 1, 2). This mechanistic worldview is claimed to have caused "the death of nature" by sanctioning unchecked commercial and industrial expansion and providing the moral permissibility of environmental destruction.

Still other ecofeminists trace historical women–nature interconnections to patriarchal dominations and conceptions of reason and rationality in classical Greek philosophy. For example, Val Plumwood argues that the culprit is "rationalism," that long-standing Western philosophical tradition that both defines rationality as the hallmark of humanness and elevates humans over nonhuman animals and nature on grounds of humans' superior abilities to reason. Plumwood argues that rationalism establishes harmful value dualisms between culture and nature that have been both human-centered (anthropocentric) and male-centered (androcentric) (1993, 1996). Plumwood criticizes environmental philosophy generally for its failure "to engage properly various positions with the rationalist tradition, which has been inimical to both women and nature" (1996, 22).

## Conceptual Interconnections

Many ecofeminists, particularly ecofeminist philosophers, have argued that ultimately, women–other human Others–nature interconnections are located in conceptual structures of unjustified domination. One account (e.g., Plumwood 1993) locates the conceptual basis in harmful value dualisms and value hierarchies. These are ways of conceptualizing diversity in terms of mutually exclusive disjunctive pairs (value dualisms) and spatial Up-Down metaphors (value hierarchies) that attribute higher status, value, or prestige to one disjunct than the other and to whatever is identified as Up in relation to whatever is identified as Down. Frequently cited examples of these hierarchically organized value dualisms include the culture/nature, human/nature, reason/emotion, mind/body, man/woman, masculine/feminine dichotomies.

A similar, second account houses the problematic value dualisms and value hierarchies in larger, oppressive conceptual frameworks—ones that are common to *all* social systems of domination (e.g., sexism, racism, classism, heterosexism, ageism, ableism, colonialism, ethnocentrism) (see Warren 1990, 2000, and essay in this section). A conceptual framework is a set of basic beliefs, values, attitudes, and assumptions that shape and reflect how one see's oneself and one's world. A conceptual framework is *oppressive* when it explains, maintains, and sanctions unjustified relationships of domination and subordination. An oppressive conceptual framework is *patriarchal* when it explains, maintains, and sanctions the subordination of women by men. Oppressive conceptual frameworks are characterized not only by harmful value dualisms and value hierarchical thinking, but also by conceptions of power and privilege which systematically advantage the Ups and by "a logic of domination." It is the logic of domination that provides the all-important moral premise that superiority (Upness) justifies subordination (Downness). In this second account, it is oppressive and patriarchal conceptual frameworks, and the behaviors they give rise to, that perpetuate women–other human Others–nature interconnections.

A third account locates the conceptual interconnections in sex-gender differences, particularly in differentiated personality formation or consciousness (see Cheney 1987; Gray 1981; Salleh 1984). Typically, the claim is that socially constructed female bodily experiences such as childbearing and child rearing, rather than biology per se, situate women differently from men with respect to nonhuman nature. These alleged sex-gender differences are manifested in different sorts of consciousness in women and men. These sociopsychological factors provide a conceptual link insofar as they are embedded in different "ways of knowing," coping strategies, and ways of relating to nature for women and men. For example, Ariel Kay Salleh argues for a way of thinking based on women's lived experience as a preferable consciousness if there is to be "any real growth towards a sane, humane, ecological future" (1998, 323).

If some such account of the conceptual interconnections among the unjustified dominations of women, other human Others, and nature is correct, then many basic Western philosophical concepts (e.g., concepts of reason and rationality, culture and nature, knowledge and objectivity, ethics and the moral self) will need to be reconceived. As such, a conceptual account of women–other human Others–nature interconnections would provide a significant challenge to mainstream Western philosophy.

## Empirical and Socioeconomic Interconnections

Many ecofeminists focus on empirical evidence that links women, people of color, the underclass, children, and colonized peoples with environmental destruction. Some ecofeminist accounts point to various health and risk factors borne disproportionately by these groups of humans—factors caused by the presence of low-level radiation, pesticides, toxins, and other pollutants (see Caldecott and Leland 1983; Curtin, 1999, this section; LaDuke 1999; Mies 1986; Mies and Shiva 1993; Shiva 1988, this section; Warren 1997, 2000, chap. 1). They provide data to show how First World development policies result in policies and practices regarding water, trees and forests, desertification and soil erosion, food production and agriculture that directly contribute to the inability of women, particularly poor women of color, to provide adequately for themselves and their families. These are cited as examples of environmental injustice.

A related, second ecofeminist account focuses on socioeconomic interconnections between the exploitation of women, women's bodies, and women's labor, on the one hand, and the exploitation of nature, on the other hand (see Mellor 1992, 1997; Shiva, this section). These accounts critique "capitalist patriarchy" for treating both women and nature as exploitable and exploited resources, without which the wealth of ruling-class men cannot be created. They also critique Western agricultural development strategies imposed on Third World countries. For example, Vandana Shiva argues that Western development is really "maldevelopment." Maldevelopment rests on several false, male-biased assumptions:

> Nature is unproductive; organic agriculture based on nature's cycles of renewability spells poverty; women and tribal and peasant societies embedded

in nature are similarly unproductive, not because it has been demonstrated that in cooperation they produce *less* goods and services for needs, but because it is assumed that "production" takes place only when mediated by technologies for commodity production, even when such technologies destroy life. A stable and clean river is not a productive resource in this view; it needs to be "developed" with dams in order to become so. Women, sharing the river as a commons to satisfy the water needs of their families and society, are not involved in productive labour: when substituted by the engineering man, water management and water use become productive activities. Natural forests remain unproductive till they are developed into monoculture plantations of commercial species. (Shiva 1988, 4)

According to Shiva, maldevelopment is a paradigm that sees all work that does not produce profits and capital as non- or unproductive work. The neglect of nature's work "in renewing herself" and of women's work in producing sustenance in the form of basic, vital needs is an essential part of the paradigm of maldevelopment fostered by industrial capitalism.

Other ecofeminist accounts focus on animal rights or on connections among violence toward animals, women, and pornography (see Adams 1990, 1994, 1996; Adams and Donovan 1995; Collard and Contrucci 1988; Gaard 1993; Kheel 1985, 1989; Slicer 1997). They argue, for example, that factory farming, animal experimentation, hunting, and meat-eating are tied to patriarchal concepts and practices. Such empirical data document the very real, felt, lived "experiential" interconnections among the dominations of women, other human Others, and nature.

## Linguistic Interconnections

Many philosophers (e.g., Ludwig Wittgenstein) have argued that the language one uses mirrors and reflects one's concept of oneself and one's world. As such, language plays a crucial role in concept formation. Some ecofeminists argue that it also plays a crucial role in keeping intact mutually reinforcing and harmful women–other human Others–nature interconnections.

Euro-American language is riddled with examples of "sexist-naturist language." Women routinely are described in pejorative animal terms: Women are dogs, cats, catty, pussycats, pussies, pets, bunnies, dumb bunnies, cows, sows, foxes, chicks, bitches, beavers, old bats, old hens, old crows, queen bees, cheetahs, vixen, serpents, bird-brains, hare-brains, elephants, and whales. Women cackle, go to hen parties, henpeck their husbands, become old biddies (old hens no longer sexually attractive or able to reproduce) and social butterflies (see Dunayer 1995, 13; Warren 2000, chaps. 1, 3). Similarly, language that feminizes nature in a patriarchal culture, where women are viewed as subordinate and inferior, reinforces and authorizes the domination of nature. Mother Nature (not Father Nature) is raped, mastered, controlled, conquered, mined. Her (not his) secrets are penetrated, and her womb (men don't have one) is put into the service of the man of science (not woman of science, or simply scientist). Virgin timber is felled, cut down. Fertile (not potent) soil is tilled, and land that lies fallow is useless or barren, like a woman unable to conceive a child. Animalizing or naturalizing women *in a patriarchal culture* where both animals and nature are seen as inferior to humans and culture, and feminizing animals and nature *in a patriarchal culture* where women are seen as inferior to men and culture, thereby reinforces and authorizes the mutually reinforcing dominations of women, animals, and nature. The exploitation of nature and animals is justified by feminizing (not masculinizing) them; the exploitation of women is justified by naturalizing or animalizing (not masculinizing) them. As Carol Adams argues in *The Sexual Politics of Meat,* language which feminizes nature and naturalizes women describes, reflects, and perpetuates unjustified patriarchal domination by failing to see the extent to which the dominations of women and nature, especially of animals, are culturally analogous and not simply metaphorically analogous (1990, 61).

## Symbolic and Literary Interconnections

Merchant's discussion of two images of nature—an older Greek notion of nature as a benevolent female and a nurturing mother, and a newer, "modern" image of nature as a (mere) machine, inert, dead—is central to her argument that the move from an organic to a mechanistic model conceptually sanctioned and ethically justified the exploitation of the (female) earth. It did so by removing the sorts of moral barriers to such treatment that the metaphor of nature as alive previously prevented. As Merchant claims:

> One does not readily slay a mother, dig into her entrails for gold or mutilate her body, although commercial mining would soon require that. As long as the earth was considered alive and sensitive, it could be considered a breach of human ethical behavior to carry out such destructive acts against it. (1980, 3)

A discussion of images of women and nonhuman nature, then, raises larger issues about symbolic patterns linking women and nature. Some ecofeminists explore these symbolic patterns in literature, art, and popular culture.

Some ecofeminists draw on "women's nature writing" to unpack the nature of the women–other human Others–nature interconnections. One of the first to do so was Susan Griffin. In the prologue to the epic poem that is her book *Woman and Nature: The Roaring Inside Her,* Griffin writes,

> He says that woman speaks with nature. That she hears voices from under the earth. That wind blows in her ears and trees whisper to her. That the dead sing through her mouth and the cries of infants are clear to her. But for him this dialogue is over. He says he is not part of this world, that he was set on this world as a stranger. He sets himself apart from woman and nature.
>
> And so it is Goldilocks who goes to the home of the three bears, Little Red Riding Hood who converses with the wolf, Dorothy who befriends a lion, Snow White who talks to the birds, Cinderella with mice as her allies, the Mermaid who is half fish, Thumbelina courted by a mole. (And when we hear in the Navajo chant of the mountain that a grown man sits and smokes with bears and

follows directions given to him by squirrels, we are surprised. We had thought only little girls spoke with animals.)

We are the bird's eggs. Bird's eggs, flowers, butterflies, rabbits, cows, sheep; we are caterpillars; we are leaves of ivy and sprigs of wallflower. We are women. We rise from the grave. We are gazelle and doe, elephant and whale, lilies and roses and peach, we are air, we are flame, we are oyster and pearl, we are girls. We are women and nature. And he says he cannot hear us speak.

But we hear. (1978, 1)

Griffin's writing is testimony to the power of literature and language to convey basic attitudes about women and nature.

A new genre of literary analysis called ecofeminist literary criticism has emerged. According to one of its main proponents, Patrick Murphy, this approach to literary criticism uses

> ecofeminism as a ground for critiquing all the literature that one reads. For literary critics in particular this would mean reevaluating the canon that constitutes the list of major works and texts, and calling for a dialogue between critical evaluations based on humanistic criteria and those based on de-homocentric criteria. This would require, for instance, reevaluating the poetic tradition of the "pastoral," which tends to be based on an idealization of nature rather than a genuine encounter with it. (1995, 25)

Ecofeminist literary criticism does not only seek "a literature that meets equally the criteria of ecological and feminist sophistication," but works "that to some extent embody both dimensions" (Murphy 1995, 29).

## Spiritual and Religious Interconnections

Ecofeminist theologian Elizabeth Dodson Gray was among the first ecofeminists to examine the roles that religious and sexual imagery play in the patriarchal heritage of the Judeo-Christian and Western intellectual traditions. In her book, *Green Paradise Lost,* first published in 1979, Gray claims that a destructive hierarchy of beings is at the heart of biblical accounts of creation:

> In this biblical view of the nature of things woman comes after and also below man. Woman was created (according to this chronologically earliest account of the creation of the world in Gen. 2) out of a man's body (rather than from a woman's body as happens naturally). . . . The come children, so derivative that they are not even in the Creation story. . . . Then come animals, who do not have the unique human spirit at all . . . Thus animals are below. Further down are plants, which do not even move about. Below them is the ground of nature itself—the hills and mountains, streams and valleys—which is the bottom of everything just as the heavens, the moon and the stars are close to God at the top of everything. (3)

In this hierarchical "pyramid of dominance and status," the higher up one goes, the closer one is to all that is spiritual and superior. Gray argues that these ancient religious creation myths are both patriarchal and naturist:

> What is clearly articulated here is a hierarchical order of *being* in which the lower orders—whether female or chid or animal or plant—can be treated, mistreated, violated, sold, sacrificed, or killed at the convenience of the higher states of spiritual being found in males and in God. Nature, being not only at the bottom of this pyramid but being the most full of dirt, blood and such nasty natural surprises as earthquakes, floods and bad storms, is obviously a prize candidate for the most ruthless "mastering" of all. (6–7)

Given Gray's account, it is not surprising that the symbols, images, and stories of traditional patriarchal religions receive the attention they do from ecofeminists. Among theologians, it has fueled a debate over whether patriarchal religions can be reformed from within to eliminate harmful patriarchal biases, or whether new or prepatriarchal religions are required in their place. It has also raised the issue, associated with "spiritual ecofeminism" ("cultural ecofeminism"), whether spirituality is a necessary aspect of any ecofeminist practice and theory (see Spretnak 1989, 1990, 1989a; Starhhawk 1989; Warren 1993).

## Epistemological Interconnections

The various alleged women–other human Other–nature interconnections (discussed in this introduction) have prompted the call for new, ecofeminist epistemologies (see Curtin, this section). Typically these emerging epistemologies build on scholarship currently under way in feminist philosophy that challenge some trademark Western philosophical views about knowledge, the knower, reason and rationality: for example, that knowledge is objective; that the "knower" is an objective, detached, independent, and rational observer; and that nonhuman nature is a passive object of knowledge. To build their case, they often turn to recent work by feminist philosophers of science, such as Sandra Harding (1986, 1991, 1993).

Harding argues that the social location of the knower is crucial to understanding and assessing epistemological claims.

> The activities of those at the bottom of . . . social hierarchies can provide starting points for thought—for *everyone's* research and scholarship—from which humans' relations with each other and the natural world can become visible. This is because the experience and lives of marginalized peoples, as they understand them, provide particularly significant *problems to be explained,* or research agendas. (1993, 54)

Many ecofeminists agree. They argue that only by listening to the perspectives of "those at the bottom of social hierarchies" can one begin to see alternative ways of viewing an environmental problem, analyzing data, or theorizing about women–other human Others–nature interconnections. The Chipko movement in India (see Curtin, this section; Shiva 1988; Warren 1997) illustrates that often local women foresters "on the bottom" have indigenous technical knowledge based on their hands-on, daily, lived experience as forest managers. This knowledge provides an invaluable perspective on what it is like to live the lives they live—information and perspectives not readily accessible to those who live outside the culture.

Ecofeminist philosopher Lori Gruen builds on work in feminist philosophy of science in developing an ecofeminist moral epistemology. She argues that ecofeminist theory always grow out of and examines the social context in which moral and epistemological claims are generated. Recognition of the interdependence of science and society, facts and values, reason and emotion "is the first step towards any legitimate knowledge" (1994, 134). Gruen writes:

> Ecofeminists recognize that claims to knowledge are always influenced by the values of the culture in which they are generated. Following the arguments made by feminist philosophers of science, Marxists, cultural critics, and others, ecofeminists believe that facts are theory-laden, theories are value-laden, and values are molded by historical and philosophical ideologies, social norms, and individual processes of categorization. (1994, 124)

Ecofeminist epistemologies often critique Western notions of objectivity and conceptions of nature as a passive object of study. Probably the most radical critique was initially given by Donna Haraway, who claimed that modern Western conceptions of objectivity and nature-as-object reflected patriarchal ideologies of domination and control (1988, 1989, 1991). Haraway argues for an alternative, pluralistic, context-dependent view of knowledge, what she calls "situated knowledges":

> Situated knowledges require that the object of knowledge be pictured as an actor and agent, not as a screen or a ground or a resource, never finally as slave to the master that closes off the dialectic in his unique agency and his authorship of "objective" knowledge. . . . A corollary of the insistence that ethics and politics covertly or overtly provide the bases for objectivity . . . is granting the status of agent/actor to the "objects" of the world. (1988, 592–93)

On this view, nature is an active subject—not a mere object or resource to be studied. Nature actively contributes to what humans know about nature. The job of the scientist, philosopher, and theorist is not to try to give accounts that "mirror nature," since mirroring assumes that nature is an unconstructed "given." Nor is it to act as if one "discovers" nature, since claims to discovery (such as "Columbus discovered America") mistakenly assume that there isn't anything (or anything important) that already exists and that has agency. Rather, the job of the scientist, philosopher, and theorist is to provide knowledge claims and accounts that are relationally "situated" in important social and material contexts.

Some ecofeminists who discuss epistemological connections appeal, instead, to the critical theory of such authors as Horkheimer, Adorno, Balbus, and the Frankfurt circle. Salleh, for instance, claims that "their epistemological and substantive analyses . . . point to a convergence of feminist and

ecological concerns, anticipating the more recent arrival of ecofeminism"
(1988, 131). Patricia Jagentowicz Mills agrees. She argues that "critical theory" provides a critique of the "nature versus culture" dichotomy and an epistemological structure for critiquing the relationships between the domination
of women and the domination of nature (1987).

## Political Interconnections

Ecofeminism has always been a grass-roots political movement motivated by
pressing pragmatic concerns. These include issues of women's and environmental health, science, development and technology, the treatment of animals,
peace, antinuclear activism, and antimilitarism. The varieties of ecofeminist
perspectives on the environment are properly seen as an attempt to take seriously such grass-roots activism and political concerns by developing analyses
of domination that explain, clarify, and guide that praxis.

Stephanie Lahar states this point well. Lahar concludes her analysis
of the links between ecofeminist theory and grass-roots political activism
as follows:

> Ecofeminism's political goals include the deconstruction of oppressive social,
> economic, and political systems and the reconstruction of more viable social
> and political forms. No version of ecofeminist theory dictates exactly what peo-
> ple should do in the face of situations they encounter in personal and public
> life, nor is it a single political platform. The relation of ecofeminist theory to
> political activism is ideally informative and generative and not one of either
> prescribing or "owning" particular actions. Ecofeminist theory advocates a
> combined politics of resistance and creative projects, but the specific enact-
> ment of these is a result of dialogue between the individuals involved and the
> actual situation or issue. (1996, 15)

Lahar claims that ecofeminism contributes to political empowerment through
understanding the effects of one's actions through multiple human and nonhuman communities.

Plumwood agrees with Lahar. Plumwood argues that if one mistakenly
construes environmental philosophy as only or primarily concerned with
ethics, one will neglect "a key aspect of the overall problem which is concerned with the definition of the human self as separate from nature, the connection between this and the instrumental view of nature, and broader
*political* aspects of the critique of instrumentalism" (1996, 162).

The political aspects of ecofeminist critiques are explicitly addressed by
Noël Sturgeon in her book *Ecofeminist Natures.* Sturgeon argues for a conception of ecofeminism as an "oppositional political discourse and set of practices imbedded in particular historical, material, and political contexts."
Sturgeon interprets ecofeminism as "a fractured, contested, discontinuous entity that constitutes itself as a social movement" (1997, 3). Sturgeon's characterization of ecofeminism as a social movement is based on her understanding
of social movements as:

contestants in hegemonic power relations, through which change is produced by numerous kinds of "action," including that of the deployment of symbolic resources, shifts in identity construction, and the production of both popular and scholarly knowledge—as well as direct action, civil disobedience, strikes, boycotts, demonstrations, lobbying, and other more traditionally recognized forms of political action. (1997, 4)

According to Sturgeon, ecofeminism is a social movement involved in both the deployment of and theorizing about concepts (e.g., of nature, women, race). Sturgeon's book is a critique of ecofeminist theory and practice "with the goal of making suggestions for the formation of a more inclusive, more politically engaged ecofeminist movement" (19).

Many ecofeminists involved in peace politics and the antinuclear movement explore theoretical connections among militarism, nuclearism, and ecofeminism. Typically, they argue that the same conceptual and theoretical structures which dominate women, colonized peoples, and the Earth breed and justify both individual and institutional violence. For example, Curtin argues (1999, this section) that the Western-imposed Green revolution in India reflects a colonialist ideology that sanctions institutional violence against women, colonized peoples, and the Earth. Spretnak argues that the ideological forces that underlie patriarchy are the same as those that "push us to war" (1989b). Warren argues that patriarchy is an unhealthy social system that, at its conceptual roots (its core beliefs and values), generates the impaired thinking and behaviors of domination that maintain, perpetuate, and "justify" militarism and nuclearism (Warren 1993, 2000, chap. 9; see also Warren and Cady, 1996). Ecofeminism thereby addresses issues of war and peace in individual, institutional, and global contexts in both theory and practice.

Notice that the debate among ecofeminists about politics often turns on the type of feminism that underlies a particular ecofeminist position. Different ecofeminist politics find different roots in, for example, liberal feminism, Marxist feminism, radical feminism, socialist feminism, psychoanalytic feminism, international and postcolonial feminisms. What is accepted as an appropriate ecofeminist political strategy or action often reflects the different and differing perspectives of these feminisms.

## Ethical Interconnections

Much of the scholarly literature of ecofeminist philosophy has focused on environmental ethics. Ecofeminist philosophers argue that the interconnections among the conceptualizations and treatment of women, other subordinated humans, animals, and the rest of nature require a feminist ethical analysis and response. Minimally, the goal of ecofeminist environmental ethics is to develop theories and practices concerning humans and the natural environment that are not male-biased and that provide a guide to action in the pre-feminist present.

Ynestra King is among the first North American theorists to defend an ecofeminist ethic based in socialist feminism. King argues that ecofeminist ethics dismantle dualisms of mind and body, reason and emotion by finding a place "in which mind and nature, heart and reason, join forces to transform the internal and external systems of domination that threaten the existence of life on earth" (1990, 117–18).

Some ecofeminists have defended an ecofeminist ethic based on the moral significance of care in human-human and human-nonhuman nature relationships (see Curtin, 1996; R. King 1996; Warren, 2000, chap. 5). Since care is a "gender-sensitive concept" (Bowden, 1997), a primary place of care in ecofeminist ethical theory and practice is as a corrective to male-bias in the conception and practice of Western philosophical and environmental ethics. Attention to the moral significance of care assumes that emotions matter for rationality and ethics, that a useful ethic must be based in human psychology, and that ethics is about the quality of relationships themselves. (and not just about the nature of relators in relationships.) (See Warren 2000, chap. 5.)

Ecofeminist philosopher Chris Cuomo argues for "ethics at the cross-roads of ethical and political theory and practice" in the form of an "ethic of flourishing." An ethic of flourishing draws on Aristotelian concepts of *eudaimonia* (translated variously as "happiness," "the good life," "living well," "excellence," and "flourishing") and the *polis* (or, "community"), as well as a commitment to the value of flourishing, or well-being, of individuals, species, and communities (1998, 70). According to Cuomo, "in ecological feminism, it is an entity's *dynamic charm*—its diffuse, 'internal' ability to adapt to or resist change, and its unique causal and motivational patterns and character—that renders it morally considerable, and that serves as a primary site for determining what is good for that being or thing" (71). Cuomo's conception of the flourishing of living things and the "dynamic charm" of systems presumes a degree of physical health and self-directedness that is achievable by both individuals in communities (both social and ecological) and communities themselves. The notion of dynamic charm thereby functions as an ecological and ethical notion with political implications.

## Theoretical Interconnections

Each of the women–other human Other–nature interconnections identified above raises theoretical issues not only for environmental ethics, but for environmental and Western philosophy generally. For example, empirical and historical data from the social sciences on relationships among women, people of color, children, geographic location, development, technology, and the domination or health of the natural environment raise important ethical issues about anthropocentric and androcentric biases in how ethics is practiced and conceived. Data on the gender division of labor in forestry, water collection, farming, and food production raise epistemological issues about "indigenous technical knowledge" and "feminist standpoint epistemologies" that challenge traditional Western notions of knowledge and knowers as objective, detached, and impersonal. Data on the cross-cultural variability of women–other human Other–nature interconnections raise metaphysical and methodological issues about the social and ecological construction of conceptions of gender, race, and class, and the viability of human–nature dualisms or culture–nature dualisms. Data on the inferior standards of living of women globally, particularly of poor women of color, raise political issues about the roles played by unequal distributions of power and privilege in the maintenance of political decision-making structures of domination. Data on the Western historical debasement of whatever is identified with women, animals, or nonhuman nature raise issues about the historical adequacy of philosophical theories on "human nature" and "human moral development." Data on the role of women in the felt, lived, hands-on activities of domestic economies, subsistence agriculture, and sustainable development in cross-cultural contexts raise ecological and scientific issues about the nature of scientific practice and theory.

However, perhaps the most serious theoretical challenges to environmental and Western philosophy are at the level of conceptual analysis and theorizing itself. Ecofeminism raises significant issues about Western philosophical conceptions of the self, knowledge and the knower, reason and rationality, objectivity, philosophical methodology, and a host of favored value dualisms that form the backbone of philosophical theorizing—indeed, of the very conception of philosophy itself. It ecofeminists are correct, these notions will need to be re-examined for possible male (and race, class) gender bias and, where such bias occurs, to be replaced by concepts, theories, and practices that are not male (or race, class) gender-biased. That is what ecofeminists generally, and the authors in this part specifically, argue is needed for any feminism, environmentalism, environmental philosophy, and philosophy to be theoretically adequate.

## THE ESSAYS IN THIS PART

As the preceding already suggests, the four essays in this section provide only a glimpse of the positions advocated by ecofeminists. Taken together, however, they raise issues across all ten categories of women–other human Others–nature interconnections. Their inclusion here provides a sample of philosophically relevant contributions that ecofeminist historians, activists, and philosophers have made to ecofeminist and environmental philosophy.

A historian of environmental science, Carolyn Merchant published her highly influential book *The Death of Nature: Women, Ecology and the Scientific Revolution* in 1980. In it she argues that the change in metaphors of the Earth from the Greek organic model of nature as benevolent female to the seventeenth-century mechanistic model of nature as (mere) machine, permitted the exploitation of the female Earth, by removing the barriers to the exploitive treatment that the previous metaphor of nature as alive had prevented. In *The*

*Death of Nature,* Merchant weaves together scholarly material from politics, art, literature, physics, technology, philosophy, and popular culture to show how this mechanistic worldview contributed to the demise of nature.

The essay by Merchant in this part, "The Death of Nature," is culled from *The Death of Nature.* It is an attempt to represent an edited version of some of the philosophically more significant aspects of Merchant's main argument in her book, sidestepping some of the more technical, literary, or scientific specifics that receive extensive attention there. Inclusion of the Merchant essay in this part ensures representation of an early and classic, although not universally accepted, historical ecofeminist position on the patriarchal nature of the dominations of women, other humans, and nature.

The second essay, "The Impoverishment of the Environment: Women and Children Last," is by Vandana Shiva, an internationally renowned Indian physicist, activist, and ecofeminist scholar. Shiva documents how the so-called Green Revolution and First World development projects have created environmental degradation and poverty for the most vulnerable in India and large portions of the Third World—women and children. Shiva argues that "patriarchal economics" and "maldevelopment" schemes have exacerbated problems of hunger and malnutrition, the availability of potable water, toxic wastes and nuclear hazards, and agriculture and food production for women, children, and the environment. Since the greatest pressure on the earth's resource "is not from large numbers of poor people but from a small number of the world's ever-consuming elite," Shiva identifies the key problem as overconsumption practices by "the world's elite," destructive technologies, unequal access to resources, and the patriarchal distribution of disproportionate environmental burdens on women, children, and the Earth. She concludes that a reversal of the logic of patriarchal destruction requires "putting women and children first."

The third essay, "Women's Knowledge as Expert Knowledge: Indian Women and Ecodevelopment," by ecofeminist philosopher Deane Curtin also initially focuses discussion on India and women's agricultural practices. However, Curtin appeals to relevant empirical data to develop an epistmological model that shows that, however well-meaning, attempts by Western and other outside agencies to "develop" modern agricultural practices in India have resulted in institutional violence. "Institutional violence is violence made possible and facilitated by social organizations having relatively explicit rules and formal status within a culture." According to Curtin, outsider developmental models that neglect traditional women's perspectives is a form of institutional violence. Curtin argues that what is needed is the inclusion of "insider' women's ecological knowledge in development practices and policies.

Part Three ends with a distinctively theoretical treatment of the sorts of ecofeminist issues raised by Merchant, Shiva, and Curtin. In her essay, "The Power and the Promise of Ecological Feminism," ecofeminist philosopher Karen J. Warren focuses on the nature of conceptual interconnections among the dominations of women, other human Others, and nature. Warren argues that because the conceptual connections are located in an oppressive patriarchal conceptual framework characterized by a logic of domination, traditional feminism must be expanded to include ecofeminist insights, and environmental ethics must include ecofeminist insights, if either is to be theoretically adequate. Appealing to the argumentative significance of first-person narrative and the moral significance of care, kinship, and appropriate reciprocity, Warren concludes that any feminism, environmentalism, or environmental philosophy that fails to recognize important interconnections among women, other human Others, and nature is simply inadequate.

## CONCLUSION

The varieties of women–other human Others–nature interconnections discussed above generate a variety of theoretical positions in all areas of feminist and environmental philosophy. Nowhere is this more evident than in the field of environmental ethics.

In some respects, the range of positions in contemporary environmental ethics reflects the range of positions in contemporary Western philosophical ethics. The latter includes traditional consequentialist ethics (such as ethical egoism, utilitarianism) and nonconsequentialist ethics (e.g., Kantian ethics of duty, the Divine Command Theory, rights-based ethics, and virtue ethics). It also includes nontraditional ethical positions (e.g., some feminist, existentialist, Marxist, multicultural, and non-Western ethics). This array of positions occurs, as well, in environmental ethics. There are *reform positions* based on traditional Western consequentialist ethics (e.g., utilitarian-based animal welfare ethics) and nonconsequentialist ethics (e.g., rights-based animal welfare ethics, Kantian-based "respect for nature" ethics, and Divine Command Theory–based "stewardship ethics"). These are "reform positions" because they extend traditional Western ethical considerations to include animals and (sometimes) nonhuman nature without significantly altering the concepts and theories of mainstream Western ethics. There are also *mixed reform and radical* positions in environmental ethics (e.g., Leopold's land ethic). They are "mixed positions" because, while they utilize familiar mainstream ethical concepts, they introduce new concepts and theoretical starting points into environmental ethics. And there are *radical* positions in Western environmental ethics that tend to be both more comprehensive in scope (e.g., not limited to ethics per se) and inclusive of multicultural, often non-Western, considerations. Texts on environmental ethics typically identify as "radical" positions deep ecology, bioregionalism, social (or political) ecology, and ecofeminism. Sometimes they also include non-European perspectives such as American Indian, Australian aborigine, and Asian positions.

Just where does ecofeminism fit in to the range of positions in environmental ethics? Not surprisingly, where ecofeminism fits in depends largely on what one means by "ecofeminism." If "ecofeminism" is an umbrella term for any feminism that raises feminist concerns about the environment, then presumably ecofeminists can be found along the *continuum* of feminist-inspired and feminist-advocated positions in environmental ethics. If, however, the term is used as I am using it in this essay and as it is used by the authors in this section, where "ecofeminism" is the umbrella term for a variety of positions expressly committed to exploring women–other human Others–nature interconnections (of the sort outlined above) and to developing feminist and environmental philosophies based on these insights, then ecofeminism is best viewed as a mixed or radical position in environmental ethics. In some respects, we are back to where the essay began: ecofeminism is the name of a variety of different, sometimes competing, positions that make visible different sorts of women–other human Others–nature interconnections, claiming that an understanding of these interconnections is necessary for any adequate feminism, environmentalism, or environmental philosophy. Whether the interconnections alleged and the arguments advanced in support of them are accepted on feminist, environmental, or philosophical grounds is a question the friendly critic must answer.

## BIBLIOGRAPHY

ADAMS, CAROL. 1990. *The Sexual Politics of Meat: A Feminist-Vegetarian Critical Theory.* New York: Continuum.

———. 1994. *Neither Man Nor Beast: Feminism and the Defense of Animals.* New York: Continuum.

———. 1996. "Ecofeminism and the Eating of Animals," in *Ecological Feminist Philosophies,* ed. Karen J. Warren. Bloomington: Indiana University Press, 114–36.

ADAMS, CAROL J., and JOSEPHINE DONOVAN, ed. 1995. *Animals and Women: Feminist Theoretical Explorations.* Durham, NC: Duke University Press.

BOWDEN, PETA. 1997. *Caring: Gender Sensitive Ethics.* London: Routledge.

CHENEY, JIM. 1987. "Eco-Feminism and Deep Ecology." *Environmental Ethics* 9 (2), 115–45.

COLLARD, ANDREE, with Joyce Contrucci. 1988. *Rape of the Wild: Man's Violence Against Animals and the Earth.* Bloomington: Indiana University Press.

CUOMO, CHRISTINE. 1998. *Feminism and Ecological Communities: An Ethic of Flourishing.* London: Routledge.

CURTIN, DEANE. 1996. "Toward an Ecological Ethic of Care," in *Ecological Feminist Philosophies,* ed. Karen J. Warren. Bloomington: Indiana University Press, 66–81.

———. 1997. *ChinnaGounder's Challenge: The Question of Ecological Citizenship.* Bloomington: Indiana University Press.

DUNAYER, JOAN. 1995. "Sexist Words, Speciesist Roots," in *Animals and Women: Feminist Theoretical Explorations,* ed. Carol J. Adams and Josephine Donovan. Durham, NC: Duke University Press, 11–31.

EISLER, RIANE. 1988. *The Chalice and the Blade: Our History, Our Future.* San Francisco: Harper & Row.

GAARD, GRETA. 1998. *Ecological Politics: Ecofeminists and the Greens.* Philadelphia: Temple University Press, 1998.

————, ed. 1993. *Ecofeminism: Women, Animals, Nature.* Philadelphia: Temple University.

GRAY, ELIZABETH DODSON. 1981. *Green Paradise Lost.* Wellesley, MA: Roundtable Press.

GRIFFIN, SUSAN. 1978. *Woman and Nature: The Roaring Inside Her.* New York: Harper & Row.

GRUEN, LORI. 1994. "Toward an Ecofeminist Moral Epistemology," in *Ecological Feminism,* ed. Karen J. Warren. New York: Routledge.

HARAWAY, DONNA. 1988. "Situated Knowledges: The Science Question in Feminism and the Privilege of Partial Perspective." *Feminist Studies* 14, no. 3 (Fall): 575–99.

————. 1989. *Primate Visions: Gender, Race and Nature in the World of Modern Science.* New York: Routledge.

————. 1991. *Simians, Cyborgs, and Women: The Reinvention of Nature.* New York: Routledge.

HARDING, SANDRA. 1986. *The Science Question in Feminism.* Ithaca, NY: Cornell University Press.

————. 1991. *Whose Science? Whose Knowledge? Thinking from Women's Lives.* Ithaca, NY: Cornell University Press.

————. 1993. "Rethinking Standpoint Epistemology: What Is 'Strong Objectivity'?" In *Feminist Epistemologies,* ed. Linda Alcoff and Elizabeth Potter. New York: Routledge, 49–82.

KHEEL, MARTI. 1985. "The Liberation of Nature: A Circular Affair." *Environmental Ethics* 7, no. 2 (Summer): 135–49.

————. 1989. "From Healing Herbs to Deadly Drugs: Western Medicine's War Against the Natural World," in *Healing the Wounds: The Promise of Ecofeminism,* ed. Judith Plant. Philadelphia: New Society, 96–114.

KING, ROGER J. H. 1996. "Caring About Nature: Feminist Ethics and the Environment," in *Ecological Feminist Philosophies,* ed. Karen J. Warren. Bloomington: Indiana University Press, 82–96.

KING, YNESTRA. 1990. "Healing the Wounds: Feminism, Ecology, and the Nature/Culture Dualism," in *Reweaving the World: The Emergence of Ecofeminism,* ed. Irene Diamond and Gloria Feman Orenstein. San Francisco: Sierra Club, 106–21.

LADUKE, WINONA. 1999. *All Our Relations.* Boston: South End Press, 1999.

Lahar, Stephanie. 1996. "Ecofeminist Theory and Grassroots Politics," in *Ecological Feminist Philosophies,* ed. Karen J. Warren. Bloomington: Indiana University Press, 1–18.

MIES, MARIA. 1986. *Patriarchy and Accumulation on a World Scale: Women in the International Division of Labor.* Atlantic Highlands, NJ: Zed Books.

MIES, MARIA, and VENDANA SHIVA. 1993. *Ecofeminism.* Atlantic Highlands, NJ: Zed Books.

MELLOR, MARY. 1992. *Breaking the Boundaries: Towards a Feminist Green Socialism.* London: Virago.

————. 1997. *Feminism and Ecology.* New York: New York University Press.

MERCHANT, CAROLYN. 1980. *The Death of Nature: Women, Ecology and the Scientific Revolution.* San Francisco: Harper & Row.

————. 1992. *Radical Ecology: The Search for a Livable World.* New York: Routledge.

————. 1995. *Earthcare: Women and the Environment.* New York: Routledge.

MILLS, PATRICIA JAGENTOWICZ. 1987. *Women, Nature and Psyche.* New Haven, CT: Yale University Press.

————. 1996. "Feminism and Ecology: On the Domination of Nature," in *Ecological Feminist Philosophies,* ed. Karen J. Warren. Bloomington: Indiana University Press, 211–227.

MURPHY, PATRICK. 1995. *Literature, Nature, and Other: Ecofeminist Critiques.* Albany, NY: State University of New York Press.

PLUMWOOD, VAL. 1993. *Feminism and the Mastery of Nature.* New York: Routledge.
———. 1996. "Nature, Self, and Gender: Feminism, Environmental Philosophy, and the Critique of Rationalism," in *Ecological Feminist Philosophies,* ed. Karen J. Warren. Bloomington: Indiana University Press, 115–80.

SALLEH, ARIEL KAY. 1998. "Working with Nature: Reciprocity or Control?" in *Environmental Philosophy: From Animal Rights to Radical Ecology,* 2nd ed., ed. Michael E. Zimmerman, J. Baird Callicott, George Sessions, Karen J. Warren, and John Clark. Upper Saddle River, NJ: Prentice Hall, 315–24.
———. 1988. "Epistemology and the Metaphors of Production: An Eco-Feminist Reading of Critical Theory," *Studies in the Humanities.* Special issue on Feminism, Ecology, and the Future of the Humanities, ed. Patrick D. Murphy. Vol. 15, no. 2, 130–39.

SHIVA, VANDANA. 1988. *Staying Alive: Women, Ecology and Development.* London: Zed Books.

SLICER, DEBORAH. 1997. "Your Daughter or Your Dog? A Feminist Assessment of the Animal Research Issue," in *Ecological Feminist Philosophies,* ed. Karen J. Warren. Bloomington: Indiana University Press, 97–113.

SPRETNAK, CHARLENE. 1985. *The Spiritual Dimension of Green Politics.* Santa Fe, NM: Bear and Company.
———. 1989a. "Toward an Ecofeminist Spirituality," in *Healing the Wounds: The Promise of Ecological Feminism,* ed. Judith Plant. Philadelphia: New Society, 127–32.
———. 1989b. "Naming the Cultural Forces That Push Us Toward War," in *Exposing Nuclear Phallacies,* ed. Diana E. H. Russell. New York: Pergamon, 53–62.
———. 1990. "Ecofeminism: Our Roots and Flowering," in *Reweaving the World: The Emergence of Ecofeminism,* ed. Irene Diamond and Gloria Feman Orenstein. San Francisco: Sierra Club Books, 3–14.

STARHAWK. 1979. *The Spiral Dance: A Rebirth of the Ancient Religion of the Great Goddess.* New York: Harper & Row.
———. 1989. *Truth or Dare: Encounters with Power, Authority, and Mystery.* San Francisco: Harper & Row.

STURGEON, NOËL. 1997. *Ecofeminist Natures: Race, Gender, Feminist Theory and Political Action.* New York: Routledge.

WARREN, KAREN J. 1987. "Feminism and Ecology: Making Connections," *Environmental Ethics* 9 (1): 3–20.
———. 1990. "The Power and the Promise of Ecological Feminism." *Environmental Ethics* 12 (2): 125–46.
———. 1991. "Feminism and the Environment: An Overview of the Issues." *American Philosophical Association Newsletter on Feminism and Philosophy* 90, no. 3 (Fall): 108–16.
———. 1993. "A Feminist Philosophical Perspective on Ecofeminist Spiritualities," in *Ecofeminism and the Sacred,* ed. Carol Adams. New York: Continuum, 119–32.
———. 1997. "Taking Empirical Data Seriously: An Ecofeminist Philosophical Perspective," in *Ecofeminism: Women, Culture, Nature,* ed. Karen J. Warren. Bloomington: Indiana University, 3–20.
———. 1999. "Care-Sensitive Ethics and Situated Universalism," in *Global Environmental Ethics,* ed. Nicholas Low. London: Routledge: 131–45.
———. 2000. *Ecofeminist Philosophy: A Western Perspective on What It Is and Why It Matters.* Lanham, MD: Rowman & Littlefield.
———. ed. *Ecological Feminism.* New York: Routledge, 1994.

―――. ed. *Ecological Feminist Philosophies.* Bloomington: Indiana University Press, 1996.

―――. ed. *Ecofeminism: Women, Culture, Nature.* Bloomington: Indiana University Press, 1997.

WARREN, KAREN J., and DUANE L. CADY. 1996. "Feminism and Peace: Seeing Connections," in *Bringing Peace Home: Feminism, Violence, and Nature,* ed. Karen J. Warren and Duane L. Cady. Bloomington: Indiana University Press, 1–15.

―――, ed. *Bringing Peace Home: Feminism, Violence, and Nature.* Bloomington: Indiana University Press, 1996.

# THE DEATH OF NATURE

*Carolyn Merchant*

Carolyn Merchant is a professor of environmental history, philosophy, and ethics in the department of conservation and resource studies at the University of California at Berkeley. She is the author of numerous publications on feminism and the environment, including *The Death of Nature: Women, Ecology and the Scientific Revolution* and *Ecological Revolutions.*

## INTRODUCTION: WOMEN AS NATURE

Women and nature have an age-old association—an affiliation that has persisted throughout culture, language, and history. Their ancient interconnections have been dramatized by the simultaneity of two recent social movements—women's liberation, symbolized in its controversial infancy by Betty Friedan's *Feminine Mystique* (1963), and the ecology movement, which built up during the 1960s and finally captured national attention on Earth Day, 1970. Common to both is an egalitarian perspective. Women are struggling to free themselves from cultural and economic contraints that have kept them subordinate to men in American society. Environmentalists, warning us of the irreversible consequences of continuing environmental exploitation, are developing an ecological ethic emphasizing the interconnectedness between people and nature. Juxtaposing the goals of the two movements can suggest new values and social structures, based not on the domination of women and nature as resources but on the full expression of both male and female talent and on the maintenance of environmental integrity.

New social concerns generate new intellectual and historical problems. Conversely, new interpretations of the past provide perspectives on the present and hence the power to change it. Today's feminist and ecological consciousness can be used to examine the historical interconnections between

Excerpted by Karen J. Warren from *The Death of Nature*, originally published by Harper & Row (New York, 1980). Reprinted with permission of HarperCollins Publishers, Inc.

women and nature that developed as the modern scientific and economic world took form in the sixteenth and seventeenth centuries—a transformation that shaped and pervades today's mainstream values and perceptions.

The ancient identity of nature as a nurturing mother links women's history with the history of the environment and ecological change. The female earth was central to the organic cosmology that was undermined by the Scientific Revolution and the rise of a market-oriented culture in early modern Europe. The ecology movement has reawakened interest in the values and concepts associated historically with the premodern organic world. The ecological model and its associated ethics make possible a fresh and critical interpretation of the rise of modern science in the crucial period when our cosmos ceased to be viewed as an organism and became instead a machine.

In investigating the roots of our current environmental dilemma and its connections to science, technology, and the economy, we must reexamine the formation of a world view and a science that, by reconceptualizing reality as a machine rather than a living organism, sanctioned the domination of both nature and women.

## NATURE AS FEMALE

The world we have lost was organic. From the obscure origins of our species, human beings have lived in daily, immediate, organic relation with the natural order for their sustenance. In 1500, the daily interaction with nature was still structured for most Europeans, as it was for other peoples, by close-knit, cooperative, organic communities.

Thus it is not surprising that for sixteenth-century Europeans the root metaphor binding together the self, society, and the cosmos was that of an organism. As a projection of the way people experienced daily life, organismic theory emphasized interdependence among the parts of the human body, subordination of individual to communal purposes in family, community, and state, and vital life permeating the cosmos to the lowliest stone.

The idea of nature as a living organism had philosophical antecedents in ancient systems of thought, variations of which formed the prevailing ideological framework of the sixteenth century. The organismic metaphor, however, was immensely flexible and adaptable to varying contexts, depending on which of its presuppositions was emphasized. A spectrum of philosophical and political possibilities existed, all of which could be subsumed under the general rubric of *organic*.

Central to the organic theory was the identification of nature, especially the earth, with a nurturing mother: A kindly beneficent female who provided for the needs of mankind in an ordered, planned universe. But another opposing image of nature as female was also prevalent: wild and uncontrollable nature that could render violence, storms, droughts, and general chaos. Both were identified with the female sex and were projections of human perceptions onto the external world. The metaphor of the earth as a nurturing mother was gradually to vanish as a dominant image as the Scientific Revolution proceeded to mechanize and to rationalize the world view. The second image, nature as disorder, called forth an important modern idea, that of power over nature. Two new ideas, those of mechanism and of the domination and mastery of nature, became core concepts of the modern world. An organically oriented mentality in which female principles played an important role was undermined and replaced by a mechanically oriented mentality that either eliminated or used female principles in an exploitative manner. As Western culture became increasingly mechanized in the 1600s, the female earth and virgin earth spirit were subdued by the machine.[1]

The change in controlling imagery was directly related to changes in human attitudes and behavior toward the earth. Whereas the nurturing earth image can be viewed as a cultural constraint restricting the types of socially and morally sanctioned human actions allowable with respect to the earth, the new images of mastery and domination functioned as cultural sanctions for the denudation of nature. Society needed these new images as it continued the processes of commercialism and industrialization, which depended on activities directly altering the earth—mining, drainage, deforestation, and assarting (grubbing up stumps to clear fields). The new activities utilized new technologies—lift and force pumps, cranes, windmills, geared wheels, flap valves, chains, pistons, treadmills, under- and overshot watermills, fulling mills, flywheels, bellows, excavators, bucket chains, rollers, geared and wheeled bridges, cranks, elaborate block and tackle systems, worm, spur, crown, and lantern gears, cams and eccentrics, ratchets, wrenches, presses, and screws in magnificent variation and combination.

These technological and commercial changes did not take place quickly; they developed gradually over the ancient and medieval eras, as did the accompanying environmental deterioration. Slowly over many centuries early Mediterranean and Greek civilization had mined and quarried the mountainsides, altered the forested landscape, and overgrazed the hills. Nevertheless, technologies were low level, people considered themselves parts of a finite cosmos, and animism and fertility cults that treated nature as sacred were numerous. Roman civilization was more pragmatic, secular, and commercial and its environmental impact more intense. Yet Roman writers such as Ovid, Seneca, Pliny, and the Stoic philosophers openly deplored mining as an abuse of their mother, the earth. With the disintegration of feudalism and the expansion of Europeans into new worlds and markets, commercial society began to have an accelerated impact on the natural environment. By the sixteenth and seventeenth centuries, the tension between technological development in the world of action and the controlling organic images in the world of the mind had become too great. The old structures were incompatible with the new activities.

Both the nurturing and domination metaphors had existed in philosophy, religion, and literature. The idea of dominion over the earth existed in Greek philosophy and Christian religion; that of the nurturing earth, in Greek and other pagan philosophies. But, as the economy became modernized and the Scientific Revolution proceeded, the dominion metaphor spread beyond the religious sphere and assumed ascendancy in the social and political spheres as well. These two competing images and their normative associations can be found in sixteenth-century literature, art, philosophy, and science.

The image of the earth as a living organism and nurturing mother had served as a cultural constraint restricting the actions of human beings. One does not readily slay a mother, dig into her entrails for gold or mutilate her body, although commercial mining would soon require that. As long as the earth was considered to be alive and sensitive, it could be considered a breach of human ethical behavior to carry out destructive acts against it. For most traditional cultures, minerals and metals ripened in the uterus of the Earth Mother, mines were compared to her vagina, and metallurgy was the human hastening of the birth of the living metal in the artificial womb of the furnace—an abortion of the metal's natural growth cycle before its time. Miners offered propitiation to the deities of the soil and subterranean world, performed ceremonial sacrifices, and observed strict cleanliness, sexual abstinence, and fasting before violating the sacredness of the living earth by sinking a mine. Smiths assumed an awesome responsibility in precipitating the metal's birth through smelting, fusing, and beating it with hammer and anvil; they were often accorded the status of shaman in tribal rituals and their tools were thought to hold special powers.

The Renaissance image of the nurturing earth still carried with it subtle ethical controls and restraints. Such imagery found in a culture's literature can play a normative role within the culture. Controlling images operate as ethical restraints or as ethical sanctions—as subtle "oughts" or "ought-nots." Thus as the descriptive metaphors and images of nature change, a behavioral restraint can be changed into a sanction. Such a change in the image and description of nature was occurring during the course of the Scientific Revolution.

## DOMINION OVER NATURE: FRANCIS BACON'S PHILOSOPHY

Francis Bacon (1561–1626), a celebrated "father of modern science," transformed tendencies already extant in his own society into a total program advocating the control of nature for human benefit. Melding together a new philosophy based on natural magic as a technique for manipulating nature, the technologies of mining and metallurgy, the emerging concept of progress and a patriarchal structure of family and state, Bacon fashioned a new ethic sanctioning the exploitation of nature.

Bacon has been eulogized as the originator of the concept of the modern research institute, a philosopher of industrial science, the inspiration behind the Royal Society (1660), and as the founder of the inductive method by which all people can verify for themselves the truths of science by the reading of nature's book.[2] But from the perspective of nature, women, and the lower orders of society emerges a less favorable image of Bacon and a critique of his program as ultimately benefiting the middle-class male entrepreneur. Bacon, of course, was not responsible for subsequent uses of his philosophy. But, because he was in an extremely influential social position and in touch with the important developments of his time, his language, style, nuance, and metaphor become a mirror reflecting his class perspective.

Sensitive to the same social transformations that had already begun to reduce women to psychic and reproductive resources, Bacon developed the power of language as political instrument in reducing female nature to a resource for economic production. Female imagery became a tool in adapting scientific knowledge and method to a new form of human power over nature. The "controversy over women" and the inquisition of witches—both present in Bacon's social milieu—permeated his description of nature and his metaphorical style and were instrumental in his transformation of the earth as a nurturing mother and womb of life into a source of secrets to be extracted for economic advance.

Much of the imagery Bacon used in delineating his new scientific objectives and methods derives from the courtroom, and, because it treats nature as a female to be tortured through mechanical inventions, strongly suggests the interrogations of the witch trials and the mechanical devices used to torture witches.

The new man of science must not think that the "inquisition of nature is in any part interdicted or forbidden." Nature must be "bound into service" and made a "slave," put "in constraint" and "molded" by the mechanical arts. The "searchers and spies of nature" are to discover her plots and secrets.[3]

This method, so readily applicable when nature is denoted by the female gender, degraded and made possible the exploitation of the natural environment. As woman's womb had symbolically yielded to the forceps, so nature's womb harbored secrets that through technology could be wrested from her grasp for use in the improvement of the human condition:

> There is therefore much ground for hoping that there are still laid up in the womb of nature many secrets of excellent use having no affinity or parallelism with anything that is now known . . . only by the method which we are now treating can they be speedily and suddenly and simultaneously presented and anticipated.[4]

Bacon transformed the magical tradition by calling on the need to dominate nature not for the sole benefit of the individual magician but for the good of the entire human race. Through vivid metaphor, he transformed the magus from nature's servant to its exploiter, and nature from a teacher to a slave. Bacon argued that it was the magician's error to consider art (technology) a mere "assistant to nature having the power to finish what nature has begun" and therefore to despair of ever "changing, transmuting, or fundamentally altering nature."[5]

The natural magician saw himself as operating within the organic order of nature—he was a manipulator of parts within that system, bringing down the heavenly powers to the earthly shrine. Agrippa . . . had begun to explore the possibility of ascending the hierarchy to the point of cohabiting with God. Bacon extended this idea to include the recovery of the power over nature lost when Adam and Eve were expelled from paradise.

Due to the Fall from the Garden of Eden (caused by the temptation of a woman), the human race lost its "dominion over creation." Before the Fall, there was no need for power or dominion, because Adam and Eve had been made sovereign over all other creatures. In this state of dominion, mankind was "like unto God." While some, accepting God's punishment, had obeyed the medieval strictures against searching too deeply into God's secrets, Bacon turned the constraints into sanctions. Only by "digging further and further into the mine of natural knowledge" could mankind recover that lost dominion. In this way, "the narrow limits of man's dominion over the universe" could be stretched "to their promised bounds."[6]

Although a female's inquisitiveness may have caused man's fall from his God-given dominion, the relentless interrogation of another female, nature, could be used to regain it. As he argued in *The Masculine Birth of Time*, "I am come in very truth leading you to nature with all her children to bind her to your service and make her your slave." "We have no right," he asserted, "to expect nature to come to us." Instead, "Nature must be taken by the forelock, being bald behind." Delay and subtle argument "permit one only to clutch at nature, never to lay hold of her and capture her."[7]

Nature existed in three states—at liberty, in error, or in bondage.

> She is either free and follows her ordinary course of development as in the heavens, in the animal and vegetable creation, and in the general array of the universe; or she is driven out of her ordinary course by the perverseness, insolence, and forwardness of matter and violence of impediments, as in the case of monsters; or lastly, she is put in constraint, molded, and made as it were new by art and the hand of man; as in things artificial.[8]

The first instance was the view of nature as immanent self-development, the nature naturing herself of the Aristotelians. This was the organic view of nature as a living, growing, self-actualizing being. The second state was necessary to explain the malfunctions and monstrosities that frequently appeared and that could not have been caused by God or another higher power acting on his instruction. Since monstrosities could not be explained by the action of form or spirit, they had to be the result of matter acting perversely. Matter in Plato's *Timaeus* was recalcitrant and had to be forcefully shaped by the demiurge. Bacon frequently described matter in female imagery, as a "common harlot." "Matter is not devoid of an appetite and inclination to dissolve the world and fall back into the old Chaos." It therefore must be "restrained and kept in order by the prevailing concord of things." "The vexations of art are certainly as the bonds and handcuffs of Proteus, which betray the ultimate struggles and efforts of matter."[9]

The third instance was the case of art (techné)—man operating on nature to create something new and artificial. Here "nature takes orders from man and works under his authority." Miners and smiths should become the model for the new class of natural philosophers who would interrogate and alter nature. They had developed the two most important methods of wresting nature's secrets from her, "the one searching into the bowels of nature, the other shaping nature as on an anvil." "Why should we not divide natural philosophy into two parts, the mine and the furnace?" For "the truth of nature lies hid in certain deep mines and caves," within the earth's bosom. Bacon, like some of the practically minded alchemists, would "advise the studious to sell their books and build furnaces" and, "forsaking Minerva and the Muses as barren virgins, to rely upon Vulcan."[10]

The new method of interrogation was not through abstract notions, but through the instruction of the understanding "that it may in very truth dissect nature." The instruments of the mind supply suggestions, those of the hand give motion and aid the work. "By art and the hand of man," nature can then be "forced out of her natural state and squeezed and molded," In this way, "human knowledge and human power meet as one."[11]

Here, in bold sexual imagery, is the key feature of the modern experimental method—constraint of nature in the laboratory, dissection by hand and mind, and the penetration of hidden secrets—language still used today in praising a scientist's "hard facts," "penetrating mind," or the "thrust of his argument." The constraints against penetration in *Natura*'s lament over her torn garments of modesty have been turned into sanctions in language that legitimates the exploitation and "rape" of nature for human good.

Scientific method, combined with mechanical technology, would create a "new organon," a new system of investigation, that unified knowledge with material power. The technological discoveries of printing, gunpowder, and the magnet in the fields of learning, warfare, and navigation "help us to think about the secrets still locked in nature's bosom." "They do not, like the old, merely exert a gentle guidance over nature's course; they have the power to conquer and subdue her, to shake her to her foundations." Under the mechanical arts, "nature betrays her secrets more fully . . . than when in enjoyment of her natural liberty."[12]

Mechanics, which gave man power over nature, consisted in motion; that is, in "the uniting or disuniting of natural bodies." Most useful were the arts that altered the materials of things—"agriculture, cookery, chemistry, dying, the manufacture of glass, enamel, sugar, gunpowder, artificial fires, paper, and the like." But in performing these operations, one was constrained to operate within the chain of causal connections; nature could "not be commanded except by being obeyed." Only by the study, interpretation, and observation of nature could these possibilities be uncovered; only by acting as the interpreter of nature could knowledge be turned into power. Of the three grades of human ambition, the most wholesome and noble was "to endeavor to establish and extend the power and dominion of the human race itself over the universe." In this way "the human race [could] recover that right over nature which belongs to it by divine bequest."[13]

The interrogation of witches as a symbol for the interrogation of nature, the courtroom as a model for its inquisition, and torture through mechanical devices as a tool for the subjugation of disorder were fundamental to the scientific method as power. For Bacon . . . , sexual politics helped to structure the nature of the empirical method that would produce a new form of knowledge and a new ideology of objectivity seemingly devoid of cultural and political assumptions.

Human dominion over nature, an integral element of the Baconian program, was to be achieved through the experimental "disclosure of nature's secrets." Seventeenth-century scientists, reinforcing aggressive attitudes toward nature, spoke out in favor of "mastering" and "managing" the earth. Descartes wrote in his *Discourse on Method* (1636) that through knowing the crafts of the artisans and the forces of bodies we could "render ourselves the masters and possessors of nature."[14] Joseph Glanvill, the English philosopher who defended the Baconian program in his *Plus Ultra* of 1668, asserted that the objective of natural philosophy was to "enlarge knowledge by observation and experiment . . . so that nature being known, it may be mastered, managed, and used in the services of humane life." To achieve this objective, arts and instruments should be developed for "searching out the beginnings and depths of things and discovering the intrigues of remoter nature."[15] The most useful of the arts were chemistry, anatomy, and mathematics; the best instruments included the microscope, telescope, thermometer, barometer, and air pump.

The new image of nature as a female to be controlled and dissected through experiment legitimated the exploitation of natural resources. Although the image of the nurturing earth popular in the Renaissance did not vanish, it was superseded by new controlling imagery. The constraints against penetration associated with the earth-mother image were transformed into sanctions for denudation. After the Scientific Revolution, *Natura* no longer complains that her garments of modesty are being torn by the wrongful thrusts of man. She is portrayed in statues by the French sculptor Louis-Ernest Barrias (1841–1905) coyly removing her own veil and exposing herself to science. From an active teacher and parent, she has become a mindless, submissive body. Not only did this new image function as a sanction, but the new conceptual framework of the Scientific Revolution—mechanism—carried with it norms quite different from the norms of organicism. The new mechanical order and its associated values of power and control would mandate the death of nature.

# THE MECHANICAL ORDER

The fundamental social and intellectual problem for the seventeenth century was the problem of order. The perception of disorder, so important to the Baconian doctrine of dominion over nature, was also crucial to the rise of mechanism as a rational antidote to the disintegration of the organic cosmos. The new mechanical philosophy of the mid-seventeenth century achieved a reunification of the cosmos, society, and the self in terms of a new metaphor—the machine. Developed by the French thinkers Mersenne, Gassendi, and Descartes in the 1620s and 1630s and elaborated by a group of English emigrés to Paris in the 1640s and 1650s, the new mechanical theories emphasized and reinforced elements in human experience developing slowly since the late Middle Ages, but accelerating in the sixteenth century.

New forms of order and power provided a remedy for the disorder perceived to be spreading throughout culture. In the organic world, order meant the function of each part within the larger whole, as determined by its nature, while power was diffused from the top downward through the social or cosmic hierarchies. In the mechanical world, order was redefined to mean the predictable behavior of each part within a rationally determined system of laws, while power derived from active and immediate intervention in a secularized world. Order and power together constituted control. Rational control over nature, society, and the self was achieved by redefining reality itself through the new machine metaphor.

As the unifying model for science and society, the machine has permeated and reconstructed human consciousness so totally that today we scarcely question its validity. Nature, society, and the human body are composed of interchangeable atomized parts that can be repaired or replaced from outside. The "technological fix" mends an ecological malfunction, new human beings replace the old to maintain the smooth functioning of industry and bureaucracy, and interventionist medicine exchanges a fresh heart for worn-out, diseased one.

The mechanical view of nature now taught in most Western schools is accepted without question as our everyday, common sense reality—matter is made up of atoms, colors occur by the reflection of light waves of differing lengths, bodies obey the law of inertia, and the sun is in the center of our solar system. None of this was common sense to our seventeenth-century counterparts. The replacement of the older, "natural" ways of thinking by a new and "unnatural" form of life—seeing, thinking, and behaving—did not occur without struggle. The submergence of the organism by the machine engaged the best minds of the times during a period fraught with anxiety, confusion, and instability in both the intellectual and social spheres.

The removal of animistic, organic assumptions about the cosmos constituted the death of nature—the most far-reaching effect of the Scientific Revolution. Because nature was now viewed as a system of dead, inert particles moved by external, rather than inherent forces, the mechanical framework itself could legitimate the manipulation of nature. Moreover, as a conceptual framework, the mechanical order had associated with it a framework of values based on power, fully compatible with the directions taken by commercial capitalism.

The mechanistic view of nature, developed by the seventeenth-century natural philosophers and based on a Western mathematical tradition going back to Plato, is still dominant in science today. This view assumes that nature can be divided into parts and that the parts can be rearranged to create other species of being. "Facts" or information bits can be extracted from the environmental context and rearranged according to a set of rules based on logical and mathematical operations. The results can then be tested and verified by resubmitting them to nature, the ultimate judge of their validity. Mathematical formalism provides the criterion for rationality and certainty, nature the criterion for empirical validity and acceptance or rejection of the theory.

The work of historians and philosophers of science notwithstanding, it is widely assumed by the scientific community that modern science is objective, value-free, and context-free knowledge of the external world. To the extent to which the sciences can be reduced to this mechanistic mathematical model, the more legitimate they become as sciences. Thus the reductionist hierarchy of the validity of the sciences first proposed in the nineteenth century by French positivist philosopher August Comte is still widely assumed by intellectuals, the most mathematical and highly theoretical sciences occupying the most revered position.

The mechanistic approach to nature is as fundamental to the twentieth-century revolution in physics as it was to classical Newtonian science, culminating in the nineteenth-century unification of mechanics, thermodynamics, and electromagnetic theory. Twentieth-century physics still views the world in terms of fundamental particles—electrons, protons, neutrons, mesons, muons, pions, taus, thetas, sigmas, pis, and so on. The search for the ultimate unifying particle, the quark, continues to engage the efforts of the best theoretical physicists.

Mathematical formalism isolates the elements of a given quantum mechanical problem, places them in a latticelike matrix, and rearranges them through a mathematical function called an *operator*. Systems theory extracts possibly relevant information bits from the environmental context and stores them in a computer memory for later use. But since it cannot store an infinite number of "facts," it must select a finite number of potentially relevant pieces of data according to a theory or set of rules governing the selection process. For any given solution, this mechanistic approach very likely excludes some potentially relevant factors.

Systems theorists claim for themselves a holistic outlook, because they believe that they are taking into account the ways in which all the parts in a given system affect the whole. Yet the formalism of the calculus of probabilities excludes the possibility of mathematizing the gestalt—that is, the ways in which each part at any given instant take their meaning from the whole. The more open, adaptive, organic, and complex the system, the less successful is the formalism. It is most successful when applied to closed, artificial, precisely defined, relatively simple systems. Mechanistic assumptions about nature push us increasingly in the direction of artificial environments, mechanized control over more and more aspects of human life, and a loss of the quality of life itself.

## HOLISM

Holism was proposed as a philosophical alternative to mechanism by J. C. Smuts in his book *Holism and Evolution* (1926), in which he attempted to define the essential characteristics of holism and to differentiate it from nineteenth-century mechanism. He attempts to show that

> Taking a plant or animal as a type of whole, we notice the fundamental holistic characters as a unity of parts which is so close and intense as to be more than a sum of its parts; which not only gives a particular conformation or structure to the parts but so relates and determines them in their synthesis that their functions are altered; the synthesis affects and determines the parts so that they function toward the "whole"; and the whole and the parts therefore reciprocally influence and determine each other and appear more or less to merge their individual characters.[16]

Smuts saw a continuum of relationships among parts from simple physical mixtures and chemical compounds to organisms and minds in which the unity among parts was affected and changed by the synthesis. "Holism is a process of creative synthesis; the resulting wholes are not static, but dynamic, evolutionary, creative. . . . The explanation of nature can therefore not be purely mechanical; and the mechanistic concept of nature has its place and justification only in the wider setting of holism."

The most important example of holism today is provided by the science of ecology. Although ecology is a relatively new science, its philosophy of nature, holism, is not. Historically, holistic presuppositions about nature have been assumed by communities of people who have succeeded in living in equilibrium with their environments. The idea of cyclical processes, of the interconnectedness of all things, and the assumption that nature is active and alive are fundamental to the history of human thought. No element of an interlocking cycle can be removed without the collapse of the cycle. The parts themselves thus take their meaning from the whole. Each particular part is defined by and dependent on the total context. The cycle itself is a dynamic interactive relationship of all its parts, and process is a dialectical relation between parts and whole. Ecology necessarily must consider the complexities and the totality. It cannot isolate the parts into simplified systems that can be studied in a laboratory because such isolation distorts the whole.

External forces and stresses on a balanced ecosystem, whether natural or man made, can make some parts of the cycle act faster than the systems' own natural oscillations. Depending on the strength of the external disturbance, the metabolic and reproductive reaction rates of the slowest parts of the cycle, and the complexity of the system, it may or may not be able to absorb the stresses without collapsing.[17] At various times in history, civilizations which have put too much external stress on their environments have caused long-term or irrevocable alterations.

## CONCLUSION

By pointing up the essential role of every part of an ecosystem, that if one part is removed the system is weakened and loses stability, ecology has moved in the direction of the leveling of value hierarchies. Each part contributes equal value to the healthy functioning of the whole. All living things, as integral parts of a viable ecosystem, thus have rights. The necessity of protecting the ecosystem from collapse due to the extinction of vital members was one argument for the passage of the Endangered Species Act of 1973. The movement toward egalitarianism manifested in the democratic revolutions of the eighteenth century, the extension of citizens' rights to blacks, and finally, voting rights to women was thus carried a step further. Endangered species became equal to the Army Corps of Engineers: the snail darter had to have a legal hearing before the Tellico Dam could be approved, the Furbish lousewort could block construction of the Dickey-Lincoln Dam in Maine, the red-cockaded woodpecker must be considered in Texas timber management, and the El Segundo Blue Butterfly in California airport expansion.

The conjunction of conservation and ecology movements with women's rights and liberation has moved in the direction of reversing both the subjugation of nature and women. In the late nineteenth and early twentieth centuries, the strong feminist movement in the United States begun in 1842 pressed for women's suffrage first in the individual states and then in the nation. Women activists also formed conservation committees in the many women's organizations that were part of the Federation of Women's Clubs established in 1890. They supported the preservationist movement for national, state, and city parks and wilderness areas led by John Muir and Frederick Law Olmsted, eventually splitting away from the managerial, utilitarian wing headed by Gifford Pinchot and Theodore Roosevelt.[18]

Today the conjunction of the women's movement with the ecology movement again brings the issue of liberation into focus. Mainstream women's groups such as the League of Women Voters took an early lead in studying and pressing for clean air and water legislation. Socialist-feminist and "science for the people" groups worked toward revolutionizing economic structures in a direction that would equalize female and male work options and reform a capitalist system that creates profits at the expense of nature and working people.

The March 1979 accident at the Three-Mile Island nuclear reactor near Harrisburg, Pennsylvania, epitomized the problems of the "death of nature" that have become apparent since the Scientific Revolution. The manipulation of nuclear processes in an effort to control and harness nature through technology backfired into disaster. The long-range economic interests and public image of the power company and the reactor's designer were set above the immediate safety of the people and the health of the earth. The hidden effects of radioactive emissions, which by concentrating in the food chain could lead to an increase in cancers over the next several years, were initially downplayed by those charged with responsibility for regulating atomic power.

Three-Mile Island is a recent symbol of the earth's sickness caused by radioactive wastes, pesticides, plastics, photochemical smog, and fluorocarbons. The pollution "of her purest streams" has been supported since the Scientific Revolution by an ideology of "power over nature," an ontology of interchangeable atomic and human parts, and a methodology of "penetration" into her innermost secrets. The sick earth, "yea dead, yea putrified," can probably in the long run be restored to health only by a reversal of mainstream values and a revolution in economic priorities. In this sense, the world must once again be turned upside down.

As natural resources and energy supplies diminish in the future, it will become essential to examine alternatives of all kinds so that, by adopting new social styles, the quality of the environment can be sustained. Decentralization, nonhierarchical forms of organization, recycling of wastes, simpler living styles involving less-polluting "soft" technologies, and labor-intensive rather than capital-intensive economic methods are possibilities only beginning to be explored.[19] The future distribution of energy and resources among communities should be based on the integration of human and natural ecosystems. Such a restructuring of priorities may be crucial if people and nature are to survive.

# NOTES

1. On the tensions between technology and the pastoral ideal in American culture, see Leo Marx, *The Machine in the Garden* (New York: Oxford University Press, 1964). On the domination of nature as female, see Annette Kolodny, *The Lay of the Land* (Chapel Hill: University of North Carolina Press, 1975); Rosemary Radford Ruether, "Women, Ecology, and the Domination of Nature," *The Ecumenist* 14 (1975): 1–5; William Leiss, *The Domination of Nature* (New York: Braziller, 1972). On the roots of the ecological crisis, see Donald Hughes, *Ecology in Ancient Civilizations* (Albuquerque: University of New Mexico Press, 1976); Lynn White, Jr., *Medieval Technology and Social Change* (New York: Oxford University Press, 1966); and L. White, Jr., "Historical Roots of Our Ecological Crisis," in White, Jr. *Machina ex Deo* (Cambridge, Mass.: M.I.T. Press, 1968), pp. 75–94; Reijer Hooykaas, *Religion and the Rise of Modern Science* (Grand Rapids, Mich.: Eerdmans, 1972); Christopher Derrick, *The Delicate Creation: Towards a Theology of the Environment* (Old Greenwich, Conn.: Devin-Adair, 1972). On traditional rituals in the mining of ores and in metallurgy, see Mircea Eliade, *The Forge and the Crucible*, trans. Stephan Corrin (New York: Harper & Row, 1962), pp. 42, 53–70, 74, 79–96. On the divergence between attitudes and practices toward the environment, see Yi-Fu Tuan,

"Our Treatment of the Environment in Ideal and Actuality," *American Scientist* (May-June 1970): 246–49.

2.  Treatments of Francis Bacon's contributions to science include Paolo Rossi, *Francis Bacon: From Magic To Science* (London: Routledge & Kegan Paul, 1968); Lisa Jardine, *Francis Bacon: Discovery and the Art of Discourse* (Cambridge, England: Cambridge University Press, 1974); Benjamin Farrington, *Francis Bacon, Philosopher of Industrial Science* (New York: Schumann, 1949); Margery Purver, *The Royal Society: Concept and Creation* (London: Routledge & Kegan Paul, 1967).

3.  Bacon, "The Great Instauration" (written 1620), *Works*, vol. 4, p. 20; "The Masculine Birth of Time," ed. and trans. Benjamin Farrington, in *The Philosophy of Francis Bacon* (Liverpool, England: Liverpool University Press, 1964), p. 62; "De Dignitate," *Works*, vol. 4, pp. 287, 294.

4.  Quoted in Moody E. Prior, "Bacon's Man of Science," in Leonard M. Marsak, ed., *The Rise of Modern Science in Relation to Society* (London: Collier-Macmillan, 1964), p. 45.

5.  Rossi, p. 21; Leiss, p. 56; Bacon, *Works*, vol. 4, p. 294; Henry Cornelius Agrippa, *De Occulta Philosophia Libri Tres* (Antwerp, 1531): "No one has such powers but he who has cohabited with the elements, vanquished nature, mounted higher than the heavens, elevating himself above the angels to the archetype itself, with whom he then becomes cooperator and can do all things," as quoted in Frances A. Yates, *Giordano Bruno and the Hermetic Tradition* (New York: Vintage Books, 1964), p. 136.

6.  Bacon, "Novum Organum," Part 2, in *Works*, vol. 4, p. 247; "Valerius Terminus," *Works*, vol. 3, pp. 217, 219; "The Masculine Birth of Time," trans. Farrington, p. 62.

7.  Bacon, "The Masculine Birth of Time," and "The Refutation of Philosophies," trans. Farrington, pp. 62, 129, 130.

8.  Bacon, "De Augmentis," *Works*, vol. 4, p. 294; see also Bacon, "Aphorisms," *Works*, vol. 4.

9.  "De Augmentis," *Works*, vol. 4, pp. 320, 325; Plato, "The Timaeus," in *The Dialogues of Plato*, trans. B. Jowett (New York: Random House, 1937), vol. 2, p. 17; Bacon, "Parasceve," *Works*, vol. 4, p. 257.

10.  Bacon, "De Augmentis," *Works*, vol. 4, pp. 343, 287, 343, 393.

11.  Bacon, "Novum Organum," *Works*, vol. 4, p. 246; "The Great Instauration," *Works*, vol. 4, p. 29; "Novum Organum," Part 2, *Works*, vol. 4, p. 247.

12.  Bacon, "Thoughts and Conclusions on the Interpretation of Nature or A Science of Productive Works," trans. Farrington, *The Philosophy of Francis Bacon*, pp. 96, 93, 99.

13.  Bacon, "De Augmentis," *Works*, vol. 4, p. 294; "Parasceve," *Works*, vol. 4, p. 257; "Plan of the Work," vol. 4, p. 32; "Novum Organum," *Works*, vol. 4, pp. 114, 115.

14.  René Descartes, "Discourse on Method," Part 4, in E. S. Haldane and G. R. T. Ross, eds., *Philosophical Works of Descartes* (New York: Dover, 1955), vol. 1, p. 119.

15.  Joseph Glanvill, *Plus Ultra* (Gainesville, Fla.: Scholar's Facsimile Reprints, 1958; first published 1668), quotations on pp. 9, 87, 13, 56, 104, 10.

16.  J. C. Smuts, *Holism and Evolution* (New York: Macmillan, 1926), pp. 86, 87. On holism in the biological sciences, see Arthur Koestler, "Beyond Holism and Reductionism: The Concept of the Holon," in *Beyond Reductionism: New Perspectives in the Life Sciences*, ed. A. Koestler and J. R. Smythies (Boston: Beacon Press, 1969).

17.  On ecological cycles, see Barry Commoner, *The Closing Circle: Nature, Man, and Technology* (New York; Bantam Books, 1971), Chap. 2.

18.  Samuel P. Hays, *Conservation and the Gospel of Efficiency: The Progressive Conservation Movement, 1890–1920* (Cambridge, Mass.: Harvard University Press, 1959), pp. 142–43.

19.  Murray Bookchin, "Ecology and Revolutionary Thought," in *Post-Scarcity Anarchism* (San Francisco: Ramparts Press, 1971), pp. 57–82, and M. Bookchin, "Toward an Ecological Solution" (Berkeley, Calif.: Ecology Center Reprint, n.d.). See also Victor Ferkiss, *Technological Man* (New York: New American Library, 1969), Chap. 9, pp. 205–11; Theodore Roszak, *Where the Wasteland Ends* (Garden City, N.Y.: Doubleday, 1973), pp. 367–71; Paul Goodman and Percival Goodman, *Communitas*, 2nd ed., rev. (New York: Vintage, 1960); Paul Goodman, *People or Personnel* (New York: Random House, 1965); E. F. Schumacher, *Small Is Beautiful: Economics as if People Mattered* (New York: Harper & Row, 1973); Ernest Callenbach, *Ecotopia* (Berkeley, Calif.: Banyan Tree Books, 1976).

# THE IMPOVERISHMENT
# OF THE ENVIRONMENT:
# WOMEN AND CHILDREN LAST

*Vandana Shiva*

Vandana Shiva, founder and director of The Research Foundation for Science, Technology, and Ecology (Dehradun, India), is an internationally renowned environmental scholar, researcher, and activist who is highly critical of multinational agriculture, reproductive technologies, and development. She has authored four books, including *Stolen Harvest: The Hijacking of the Global Food Supply.*

Ruth Sidel's book, *Women and Children Last,*[1] opens with an account of the sinking of the unsinkable *Titanic.* Women and children were, indeed, the first to be saved on that dreadful night—that is, those in the first and second class. But the majority of women and children did not survive—they were in the third class.

The state of the global economy is in many ways comparable to the *Titanic:* glittering and affluent and considered unsinkable. But as Ruth Sidel observed, despite our side-walk cafes, our saunas, our luxury boutiques, we, too, lack lifeboats for everyone when disaster strikes. Like the *Titanic,* the global economy has too many locked gates, segregated decks and policies ensuring that women and children will be first—not to be saved, but to fall into the abyss of poverty.

## ENVIRONMENTAL DEGRADATION AND POVERTY CREATION

Development was to have created well-being and affluence for all in the Third World. For some regions, and some people, it has delivered that promise, but

This essay originally appeared in Maria Mies and Vandana Shiva, *Ecofeminism* (Atlantic Highlands, N.J.: Zed Books, 1993). Reprinted with permission.

for most regions and people, it has instead brought environmental degradation and poverty. Where did the development paradigm go wrong?

Firstly, it focused exclusively on a model of progress derived from Western industrialized economies, on the assumption that Western style progress was possible for all. Development, as the improved well-being of all, was thus equated with the Westernization of economic categories—of human needs, productivity, and growth. Concepts and categories relating to economic development and natural resource utilization that had emerged in the specific context of industrialization and capitalist growth in a centre of colonial power, were raised to the level of universal assumptions and thought to be successfully applicable in the entirely different context of basic-needs satisfaction for the people of the erstwhile colonies—newly independent Third World countries. Yet, as Rosa Luxemburg[2] has pointed out, early industrial development in Western Europe necessitated permanent occupation of the colonies by the colonial powers, and the destruction of the local "natural economy." According to Luxemburg, colonialism is a constant, necessary condition for capitalist growth: without colonies, capital accumulation would grind to a halt. "Development" as capital accumulation and the commercialization of the economy for the generation of 'surplus' and profits thus involved the reproduction of not only a particular form of wealth creation, but also of the associated creation of poverty and dispossession. A replication of economic development based on commercialization of resource-use for commodity production in the newly independent countries created internal colonies and perpetuated old colonial linkages. Development thus became a continuation of the colonization process; it became an extension of the project of wealth creation in modern, Western patriarchy's economic vision.

Secondly, development focused exclusively on such financial indicators as GNP (gross national product). What these indicators could not demonstrate was the environmental destruction and the creation of poverty associated with the development process. The problem with measuring economic growth in GNP is that it measures some costs as benefits (for example, pollution control) but fails to fully measure other costs. In GNP calculations, clear-felling a natural forest adds to economic growth, even though it leaves behind impoverished ecosystems which can no longer produce biomass or water, and thus also leaves impoverished forest and farming communities.

Thirdly, such indicators as GNP can measure only those activities that take place through the market mechanism, regardless of whether or not such activities are productive, unproductive or destructive.

In the market economy, the organizing principle for natural resource use is maximization of profits and capital accumulation. Nature and human needs are managed through market mechanisms. Natural resources demands are restricted to those registering on the market; the ideology of development is largely based on a notion of bringing all natural resources into the market economy for commodity production. When these resources are already being used by nature to maintain production of renewable resources, and by women for sustenance and livelihood, their diversion to the market economy generates a scarcity condition for ecological stability and creates new forms of poverty for all, especially women and children.

Finally, the conventional paradigm of development perceives poverty only in terms of an absence of Western consumption patterns, or in terms of cash incomes and therefore is unable to grapple with self-provisioning economies, or to include the poverty created by their destruction through development. In a book entitled *Poverty: the Wealth of the People,*[3] an African writer draws a distinction between poverty as subsistence, and poverty as deprivation. It is useful to separate a cultural conception of subsistence living as poverty from the material experience of poverty resulting from dispossession and deprivation. Culturally perceived poverty is not necessarily real material poverty: subsistence economies that satisfy basic needs through self-provisioning are not poor in the sense of deprivation. Yet the ideology of development declares them to be so because they neither participate overwhelmingly in the market economy nor consume commodities produced for and distributed through the market, even though they might be satisfying those basic needs through self-provisioning mechanisms. People are perceived as poor if they eat millets (grown by women) rather than commercially produced and distributed processed foods sold by global agribusiness. They are seen as poor if they live in houses self-built with natural materials like bamboo and mud rather than concrete. They are seen as poor if they wear home-made garments of natural fibre rather than synthetics. Subsistence, as culturally perceived poverty, does not necessarily imply a low material quality of life. On the contrary, millets, for example, are nutritionally superior to processed foods, houses built with local materials rather than concrete are better adapted to the local climate and ecology, natural fibres are generally preferable to synthetic ones—and often more affordable. The cultural perception of prudent subsistence living as poverty has provided legitimization for the development process as a "poverty-removal" project. "Development," as a culturally biased process destroys wholesome and sustainable lifestyles and instead creates real material poverty, and misery, by denying the means of survival through the diversion of resources to resource-intensive commodity production. Cash crop production and food processing, by diverting land and water resources away from sustenance needs, deprive increasingly large numbers of people from the means of satisfying their entitlements to food.

The resource base for survival is being increasingly eroded by the demand for resources by the market economy, dominated by global forces. The creation of inequality through ecologically disruptive economic activity arises in two ways: first, inequalities in the distribution of privileges and power make for unequal access to natural resources—these include privileges of both a political and economic nature. Second, government policy enables resource intensive production processes to gain access to the raw material that many people, especially from the less privileged economic groups, depend upon for their survival. Consumption of this raw material is determined solely by market forces, unimpeded by any consideration of the social or ecological impact. The costs of resource destruction are externalized and divided unequally among various economic groups in society, but these costs are borne largely by women and those who, lacking the purchasing power to register their demands on the modern production system's goods and services, provide for their basic material needs directly from nature.

The paradox and crisis of development results from mistakenly identifying culturally perceived poverty with real material poverty, and of mistaking the growth of commodity production as better satisfying basic needs. In fact, however, water, soil fertility, and genetic wealth are considerably diminished as a result of the development process. The scarcity of these natural resources, which form the basis of nature's economy and especially women's survival economy, is impoverishing women, and all marginalized peoples to an unprecedented extent. The source of this impoverishment is the market economy, which has absorbed these resources in the pursuit of commodity production.

## IMPOVERISHMENT OF WOMEN, CHILDREN AND THE ENVIRONMENT

The UN Decade for Women was based on the assumption that the improvement of women's economic position would automatically flow from an expansion and diffusion of the development process. By the end of the Decade, however, it was becoming clear that development itself was the problem. Women's increasing underdevelopment was not due to insufficient and inadequate "participation" in "development." Rather, it was due to their enforced but asymmetric participation, whereby they bore the costs but were excluded from the benefits. Development and dispossession augmented the colonial processes of ecological degradation and the loss of political control over nature's sustenance base. Economic growth was a new colonialism, draining resources away from those who most needed them. But now, it was not the old colonial powers but the new national elites that masterminded the exploitation on grounds of "national interest" and growing GNPs, and it was accomplished by more powerful technologies of appropriation and destruction.

Ester Boserup[4] has documented how women's impoverishment increased during colonial rule; those rulers who had for centuries subjugated and reduced their own women to the status of de-skilled, de-intellectualized appendages, discriminated against the women of the colonies on access to land, technology and employment. The economic and political processes of colonial underdevelopment were clear manifestations of modern Western patriarchy, and while large numbers of men as well as women were impoverished by these processes, women tended to be the greater losers. The privatization of land for revenue generation affected women more seriously, eroding their traditional land-use rights. The expansion of cash crops undermined food production, and when men migrated or were conscripted into forced labour by the colonizers, women were often left with meagre resources to feed and care for their families. As a collective document by women activists, organizers and researchers stated at the end of the UN Decade for Women:

> The almost uniform conclusion of the Decade's research is that with a few exceptions, women's relative access to economic resources, incomes and employment has worsened, their burden of work has increased, and their relative and even absolute health, nutritional and educational status has declined.[5]

Women's role in the regeneration of human life and the provisioning of sustenance has meant that the destructive impact on women and the environment extends into a negative impact on the status of children.

The exclusive focus on incomes and cash-flows as measured in GNP has meant that the web of life around women, children and the environment is excluded from central concern. The status of women and children and the state of the environment have never functioned as "indicators" of development. This exclusion is achieved by rendering invisible two kinds of processes. Firstly, nature's, women's and children's contribution to the growth of the market economy is neglected and denied. Dominant economic theories assign no value to tasks carried out at subsistence and domestic levels. These theories are unable to encompass the majority in the world—women and children—who are statistically "invisible." Secondly, the negative impact of economic development and growth on women, children and environment goes largely unrecognized and unrecorded. Both these factors lead to impoverishment.

Among the hidden costs generated by destructive development are the new burdens created by ecological devastation, costs that are invariably heavier for women, in both the North and South. It is hardly surprising, therefore, that a rising GNP does not necessarily mean that either wealth or welfare increase proportionately. I would argue that GNP is becoming increasingly a measure of how real wealth—the wealth of nature and the life sustaining wealth produced by women—is rapidly decreasing. When commodity production as the prime economic activity is introduced as development, it destroys the potential of nature and women to produce life and goods and services for basic needs. More commodities and more cash mean less life—in nature through ecological destruction and in society through denial of basic needs. Women are devalued, first, because their work co-operates with nature's processes, and second, because work that satisfies needs and ensures sustenance is devalued in general. More growth in what is maldevelopment has meant less nurturing of life and life support systems.

Nature's economy—through which environmental regeneration takes place—and the people's subsistence economy—within which women produce the sustenance for society through "invisible" unpaid work called non-work—are being systematically destroyed to create growth in the market economy.

Closely reflecting what I have called the three economies, of nature, people and the market in the Third World context, is Hilkka Pietila's[6] categorization of industrialized economies as: the free economy; the protected sector; and the fettered economy.

*The Free Economy:*   The non-monetary core of the economy and society, unpaid work for one's own and family needs, community activities, mutual help and co-operation within the neighbourhood and so on.

*The Protected Sector:*   Production, protected and guided by official means for domestic markets; food, constructions, services, administration, health, schools and culture, and so on.

*The Fettered Economy:*   Large-scale production for export and to compete with imports. The terms dictated by the world market, dependency, vulnerability, compulsive competitiveness and so forth.

For example, in 1980, the proportions of time and money value that went into running each category of the Finnish economy were as follows!

**TABLE 20.1**

|                                          | Time | Money |
|------------------------------------------|------|-------|
| A. The free economy, informal economy    | 54%  | 35%   |
| B. Protected sector                       | 36%  | 46%   |
| C. The fettered economy                   | 10%  | 19%   |

In patriarchal economics, B and C are perceived as the primary economy, and A as the secondary economy. In fact as Marilyn Waring[7] has documented, national accounts and GNP actually exclude the free economy as lying outside the production boundary. What most economists and politicians call the "free" or "open" economy is seen by women as the "fettered" economy. When the fettered economy becomes "poor"—that is, runs into deficit—it is the free economy that pays to restore it to health. In times of structural adjustment and austerity programmes, cuts in public expenditure generally fall most heavily on the poor. In many cases reduction of the fiscal deficit has been effected by making substantial cuts in social and economic development expenditure, and real wages and consumption decrease considerably.

The poverty trap, created through the vicious cycle of "development," debt, environmental destruction and structural adjustment, is most significantly experienced by women and children. Capital flows from North to South have been reversed. Ten years ago, a net $40 billion flowed from the Northern hemisphere to the countries of the South. Today in terms of loans, aid, repayment of interest and capital, the South transfers $20 billion a year to the North. If the effective transfer of resources implied in the reduced prices industrialized nations pay for the developing world's raw materials is taken into account, the annual flow from the poor to the rich countries could amount to $60 billion annually. This economic drain implies a deepening of the crisis of impoverishment of women, children and the environment.

According to UNICEF estimates, in 1988[8] half-a-million children died as a direct result of debt-related adjustment policies that sustain the North's economic growth. Poverty, of course, needs to be redefined in the emerging context of the feminization of poverty on the one hand, and the link to environmental impoverishment on the other.

Poverty is not confined to the so-called poor countries; it exists in the world's wealthiest society. Today, the vast majority of poor people in the US are women and children. According to the Census Bureau, in 1984, 14.4 percent of all Americans (33.7 million) lived below the poverty line. From 1980 to 1984 the number of poor people increased by four-and-a-half million. For female-headed households in 1984, the poverty rate was 34.5 percent—five times that for married couples. The poverty rate for white, female-headed families was 27.1 percent; for black, women-headed families, 51.7 percent; and for women-headed Hispanic families, 53.4 percent. The impact of women's poverty on the economic status of children is even more shocking: in 1984, the poverty rate for children under six was 24 percent, and in the same year, for children living in women-headed households it was 53.9 percent. Among black children the poverty rate was 46.3 percent; and for those living in female-headed families, 66.6 percent. Among Hispanic children 39 percent were poor, and for those living in female-headed families, the poverty rate was 70.5 percent.[9]

Theresa Funiciello, a welfare rights organizer in the US, writes that "By almost any honest measure, poverty is the number one killer of children in the U.S." (Waring, 1988). In New York City, 40 percent of the children (700,000) are living in families that the government classifies deprived as 7,000 children are born addicted to drugs each year, and 12,000 removed to foster homes because of abuse or neglect (Waring, 1988).

The first right mentioned in the Convention of the Rights of the Child is the inherent right to life. Denial of this right should be the point of departure for evolving a definition of poverty. It should be based on denial of access to food, water and shelter in the quality and quantity that makes a healthy life possible.

Pure income indicators often do not capture the poverty of life to which the future generations are being condemned, with threats to survival from environmental hazards even in conditions otherwise characterized by "affluence." Poverty has so far been culturally perceived in terms of life styles that do not fit into the categories of Western industrial society. We need to move away from these restricted and biased perceptions to grapple with poverty in terms of threats to a safe and healthy life either due to denial of access to food, water and shelter, or due to lack of protection from hazards in the form of toxic and nuclear threats.

Human scale development can be a beginning of an operational definition of poverty as a denial of vital human needs. At the highest level, the basic needs have been identified as subsistence, protection, affection, understanding, participation, leisure, creation, identity, freedom. These needs are most clearly manifest in a child, and the child can thus become our guide to a humane, just and sustainable social organization, and to a shift away from the destructiveness of what has been construed as "development."[10]

While producing higher cash flows, patriarchal development has led to deprivation at the level of real human needs. For the child, these deprivations can become life threatening, as the following illustrates.

## THE FOOD AND NUTRITION CRISIS

Both traditionally, and in the context of the new poverty, women and children have been treated as marginal to food systems. In terms of nutrition the girl-child is doubly discriminated against in such countries as India (see Table 20.2).[11]

The effects of inadequate nourishment of young girls continue into their adulthood and are passed on to the next generation. Complications during pregnancy, premature births and low birth weight babies with little chance of survival result when a mother is undernourished; and a high percentage of deaths during pregnancy and childbirth are directly due to anaemia, and childhood undernourishment is probably an underlying cause.[12] Denial of nutritional rights to women and children is the biggest threat to their lives.

Programmes of agricultural "development" often become programmes of hunger generation because fertile land is diverted to grow export crops, small peasants are displaced, and the biological diversity, which provided much of the poor's food entitlements, is eliminated and replaced by cash crop monocultures, or land-use systems ill suited to the ecology or to the provision of people's food entitlements. A permanent food crisis affects more than a 100 million people in Africa; famine is just the tip of a much bigger underlying crisis. Even when Ethiopia is not suffering from famine, 1,000 children are thought to die each day of malnutrition and related illnesses.[13]

Everywhere in the South, the economic crisis rooted in maldevelopment is leading to an impoverishment of the environment and a threat to the survival of children. It is even possible to quantify the debt mortality effect: over the decade of 1970 to 1980, each additional $10 a year interest payments per capita reflected 0.39 of a year less in life expectancy improvement. This is an average of 387 days of life foregone by every inhabitant of the 73 countries studied in Latin America.[14] Nutritional studies carried out in Peru show that in the poorest neighbourhoods of Ijma and surrounding shanty towns, the percentage of undernourished children increased from 24 percent in 1972 to 28 percent in 1978 and to 36 percent in 1983.

**TABLE 20.2   FOODS RECEIVED BY MALE AND FEMALE CHILDREN 3–4 AND 7–9 YEARS (INDIA)**

| Food Items in Grams | Age in Years | | | | | |
| | 3–4 | | | 7–9 | | |
| | RDA | Male | Female | RDA | Male | Female |
|---|---|---|---|---|---|---|
| Cereals | 173 | 118 | 90 | 250 | 252 | 240 |
| Pulses | 55 | 22 | 18 | 70 | 49 | 25 |
| Green leafy vegetables | 62 | 3 | 0 | 75 | 0 | 0 |
| Roots and tubers | 40 | 15 | 13 | 50 | 42 | 0 |
| Fruits | 50 | 30 | 17 | 50 | 17 | 6 |
| Milk | 225 | 188 | 173 | 250 | 122 | 10 |
| Sugar and jaggery | 22 | 13 | 16 | 30 | 30 | 12 |
| Fats and oils | 30 | 5 | 2 | 50 | 23 | 8 |

*Source:* Devadas, R. and G. Kamalanathan, "A Women's First Decade." Paper presented at the Women's NGO Consultation and Equality, Development and Peace, New Delhi, 1985.

In Argentina, according to official sources, in 1986 685,000 children in greater Buenos Aires and a further 385,000 in the province of Buenos Aires did not eat enough to stay alive; together constituting one-third of all children under 14.[15]

Starvation is endemic in the ultra-poor northeast of Brazil, where it is producing what IBASE (a public interest research group in Brazil) calls a "sub-race" and nutritionists call an epidemic of dwarfism. The children in this area are 16 percent shorter and weigh 20 percent less than those of the same age elsewhere in Brazil—who, themselves, are not exactly well nourished.

In Jamaica, too, food consumption has decreased as is shown:

**TABLE 20.3**

| Item | No. of Calories August 1984 | No. of Calories November 1985 | Change % |
|---|---|---|---|
| Flour | 2,232 | 1,443 | −35 |
| Cornmeal | 3,669 | 2,013 | −45 |
| Rice | 1,646 | 905 | −45 |
| Chicken | 220 | 174 | −20 |
| Condensed milk | 1,037 | 508 | −51 |
| Oil | 1,003 | 823 | −18 |
| Dark sugar | 1,727 | 1,253 | −27 |

*Source:* Susan George, *A Fate Worse than Debt, 1988,* p. 188.

As the price of food rose beyond people's ability to pay, children's health demonstratively declined. In 1978, fewer than 2 percent of children admitted to the Bustamente Children's Hospital were suffering from malnutrition, and 1.6 percent from malnutrition-related gastroenteritis. By 1986, when the full effects of the adjustment policies were being felt, the figures for malnutrition-related admissions had doubled, to almost four percent; gastroenteritis admissions were almost five percent.[16]

Numerical malnutrition is the most serious health hazard for children, particularly in the developing countries. Surveys in different regions of the world indicate that at any moment an estimated ten million children are suffering from severe malnutrition and a further 200 million are inadequately nourished.[17]

The increase in nutritional deprivation of children is one result of the same policies that lead to the nutritional deprivation of soils. Agriculture policies which extract surplus to meet export targets and enhance foreign exchange earnings generate that surplus by creating new levels of nutritional impoverishment for women, children and the environment. As Maria Mies has pointed out,[18] this concept of surplus has a patriarchal bias because, from the point of view of nature, women and children, it is based not on material surplus produced *over and above* the requirements of the environment or of the community, it is violently stolen and appropriated from nature (which needs a share of her produce to reproduce herself) and from women (who need a share of nature's produce to sustain and to ensure the survival of themselves and their children). Malnutrition and deficiency diseases are also caused by the destruction of biodiversity which forms the nutritional base in subsistence communities. For example, *bathua* is an important green leafy vegetable with very high nutritive value which grows in association with wheat, and when women weed the wheat field they not only contribute to the productivity of wheat but also harvest a rich nutritional source for their families. With the intensive use of chemical fertilizer, however, *bathua* becomes a major competitor of wheat and has been declared a "weed" to be eliminated by herbicides. Thus, the food cycle is broken; women are deprived of work; children are deprived of a free source of nutrition.

## THE WATER CRISIS

The water crisis contributes to 34.6 percent of all child deaths in the Third World. Each year, 5,000,000 children die of diarrhoeal diseases.[19] The declining availability of water resources, due to their diversion for industry and industrial agriculture and to complex factors related to deforestation, desertification and drought, is a severe threat to children's health and survival. As access to water decreases, polluted water sources and related health hazards, increase. "Development" in the conventional paradigm implies a more intensive and wasteful use of water—dams and intensive irrigation for green revolution agriculture, water for air-conditioning mushrooming hotels and urban-industrial complexes, water for coolants, as well as pollution due to the dumping of industrial wastes. And as development creates more water demands, the survival needs of children—and adults—for pure and safe water are sacrificed.

Antonia Alcantara, a vendor from a slum outside Mexico City, complains that her tap water is "yellow and full of worms." Even dirty water is in short supply. The demands of Mexico City's 20 million people have caused the level of the main aquifer to drop as much as 3.4 metres annually.[20] Those with access to Mexico City's water system are usually the wealthy and middle classes. They are, in fact, almost encouraged to be wasteful by subsidies that allow consumers to pay as little as one-tenth the actual cost of water. The poor, on the other hand, are often forced to buy from *piperas,* entrepreneurs, who fix prices according to demand.

In Delhi, in 1988, 2,000 people (mainly children) died as a result of a cholera epidemic in slum colonies. These colonies had been "resettled" when slums were removed from Delhi to beautify India's capital. This dispensable population was provided with neither safe drinking water nor adequate sewage facilities; it was only the children of the poor communities who died of cholera. Across the Yamuna river, the swimming pools had enough chlorinated water to protect the tourists, the diplomats, the elite.[21]

## TOXIC HAZARDS

In the late twentieth century it is becoming clear that our scientific systems are totally inadequate to counteract or eliminate the hazards—actual and potential—to which children, in particular, are subjected. Each disaster seems like an experiment, with children as guinea pigs, to teach us more about the effects of deadly substances that are brought into daily production and use. The patriarchal systems would like to maintain silence about these poisonous substances, but as mothers women cannot ignore the threats posed to their children. Children are the most highly sensitive to chemical contamination, the chemical pollution of the environment is therefore most clearly manifested in their ill-health.

In the Love Canal and the Bhopal disasters, children were the worst affected victims. And in both places it is the women who have continued to resist and have refused to be silenced as corporations and state agencies would wish.

Love Canal was a site where, for decades, Hooker Chemical Company had dumped their chemical wastes, over which houses were later built. By the 1970s it was a peaceful middle-class residential area but its residents were unaware of the toxic dumps beneath their houses. Headaches, dizziness, nausea, and epilepsy were only a few of the problems afflicting those near the Canal. Liver, kidney, or recurrent urinary strictures abounded. There was also an alarmingly high rate of 56 percent risk of birth defects, including childhood deafness, and children suffered an unusually high rate of leukemia and other cancers.[22] There was a 75 percent above normal rate of miscarriage, and among 15 pregnancies of Love Canal women, only two resulted in healthy babies.

It was the mothers of children threatened by death and disease who first raised the alarm and who kept the issue alive.

In Japan, the dependence of Minamata Bay's fishermen and their families on a fish diet had disastrous results as the fish were heavily contaminated with methylmercury, which had been discharged into the Bay over a period of 30 years by the Chissio chemical factory.

In Bhopal, in 1984, the leak from Union Carbide's pesticide plant led to instant death for thousands. A host of ailments still afflicts many more thousands of those who escaped death. In addition women also suffer from gynaecological complications and menstrual disorders. Damage to the respiratory, reproductive, nervous, musculo-skeletal and immune systems of the gas victims has been documented in epidemiological studies carried out so far. The 1990 report of the Indian Council of Medical Research[23] states that the death rate among the affected population is more than double that of the unexposed population. Significantly higher incidences of spontaneous abortions, still-births and infant mortality among the gas victims have also been documented.

> A few months after the gas disaster, I had a son. He was alright. After that I had another child in the hospital. But it was not fully formed. It had no legs and no eyes and was born dead. Then another child was born but it died soon after. I had another child just one and a half months back. Its skin looked scalded and only half its head was formed. The other half was filled with water. It was born dead and was white all over. I had a lot of pain two months before I delivered. My legs hurt so much that I couldn't sit or walk around. I got rashes all over my body. The doctors said that I will be okay after the childbirth, but I still have these problems.[24]

## NUCLEAR HAZARDS

Hiroshima, Three Mile Island, the Pacific Islands, Chernobyl—each of these nuclear disasters reminds us that the nuclear threat is greater for future generations than for us.

Lijon Eknilang was seven years old at the time of the Bravo test on Bikini Island. She remembers her eyes itching, nausea and being covered by burns. Two days after the test, Lijon and her people were evacuated to the US base on Kwajalein Atoll. For three years they were kept away because Rongelap was too dangerous for life. Lijon's grandmother died in the 1960s due to thyroid and stomach cancer. Her father died during the nuclear test. Lijon reports that:

> I have had seven miscarriages and still births. Altogether there are eight other women on the island who have given birth to babies that look like blobs of jelly.

Some of these things we carry for eight months, nine months, there are no legs, no arms, no head, no nothing. Other children are born who will never recognise this world or their own parents. They just lie there with crooked arms and legs and never speak.[25]

Every aspect of environmental destruction translates into a severe threat to the life of future generations. Much has been written on the issue of sustainability as "intergenerational equity," but what is often overlooked is that the issue of justice between generations can only be realized through justice between sexes. Children cannot be put at the centre for concern if their mothers are meantime pushed beyond the margins of care and concern.

Over the past decades, women's coalitions have been developing survival strategies and fighting against the threat to their children that results from threats to the environment.

## SURVIVAL STRATEGIES OF WOMEN AND CHILDREN

As survival is more and more threatened by negative development trends, environmental degradation and poverty, women and children develop new ways to cope with the threat.

Today, more than one-third of the households in Africa, Latin America and the developed world are female headed; in Norway the figure is 38 percent, and in Asia 14 percent.[26] Even where women are not the sole family supporters they are primary supporters in terms of work and energy spent on providing sustenance to the family. For example, in rural areas women and children must walk further to collect the diminishing supplies of firewood and water, in urban areas they must take on more paid outside work. Usually, more time thus spent on working to sustain the family conflicts with the time and energy needed for child care. At times girls children take on part of the mother's burden: in India, the percentage of female workers below 14 years increased from four to eight percent. In the 15–19 year age group, the labour force participation rate increased by 17 percent for females, but declined by eight percent for males.[27] This suggests that more girls are being drawn into the labour force, and more boys are sent to school. This sizeable proportion perhaps explains high female school dropout rates, a conclusion that is supported by the higher levels of illiteracy among female workers, compared with 50 percent for males. It has been projected that by the year 2001 work participation among 0–14 year old girls will increase by a further 20 percent and among 15–19 year olds by 30 percent.[28]

The International Labour Organization (ILO) has estimated that at the beginning of the 1980s the overall number of children under 15 who were "economically active" was around 50 million; the World Health Organization (WHO) estimates put it at 100 million. There are another 100 million "street" children, without families or homes. These are victims of poverty, underdevelopment, and poor environmental conditions—society's disposable people—surviving entirely on their own, without any rights, without any voice.

Chipko women of Himalaya have organized to resist the environmental destruction caused by logging.

The Love Canal home owner's association is another well-known example of young housewives' persistent action to ensure health security for their families; this has now resulted in the Citizens' Clearinghouse for Hazardous Waste.

The Bhopal Gas Peedit Mahila Udyog Sangathan, a group of women victims of the Bhopal disaster, has continued to struggle for seven years to obtain justice from Union Carbide Corporation.

Across different contexts, in the North and in the South, in ecologically eroded zones and polluted places, women identify with the interest of the earth and their children in finding solutions to the crisis of survival. Against all odds they attempt to reweave the web which connects their life to the life of their children and the life of the planet. From women's perspective, sustainability without environmental justice is impossible, and environmental justice is impossible without justice between sexes and generations.

To whom will the future belong? to the women and children who struggle for survival and for environmental security? or to those who treat women, children and the environment as dispensable and disposable? Gandhi proposed a simple test for making decisions in a moment of doubt. "Recall the face of the least privileged person you know," he said, "and ask if your action will harm or benefit him/her."[29] This criterion of the "last person" must be extended to the "last child" if we are serious about evolving a code of environmental justice which protects future generations.

## DISPENSABILITY OF THE LAST CHILD: THE DOMINANT PARADIGM

From the viewpoint of governments, intergovernmental agencies, and power elites, the "last child" needs no lifeboat. This view has been explicitly developed by Garrett Hardin in his "life-boat ethics":[30] the poor, the weak are a "surplus" population, putting an unnecessary burden on the planet's resources. This view, and the responses and strategies that emerge from it, totally ignore the fact that the greatest pressure on the earth's resources is not from large numbers of poor people but from a small number of the world's ever-consuming elite.

Ignoring these resource pressures of consumption and destructive technologies, "conservation" plans increasingly push the last child further to the margins of existence. Official strategies, reflecting elite interests, strongly imply that the world would be better off if it could shed its "non-productive" poor through the life-boat strategy. Environmentalism is increasingly used in the rhetoric of manager-technocrats, who see the ecological crises as an opportunity for new investments and profits. The World Bank's Tropical Action Plan, the Climate Convention, the Montreal Protocol are often viewed as new means of dispossessing the poor to "save" the forests and atmosphere and biological commons for exploitation by the rich and powerful. The victims are transformed into villains in these ecological plans—and women, who have struggled most to protect their children in the face of ecological threats, become the elements who have to be policed to protect the planet.[31]

"Population explosions" have always emerged as images created by modern patriarchy in periods of increasing social and economic polarizations. Malthus[32] saw populations exploding at the dawn of the industrial era; between World War I and II certain groups were seen as threatening deterioration of the human genetic stock; post–World War II, countries where unrest threatened US access to resources and markets, became known as the "population powderkegs." Today, concern for the survival of the planet has made pollution control appear acceptable and even imperative, in the face of the popularized pictures of the world's hungry hordes.

What this focus on numbers hides is people's unequal access to resources and the unequal environmental burden they put on the earth. In global terms, the impact of a drastic decrease of population in the poorest areas of Asia, Africa and Latin America would be immeasurably smaller than a decrease of only five percent in the ten richest countries at present consumption levels.[33]

Through population control programmes, women's bodies are brutally invaded to protect the earth from the threat of overpopulation. Where women's fertility itself is threatened due to industrial pollution, their interest is put in opposition to the interests of their children. This divide and rule policy seems essential for managing the eco-crisis to the advantage of those who control power and privilege.

The emerging language of manager-technocrats describes women either as the passive "environment" of the child, or the dangerous "bomb" threatening a "population explosion." In either case, women whose lives are inextricably a part of children's lives have to be managed to protect children and the environment.

The mother's womb has been called the child's "environment." Even in the relatively sheltered environment of the mother's uterus the developing baby is far from completely protected. The mother's health, so intimately linked to the child's well-being, is reduced to a "factor within the foetus's environment."

Similar decontextualized views of the women-child relationship are presented as solutions to managing environmental hazards in the workplace. "Foetal protection policies" are the means by which employers take the focus off their own hazardous production by offering to "protect the unborn" by removing pregnant (or wanting-to-be pregnant) women from hazardous zones.[34] In extreme cases, women have consented to sterilization in order to keep their jobs and keep food on the table. More typically, practices include surveillance of women's menstrual cycle, of waiting for a woman to abort her pregnancy before employing her. As Lin Nelson has stated: "It is all too easy to 'assume pollution' and accept industrial relocation and obstetrical intervention, but they are responses to the symptoms, not the disease."[35]

## GRASSROOTS RESPONSE

Community groups, NGOs, ecology movements and women's movements begin the reversal of environmental degradation by reversing the trends that push women and children beyond the edge of survival. As mentioned earlier, the Chipko movement in India has been one such response. In Kenya, the Green Belt movement has fostered 1,000 Community Green Belts. In Malaysia, the Sahabal Alain Malaysia (SAM) and Consumer Association of Penang have worked with tribal, peasant, and fishing communities to reverse environmental decline. Tribals' blockades against logging in Sarawak are another important action in which these organizations have been involved. In Brazil the Acao Democratica Feminina Gaucha (ADFG) has been working on sustainable agriculture, indigenous rights, debt and structural adjustment.

What is distinctive about these popular responses is that they put the last child at the centre of concern, and work out strategies that simultaneously empower women and protect nature. Emerging work on women, health and ecology, such as the dialogue organized by the Research Foundation of India and the Dag Hammarskjold Foundation of Sweden,[36] the Planeta Femea at the Global Forum in Rio 1992[37] are pointing to new directions in which children's, women's and nature's integrity are perceived in wholeness, not fragmentation.

## PUTTING WOMEN AND CHILDREN FIRST

In 1987, at the Wilderness Congress, Oren Lyons of the Onondaga Nation said: "Take care how you place your moccasins upon the earth, step with care, for the faces of the future generations are looking up from the earth waiting for their turn for life."[38]

In the achievements of growing GNPs, increasing capital accumulation, it was the faces of children and future generations that receded from the minds of policy makers in centres of international power. The child had been excluded from concern, and cultures which were child-centred have been destroyed and marginalized. The challenge to the world's policy makers is to learn from mothers, from tribals and other communities, how to focus decisions on the well-being of children.

Putting women and children first needs above all, a reversal of the logic which has treated women as subordinate because they create life, and men as superior because they destroy it. All past achievements of patriarchy have been based on alienation from life, and have led to the impoverishment of women, children and the environment. If we want to reverse that decline, the creation, not the destruction of life must be seen as the truly human task, and the essence of being human has to be seen in our capacity to recognize, respect and protect the right to life of all the world's miltifarious species.

## NOTES

1. Sidel, Ruth, *Women and Children Last.* Penguin, New York, 1987.
2. Luxemburg, Rosa, *The Accumulation of Capital.* Routledge and Kegan Paul, London, 1951.
3. Quoted in R. Bahro, *From Red to Green.* Verso, London, 1984, p. 211.
4. Boserup, Ester, *Women's Role in Economic Development.* Allen and Unwin, London, 1960.
5. DAWN, 1985, *Development Crisis and Alternative Visions: Third World Women's Perspectives.* Christian Michelsen Institute, Bergen.
6. Pietila, Hilkka, *Tomorrow Begins Today.* ICDA/ISIS Workshop, Nairobi, 1985.
7. Waring, Marilyn, *If Women Counted.* Harper & Row, San Francisco, 1988.
8. UNICEF, *State of the World's Children,* 1988.
9. Quoted in Marilyn Waring, op. cit. p. 180; and Ruth Sidel, op. cit.
10. Max-Neef, Manfred, *Human Scale Development: Development Dialogue.* Dag Hammarskjold Foundation, 1989.
11. Chatterjee, Meera, *A Report on Indian Women from Birth to Twenty.* National Institute of Public Cooperation and Child Development, New Delhi, 1990.
12. Timberlake, Lloyd, *Africa in Crisis.* Earthscan, London, 1987.
13. Susan George, *A Fate Worse than Debt.* Food First, San Francisco, 1988.
14. Ibid.
15. Ibid.
16. Ibid.
17. UNICEF, *Children and the Environment,* 1990.
18. Mies, Maria, *Patriarchy and Accumulation on a World Scale.* Zed Books, London, 1987.
19. UNICEF, op. cit., 1990.
20. Moser, Caroline, Contribution on OECD Workshop on Women and Development. Paris, 1989.
21. Shiva, Maria, "Environmental Degradation and Subversion of Health" in Vandana Shiva (ed.) *Minding Our Lives: Women from the South and North Reconnect Ecology and Health,* Kali for Women, Delhi, 1993.
22. Gibbs, Lois, *Love Canal, My Story.* State University of New York, Albany, 1982.
23. Bhopal Information and Action Group, Voices of Bhopal. Bhopal, 1990.
24. Ibid.
25. *Pacific Women Speak,* Women Working for a Nuclear Free and Independent Pacific, 1987.
26. United Nations, *World's Women, 1970–1990.*
27. Chatterjee, Meera op. cit.
28. UNICEF, op. cit., 1990.
29. Kothari, Rajni, Vandana Shiva, "The Last Child," Manuscript for United Nations University Programme on Peace and Global Transformation.
30. Hardin, Garrett, in *Bioscience,* Vol. 24, (1974) p. 561.
31. Shiva, Vandana, "Forestry Crisis and Forestry Myths: A Critical Review of Tropical Forests: A Call for Action," World Rainforest Movement, Penang, 1987.
32. Malthus, in Barbara Duden, "Population," in Wolfgang Sachs (ed.), *Development Dictionary.* Zed Books, London, 1990.
33. UNICEF, op. cit., 1990.
34. Nelson, Lin, "The Place of Women in Polluted Places" in *Reweaving the World: The Emergence of Ecofeminism,* Irene Diamond and Gloria Orenstein (eds.). Sierra Club Books, 1990.
35. Ibid.

36. "Women, Health and Ecology," proceedings of a Seminar organized by Research Foundation for Science, Technology and Natural Resource Policy, and Dag Hammarskjold Foundation, in *Development Dialogue,* 1992.

37. "Planeta Femea" was the women's tent in the Global Forum during the UN Conference on Environment and Development, 1992.

38. Lyons, Oren 4th World Wilderness Conference, 11 September 1987, Eugene, Oregon.

# RECOGNIZING WOMEN'S ENVIRONMENTAL EXPERTISE

*Deane Curtin*

Deane Curtin holds the Raymond and Florence Sponberg chair of ethics at Gustavus Adolphus College. He has lived and taught in India, Japan, and Italy, and has published articles on deep ecology, ecofeminism, and Gandhian resistance to development. Curtin is the author of *Chinnagounder's Challenge: The Questions of Ecological Citizenship*.

## INSTITUTIONAL AND SYSTEMIC VIOLENCE

In addition to their more widely recognized roles as mothers and caretakers, women are the world's agriculturists. Women also provide most of the world's medical care. All three of these critical roles require dependable access to, and knowledge of, natural and human processes. One of the reasons we in the "First World"[1] may have difficulty in recognizing women's environmental expertise is that we view their practices through a conceptual lens that systematically distorts women's practices. It thereby makes it difficult for us to focus on the value of such practices. I suggest that such lenses are, in a philosophically important sense, violent.

Whether or not we can define violence, we in the First World are good at recognizing *individual violence*. Individual violence such as the abuse of a child is one-on-one violence, and it can be either overt or covert. For example, child abuse can be either overt and physical, resulting in broken bones and bruised faces, or it can be more subtle, covert violence, as in a parent's pattern of psychological abuse that robs a child of self-esteem. Westerners are good at recognizing individual violence, I suggest, because we are the heirs of a type of liberal individualism, one of whose defining beliefs is in the sovereignty of the

A slightly different version of this essay appeared in *Chinnagounder's Challenge: The Questions of Ecological Citizenship* (Bloomington: Indiana University Press, 1999). Reprinted with permission.

individual. It is not an accident, for example, that the utilitarian philosophers who ruled India for the East India Company regarded community as a "fictitious *body*" whose interests were nothing more than the sum of the interests of individual members.[2]

However, liberal individualism makes it difficult to recognize two other forms of violence, *systemic* and *institutional violence.*[3] "Systemic violence" refers to a pervasive, hierarchical pattern of thinking, a form of "arrogant perception" that privileges some groups and marginalizes or subordinates others, for no morally justifiable reason. Racism and sexism, colonialism and naturism, are forms of systemic violence. "Institutional violence" refers to violence facilitated by well organized cultural institutions. Systemic violence like racism may necessitate the creation of violent institutions: racist schools, police forces, and legal systems.

Unlike individual violence, systemic and institutional violence are rarely the result of any individual's conscious intentions. If I am guilty of mugging or murdering another person, it is likely that I will be able to introspect and find myself responsible for these acts of individual violence. However, it is very unlikely that we would hold any individual responsible for a system of violence or the related institution. A racist police officer may be "part of the system" of institutional violence, but it is unlikely that we could hold any individual responsible for the system or the institution. In opposition to attempts to address systemic violence, for example, by affirmative action programs in the United States, we often hear people say, "I didn't personally endorse past injustices so I can't be held responsible for contemporary inequalities." Such a view makes sense in the context of a strict form of liberal individualism where only culpability for individual violence counts. However, it fails to recognize institutional and systemic forms of violence. These are forms of violence that *no individual intended.* If we are benefited by these systems of exclusion, we are likely to think such systems are just. Those who are excluded know better.

The taxonomy of violence suggested here can be schematized as follows:

| Type | Overt | Covert |
|---|---|---|
| *Individual:* | muggings<br>murder | personal threats<br>character assassination |
| *Institutional:* | police brutality<br>terrorism | institutions of slavery<br>institutions of apartheid |
| *Systemic:* | domestic violence<br>genocidal violence<br>land disenfranchisement | sexism<br>racism<br>colonialism |

Granted, there are problems with naming in a taxonomy like this. "Colonialism," for example, may refer either to a systemic set of attitudes, or to an actual set of institutions created to support and foster the basic attitudes.

Similarly, a murder may be simply an act of one-on-one violence, or it may be a form of systemic violence that has resulted in violent institutions. The fact that these verbal shifts are possible is philosophically interesting and important. The lack of firm ground in discussing violence suggests that we may still not understand very well what violence is.

My particular concern in this essay is to ask why women's critical contributions to food production are often overlooked. Drawing on the distinctions among individual, institutional, and systemic violence, I suggest that neglect of traditional women's perspectives is best understood as a form of institutional and systemic violence. That is, while there are certainly individuals who consciously want to marginalize traditional women's perspectives, a much more powerful analysis is to recognize that certain features of the developmentalist story make it exceedingly difficult to recognize and value women's agricultural labor.

My conclusion is that what might be called developmentalism is a form of systemic violence that facilitated the creation of violent institutions. With regard to agriculture, those in the First World who have benefited from systems of marginalization are likely to think of agricultural development programs like the Green Revolution as progress.[4] Those in the First World who have benefited from this system of marginalization are likely to think of the Green Revolution as progress. Those who experience the Green Revolution from the other side know better.

## INSTITUTIONS AND MATERIAL CULTURE

A frequent theme of ecofeminism is the importance of recognizing the roles that women traditionally play in mediating between nature and human culture. Women do this in many ways, but their roles as farmers, or traditional cultivators, are particularly critical to an accurate rendering of the environmental crisis we face. In this regard, it is important to contrast traditional agriculture, which is often the primary responsibility of women, with the agriculture of the Green Revolution, which almost always defines agriculture as men's work. The contrast is stark: traditional agriculture tends to be small in scale. It depends on adapting seed genetics to local conditions. It is diverse, requiring a mixture of crops with livestock. In turn, agriculture is only part of a larger system that includes a biological commons which provides building materials and medicines.

In contrast, Green Revolution agriculture is massive in scale, and this requires a major investment in farm machinery. Its seed genetics come from the multinational corporation, and the entire package of inputs is designed to make the land adapt to the requirements of the inputs. This necessitates massive irrigation. It is a system of plant monoculture, and therefore defines everything that does not contribute to the production of this single crop as waste. The biological commons become wasteland in need of "development."

Given that, despite fifty years of the Green Revolution, most food is still produced by women's labor in the traditional way, it is surprising that women's agriculture is still defined as needing "development." Modernization is still synonymous with the process of dislodging the poor from their land which, in turn, causes migration to the urban slums. The General Agreement on Tariffs and Trade (GATT) and the North American Free Trade Agreement (NAFTA), including their new instruments for privatizing the biological commons, clearly indicate that we have not learned to work with the land, or with indigenous cultures. Nothing, really, has changed since the days of the utilitarians.

Yet, a problem emerges in attempts to correct this developmentalist bias: how *can* we generalize about women's ecological practices, their material cultures, to the point that their roles become recognizable, without thereby losing sight of the enormous diversity of their lives? In India alone, for example, Dalit (Untouchable) women suffer the worst effects of the caste system, while tribal (Adivasi) women come from cultures that have traditionally been outside the caste system, and often fare better. Even among tribal groups, however, some have matrilineal social structures, others patrilineal. This means that social arrangements differ considerably, even among neighboring villages.

Western feminists have learned how difficult it is to generalize about "women." It is easy for race and class biases to slip into generalizations about the conditions of Western women. The attempt to generalize across a deeply contentious and artificial category like "Third World women" is surely more risky. Not to enter into this hazardous territory, however, risks something even greater: that the lives of women will continue to occupy conceptually marginal places. The challenge is to make true and useful generalizations about women which permits meaningful and central talk of the diversities of Third World women's lives.

It is often charged in the Third World, even by self-described feminist women, that feminism is a First World phenomenon that is inappropriately projected onto the Third World. But this misses the importance of international feminism as evolving toward pluralistic perspectives that include relations between First and Third, as well as relations among race, class, caste, and gender. Moreover, there are development perspectives that arise from the lives of Third World women. In India, for example, these include the famed Chipko movement, the feminist journal *Manushi,* and Kali for Women, which publishes important feminist development books in association with Zed Books. To dismiss feminism as a First World perspective denies that there are self-identified Third World feminists.

This is not to suggest that Third World feminists who complain of being marginalized by First World liberal feminists do not raise important worries about the conception and practice of feminism. One key source of tension is the perception that First World liberal feminism is corrosively individualistic. It attempts to put the needs of individual women ahead of, and in opposition to, the needs of their communities. If there is a common theme among Indian feminists, at least, it is that they will not define feminist aspirations in terms abdicating responsibility for roles that hold together traditional societies.[5]

Partly because of important problems with generalizations about women, the approach I employ here is empirical and nonessentialist. It does not resort to abstractions about the supposed inherent natures of women and the environment. Such depictions of "women's nature" are often self-defeating. A famous bumper sticker that pictures the earth viewed from outer space reads "Love Your Mother." Read in a sexist culture, however, it has an unintended double meaning if we think it is our mother's job to pick up after us. Such images only tend to reinforce stereotypes of "man" as the builder of culture out of nature. "Woman" is left with the dirty work (see Murphy 1988).

While women are not *essentially* more "natural," closer to nature, than men, while nature is no more female than male, the *actual practices* typically demanded of women by institutional structures, involve direct mediation between culture and nature. This is particularly evident in the material lives of Third World women farmers. We begin to remedy this situation when we stress the need for a philosophy of material culture. We need to attend to what women *do,* their self-explanations. Most important, we need to set aside comfortable assumptions about what counts as expertise.

## LITTLE IS KNOWN OF THEIR CONDITION

An Indian woman and scholar gave this description of the daily lives of village women in her country:

> While they work on an average many more hours than their men, they eat much less. When there is little food, it is the woman who has to go without. . . . She works in the fields, looks after the children, comes home and prepares the family meal and then has to be available for her man whenever she is required. . . . rural women endure childbirth after childbirth which drains them of physical energy and destroys their health. They have little or no access to health care and such facilities as there are pitifully inadequate. In any militant struggle that they, or their men, have been involved in, they are the ones who are most vulnerable to police and state repression. They suffer violence and abuse within their own homes. Yet little is known of their condition. (Butalia 1985, 132–133)

Reading this, one could easily conclude that there is little hope for rural women's development in the Third World, much less for an approach to eco-development based on their distinctive practices.

As deeply troubling as these acts of gendered violence are, I suggest that a deeper question raised by this passage is institutional: what are the institutionalized ways of thinking that allow both developmentalist and local cultures to put women last? Even attempts to help women often go disastrously wrong. It made good sense to well-intended development experts, for example, that women in a sunny continent like Africa could benefit from solar stoves.[6] Experts' ignorance of what women know, however, caused them to ignore the fact that women are not likely to cook in the heat of the day, nor are they often able to cook during the valuable daylight hours given the other demands that claim their time. In a First World culture in which women are expected to do most of the cooking, it would not be a very bright business policy to have men design stoves for use by women without consulting their needs. Yet, this happens all the time in the attempt to "develop" Third World women. Much of this tendency to look past Third World women derives from our thinking about what counts as expertise. The sorts of biases I hope to capture in the term "developmentalism" are elucidated through what Richard Levins has called "seven developmentalist myths in agriculture."

1.  Backward is labor-intensive, modern is capital-intensive agriculture.
2.  Diversity is backward, uniform monoculture is modern.
3.  Small scale is backward, large scale is modern.
4.  Backward is subjection to nature, modern implies increasingly complete control over everything that happens in the field or orchard or pasture.
5.  Folk knowledge is backward, scientific knowledge is modern.
6.  Specialists are modern, generalists backward.
7.  The smaller the object of study, the more modern. (Levins 1986, 13–20)

Since women are at the bottom of the developmentalist pecking order they often experience the force of these myths most directly. Women are regarded as backward because what they do is labor-intensive rather than capital-intensive; their labors are committed to maintaining diversity on a small scale, and this is surely an indication of subjection to nature rather than complete control over it; since their knowledge is the accumulation of centuries of village-based genetic experimentation, what they know is dismissed as superstition, folk-knowledge.

Vandana Shiva is particularly effective in challenging assumptions such as these about what counts as expertise. Describing traditional agricultural production, she says, "The backyard of each rural home was a nursery, and each peasant woman the sylviculturalist. The invisible, decentred agroforestry model was significant because the humblest of species and the smallest of people could participate in it . . ." This plant diversity, and the mixture of private and public tree stands, provides "food and fodder, fertilizer and pesticide, fuel and small timber."

In masculinist development projects, this kind of agricultural production and the knowledge it requires is replaced, she says, by the "reductionist mind" of outside experts who do not understand the multiple uses of traditional plantings, nor their uses in traditional culture. According to Shiva:

> The experts decided that indigenous knowledge was worthless and "unscientific," and proceeded to destroy the diversity of indigenous species by replacing them with row after row of eucalyptus seedlings in polythene bags, in government

nurseries. Nature's locally available seeds were laid waste; people's locally available knowledge and energies were laid waste. With imported seeds and expertise came the import of loans and debt and the export of wood, soils—and people. Trees, as a living resource, maintaining the life of the soil and water and of local people, were replaced by trees whose dead wood went straight to a pulp factory hundreds of miles away. (Shiva 1988, 79)

The eucalyptus is valuable as a cash-crop because it grows fast and straight, putting most of its energy into wood pulp instead of into branches and leafy matter. But it is also an ecological disaster whose impact is felt particularly by women. Its lack of leaves and small branches mean there is very little to return to the land to conserve moisture and fertility. Neither does it provide wood for housing. The fact that it grows quickly means that it places heavy demand on water supplies. In arid regions the demand on water and its lack of contribution to humus, which maintains soil moisture, have contributed directly to the oppression of women, who must walk further and further each year to obtain drinking water.

The eucalyptus has become a symbol for the many ways in which women's ecological knowledge is marginalized. Today in India one cannot drive far along a major road without seeing advertisements calling for investments in new eucalyptus plantations. When cash-crops such as these drive out traditional crops (crops like pulses) that return nitrogen to the soil without expensive inorganic fertilizers, this is a gender bias. When herbicides kill grasses that are used to make baskets and mats, grasses that are defined by outside experts as worthless, this is a gender bias. When plants are genetically engineered to produce only cash value, thereby reducing byproducts that go to fuel and fodder, this is gender bias. When so-called undeveloped lands to which everyone has access are privatized and dedicated to plant monoculture, this is gender bias.

Technological innovations, such as hydroelectric dams to support large-scale irrigation and plant monoculture, are typical of men's agriculture. The impact of these and other Green Revolution techniques has often been devastating for women. The scarcity of water in the Third World, for example, reveals much. Though 73 percent of the world's water use is dedicated to irrigation, only 20–30 percent gets to its destination. Such waste has a tragic impact on women's lives. Women are still overwhelmingly responsible for collecting water for drinking and cooking. Yet, in India, 23,000 villages are without drinking water due to deforestation and irrigation. Seventy percent of the ground water that is available is polluted. (Dankelman and Davidson 1988, 21 and 33) Water collection increasingly demands women's time. The need to carry water over greater distances affects women's health, particularly the health of girls whose bodies are still developing.

Despite misguided attempts at development, many Third World women and their communities have not stood aside as their communities have been destroyed. The experiences of Chipko women in the Himalayan foothills are justly celebrated. The modern Chipko movement began as a response to flooding due to deforestation in the mountains above Chipko villages. The response to deforestation varied by gender. Men were drawn to wage-labor jobs in the forestry industry. Women were drawn to reforestation since their concerns were different. These include the entire cycle of concerns that depend on forests, from adequate water supplies, to fuel and fodder, and sources of traditional medicines. A healthy ecosystem is a necessity for the safety of children and for the possibility of future generations. When villagers were asked about which trees should be planted as part of a reforestation plan, the men immediately chose fruit trees, a cash crop. The women responded, however, "The men would take the fruits and sell them by the roadside. The cash will only go to buy liquor and tobacco. We women prefer fuel and fodder trees." (Dankelman and Davidson 1988, 50–51). The demonstrated effectiveness of women's projects that involve caring labor cannot be doubted. In a ten-year study of trees planted and cared for by Chipko women, it was found that their survival rate had increased from 10 percent to the 80–90 percent range (50). Similar statistics on women's reforestation projects can be found for other locations in India and in the Green Belt Movement in Kenya.

Social forestry is a feminist issue. Tree-hugging by Chipko women is more than the simple attempt to save trees from logging companies. It is a political act growing out of women's local knowledge of the forest. Tree hugging represents the broad circle of concerns that women understand. Trees mean water for Chipko women. Trees mean safety from flooding. Forests, not simply plant monoculture, mean food, fodder, building materials, and medicines. Trees hugging is as much a defense of culture and future generations as it is a defense of nature.

Development theory has progressed from what can only be described as racist and sexist beginnings. Ester Boserup, for example, has documented the impact of colonial attitudes on development practices in Africa. Her work serves as an example of how sexist (and racist) categories have affected the concept of development historically. Prior to the arrival of European culture, men's traditional activities in Africa were tree-felling, hunting, and war. All were curbed by Europeans. Forcibly deprived of their traditional roles, African males were left with little to do, thus the Western stereotype of the "lazy African male." African women were responsible for most agricultural work and food gathering. Development might have begun, therefore, with women's traditional knowledge. However, because of the European bias that farming is men's work, most European efforts were addressed solely to men (Boserup 1970, 19 and 55). Such biases certify masculine knowledge as official—they also certify indigenous men as ignorant—while challenging and marginalizing traditionally women's knowledge.

Nevertheless, contemporary programs that are advertised as profamily often remain antiwoman. Masculinity and the culture of high technology are connected through the division of labor. Men's cultural status tends to increase under the influence of technology, while women's status tends to decrease. Young men, in particular, can insist on becoming "modern," often wearing Western clothes and sporting Western electronic goods. Women are expected to maintain traditional values and dress (Mies 1988, 138).

Many international agents—even the World Bank—now include women's issues in their programs. Yet programs directed at the male "head of household" are conceptually flawed when they assume equity and identity of interests within the family. Because equity is rare, these programs pull the family apart. The effort to involve Third World communities in international markets through introduction of technologies to produce cash-crops is one example. This tends to cause dual economies with men working in the for-profit sector, while women continue with traditional agriculture to meet the needs of the family. Such programs rarely improve the lives of women and children.

## TAKING WOMEN'S PRACTICES SERIOUSLY

This tendency of many development schemes to elevate men while further marginalizing women depends on a familiar set of normative categories. Expertise requires the mind, not bodily labor; it requires reason, not feeling; it requires theorizing out of any social context, not concrete practice within a historied community. The masculine bias in these dualisms favors the "modern," scientific, rational, global, and the high-tech over the traditional, small-scale, and the low-tech. Developmentalism constructs masculinity as independent, autonomous, rational; women are constructed as dependent or interdependent. Men's agriculture, which can hardly be understood as anything but a practical activity, is, nevertheless, represented as a "theoretical practice," that is, as an applied *science*. Women's expert knowledge of soil, climate, and seeds is marginalized as anecdotal; it is often dismissed as mere "wive's tales."

The patriarchal story of development is based on a linear narrative according to which culture emerged out of, and then decisively departed from, nature. Practices that involve caring for others—mothering, cooking, traditional health care, and certain kinds of simple, traditional agricultural labor that are low-paid or unpaid, such as weeding and tending to livestock—are the spots at which nature is nurtured into culture.

This creates a dilemma: the "public face" of women's labor is a systematic distortion. Yet, Third World women are emphatic that they will not define authentic development in terms of what they regard as the First World feminist narrative of liberal individualism. They will not abdicate responsibility for traditional roles that hold communities together. Children's health and safety depend on regular access to clean water. Traditional medicine and agriculture depend on the biodiversity of an environment that can supply medicines as well as fuel, fodder, and food. Caring labor holds together the family and the environment, and is inherently interested in future generations. As with Liberation and Dalit theologies, Third World women are calling for a localized expression of their aspirations.

The issue, then, is how an epistemology can be constructed that is faithful to *what* Third World women know, as well as to the *ways* in which they know. First, some clarifications. In emphasizing gender-bias in the construction of what is counted as knowledge, I am speaking about the construction of gender categories, not about particular individuals. While gender does have a powerful hold on individuals, there are other forces that intersect in the individual as well, including race, caste, class, and religion. This means that some men are nonsexist despite sexist constructions of gender; some women are implicated in the destruction of the environment even though traditional women's praxis involves caring. Consequently, my argument is that recognition of gender is a *necessary* condition—not a sufficient condition—for sustainable development.

Neither is gender the same as sex. If we take sex to be a matter of chromosomes, a biological distinction between males and females, gender, like race, caste, or class, is a social construction. It is a set of institutional signals that shape what can and cannot be done in a particular social context. Constructions of gender shape the ways in which social powers are granted or withheld.

It would be a mistake, furthermore, to look to the traditional philosophical distinction between propositional (the belief that a proposition is true) and nonpropositional attitudes to clarify the distinction between men's and women's ways of knowing. I would say, rather, that such forms of knowledge are *constructed* by gendered categories as propositional and nonpropositional to the disadvantage of both. As medicine has been masculinized, for example, it has been important to construct medical knowledge as propositional (abstract, theoretical) despite the evident hands-on expertise required by the skilled surgeon. Cooking, a clear case of hands-on epistemic practice, is diminished if it is reduced simply to knowing-how.

This brief overview of the construction of gendered agricultural knowledge leads me, instead, to focus on *practices* as a way of getting at a reconstructed conception of women's agricultural labor. Practices, as I understand them, are much more than sets of individual actions. They are fundamental ways of categorizing, experiencing, and valuing the world. In turn, the requirements of a practice generate distinctive forms of *knowledge*. Mothering, for example, is a practice that generates its own epistemology[7] (see Ruddick 1989). There are also epistmologies of cooking (see Curtin and Heldke 1992, section 3) and land cultivation. Epistemic attitudes derive from doing. If women have been assigned agricultural tasks throughout history, and knowledge derives from the requirements of a particular kind of practice, should we not expect to find that women have been responsible for the advances required by that practice? If women have been located at the intersection of the environment and those practices that sustain the community, such as mothering, health care, and care for the land, would we not expect them to be sources of traditional knowledge on these matters? Simply put, attention to practices has a better chance of capturing "thoughtful actions" like traditional farming than philosophical distinctions between propositional and nonpropositional attitudes.

A sympathetic and accurate portrayal of women's actual involvement in agricultural production might begin with some revisionist history. In a review of anthropological and mythological sources, Autumn Stanley says, "From the earliest times until at least the horticultural period . . . women were largely responsible for the gathering, processing, storing, and eventually for the cultivation of plant foods." In contrast to the hunter-gatherer myth, according to which man-the-hunter provides most of the food, anthropological evidence indicates that until recent times 60–80 percent of food was provided by women. While both women and men must have been involved in food gathering, "female's gathering would be different from males'— more highly motivated, and more of a 'social role' from the start in that females were usually gathering for one or more offspring as well as for themselves. Females . . . would thus be more likely to innovate and improve" (Stanley 1982, 290).

Women have been farmers for more than forty centuries. Given the assumption that *"the workers invented their tools,"* it makes sense to assume that women were responsible for:

> (1) food-gathering inventions such as the digging stick, the carrying sling or bag, the reaping knife or sickle, and other knives; (2) food processing inventions such as the mortar and pestle or pounder, winnowing methods, grain-roasting tray, querns . . . , washing to remove grit, detoxification . . . , and some forms of cooking . . . and (3) food-storage inventions such as baskets, clay-lined storage pits, drying and smoking of food, and preservation with honey.

Stanley also argues that women were responsible for domestication of wheat, rice, maize, barley, oats, sorghum, millet, and rye. These cereals still provide 75 percent of all human food energy (Stanley 1982, 293–294). The same pattern can be found in the development of traditional medicines. Still today, women are responsible for 80 percent of the world's medical care (see Kheel 1989).

We should not expect to find women's expert knowledge at work everywhere in the contemporary world. The ancient patterns of women's knowledge have been distorted and disrupted. Women struggle to invent and reinvent forms of knowledge that are appropriate to their complex situations as mothers, wives, traditional farmers, health-care workers, and last line of environmental defense. If their indigenous knowledge of the sustainable ecological community has often been destroyed by maldevelopment, women are still invested by their daily practices in the reinvention of such knowledge. That women are dedicated to saving and restoring their knowledge is shown in the many organizations worldwide that are doing just this, organizations such as Chipko in India, Development Alternatives with Women for a New Era (DAWN) based in Brazil, The Third World Network in Malaysia, the Green Belt Movement in Kenya, and Women of All Red Nations (WARN) in Chicago.

The work of these organizations demonstrates it would be a mistake to think that women's knowledge is backward-looking, that it is antitechnology, or antiprogress. In fact, if Stanley is correct, women have been responsible for most technological innovation. Women can hardly afford to be against progress if it is genuinely life-nurturing progress. It is simply that genuine progress for women and their communities is always judged by its relevance to a context.

This historical account of women's agricultural labor undercuts the typical reductionist accounts of the relation between nature and culture. Women are often pressed in two ways by this distinction. The first claims that nature ought to be preserved museumlike, free from human interaction. This mistake has caused some Third World countries to remove indigenous people from their traditional lands to create American-style national parks. The second version claims that nature is only here for human manipulation and consumption, one cause of the tragedy of development. Both are forms of the myth that "man' lives apart from nature. Because of their traditional practices, women are typically well positioned to know that ecodevelopment inevitably changes nature, and that changes that constitute real progress must be measured against the welfare of whole ecocommunities and future generations.

What, then, is distinctive about women's ecological knowledge? Based on the cases previously considered, I offer several generalizations. Since we are talking of constructions of gender, we need to keep in mind that these are, indeed, generalizations, not universal rules. No set of generalizations can capture the complexity of women's lives.

- Because women have been charged with many kinds of caring labor, *traditional women's knowledge tends to be relational.* Women tend to locate knowledge in the concrete, relational space between individuals and their communities, not in the abstraction of isolated, autonomous individuals. The relations that define community are broader than the human community. They include the entire ecological community, *this* place.

- *Traditional women's knowledge tends to be collaborative.* It is the project of the whole ecological *community* that is engaged by caring practices. A familiar example of this is home cooking. We tend not to even think of cooking as an epistemic practice that has its own rules and procedures. Yet, sharing family and community culinary traditions is a perfect example of a collaborative epistemic community. A less familiar example is sharing seeds over generations of women farmers. Such patient development of ecological knowledge reflects the complexity of local ecosystems. Within a single valley, women often plant dozens of genetically different strains of a single crop to take advantage of subtle changes in growing conditions.

- *Traditional women's knowledge tends to be transparently situated,* not abstract and rule-bound. To form an opinion, women need to know the life histories of the people and contexts they are speaking about. Concretely, we have seen this often means that what the outsider dismisses as waste has value within a context, for example, grasses at the edges of a field, or commons areas used by an entire village.

- *Traditional women's knowledge tends to be temporal.* If it grows out of actual contexts and histories. It is also future-directed. As those who have been defined in terms of their responsibility for children and future generations, women cannot help but test their knowledge against a criterion of sustainability. Women's knowledge is not only knowledge that operates in the spaces between individuals, but in the times between generations.

- Finally, *traditional women's knowledge tends to be bodily knowledge.* Because cultural dualisms have defined women in terms of the body and nature, women tend to cultivate knowledge that integrates head and hand. Their knowledge consists more in "thoughtful ways of doing" than in "ways of thinking about."

Given these general ways of characterizing traditional women's knowledge, we can understand why it is easy to miss women's knowledge, and thereby to abuse it. To those who look for knowledge as a decisive intervention from above, a self-confident declaration, women's relational knowledge can appear indecisive. It appears to the outsider as what Plato would have called "accidentally true belief" rather than knowledge. Women often have difficulty saying what they know about *all* situations just because they know how complex *this* situation is. Growing out of practices that cannot escape their temporality, women's knowledge has the appearance to outsiders of being qualified or tentative. One task required by the revaluation of caring labor is to value this apparent tentativeness as a positive quality. Since women's knowledge is marked by its group collaboration, for example, we should expect that Third World women's knowledge is expressed through the group rather than through the individual.

Because knowledge varies in relation to different forms of practice, moving between forms of knowledge involves what María Lugones calls "world-travelling" (Lugones 1987). Her term is useful because it emphasizes that entire worlds must be traversed for communication to occur. If we assume, for example, that the epistemic world of the outsider, the (male) scientific expert, is the standard against which all others are measured, it is impossible to cross over into the world of hands-on expertise that is characteristic of women's ecological knowledge.

Since we are talking about different worlds of discourse, each having its own standards for knowledge and success, there is an important distinction between those who function as "insiders" to the practice and those who come to it as outsiders. The rules of the practice are, by definition, known to the insiders, those who engage in the practice. To outsiders, it may appear there is no knowledge at all. The outsider, particularly when motivated by institutional biases, can easily dismiss the real inside knowledge that motivates and sustains the practice, as mere superstition. Gender-biased development programs, therefore, are not always reducible to simple malice. It may well be that, from the perspective of another "world," the insider's knowledge is not, or cannot be revealed as, knowledge. The work of those concerned with the lives of

Third World women is a matter of devising strategies for making these forms of practice and knowledge visible.

While insider's knowledge may be initially invisible to the outsider, that does not mean it lacks power. If it is true that "real knowledge is history that comes from below," (Rose 1986, 162), then we must learn to recognize the intersection of forces in tribal or Dalit women that makes their forms of knowledge conceptually central to the task of reconstructing caring labor. In the "lowest of the low," in those who must care for others without being cared for themselves, there is a praxis that is the key to sustainable development. Those who are marginalized and charged with responsibility for caring labor cannot fail to know the lives of those who marginalized them. The converse is not true. The master need not know the servant. Simply stated, because of their caring practices, Third World women of low caste and class know things that others—including outside development experts—do not know.[8]

Poor Third World women cannot even pretend to escape the temporal reality of life that is demanded by caring labor. They do not have secretaries to reschedule appointments; they do not have servants to whom work can be delegated when they are tired or busy. Meals must come with predictable regularity, therefore food and fuel must be gathered *now*. Need for medical care is unpredictable; the need is immediate and cannot wait.

Women cannot afford the illusion that it is possible to escape time and place. This is one reason for calling typically women's knowledge "expert knowledge." Caring labor produces relational knowledge that must be open to its context. Survival often depends on it. In contrast, there is delusion in constructions of life that claim to be free of time and place. While men are inevitably dependent on many forms of caring labor, they have the power to construct the self-serving myth of themselves as independent, autonomous, and atemporal. Patriarchal constructions work to bolster this delusive self-construction.

Liberated from patriarchal distortions, caring contexts are potentially those in which women and men can experience themselves as citizens in a broadly ecological community. This space, which is normally an ambiguous borderland, neither fully culture, nor fully nature, can become a context in which the dualistic opposition between culture and nature is transformed. Such spaces can be transformed and reconstructed, that is, as small-scale contexts in which citizenship for women and men is defined in relation to an environment that can produce safe food and water, sustainable fuels, and health care that works toward the well-being of this and future generations.

It does make sense, therefore, to say that traditional women's knowledge of the environment is privileged. It is privileged, not in the sense that women "know nature by nature." Rather, engagement in a practice requires development of localized expertise. Of course, this does not mean that such localized expertise is infallible, or that it would not benefit from context-sensitive change. Women do not often think of themselves as infallible, and they often have no choice but to recognize localized change that makes sense. When I describe traditional women's environmental knowledge as privileged, I mean that they are the primary experts, the people whose opinions must come first.

Though much can be said about the practical consequences of the practice-oriented approach I have developed here, I will mention only one. There is the tendency to assume that one aspect of development must come first. It has been argued, for example, that the development of the head of household should come first, or that race or class must take precedence. A nonreductionist perspective indicates that race, caste, class, and other issues are intricately woven into a quilt whose patterns vary subtly. Women's issues within the community should not be delayed for the sake of solidarity with another group. From the beginning, women need the resource of other women in groups whose purpose is to articulate their distinctive concerns. This is required not only because of the character of women's knowledge as collaborative, but simply for the safety of women who risk much by speaking out alone. If development is to be truly dialogical, then all aspects of development must move together. Dialogue can only take place among dialogical equals.

I have described the tragic neglect of women's environmental expertise as a form systemic violence. These broad, hierarchical patterns of thought, in turn, encourage the creation of violent institutions. More often than not, the institutions created since World War II to "develop" the Third World have, in fact, made women's lives, as well as their ecocommunities, more precarious. Since this is institutional and systemic violence, not individual violence, we probably waste valuable time when we seek *individuals* against whom we can assign blame for this system of marginalization. Much violence against women has been offered out of a sincere, though misguided, desire to help.

However, the fact that we never intended to inflict these forms of violence on women does not relieve us in the First World of the obligation to change the institutions and systemic patterns of thought that cause violence against women. Those who experience institutional and systemic violence will tell us that these forms of violence, though perhaps harder for us to identify, harm every bit as much as individual violence.[9]

## NOTES

1. I continue to use the terms "First World" and "Third World" as a way of making the conceptual hierarchy that concerns me here more visible. It is worth thinking about what a linguistic substitute might be. The most common substitute, "developing world," begs the question "Developing into what?"
2. See Curtin 1999, chap. 2, "The British Utilitarians and the Invention of the 'Third World'" for a detailed account of the Utilitarian legacy in establishing colonial policy in India.
3. The account of violence here resembles Karen Warren's account of oppressive conceptual frameworks. (See Warren 1990.) My thinking on violence has benefited from my work with Bob Litke in Curtin and Litke 1999.
4. For a more detailed account of the Green Revolution see Curtin, 1995.
5. For an important account of this sort of dispute in feminism see Shiva and Shiva 1994.

6. I owe this example to Kristin Cashman, Center for Indigenous Knowledge for Agriculture and Rural Development, Iowa State University.
7. This article takes its inspiration from feminist standpoint theory (Hartsock 1983), which argues that there are typically women's ways of categorizing, experiencing, and valuing the world. Hilary Rose has said, ". . . feminist epistemology derives from women's lived experience, centred on the domains of interconnectedness and affectual rationality. It emphasizes holism and harmonious relationships with nature, which is why feminism has links with that other major social movement of our time, ecology" (Rose 1986, 162–163). A feminist standpoint values and organizes the world precisely through a revaluation of those practices that sexist categories marginalize, practices that are pushed to the periphery of what has counted as important. Thus, like the meal that miraculously appears on the table every night and only becomes important when it is not there, these practices are often invisible to those who benefit from them.
8. For an extended account of what it means to function within a practice see Curtin 1999, chap. 9, "Democratic Discourse in a Morally Pluralistic World."
9. An earlier version of this article was published in Warren 1997. My deep appreciation to Karen Warren for her help with both versions of this essay.

# BIBLIOGRAPHY

BOSERUP, E. (1970). *Woman's Role in Economic Development.* London: Allen and Unwin.

BUTALIA, U. (1985). "Indian Women and the New Movement." *Women's Studies International Forum* 8(2): 131–133.

CURTIN, D. (1999). *Chinnagounder's Challenge: The Question of Ecological Citizenship.* Bloomington: Indiana University Press.

_____. (1995). "Making Peace with the Earth: Indigenous Agriculture and the Green Revolution." *Environmental Ethics* 17(Spring): 59–73.

CURTIN, D., and L. HELDKE, Eds. (1992). *Cooking, Eating, Thinking: Transformative Philosophies of Food.* Bloomington: University of Indiana Press.

CURTIN, D., and R. LITKE, Eds. (1999). *Institutional Violence.* Amsterdam: Editions Rodopi.

DANKELMAN, I., and J. DAVIDSON, Eds. (1988). *Women and Environment in the Third World.* London: Earthscan.

HARTSOCK, N. (1983). "The Feminist Standpoint: Developing the Ground for a Specifically Feminist Historical Materialism." *Discovering Reality;* and London: D. Reidel, 283–310.

KHEEL, M. (1989). "From Healing Herbs to Deadly Drugs: Western Medicine's War Against the Natural World." *Healing the Wounds: The Promise of Ecofeminism.* Philadelphia: New Society.

LEVINS, R. (1986). "Science and Progress: Seven Developmentalist Myths in Agriculture." *Monthly Review* 38(3): 13–20.

LUGONES, M. (1987). "Playfulness, World-Traveling, and Loving Perception." *Hypatia* 2(2): 3–18.

MIES, M. (1988). "Class Struggles and Women's Struggles in Rural India. *Women: The Last Colony*"; and London: Zed Books.

MURPHY, P. (1988). "Sex-Typing the Planet: Gaia Imagery and the Problem of Subverting Patriarchy." *Environmental Ethics* 10(2): 155–168.

ROSE, H. (1986). "Women's Work, Women's Knowledge." *What Is Feminism?* and New York: Pantheon.

RUDDICK, S. (1989). *Maternal Thinking: Toward a Politics of Peace.* New York: Ballantine Books.

SHIVA, V. (1988). *Staying Alive: Women, Ecology and Development.* London: Zed Books.

SHIVA, V, and M. SHIVA. (1994). "Was Cairo a Step Forward for Third World Women?" *Third World Resurgence* (50): 13–16.

STANLEY, A. (1982). Daughters of Isis, Daughters of Demeter: When Women Sowed and Reaped. *Women, Technology and Innovation.* New York: Pergamon.

WARREN, K., Ed. (1997). *Ecofeminism: Women, Nature, Culture.* Bloomington: Indiana University Press.

WARREN K. (1990). "The Power and Promise of Ecological Feminism." *The Journal of Environmental Ethics* 12 (Summer): 125–146.

# THE POWER AND THE PROMISE
# OF ECOLOGICAL FEMINISM

*Karen J. Warren*

Karen J. Warren is professor of philosophy at Macalester College in St. Paul,
Minnesota. She has published numerous articles, edited three anthologies, and
written a book on ecofeminist philosophy, *Ecofeminist Philosophy: A Western Perspective on What It Is and Why It Matters*. Warren's wilderness experiences include rock
climbing, backpacking, canoeing, hiking, all weather camping, and swimming
with wild spotted bottlenose dolphins. Warren has received several teaching
awards for both her college-level and pre-college level teaching of philosophy
and critical thinking.

## INTRODUCTION

Ecological feminism (ecofeminism) has begun to receive a fair amount of attention lately as an alternative feminism and environmental ethic.[1] Since
Françoise d'Eaubonne introduced the term *ecoféminisme* in 1974 to bring attention to women's potential for bringing about an ecological revolution,[2] the
term has been used in a variety of ways. As I use the term in this paper, ecological feminism is the position that there are important connections—historical, experiential, symbolic, theoretical—between the domination of women
and the domination of nature, an understanding of which is crucial to both
feminism and environmental ethics. I argue that the promise and power of
ecological feminism is that *it provides a distinctive framework both for reconceiving
feminism and for developing an environmental ethic which takes seriously connections
between the domination of women and the domination of nature*. I do so by discussing the nature of a feminist ethic and the ways in which ecofeminism provides a feminist and environmental ethic. I conclude that any feminist theory

This essay originally appeared in *Environmental Ethics* 12, 3 (Summer 1990): 125–46. Reprinted
with permission.

*and* any environmental ethic which fails to take seriously the twin and inter-connected dominations of women and nature is at best incomplete and at worst simply inadequate.

## FEMINISM, ECOLOGICAL FEMINISM, AND CONCEPTUAL FRAMEWORKS

Whatever else it is, feminism is at least the movement to end sexist oppression. It involves the elimination of any and all factors that contribute to the continued and systematic domination or subordination of women. While feminists disagree about the nature of and solutions to the subordination of women, all feminists agree that sexist oppression exists, is wrong, and must be abolished.

A "feminist issue" is any issue that contributes in some way to understanding the oppression of women. Equal rights, comparable pay for comparable work, and food production are feminist issues wherever and whenever an understanding of them contributes to an understanding of the continued exploitation or subjugation of women. Carrying water and searching for firewood are feminist issues wherever and whenever women's primary responsibility for these tasks contributes to their lack of full participation in decision making, income producing, or high status positions engaged in by men. What counts as a feminist issue, then, depends largely on context, particularly the historical and material conditions of women's lives.

Environmental degradation and exploitation are feminist issues because an understanding of them contributes to an understanding of the oppression of women. In India, for example, both deforestation and reforestation through the introduction of a monoculture species tree (e.g., eucalyptus) intended for commercial production are feminist issues because the loss of indigenous forests and multiple species of trees has drastically affected rural Indian women's ability to maintain a subsistence household. Indigenous forests provide a variety of trees for food, fuel, fodder, household utensils, dyes, medicines, and income-generating uses, while monoculture-species forests do not.[3] Although I do not argue for this claim here, a look at the global impact of environmental degradation on women's lives suggests important respects in which environmental degradation is a feminist issue.

Feminist philosophers claim that some of the most important feminist issues are *conceptual* ones: these issues concern how one conceptualizes such mainstay philosophical notions as reason and rationality, ethics, and what it is to be human. Ecofeminists extend this feminist philosophical concern to nature. They argue that, ultimately, some of the most important connections between the domination of women and the domination of nature are conceptual. To see this, consider the nature of conceptual frameworks.

A *conceptual framework* is a set of *basic* beliefs, values, attitudes, and assumptions which shape and reflect how one views oneself and one's world. It is a socially constructed lens through which we perceive ourselves and others. It is affected by such factors as gender, race, class, age, affectional orientation, nationality, and religious background.

Some conceptual frameworks are oppressive. An *oppressive conceptual framework* is one that explains, justifies, and maintains relationships of domination and subordination. When an oppressive conceptual framework is *patriarchal*, it explains, justifies, and maintains the subordination of women by men.

I have argued elsewhere that there are three significant features of oppressive conceptual frameworks: (1) value-hierarchical thinking, i.e., "up-down" thinking which places higher value, status, or prestige on what is "up" rather than on what is "down"; (2) value dualisms, i.e., disjunctive pairs in which the disjuncts are seen as oppositional (rather than as complementary) and exclusive (rather than as inclusive), and which place higher value (status, prestige) on one disjunct rather than the other (e.g., dualisms which give higher value or status to that which has historically been identified as "body," "emotion," and "female"); and (3) logic of domination, i.e., a structure of argumentation which leads to a justification of subordination.[4]

The third feature of oppressive conceptual frameworks is the most significant. A logic of domination is not *just* a logical structure. It also involves a substantive value system, since an ethical premise is needed to permit or sanction the "just" subordination of that which is subordinate. This justification typically is given on grounds of some alleged characteristic (e.g., rationality) which the dominant (e.g., men) have and the subordinate (e.g., women) lack.

Contrary to what many feminists and ecofeminists have said or suggested, there may be nothing *inherently* problematic about "hierarchical thinking" or even "value-hierarchical thinking" in contexts other than contexts of oppression. Hierarchical thinking is important in daily living for classifying data, comparing information, and organizing material. Taxonomies (e.g., plant taxonomies) and biological nomenclature seem to require *some* form of "hierarchical thinking." Even "value-hierarchical thinking" may be quite acceptable in certain contexts. (The same may be said of "value dualisms" in non-oppressive contexts.) For example, suppose it is true that what is unique about humans is our conscious capacity to radically reshape our social environments (or "societies"), as Murray Bookchin suggests.[5] Then one could truthfully say that humans are better equipped to radically reshape their environments than are rocks or plants—a "value-hierarchical" way of speaking.

The problem is not simply *that* value-hierarchial thinking and value dualisms are used, but *the way* in which each has been used in *oppressive conceptual frameworks* to establish inferiority and to justify subordination.[6] It is the logic of domination, *coupled with* value-hierarchical thinking and value dualisms, which "justifies" subordination. What is explanatorily basic, then, about the nature of oppressive conceptual frameworks is the logic of domination.

For ecofeminism, that a logic of domination is explanatorily basic is important for at least three reasons. First, without a logic of domination, a description of similarities and differences would be just that—a description of similarities and differences. Consider the claim, "Humans are different from plants and rocks in that humans can (and plants and rocks cannot) consciously and radically reshape the communities in which they live; humans are similar to plants and rocks in that they are both members of an ecological community." Even if humans are "better" than plants and rocks with respect to the conscious ability of humans to radically transform communities, one does not *thereby* get any *morally* relevant distinction between humans and non-humans, or an argument for the domination of plants and rocks by humans. To get *those* conclusions one needs to add at least two powerful assumptions, viz., (A2) and (A4) in argument A below:

**(A1)**  Humans do, and plants and rocks do not, have the capacity to consciously and radically change the community in which they live.

**(A2)**  Whatever has the capacity to consciously and radically change the community in which it lives is morally superior to whatever lacks this capacity.

**(A3)**  Thus, humans are morally superior to plants and rocks.

**(A4)**  For any X and Y, if X is morally superior to Y, then X is morally justified in subordinating Y.

**(A5)**  Thus, humans are morally justified in subordinating plants and rocks.

Without the two assumptions that *humans are morally superior* to (at least some) nonhumans, (A2), and that *superiority justifies subordination*, (A4), all one has is some difference between humans and some nonhumans. This is true *even if* that difference is given in terms of superiority. Thus, it is the logic of domination, (A4), which is the bottom line in ecofeminist discussions of oppression.

Second, ecofeminists argue that, at least in Western societies, the oppressive conceptual framework which sanctions the twin dominations of women and nature is a patriarchal one characterized by all three features of an oppressive conceptual framework. Many ecofeminists claim that, historically, within at least the dominant Western culture, a patriarchal conceptual framework has sanctioned the following argument B:

**(B1)**  Women are identified with nature and the realm of the physical; men are identified with the "human" and the realm of the mental.

**(B2)**  Whatever is identified with nature and the realm of the physical is inferior to ("below") whatever is identified with the "human" and the realm of the mental; or, conversely, the latter is superior to ("above") the former.

**(B3)**  Thus, women are inferior to ("below") men; or, conversely, men are superior to ("above") women.

**(B4)** For any X and Y, if X is superior to Y, then X is justified in subordinating Y.

**(B5)** Thus, men are justified in subordinating women.

If sound, argument B establishes *patriarchy*, i.e., the conclusion given at (B5) that the systematic domination of women by men is justified. But according to ecofeminists, (B5) is justified by just those three features of an oppressive conceptual framework identified earlier: value-hierarchical thinking, the assumption at (B2); value dualisms, the assumed dualism of the mental and the physical at (B1) and the assumed inferiority of the physical vis-à-vis the mental at (B2); and a logic of domination, the assumption at (B4), the same as the previous premise (A4). Hence, according to ecofeminists, insofar as an oppressive patriarchal conceptual framework has functioned historically (within at least dominant Western culture) to sanction the twin dominations of women and nature (argument B), both argument B and the patriarchal conceptual framework from whence it comes ought to be rejected.

Of course, the preceding does not identify which premises of B are false. What is the status of premises (B1) and (B2)? Most, if not all, feminists claim that (B1), and many ecofeminists claim that (B2), have been assumed or asserted within the dominant Western philosophical and intellectual tradition.[7] As such, these feminists assert, as a matter of historical fact, that the dominant Western philosophical tradition has assumed the truth of (B1) and (B2). Ecofeminists, however, either deny (B2) or do not affirm (B2). Furthermore, because some ecofeminists are anxious to deny any ahistorical identification of women with nature, some ecofeminists deny (B1) when (B1) is used to support anything other than a strictly historical claim about what has been asserted or assumed to be true within patriarchal culture—e.g., when (B1) is used to assert that women properly are identified with the realm of nature and the physical.[8] Thus, from an ecofeminist perspective, (B1) and (B2) are properly viewed as problematic though historically sanctioned claims: they are problematic precisely because of the way they have functioned historically in a patriarchal conceptual framework and culture to sanction the dominations of women and nature.

What *all* ecofeminists agree about, then, is the way in which *the logic of domination* has functioned historically within patriarchy to sustain and justify the twin dominations of women and nature.[9] Since *all* feminists (and not just ecofeminists) oppose patriarchy, the conclusion given at (B5), all feminists (including ecofeminists) must oppose at least the logic of domination, premise (B4), on which argument B rests—whatever the truth-value status of (B1) and (B2) *outside of* a patriarchal context.

That *all* feminists must oppose the logic of domination shows the breadth and depth of the ecofeminist critique of B: it is a critique not only of the three assumptions on which this argument for the domination of women and nature rest, viz., the assumptions at (B1), (B2), and (B4); it is also a critique of patriarchal conceptual frameworks generally, i.e., of those oppressive conceptual frameworks which put men "up" and women "down," allege some way in which women are morally inferior to men, and use that alleged difference to justify the subordination of women by men. Therefore, ecofeminism is necessary to *any* feminist critique of patriarchy, and, hence, necessary to feminism (a point I discuss again later).

Third, ecofeminism clarifies why the logic of domination, and any conceptual framework which gives rise to it, must be abolished in order both to make possible a meaningful notion of difference which does not breed domination and to prevent feminism from becoming a support movement based primarily on shared experiences. In contemporary society, there is no one "woman's voice," no *woman* (or *human*) *simpliciter.* Every woman (or human) is a woman (or human) of some race, class, age, affectional orientation, marital status, regional or national background, and so forth. Because there are no monolithic experiences that all women share, feminism must be a "solidarity movement" based on shared beliefs and interests rather than a "unity in sameness" movement based on shared experiences and shared victimization.[10] In the words of Maria Lugones, "Unity—not to be confused with solidarity—is understood as conceptually tied to domination."[11]

Ecofeminists insist that the sort of logic of domination used to justify the domination of humans by gender, racial or ethnic, or class status is also used to justify the domination of nature. Because eliminating a logic of domination is part of a feminist critique—whether a critique of patriarchy, white supremacist culture, or imperialism—ecofeminists insist that *naturism* is properly viewed as an integral part of any feminist solidarity movement to end sexist oppression and the logic of domination which conceptually grounds it.

## ECOFEMINISM RECONCEIVES FEMINISM

The discussion so far has focused on some of the oppressive conceptual features of patriarchy. As I use the phrase, the "logic of traditional feminism" refers to the location of the conceptual roots of sexist oppression, at least in Western societies, in an oppressive patriarchal conceptual framework characterized by a logic of domination. Insofar as other systems of oppression (e.g., racism, classism, ageism, heterosexism) are also conceptually maintained by a logic of domination, appeal to the logic of traditional feminism ultimately locates the basic conceptual interconnections among *all* systems of oppression in the logic of domination. It thereby explains at a *conceptual* level why the eradication of sexist oppression requires the eradication of the other forms of oppression.[12] It is by clarifying this conceptual connection between systems of oppression that a movement to end sexist oppression—traditionally the special turf of feminist theory and practice—leads to a reconceiving of feminism as *a movement to end all forms of oppression.*

Suppose one agrees that the logic of traditional feminism requires the expansion of feminism to include other social systems of domination (e.g., racism and classism). What warrants the inclusion of nature in these "social systems of domination"? Why must the logic of traditional feminism include the abolition of "naturism" (i.e., the domination of nonhuman nature) among the "isms" feminism must confront? The conceptual justification for expanding feminism to include ecofeminism is twofold. One basis has already been suggested: By showing that the conceptual connections between the dual dominations of women and nature are located in an oppressive and, at least in Western societies, patriarchal conceptual framework characterized by a logic of domination, ecofeminism explains how and why feminism, conceived as a movement to end sexist oppression, must be expanded and reconceived as also a movement to end naturism. This is made explicit by the following argument C:

**(C1)** Feminism is a movement to end sexism.

**(C2)** But Sexism is conceptually linked with naturism (through an oppressive conceptual framework characterized by a logic of domination).

**(C3)** Thus, Feminism is (also) a movement to end naturism.

Because, ultimately, these connections between sexism and naturism are conceptual—embedded in an oppressive conceptual framework—the logic of traditional feminism leads to the embracement of ecological feminism.[13]

The other justification for reconceiving feminism to include ecofeminism has to do with the concepts of gender and nature. Just as conceptions of gender are socially constructed, so are conceptions of nature. Of course, the claim that women and nature are social constructions does not require anyone to deny that there are actual humans and actual trees, rivers, and plants. It simply implies that *how* women and nature are conceived is a matter of historical and social reality. These conceptions vary cross-culturally and by historical time period. As a result, any discussion of the "domination of nature" involves reference to historically specific forms of social domination of nonhuman nature by humans, just as discussion of the "domination of women" refers to historically specific forms of social domination of women by men. Although I do not argue for it here, an ecofeminist defense of the historical connections between the dominations of women and of nature, claims (B1) and (B2) in argument B, involves showing that within patriarchy the feminization of nature and the naturalization of women have been crucial to the historically successful subordinations of both.[14]

If ecofeminism promises to reconceive traditional feminism in ways which include naturism as a legitimate feminist issue, does ecofeminism also promise to reconceive environmental ethics in ways which are feminist? I think so. This is the subject of the remainder of the paper.

# CLIMBING FROM ECOFEMINISM
# TO ENVIRONMENTAL ETHICS

Many feminists and some environmental ethicists have begun to explore the use of first-person narrative as a way of raising philosophically germane issues in ethics often lost or underplayed in mainstream philosophical ethics. Why is this so? What is it about narrative which makes it a significant resource for theory and practice in feminism and environmental ethics? Even if appeal to first-person narrative is a helpful literary device for describing ineffable experience or a legitimate social science methodology for documenting personal and social history, how is first-person narrative a valuable vehicle of argumentation for ethical decision making and theory building? One fruitful way to begin answering these questions is to ask them of a particular first-person narrative.

Consider the following first-person narrative about rock climbing:

For my very first rock climbing experience, I chose a somewhat private spot, away from other climbers and on-lookers. After studying the chimney, I focused all my energy on making it to the top. I climbed with intense determination, using whatever strength and skills I had to accomplish this challenging feat. By midway I was exhausted and anxious. I couldn't see what to do next—where to put my hands or feet. Growing increasingly more weary as I clung somewhat desperately to the rock, I made a move. It didn't work. I fell. There I was, dangling midair above the rocky ground below, frightened but terribly relieved that the belay rope had held me. I knew I was safe. I took a look up at the climb that remained. I was determined to make it to the top. With renewed confidence and concentration, I finished the climb to the top.

On my second day of climbing, I rappelled down about 200 feet from the top of the Palisades at Lake Superior to just a few feet above the water level. I could see no one—not my belayer, not the other climbers, no one. I unhooked slowly from the rappel rope and took a deep cleansing breath. I looked all around me—really looked—and listened. I heard a cacophony of voices—birds, trickles of water on the rock before me, waves lapping against the rocks below. I closed my eyes and began to feel the rock with my hands—the cracks and crannies, the raised lichen and mosses, the almost imperceptible nubs that might provide a resting place for my fingers and toes when I began to climb. At that moment I was bathed in serenity. I began to talk to the rock in an almost inaudible, child-like way, as if the rock were my friend. I felt an overwhelming sense of gratitude for what it offered me—a chance to know myself and the rock differently, to appreciate unforeseen miracles like the tiny flowers growing in the even tinier cracks in the rock's surface, and to come to know a sense of *being in relationship* with the natural environment. It felt as if the rock and I were silent conversational partners in a longstanding friendship. I realized then that I had come to care about this cliff which was so different from me, so unmovable and invincible, independent and seemingly indifferent to my presence. I wanted to be with the rock as I climbed. Gone was the determination to conquer the rock, to forcefully impose my will on it; I wanted simply to work respectfully with the rock as I climbed. And as I climbed, that is what I felt. I felt myself *caring* for this rock and feeling thankful that climbing provided the opportunity for me to know it and myself in this new way.

There are at least four reasons why use of such a first-person narrative is important to feminism and environmental ethics. First, such a narrative gives voice to a felt sensitivity often lacking in traditional analytical ethical discourse, viz., a sensitivity to conceiving of oneself as fundamentally "in relationship with" others, including the nonhuman environment. It is a modality which *takes relationships themselves seriously.* It thereby stands in contrast to a strictly reductionist modality that takes relationships seriously only or primarily because of the nature of the *relators* or parties to those relationships (e.g., relators conceived as moral agents, right holders, interest carriers, or sentient beings). In the rock-climbing narrative above, it is the climber's relationship with the rock she climbs which takes on special significance—which is itself a locus of value—in addition to whatever moral status or moral considerability she or the rock or any other parties to the relationship may also have.[15]

Second, such a first-person narrative gives expression to a variety of ethical attitudes and behaviors often overlooked or underplayed in mainstream Western ethics, e.g., the difference in attitudes and behaviors toward a rock when one is "making it to the top" and when one thinks of oneself as "friends with" or "caring about" the rock one climbs.[16] These different attitudes and behaviors suggest an ethically germane contrast between two different types of relationship humans or climbers may have toward a rock: An imposed conqueror-type relationship, and an emergent caring-type relationship. This contrast grows out of, and is faithful to, felt, lived experience.

The difference between conquering and caring attitudes and behaviors in relation to the natural environment provides a third reason why the use of first-person narrative is important to feminism and environmental ethics: it provides a way of conceiving of ethics and ethical meaning as *emerging out of* particular situations moral agents find themselves in, rather than as being *imposed on* those situations (e.g., as a derivation or instantiation of some predetermined abstract principle or rule). This emergent feature of narrative centralizes the importance of *voice.* When a multiplicity of cross-cultural *voices* are centralized, narrative is able to give expression to a range of attitudes, values, beliefs, and behaviors which may be overlooked or silenced by imposed ethical meaning and theory. As a reflection on a felt, lived experience, the use of narrative in ethics provides a stance from which ethical discourse can be held accountable to the historical, material, and social realities in which moral subjects find themselves.

Lastly, and for our purposes perhaps most importantly, the use of narrative has argumentative significance. Jim Cheney calls attention to this feature of narrative when he claims, "To contextualize ethical deliberation is, in some sense, to provide a narrative or story, from which the solution to the ethical dilemma emerges as the fitting conclusion."[17] Narrative has argumentative force by suggesting *what counts* as an appropriate conclusion to an ethical situation. One ethical conclusion suggested by the climbing narrative is that what counts as a proper ethical attitude toward mountains and rocks is an attitude of respect and care (whatever that turns out to be or involve), not one of domination and conquest.

In an essay entitled "In and Out of Harm's Way: Arrogance and Love," feminist philosopher Marilyn Frye distinguishes between "arrogant" and "loving" perception as one way of getting at this difference in the ethical attitudes of care and conquest.[18] Frye writes:

> The loving eye is a contrary of the arrogant eye.
>
> The loving eye knows the independence of the other. It is the eye of a seer who knows that nature is indifferent. It is the eye of one who knows that to know the seen, one must consult something other than one's own will and interests and fears and imagination. One must look at the thing. One must look and listen and check and question.
>
> The loving eye is one that pays a certain sort of attention. This attention can require a discipline but *not* a self-denial. The discipline is one of self-knowledge, knowledge of the scope and boundary of the self. . . . In particular, it is a matter of being able to tell one's own interests from those of others and of knowing where one's self leaves off and another begins. . . .
>
> The loving eye does not make the object of perception into something edible, does not try to assimilate it, does not reduce it to the size of the seer's desire, fear and imagination, and hence does not have to simplify. It knows the complexity of the other as something which will forever present new things to be known. The science of the loving eye would favor The Complexity Theory of Truth [in contrast to The Simplicity Theory of Truth] and presuppose The Endless Interestingness of the Universe.[19]

According to Frye, the loving eye is not an invasive, coercive eye which annexes others to itself, but one which "knows the complexity of the other as something which will forever present new things to be known."

When one climbs a rock as a conqueror, one climbs with an arrogant eye. When one climbs with a loving eye, one constantly "must look and listen and check and question." One recognizes the rock as something very different, something perhaps totally indifferent to one's own presence, and finds in that difference joyous occasion for celebration. One knows "the boundary of the self," where the self—the "I," the climber—leaves off and the rock begins. There is no fusion of two into one, but a complement of two entities *acknowledged* as separate, different, independent, yet *in relationship*; they are in relationship *if only* because the loving eye is perceiving it, responding to it, noticing it, attending to it.

An ecofeminist perspective about both women and nature involves this shift in attitude from "arrogant perception" to "loving perception" of the nonhuman world. Arrogant perception of nonhumans by humans presupposes and maintains *sameness* in such a way that it expands the moral community to those beings who are thought to resemble (be like, similar to, or the same as) humans in some morally significant way. Any environmental movement or ethic based on arrogant perception builds a moral hierarchy of beings and assumes some common denominator of moral considerability in virtue of which like beings deserve similar treatment or moral consideration and unlike beings do not. Such environmental ethics are or generate a "unity in sameness." In contrast, "loving perception" presupposes and maintains *difference*—a distinction between the self and other, between human and at least some non-humans—in such a way that perception of the other as other *is* an expression of love for one who/which is recognized at the outset as independent, dissimilar, different. As Maria Lugones says, in loving perception, "Love is seen not as fusion and erasure of difference but as incompatible with them."[20] "Unity in sameness" alone is an *erasure of difference.*

"Loving perception" of the nonhuman natural world is an attempt to understand what it means *for humans* to care about the nonhuman world, a world *acknowledged* as being independent, different, perhaps even indifferent to humans. Humans *are* different from rocks in important ways, even if they are also both members of some ecological community. A moral community based on loving perception of oneself *in relationship with* a rock, or with the natural environment as a whole, is one which acknowledges and respects difference, whatever "sameness" also exists.[21] The limits of loving perception are determined only by the limits of one's (e.g., a person's, a community's) ability to respond lovingly (or with appropriate care, trust, or friendship)—whether it is to other humans or to the nonhuman world and elements of it.[22]

If what I have said so far is correct, then there are very different ways to climb a mountain; *how* one climbs it and *how* one narrates the experience of climbing it matter ethically. If one climbs with "arrogant perception," with an attitude of "conquer and control," one keeps intact the very sorts of thinking that characterize a logic of domination and an oppressive conceptual framework. Since the oppressive conceptual framework which sanctions the domination of nature is a patriarchal one, one also thereby keeps intact, even if unwittingly, a patriarchal conceptual framework. Because the dismantling of patriarchal conceptual frameworks is a feminist issue, *how* one climbs a mountain and *how* one narrates—or tells the story—about the experience of climbing also are *feminist issues.* In this way, ecofeminism makes visible why, at a conceptual level, environmental ethics is a feminist issue. I turn now to a consideration of ecofeminism as a distinctively feminist and environmental ethic.

## ECOFEMINISM AS A FEMINIST AND ENVIRONMENTAL ETHIC

A feminist ethic involves a twofold commitment to critique male bias in ethics wherever it occurs, and to develop ethics which are not male-biased. Sometimes this involves articulation of values (e.g., values of care, appropriate trust, kinship, friendship) often lost or underplayed in mainstream ethics.[23]

Sometimes it involves engaging in theory building by pioneering in new directions or by revamping old theories in gender sensitive ways. What makes the critiques of old theories or conceptualizations of new ones "feminist" is that they emerge out of sex-gender analyses and reflect whatever those analyses reveal about gendered experience and gendered social reality.

As I conceive feminist ethics in the pre-feminist present, it rejects attempts to conceive of ethical theory in terms of necessary and sufficient conditions, because it assumes that there is no essence (in the sense of some transhistorical, universal, absolute abstraction) of feminist ethics. While attempts to formulate joint necessary and sufficient conditions of a feminist ethic are unfruitful, nonetheless, there are some necessary conditions, what I prefer to call "boundary conditions," of a feminist ethic. These boundary conditions clarify some of the minimal conditions of a feminist ethic without suggesting that feminist ethics has some ahistorical essence. They are like the boundaries of a quilt or collage. They delimit the territory of the piece without dictating what the interior, the design, the actual pattern of the piece looks like. Because the actual design of the quilt emerges from the multiplicity of voices of women in a cross-cultural context, the design will change over time. It is not something static.

What are some of the boundary conditions of a feminist ethic? First, nothing can become part of a feminist ethic—can be part of the quilt—that promotes sexism, racism, classism, or any other "isms" of social domination. Of course, people may disagree about what counts as a sexist act, racist attitude, classist behavior. What counts as sexism, racism, or classism may vary cross-culturally. Still, because a feminist ethic aims at eliminating sexism and sexist bias, and (as I have already shown) sexism is intimately connected in conceptualization and in practice to racism, classism, and naturism, a feminist ethic must be anti-sexist, anti-racist, anti-classist, anti-naturist and opposed to any "ism" which presupposes or advances a logic of domination.

Second, a feminist ethic is a *contextualist* ethic. A contextualist ethic is one which sees ethical discourse and practice as emerging from the voices of people located in different historical circumstances. A contextualist ethic is properly viewed as a *collage* or *mosaic*, a *tapestry* of voices that emerges out of felt experiences. Like any collage or mosaic, the point is not to have *one picture* based on a unity of voices, but a *pattern* which emerges out of the very different voices of people located in different circumstances. When a contextualist ethic is *feminist*, it gives central place to the voices of women.

Third, since a feminist ethic gives central significance to the diversity of women's voices, a feminist ethic must be structurally pluralistic rather than unitary or reductionistic. It rejects the assumption that there is "one voice" in terms of which ethical values, beliefs, attitudes, and conduct can be assessed.

Fourth, a feminist ethic reconceives ethical theory as theory in process which will change over time. Like all theory, a feminist ethic is based on some generalizations.[24] Nevertheless, the generalizations associated with it are themselves a pattern of voices within which the different voices emerging out of concrete and alternative descriptions of ethical situations have meaning. The coherence of a feminist theory so conceived is given within a historical and conceptual context, i.e., within a set of historical, socioeconomic circumstances (including circumstances of race, class, age, and affectional orientation) and within a set of basic beliefs, values, attitudes, and assumptions about the world.

Fifth, because a feminist ethic is contextualist, structurally pluralistic, and "in-process," one way to evaluate the claims of a feminist ethic is in terms of their *inclusiveness*: those claims (voices, patterns of voices) are morally and epistemologically favored (preferred, better, less partial, less biased) which are more inclusive of the felt experiences and perspectives of oppressed persons. The condition of inclusiveness requires and ensures that the diverse voices of women (as oppressed persons) will be given legitimacy in ethical theory building. It thereby helps to minimize empirical bias, e.g., bias rising from faulty or false generalizations based on stereotyping, too small a sample size, or a skewed sample. It does so by ensuring that any generalizations which are made about ethics and ethical decision making include—indeed cohere with—the patterned voices of women.[25]

Sixth, a feminist ethic makes no attempt to provide an "objective" point of view, since it assumes that in contemporary culture there really is no such point of view. As such, it does not claim to be "unbiased" in the sense of "value-neutral" or "objective." However, it does assume that whatever bias it has as an ethic centralizing the voices of oppressed persons is a *better bias*—"better" because it is more inclusive and therefore less partial—than those which exclude those voices.[26]

Seventh, a feminist ethic provides a central place for values typically unnoticed, underplayed, or misrepresented in traditional ethics, e.g., values of care, love, friendship, and appropriate trust.[27] Again, it need not do this at the exclusion of considerations of rights, rules, or utility. There may be many contexts in which talk of rights or of utility is useful or appropriate. For instance, in contracts or property relationships, talk of rights may be useful and appropriate. In deciding what is cost-effective or advantageous to the most people, talk of utility may be useful and appropriate. In a feminist *qua* contextualist ethic, whether or not such talk is useful or appropriate depends on the context; *other values* (e.g., values of care, trust, friendship) are *not* viewed as reducible to or captured solely in terms of such talk.[28]

Eighth, a feminist ethic also involves a reconception of what it is to be human and what it is for humans to engage in ethical decision making, since it rejects as either meaningless or currently untenable any gender-free or gender-neutral description of humans, ethics, and ethical decision making. It thereby rejects what Alison Jaggar calls "abstract individualism," i.e., the position that it is possible to identify a human essence or human nature that exists independently of any particular historical context.[29] Humans and human moral conduct are properly understood essentially (and not merely accidentally) in terms of networks or webs of historical and concrete relationships.

All the props are now in place for seeing how ecofeminism provides the framework for a distinctively feminist and environmental ethic. It is a feminism that critiques male bias wherever it occurs in ethics (including environmental ethics) and aims at providing an ethic (including an environmental ethic) which is not male biased—and it does so in a way that satisfies the preliminary boundary conditions of a feminist ethic.

First, ecofeminism is quintessentially anti-naturist. Its anti-naturism consists in the rejection of any way of thinking about or acting toward nonhuman nature that reflects a logic, values, or attitude of domination. Its anti-naturist, anti-sexist, anti-racist, anti-classist (and so forth, for all other "isms" of social domination) stance forms the outer boundary of the quilt: nothing gets on the quilt which is naturist, sexist, racist, classist, and so forth.

Second, ecofeminism is a contextualist ethic. It involves a shift *from* a conception of ethics as primarily a matter of rights, rules, or principles predetermined and applied in specific cases to entities viewed as competitors in the contest of moral standing, *to* a conception of ethics as growing out of what Jim Cheney calls "defining relationships," i.e., relationships conceived in some sense as defining who one is.[30] As a contextualist ethic, it is not that rights, or rules, or principles are *not* relevant or important. Clearly they are in certain contexts and for certain purposes.[31] It is just that what *makes* them relevant or important is that those to whom they apply are entities *in relationship with* others.

Ecofeminism also involves an ethical shift *from* granting moral consideration to nonhumans *exclusively* on the grounds of some similarity they share with humans (e.g., rationality, interests, moral agency, sentiency, right-holder status) *to* "a highly contextual account to see clearly what a human being is and what the nonhuman world might be, morally speaking, *for* human beings."[32] For an ecofeminist, *how* a moral agent is in relationship to another becomes of central significance, not simply *that* a moral agent is a moral agent or is bound by rights, duties, virtue, or utility to act in a certain way.

Third, ecofeminism is structurally pluralistic in that it presupposes and maintains difference—difference among humans as well as between humans and at least some elements of nonhuman nature. Thus, while ecofeminism denies the "nature/culture" split, it affirms that humans are both members of an ecological community (in some respects) and different from it (in other respects). Ecofeminism's attention to relationships and community is not, therefore, an erasure of difference but a respectful acknowledgement of it.

Fourth, ecofeminism reconceives theory as theory in process. It focuses on patterns of meaning which emerge, for instance, from the storytelling and first-person narratives of women (and others) who deplore the twin dominations of women and nature. The use of narrative is one way to ensure that the content of the ethic—the pattern of the quilt—may/will change over time, as the historical and material realities of women's lives change and as more is learned about women-nature connections and the destruction of the non-human world.[33]

Fifth, ecofeminism is inclusivist. It emerges from the voices of women who experience the harmful domination of nature and the way that domination is tied to their domination as women. It emerges from listening to the voices of indigenous peoples such as Native Americans who have been dislocated from their land and have witnessed the attendant undermining of such values as appropriate reciprocity, sharing, and kinship that characterize traditional Indian culture. It emerges from listening to voices of those who, like Nathan Hare, critique traditional approaches to environmental ethics as white and bourgeois, and as failing to address issues of "black ecology" and the "ecology" of the inner city and urban spaces.[34] It also emerges out of the voices of Chipko women who see the destruction of "earth, soil, and water" as intimately connected with their own inability to survive economically.[35] With its emphasis on inclusivity and difference, ecofeminism provides a framework for recognizing that what counts as ecology and what counts as appropriate conduct toward both human and non-human environments is largely a matter of context.

Sixth, as a feminism, ecofeminism makes no attempt to provide an "objective" point of view. It is a social ecology. It recognizes the twin dominations of women and nature as social problems rooted both in very concrete, historical, socioeconomic circumstances and in oppressive patriarchal conceptual frameworks which maintain and sanction these circumstances.

Seventh, ecofeminism makes a central place for values of care, love, friendship, trust, and appropriate reciprocity—values that presuppose that our relationships to others are central to our understanding of who we are.[36] It thereby gives voice to the sensitivity that in climbing a mountain, one is doing something in relationship with an "other," an "other" whom one can come to care about and treat respectfully.

Lastly, an ecofeminist ethic involves a reconception of what it means to be human, and in what human ethical behavior consists. Ecofeminism denies abstract individualism. Humans are who we are in large part by virtue of the historical and social contexts and the relationships we are in, including our relationships with nonhuman nature. Relationships are not something extrinsic to who we are, not an "add on" feature of human nature; they play an essential role in shaping what it is to be human. Relationships of humans to the nonhuman environment are, in part, constitutive of what it is to be a human.

By making visible the interconnections among the dominations of women and nature, ecofeminism shows that both are feminist issues and that explicit acknowledgement of both is vital to any responsible environmental ethic. Feminism *must* embrace ecological feminism if it is to end the domination of women because the domination of women is tied conceptually and historically to the domination of nature.

A responsible environmental ethic also *must* embrace feminism. Otherwise, even the seemingly most revolutionary, liberational, and holistic ecological ethic will fail to take seriously the interconnected dominations of nature and women that are so much a part of the historical legacy and conceptual framework that sanctions the exploitation of nonhuman nature. Failure to make visible these interconnected, twin dominations results in an inaccurate account of how it is that nature has been and continues to be dominated and exploited and produces an environmental ethic that lacks the depth necessary to be truly *inclusive* of the realities of persons who, at least in dominant Western culture, have been intimately tied with that exploitation, viz., women. Whatever else can be said in favor of such holistic ethics, a failure to make visible ecofeminist insights into the common denominators of the twin oppressions of women and nature is to perpetuate, rather than overcome, the source of that oppression.

This last point deserves further attention. It may be objected that as long as the end result is "the same"—the development of an environmental ethic which does not emerge out of or reinforce an oppressive conceptual framework—it does not matter whether that ethic (or the ethic endorsed in getting there) is feminist or not. Hence, it simply is *not* the case that any adequate environmental ethic must be feminist. My argument, in contrast, has been that it *does* matter, and for three important reasons. First, there is the scholarly issue of accurately representing historical reality, and that, ecofeminists claim, requires acknowledging the historical feminization of nature and naturalization of women as part of the exploitation of nature. Second, I have shown that the conceptual connections between the domination of women and the domination of nature are located in an oppressive and, at least in Western societies, patriarchal conceptual framework characterized by a logic of domination. Thus, I have shown that failure to notice the nature of this connection leaves at best an incomplete, inaccurate, and partial account of what is required of a conceptually adequate environmental ethic. An ethic which *does not* acknowledge this is simply *not* the same as one that does, whatever else the similarities between them. Third, the claim that, in contemporary culture, one can have an adequate environmental ethic which is *not* feminist assumes that, in contemporary culture, the label *feminist* does not add anything crucial to the nature or description of environmental ethics. I have shown that at least in contemporary culture this is false, for the word *feminist* currently helps to clarify just *how* the domination of nature is conceptually linked to patriarchy and, hence, how the liberation of nature is conceptually linked to the termination of patriarchy. Thus, because the word feminist has critical bite in contemporary culture, it serves as an important reminder that in contemporary sex-gendered, raced, classed, and naturist culture, an unlabeled position functions as a privileged and "unmarked" position. That is, without the addition of the word *feminist,* one presents environmental ethics as if it has no bias, including male-gender bias, which is just what ecofeminists deny: failure to notice the connections between the twin oppressions of women and nature *is* male-gender bias.

One of the goals of feminism is the eradication of all oppressive sex-gender (and related race, class, age, affectional preference) categories and the creation of a world in which *difference does not breed domination*—say, the world of 4001. If in 4001 an "adequate environmental ethic" is a "feminist environmental ethic," the word *feminist* may then be redundant and unnecessary. However, this is *not* 4001, and in terms of the current historical and conceptual reality the dominations of nature and of women are intimately connected. Failure to notice or make visible that connection in 1990 perpetuates the mistaken (and privileged) view that "environmental ethics" is *not* a feminist issue, and that *feminist* adds nothing to environmental ethics.[37]

## CONCLUSION

I have argued in this paper that ecofeminism provides a framework for a distinctively feminist and environmental ethic. Ecofeminism grows out of the felt and theorized about connections between the domination of women and the domination of nature. As a contextualist ethic, ecofeminism refocuses environmental ethics on what nature might mean, morally speaking, *for* humans, and on how the relational attitudes of humans to others—humans as well as nonhumans—sculpt both what it is to be human and the nature and ground of human responsibilities to the nonhuman environment. Part of what this refocusing does is to take seriously the voices of women and other oppressed persons in the construction of that ethic.

A Sioux elder once told me a story about his son. He sent his seven-year-old son to live with the child's grandparents on a Sioux reservation so that he could "learn the Indian ways." Part of what the grandparents taught the son was how to hunt the four leggeds of the forest. As I heard the story, the boy was taught,

> to shoot your four-legged brother in his hind area, slowing it down but not killing it. Then, take the four-legged's head in your hands, and look into his eyes. The eyes are where all the suffering is. Look into your brother's eyes and feel his pain. Then, take your knife and cut the four-legged under his chin, here, on his neck, so that he dies quickly. And as you do, ask your brother, the four-legged, for forgiveness for what you do. Offer also a prayer of thanks to your four-legged kin for offering his body to you just now, when you need food to eat and clothing to wear. And promise the four-legged that you will put yourself back into the earth when you die, to become nourishment of the earth, and for the sister flowers, and for the brother deer. It is appropriate that you should offer this blessing for the

four-legged and, in due time, reciprocate in turn with your body in this way, as the four-legged gives life to you for your survival.

As I reflect upon that story, I am struck by the power of the environmental ethic that grows out of and takes seriously narrative, context, and such values and relational attitudes as care, loving perception, and appropriate reciprocity, and doing what is appropriate in a given situation—however that notion of appropriateness eventually gets filled out. I am also struck by what one is able to see, once one begins to explore some of the historical and conceptual connections between the dominations of women and of nature. A *re-conceiving* and *re-visioning* of both feminism and environmental ethics, is, I think, the power and promise of ecofeminism.

# NOTES

1. Explicit ecological feminist literature includes works from a variety of scholarly perspectives and sources. Some of these works are Jim Cheney, "Eco-Feminism and Deep Ecology," *Environmental Ethics* 9 (1987): 115–45; Katherine Davies, "Historical Associations: Women and the Natural World," *Women & Environments* 9, no. 2 (Spring 1987): 4–6; Sharon Doubiago, "Deeper than Deep Ecology: Men Must Become Feminists," in *The New Catalyst Quarterly*, no. 10 (Winter 1987/88): 10–11; Brian Easlea, *Science and Sexual Oppression: Patriarchy's Confrontation with Women and Nature* (London: Weidenfeld & Nicholson, 1981); Ynestra King, "Feminism and the Revolt of Nature," in *Heresies #13: Feminism and Ecology* 4, no. 1 (1981): Greater King 12–16, and "What Is Ecofeminism?" *The Nation*, 12 December 1987; Abby Peterson and Carolyn Merchant, "Peace with the Earth: Women and the Environmental Movement in Sweden," *Women's Studies International Forum* 9, no. 5–6. (1986): 465–79; Judith Plant, ed., *Healing Our Wounds: The Power of Ecological Feminism* (Boston: New Society Publishers, 1989); Kirkpatrick Sale, "Ecofeminism—A New Perspective," *The Nation*, 26 (September 1987): 302–05; Ariel Kay Salleh, "Deeper than Deep Ecology: The Eco-Feminist Connection," *Environmental Ethics* 6 (1984): 339–45, and "Epistemology and the Metaphors of Production: An Eco-Feminist Reading of Critical Theory," in *Studies in the Humanities* 15 (1988): 130–39; Karen J. Warren, "Feminism and Ecology: Making Connections," *Environmental Ethics* 9 (1987): 3–21; Miriam Wyman, "Explorations of Eco-Feminism," *Women & Environments* (Spring 1987): 6–7; Iris Young, "'Feminism and Ecology' and 'Women and Life on Earth: Eco-Feminism in the 80's,'" *Environmental Ethics* 5 (1983): 173–80.
2. Françoise d'Eaubonne, *Le Féminisme ou la Mort* (Paris: Pierre Horay, 1974), pp. 213–52.
3. I discuss this in my paper "Toward an Ecofeminist Ethic."
4. The account offered here is a revision of the account given earlier in my paper "Feminism and Ecology: Making Connections." I have changed the account to be about "oppressive" rather than strictly "partriarchal" conceptual frameworks in order to leave open the possibility that there may be some patriarchal conceptual frameworks (e.g., in non-Western cultures) which are *not* properly characterized as based on value dualisms.
5. Murray Bookchin, "Social Ecology versus 'Deep Ecology,'" in *Green Perspectives: Newsletter of the Green Program Project*, no. 4–5 (Summer 1987): 9.
6. It may be that in contemporary Western society, which is so thoroughly structured by categories of gender, race, class, age, and affectional orientation, that there simply is no meaningful notion of "value-hierarchical thinking" which does not function in an oppressive context. For purposes of this paper, I leave that question open.
7. Many feminists who argue for the historical point that claims (B1) and (B2) have been asserted or assumed to be true within the dominant Western philosophical tradition do so by discussion of that tradition's conceptions of reason, rationality, and science. For a

sampling of the sorts of claims made within that context, see "Reason, Rationality, and Gender," ed. Nancy Tuana and Karen J. Warren, a special issue of the American Philosophical Association's *Newsletter on Feminism and Philosophy* 88, no. 2 (March 1989): 17–71. Ecofeminists who claim that (B2) has been assumed to be true within the dominant Western philosophical tradition include: Gray, *Green Paradise Lost*; Griffin, *Woman and Nature*; Merchant, *The Death of Nature*; Ruether, *New Woman/New Earth*. For a discussion of some of these ecofeminist historical acounts, see Plumwood, "Ecofeminism." While I agree that the historical connections between the domination of women and the domination of nature is a crucial one, I do not argue for that claim here.

8. Ecofeminists who deny (B1) when (B1) is offered as anything other than a true, descriptive, historical claim about patriarchal culture often do so on grounds that an objectionable sort of biological determinism, or at least harmful female sex-gender stereotypes, underlie (B1). For a discussion of this "split" among those ecofeminists ("nature feminists") who assert and those ecofeminists ("social feminists") who deny (B1) as anything other than a true historical claim about how women are described in patriarchal culture, see Griscom, "On Healing the Nature/History Split."

9. I make no attempt here to defend the historically sanctioned truth of these premises.

10. See, e.g., Bell Hooks, *Feminist Theory: From Margin to Center* (Boston: South End Press, 1984), pp. 51–52.

11. Maria Lugones, "Playfulness, 'World-Travelling,' and Loving Perception," *Hypatia* 2, no. 2 (Summer 1987): 3.

12. At an *experiential* level, some women are "women of color," poor, old, lesbian, Jewish, and physically challenged. Thus, if feminism is going to liberate these women, it also needs to end the racism, classism, heterosexism, anti-Semitism, and discrimination against the handicapped that is constitutive of their oppression as black, or Latina, or poor, or older, or lesbian, or Jewish, or physically challenged women.

13. This same sort of reasoning shows that feminism is also a movement to end racism, classism, age-ism, heterosexism and other "isms," which are based in oppressive conceptual frameworks characterized by a logic of domination. However, there is an important caveat: ecofeminism is *not* compatible with all feminisms and all environmentalisms. For a discussion of this point, see my article "Feminism and Ecology: Making Connections." What it *is* compatible with is the minimal condition characterization of feminism as a movement to end sexism that is accepted by all contemporary feminisms (liberal, traditional Marxist, radical, socialist, Blacks and non-Western).

14. See, e.g., Gray, *Green Paradise Lost;* Griffin, *Women and Nature;* Merchant, *The Death of Nature;* and Ruether, *New Woman/New Earth.*

15. Suppose, as I think is the case, that a necessary condition for the existence of a moral relationship is that at least one party to the relationship is a moral being (leaving open for our purposes what counts as a "moral being"). If this is so, then the Mona Lisa cannot properly be said to have or stand in a moral relationship with the wall on which she hangs, and a wolf cannot have or properly be said to have or stand in a moral relationship with a moose. Such a necessary-condition account leaves open the question whether *both* parties to the relationship must be moral beings. My point here is simply that however one resolves *that* question, recognition of the relationships themselves as a locus of value is a recognition of a source of value that is different from and not reducible to the values of the "moral beings" in those relationships.

16. It is interesting to note that the image of being friends with the Earth is one which cytogeneticist Barbara McClintock uses when she describes the importance of having "a feeling for the organism," "listening to the material [in this case the corn plant]," in one's work as a scientist. See Evelyn Fox Keller, "Women, Science, and Popular Mythology," in *Machina Ex Dea: Feminist Perspectives on Technology*, ed. Joan Rothschild (New York: Pergamon Press, 1983), and Evelyn Fox Keller, *A Feeling for the Organism: The Life and Work of Barbara McClintock* (San Francisco: W. H. Freeman, 1983).

17. Cheney, "Eco-Feminism and Deep Ecology," 144.

18. Marilyn Frye, "In and Out of Harm's Way: Arrogance and Love," *The Politics of Reality* (Trumansburg, N.Y.: The Crossing Press, 1983), pp. 66–72.

19. Ibid., pp. 75–76.

20. Maria Lugones, "Playfulness," p. 3.

21. Cheney makes a similar point in "Eco-Feminism and Deep Ecology," p. 140.

22. Ibid., p. 138.
23. This account of a feminist ethic draws on my paper "Toward an Ecofeminist Ethic."
24. Marilyn Frye makes this point in her illuminating paper, "The Possibility of Feminist Theory," read at the American Philosophical Association Central Division Meetings in Chicago, 29 April–1 May 1986. My discussion of feminist theory is inspired largely by that paper and by Kathryn Addelson's paper "Moral Revolution," in *Women and Values: Reading in Recent Feminist Philosophy,* ed. Marilyn Pearsall (Belmont, Calif.: Wadsworth, 1986), pp. 291–309.
25. Notice that the standard of inclusiveness does not exclude the voices of men. It is just that those voices must cohere with the voices of women.
26. For a more in-depth discussion of the notions of impartiality and bias, see my paper, "Critical Thinking and Feminism," *Informal Logic* 10, no. 1 (Winter 1988): 31–44.
27. The burgeoning literature on these values is noteworthy. See, e.g., Carol Gilligan, *In a Different Voice: Psychological Theories and Women's Development* (Cambridge, Mass.: Harvard University Press, 1982); *Mapping the Moral Domain: A Contribution of Women's Thinking to Psychological Theory and Education,* ed. Carol Gilligan, Janie Victoria Ward, and Jill McLean Taylor, with Betty Bardige (Cambridge, Mass.: Harvard University Press, 1988); Nel Nodings, *Caring: A Feminine Approach to Ethics and Moral Education* (Berkeley: University of California Press, 1984); Maria Lugones and Elizabeth V. Spelman, "Have We Got a Theory for You! Feminist Theory, Cultural Imperialism, and the Women's Voice," *Women's Studies International Forum* 6 (1983): 573–81; Maria Lugones, "Playfulness"; Annette C. Baier, "What Do Women Want in a Moral Theory?" *Nous* 19 (1985): 53–63.
28. Jim Cheney would claim that our fundamental relationships to one another as moral agents are not as moral agents to rights holders, and that whatever rights a person properly may be said to have are relationally defined rights, not rights possessed by atomistic individuals conceived as Robinson Crusoes who do not exist essentially in relation to others. On this view, even rights talk itself is properly conceived as growing out of a relational ethic, not vice versa.
29. Alison Jaggar, *Feminist Politics and Human Nature* (Totowa, N.J.: Rowman and Allanheld, 1980), pp. 42–44.
30. Henry West has pointed out that the expression "defining relations" is ambiguous. According to West, "the defining" as Cheney uses it is an adjective, not a principle—it is not that ethics defines relationships; it is that ethics grows out of conceiving of the relationships that one is in as defining what the individual is.
31. For example, in relationships involving contracts or promises, those relationships might be correctly described as that of moral agent to rights holders. In relationships involving mere property, those relationships might be correctly described as that of moral agent to objects having only instrumental value, "relationships of instrumentality." In comments on an earlier draft of this paper, West suggested that possessive individualism, for instance, might be recast in such a way that an individual is defined by his or her property relationships.
32. Cheney, "Eco-Feminism and Deep Ecology," p. 144.
33. One might object that such permission for change opens the door for environmental exploitation. This is not the case. An ecofeminist ethic is anti-naturist. Hence, the unjust domination and exploitation of nature is a "boundary condition" of the ethic; no such actions are sanctioned or justified on ecofeminist grounds. What it *does* leave open is some leeway about what counts as domination and exploitation. This, I think, is a strength of the ethic, not a weakness, since it acknowledges that *that* issue cannot be resolved in any practical way in the abstract, independent of a historical and social context.
34. Nathan Hare, "Black Ecology," in *Environmental Ethics,* ed. K. S. Shrader-Frechette (Pacific Grove, Calif.: Boxwood Press, 1981), pp. 229–36.
35. For an ecofeminist discussion of the Chipko movement, see my "Toward an Ecofeminist Ethic," and Shiva's *Staying Alive.*
36. See Cheney, "Eco-Feminism and Deep Ecology," p. 122.
37. I offer the same sort of reply to critics of ecofeminism such as Warwick Fox who suggest that for the sort of ecofeminism I defend, the word *feminist* does not add anything significant to environmental ethics and, consequently, that an ecofeminist like myself might as well call herself a deep ecologist. He asks: "Why doesn't she just call it [i.e., Warren's vision of a transformative feminism] deep ecology? Why specifically attach

the label *feminist* to it . . . ?" (Warwick Fox, "The Deep Ecology-Ecofeminism Debate and Its Parallels," *Environmental Ethics* 11, no. 1 [1989]: 14, n. 22). Whatever the important similarities between deep ecology and ecofeminism (or, specifically, my version of ecofeminism)—and, indeed, there are many—it is precisely my point here that the word *feminist* does add something significant to the conception of environmental ethics, and that any environmental ethic (including deep ecology) that fails to make explicit the different kinds of interconnections among the domination of nature and the domination of women will be, from a feminist (and ecofeminist) perspective such as mine, inadequate.

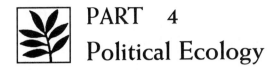

# PART 4
# Political Ecology

# INTRODUCTION

*John Clark*

John Clark is professor of philosophy at Loyola University, New Orleans, and currently chairs the Environmental Studies Program. He has long been active in the green and bioregionalism movements. His books include *The Anarchist Moment: Reflection on Culture, Nature, and Power; Liberty, Ecology, Geography: The Social Thought of Elisee Reclus;* and a forthcoming reinterpretation of social ecology.

The field of political ecology has developed rapidly in recent times as political theorists and philosophers have sought to redefine their subject matter in response to an increasing interest in environmental issues, to the intensifying ecological crisis, and to the emergence of the ecological worldview as a major paradigm in contemporary thought. In recent ethical theory, these same factors have produced forms of "moral extensionism," in which the principles and methodologies of various traditional ethical theories are applied to environmental questions. They have also inspired the emergence of new ethical theories that are more fundamentally transformed through ecological thinking. Similar developments are now taking place in political theory and social ethics, producing a spectrum of positions that express ecological concerns and embody ecological concepts to widely varying degrees.

The term "environmentalism" is sometimes used to refer to a traditional, instrumentalist view that conceives of "nature" as that which *surrounds* human beings, and reduces the natural world to a stock of resources that ought to be used wisely for the benefit of humanity. The term "ecology" may accordingly be reserved for a more critical and transformative perspective that reconceptualizes the place of humanity *within* the larger system or whole. According to such a distinction, most ventures into "political ecology" have thus far remained at the environmental or moral extensionist level. Most discussions of ecological questions from conservative, liberal, libertarian, and socialist perspectives have merely applied preexisting categories to environmental issues with little reflection on the challenge that ecological thinking might pose for these categories.

There are, however, some notable exceptions. For example, some Marxist theorists have moved in a more ecological direction by exploring the affinities between dialectical and ecological thought. In addition, many exponents of ecofeminism, social ecology, and bioregionalism have consciously sought to develop a political approach that is explicitly grounded in an ecological worldview. As a result of such efforts, political ecology has become a vibrant and rapidly evolving field.

As the severity, complexity, and global nature of today's ecological problems has become increasingly more apparent, the need for a political approach to them has gained wider recognition. The growth of political ecology has perhaps been most evident in the various environmental justice movements around the world. Many of these ecological struggles have centered around the conflict between indigenous or traditional peoples and the expanding global corporate economy. Widespread public attention has focused on struggles such as those of the Chipko ("tree-huggers") movement in India, of Chico Mendes and the rubber tappers of the Amazon basin, and of the Ogoni people in Nigeria. Indeed, one finds that throughout the world, political movements among peasants and the urban poor that once seemed focused primarily on social justice issues increasingly define themselves as both social and ecological. Furthermore, the central role of women in ecological politics has become increasingly evident, and women have constituted a majority of activists in many ecological movements of both North and South. The connection between ecological destruction, the oppression of women, and other forms of social injustice has gained increasing recognition by both theorists and activists. The American environmental movement has undergone a transformation that parallels global developments. While environmentalism was long stereotyped as an exclusive preserve of the white middle class, a very large proportion of ecological activism in the United States now occurs in poor, working class and minority communities.[1]

The growing international Green movement has also been an important expression of interest in political ecology. While the United States has lagged behind many other countries, ecological politics in much of the world is now represented through significant Green political parties and movements, a few of which have entered into governing coalitions, and many of which have exerted significant influence at the national level. Such political developments have been accompanied by a rapidly growing literature in Green political theory.[2] An even larger context for developments in political ecology is the reconfiguration of the post-colonial, post–Cold War world political culture in relation to economic globalization. Increasingly, the discourse of environmental politics focuses on the role of transnational corporations and neo-liberal state policies in relation to such issues as global warming, deforestation, biodiversity loss, species extinction, and air and water pollution.[3]

In view of these developments, the field of political ecology promises to become an important area of political theory and social philosophy, just as environmental ethics has moved to the center of discussion in applied ethics. While a thorough survey of the topic of political ecology would require a sizable work in itself, this part of the text offers an introduction to the field through introductory comments and reading selections discussing some of the most important viewpoints in the field. These positions include "free market" environmentalism, traditionalist conservative environmentalism, Green market environmentalism, liberal environmentalism, socialist ecology, social ecology, ecofeminism, and bioregionalism.[4]

## FREE MARKET ENVIRONMENTALISM

Free market environmentalism applies to environmental issues the general principle that the greatest good can be promoted and justice can be achieved best through the unrestricted operation of the market economy. Whether grounding their position in utility or in rights theory, its proponents usually contend that the proper function of government is the protection of life, liberty, and property. They support a minimal or negative state in which governmental activity is limited to such functions as police protection, military defense, adjudication of civil and criminal cases, and the provision of a stable monetary framework within which the market can operate efficiently and productively.

Free market advocates reject the view that market forces have led to ecological degradation in the past or that they will produce any severe ecological crisis in the future. Terry L. Anderson and Donald R. Leal contend that predictions of "serious stresses involving population, resources, and environment" are inaccurate because "[a]ll of these forecasts fail to take account of the ability of humans to react to problems of scarcity by reducing consumption, finding substitutes, and improving productivity."[5] Their position is thus close to the well-known "cornucopian" viewpoint of economist Julian Simon, who argues that resources and possibilities for growth are unlimited.[6]

Writers such as Anderson and Leal maintain that clearly defined property rights are the best assurance of optimal environmental decision-making (and, indeed, of the best decision-making in every area related to the rational allocation of resources). In their view, ecological problems seldom result from the exercise of property rights in ways that are (as critics of the market often charge) individually rational but socially and ecologically irrational. Rather, they see these problems as the result of an inadequate definition of property rights, or of the absence of such rights over certain natural resources, which are consequently not protected. They accept the economic model of human beings as self-interested rational calculators and consider any reliance on altruistic motivation such as civic responsibility or moral values to be ineffectual.

Accordingly, Anderson and Leal argue that because of the complexity of ecosystems they cannot be effectively managed by the state, but only by private owners who are more familiar with natural resources in which they have a personal stake. Owners will make wise decisions if they are allowed to benefit fully from their property, if they are required to pay the costs incurred in the exercise of their property rights, and if price mechanisms are not "distorted" through political intervention. Furthermore, they claim that political decision-making will be biased in favor of groups that are more organized and better informed than the majority of the public, which may not have a strong interest in most decisions and may be "rationally ignorant" concerning the issues. According to this analysis, the market assures efficiency (which is taken as the major criterion by which to judge decision-making), while state activity does not, even when democratic electoral processes are utilized.

As a major alternative to government regulatory agencies, free market advocates support the idea of holding polluters legally responsible for the effects of their actions. For example, the government might "register pollutants, monitor the flow of pollutants in the atmosphere, and enforce liability for damages."[7] Governmental activity would thus follow the minimal state model of using policing powers and the court system to protect life and property rights from invasion.

While most free market approaches exhibit little evidence of the influence of ecological thought, the recent work of Gus diZerega is an exception.[8] DiZerega claims, following Hayek, that societies in which limited governmental activity takes place constitute "spontaneous orders" and "self-regulating systems" comparable to naturally functioning ecosystems. This outlook assumes that there are "processes of mutual adjustment maintaining the system as a whole," that are upset by governmental regulatory activity.[9] DiZerega is also atypical of free market advocates in his strong rejection of certain property rights. In his view, the "right to ruin soil, create nonrecyclable waste, or seriously reduce genetic diversity within a species are all examples of inappropriate property rights."[10] In general, free market advocates contend that these activities do not violate any rights if they are carried out by property owners, but argue that they will be eliminated to the extent that the public develops a demand for environmental goods, so that it will be in the interest of owners to "produce" these commodities.

## TRADITIONALIST CONSERVATIVE ENVIRONMENTALISM

The term "conservative" in American political discourse encompasses two distinct political tendencies.[11] The first comes out of the tradition of Adam Smith, John Locke, and classical liberalism, and emphasizes the importance of individualism, "negative liberty" (that is, freedom from coercion), a substantially unregulated market, social progress through material production, and limitation of the state to a protective "night-watchman" role. This tendency is often called libertarian or "free market" conservatism. The other, rather neglected tradition in American conservatism is traditionalism. It traces its lineage to figures such as Alexander Hamilton, John Adams, Alexis de Tocqueville, John Calhoun, and, above all, Edmund Burke, the father of Anglo-American conservatism.[12] It stresses the importance of inherited values, practices and institutions, religious traditions, cultural continuity, social order, organic community, and gradual social change. It is skeptical of the idea of progress and focuses on the community more than the individual. John R. E. Bliese argues that the latter, traditionalist conservatism offers a strong basis for environmentalism. Traditionalists diverge from libertarians in rejecting the economistic focus of the latter and emphasizing instead such values as "the health of our human spirits and the state of our culture."[13] Bliese sees as fundamental to the traditionalist position five guiding principles, which he identifies as: "rejection of materialism"; "rejection of ideology"; "piety toward nature"; "social contract across generations"; and "prudence, the prime political virtue."[14]

Bliese finds in traditionalism a powerful critique of the central modern project of the conquest of nature in the name of progress and productivity. Such a project, he notes, sins against the cardinal conservative virtue of piety, "which respects the mystery of nature," and connects human spiritual development with "an acceptance of nature."[15] The traditionalist Burkean view of society as a sacred "partnership between those who are living, those who are dead, and those who are yet to be born" is the basis for a strong stewardship ethic, in which the present generation is morally bound to pass its natural heritage on to future generations in at least as good a condition as that in which it was received. Furthermore, the conservative virtue of prudence might be compared to the "precautionary principle" that is much discussed in contemporary environmentalism. While today innovations are introduced casually for economic, political, or technological ends, the traditionalist conservative concludes that "we need to be very careful, humble and prudent" in making any social changes, but "much more so in changing the environment."[16]

The specific environmental policy implications of such a position are far-reaching. For Bliese the application of conservative principles of prudence and piety to such phenomena as global warming and biodiversity loss would require us to "cut our energy use dramatically,"[17] and to end practices that result in species extinction. Furthermore, the conservative stewardship ethic demands not only that the cost of pollution be "internalized" to production, but that pollution be eliminated when human beings or nature are significantly harmed for the sake of mere material consumption. According to Bliese, in pursuing these goals, the traditionalist conservative does not dogmatically oppose governmental environmental legislation, but prefers to use market mechanisms rather than "bureaucratic command-and-control techniques" for conservation.[18]

Bliese does not spell out the specific policy implications of the traditionalist environmentalism he outlines. However, it seems likely that the attainment of such goals as stopping needless species extinction, reversing the causes of global warming, and ending pollution for nonessential purposes, would require much more far-ranging economic, political, and technological changes in the near future than those proposed by mainstream environmentalists, whether conservative or liberal. Traditionalists are thus perhaps faced with a dilemma: their end of protecting the heritage of nature from reckless destruction may require means that are at odds with their social and political gradualism.

## GREEN MARKET ENVIRONMENTALISM

The best-known advocate of "greening the market" is Paul Hawken, who proposes a market-based approach that differs considerably from that of the "free market" theorists. Hawken believes that the ecological crisis is much more severe and the risks for the future much greater than the free market theorists are willing to admit. He argues that an unregulated market inevitably creates ecological crisis because enterprises have an economic incentive to reduce expenditures and gain a competitive advantage by externalizing costs as environmental damage. Hawken believes that as a result of this tendency, significant governmental action is necessary. However, he argues that as little as possible of it should consist of administrative regulation and government planning, since in his view these approaches cause inefficiencies and undermine the benefits of market mechanisms.

Hawkens proposes instead the enactment of "green taxes" that would internalize ecological costs (the cost of "externalities") in prices. On this he follows British economist A. C. Pigou, who proposed the idea of "a 'tax to correct maladjustments' on producers, a tax that would be comparable to the avoided cost or unborne expense."[19] Under such a system, producers would have the same kind of incentives as they presently do to produce profitably and efficiently, but the incentives would work to produce cleaner, more ecologically sound products. In Hawken's view, such a system would make sustainability profitable, while harnessing what he sees as the vast creative potential of the competitive market and individual initiative. It would also permit the phasing out of much of the present tax system, as green taxation is introduced over a twenty-year period.

There are several other important elements in Hawken's green market system. One is "an intelligent product system," which consists of several strategies, including a system of licensing "durables" such as cars and household appliances to the consumer for use, while the producer retains ownership and responsibility for ecological consequences during the life of the product. He claims that under such a system "products of service would be designed for complete and easy disassembly for reuse, remanufacture, or reclaiming."[20] Another of his innovative economic proposals is the formation of public "utilities" that are a "hybrid of public-private interests"[21] in areas of important "natural resources." These entities would receive levels of return on investments proportional to their fulfillment of society's needs in an eco-logically sound manner.[22] According to Hawken, the result of all these poli-cies would be a market that is both substantially "free" in its principles of operation, and ecologically sustainable in its functioning.

## LIBERAL ENVIRONMENTALISM

Liberal environmentalism rejects the idea that unrestrained market activity can solve ecological problems, and contends that significant governmental regulatory activity is necessary to prevent environmental damage while re-specting human rights and maintaining justice. Liberalism (in the American sense of a moderate social democracy) is the guiding ideological orientation of much of contemporary environmental thinking. This is exemplified, for ex-ample, in the extensive publications of the Worldwatch Institute and its direc-tor Lester R. Brown, which call for expanded government regulatory activity and more effective international environmental agreements, in addition to expanded use of market-based incentives.[23]

In view of the fact that mainstream environmentalism in the United States and many Western countries has remained steadfastly in the liberal tradition, it is rather surprising that an extensive literature in liberal environ-mental political theory has not yet developed. A notable contribution, how-ever, is Avner de-Shalit's forthright defense of this position, in which he makes a case for broad governmental environmental regulation in the context of a strong welfare state based on a liberal conception of the general good.[24] In de-Shalit's view, this conception can be given a more ecological dimension. He contends that the idea of "antichauvinism" is basic to liberalism and that it can, through a kind of moral and political extension, yield an effective envi-ronmental politics. According to such a problematic, the liberal principle of concern for the interest and welfare of others can reasonably be expanded "to include nonhuman animals, 'all sentient creatures,' or even 'all living objects' or 'ecosystems.'"[25]

De-Shalit rejects the green market approach to ecological problems on the grounds that Pigovian taxes are regressive and therefore unjust. In his view, if producers are charged for "externalities," they will pass the cost on to consumers, and the poor will bear a disproportionate burden, since they spend much more of their income on energy and other goods that will be taxed most heavily. Advocates of green taxes respond that other taxes and even some of the green fees themselves could be made progressive to offset the otherwise regressive nature of taxes on energy and other necessities. Eq-uity could thus be reconciled with full-cost pricing, as some liberals are will-ing to admit.

However, de-Shalit has a stronger criticism of the very idea that "costs" can be internalized in the market price of a commodity. He points out the dif-ficulty of placing a price on human sickness and suffering or the destruction of animal life, and the obvious impossibility of assigning a monetary value to human lives, not to mention species loss and ecosystem destruction. He also notes that cost-benefit analysis irrationally "discounts" the value of the lives and experience of future generations. His point, like that of many critics of cost-benefit analysis, is that determination of value is an ethical and political question. Neither an unrestricted market nor even a market that theoretically internalizes estimated external costs can assess value in any "objective" manner.

De-Shalit advocates a process of public debate and political decision-making to limit the amount of pollution and environmental destruction in accord with the public's view of its own interest, whatever the market might otherwise have dictated. He rejects the idea that the community's interest is served by the "free market" approach of litigation after the fact by specific individuals whose "property rights" are violated by polluters. He asks why the public should not "prevent pollution before workers breathe in smog, or before people are hurt and the environment is damaged."[26]

Such a liberalism espouses a concept of citizenship that has a significant communitarian dimension. De-Shalit holds that "environmental imperatives are basically matters of principle that cannot be bargained away in an economic fashion," and that "not all of us think of ourselves primarily as consumers; many of us regard ourselves as citizens as well."[27] He strongly rejects the putative value-neutrality of the kind of liberalism popularized by John Rawls, Bruce Ackerman, Ronald Dworkin, and other recent theorists. Rather, he believes that liberalism should be committed to a common "idea of the good" based on "a theory of value, that is, on the idea of an intrinsic, noninstrumental value."[28]

However, other recent liberal theorists have tried to construct a liberal environmentalism based on the principles of justice developed by Rawls in his landmark work *A Theory of Justice.*[29] Rawls's own recent restatement of his position in *Political Liberalism* gives little encouragement to those interested in moving his theory in a strongly ecological direction. He states, in fact, that his concept of justice as fairness does not offer guidance concerning obligations to other species and to "the rest of nature."[30] Later he notes that his principles would justify appeals to human survival, health, aesthetic, recreational, and intellectual needs, in the present and the future, on behalf of the protection of animals and the natural world. Beyond this we enter the realm of "natural religion," in which "public reason" can be of no assistance.[31]

Nevertheless, Brent A. Singer has attempted to develop a Rawlsian liberal environmentalism that goes beyond the limits prescribed by Rawls himself. He begins with an environmentally oriented reformulation of Rawls's "original position" in which hypothetical contracting agents determine the nature of just political institutions and social practices.[32] According to Rawls, there are certain primary goods that any rationally self-interested person will desire. Singer argues that among these goods will be "regular access to potable water, shelter from freezing temperatures, uncontaminated food supplies, and safe air to breathe."[33] Such goods, in Singer's view, are as fundamental as are political liberties such as free speech or the right to vote, in that they cannot rationally be traded for "social and economic privileges."[34] He contends further that Rawlsian assumptions require the consideration of future generations in an assessment of the need for these primary goods, in addition to a consideration of the interests of "many species of animals as well."[35] Finally, he argues that since many people consider "places of great natural beauty" to have spiritual value, a Rawlsian liberal argument can be made for preserving wilderness and various natural sites on grounds of "spiritual freedom" and "liberty of conscience," unless there are overriding considerations of justice.[36] Such an attempt to apply liberalism to environmental issues may have a somewhat more ecological dimension than the "free market" approaches they hope to correct, yet the concern for nature seems much closer to the "moral extensionism" of animal rights theories than the more thoroughgoing ecological viewpoints (as proposed by various "ecocentric," "holistic," "organicist," and "relational" theories).

It is noteworthy that while neither free market environmentalism nor liberalism has been at the center of theoretical discussion in political ecology, their basic assumptions remain dominant in most analyses of the political dimensions of environmental issues. Most analysts have assumed that some balance between the decision-making processes within a corporate capitalist market economy, planning and regulation by centralized nation-states, and agreements between such states is the context in which approaches to environmental issues and growing ecological crisis must be discussed. However, there are several tendencies in ecological thought that propose deeper changes in political and economic systems and a more radically ecological rethinking of political categories.

# SOCIALIST ECOLOGY

In recent years, a variety of ecosocialist theories have sought to demonstrate the relevance of Marxian theory to ecological issues, and a large body of theoretical work has emerged in the process.[37] Much of it can be found in the journal *Capitalism, Nature, Socialism,* which in over a decade of publication has become a major forum for the development of socialist ecology. In fact, its level of ongoing theoretical discussion of issues in political ecology is unsurpassed by any English-language publication dealing with such issues.

One of the most notable developments in ecosocialist theory is James O'Connor's application of Marx's analysis of conditions of production to environmental issues, and his resulting thesis that ecological crisis is "the second contradiction of capitalism." O'Connor explains that "red green politics" assumes that "the ecological crisis cannot be resolved without a radical transformation of capitalist production relationships" and that "economic crisis cannot be resolved without an equally radical transformation of capitalist productive forces."[38] Ecosocialists contend that global competition has led to the "externalization of social and environmental costs," which has resulted in a deterioration of environmental and labor conditions. Since these problems are widespread and overstep regional and national boundaries, they cannot be solved through action at the local level to the extent that many greens, bioregionalists, and social ecologists contend. Even seemingly local problems such as transportation, housing costs, and the drug trade are in fact "global issues pertaining to the way that money capital is allocated worldwide" and therefore require globally coordinated political action.[39] O'Connor concludes that "the only political form" that "might be eminently suited to both ecological problems of site specificity and global issues, is a democratic state—a state in which the administration of the division of social labor is democratically organized."[40]

John Bellamy Foster applies Barry Commoner's well-known "Four Laws of Ecology" to the Marxist critique of capitalism.[41] Commoner summarizes these principles as asserting that: (1) everything is connected to everything else; (2) everything must go somewhere; (3) nature knows best; and (4) nothing comes from nothing.[42] Foster argues that capitalism "breaks" all these "laws" and follows instead the principles that: "(1) the only lasting connection between things is the cash nexus; (2) it doesn't matter where something goes as long as it doesn't reenter the circuit of capital; (3) the self-regulating market knows best; and (4) nature's bounty is a free gift to the property owner."[43] In Foster's view, the basic rules of capitalist decision-making inevitably lead to ecological crisis. Under capitalism, the maintenance of a given level of profit requires constant growth, so that any measures to deal with ecological crisis will only contribute to economic crisis.[44] The only real solution to this problem is therefore "the socialization of nature," by which Foster means environmental protection through "centralized management . . . on a national scale," and, ultimately, a worldwide social revolution which achieves "the democratically organized social governance of both production and nature on a global scale."[45]

David Harvey has developed one of the most sophisticated versions of ecological Marxism to date.[46] Harvey notes that in a capitalistic money economy much of what is thought of as "the environment" is assigned a monetary value that has no necessary relationship to any other kind of value it may have. Monetary value becomes the only universal standard of value available, and is the one given most recognition by those who hold decision-making power. This dominance of monetary value does not result from its adequacy as a means of evaluation. It is generally agreed that many realities cannot be quantified in monetary terms, if by any means at all, and many people intuitively find the assessment of human life, species survival, or ancient ecosystems in monetary terms to be morally objectionable.

Harvey argues that the inappropriateness of economistic values becomes increasingly evident the more we consider realities that are complex wholes, rather than discrete entities. While monetary values can be attributed, however inadequately, to individual parts of an ecosystem, they can never correspond to ecological value, which is a function of the complex relationship between the various parts of the whole, and of the relation of all these parts to the whole. Harvey argues that economistic value also fails when we expand our evaluation over time. He contends that the economic practice of discounting the value of any goods that might exist in the future is irrational ecologically, since biologically essential natural goods are the precondition for the existence of any other kind of value, including the economic ones. Finally, he argues that the fundamental economistic conceptualization of "environmental consequences" as "externalities" is in basic contradiction to an ecological analysis, which looks upon natural processes as intrinsically interrelated parts of a whole.

Harvey focuses much more directly on the project of a radically dialectical approach than do most thinkers in the Marxist tradition, for whom issues of class, economic exploitation, ideology, social crisis, historical agency, and revolutionary social transformation often take theoretical priority. This emphasis gives Harvey's analysis a strongly ecological flavor that is missing in many versions of political ecology, whether socialist or not. As he points out, "[d]ialectical thinking prioritizes the understanding of processes, flows, fluxes and relations over the analysis of elements, things, structures and organised systems."[47] Ecological thinking gives priority to these same realities, and his efforts to make a connection between the two makes Harvey's approach one of the most successful attempts at ecologizing Marxism.

At the other end of the ecosocialist spectrum, David Pepper has presented an extensive defense of an ecosocialism that remains much closer in many ways to more traditional Marxism. Marxism is "ecological," in his view, precisely because of its completely anthropocentric concern for human welfare. It is because socialist economic growth "must be rational, planned development for everyone's benefit," that it must of necessity be "ecologically benign."[48] Pepper lays claim to the Enlightenment heritage of Marxism and rejects the "green postmodernist" critique of both anthropocentrism and the project of the domination of nature. Marxism, he says, rejects a "mastery" of nature that implies "subjection or destruction," but proposes a form of "domination" of nature that will in fact solve ecological problems. This "domination" consists of *"collective conscious control by humans of their relationship with nature"* and "implies stewardship rather than destruction."[49] For Pepper, it is not anthropocentrism but rather "short-term individualist anthropocentrism" that is ecologically destructive. Pepper espouses the traditional socialist commitment to centralized planning for implementing policies that are in the long-term interest of humanity, and he rejects decentralist solutions as naively utopian. He emphasizes the centrality of working-class organizations in the development of an ecosocialist movement, though he also sees an important role for such transitional steps as municipal socialism and local currency systems.[50]

While some ecosocialist thinkers such as Pepper seek to hold on to much of traditional Marxism while attempting to ecologize it, more strongly ecological socialisms continue to emerge.[51] With the collapse of "actually existing social-ism," Marxist and socialist ideas of praxis are in a state that one might see as either disarray or creative ferment. Accordingly, we find some ecosocialisms that look much like environmental liberalism or social democracy, others that propose radical decentralism and participatory democracy reminiscent of so-cial ecology, some that incorporate more traditional Marxist ideas in the con-cept of an ecologically responsible centralized workers' state, and still others that propose an eclectic "post-modern" socialism inspired by environmental-ism and other "new social movements."

# SOCIAL ECOLOGY

Social ecology also pursues a dialectical approach to ecopolitics. This ecophi-losophy comes out of the tradition of social geography and ecological region-alism of Elisée Reclus, Patrick Geddes, and Lewis Mumford; the libertarian communitarianism of Peter Kropotkin, Gustav Landauer, and Martin Buber, and the tradition of dialectical philosophy of Aristotle, Hegel, and Marx. It is also related to recent evolutionary and process philosophies, and to holistic and organismic traditions of both East and West.

Some have identified social ecology narrowly with the ideas of social the-orist Murray Bookchin,[52] while others use the term in a rather amorphous and generic sense. Thus, Carolyn Merchant, in *Radical Ecology*, subsumes under social ecology not only those who explicitly use the term, but also those who call themselves "socialist ecologists, green Marxists, and red greens."[53] Con-trary to both these views, there is a coherent social ecological tradition that is much larger than any one writer's ideas, but that is still quite distinct from most (but not all) socialist and Marxist views.

Social ecology applies an evolutionary, developmental view of history and a holistic conception of social unity-in-diversity to social and political is-sues. As a dialectic theory, it does not dissolve the parts into the whole (as var-ious forms of holism are regularly accused by critics of doing). Rather, it studies the mutual interaction between parts and wholes, while reducing nei-ther dimension to the other. Accordingly, social ecology as a social theory is concerned with the development in society of both individuality and commu-nity, so that each member can achieve personal self-realization while develop-ing a sense of identification with and responsibility toward the larger social whole. As an ecological social theory, it is concerned with the relationship between the flourishing of individual organisms, species, populations, and larger ecological wholes.

Social ecologists often stress the fact that politics is a branch of ethics, and that it has as its goal the pursuit of the self-realization of both the indi-vidual person and the larger community. Some social ecologists conceive of this project not only in relation to the various forms of human community in which we participate, but also incorporate into it the diverse ecological com-munities of which we are also members, up to the level of the entire biosphere or earth community. Critics have sometimes argued that social ecologists naively construct a view of ethics or politics on the model of what is found "in nature." But in fact it is often a much more sophisticated view that reinterprets ethics in the light of a holistic outlook and attempts to avoid a dualistic split between humanity and nature. A social ecology of value situates human processes of self-realization and value-experience within a wider context of self-realization, experience of value, and attainment of good. When social ecology is consistent, it holds that there is no purely external nature that could serve as a model for human activity or social organization, since not only are both the person and society themselves "nature," but looked at dialectically, even what we might see as their "internal nature" is itself an expression of "external nature."

A central concern of social ecological theory is the critique of all forms of domination that hinder the evolutionary processes of human and planetary self-realization. The objects of this critique include the centralized nation-state, concentrated economic power, patriarchy, the technological megamachine, and various authoritarian and repressive ideologies. While social ecologists hold that there is a *system* of domination in which various hierarchical and authoritarian institutions interact, they find some of these to be more central to the social and ecological crisis than others. They usually see the dominance of economic power as the most powerful determinant of both social injustice and ecological crisis in our present historical epoch. Moreover, they find this power to be embodied in a vast economic and technological machine (globalized corporate capital), and in an all-pervasive, nihilistic culture of consumption.

The political goal of social ecology is the creation of a free, communitarian society in harmony with the natural world. The means to this end are, however, vigorously debated. The politics of social ecology has sometimes been equated with Murray Bookchin's "libertarian municipalism," which aims at creating a movement to establish municipalities governed by sovereign municipal or neighborhood assemblies. According to this viewpoint, the municipalities are to remain politically sovereign, but will form voluntary "confederations" to organize themselves politically and economically beyond the local level. In Bookchin's view, these confederations will eventually create a condition of "dual power" in which they will be able to challenge the power of the nation-state and the global corporate economic power with which it is allied. A system of libertarian communism, in which distribution will be according to need, will then be established. Private ownership of the means of production will be abolished and replaced by community-controlled enterprises. Hierarchical social institutions, including patriarchy, will be destroyed and the quest for human domination of nature will come to an end.

Although most social ecologists are strong advocates of decentralized direct democracy, some question libertarian municipalism as both an effective practical politics and as an adequate vision of a future society.[54] Rather, they incorporate proposals similar to Bookchin's municipalism into a broader ecological communitarianism. There is general agreement among social ecologists that there must be a radical decentralization of political power away from the centralized state and of economic power away from large corporations, and that more human-scale technologies are essential both socially and ecologically. However, many support a variety of social, political, and economic strategies as a means of working toward a free, ecological society. Social ecologists are often interested in creating and promoting producer and consumer cooperatives, land trusts and housing cooperatives, ecological agriculture, ecologically sound technologies, municipal citizens' movements, Green political parties, environmental justice groups, environmental defense alliances, cultural and educational projects, ecologically oriented labor organizations, bioregional groups, and many other efforts aimed at social and ecological regeneration.

Social ecologists often take a comprehensive, theoretically grounded but experimental approach to social transformation. They base their efforts on the needs and interests of local communities, the possibilities for social creativity that exist in historically determinate situations, and the relationship between such diverse particularity and the evolving global society. Such a nondogmatic, experimental social ecology takes as the measure of its success the organic growth of a compassionate, cooperative, ecological culture, rooted in the specificity of history and place, but developing growing interconnections within the entire earth community.

Over the past decade, social ecology has gained some notoriety through Murray Bookchin's often bitter attacks on other philosophical positions, including, most notably, deep ecology, but also ecofeminism and ecosocialism, and more recently bioregionalism, ecocommunitarianism, and various competing forms of ecoanarchism. Bookchin gained some attention for his views through his claims of links between deep ecology and racist and politically reactionary ideas.[55] His argument was based primarily on statements made by several deep ecologists supporting withholding of aid to famine victims, opposing immigration on both ecological and cultural grounds, and holding that AIDS and other diseases were a natural process of controlling human overpopulation. Ironically, Bookchin's attacks have been directed at theorists of deep ecology in general, although very few of them support any of the views he attributes to them, rather than thinkers such as Garrett Hardin, who is well known for his essays opposing immigration and aid to famine victims, and who has proposed a world government with powers to control population.[56]

The major substantive political divergence between social and deep ecologists has not stemmed from the supposed ecofascist tendencies of the latter, which is at most a marginal phenomenon. Rather, it can be traced to the fact that most social ecologists have engaged in the systematic analysis of social institutions and their relationship to ecological problems and have been committed to a radical decentralist, antistate and anticapitalist politics. On the other hand, many deep ecologists have devoted little attention to social analysis, and others have adopted a spectrum of political positions, ranging from a rather apolitical emphasis on the need for changes in personal values and "lifestyle," to a liberal reformist politics, and even to a revolutionary opposition to the megamachine that aims at the overthrow of industrial civilization.

Recently, an increasing number of deep ecologists have begun to undertake a deeper analysis of social and political issues, as exhibited in the work of theorists such as Robyn Eckersley and Andrew McLaughlin, and the theoretical gap between social and deep ecology has narrowed considerably.[57] In addition, nondogmatic social and deep ecologists have begun to discuss their commonalities and useful dialogue has begun to replace sectarian quarreling.[58] The existence of such common ground is indicated by the emergence of a "left biocentrism" that combines a theoretical commitment to deep ecology with a radical decentralist, anticapitalist politics having much in common with social ecology.[59]

# ECOFEMINISM

Ecofeminism has emerged as one of the most sophisticated and creative political ecologies. Karen Warren notes that ecofeminism has always been a grassroots political movement with concerns such as issues of women's health, science, development, and technology, the treatment of animals, and peace and antinuclear, antimilitarist activism.[60] In recent years, ecofeminism has become even more highly politicized. Nevertheless, ecofeminist theory (or at least the Anglo-American varieties that have received the most attention) has been thought of as focusing primarily either on conceptual issues such as the link between patriarchy and the domination of nature, or as emphasizing issues of personal life, values, and spirituality. Social and political theory has not been recognized as a major strength of the movement. Nevertheless, impressive advances in these areas have been made within ecofeminist thought, particularly as it has confronted globalization and theorized the central position of women in the world economy. Two notable examples of such advances are the work of Indian ecofeminist Vandana Shiva and Australian ecofeminist Ariel Salleh.[61]

Shiva is one of the world's most important theoretical critics of development and globalization. She sees the dominant forms of development as a continuation of the project of domination of the "other" (nature, woman, indigenous peoples, subordinate classes) that spans the history of patriarchal, hierarchical civilization. More specifically, development is seen as a transformation of colonialism. While classical colonialism was carried out by the dominant powers through military conquest and occupation, bureaucratic administration, and ruthless industrial exploitation, neocolonial development achieves many of the same goals by means of national elites and more powerful and advanced technologies. And despite its use of nationalist ideology, it continues the colonialist project of annihilation of traditional culture and methods of production. As Shiva points out, the existence of "production" is recognized only "when mediated by technologies for commodity production."[62]

Such development, according to Shiva, presupposes the reduction of both women and nature as passive objects acted upon by economic and technological forces. This reduction does not take place merely in the realm of ideas and values; it encompasses a material practice of pacification and disempowerment of women. While the conventional wisdom holds that women are more oppressed in traditional societies, and that Westernization and technological and economic development improve their position in many ways, Shiva argues that the reverse is usually the case. Traditional subsistence production accepts "the interdependence and complementarity of the separate male and female domains of work,"[63] while development marginalizes women, reduces their status and that of their labor, and increases male dominance.

Moreover, so-called technological advances impose ecological costs that disproportionately affect women, and that are not recognized in official indicators. There is "less water, less fertile soil, less genetic wealth as a result of the development process. Since these natural resources are the basis of nature's economy and woman's survival economy, their scarcity is impoverishing women and marginalized peoples in an unprecedented manner."[64] A superb case study of the details of these processes from an implicitly ecofeminist perspective is presented in Helena Norberg-Hodge's analysis of the transformation of Ladakhi society in *Ancient Futures: Learning from Ladakh.*[65]

Ariel Salleh's work also makes a major contribution to ecofeminist political ecology. Salleh seeks a material basis for ecofeminist politics in the real-world, historically situated condition of women. Her dialectical analysis takes into account the complex interplay between biological, psychological, historical, and cultural factors, while avoiding one-sided essentialist and reductionist explanations. For Salleh, "[t]he case for women as historical actors in a time of environmental crisis rests not on universal essences but on how the majority of women actually work and think now."[66]

Salleh's analysis focuses on the magnitude of women's work, the nature of that work, and the level of exploitation of women's labor globally. Marxist analyses have usually had a rather generalized, economic, class-based conception of exploitation. Other leftist positions have substituted for exploitation rather vague conceptions of "domination" that are also inadequate. In neither case has the sexual politics of exploitation been given adequate attention. Salleh points out that "on an international scale, women, undertaking 65 percent of the world's work for 5 percent of its pay, effectively are 'the proletariat.'"[67]

At least as significant as this striking fact is the qualitative dimension of women's labor as it relates to the concept of care. For Salleh, care involves an openness to its objects and to the web of relationships in which those objects exist and which constitute them. She cites Sara Ruddick's concept of "holding" as being of particular relevance to ecopolitics. "Holding" is associated with efforts "to minimize risk and to reconcile differences rather than to sharply accentuate them," with "maintaining the minimal harmony, material resources, and skills necessary for sustaining a child in safety," and (in Ruddick's words) with processes of "world protection, world-preservation, world repair . . . the invisible weaving of a frayed and threadbare family life."[68] Salleh sees much of women's labor, both inside and outside the home, as having such aims. The concept of "holding labor" deepens the "ethics of care" into an ecopolitics of care by giving it a material basis in the life-activities of women throughout the world.

Salleh points out that empirical evidence from social change movements around the world indicates that women's caring sensibility and caring labor are a powerful force for the defense of human communities and nature. Women have played a central (and often a predominant) role in environmental justice movements in both the industrialized North and the nonindustrial South. There is often evident in their activities deep commitment, tireless energy, and political passion that arise not merely from abstract ideology but rather from profound, complex, experiential relationships to specific persons and places.

## BIOREGIONALISM

"Bioregionalism," like ecofeminism, is one of the tendencies in political ecology that has gone furthest in taking account of the ecological in the most concrete sense. Bioregionalism focuses on the process of "reinhabitation": the creation of a culture and way of life based on a very specific, detailed knowledge of the ecological realities of the larger natural community in which the human community participates.[69] Furthermore, it explores forms of governance based on such a bioregional consciousness. It calls into question the primacy of the nation-state and political boundaries on the one hand, and the homogenizing culture of consumption on the other. Its vision of social transformation does not appeal to any abstract principles of rights or justice, or contentious ideas of individual or group interest. Rather, it is rooted in realities that are very concrete and experiential and which might form a strong basis for an ecologically sound culture and way of life.

For two decades there has been in North America an organized bioregional movement advocating the rediscovery of a sense of place (reinhabitation), the rooting of culture in the particularities of natural regions, and the development of social and political institutions reflecting bioregional realities. The term "bioregionalism" was first used to describe such an approach by Peter Berg and Raymond Dasmann of the Planet Drum Foundation in San Francisco.[70] That organization's journal, *Raise the Stakes,* has been the most important ongoing arena for discussion of bioregional ideas. In addition, a series of semiannual Turtle Island (North American) Bioregional congresses have contributed to the movement's growing cultural and political significance.

Donald Alexander, in "Bioregionalism: Science or Sensibility?" argues that there is a need to overcome the split between those who see bioregionalism, sometimes rather reductively, as a science, and those who see it primarily "as an environmental ethic and as a cultural sensibility."[71] Alexander sees

Lewis Mumford as the inspiration for a bioregionalism that combines these two aspects in a "dialectical manner." He recommends Mumford's view of the region as "a complex of geographic, economic, and cultural elements. Not found as a finished product in nature, not solely the creation of human will and fantasy, the region, like its corresponding artifact, the city, is a collective work of art."[72]

It is true that Mumford's ecological regionalism, with its sweeping historical vision and broadly synthesizing scope has much to offer to the bioregional perspective. However, the kind of regional vision that Mumford expresses is already present to a considerable degree within the bioregional tradition. The work of poet and essayist Gary Snyder, the major intellectual influence on the bioregional movement, expresses just such a rich conception of natural and cultural regions.[73] Synder encourages us to learn from the wisdom of "peoples for whom there is no great dichotomy between their culture and nature," and for whom "[t]o be well educated is to have learned the songs, proverbs, stories, sayings, myths (and technologies) that come with [an] experiencing of the nonhuman members of the local ecological community."[74] Bioregional reinhabitation means becoming part of such a culture of nature rooted in a specific place.

Snyder does not spell out the political implications of his regionalism in a programmatic manner; however, a strong political critique is implicit in it. For Snyder, it is wild nature and organically rooted local and regional culture that are the source of ecological and social order. On the other hand, "it is the State itself which is inherently greedy, destabilizing, entropic, disorderly, and illegitimate," so that the political question becomes "how the whole human race can regain self-determination in place after centuries of having been disenfranchised by hierarchy and/or centralized power."[75]

Some bioregional theorists have sought to draw out the more explicit political implications of the outlook expressed by Snyder. For example, Kirkpatrick Sale discusses a "bioregional paradigm" that challenges the dominant "industrio-scientific" one in every important area, including its conception of the "polity." While the dominant paradigm emphasizes "centralization, hierarchy, and uniformity," bioregionalism espouses a politics of "decentralization, complementarity, and diversity."[76]

Sale's conception of bioregional political institutions is in many ways very similar to that of social ecologist Murray Bookchin (despite harsh attacks on Sale by Bookchin and his colleague Janet Biehl). Sale states that bioregionalism rejects social hierarchy and domination as "unecological," and proposes an egalitarian, decentralized form of social organization. Such an approach would include community ownership of productive enterprises and decision-making at the local level, with local units ranging from villages of perhaps one thousand people up to larger towns and neighborhoods of five to ten thousand inhabitants.

Bioregional politics is to be based on informal decision-making by those with competence and experience, the election of a small number of community officials, and the retention of ultimate power by the whole body of citizens.[77] Cooperation on a larger scale would be achieved through voluntary confederations, the boundaries of which would be determined bioregionally.[78] Sale foresees the persistence of some monetary market exchange between communities, although barter and cooperative sharing would become increasingly important among bioregional communities. The monopolistic dominance of the exchange economy would be broken.

Sale does not present any detailed picture of how such a decentralized cooperative economy might operate. He assumes, however, that bioregionalism would require a decentralization not only of political and economic power, but also of population. He advocates the voluntary resettlement of the urban population into ecologically balanced cities of much smaller scale than at present.[79] He contends that "division" is "nature's way" of achieving "salubrity and balance,"[80] and that a decentralized, democratic, bioregionally based society would be the social equivalent of a thriving, health ecosystem.

# NOTES

1. For a survey of this phenomenon, see Jim Schwab, *Deeper Shades of Green: The Rise of Blue-Collar and Minority Environmentalism in America* (San Francisco: Sierra Club Books, 1994). On environmental justice issues, see Robert Bullard, ed. *Unequal Protection* (San Francisco: Sierra Club Books, 1994) and Laura Westra and Peter Wenz, *Faces of Environmental Racism* (Totowa, NJ: Rowman and Littlefield, 1995).

2. See Dan Coleman, *Ecopolitics: Building a Green Society* (New Brunswick, NJ: Rutgers University Press, 1994), Peter Dickens, *Society and Nature: Toward a Green Social Theory* (London: Harvester Wheatsheaf, 1992), Andrew Dobson, *Green Political Thought* (London: HarperCollins, 1991), Robert Goodin, *Green Political Theory* (Oxford: Polity Press, 1992), Roy Morrison, *Ecological Democracy* (Boston: South End Press, 1995), and Brian Tokar, *The Green Alternative: Creating an Ecological Future* (Philadelphia: New Society, 1992).

3. See Tom Athanasiou, *Divided Planet: The Ecology of Rich and Poor* (Boston: Little, Brown, 1996); Joshua Karliner, *The Corporate Planet: Ecology and Politics in the Age of Globalization* (San Francisco: Sierra Club Books, 1997); and David C. Korten, *When Corporations Rule the World* (West Harford, CT and San Francisco: Kumarion Press and Berrett-Koehler Publishers, 1995), especially chap. 21, "The Ecological Revolution." See also Lisa H. Newton and Catherine K. Dillingham, *Watersheds 2: Ten Cases in Environmental Ethics* (Belmont, CA: Wadsworth, 1997), which shows how such developments are reflected in contemporary environmental ethics debates.

4. The order of the selections indicates, in general, a spectrum of approaches ranging from the more conservative to the more radical, in political terms, and from the more anthropocentric to the more ecological, in terms of ontology and axiology. However, in view of the complexities and even internal tensions found in various theories, the idea of a spectrum should not be taken in too literal a sense.

5. Terry L. Anderson and Donald R. Leal, *Free Market Environmentalism* (San Francisco: Pacific Research Institute for Public Policy, 1991), p. 2.

6. See Julian L. Simon, *The Ultimate Resource* (Princeton, NJ: Princeton University Press, 1981), especially the widely reprinted third chapter, "Can the Supply of Natural Resources Really Be Infinite? Yes!"

7. Anderson and Leal, *Free Market Environmentalism*, p. 166.

8. See Gus DiZerega, "Empathy, Society, Nature, and the Relational Self: Deep Ecology and Liberal Modernity" in *Social Theory and Practice* 21 (1995): 239–269.

9. Ibid., p. 264.

10. Ibid., pp. 265–266.

11. There is a sizable literature on this topic, going back to such classic works as Clinton Rossiter's *Conservatism in America: The Thankless Persuasion* (New York: Random House, 1962) and Frank Meyer's anthology, *What Is Conservatism?* (New York: Holt, Rinehart & Winston, 1964). John R. E. Bliese invokes two of the most important intellectual figures in American traditionalist conservatism, Richard Weaver and Russell Kirk, in addition to John Grey, a contemporary British political theorist, on behalf of a conservative environmentalism. See his discussion of "Traditionalist Political Philosophy" in "Traditionalist Conservatism and Environmental Ethics," in *Environmental Ethics* 19 (1997): 139–147.

12. See especially Russell Kirk, *The Conservative Mind: From Blake to Eliot,* third revised edition (Chicago: Henry Regnery, 1960).

13. Bliese, p. 139.

14. Ibid., p. 141. It should be noted that the traditionalist conservative definition of "ideology" is unusual, for it connotes neither a system of ideas that motivates social action, as in the usual social scientific definition, nor a form of false consciousness that legitimates a system of power, as the term is often used in political theory. Rather, it refers to "attempts to refashion society after abstract notions" as Bliese states it in rather Burkean terminology. Needless to say, traditionalist conservatism itself turns out to be nonideological in such terms, though the "free market" variety is reproached (as is the Left) for its tendency to succumb to the ideology of progress and materialism.

15. Ibid., p. 144.

16. Ibid., p. 147.

17. Ibid., p. 148.

18. Ibid., p. 147. However, most traditional communities (especially hunting and gathering societies, but also many later peasant societies) depended neither on market mechanisms nor on state control to achieve a balanced relationship with the natural world. Yet the traditionalist Bliese seems to find no inspiration in approaches that preceded those of both the modern market economy and the modern nation-state.

19. Paul Hawken, *The Ecology of Commerce: A Declaration of Sustainability* (New York: Harper-Business, 1993), p. 82.

20. Ibid., p. 68.

21. Paul Hawken, "A Declaration of Sustainability," in *Utne Reader* #59 (Sept./Oct. 1993): 57.

22. It is not clear how Hawken's desire for minimal regulatory activity can be reconciled with such a proposal.

23. See the annual editions of *State of the World* (New York: W. W. Norton, 1984–present). Robert C. Paehlke's analysis of the possibilities for a "progressive environmentalism" is typical of a somewhat greener, less bureaucratic version of liberalism that has increasingly been adopted by environmentalists. See Robert C. Paehlke, *Environmentalism And the Future of Progressive Politics* (New Haven, CT: Yale University Press, 1989), especially his "core priorities for a contemporary environmental progressivism" (pp. 270–272), and his list of ways that environmentalists can be distinguished from "neo-conservatives" and "traditional progressives" (pp. 276–277). Paehlke identifies himself as a "moderate social democrat" (p. 311) a term that is much clearer than "liberal," in view of the contemporary use of that term and the term "neo-liberal" to refer to positions defending market expansionism and corporate interests.

24. Avner de-Shalit, "Is Liberalism Environment-Friendly?" in *Social Theory and Practice* 21 (1995): 287–314.

25. Ibid., p. 289.

26. Ibid., p. 301.

27. Ibid., p. 306.

28. Ibid., p. 307.

29. John Rawls, *A Theory of Justice* (Cambridge, MA: Harvard University Press, 1971).

30. John Rawls, *Political Liberalism* (New York: Columbia University Press, 1993), p. 21.

31. Ibid., pp. 245–246.

32. Brent A. Singer, "An Extension of Rawls' Theory of Justice to Environmental Ethics" in *Environmental Ethics* 10 (1988): 217–231. See also Marcel Wissenberg, *Green Liberalism: The Free and the Green Society* (London: University College London Press, 1998), pp. 76–80, 127–136, and 173–174, for an attempt to apply Rawls' "savings principle" to the question of sustainability. Wissenberg's approach is forthrightly anthropocentric and methodologically individualist and shows no evidence of any theoretical accommodation with ecological

thought. As is typical in contemporary liberal thought, he rejects the idea that there can be any intrinsic good independent of human valuation (p. 97) and holds that "there is no higher standard of the good than that of the individuals' plans of life" (p. 98).

33. Singer, p. 219.

34. Ibid.

35. On future generations, see Singer, p. 220. Singer argues interestingly that the original contractors would have to consider the possibility that they might be embodied as "anencephalic children, Tay-Sachs children, and serious psychotics," and that if so "it is arbitrary to insist that they cannot turn out to be healthy pandas, llamas, seals, whales, lions, horses, gorillas, otters, or any other animal with interests" (p. 223).

36. Ibid., p. 230.

37. For defenses of the ecological nature of Marx's own thought, see Howard L. Parson's, ed., *Marx and Engels on Ecology* (Westport, CT: Greenwood Press, 1977), and Donald C. Lee, "On the Marxian View of the Relationship Between Man and Nature," in *Environmental Ethics* 2 (1980): 3–16. For critiques of this view, see Val Routley [Plumwood], "On Karl Marx as Environmental Hero" in *Environmental Ethics* 3 (1981): 237–244, and John Clark, "Marx's Inorganic Body" in *Environmental Ethics* 11 (1989): 243–258. Many eco-Marxists now recognize the problematical character of Marx's concept of nature and are attempting to develop a more consistently dialectical view.

38. James O'Connor, "Socialism and Ecology," in *Capitalism Nature Socialism* 2 (1991): 1. See also O'Connor's essay "Capitalism, Nature, Socialism: A Theoretical Introduction" in *Capitalism, Nature, Socialism* 1 (1988): 11–38, and his collection *Natural Causes: Essays in Ecological Marxism* (New York: Guilford Press, 1998).

39. O'Connor, "Socialism and Ecology," in *Natural Causes,* p. 274.

40. Ibid., p. 277.

41. John Bellamy Foster, *The Vulnerable Planet: A Short Economic History of the Environment* (New York: Monthly Review Press, 1995).

42. Barry Commoner, *The Closing Circle: Nature, Man and Technology* (New York: Knopf, 1971), pp. 33–46.

43. Foster, *The Vulnerable Planet,* p. 120.

44. Ibid., p. 133.

45. Ibid., p. 142.

46. David Harvey, "The Nature of Environment: The Dialectics of Social and Environmental Change" in Ralph Miliband and Leo Panich, eds. *Real Problems, False Solutions: Socialist Register* 1993 (London: Merlin Press, 1993).

47. Ibid., p. 34.

48. David Pepper, *Ecosocialism: From Deep Ecology to Social Justice* (London: Routledge, 1993), p. 219.

49. Ibid., p. 221, italics in the original.

50. Ibid., pp. 222, 229–231.

51. Robyn Eckersley explores the possibility of a convergence between deep ecology and ecosocialism in "The Political Challenge of Left-Green Reconciliation" in *Capitalism, Nature, Socialism* 6 (1995): 24. A theoretical development of considerable importance is Joel Kovel's synthesis of ecosocialism with aspects of psychoanalytic theory, existential and phenomenological philosophy, social ecology, and spiritual traditions of East and West. See *History and Spirit: An Inquiry into the Philosophy of Liberation* (Boston: Beacon Press, 1991) and "Ecological Marxism and Dialectic" in *Capitalism, Nature, Socialism* 6 (1995): 31–50. See also Ted Benton, ed., *The Greening of Marxism* (New York: Guilford Press, 1996) for a spectrum of ecosocialist approaches, including Eckersley's essay, "Socialism and Ecocentrism: Toward a New Synthesis."

52. See Peter List, *Radical Environmentalism: Philosophy and Tactics* (Belmont, CA: Wadsworth, 1993), p. 11.

53. Carolyn Merchant, *Radical Ecology: The Search for a Livable World* (New York: Routledge, 1992), p. 134.

54. In fact, criticism of Bookchin from within social ecology has extended not only to his politics but to many aspects of his "dialectical naturalism," which, according to critics, has become an increasingly rigid and nondialectical. For social ecological critiques of Bookchin's ideas, see David Watson, *Beyond Bookchin: Preface for a Future Social Ecology* (Brooklyn, NY: Autonomedia, 1996), Andrew Light, ed., *Social Ecology After Bookchin* (New

York: Guilford Press, 1998) and "The Matter of Freedom: Some Ecofeminist Lessons for Social Ecology," below.

55. See, for example, Bookchin's "Social Ecology Versus Deep Ecology" in *Socialist Review* 88 (1988): 11–29.

56. See Garrett Hardin, "The Tragedy of the Commons" in *Science*, Vol. 162 (Dec. 1968): 1243–1248 and "Living on a Lifeboat" (one of the most frequently reprinted articles in current applied ethics texts) in *Bioscience* 24 (1974): 561–568. For a careful response to what might be seen as ecofascist tendencies in recent ecological thought, see Michael E. Zimmerman, "The Threat of Ecofascism" in *Social Theory and Practice* 21 (1995): 207–238.

57. See Robyn Eckersley, *Environmentalism and Political Theory* (Albany, NY: SUNY Press, 1992), and Andrew McLaughlin, *Regarding Nature: Industrialism and Deep Ecology* (Albany, NY: SUNY Press, 1993).

58. See Joel Kovel, "The Marriage of Radical Ecologies" in Michael Zimmerman, et al. *Environmental Philosphy: From Animal Rights to Radical Ecology,* first edition (Englewood Cliffs, NJ: Prentice Hall, 1993), pp. 406–417; George Bradford, "Toward a Deep Social Ecology" in Ibid., pp. 418–437; and John Clark, "How Wide is Deep Ecology?" in *Inquiry* 39 (June 1996): 189–201.

59. The Green Web Bulletins of the left biocentrists and a "Primer of Left Biocentrism" can be found on Green Web at <*http://fox.nstn.ca/~greenweb/index.htm*>.

60. See Karen Warren, "Introduction" to "Part Three: Ecofeminism," above, pp. 281–283.

61. In addition to the works cited below, see also the articles in the section of this text on ecofeminism, which are relevant to its contribution to political ecology.

62. Vandana Shiva, *Staying Alive: Women, Ecology and Development* (London: Zed Books, 1989), p. 4.

63. Ibid., p. 5.

64. Ibid., p. 13.

65. Helena Norberg-Hodge, *Ancient Futures: Learning from Ladakh* (San Francisco: Sierra Club Books, 1991). There is also a video with the same title that is based on the book and produced by the International Society for Ecology and Culture (Bristol, UK: ISEC, 1993).

66. Salleh, Ariel. *Ecofeminism As Politics: Nature, Marx and the Postmodern* (London and New York: Zed Books, 1997), p. 6.

67. Ibid.

68. Ibid., p. 144. See Sara Ruddick, *Maternal Thinking: Toward a Politics of Peace* (Boston: Beacon Press, 1989).

69. For a good sample of bioregional writings, see C. Plant et al., *Home! A Bioregional Reader* (Philadelphia: New Society, 1990).

70. See Peter Berg, ed. *Reinhabiting A Separate Country: A Bioregional Anthology of Northern California* (San Francisco: Planet Drum Foundation, 1978).

71. Donald Alexander, "Bioregionalism: Science or Sensibility?" in *Environmental Ethics* 12 (1990): 164.

72. Ibid., p. 172.

73. Snyder's work plays a very important role in contemporary ecophilosophy and political ecology. While he is a major figure in bioregionalism, he has also had enormous influence on many deep and social ecologists. His broad ecological vision, his exploration of the complex interconnections between nature and culture, his critique of centralized power, and his synthesis of Eastern, Western and indigenous traditions help one find the common ground in ecophilosophy.

74. Gary Snyder, *The Practice of the Wild* (San Francisco: North Point Press, 1990), p. 18.

75. Ibid., pp. 41–43.

76. Kirkpatrick Sale, *Dwellers in the Land: The Bioregional Vision* (San Francisco: Sierra Club Books, 1985), p. 50.

77. Ibid., p. 94.

78. Ibid., p. 96.

79. Ibid., p. 116.

80. Ibid., p. 127.

# FREE MARKET VERSUS POLITICAL ENVIRONMENTALISM

*Terry L. Anderson and Donald R. Leal*

Terry L. Anderson is executive director for the Political Economy Research Center (PERC) in Bozeman, Montana. David R. Leal is a senior associate at PERC.

In the West it is often said, "Whiskey is for drinkin' and water is for fightin'." These words ring loud and clear when environmental and other demands compete with agricultural needs for water. Fortunately, market-based solutions represent an alternative to this prescription and a possible solution to broader problems of water resource allocation.

A recent incident on Montana's Ruby River illustrates part of the difficulty with present approaches to water resource management. By May of 1987, minimal snowpack, little spring rain, and a heavy demand for irrigation had reduced a 1.5 mile section of the Ruby to a trickle. Hundreds of trout were stranded in overheated pools.[1] Sadly, as fish were dying in the Ruby River, six inches of water was standing in nearby fields, where it was of little or no use. This water could have kept the Ruby flowing and the fish alive if it had been transferred from irrigation to instream flows. Montana's Department of Natural Resources and Conservation and the irrigators eventually agreed to get water flowing again in the Ruby. Unfortunately, the effort was too little and too late to save many of the trout.

Because of the urgency of the situation, legal action would have been largely futile. An alternative would have been to lease from the irrigators some of the water that they were diverting from the river. It would have been relatively easy and inexpensive for a private conservation group like Trout Unlimited to lease the water from irrigators and transfer it to instream flows. Indeed, the amount of water needed to keep the fish alive could have been

This essay originally appeared in the *Harvard Journal of Law and Public Policy*, 15, 2 (Spring 1992), 297–310. Reprinted with permission.

rented for less than $4,000.[2] With an annual budget of several million dollars, Trout Unlimited could have purchased the water if it had been permitted to do so.[3] Herein lies the problem. At the time of the incident, legitimate use of the water required diversion. Under western water law, private parties were not permitted to use water for instream purposes, except for hydroelectric power generation.[4] Today, the good news is that water marketing is becoming increasingly acceptable in the West. In 1989, conservation groups sought legislation in Montana that would allow water to be purchased or leased from appropriators on a "willing buyer, willing seller" basis. While the groups failed to convince legislators to allow private parties to engage in such transactions, new legislation does allow the Department of Fish, Wildlife, and Parks to experiment with water leasing to enhance instream flows. Colorado, Utah, and Arizona permit private and public entities to acquire existing consumptive rights to augment instream flows.[5]

The market for federal water is also expanding, although much remains to be done.[6] The U.S. Department of Interior in 1987 adopted a policy in support of voluntary transfers of reclamation water, including water markets.[7] Without the typical restrictions on end-use and location, the markets for federal water will ensure correct water prices, thereby promoting greater efficiency and conservation.[8]

Support for water marketing has increased substantially over the last decade, with some of the strongest support coming from environmental groups like the Environmental Defense Fund (EDF). EDF's economist Zach Willey and others have endorsed water markets as a key step in reforming water policy.[9] Even Sandra Postel of Worldwatch Institute, a group not noted for its support of free market environmentalism, has suggested that water markets offer a "promising remedy."[10]

## I. "BLISS POINT" ECONOMICS

Despite the growing acceptance of water markets, some environmental officials have failed to embrace the idea. A recent statement by South Africa's Department of Water Affairs (DWA) is one example of this reluctance:

> With the increasing scarcity of water, the hierarchy of priorities for allocation must be further refined by means of appropriate benefit-cost and other economic studies. Within the requirements of contributing to the quality of life, the allocation of water must be based on the economic interests and the social demands of the country as a whole. The optimal utilization of resources, balanced growth and the minimal disruption of the economy are the most important criteria in this regard. . . . The DWA does, however, endeavour to provide for all rightful and reasonable demands within a particular catchment area before considering exports to other areas. The fairness of demands within catchment areas will, however, always be weighed against national requirements.[11]

This analytic approach is rooted in "scientific management," an economic paradigm that stresses marginal analysis by dispassionate "experts," who measure the benefits and costs of alternative allocations with the goal of maximizing social welfare.[12] The paradigm does not consider parties' intentions or the costs of information. Instead, it assumes that benefits and costs are known, and that the process of decisionmaking is simple, if one uses the appropriate model to reach the desired "bliss point" for society.

This same paradigm emphasizes the potential for market failure. In the dominant economics textbook used during the 1960s and the 1970s, Paul Samuelson states:

> Wherever there are externalities, a strong case can be made for supplanting complete individualism by some kind of group action. . . . The reader can think of countless . . . externalities where economics would suggest some kind of limitations on individual freedom in the interest of all.[13]

The emphasis on externalities "contains an implicit bias toward 'intervention solutions' for externalities in the form of taxes, subsidies, regulations, and prohibitions" because it suggests "that externalities necessitate 'corrective' government action."[14]

This emphasis on corrective action often explicitly assumes that governmental decisions will maximize social welfare. In a resource economics textbook, Hartwick and Olewiler write: "'[T]he government' is a separate agent acting in the social interest when activity by individuals fails to bring about a social optimum. . . [W]e discuss some limits of this approach, but it permits us to abstract from the details of the political process."[15] By abstracting from the details of the political process, however, they ignore the incentives inherent in that process. Because politicians and bureaucrats are rewarded for responding to political pressure groups, there is no guarantee that the values of unorganized interests will be taken into account. Daniel Bromley claims that governmental agencies are

> politically responsible to the citizenry through . . . elections and ministerial direction. However imperfectly this may work, the presumption must be that the wishes of the full citizenry are more properly catered to than would be the case if all environmental protection were left to the ability to pay by a few members of society given to philanthropy.[16]

Compare, however, the factors that influence the relationship between policymakers and bureaucrats with those that influence the relationship between policymakers and voters. First, with most issues, voters face relatively high information costs, creating the phenomenon of "rational ignorance." Second, the only exceptions to this general rule are issues that directly concern the voter. For example, the average urban dweller will likely know more about mass transit issues than agricultural matters. Third, those who are directly affected by policies often find it in their interest to spend time and money trying to influence decision making in the political arena. Thus, because the costs of policies are often diffused and the benefits concentrated, special interest groups (that is, people whose interests are directly affected by a policy) will be well organized and highly influential in the political arena. Those who have only an indirect or perhaps no interest at stake will remain largely indifferent. This rational indifference and the special interest groups combine to undermine the presumption that in the political arena the full citizenry are more properly catered to by intervention than by market-based incentives.

Government decisionmakers do not necessarily have access to the full information required to maximize society's welfare. As F. A. Hayek has pointed out,

> [T]he economic problem of society is . . . not merely a problem of how to allocate "given" resources—if "given" is taken to mean given to a single mind which deliberately solves the problem set by these "data." It is rather a problem of how to secure the best use of resources known to any of the members of society, for ends whose relative importance only those individuals know. Or, to put it briefly, it is a problem of the utilization of knowledge not given to anyone in its totality.[17]

Assessing the government's "corrective ability" requires only that we examine the record of bureaucratic control of land and water resources in this country. Millions of acres that the U.S. Forest Service manages are denuded of trees at tremendous expense to the environment and to the taxpayer. In Alaska's Tongass National Forest, for example, the federal government spends 98 cents for every 2 cents worth of timber harvested.[18] Another example is water policy. The Bureau of Reclamation built huge dams, flooding vast tracts of land, and delivered the water to farms growing mostly subsidized products. Prices charged for the water seldom cover even the incremental cost of delivering the water, let alone the capital or environmental costs associated with the project. As a result, farmers demand more and more water to produce surplus crops.[19]

Government is not infallible. It is clear, as Castle writes, that "[m]arket 'failure' in some abstract sense does not mean that a nonmarket [*sic*] alternative will not also fail in the same or in some other abstract sense."[20]

## II. FREE MARKET ENVIRONMENTALISM

Free market environmentalism considers the potential for market solutions and the problems with political ones. Anthony Fisher summarizes the change in emphasis:

> We have already abandoned the assumption of a complete set of competitive markets. . . . But if we now similarly abandon the notion of a perfect planner, it is not clear, in my judgement, that the government will do any better. Apart from the question of the planner's motivation to behave in the way assumed in our models, to allocate resource [*sic*] efficiently, there is the question of his ability to do so.[21]

Free market environmentalism challenges both the government planner's motivation and his ability. The approach recognizes two facts. First, *incentives affect all human behavior.* Professional managers, no matter how well-intended, respond to the incentives they face. This holds as true for bureaucrats as it does for profit-maximizing owners of firms. We readily accept the argument that business operators would dump wastes into the airways if they did not have to pay for the costs of their action. We often fail, however, to recognize the same elements at work in the political sector. If a politician is not personally accountable for allowing oil development on federal lands or for permitting an agency to dump hazardous wastes into the environment, then we can expect too much development and too much dumping. Moreover, when the beneficiaries of these activities do not have to pay the full costs, they will demand more of each from their political representatives.

Second, *information costs are positive.* In a world of scarcity, private and public decisionmakers must obtain information on the relative values of resource uses. When one use competes with another, tradeoffs are inevitable. Unfortunately, these tradeoffs are complicated when decisionmakers lack value information. In the absence of markets, a resource manager must rely on his own personal valuation of the tradeoffs or on information provided by special interest groups. In either case, there is little reason to believe that these values will necessarily reflect the social good.

With markets for commodities and amenities, prices provide the necessary information for making tradeoffs. Consider the influence a market for recreational and environmental amenities has had on International Paper (IP), one of the nation's largest private timber landowners. When leasing recreational opportunities on its land, IP has systematically improved wildlife habitats. IP's fee hunting and fee recreation programs yield approximately twenty-five percent of the operating profits in the mid-South region, with timber making up the rest. Populations of white-tailed deer, turkeys, rabbits, bobwhite quail, and mourning dove benefit from controlled burns that stimulate forage and from protected riparian zones that preserve cover and food. According to IP's wildlife managers, profits from these programs induced company executives to listen to proposals for improving habitats at the expense of timber production.[22] In contrast, political managers in the Forest Service, who "give away" recreational activities on federal lands, lack this price information and have less incentive to react to changing values.

Free market environmentalism stresses the importance of well-specified property rights as the proper mechanism to provide the incentive for entrepreneurs acting on specific time and space information. Before a landowner can sell access to those interested in recreation or an easement to a land trust, there must be clearly defined and enforceable property rights to the resources. With such rights, imaginative entrepreneurs can capture the value of environmental amenities. For example, a stream owner who can devise ways of charging fishermen can internalize the benefits and costs of improving fishing quality. Similarly, a subdivider who puts covenants on deeds to preserve open space, improve views, and harmonize development with the environment, establishes property rights to these values and captures value in higher asset-prices.

## III. FROM THE IMAGINABLE TO THE IMAGINATIVE

Skeptics are quick to point out that harmonizing wildlife needs with timber harvesting or livestock grazing is an easy solution and that free market environmentalism fails to provide solutions to the tougher problems. For example, although wildlife migrate across boundaries, landowners can at least benefit by improved management; in *the open ocean, however, there are no boundaries and no ways to fence in fish.* The result is over-fishing like that which occurs in the North Sea.[23]

The free market environmentalist approach to this problem would establish property rights through individual transferable quotas (ITQs). ITQs give each fisherman a right to a proportion of the catch, thereby eliminating the incentive to over-fish the resource. The market establishes a price for the quota and more efficient fishermen buy quotas from those who are less efficient. The ITQ system has been successfully applied in Australia and New Zealand. Six months after ITQs were applied to Australia's bluefin tuna fishery, fleet capacity dropped by sixty percent, the value of quotas doubled, and the average size of the catch rose as operators with access to larger fish bought out operators with access to smaller fish.[24] Similarly, two years after ITQs were applied to New Zealand's abalone fishery, the value of quotas increased nearly six-fold and abalone numbers increased with the aid of a new breeding program which fishermen financed.[25]

Free market environmentalism can also solve pollution problems through common law tort remedies if property rights are established and polluters can be identified. In England, an association of anglers and clubs has monitored pollution since the 1960s. Angler's Cooperative Association officials point out that the organization was protecting the environment twenty years before the general public became concerned and pressured the government to act:

> The A.C.A. has had an extraordinary record of success. It has fought hundreds of pollution cases (not all of which have gone to court) and only lost one minor one on a legal technicality. The damages it has secured on behalf of members, and member clubs, runs [*sic*] into hundreds of thousands of pounds.[26]

The British experience suggests that pollution could be reduced if private fishing rights were established in the United States. Liability rules would evolve so that owners of fishing rights could bring suit against an upstream polluter whose effluent damaged their fishing resource.[27]

The challenge to the property rights approach occurs when the polluter cannot be identified and damages cannot be assessed. For example, with acid rain, it is clear that sulfur dioxide is the cause, but the actual damage caused by a specific polluter will vary with air currents, moisture, and other climatic conditions. A free market environmentalist solution would require "branding" the pollutants so it would be clear who is causing what damage.

New technology offers the potential for such branding by introducing tracers into the smoke stacks of suspected polluters. This technology was applied in the Winter Haze Intensive Tracer Experiment in Canyonlands National Park, Utah. The park commonly experiences a haze-causing pollutant that some suspected originated from a coal-fired generating plant several hundred miles away. To identify the source, chemical tracers that mimicked the pollutant were introduced into the stack of the plant and a battery of air monitoring stations was set up around the park. The experiment concluded that the plant was contributing to the haze.[28]

The possibility of using tracers has enormous potential for tracking a variety of effluents and media. Tracers can identify users of pesticides and fertilizers, growing contributors to nonpoint sources of pollution. Tracers can also brand chemicals that contaminate groundwater basins. Just as the government requires registration and monitoring of pets to minimize nuisances, the government can require the branding and monitoring of emissions.[29]

Technology has played a key in the evolution of free market environmentalism solutions. Technology provided the means to change dramatically the face of the American West. In the 1870s, homesteaders and ranchers began using barbed wire to define property rights to their land. Previously, the lack of trees and other materials made it very costly to establish property rights. Barbed wire, however, lowered the cost of fencing the western range dramatically.[30]

## IV. FROM THEORY TO PRACTICE: ENDANGERED SPECIES

The opening vignette on Montana's Ruby River introduced the free market environmentalism approach as an alternative to political conflicts over water. Similar potential exists in the resource-rich Pacific Northwest, where two major controversies have been brewing over efforts to save several declining species.

The first dispute involves the Northern Spotted Owl, which was declared a threatened species under the Endangered Species Act of 1973[31] in June of 1990.[32] The controversy concerns the amount of federal timberland that would be removed from timber harvesting because of the Act. A government-sponsored plan to increase breeding owl pairs from 739 to 1,180 in the long term would remove from logging perhaps three million acres of timberland.

If the plan were implemented, it is estimated that 25,000 to 40,000 timber-related jobs would be lost.[33]

The second controversy surrounds the potential declaration of the sockeye salmon (and possibly other salmon species on the Columbia River) as endangered. Eight federal mainstem dams are located along the Columbia and Snake Rivers, where over ninety percent of the juvenile salmon are killed trying to migrate from their spawning grounds to the ocean. Salmon die when they are shredded or shocked as they are sucked into the giant turbines. They also fall victim to predators, high temperatures, and disease when they are trapped in the slack water behind the dams. According to salmon proponents, the solution is to increase river flows for several months during the spring, the period when juvenile salmon migrate to the sea.

Use of the Endangered Species Act to force a solution has sparked controversy. If sockeye and other salmon are declared endangered, their safety would be given highest priority relative to other uses of the Columbia Basin, such as hydroelectric power generation, shipping, and irrigation. Both hydroelectric power generation and shipping would be severely limited if water is released from the dams to increase river flows. Furthermore, these flows would not be available to fill reservoirs for later power production and irrigation.[34] The Bonneville Power Administration also estimates that rates for Northwestern power could rise by thirty percent or more. Columbia River barge operators predict the possible demise of their industry, and irrigators say farming in Washington and southern Idaho will be devastated if water for irrigation is confiscated.[35]

Why are the Northern Spotted Owl and Columbia River salmon in trouble? The answer is simple: No one owns them or their habitat; thus, no one has the incentive to protect them. In both cases, the federal government controls most of their habitats. The Forest Service and the Bureau of Land Management control the forests that the spotted owl inhabits, and the Bureau of Reclamation and the Army Corps of Engineers control the dams that kill the salmon.

The two cases do differ, however, in the extent of the subsidized destruction of the respective habitats. While federal timber programs run million-dollar deficits or more on many national forests, forests in the Pacific Northwest are moneymakers. The thirteen national forests in Oregon and Washington affected by the spotted owl decision net more than $500 million in timber revenues each year.[36] The government will lose $150 million in revenues on these forests alone, where forest planners project a thirty percent harvest reduction.[37]

The economics of water development in the Columbia River basin are quite different. Here the rule of subsidized development applies to the 6.5 million acre-feet of water used annually for irrigation. The costs of development allocated to irrigation are $745 million. Of this amount, irrigators pay $136 million, while hydroelectric power consumers pay the rest. In addition to the power subsidy, irrigators receive an implicit interest subsidy: They have a ten-year grace period during which they do not have to repay their reclamation loans and they are not charged interest during the forty-year repayment period; this amounts to an interest subsidy of seventy-nine percent.[38] Water supplied for irrigation has made the "desert bloom like a rose," but only at a tremendous cost.

Free market environmentalism can correct these problems. Short of privatizing the national forests, timber leases could be put up for competitive bid with no requirement that timber be harvested; environmentalists could then bid with timber companies. Environmental groups could lease the most critical owl habitat and allow no logging there. On other tracts, they might allow some logging, thus partially offsetting lease costs, but require that logging be done with minimal impact on the owls. Because it owns its timberlands, International Paper has successfully minimized impacts on endangered species such as the red-cockaded woodpecker, and the Audubon Society has demonstrated that oil development can occur on its private preserves without significant damage to bird habitat.[39]

Similarly, efforts to save the sockeye and other species of salmon in the Columbia River basin can be enhanced through water marketing. Environmentalists have embraced water marketing because it raises water prices and reduces water consumption. As the Ruby River example indicates, water leasing for instream purposes offers an innovative way of increasing stream flows to help migrating salmon. If environmental groups, commercial and sports fishermen, and the U.S. Fish and Wildlife Service could negotiate with power producers and irrigators for increased water flows, cooperation would replace conflict. This has happened elsewhere. On the Gunnison River in Colorado, the Nature Conservancy has obtained the rights to 20,000 acre-feet of water to maintain flows for the hump-backed chub, an endangered species with no commercial or sport value.[40] If those who care about the fate of the salmon could lease water for instream flows, they could directly invest their dollars where the salmon are threatened instead of spending time and money on costly lobbying efforts or litigation.

# V. CONCLUSION

Critics of free market environmentalism contend that it does not offer a solution to all environmental problems. They contend that although free market environmentalism may work for some recreational and environmental amenities produced from land, it is inconceivable that property rights can be used to solve problems such as ozone depletion or global warming.[41]

If free market environmentalism stimulates environmentalists to apply free market solutions to the easier problems, it can free political resources to work on the tougher problems that, at the moment, seem to be the domain of government. If free market environmentalist solutions spark the imagination of environmental entrepreneurs, technological progress toward fencing the atmosphere may be accelerated. The "free" in free market environmentalism refers to the individual liberty that only markets can provide; and without that human freedom, environmental quality will be of little consequence.

## NOTES

1. Eric Wiltse, *Irrigation Spells Death for Hundreds of Ruby River Trout*, BOZEMAN DAILY CHRON., May 12, 1987, at 3.
2. Terry L. Anderson & Donald R. Leal, *A Private Fix for Leaky Trout Streams*, FLY FISHERMAN, June 1988, at 28–31.
3. *Id.*
4. *See* Terry L. Anderson & Ronald N. Johnson, *The Problem of Instream Flows*, 24 ECON. INQUIRY 535 (1986).
5. Terry L. Anderson, *Water Rights and the Market for Water: The Western USA Experience* 21–22 (June 4, 1991). Unpublished manuscript on file with Political Economy Research Center, Bozeman, Montana.
6. Zach Willey, Statement before the Joint Select Committee on Water Resource Policy, Washington State Legislature 6–7 (September 11, 1990). Transcript available from the Environmental Defense Fund, Oakland, California.
7. Richard Wahl, *Markets for Federal Water: Subsidies, Property Rights, and the Bureau of Reclamation* 120–129 (1989).
8. *Id.*
9. *See* Zach Willey, *supra* note 6, at 6–7.
10. Sandra Postel, *Water, Water Everywhere, But Not For Long*, WASHINGTON POST, November 6, 1989, at 23 (National Weekly Edition).
11. Department of Water Affairs, *Management of the Water Resources of the Republic of South Africa* 2.8 (1986).
12. *See* Alan Randall, RESOURCE ECONOMICS 36 (1981).
13. Paul A. Samuelson, ECONOMICS 450 (11th ed. 1980).
14. John Burton, *Epilogue* to STEVEN N.S. CHEUNG, THE MYTH OF SOCIAL COSTS 76 (1978).
15. John M. Hartwick & Nancy D. Olewiler, T*he Economics of Natural Resource Use* 18 (1986).
16. Daniel W. Bromley, *Property Rights and the Environment: Natural Resource Policy in Transition* 55 (1988).
17. F. A. Hayek, *The Use of Knowledge in Society*, 35 AMER. ECON. REV. 519–520 (1945).
18. U.S. Forest Service, *Region 10 Statement of Obligations* (1984); U.S. Forest Service, *Timber Sale Program Annual Report* 8–9 (1989).
19. Wahl, *supra* note 7, at 47–67 (1989).
20. Emery N. Castle, *The Market Mechanism, Externalities, and Land Economics*, FARM ECON. 542, 552 (1965).
21. Anthony C. Fisher, RESOURCE AND ENVIRONMENTAL ECONOMICS 54 (1981).
22. Telephone interview with Tom Bourland, Wildlife Biologist, International Paper Company (Sept. 23, 1989); *see also* President's Council on Envtl. Quality, 15TH ANNUAL REPORT OF THE COUNCIL ON ENVIRONMENTAL QUALITY 426 (1984).
23. There, British fishermen's income has fallen by six percent in real terms since 1980 and stocks of cod and haddock have fallen by one-half and two-thirds, respectively. *A Sustainable Stock of Fishermen*, ECONOMIST, January 19, 1991, at 17–18.
24. William L. Robinson, *Individual Transferable Quotas in the Australian Southern Bluefin Tuna Fishery*, in FISHERY ACCESS CONTROL PROGRAMS: WORLDWIDE PROCEEDINGS OF THE WORKSHOP IN MANAGEMENT OPTIONS FOR THE NORTH PACIFIC LONGLINE FISHERS 186–205 (Alaska Sea Grant Report No. 86–4, 1986).
25. Rodney P. Hide & Peter Ackroyd, DEPOLITICISING FISHERIES MANAGEMENT: CHATHAM ISLANDS' PAUA (ABALONE) AS A CASE STUDY 42, 44 (March 1990). Unpublished report for R. D. Beattie, Ltd., Kaikoura, New Zealand.
26. Esmond Drury, *John Eastwood and the A.C.A.*, ANGLERS' COOPERATIVE ASS'N REV., Summer 1984, at 12, 13.
27. *See, e.g.*, A Mitchell Polinsky, AN INTRODUCTION TO LAW AND ECONOMICS 89–94 (1983). With well-specified rights, owners have an incentive to discover innovative ways to detect

and monitor pollution. In Britain, the water company for Bournemouth has enlisted the services of twenty West African elephant fish, *Gnathonemus petersii*, to monitor water pollution. The four-inch creature emits an easily tracked electrical discharge, the rate of which depends on the pollution level of the water. A contented fish puts out 300 to 500 pulses a minute, but if it becomes distressed by the presence of pollutants, the rate shoots up to more than 1,000 pulses a minute. Sensors in the water supply pick up the pulse rate and pass them on to a computer. If more than half of the fish suddenly increase their pulse rate, an alarm is sounded and scientists step in to assay the water. *See, A Fishy Kind of Pollution Detector*, 249 SCIENCE 983 (1990).

28. Mark Crawford, *Scientists Battle Over Grand Canyon Pollution*, 247 Science. 911–912 (1990).
29. Former EPA analyst Fred Smith suggests the possibilities:

> Detection and monitoring schemes would evolve as environmental values mounted and it became appropriate to expend more on fencing. There are exotic technologies that might well play a fencing role even for resources as complex as airsheds. For example, lasimetrics, a technology which can already map atmospheric chemical concentrations from orbit, might in time provide a sophisticated means of tracking transnational pollution flows.

> Fred L. Smith, Jr., *Controlling the Global Threat to the Global Liberal Order 10* (November 1989). Unpublished manuscript, on file with the Competitive Enterprise Institute, Washington, D.C.

30. *See* Walter Prescott Webb, THE GREAT PLAINS 309 (1931).
31. Pub. L. No. 93-205, §§ 2–15, 17, 87 Stat. 884 (1973) (codified as amended in scattered sections of 16 U.S.C. (1988)).
32. *Determination of Threatened Status for the Northern Spotted Owl*, 55 FED. REG. 26,114 (1990) (codified in Endangered and Threatened Wildlife, 50 C.F.R. § 17.11 (1991)). *See* David Schaefer & Sylvia Nogaki, *Threatened Wildlife—Agency Makes It Official on Spotted Owl*, SEATTLE TIMES, June 22, 1990, at A1.
33. Robert Nelson, *Rethinking Federal Forest Management: A Response to the Designation of the Spotted Owl as a Threatened Species* 8–9 (Political Economy Research Center Working Paper No. 90–34, Jan. 1991). Unpublished manuscript, on file at the Political Economy Research Center, Bozeman, Montana.
34. Pat Ford, *How the Basin's Salmon-Killing System Works*, HIGH COUNTRY NEWS, April 22, 1991, at 14–15.
35. Pat Ford, *We've Got An Economic Opportunity Here*, HIGH COUNTRY NEWS, April 22, 1991, at 15.
36. U.S. Forest Service, TIMBER SALE PROGRAM ANNUAL REPORT 115–16, 162 (1989).
37. When all affected federal forests in Washington, Oregon, and California are taken into account, the loss could be as high as $625 million per year. *See* Nelson, *supra* note 33.
38. Randal R. Rucker & Price V. Fishback, *The Federal Reclamation Program: An Analysis of Rent-Seeking Behavior*, in WATER RIGHTS: SCARCE RESOURCE ALLOCATION, BUREAUCRACY, AND THE ENVIRONMENT 45, 52–63 (Terry L. Anderson ed., 1983). Using a discount rate of 8%.
39. *See* President's Council on Envtl. Quality, *supra* note 21, at 425; *see also* John Baden & Richard Stroup, *Saving the Wilderness*, REASON, July 1981, at 28–36.
40. Steven J. Shupe & John A. Folk-Williams, *Public Interest Perspective*, WATER MARKET UPDATE, March 1987, at 9–10.
41. *But see* Robert Stavins et al., PROJECT 88: HARNESSING MARKET FORCES TO PROTECT OUR ENVIRONMENT 10–23 (1988) (recommending a tradeable permit system for phasing out potential ozone depleters, international emissions trading in greenhouse gases, and prevention of deforestation through debt-forest swaps).

# TRADITIONALIST CONSERVATISM AND ENVIRONMENTAL ETHICS

*John R. E. Bliese*

John R. E. Bliese has a long-standing interest in the American conservative essayist Richard Weaver, and has published several articles on that writer's rhetorical theory and conservative philosophy.

## INTRODUCTION

Environmentalists are usually thought of as liberals, and environmentalism is often thought to be a liberal political position. However, this perception is in large part merely an historical accident. Environmentalism does not have any single political home.[1] In fact, the philosophical foundations of conservatism also support environmental protection and resource conservation.

The term *conservative* is one of the most abused in our political vocabulary. Here I am concerned only with the conservative intellectual movement in America and England that began shortly after World War II.[2] Within that movement there are two primary schools of thought: libertarian, free market advocates who trace their lineage back to Adam Smith, and traditionalists who are the intellectual heirs of Edmund Burke.[3]

Before considering their respective principles in relation to environmental ethics, I need to consider briefly one of the most unfortunate abuses of the term *conservatism,* which simply equates it with "business interests." The belief that conservatism endorses whatever the business community wants is all too common, and often politically useful to the business community and its supporters in politics and the press, but it is completely false.[4] Clinton Rossiter rightly calls it "the Great Train Robbery of American intellectual history."[5] The modern conservative movement has had to confront it from the beginning.

This essay originally appeared in *Environmental Ethics*, Vol. 19, No. 2 (Summer 1997), 135–151. Reprinted with permission.

Neither school of conservative thought is "pro-business" in the ordinary sense. Advocates of the free market have realized ever since the days of Adam Smith that businessmen (and now businesswomen) hate the idea. They think it is a fine theory, of course, but only when applied to everyone else. Their own cases are exceptional and require exemption from the rigors of the market. Adam Smith observed that whenever businessmen gather together, they invariably conspire to fix prices.[6] Today, the game has changed somewhat and what businessmen and women usually want is governmental protection, either as direct subsidies or import quotas and the like. As Francis Graham Wilson notes, "the day-to-day exponents of modern industrialism have been generally in favor of having the government on their side."[7] For the advocate of the free market, the task of policy, therefore, is to design a system in which businesses must compete, whether they want to or not.

While free market advocates are not simply "pro-business," traditionalists are sometimes even hostile. They have always insisted that they are not to be identified with business interests. According to Stephen Tonsor, "the leaders of the new conservatism are not now, nor will they be, identified with the American business community." This conservatism is to be defined "in religious and moral terms."[8] Peter Viereck argues that conservatives wish "to conserve the humane and ethical values of the west rather than the economic privileges of a fraction of the west."[9] Russell Kirk claims that "conservatism is something more than mere solicitude for tidy incomes,"[10] and that "a doctrinaire attachment to the accumulation of private wealth" is not an "article of conservative conviction."[11]

Kirk acknowledges that "the American businessman . . . is immensely important . . . to the cause of American conservatism." Nevertheless, he then proceeds to issue a severe critique of the typical business mentality. "For a long while, the American man of business, generally speaking, has been intent upon getting and spending to the exclusion of almost every cultural and social interest. . . . In the whole American nation, perhaps, there are not a hundred important businessmen who take an intelligent interest in the problems of modern society." After condemning the American businessman for being "inordinately vain," a "Philistine" who is ignorant of general ideas, Kirk concludes: "A conservative order is not the creation of the free entrepreneur."[12]

Likewise, Richard Weaver condemns "the dominance of the businessman type. . . . [N]ever before in history had this type of person formed a class enjoying social prestige" because in the business mentality "all the virtues are subordinated to successful gain-getting." This obsession "does constant damage" to "the spirit which creates culture."[13]

When business and industry oppose policies to protect the environment, conservatives, to be consistent with their underlying philosophy, should not automatically offer their support. Quite the contrary, as I show, both libertarian and traditionalist principles give the conservative good reason to suspect that they are getting away with something.

Indeed, both conservative schools of thought provide a basis for resource conservation and environmental protection. The free market perspective is now receiving considerable attention for its potential to solve environmental problems. A good example is Terry Anderson and Donald Leal's recent book, *Free Market Environmentalism.*[14] The Heritage Foundation has published a number of articles in *Policy Review* that argue for environmental protection from a market perspective,[15] as do its recommendations in *Mandate for Leadership III.*[16] The two volumes of *Project 88* propose numerous ways to use market mechanisms to curb pollution, conserve resources, and protect the environment.[17] Moreover, there are now several organizations, such as John Baden's FREE (Foundation for Research on Economics and the Environment), that are engaged in promoting "free market environmentalism." With the increasing number of advocates for the market perspective, the approach is also receiving careful attention by critics, and indeed one of the best such analyses appeared in the pages of *Environmental Ethics.*[18]

However, while the libertarian school of conservative thought is receiving considerable attention in relation to environmental issues, the traditionalist one is not. For this reason, I consider this branch of conservatism and its implications for environmental ethics. But before turning to the principles of traditionalist conservatism, a brief summary of the market based approach to environmentalism is appropriate, for the traditionalist also believes that the free market has an important role to play in a proper, conservative society.

Free market conservatives are environmentalists in many policy areas simply because so many of our environmental problems have been created by "market failures" or by governmental interventions, all of which disciples of Adam Smith would try to correct. Consistent free market conservatives oppose all of the governmental subsidies that have devastated so much of our land: by means of below-cost timber sales, below-market grazing fees, subsidized irrigation water, and the like. Without such subsidies, they contend, most of our national forests would still be intact, our western lands would not be overgrazed, and a lot of rivers would still flow freely.

A consistent free market conservative would also insist on "internalizing externalities." They would argue that all costs of production and consumption should be paid by the producer and consumer of a product, not imposed on innocent third parties. All forms of pollution are "externalities"; the producers are avoiding some of the costs of production by fouling the air and water, thereby imposing those costs on others, infringing on their freedom and violating their property rights. A free market advocate would insist that the producer should clean up those emissions and "internalize" the costs of doing so in the price of the product. If such externalities had not been allowed, most of our air and water pollution would never have occurred.

Free market conservatives also advocate using pricing mechanisms to create incentives for environmental protection. For example, bottle and can deposits, refunded for recycling, reduce litter, save space in land fills, and save energy as well. A similar system could be used for toxic or hazardous materials. Pollution taxes or effluent charges could be imposed to create incentives to reduce pollution. Moreover, tradeable emission permits could be used to reduce pollution efficiently.

In general, the libertarians focus their concerns almost entirely on the market place. They believe that allowing it to function properly would have many beneficial effects on the environment. By contrast, while the traditionalists agree that a free market has an important role in society, they are by and large not much concerned with economics. Their focus, instead, is on the health of our human spirits and the state of our culture. They believe that a civilization is dearly won and requires generations to create. Civilization, they contend, is at best a fragile thing that, once broken, leaves mankind at the mercy of all its brutish instincts and tendencies. They look to tradition to provide guidance based on the wisdom of our ancestors. Tradition, in which religion plays a major role, creates the continuity and social stability in which the individual is best able to develop as a fully human being. Several important aspects of traditionalism have a direct bearing on environmental policy.[19]

## TRADITIONALIST POLITICAL PHILOSOPHY

In analyzing traditionalist political thought, it is not my purpose to advocate this philosophy or to argue that it is superior to any other. All I want to do here is to indicate that this political position, with a venerable heritage and a significant number of intellectually respectable advocates, has important implications for environmental ethics.

In considering the traditionalist political philosophy, although I refer to a number of authors, I focus primarily on the works of three outstanding scholars—Richard Weaver, Russell Kirk, and John Gray—whose careers in combination span the modern conservative movement, from the revival of conservatism in the 1950s to today.

Richard Weaver was a Southerner, from North Carolina. Born in 1910, he attended the University of Kentucky during the Depression. In his graduate study in English at Vanderbilt and Louisiana State University, he was profoundly influenced by the Southern Agrarians. After receiving his doctorate, the rest of his academic career was spent in the English Department at the University of Chicago. Some of his works were in the field of rhetoric, but he devoted much of his life to a defense of traditional Southern culture and a critique of the cultural tendencies of modern America. His first book, *Ideas Have Consequences,* appeared in 1948 and was the opening shot in the postwar attack on liberalism.[20] Frank Meyer calls the book "the *fons et origo* of the contemporary American conservative movement."[21] When Weaver died in 1963, he left the manuscript of *Visions of Order,* which was published posthumously. Willmoore Kendall contends that this book should have "biblical status" on the bookshelves of all conservatives.[22] Weaver wrote many articles for Southern reviews and conservative journals, and served on the editorial board of *Modern Age.*

Russell Kirk was a Northerner, from Michigan. Born in 1918, he died in April 1994. He earned a doctorate from St. Andrews in Scotland and taught briefly at Michigan State College. For most of his life, however, he was an outstanding example of that most endangered species, the private scholar. Based in the rural village of Mecosta, Michigan, Kirk was an incredibly prolific writer. Charles Brown's bibliography of his works is over eighty pages long, and Kirk still had some thirteen productive years after it was compiled.[23] His best-known book, *The Conservative Mind*, appeared in 1953 and became an instant classic in the conservative movement, and so it remains today, now in its seventh edition.[24] This book, more than any other single work, established traditionalist conservatism as an intellectually respectable position in England and America. In 1957 Kirk founded *Modern Age*, which to this day is still the leading American journal of traditionalist conservative thought.

Weaver and Kirk, thus, were historically important figures in the origin and development of the conservative movement. The British scholar John Gray is a contemporary counterpart. Gray is a fellow of Jesus College, Oxford, and "one of Britain's foremost political theorists. During the 1980s he was closely associated with the ideas and think-tanks of . . . Thatcherism."[25] His recent book, *Beyond the New Right*, is an important, closely reasoned critique of politics, especially of free market conservatism, from a traditionalist, Tory perspective.[26]

At the heart of traditionalist philosophy are several crucial principles that have profound implications for environmentalism, and our three authors are noteworthy among leading theoreticians of the traditionalist position for explicitly applying them to environmental issues.[27] The principles to be discussed here are:

**(1)** Rejection of materialism
**(2)** Rejection of ideology
**(3)** Piety toward nature
**(4)** Social contract across generations
**(5)** Prudence, the prime political virtue

(1) *Rejection of materialism.* I start with a negative statement as principle number one because it is perhaps the most prominent aspect of all traditionalist writings: traditionalists are not materialists. According to Rossiter, the conservative "places moral above material values and ends. . . . The state of culture, learning, law, charity, and morality are of more concern to the Conservative than the annual output of steel and aluminium."[28] Kirk insists that the conservative rejects the "reduction of human striving to material production and consumption."[29]

Weaver contends that civilization is not to be equated with material success.[30] "There is no correlation between the degree of comfort enjoyed and the achievement of a civilization. On the contrary, absorption in ease is one of the most reliable signs of present or impending decay."[31] A person's character develops in response to inner and outer checks on appetites and desires, so what is really needed is not more consumer goods but training that includes "the disciplines of rigor and denial."[32] In stark contrast to the "spoiled child psychology" of modern America, "self-denial [is] the greatest lesson to be learned."[33] Weaver was a student of the culture of the Old South, and while he well realized its faults, he thought it admirable in one overriding respect: it was *"the last non-materialist civilization in the Western World"* and it stands as a challenge: "to save the human spirit by re-creating a non-materialist society."[34] Whether his historical judgment is accurate or not, the conservative principle that he advocates is clear.

For the traditionalist conservative, because production and consumption are very low level concerns, economics does not provide the standard for life, or even for government.[35] Edmund Burke, after all, put economists in the same category with "sophisters."[36]

The traditionalists are especially critical of modern industrial capitalism. "They view unregulated capitalism as an integral part of the materialism and hedonism they so dislike in the modern Western world; they spurn the civilization that has grown up around the capitalist order. They believe that unregulated capitalism has placed great burdens on the way of life they think necessary for the development of human freedom along virtuous lines."[37] Rossiter notes their "outspoken distaste for the excesses, vulgarities, and dislocations of the industrial way of life."[38] Kirk contends that "industrialism was a harder knock to conservatism than the books of the French egalitarians," for it "turned the world inside out," replacing personal loyalties with financial relationships, turning the wealthy from being patrons to pursuing mere aggrandizement, and destroying community.[39]

Industrial capitalism has destroyed the world that the traditionalist conservative prefers, but Kirk is realistic: ". . . once in an industrial society, we cannot get out of it without starving half the world's population. What we can do, nevertheless, is to humanize the industrial system, so far as lies in our power," and "to stand guard against over-industrialism, a real menace nowadays."[40]

The rejection of materialism can have wide-ranging implications for environmentalism. For example, at the most basic level, a traditionalist is not willing to sacrifice environmental quality merely to get more consumer goods. At the macro level, environmentalists often see the crux of many problems in the current "worship" (for that is what it must be called) of economic growth. Ecologists would perhaps universally agree that unlimited growth on a finite planet is a recipe for disaster. Traditionalist conservatives would also reject the policy of growth as an end in itself because it is a manifestation of materialism pure and simple.[41] Where Edward Abbey calls the desire for unlimited growth "the ideology of the cancer cell,"[42] Gray calls it "the most vulgar ideal ever put before suffering humankind."[43] If some restrictions on growth are needed to preserve environmental quality, the traditionalist is quite willing to accept them.

(2) *Rejection of ideology.* A second negative principle may also be found throughout the writings of the traditionalists: a rejection of all ideology, and a corresponding humility in the face of the limits of human reason. Traditionalists reject all attempts to refashion society after abstract notions. Society is

infinitely complex, always a historical creation, and therefore is not malleable for the creation of utopias, as ideologists believe. John Gray rejects rationalism in politics, because it

> . . . represents political reasoning as an application of first principles of justice or rights, rather than as circumstantial reasoning aiming at the achievement of a *modus vivendi.* It supposes that the functions and limits of state activity can be specified, once and for all, by a theory, instead of varying with the history, traditions, and circumstances that peoples and their governments inherit. . . . It thereby contributes to the corruption of political practice of ideological hubris, which is one of the most distinctive vices of an age wedded to political religions.[44]

Similarly, Gerhart Niemeyer condemns "the ideological mind building thought systems around utopian fantasies with which to manipulate human beings into false hopes."[45]

Imposing abstract ideologies on a society invariably produces disaster. Burke saw that the attempt to remold France produced not a utopia but a revolution, vast amounts of human suffering, and eventually tyranny. The scholars who revived traditionalism after World War II had the example of Stalin's Russia as a stark warning of how much suffering an abstract ideology, attempting to create a new type of human being, can bring upon a vast nation.

The other side of this coin, of course, is an insistence that conservatism is non-ideological. Niemeyer contends that "no conservative ideology can be dreamed into existence."[46] Gray claims that "it is by returning to the homely truths of traditional conservatism that we are best protected from the illusions of ideology."[47]

This rejection of ideology (as they define it) has some important implications for environmental policies. It provides a basis from within conservatism for limiting the excesses of free market thinking, where that has itself become an ideology, i.e., an abstract theory to be imposed on society, promising utopia. Much of Gray's *Beyond the New Right* is devoted to precisely this type of a critique, including the very long chapter on environmental policies. It should be valuable to environmentalists, especially in America today, to find such a critique firmly within the conservative intellectual movement.

To this point, I have been dealing with things that the traditionalist opposes. I now turn to a consideration of principles that the traditionalist advocates. Some of the major virtues for conservatism have profound implications that would lead the traditionalist conservative to be an environmentalist.

(3) *Piety toward nature.* I begin with what Weaver calls "a crowning concept which governs [a person's] attitude toward the totality of the world": the capstone virtue, piety. Weaver defines piety as "a discipline of the will through respect. It admits the right to exist of things larger than the ego, of things different from the ego." In order to bring harmony back into our world, we need to regard three things "with the spirit of piety": nature, other people, and the past.[48] It is the first of these, of course, that is most important here.

Weaver explains the proper, pious attitude toward nature in several of his works. The point is a crucial one, so we need to consider it, in his own words, at some length. He contends that

> ... the attitude toward nature ... is a matter ... basic to one's outlook or phi-
> losophy of life ... [A pious person] tends to look upon nature as something
> which is given and something which is finally inscrutable. This is equivalent to
> saying that he looks upon it as the creation of a Creator. There follows from this
> attitude an important deduction, which is that man has a duty of veneration to-
> ward nature and the natural. Nature is not something to be fought, conquered
> and changed according to any human whims. To some extent, of course, it has
> to be used. But what man should seek in regard to nature is not a complete do-
> minion but a *modus vivendi*—that is, a manner of living together, a coming to
> terms with something that was here before our time and will be here after it.
> The important corollary of this doctrine, it seems to me, is that man is not the
> lord of creation, with an omnipotent will, but a part of creation, with limita-
> tions, who ought to observe a decent humility in the face of the inscrutable.[49]

In his only autobiographical essay, Weaver traces the development of his thought toward conservatism: "I found myself in decreasing sympathy with those social and political doctrines erected upon the concept of a man-dominated universe." "Creation," he concludes, "is not our and [it] exhibits the marks of a creative power that we do not begin to possess."[50]

In one of his last works, he returns to this theme: "Civilized man carries a sense of restraint into his behavior both toward nature and his fellow beings. The first of these is piety: the second ethics. Piety comes to us as a warning voice that we must think as mortals, that it is not for us either to know all or to control all. It is a recognition of our own limitations and a cheerful accep-tance of the contingency of nature, which gives us the protective virtue of humility. . . . [Nature] is the matrix of our being." "Piety respects the mystery of nature," and an "acceptance of nature, with an awareness of the persistence of tragedy, is the first element of spirituality."[51]

A similar conclusion may be found in an analysis of Christian society by T. S. Eliot. "We may say that religion . . . implies a life in conformity with na-ture. It may be observed that the natural life and the supernatural life have a conformity to each other which neither has with the mechanistic life . . . a wrong attitude towards nature implies, somewhere, a wrong attitude towards God, and . . . the consequence is an inevitable doom."[52]

The dominant attitude toward nature, traditionalist conservatives be-lieve, is completely wrong. Weaver sums up "the offense of modern man" by saying that "he is impious," and this impiety is nothing less than a "sin."[53] Con-cerning the modern attitude toward the natural world, he writes:

> For centuries now we have been told that our happiness requires an unrelent-
> ing assault upon [nature]: dominion, conquest, triumph—all these names
> have been used as if it were a military campaign. Somehow the notion has been
> loosed that nature is hostile to man or that her ways are offensive or slovenly,
> so that every step of progress is measured by how far we have altered these.

Nothing short of a recovery of the ancient virtue of *pietas* can absolve man from this sin. . . . [The attempt to win] an unconditional victory over nature . . . is impious, for . . . it violates the belief that creation or nature is fundamentally good, that the ultimate reason for its laws is a mystery, and that acts of defiance such as are daily celebrated by the newspapers are subversive of cosmos. Obviously a degree of humility is required to accept this view.[54]

Weaver maintained this position throughout his life. In *Visions of Order,* he again rejects the notion of conquering nature. "If nature is something ordained by a creator, one does not speak of 'conquering' it. The creation of a benevolent creator is something good, and conquest implies enmity and aggression." And he again denounces industrialism for "constantly making war upon nature, disfiguring and violating her."[55]

Kirk also condemns the consequences of impiety toward nature. "The modern spectacle of vanished forests and eroded lands, wasted petroleum and ruthless mining . . . is evidence of what an age without veneration does to itself and its successors."[56] Those words were originally written in the 1950s. How much worse must a traditionalist believe we are today, considering, for instance, the national forests "hammered" by clear-cutting, the "cow bombed" grazing lands of the west, the lunar landscapes created by heap leach mining, or the fragile deserts torn up by ORVs. Those are not just the results of poor policies; they are impieties toward nature which, as the traditionalist insists, are nothing less than sins—a conclusion with which environmentalists would certainly concur.

(4) *Social contract across generations.* A fundamental tenet of traditionalist conservatism is that society is intergenerational, "joined in perpetuity by a moral bond among the dead, the living, and those yet to be born—the community of souls."[57] Of all of Burke's magnificent prose, the passage perhaps most often quoted by conservatives elaborates this principle: "Society is indeed a contract. . . . It is a partnership in all science; a partnership in all art; a partnership in every virtue, and in all perfection. As the ends of such a partnership cannot be obtained in many generations, it becomes a partnership not only between those who are living, but between those who are living, those who are dead, and those who are to be born."[58]

In this partnership, we who are now alive have an obligation to posterity. Our fundamental role toward future generations is one of stewardship: "The spirit of trusteeship—the sense of receiving a precious heritage and handing it on intact and perhaps even slightly strengthened—pervades Conservatism."[59]

The conservative principle of trusteeship for future generations has obvious links with environmentalism. Indeed, as Carl Pope, Executive Director of the Sierra Club, states, "If there is anything that has distinguished the environmental movement during the past 100 years, it has been our insistence that we not plan for a one-generation society, that the future matters."[60]

(5) *Prudence, the prime political virtue.* According to Burke, "prudence is not only first in rank of the virtues political and moral, but she is the director of all the others."[61] Rossiter explains that prudence "represents a cluster of urges—toward caution, deliberation, and discretion, toward moderation and

calculation, toward old ways and good form—which gives every other standard virtue a special look when displayed by a true Conservative."[62]

One basic reason that the traditionalist insists on prudence in altering or "reforming" society is because of its complexity. In Burke's words, "the nature of man is intricate; the objects of society are of the greatest possible complexity,"[63] so complex that individual human reason is not able to grasp them. Our culture has been created over many generations, with contributions from countless minds and hearts. Therefore, says the traditionalist, we need to be very careful when trying to change society on the basis of some new notion an individual has dreamed up. We need to remember that the individual is foolish, but the species is wise.[64]

Such reasoning, of course, applies *a fortiori* to the environment. As Forest Service Chief Jack Ward Thomas is fond of quoting: "ecosystems are not only more complex than we think: they are more complex than we *can* think."[65] If we need to be very careful, humble and prudent in introducing social and political changes and reforms, we need to be much more so in changing the environment.

## IMPLICATIONS FOR POLICY

The political philosophy of traditionalist conservatism, we have seen, contains several important principles that support environmental protection and resource conservation. While this is not the place for a detailed analysis of specific policies, we may consider briefly a few general implications of the traditionalist perspective for environmental policy.[66]

*(1) Conservation of Natural Resources and Sustainable Development.*    The conservative notions of stewardship, of obligation for the future, of holding our world and our civilization in trusteeship, have some important implications for environmental policies. Both environmentalists and traditionalist conservatives reject many current practices as "unconscionable effort[s] to transfer . . . costs and risks from the present to future generations."[67] Thus, T. S. Eliot objects "to the exhaustion of natural resources." He contends that "a good deal of our material progress is a progress for which succeeding generations may have to pay dearly." He illustrates this contention by pointing to soil erosion, a result of "the exploitation of the earth, on a vast scale for two generations, for commercial profit: immediate benefits leading to dearth and desert."[68]

Kirk likewise objects to squandering natural resources that future generations will need. "In America especially, we live beyond our means by consuming the portion of posterity, insatiably devouring minerals and forests and the very soil, lowering the water-table, to gratify the appetites of the present tenants of the country." He recommends "turning away from the furious depletion of natural resources, we ought to employ our techniques of efficiency in the interest of posterity, voluntarily conserving our land and our minerals and our forests and our water and our old towns and our countryside for the future partners in our contract of eternal society."[69]

The current concept of "sustainable development" is an eminently conservative idea. Traditionalists would favor measures to ensure that renewable resources are used no faster than they can be replenished and that nonrenewable resources are used very carefully and efficiently, ideally no faster than substitutes can be found and introduced. An economy designed on these lines would meet our obligations to future generations.

Two of the most daunting problems that we face—global warming and the collapse of biodiversity—call for the prime conservative virtue of prudence above all. In both cases, we are conducting uncontrolled and irreversible experiments with the entire planet, surely the height of imprudence.

*(2) Climate Change.* Our massive use of fossil fuels has significantly changed the composition of the atmosphere by increasing the amount of greenhouse gases. The ultimate consequences are not at all clear, but they could be devastating. It may take another decade or more for scientists to study the question.

Thus, what policies should we pursue now? Prudence would surely dictate that we not continue blindly with the status quo. We should cut our energy use dramatically, in order to reduce the addition of greenhouse gases until we have greater knowledge about their ultimate effects. Nor would this require drastic, imprudent policies. Quite the contrary, it could be done rather easily because we now use energy very inefficiently. Major improvements in efficiency would be worth making even in the absence of concern over climate change.

*(3) Declining Biodiversity: The Need for Prudent and Pious Action.* The incredible diversity of life is one of the most outstanding features of our marvelous, and so far as we know, unique planet. These myriads of life forms have evolved over hundreds of millions of years. In the natural course of events, species are constantly becoming extinct and other species evolving. But we are now causing extinctions at rates hundreds or thousands of times higher than normal.[70] We are causing the loss of untold numbers of species without knowing what potential value they might be to us—as say, medicines or food—without knowing anything about their roles in their ecosystems and without knowing at what point whole ecosystems will simply collapse, as one after another of their important elements are destroyed. This loss surely is the height of impiety, but it is also enormously imprudent. In the often quoted words of biologist Edward O. Wilson, "this is the folly our descendants are least likely to forgive us."[71] A traditionalist conservative would appreciate the homely advice of Aldo Leopold, that it is the first rule of the tinkerer, when you take something apart, to save all the pieces.[72]

Moreover, traditionalist conservatism, with its veneration for religion, would find support for preserving biodiversity in the *Bible*. The story of Noah is a relevant allegory for our time: God may have given humans "dominion" over the Earth, but He also ordered Noah to save *all* the creatures, not just the charismatic megafauna. A traditionalist would see no reason to believe that God expects less of us today.[73]

To be prudent and pious, we should do everything we can to preserve the diversity of life on Earth. The key is to preserve sufficient habitat intact and unpolluted. If that means some restrictions on "development," so be it. For the traditionalist, piety and prudence in preserving God's creatures would be far more important than a few more golf courses or shopping malls.

*(4) Costs of Environmental Protection.* The business community often objects to pollution abatement measures because they increase costs of production. The traditionalist would here agree with the libertarian that precisely those costs *ought* to be borne by the polluter. But the traditionalist would go even farther and add that there is a basic duty, a moral responsibility on the part of industry, and everyone else for that matter, not to pollute the environment. No one has the right to hurt his or her neighbors or to damage creation just to save a little money—a position shared with environmentalists.

*(5) Role of Government and Restrictions on the Market.* Traditionalist conservatives apply their rejection of ideology to free market theory as well, for it has too often become the ideology of the libertarian.[74] Traditionalists, to be sure, accept the importance of a free market as a means of ensuring freedom.[75] But the traditionalist conservative "would . . . resist making a fetish of market institutions" and "would also be ready to curb them when their workings are demonstrably harmful."[76] The traditionalist is perfectly willing to grant government a role, especially in solving environmental problems. John Gray contends that "market institutions, although they are indispensably necessary, are insufficient as guarantors of the integrity of the environment, human as well as natural. They must be supplemented by governmental activity when . . . private investment cannot by itself sustain the public environment of the common life."[77]

When confronting specific environmental problems, Kirk in similar fashion looks to the government for solutions. In a newspaper column about the damages caused by pesticides, Kirk concludes that "the public needs to bring pressure upon state authorities, everywhere, to take measures against polluters of every sort."[78] In another column he laments the loss of "farmlands, woodlands and wetlands" to urban sprawl, industrial expansion and tourist development. Arguing that "restraining action has become necessary," he praises a policy adopted by the government of Vermont to "restrain thoughtless development by bulldozer and speculator."[79]

Traditionalist principles would call for limits on some specific systemic elements in our economy that can be particularly damaging to the environment. For example, a traditionalist conservative would want to put checks on the market in those areas where it can be used to "justify" harvesting naturally renewable resources to depletion. Our economic system can lead a company to view a resource as simply an investment, and if an alternative investment offers higher returns, the company can find it "economical" to deplete the resource and put its money elsewhere.[80] With equally damaging results, "discount rates" can be used to justify immediate consumption and destruction of natural resources, leaving nothing to the future. A traditionalist would want to devise checks on such workings of the market, where they violate our moral obligations of piety and stewardship.

*(6) Preservation of Wilderness.*   There are many other areas in which traditionalist conservative ideas coincide with and reinforce those of environmentalists. It may suffice here to mention just a couple that relate to preservation of natural areas.

Now that our wilderness is virtually all gone, we need to preserve what little is left for a wide variety of reasons, one of which is for its heritage value.[81] Aldo Leopold claims that "many of the attributes most distinctive of America and Americans are [due to] the impress of the wilderness and the life that accompanied it."[82] Because traditionalists are interested in preserving those things that have shaped what is best in the American character, their preservation is the basis for an argument for wilderness preservation that they would support.

Environmentalists believe that natural areas should be preserved for their aesthetic and spiritual values. We need periodically to get back to nature for spiritual renewal, to recover from the stresses of modernity and our hectic urban lives. With his belief that nature is to be venerated, it is not surprising to find a similar sentiment expressed by Weaver: "What humane spirit, after reading a newspaper or attending a popular motion picture or listening to the farrago of nonsense on a radio program, has not found relief in fixing his gaze upon some characteristic bit of nature? It is escape from the sickly metaphysical dream. Out of the surfeit of falsity born of technology and commericalism we rejoice in returning to primary data."[83] And he wrote these remarks before the age of television.

The political philosophy of traditionalist conservatism, we have seen, contains several important principles that support conservation of natural resources and protection of the environment. They establish a basis for limiting some of the excesses of rampant industrialism and thoughtless "development." And they offer, from within the conservative movement, grounds for curbing some of the excesses that result from a doctrinaire or ideological application of free market theory. In the political climate of America in the mid-1990s, environmentalists might find it very useful to discover these intellectual resources from impeccably conservative sources.[84]

## NOTES

1. Frances Cairncross, "Costing the Earth (Survey)," *The Economist,* 2 September 1989, p. 5; Russell Kirk, "Common Reader for Everyday Ecologists," *New Orleans Times-Picayune* 20 September 1971, sec. 1, p. 11.

2. The Anglo-American conservative intellectual movement has generally been seen as separate from Continental conservatism and other related political philosophies; see, e.g., William R. Harbour, *The Foundations of Conservative Thought: An Anglo-American Tradition in Perspective* (Notre Dame, Indiana: University of Notre Dame Press, 1982); Gregory Wolfe, "The Catholic as Conservative." *Crisis* 11 (October 1993): 29.

3. The specific relationships, and the disputes, between these two schools of thought need not detain us here. For those who may be interested, they are traced in detail by George H. Nash. *The Conservative Intellectual Movement in America since 1945* (New York: Basic Books, 1976, rev. ed., Wilmington, Del.: Intercollegiate Studies Institute, 1996) and may be followed, *in situ* as it were, in the pages of *National Review* in its early years. Frank S. Meyer perhaps best analyzed the overlap between the two perspectives, and the extent to which each logically needs the other: "Freedom, Tradition, Conservatism," *Modern Age* 4 (1960): 355–63. Within contemporary conservatism one will also find several other groups (e.g., neo-conservatives, populists) that have adopted part or all of these two schools of thought, in various combinations and sometimes with additions from other political views. For purposes of analysis here, we can take libertarian and traditionalist as the "pure" forms, and the conclusions can then be applied to other conservative tendencies accordingly.

4. *The Economist* contends that "pursuing corporate favouritism instead of competitive markets" is "a basic right-wing error," 13 April 1996, p. 14.

5. Clinton Rossiter, *Conservatism in America*, 2d ed. (Cambridge, Mass.: Harvard University Press, 1982), p. 204.

6. Adam Smith, *An Inquiry into the Nature and Causes of the Wealth of Nations* (New York: Modern Library, 1937), p. 128.

7. Francis Graham Wilson, *The Case for Conservatism* (Seattle: University of Washington Press, 1951), p. 65.

8. Stephen J. Tonsor, letter to the editor, *The Reporter* 13 (11 August 1955): 8.

9. Peter Viereck, *Conservatism Revisited* (New York: Charles Scribner's Sons, 1949), p. x.

10. Russell Kirk, *A Program for Conservatives*, rev. ed. (Chicago: Henry Regnery, 1962), p. 23.

11. Russell Kirk, "The American Conservative Character." *The Georgia Review* 8 (1954): 251.

12. Ibid., pp. 253–55.

13. Richard M. Weaver, *Visions of Order* (Baton Rouge: Louisiana State University Press, 1964), pp. 32–33.

14. Terry L. Anderson and Donald R. Leal, *Free Market Environmentalism* (San Francisco: Pacific Research Institute for Public Policy, 1991).

15. For example, see: John Miller, "Land of the Free: An Environmental Strategy for Republicans," *Policy Review* 63 (Winter 1993): 66–70; Robert N. Stavins, "Clean Profits: Using Economic Incentives to Protect the Environment," *Policy Review* 48 (Spring 1989): 58–63; John Baden, "Crimes Against Nature: Public Funding of Environmental Destruction," *Policy Review* 39 (Winter 1987): 36–40.

16. Charles L. Heatherly and Burton Yale Pines, ed., *Mandate for Leadership III: Policy Strategies for the 1990s* (Washington, D.C.: Heritage Foundation, 1989).

17. *Project 88*, 2 vols., sponsored by Senators Timothy E. Wirth and John Heinz, directed by Robert N. Stavins (Washington, D.C., 1988, 1991).

18. John M. Gowdy and Peg R. Olsen, "Further Problems with Neoclassical Environmental Economics," *Environmental Ethics* 16 (1994): 161–71.

19. I make no attempt here to give a complete summary of the traditionalist philosophy; for that, the interested reader may consult Harbour, *Foundations of Conservative Thought* and Rossiter, *Conservatism in America*.

20. Richard M. Weaver, *Ideas Have Consequences* (Chicago: University of Chicago Press, 1948).

21. Frank S. Meyer, "Richard M. Weaver: An Appreciation," *Modern Age* 14 (1970): 243.

22. Willmoore Kendall, "How to Read Richard Weaver: Philosopher of 'We the (Virtuous) People,'" *The Intercollegiate Review* 2 (1965): 81.

23. Charles Brown, *Russell Kirk: A Bibliography* (Mount Pleasant: Central Michigan University, 1981).

24. Russell Kirk, *The Conservative Mind*, 7th ed. (Chicago: Regnery Books, 1986).

25. *The Economist* (August 14, 1993): 85.

26. John Gray, *Beyond the New Right* (London: Routledge, 1993).

27. Gray goes so far as to claim that "concern for the integrity of the common environment, human as well as ecological, is most in harmony with the outlook of traditional conservatism" (ibid., p. 124).

28. Rossiter, *Conservatism in America*, p. 47.
29. Kirk, *Conservative Mind*, p. iii.
30. Weaver, *Ideas Have Consequences*, p. 17.
31. Ibid., pp. 116–17.
32. Richard M. Weaver, "Mass Plutocracy," *National Review* 9 (5 November 1960): 275–290.
33. Richard M. Weaver, *The Southern Tradition at Bay*, ed. George Core and M. F. Bradford (New Rochelle, New York: Arlington House, 1968), pp. 33–34.
34. Ibid., p. 391; emphasis in the original.
35. Rossiter, *Conservatism in America*, p. vii.
36. Russell Kirk, "Ideology and Political Economy," *America* 96 (5 January 1957): 389.
37. Harbour, *Foundations of Conservative Thought*, p. 110.
38. Rossiter, *Conservatism in America*, p. 226.
39. Kirk, *Conservative Mind*, p. 228.
40. Russell Kirk, *Prospects for Conservatives* (Washington, D.C.: Regnery Gateway, 1989), pp. 178–79.
41. John Crowe Ransom, "Reconstructed but Unregenerate," in Twelve Southerners, *I'll Take My Stand* (New York: Peter Smith, 1951), pp. 5–10; Richard M. Weaver, "The Southern Tradition," *New Individualist Review* 3 (1964): 14; reprinted in George M. Curtis III and James J. Thompson, Jr., ed., *The Southern Essays of Richard M. Weaver* (Indianapolis: Liberty Press, 1987), p. 223; Weaver, *Ideas Have Consequences*, p. 51.
42. Edward Abbey, *One Life at a Time, Please* (New York: Henry Holt, 1987), p. 21.
43. Gray, *Beyond the New Right*, p. 127.
44. Ibid., p. viii.
45. Gerhart Niemeyer, "Kirk and Ideology," *National Review*, 13 June 1994, p. 54.
46. Ibid.
47. Gray, *Beyond the New Right*, p. xi.
48. Weaver, *Ideas Have Consequences*, pp. 170, 172.
49. Weaver, "Southern Tradition," p. 13; Thompson, *Southern Essays*, pp. 220–21.
50. Richard M. Weaver, "Up From Liberalism," in *Life Without Prejudice and Other Essays* (Chicago: Henry Regnery, 1965), pp. 141–42. In his college days, he was a socialist.
51. Weaver, *Southern Tradition at Bay*, pp. 32, 34.
52. T. S. Eliot, *Christianity and Culture* (New York: Harcourt, Brace and World, 1949), pp. 48–49.
53. Weaver, *Ideas Have Consequences*, pp. 170–71.
54. Ibid., pp. 171–72.
55. Weaver, *Visions of Order*, pp. 121, 123. For the equivalent sentiment from an environmentalist, see the works of Wendell Berry, e.g., "The Obligation of Care," *Sierra*, September/October 1995, pp. 62–67, 102.
56. Kirk, *Conservative Mind*, pp. 44–45; see also Russell Kirk, "Impious Generations Are Often Rebuked," *New Orleans Times-Picayune*, 26 February 1968, sec. 1, p. 9.
57. Kirk, *Conservative Mind*, p. 10.
58. Quoted in Harbour, *Foundations of Conservative Thought*, p. 114.
59. Rossiter, *Conservatism in America*, p. 52.
60. Carl Pope, "Clinton's Layaway Plan," *Sierra*, May/June, 1994, p. 16.
61. Quoted in Rossiter, *Conservatism in America*, p. 26.
62. Ibid.
63. Quoted in C. A. Bowers, "The Conservative Misinterpretation of the Educational Ecological Crisis," *Environmental Ethics* 14 (1992): 121.
64. Kirk, *Prospects for Conservatives*, p. 6.
65. *High Country News*, 13 December 1993, p. 10: the quotation comes from Frank Egler, a pioneer in the field of ecology. For a classic statement of the need for humility for similar reasons from an environmentalist perspective, see David Ehrenfeld, *The Arrogance of Humanism* (New York: Oxford University Press, 1978).
66. The specific policy choices a conservative of either school would make to protect the environment would often be different from those a liberal would choose. The conservative would normally be inclined to use market mechanisms whenever possible to provide incentives for environmentally sound behavior, where the liberal, historically at least, has been inclined to turn first to bureaucratic command-and-control techniques. In suggesting policy implications here, my concern is still solely with the conservative intellectual movement, rather than with politicians who call themselves conservatives. Although the

conservative philosophy supports protecting the environment and conserving natural resources, "conservative" politicians (and pundits in the business press) have, in general, been notoriously hostile to environmental policies. The reasons for this discrepancy are many, and to consider the question in detail would require a separate essay. Here it may suffice to note a couple of points. In part, environmental activists may be at fault, to the extent that from the beginning they gave the environmental movement an anticapitalist tone. In large part, however, the politicians and commentators seem to be victims of Rossiter's "Great Train Robbery" noted above. And, of course, politicians are probably far more concerned with financing their campaigns and providing benefits to their constituents in order to get reelected than they are with philosophical consistency. There are, however, some notable exceptions, Margaret Thatcher is a convert to environmentalism (Cairncross, "Costing the Earth," p. 3). Barry Goldwater considers himself to be an environmentalist and there is now a growing group of conservative and moderate "Republicans for Environmental Protection" (Brad Knickerbocker, "GOP Lawmakers' New Shade of Green," *Christian Science Monitor* [October 20, 1995]: 4; see, for example, the op-ed piece on "Conservative Conservation" by Representative Connie Morella, Republican from Maryland, in the *Christian Science Monitor,* 3 August 1995, p. 20).

67. Pope, "Clinton's Layaway Plan," p. 14.
68. Eliot, *Christianity and Culture,* pp. 48–49.
69. Kirk, *Prospects for Conservatives,* pp. 81, 173.
70. Edward O. Wilson, *The Diversity of Life* (Cambridge: Harvard University Press, 1992), p. 346.
71. Edward O. Wilson, "Resolutions for the 80s," *Harvard Magazine,* January–February 1980, p. 21.
72. Aldo Leopold, "The Round River," in *A Sand County Almanac with Other Essays on Conservation from Round River* (New York: Oxford University Press, 1966), p. 177.
73. Russell Kirk, "Man Undoing Noah's Preservation Program," *New Orleans Times–Picayune,* 1 June 1965, sec. 1, p. 9. This column is a good illustration of Kirk's "literary" approach to issues. He begins, not with a biological or political analysis, but with a reference to a "fantasy" by C. S. Lewis, in which a diabolical power tries to overthrow God's universe. One of its first projects is "the extirpation of the great diversity and charm of animal life on this planet."
74. Gerhart Niemeyer notes that many American conservatives today are "laissez-faire economists who adhere to something like an ideology"; "The Burke-Kirk Phenomenon," *Crisis* 11 (October 1993): 26.
75. Kirk, "Ideology and Political Economy," p. 390.
76. Gray, *Beyond the New Right,* p. 128. Adam Smith himself was, apparently, no ideologue but was quite willing to turn to the state to correct market failures: Denis Collins and John Barkdull, "Capitalism, Environmentalism and Mediating Structures: From Adam Smith to Stakeholder Panels," *Environmental Ethics* 17 (1995): 227–44.
77. Gray, *Beyond the New Right,* p. 126.
78. Russell Kirk, "Pollution Might Be Spreading Over Land," *Los Angeles Times,* morning edition, 26 November 1962, sec. 2, p. 5.
79. Russell Kirk, "America the Beautiful? Not Without Some Countryside," *Detroit News,* 22 March 1973, p. B15.
80. For a detailed economic analysis, see Colin W. Clark, "The Economics of Overexploitation," *Science* 181 (1973): 630–34.
81. John L. Hammond, "Wilderness and Heritage Values," *Environmental Ethics* 7 (1985): 165–70.
82. Aldo Leopold, "Wilderness as a Form of Land Use," in *The River of the Mother of God and Other Essays,* ed. Susan L. Flader and J. Baird Callicott (Madison: University of Wisconsin Press, 1991), p. 138.
83. Weaver, *Ideas Have Consequences,* p. 112.
84. For similar conclusions about the implications of traditionalism, but from an analysis with a very different focus from the one used here, see R. V. Young, Jr., "A Conservative View of Environmental Affairs," *Environmental Ethics* 1 (1979): 241–54.

# A DECLARATION OF SUSTAINABILITY

*Paul Hawken*

Paul Hawken is author of the best-selling book *The Ecology of Commerce* and of other publications that promote sustainable economic development.

I recently performed a social audit for Ben and Jerry's Homemade Inc., America's premier socially responsible company. After poking and prodding around, asking tough questions, trying to provoke debate, and generally making a nuisance of myself, I can attest that their status as the leading social pioneer in commerce is safe for at least another year. They are an outstanding company. Are there flaws? Of course. Welcome to planet Earth. But the people at Ben & Jerry's are relaxed and unflinching in their willingness to look at, discuss, and deal with problems.

In the meantime, the company continues to put ice cream shops in Harlem, pay outstanding benefits, keep a compensation ratio of seven to one from the top of the organization to the bottom, seek out vendors from disadvantaged groups, and donate generous scoops of their profits to others. And they are about to overtake their historic rival Häagen-Dazs, the ersatz Scandinavian originator of super-premium ice cream, as the market leader in their category. At present rates of growth, Ben & Jerry's will be a $1 billion company by the end of the century. They are publicly held, nationally recognized, and rapidly growing, in part because Ben wanted to show that a socially responsible company could make it in the normal world of business.

Ben and Jerry's is just one of a growing vanguard of companies attempting to redefine their social and ethical responsibilities. These companies no longer accept the maxim that the business of business is business. Their premise is simple: Corporations, because they are the dominant institution on the planet, must squarely face the social and environmental problems that afflict

This essay originally appeared in *Utne Reader,* #59 (September/October 1993), 54–61. Reprinted with permission.

humankind. Organizations such as Business for Social Responsibility and the Social Venture Network, corporate "ethics" consultants, magazines such as *In Business* and *Business Ethics,* non-profits including the Council on Economic Priorities, investment funds such as Calvert and Covenant, newsletters like *Greenmoney,* and thousands of unaffiliated companies are drawing up new codes of conduct for corporate life that integrate social, ethical, and environmental principles.

Ben and Jerry's and the roughly 2,000 other committed companies in the social responsibility movement here and abroad have combined annual sales of approximately $2 billion, or one-hundredth of 1 percent of the $20 trillion sales garnered by the estimated 80 million to 100 million enterprises worldwide. The problems they are trying to address are vast and unremittingly complex: 5.5 billion people are breeding exponentially, and fulfilling their wants and needs is stripping the earth of its biotic capacity to produce life; a climactic burst of consumption by a single species is overwhelming the skies, earth, waters, and fauna.

As the Worldwatch Institute's Lester Brown patiently explains in his annual survey *State of the World,* every living system on earth is in decline. Making matters worse, we are having a once-in-a-billion-year blowout sale of hydrocarbons, which are being combusted into the atmosphere, effectively double glazing the planet within the next 50 years with unknown climatic results. The cornucopia of resources that are being extracted, mined, and harvested is so poorly distributed that 20 percent of the earth's people are chronically hungry or starving, while the top 20 percent of the population, largely in the north, control and consume 80 percent of the world's wealth. Since business in its myriad forms is primarily responsible for this "taking," it is appropriate that a growing number of companies ask the question, How does one honorably conduct business in the latter days of industrialism and the beginning of an ecological age? The ethical dilemma that confronts business begins with the acknowledgment that a commercial system that functions well by its own definitions unavoidably defies the greater and more profound ethic of biology. Specifically, how does business face the prospect that creating a profitable, growing company requires an intolerable abuse of the natural world?

Despite their dedicated good work, if we examine all or any of the businesses that deservedly earn high marks for social and environmental responsibility, we are faced with a sobering irony: If every company on the planet were to adopt the environmental and social practices of the best companies—of, say, the Body Shop, Patagonia, and Ben and Jerry's—the world would still be moving toward environmental degradation and collapse. In other words, if we analyze environmental effects and create an input-output model of resources and energy, the results do not even approximate a tolerable or sustainable future. If a tiny fraction of the world's most intelligent companies cannot model a sustainable world, then that tells us that being socially responsible is only one part of an overall solution, and that what we have is not a management problem but a design problem.

At present, there is a contradiction inherent in the premise of a socially responsible corporation: to wit, that a company can make the world better, can grow, and can increase profits by meeting social and environmental needs. It is a have-your-cake-and-eat-it fantasy that cannot come true if the primary cause of environmental degradation is overconsumption. Although proponents of socially responsible business are making an outstanding effort at reforming the tired old ethics of commerce, they are unintentionally creating a new rationale for companies to produce, advertise, expand, grow, capitalize, and use up resources: the rationale that they are doing good. A jet flying across the country, a car rented at an airport, an air-conditioned hotel room, a truck full of goods, a worker commuting to his or her job—all cause the same amount of environmental degradation whether they're associated with the Body Shop, the Environmental Defense Fund, or R. J. Reynolds.

In order to approximate a sustainable society, we need to describe a system of commerce and production in which each and every act is inherently sustainable and restorative. Because of the way our system of commerce is designed, businesses will not be able to fulfill their social contract with the environment or society until the system in which they operate undergoes a fundamental change, a change that brings commerce and governance into alignment with the natural world from which we receive our life. There must be an integration of economic, biologic, and human systems in order to create a sustainable and interdependent method of commerce that supports and furthers our existence. As hard as we may strive to create sustainability on a company level, we cannot fully succeed until the institutions surrounding commerce are redesigned. Just as every act of production and consumption in an industrial society leads to further environmental degradation, regardless of intention or ethos, we need to imagine—and then design—a system of commerce where the opposite is true, where doing good is like falling off a log, where the natural, everyday acts of work and life accumulate into a better world as a matter of course, not a matter of altruism. A system of sustainable commerce would involve these objectives:

1. It would reduce absolute consumption of energy and natural resources among developed nations by 80 percent within 40 to 60 years.
2. It would provide secure, stable, and meaningful employment for people everywhere.
3. It would be self-actuating as opposed to regulated, controlled, mandated, or moralistic.
4. It would honor human nature and market principles.
5. It would be perceived as more desirable than our present way of life.
6. It would exceed sustainability by restoring degraded habitats and ecosystems to their fullest biological capacity.
7. It would rely on current solar income.
8. It should be fun and engaging, and strive for an aesthetic outcome.

# STRATEGIES FOR SUSTAINABILITY

At present, the environmental and social responsibility movements consist of many different initiatives, connected primarily by values and beliefs rather than by design. What is needed is a conscious plan to create a sustainable future, including a set of design strategies for people to follow. For the record, I will suggest 12.

## 1. Take Back the Charter

Although corporate charters may seem to have little to do with sustainability, they are critical to any long-term movement toward restoration of the planet. Read *Taking Care of Business: Citizenship and the Charter of Incorporation*, a 1992 pamphlet by Richard Grossman and Frank T. Adams (Charter Ink, Box 806. Cambridge, MA 02140). In it you find a lost history of corporate power and citizen involvement that addresses a basic and crucial point: Corporations are chartered by, and exist at the behest of, citizens. Incorporation is not a right but a privilege granted by the state that includes certain considerations such as limited liability. Corporations are supposed to be under our ultimate authority, not the other way around. The charter of incorporation is a revocable dispensation that was supposed to ensure accountability of the corporation to society as a whole. When Rockwell criminally despoils a weapons facility at Rocky Flats, Colorado, with plutonium waste, or when any corporation continually harms, abuses, or violates the public trust, citizens should have the right to revoke its charter, causing the company to disband, sell off its enterprises to other companies, and effectively go out of business. The workers would have jobs with the new owners, but the executives, directors, and management would be out of jobs, with a permanent notice on their resumes that they mismanaged a corporation into a charter revocation. This is not merely a deterrent to corporate abuse but a critical element of an ecological society because it creates feedback loops that prompt accountability, citizen involvement, and learning. We should remember that the citizens of this country originally envisioned corporations to be part of a public-private partnership, which is why the relationship between the chartering authority of state legislatures and the corporation was kept alive and active. They had it right.

## 2. Adjust Price to Reflect Cost

The economy is environmentally and commercially dysfunctional because the market does not provide consumers with proper information. The "free market" economies that we love so much are excellent at setting prices but lousy when it comes to recognizing costs. In order for a sustainable society to exist, every purchase must reflect or at least approximate its actual cost, not only the direct cost of production but also the costs to the air, water, and soil; the cost to future generations; the cost to worker health; the cost of waste, pollution, and toxicity. Simply stated, the marketplace gives us the wrong information. It tells us the flying across the country on a discount airline ticket is cheap when it is not. It tells us that our food is inexpensive when its method of production destroys aquifers and soil, the viability of ecosystems, and workers' lives. Whenever an organism gets wrong information, it is a form of toxicity. In fact, that is how pesticides work. A herbicide kills because it is a hormone that tells the plant to grow faster than its capacity to absorb nutrients allows. It literally grows itself to death. Sound familiar? Our daily doses of toxicity are the prices in the market place. They are telling us to do the wrong thing for our own survival. They are lulling us into cutting down old-growth forests on the Olympic Peninsula for apple crates, into patterns of production and consumption that are not just unsustainable but profoundly short-sighted and destructive. It is surprising that "conservative" economists do not support or understand this idea, because it is they who insist that we pay as we go, have no debts, and take care of business. Let's do it.

## 3. Throw Out and Replace the Entire Tax System

The present tax system sends the wrong messages to virtually everyone, encourages waste, discourages conservation, and rewards consumption. It taxes what we want to encourage—jobs, creativity, payrolls, and real income—and ignores the things we want to discourage—degradation, pollution, and depletion. The present U.S. tax system costs citizens $500 billion a year in record-keeping, filing, administrative, legal, and governmental costs—more than the actual amount we pay in personal income taxes. The only incentive in the present system is to cheat or hire a lawyer to cheat for us. The entire tax system must be incrementally replaced over a 20-year period by "Green fees," taxes that are added onto existing products, energy, services, and materials so that prices in the marketplace more closely approximate true costs. These taxes are not a means to raise revenue or bring down deficits, but must be absolutely revenue neutral so that people in the lower and middle classes experience no real change of income, only a shift in expenditures. Eventually, the cost of non-renewable resources, extractive energy, and industrial modes of production will be more expensive than renewable resources, such as solar energy, sustainable forestry, and biological methods of agriculture. Why should the upper middle class be able to afford to conserve while the lower income classes cannot? So far the environmental movement has only made the world better for upper middle class white people. The only kind of environmental movement that can succeed has to start from the bottom up. Under a Green fee system the incentives to save on taxes will create positive, constructive acts that are affordable for everyone. As energy prices go up to three to four times their existing levels (with commensurate tax reductions to offset the increase), the natural inclination to save money will result in carpooling, bicycling, telecommuting, public transport, and more efficient houses. As taxes on artificial fertilizers, pesticides, and fuel go up, again with offsetting reductions in income and payroll taxes, organic farmers will find that their produce and methods are the cheapest means of production (because they truly are), and customers will find that organically grown food is less expensive than its commercial cousin. Eventually, with the probable exception of taxes on the rich, we will find ourselves in a position where we pay no taxes, but spend our money with a practiced and constructive discernment. Under an enlightened and redesigned tax system, the cheapest product in the marketplace would be best for the customer, the worker, the environment, and the company. That is rarely the case today.

## 4. Allow Resource Companies to Be Utilities

An energy utility is an interesting hybrid of public-private interests. A utility gains a market monopoly in exchange for public control of rates, open books, and a guaranteed rate of return. Because of this relationship and the pioneering work of Amory Lovins, we now have markets for "negawatts." It is the first time in the history of industrialism that a corporation has figured out how to make money by selling the absence of something. Negawatts are the opposite of energy: They represent the collaborative ability of a utility to harness efficiency instead of hydrocarbons. This conservation-based alternative saves ratepayers, shareholders, and the company money—savings that are passed along to everyone. All resource systems, including oil, gas, forests, and water, should be run by some form of utility. There should be markets in negabarrels, negatrees, and negacoal. Oil companies, for example, have no alternative at present other than to lobby for the absurd, like drilling in the Arctic National Wildlife Refuge. That project, a $40 billion to $60 billion investment for a hoped-for supply of oil that would meet U.S. consumption needs for only six months, is the only way an oil company can make money under our current system of commerce. But what if the oil companies formed an oil utility and cut a deal with citizens and taxpayers that allowed them to "invest" in insulation, super-glazed windows, conservation rebates on new automobiles, and the scrapping of old cars? Through Green fees, we would pay them back a return on their conservation investment equal to what utilities receive, a rate of return that would be in accord with how many barrels of oil they save, rather than how many barrels they produce. Why should they care? Why should we? A $60 billion investment in conservation will yield, conservatively, four to ten times as much energy as drilling for oil. Given Lovins' principle of efficiency extraction, try to imagine a forest utility, a salmon utility, a copper utility, a Mississippi River utility, a grasslands utility. Imagine a system where the resource utility benefits from conservation, makes money from efficiency, thrives through restoration, and profits from sustainability. It is possible today.

## 5. Change Linear Systems to Cyclical Ones

Our economy has many design flaws, but the most glaring one is that nature is cyclical and industrialism is linear. In nature, no linear systems exist, or they don't exist for long because they exhaust themselves into extinction. Linear industrial systems take resources, transform them into products or services, discard waste, and sell to consumers, who discard more waste when they have consumed the product. But of course we don't consume TVs, cars, or most of the other stuff we buy. Instead, Americans produce six times their body weight every week in hazardous and toxic waste water, incinerator fly ash, agricultural wastes, heavy metals, and waste chemicals, paper, wood, etc. This does not include $CO_2$, which if it were included would double the amount of waste. Cyclical means of production are designed to imitate natural systems in which waste equals food for other forms of life, nothing is thrown away, and symbiosis replaces competition. Bill McDonough, a New York architect who has pioneered environmental design principles, has designed a system to retrofit every window in a major American city. Although it still awaits final approval, the project is planned to go like this: The city and a major window manufacturer form a joint venture to produce energy-saving super-glazed windows in the town. This partnership company will come to your house or business, measure all windows and glass doors, and then replace them with windows with an R-8 to R-12 energy-efficiency rating within 72 hours. The windows will have the same casements, molding, and general appearance as the old ones. You will receive a $500 check upon installation, and you will pay for the new windows over a 10- to 15-year period in your utility or tax bill. The total bill is less than the cost of the energy the windows will save. In other words, the windows will cost the home or business owner nothing. The city will pay for them initially with industrial development bonds. The factory will train and employ 300 disadvantaged people. The old windows will be completely recycled and reused, the glass melted into glass, the wooden frames ground up and mixed with recycled resins that are extruded to make the casements. When the city is reglazed, the residents and businesses will pocket an extra $20 million to $30 million every year in money saved on utility bills. After the windows are paid for, the figure will go even higher. The factory, designed to be transportable, will move to another city, the first city will retain an equity interest in the venture. McDonough has designed a win-win-win-win-win system that optimizes a number of agendas. The ratepayers, the homeowners, the renters, the city, the environment, and the employed all thrive because they are "making" money from efficiency rather than exploitation. It's a little like running the industrial economy backwards.

## 6. Transform the Making of Things

We have to institute the Intelligent Product System created by Michael Braungart of the EPEA (Environmental Protection Encouragement Agency) in

Hamburg, Germany. The system recognizes three types of products. The first are *consumables*, products that are either eaten, or, when they're placed on the ground, turn into dirt without any bio-accumulative effects. In other words, they are products whose waste equals food for other living systems. At present, many of the products that should be "consumable," like clothing and shoes, are not. Cotton cloth contains hundreds of different chemicals, plasticizers, defoliants, pesticides, and dyes: shoes are tanned with chromium and their soles contain lead: neckties and silk blouses contain zinc, tin, and toxic dye. Much of what we recycle today turns into toxic by-products, consuming more energy in the recycling process than is saved by recycling. We should be designing more things so that they can be thrown away—into the compost heap. Toothpaste tubes and other non-degradable packaging can be made out of natural polymers so that they break down and become fertilizer for plants. A package that turns into dirt is infinitely more useful, biologically speaking, than a package that turns into a plastic park bench. Heretical as it sounds, designing for decomposition, not recycling, is the way of the world around us.

The second category is *durables*, but in this case, they would not be sold, only licensed. Cars, TVs, VCRs, and refrigerators would always belong to the original manufacturer, so they would be made, used, and returned within a closed-loop system. This is already being instituted in Germany and to a lesser extent in Japan, where companies are beginning to design for disassembly. If a company knows that its products will come back someday, and that it cannot throw anything away when they do, it creates a very different approach to design and materials.

Last, there are *unsalables*—toxins, radiation, heavy metals, and chemicals. There is no living system for which these are food and thus they can never be thrown away. In Braungart's Intelligent Product System, unsalables must always belong to the original maker, safeguarded by public utilities called "parking lots" that store the toxins in glass-lined barrels indefinitely, charging the original manufacturers rent for the service. The rent ceases when an independent scientific panel can confirm that there is a safe method to detoxify the substances in question. All toxic chemicals would have molecular markers identifying them as belonging to their originator, so that if they are found in wells, rivers, soil, or fish, it is the responsibility of the company to retrieve them and clean up. This places the problem of toxicity with the makers, where it belongs, making them responsible for full–life-cycle effects.

## 7. Vote, Don't Buy

Democracy has been effectively eliminated in America by the influence of money, lawyers, and a political system that is the outgrowth of the first two. While we can dream of restoring our democratic system, the fact remains that we live in a plutocracy—government by the wealthy. One way out is to vote with your dollars, to withhold purchases from companies that act or respond inappropriately. Don't just avoid buying a Mitsubishi automobile because of the company's participation in the destruction of primary forests in Malaysia, Indonesia, Ecuador, Brazil, Bolivia, Canada, Chile, Canada, Siberia, and Papua New Guinea. Write and tell them why you won't. Engage in dialogue, send one postcard a week, talk, organize, meet, publish newsletters, boycott, patronize, and communicate with companies like General Electric. Educate non-profits, organizations, municipalities, and pension funds to act affirmatively, to support the ecological CERES (formerly *Valdez*) Principles for business, to invest intelligently, and to *think* with their money, not merely spend it. Demand the best from the companies you work for and buy from. You deserve it and your actions will help them change.

## 8. Restore the "Guardian"

There can be no healthy business sector unless there is a healthy governing sector. In her book *System of Survival,* author Jane Jacobs describes two overarching moral syndromes that permeate our society: the commercial syndrome, which arose from trading cultures, and the governing, or guardian, syndrome that arose from territorial cultures. The guardian system is hierarchical, adheres to tradition, values loyalty, and shuns trading and inventiveness. The commercial system, on the other hand, is based on trading, so it values trust of outsiders, innovation, and future thinking. Each has qualities the other lacks. Whenever the guardian tries to be in business, as in Eastern Europe, business doesn't work. What is also true, but not so obvious to us, is that when business plays government, governance fails as well. Our guardian system has almost completely broken down because of the money, power, influence, and control exercised by business and, to a lesser degree, other institutions. Business and unions have to get out of government. We need more than campaign reform: We need a vision that allows us all to see that when Speaker of the House Tom Foley exempts the aluminum industry in his district from the proposed Btu tax, or when Philip Morris donates $200,000 to the Jesse Helms Citizenship Center, citizenship is mocked and democracy is left gagging and twitching on the Capitol steps. The irony is that business thinks that its involvement in governance is good corporate citizenship or at least is advancing its own interests. The reality is that business is preventing the economy from evolving. Business loses, workers lose, the environment loses.

## 9. Shift from Electronic Literacy to Biologic Literacy

That an average adult can recognize one thousand brand names and logos but fewer than ten local plants is not a good sign. We are moving not to an information age but to a biologic age, and unfortunately our technological education is equipping us for corporate markets, not the future. Sitting at home with virtual reality gloves, 3D video games, and interactive cable TV shopping is a barren and impoverished vision of the future. The computer revolution is not the totem of our future, only a tool. Don't get me wrong. Computers are great. But they are not an uplifting or compelling vision for culture or society.

They do not move us toward a sustainable future any more than our obsession with cars and televisions provided us with newer definitions or richer meaning. We are moving into the age of living machines, not, as Corbusier noted, "machines for living in." The Thomas Edison of the future is not Bill Gates of Microsoft, but John and Nancy Todd, founders of the New Alchemy Institute, a Massachusetts design lab and think tank for sustainability. If the Todds' work seems less commercial, less successful, and less glamorous, it is because they are working on the real problem—how to live—and it is infinitely more complex than a microprocessor. Understanding biological processes is how we are going to create a new symbiosis with living systems (or perish). What we can learn on-line is how to model complex systems. It is computers that have allowed us to realize how the synapses in the common sea slug are more powerful than all of our parallel processors put together.

## 10. Take Inventory

We do not know how many species live on the planet within a factor of ten. We do not know how many are being extirpated. We do not know what is contained in the biological library inherited from the Cenozoic age. (Sociobiologist E. O. Wilson estimates that it would take 25,000 person-years to catalog most of the species, putting aside the fact that there are only 1,500 people with the taxonomic ability to undertake the task.) We do not know how complex systems interact—how the transpiration of the giant lily, *Victoria amazonica*, of Brazil's rainforests affects European rainfall and agriculture, for example. We do not know what happens to 20 percent of the $CO_2$ that is offgassed every year (it disappears without a trace). We do not know how to calculate sustainable yields in fisheries and forest systems. We do not know why certain species, such as frogs, are dying out even in pristine habitats. We do not know the long-term effects of chlorinated hydrocarbons on human health, behavior, sexuality, and fertility. We do not know what a sustainable life is for existing inhabitants of the planet, and certainly not for future populations. (A Dutch study calculated that your fair share of air travel is one trip across the Atlantic in a lifetime.) We do not know how many people we can feed on a sustainable basis, or what our diet would look like. In short, we need to find out what's here, who has it, and what we can or can't do with it.

## 11. Take Care of Human Health

The environmental and socially responsible movements would gain additional credibility if they recognized that the greatest amount of human suffering and mortality is caused by environmental problems that are not being addressed by environmental organizations or companies. Contaminated water is killing a hundred times more people than all other forms of pollution combined. Millions of children are dying from preventable diseases and malnutrition.

The movement toward sustainability must address the clear and present dangers that people face worldwide, dangers that ironically increase population levels because of their perceived threat. People produce more children when they're afraid they'll lose them. Not until the majority of the people in the world, all of whom suffer in myriad preventable yet intolerable ways, understand that environmentalism means improving their lives directly will the ecology movement walk its talk. Americans will spend more money in the next 12 months on the movie and tchotchkes of *Jurassic Park* than on foreign aid to prevent malnutrition or provide safe water.

## 12. Respect the Human Spirit

If hope is to pass the sobriety test, then it has to walk a pretty straight line to reality. Nothing written, suggested, or proposed here is possible unless business is willing to integrate itself into the natural world. It is time for business to take the initiative in a genuinely open process of dialogue, collaboration, reflection, and redesign. "It is not enough," writes Jeremy Seabrook of the British Green party, "to declare, as many do, that we are living in an unsustainable way, using up resources, squandering the substance of the next generation however true this may be. People must feel subjectively the injustice and unsustainability before they will make a more sober assessment as to whether it is worth maintaining what is, or whether there might not be more equitable and satisfying ways that will not be won at the expense either of the necessities of the poor or of the wasting fabric of the planet."

Poet and naturalist W. S. Merwin (citing Robert Graves) reminds us that we have one story, and one story only, to tell in our lives. We are made to believe by our parents and businesses, by our culture and televisions, by our politicians and movie stars that it is the story of money, of finance, of wealth, of the stock portfolio, the partnership, the country house. These are small, impoverished tales and whispers that have made us restless and craven: they are not stories at all. As author and garlic grower Stanley Crawford puts it, "The financial statement must finally give way to the narrative, with all its exceptions, special cases, imponderables. It must finally give way to the story, which is perhaps the way we arm ourselves against the next and always unpredictable turn of the cycle in the quixotic dare that is life: across the rock and cold of lifelines, it is our seed, our clove, our filament cast toward the future." It is something deeper than anything commercial culture can plumb, and it is waiting for each of us.

Business must yield to the longings of the human spirit. The most important contribution of the socially responsible business movement has little to do with recycling, nuts from the rainforest, or employing the homeless. Their gift to us is that they are leading by trying to do something, to risk, take a chance, make a change—any change. They are not waiting for "the solution," but are acting without guarantees of success or proof of purchase. This is what all of us must do. Being visionary has always been given a bad rap by commerce. But without a positive vision for humankind we can have no meaning, no work, and no purpose.

# IS LIBERALISM
# ENVIRONMENT-FRIENDLY?

*Avner de-Shalit*

Avner de-Shalit, senior lecturer in political science at the Hebrew University in Jerusalem, is the author of *Why Posterity Matters*.

The state of the environment is a novel issue on the political agenda, yet it is one of the most important. People the world over have begun to realize that the damage to the environment caused by human activities is drastic and at times even irreversible. The pollution of the soil, contamination of water by chemicals, air pollution, the damage to the ozone layer, acid rain, the complications in radioactive waste management, the extinction of certain animal species, deforestation, misguided urban development—all these and other phenomena constitute what is now widely called "the environmental problem."

Some people tend to think that scientists, or engineers, can solve, or at least suggest solutions to all these problems.[1] But although theoretically speaking most environmental problems have scientific solutions, in practice these solutions are thrust aside by economic criteria and considerations. Now, the latter are simply the reflection of social and political ideologies, and so, in fact, environmental policies involve decisions on the allocation of financial resources and time, the distribution of money and political power, and on public priorities. Consequently, the solution to these problems is political,[2] with the result that philosophers and political theorists have tried to find the moral grounds for environment-friendly policies. This paper deals with this attempt. My argument is two-fold: first, that liberalism, for a number of reasons that will be investigated here, has provided a good framework for the evolution of the "Green" ideas and environmental philosophy. But second, that with regard to environmental policies, liberalism nevertheless faces difficulties: while it allows and encourages discussion of environmental issues, it cannot permit its outcome, namely the implementation, maintenance, and justification of environmental policies, and therefore it precludes constructive public action to secure environmental protection.

This ambivalent attitude may confuse the reader, since there is no sharp and unequivocal assertion in favor of or against liberalism in the context of the environment. On the contrary, the intrinsic complexity of liberalism and the gap between the theoretical discussion and praxis reveal the complexity of liberalism's relationship with environmentalism. But this paper may speak to the suggestion that a more "social" liberalism could, perhaps, deliver the goods.[3] In that respect my project calls for further research; however, I am suggesting that theory about the politics of the environment should be placed not merely in its "Greens" or "movement" context, but in a wider framework, that of the liberal tradition in political theory.[4]

## LIBERALISM AND ENVIRONMENTAL PHILOSOPHY

It may be argued that at first appearance liberalism and environmental philosophy do not tie in with each other because liberalism's most fundamental feature—the contract—leaves out those who cannot join it, that is, trees, rocks, rivers, animals, and so on. The most prominent of contemporary liberal theorists, John Rawls, for instance, leaves this issue to metaphysics.[5] Others have tried to follow Rawls's path, and yet modify it so that it generates an animal rights ethics,[6] or show that his theory implicitly requires extensive environmental policies.[7] But in this section my aim is not so much to show how liberalism and environmental philosophy can be seen as identical twins or as ideal ideological bedfellows, but rather to argue that liberal societies have become a fertile ground for the promotion of ecological attitudes and environmental philosophy. There are four main reasons for this: the first two reasons lie in the sphere of philosophy, or theory, and involve both the content of the liberal idea and the tradition of liberal thought.

Let us start with the former. One of the main components of liberalism is antichauvinism: the moral agent does not automatically exalt its own virtues and discredit those of others. (The moral agent could be a single person or a collective body to which the person belongs, whether it is a voluntary body, for example, a party, firm, or a body into which the person was born, for example, a nation, race, gender, class.) Chauvinists do not consider "others" on equal terms, but liberals have rejected such attitudes and instead propound the idea that all people are equal since they are all human beings cast in the same mold. Hence liberals have contended that all humans deserve equal rights, and that we should follow a policy of "respect for others" and "respecting others as equals."[8] In short, liberalism as a social philosophy has rejected all expressions of chauvinism from national to male chauvinism.

At the same time the situation in which humans deplete resources and damage the environment has been described on several occasions, and quite rightly, as "man (or human) chauvinism"[9] with respect to the ill-treatment of nonhuman animals (sometimes even plants or ecosystems) and their exclusion from the ethical community.

It is only natural, then, that many liberals, both theorists and politicians, have adopted Green ideas and ecological attitudes: the essence of liberalism, as indicated above, is the philosophy of "respect for others." An environmental attitude implies extending the notion of "others" to include nonhuman animals, "all sentient creatures," or even "all living objects" or "ecosystems."

> A land ethic changes the role of homo sapiens from conqueror of the land-community to plain member and citizen of it. It implies respect for his fellow members, and also respect for the community as such.[10]

Most liberals would find it difficult to adhere to "holism" or to Aldo Leopold's "Land Ethic," which rests upon the premise that the individual is a member of a community of interdependent parts; but it is arguable that the elements of antichauvinism and "respect for others" that have characterized liberal thought have influenced and contributed to the emergence of "Green" ideas, at least in their defense of individual entities in the environment. Admittedly, many greens are keener on collections of living objects, for example, species, rather than individual entities. This will be discussed below, where I suggest that a more social type of liberalism suits environmental issues. It also remains to develop a theory of humans' relationship with the nonsentient objects; Christopher Stone has perhaps shown the way.[11] Nevertheless, Roderick Nash has drawn an interesting analogy in this connection between the liberal political campaign against slavery in America and the environmentalists' attempt to persuade the public that the circle of the ethical community should be enlarged to include animals, and even plants, or ecosystems. Just as the Abolitionists were considered radical when they claimed that blacks were being ill–treated and denied any moral status, so the environmentalists are regarded as radical today. Consequently, Nash may be right in claiming that environmental ethics is a "logical extrapolation of the powerful liberal tradition."[12] Liberals in the nineteenth century passed from male chauvinism and racism to moral universalism, environmentalists today pass from a human chauvinism to a broader moral universalism, arguing that "the conscious suffering of a sentient creature is indeed intrinsically bad from that creature's standpoint." Thus, we look at other species

> [as] we look at ourselves, seeing them as beings which have a good they are striving to realize just as we have a good we are striving to realize. . . . [Hence] their lives can be made better or worse by the way humans treat them, and it is possible for humans to take their standpoint and judge what happens to them in terms of *their* well-being [emphasis in original].[13]

Now while liberals in the nineteenth century wished to protect the vulnerable, that is, the potential victims of modernity and progress, environmentalists towards the end of the twentieth century still protect the victims of modernity, but unlike progressive forces in the nineteenth century, they extend the circle of protection to include the natural environment.

So much for the content of liberalism. But there is a second aspect of liberal theory that is built into the tradition of liberal philosophy. Liberals have always subjected their positions, values, ideas and theories to critical scrutiny, and have been the proponents of openness and tolerance, not only in political life, but in the academic and philosophical debate as well.[14] Even philosophers and theorists who attack the liberal tradition for its inability to tackle, understand, or solve ecological problems[15] must admit that they can do so because they live and work in a liberal and tolerant society.

Moreover, in order to accept environmental philosophy one must be relatively open to new ideas and tolerant of criticism—not only of one's own theory, but also of one's methodology. This is because environmental philosophy is (mostly) biocentric or ecocentric, rather than anthropocentric: that is, it considers nonhuman objects (individual animals, plants, or ecosystems) as moral "clients" as well as human beings, and unlike traditional morality, it discusses the moral relationship between humans and nonhuman entities. So while one should be careful in claiming similarity between liberalism and environmental philosophy (just because the former argues for tolerance), it seems fair to maintain that it is at least partly due to liberalism's rejection of methodological monism and fostering of a philosophical and intellectual milieu in which new ideas can flourish, that environmental philosophy has emerged.[16]

The third reason why liberalism became the breeding ground for a flourishing of ecological attitudes lies in the sphere of internal politics. I refer here to a tradition of defending the individual against the church, the state, large-scale industries and firms. This started in the eighteenth century with the defense of the individual against the state or church, followed by a warning that democracy might still yield despotism. A suspicion of the despotic rule of the majority (thus, liberals defended the minorities—especially the intellectuals—from the masses) grew into the ideology of citizens' rights in the twentieth century. Recently liberalism became the defender of the underdog, a crusader against monopolies and for proper government and universal law.[17]

The same stand is taken today by environmentalists: they must challenge the activities of huge industries and firms, mainly because they are unsustainable. Such firms, for purely profit-making motives, often pollute the air or the water, decimate forests, and in general neglect the right of individuals to a clean environment. The state must impose regulations, but very often the state, for economic and other reasons, also ignores the dangers to individuals. The role of environmentalists, then, is to document the situation, publish warnings, and sometimes take the liberty to act.[18]

Indeed, this stand is taken by many environmentalists. Even Jonathon Porritt, ex-director of Friends of the Earth in Britain and one of the leaders of the British Green Party, who attacks liberal politicians for their lack of support for the Green cause,[19] employs the liberal terminology of rights when presenting his Green philosophy.

The fact that people's *rights* are being denied is in itself a serious enough problem. . . . And the fact that there are so few . . . who are prepared either to inform people of the denial of their *rights* or to help them to fight for those *rights*, turns a problem of indifference into crisis of inaction [emphasis added].[20]

Last, a fourth reason why ecological attitudes have taken root in liberal societies lies in the sphere of international relations. Here one particular element inherent in liberal thought should be highlighted: internationalism. Admittedly this notion sometimes stands for "free trade," which is not environment-friendly, according to many environmentalists. But at the same time, internationalism embodies a strong belief in and reliance on multilateral agreements and international organizations, together with the conviction that political problems may be solved by sometimes tiresome negotiations and that national interests do not necessarily run counter to international cooperation. While many people consider the international arena as a place where "might is right," and where those whose interests are harmed can only complain post factum, liberals have regarded international relations as a sphere in which it is possible to foresee problems and apply the treatment before the damage is caused.

All these elements are crucial, because environmental problems can and must of course be tackled only through international cooperation. This is precisely the element that is both lacking and needed in contemporary politics in regard to the solution of environmental problems, which are rarely entirely local in character.[21] Indeed, the idea that prevention is better than cure has been the underlying rationale for the 1972 Stockholm Conference on the Human Environment, the Toronto Declaration, the London Dumping Convention, *Our Common Future*, the 1992 UNCED in Rio de Janeiro, and other notable international agreements.

At this point it may be argued that at least a few of the features of liberalism, discussed so far, characterize other currents of thought and ideologies as well, for example, socialism. This may be true, although the second feature, that is, the rejection of methodological monism and advancing academic pluralism is, I believe, characteristic mainly of liberalism. But even if not, my argument is neither that liberalism is a necessary condition for the emergence of environmental philosophy, nor that it is a sufficient condition, but rather that liberalism—as a philosophy and a political attitude—influences, stimulates, and encourages the environmental deliberation and the rise of Green thought.

## THE POLITICAL TASK

While in recent years much thought has been given to ecology, it seems that it has nevertheless been too little. The damages to the environment are now of such horrifying proportions that many people think that these problems call for radical and urgent solutions, an approach not necessarily compatible with traditional liberal democracy's reluctance to undertake dramatic changes. And yet, now, in the 1990s the world is witnessing a worldwide democratization and the flourishing of liberal–democratic ideas, and no one should be required to abandon this trend.

The extremely complex political mission for the 1990s, then is twofold: on the one hand, no longer to relieve ecological "suffering," but rather to introduce reforms radical enough to save the environment and reverse what is still reversible; and on the other hand, to ensure this should not come about at the price of imposing regulations that limit or reduce liberties. Thus, there are two dimensions to this mission: to sustain the growing enthusiasm for democracy and liberty and at the same time to save the environment.

As already indicated above, these two dimensions are closely correlated. Many environmentalists, political theorists, and philosophers, in the light of environmental problems, among them scarcity of resources and pollution, have expressed pessimism and anxiety regarding the future of liberal democracy. Lack of resources on the one hand, and selfish, or self-interested, behavior on the other, has caused them to believe that the only solution might be the imposition of regulations and policies against people's wills. William Ophuls, for example, wrote that "the return of scarcity portends the revival of age-old political evils, for our descendants if not ourselves."[22] As Paehlke points out, all these writers fear that the only possible outcome will be "severe economic restraints, self-discipline beyond that which is likely to develop voluntarily."[23]

But Ophuls's prophecy need not necessarily come to pass. For instance, while his suggestion of replacing the market by political action is, I believe, welcome (see below), it is still questionable whether liberty should give way to authority and egalitarian democracy should be abandoned for the sake of "political competence and status."[24] Ophuls's appeal for a strong leadership[25]— reminiscent of George Bernard Shaw's *Man and Superman*—is not the only alternative.

It seems that democratic societies should be looking for a middle path, which might include, at least prima facie, noncoercive, but planned and consistent policies. These policies must be in line with sustaining and promoting democracy and people's liberties, and yet they may also imply a shift from discussing environmental issues politically to a politics of the environment, and hence state intervention. This leads us to the second main question of the paper.

## ENVIRONMENTALISM AND LIBERALISM: INDIVIDUALS' ECONOMIC BEHAVIOR

Why does liberalism outside the debate in the universities fail to justify environmental policies? What happens when it comes to real politics? The debate in the universities has been mainly focused on the question of whether or not there are intrinsic values in nature, or on the issue of animals' rights, because it has never been faced with the actual need to convince the other side, for example, developers, vivisectionists, and so forth. But when politicians come to justify their policies to the general public, they must do this in more traditional, general, and popular terms[26] and it is at this point that liberalism runs into difficulties.

Now, in order to demonstrate this, a distinction should be made between two conceptions of politics that represent two interpretations of liberalism. One, which generally speaking is more common in contemporary mainstream American liberalism, is based on the values of neutrality, minimal state intervention, an opposition to regulations, and a concept of politics as an aggregate of autonomous decisions—all of which are antithetical to environmental policies. The other interpretation, sometimes called "social liberalism," is not hostile to advancing certain ideas of the good (for example, conservation), and is more open to state intervention.[27]

But before we discuss the best conception of politics in the context of ecology, a more radical liberal argument, that the state should not intervene at all because individuals' economic behavior is the best foundation for solving environmental policies, needs to be refuted. I deliberately refrain from claiming to refute the "market approach" to the environment. This is a much debated issue, and had I set out to do this, I should have written a separate article. But I would like to examine the literature on the premises of the market approach in our context, with special attention to the "correct" (not in the sense of politically correct) role of politics.

First of all, many arguments have been put forward against the economic behavior approach with respect to the environment. According to several ecosocialists, we can no longer trust the magic and the invisible hand of the market to do the work for us; we must plan and initiate. Individuals' economic behavior has proved to be both inefficient and inequitable in coping with ecology.

For instance, Jeremy Seabrook, an ex-member of the British Labour Party and currently a Green activist, contends that the market is the best and most efficient mechanism to ruin the entire universe. In spite of this, people all over the world have been attracted to the idea of the market and its promise of a better material future, and so forth, because "the economy became the arena in which the guilt for what had happened [in WW II] was to be assuaged." The market, he argues, became "the object of a superstitious reverence: if only this could be made to work, to grow, to provide, we would surely gain exemption from any recurrence of the barbarities of the recent past." The market, he contends, was successful in doing just this, but it cannot provide what people really need and long for: a pleasant and harmonious life. In the east, he claims, the imported idea of the market ruined the traditional rural way of life and its social manifestations, through the process of urbanization, whereas in the west the market ruined our conception of nature.[28]

But the critique of the economic behavior approach in relation to the environment is also based on economic arguments, using "market" terminology to demonstrate that individuals' behavior cannot tackle the environmental issue. According to those arguments, this will always result in more pollution, because the costs of this pollution are borne by nature as well as by other people who share the environment, rather than by the polluter itself.[29] The polluter does not have to be motivated by ill will: this problem is ingrained in the idea of the market and its very "imperative," as Eckersley calls it—"grow or die."[30] Such private attitudes cannot respect environmental notions of limits to growth and carrying capacity. An environment-friendly product is likely to be more expensive than its rival product, and hence no "rational" (that is, profit-seeking) entrepreneur will consider such products.

At this point, market advocates put forward the idea of penalties for the polluter. Let us intervene slightly in the market, they say, and charge the polluter for what he or she has done.[31] So anybody who pollutes, depletes, or utilizes a certain natural resource beyond a certain degree will have to pay for it one way or another. But how can we assess the damages? Can we do this when the damage is not local, or within national borders, but rather international, for example, acid rain in Canada due to air pollution in the U.S.A.? How do we assess the damage when only a small and very specific section of the society is hurt (for example, the workers in a factory, or those who used to play golf on a ground that is now to be developed)? Moreover, it is very likely that the consumers themselves have to pay for the pollution that the manufacture causes, especially in the cases of monopolies or special products that very few firms, or even only one firm produces. So if all polluting manufacturers are charged for the pollution they cause, they will transfer the cost to the consumers. All consumers will then pay the real and full price of energy (including cleaning costs). This, in turn, will increase inequality, because the proportion of income spent on energy declines as income increases, although the use of energy increases. Thus, paying the full price of energy seems unfair for the worst-off.

But there is a further problem with regard to assessing environmental damages. While perhaps it is possible to determine the cost of a certain illness (for example, it is equal to the cost of hospital treatment plus a certain amount for compensations), how can we determine the "cost" of a life? Indeed the very term is strange. We are thinking of the value of life, but can it be translated into the "cost" of life? To estimate a person's probable future earnings or any other criterion of the value of life is obnoxious, because in that case someone who possesses this amount of money would be able to purchase another person's life. But, if, as some advocates of the individuals' economic behavior approach have maintained, this question is too artificial or even irrelevant (for instance, because most environmental problems do not cause death), there is still the question of assessing the value of the lives of nonhumans. Thus, how much is the life of a sea otter worth? David Moberg comments that surveying people about how much the animals are worth to them or measuring lost income if sea otters disappeared may keep a few economists employed, but it does not answer the question.

This is indeed a cynical, although a serious reply.

> If only one respondent said it was of infinite value, that would throw off the survey. If you limit the response to how much a person would be willing to spend, the result would obviously be affected by how much money people have, a standard flaw of market preference analysis.[32]

Yet Moberg's response is only part of the answer. The truth of the matter is that any calculation or assessment of the cost/value of animals' lives is, at the end of the day, anthropocentric, and any value in the world of nature is instrumental,[33] just as in the Lockean theory only by mixing human labor with natural objects could these object have some (instrumental) value. Preservation, according to this approach, is a problem only because if humans want to enjoy, say, sea otters, they must first "possess" them. What we should have done instead is to ask the animal itself for the value of its life (for itself). Just as, in the case of human lives, we do not ask a murderer what the value of his victim's life is, but rather ask the victim herself or himself, so should we do in the case of animals' lives. Now I do not wish to slip into the heavily discussed question of the degrees of life, the difference between a virus and a horse, and so on. But if, as indicated above, liberalism has enabled biocentrism to flourish, this is not the right moment to retreat to anthropocentrism. Indeed, this is true not only in cases resulting in the death of animals, but in any case of environmental damage. Evaluating the cost in terms of how much people would pay is totally anthropocentric, and if liberalism follows this path it will not be able to genuinely emerge as "environment-friendly" because environmentalists' criticism of the market approach to valuing is that what makes a certain good valuable is not the state of mind of the consumer who wants that good, but rather something inherent in that good.[34]

Now, some "economic behavior" advocates may remain skeptical with regard to biocentrism. Nonetheless, it is undeniable that these calculations fail to evaluate the cost for some other human beings: those of future generations. The not-yet-born are either ignored or "discounted." The main reason for the latter is that these economists tend to discount the future: a value $x$ in the future is less than $x$ now, because it would be equal to the amount that $x$ would yield in this future if it were invested now and benefited from the interest rate. This, of course, is incompatible with any notion of intergenerational equity.[35]

In addition to the above difficulties with the evaluation of the cost of environmental damages, there is a serious difficulty with the notion that serves the market advocates in their approach to this issue. They assume that all we have to do when we decide on environmental policies is ask people how much they will pay to conserve a forest, save the life of three whales, preserve a certain building, and so forth. Economists call this mechanism the WTP (willingness to pay) test.

But following psychological research that Amos Twersky and Danny Kahaneman conducted in the U.S.A. and Maya Bar-Hillel in Israel, I conducted a simple experiment that reveals the fallacy of the concept of WTP. I told a group of forty students that they should imagine that an ecological disaster has occurred, and that there is an urgent need to clean our country's coast. The first twenty students were given papers in which they were asked whether they would contribute 1 percent of their salaries this month to clean the coast. All of them replied positively. Then they were asked whether they thought it would be possible to know the average amount that their fellow students would be willing to pay. Ninety percent replied that it would be possible; the average WTP predicted was 1.85 percent of one's salary.

The second group of twenty students were told the same story, and yet they were asked whether they would be willing to pay 4 percent of their salaries. They all asserted that they would contribute this amount, and thought that the average WTP would be 6.16 percent of one's salary.

The results are clear: the concept of WTP reflects nothing about "individuals' autonomous wills." Rather we see that the format of the question and the starting point affect the WTP. Is there no consistent notion of WTP?

So I conducted a similar experiment. This time I told forty students that the department had decided to allow them to use our common room for their coffee breaks. Each student would contribute as much as he or she wishes, in order to run this "coffee shop." They were asked whether they would pay $6 a month. They all answered "yes." When asked about the WTP of their fellow students, their answers varied from $2 to $16 with the average of $7.42.

The second group of twenty students were given the same story, but were asked to contribute $30 a month. Twenty percent agreed, whereas 80 percent disagreed, but the average evaluations of their fellow students' WTP was $15! My conclusion is that WTP is perhaps interesting, theoretically speaking, but it is not a reliable mechanism for revealing preferences.

It goes without saying that this technical question does not exhaust the discussion of the relationship of liberalism with environmental concern, but it does point to the difficulties with regard to the political and practical implications of liberalism in this context. And beyond all these difficulties with the "economic behavior" approach, there is—according to the critique of the market theory—another, perhaps greater, difficulty. This is the belief that individuals' economic behavior yields the best (sometimes defined in terms of being the most rational) results. Do such results include the difficulties that the people of Athens have in breathing every summer, because of traffic pollution? The problem with the market is that even if it corrects itself, it may be too late, because the damage—sometimes to humans—is irreversible.

Some market advocates answer that the question is not one of metaphysical beliefs, but rather of an ethical belief in the idea of freedom. Since they are aware of the environmental damages in our world, they have suggested that firms should be allowed to react in their own ways and according to their own methods to the changing needs of the market, including the need to be more environment-friendly. This, as Eckersley notes, "is not simply a defense of economic efficiency; it is also linked to a defense of political freedom."[36] Thus, for example, if there must be less pollution, then a system of selling pollution rights should be introduced. Pollution rights will be distributed to firms: if $x$ is the degree of pollution that is tolerable, and $n$ is the number of firms, each firm will get $x/n$ pollution rights. Those who can continue manufacturing and limit the resulting pollution will so do, and cover the cost of doing so by selling pollution rights to other firms.[37]

But while some firms adjust to the new circumstances by limiting pollution, others buy pollution rights, and the problem that remains is the distribution of exposure to hazardous waste and pollution. Third World countries have long been disproportionally exposed to dangerous waste. For instance, in the 1970s it was quite common for African countries to "export" land to Western firms for burying toxic and radioactive waste. And in the Western world the poor find themselves unable to buy houses located in safer areas or to look for safer jobs. Even if taxes are introduced, those who find it most difficult to cope will be, again, the least advantaged.[38] Indeed, why should we wait until the dirt is produced in order to clean it up? Why not prevent pollution before workers breathe in smog, or before people are hurt and the environment is damaged? Why should we let the private sector make the decisions on where to pollute? Are such decisions private at all? Should they be in the hands of those who run the industries and pollute rivers, meadows, and seas?

However, to some Greens and other advocates of the environmental case, the above approach seems too superficial and simplistic. In the final analysis, the world is not ready to give up any form of private initiative, or any expression of political freedom in the sphere of economics. The ultimate opposite to an economy that lacks any state action at all would be an economy lacking any profit-making motive, but many people doubt not only whether full state or public ownership is congruent with liberty, but also whether such a system is better for the environment. As Goodin notes, "the environmental consequences of public ownership in Eastern Europe do not serve as a happy precedent."[39] Thus these people seek to modify, refine, or correct the market, to make it more environment-friendly. They do not reject all that liberalism stands for, but still think that if liberalism implies an "individuals' economic behavior" type of economics, then it is inadequate in the sense that it neglects aspects of ecology, wilderness preservation, and so on. The right question to be asked, these Greens argue, is not how to get rid of the market, but what sort of environmental goods it can deliver, and what it cannot.

The market economy, to start with, does not compensate or reward individuals and firms that do act to conserve the environment. A person who lives in an historic house and preserves it is not usually paid to do so. However, if she sells the house to a developer she may make a lot of money. Similarly, the capitalist who invests huge sums of money in order to recycle his or her industry's waste is not rewarded by his or her neighbor capitalist who pollutes the river that runs next to this industry.

Admittedly the market finds solutions to environmental problems: the quality of the water is bad, so we switch to drinking mineral water; there are no green spots left in town, so a farmer opens her land to the public, and we take our car, drive out into the country, and pay the farmer to enjoy nature; there is too much noise, so there are glass factories that offer us cheaper double windows. But the serious question remains: are we satisfied with these solutions? Is this what we wanted? Can we all afford them? And can the market, even if it does solve one or two problems, become the right solution to the ecological crisis in general?[40]

Moreover, the market may suggest theoretical ways of coping with environmental damages; but can it enforce them? Pollution is a good example. All the more litter and a clean environment is a good that (almost) everybody wants. But some environmental goods (for example, leaving a remote forest untouched) are desired by only a part of the population. Individuals' economic behavior will not save this forest, because its economic value to timber merchants is much greater than the amount that some environmentalists are able to pay to save it for aesthetic reasons.[41]

It seems that this list of goods that individuals' behavior cannot supply in the environmental context is quite long and includes some significant examples. So even if we accept the market as a system relevant to the "environmental era," there is still a strong need for "politics." In other words, we shall eventually realize that the economy is not a genuinely market one. But then, the pro-market economists fail not so much in their economic theory as in their political theory. Therefore, instead of dealing with the issue of a "market or non-market" economy, the right question to consider is that of the more suitable type of politics.

So I now want to return to this question, and argue that liberals must come to terms with the political fact that the need to promote environmental policies reveals: namely, that the state of the environment is closely related to our view of "the political" and the political process, including the debate over the good life, and that the issue of the environment involves the goals of our political life rather than merely the means of achieving certain goals.

## ENVIRONMENTALISM AND LIBERALISM: CONCEPTIONS OF POLITICS

When discussing the inadequacy of liberalism's image of politics in the context of ecological policies, I must refer first to the impossibility of neutrality in the context of conservation or any other environmental policy.

The idea of neutrality, as advanced by many prominent liberal theorists, is that the state should stay out of the debate on the nature of the good. Official policies should not promote or reflect any conception of what constitutes the good life; on the contrary, the state should be indifferent to any discrepancies between those ideas. For example, while discussing distributive justice, Gauthier writes:

> An essentially just society . . . does not need to shape individuals in order to afford them justice. . . . In saying that an essentially just society is neutral with respect to the aims of its members, we deny that justice is linked to any substantive conception of what is good, either for the individual or for society.[42]

But can one remain neutral in matters of conservation? A neutral argument in favor of conservation must make a fair political procedure the only criterion for choosing a policy. Suppose a liberal, it is argued, holds a belief about the importance of preservation. This person may hope that a way of life, which in one way or another is related to the environment (for example, to a beautiful forest), will be available to posterity. But this liberal fears that, owing to the destruction of the environment, this way of life will disappear. The destruction of natural objects is, in fact, destructive of the very possibility of certain competing ideas of the good life. The liberal fears that in the future one (that is future generations) may not be in a position to make a neutral choice amongst the ideas of the good life now available.[43]

But this way of reasoning is misleading. If you and I are choosing between $x$ ideas and I assert that we should choose between $(x + 1)$ ideas, you will probably ask me why I insist upon idea $(x + 1)$. I cannot answer "because it exists," because then you may wonder why I do not advocate idea $(x + 2)$. I therefore have no other choice than to explain why $(x + 1)$ is especially desirable, significant, important and so forth. We wish posterity to enjoy a certain object precisely because it has been "desired and found satisfying in the past." Moreover, we do not preserve—indeed we sometimes try to destroy—what we think is wrong or bad, for example, nuclear weapons. Ironically, according to the above liberal argument we should conserve nuclear weapons—perhaps the idea of war itself as a way of life—so that future generations will be aware of it and have the opportunity to choose between a larger variety of ideas of the good. This, of course, is unwise, if not outrageous. In short, an argument in favor of the conservation of a certain object must be based on the claim that this object is in itself good, especially when conserving it contradicts the interests of certain people at the present time (for example, higher salaries, more jobs, and so on).

It is possible at this point to defend the "neutral liberal" stand by distinguishing between those things that are good in themselves, and those things that are instrumentally valuable, arguing that nuclear weapons fall into the latter category. Leaving aside the empirical question of whether or not there are people who regard nuclear weapons, or wars, as a good, this is exactly the point: "neutral" liberals usually find individuals' well-being the most proper—if not the only—moral basic consideration for social policies. They then tend to define individuals' well-being in terms of satisfying personal individual wants, interpreted as those individuals' subjective wants. But they could have defined them according to objective wants (preferences a person would hold if (s)he were fully informed, not confused and rational).[44] Otherwise it is enough to assume that there may be someone who thinks that wars are good to imply the preservation of this idea. We must therefore assert that wars are not good, but then we should do this according to objective wants. In other words, the challenge of the environment is such that objective wants should also be considered and well-being should be an account of final goods.

In the above liberal argument, however, the concept of neutrality is, in fact, derived from the more fundamental values of choice and autonomy, which are, it has been suggested, basic to American liberalism.[45] The latter is therefore considered very democratic inasmuch as, according to its doctrines, political decisions should reflect nothing other than the aggregate of people's preferences, and respect their choices. For example, environmental policies are congruent with liberalism if and only if a majority (or a winning coalition) is in favor. Thus, private preferences and economic measures, backed by the legitimacy of "rational behavior," have supplanted the debate on political ideals and the image of the good life.[46] This philosophy holds that society is an instrument for the benefit of individuals; all the more, therefore, should nature be subjugated by humans, who through its progressive transformation fulfill their individualistic desires.[47] And according to this idea of politics, everything is reduced to private interests, which are held in balance of a market or exchange.[48]

But if there is any methodological innovation in Green philosophy it is that the wall between what has been considered nature or the environment on the one side and culture on the other side falls. The concept of the environment becomes part of our culture, or political. Therefore it is repeatedly argued and widely accepted that what is now needed in environmental politics (which are more than the political discussion of environmental matters) is something more sophisticated: not merely policies that are responsive, whatever the individual preferences are or whatever the outcome may be, but policies that, while responsive, take into account the good of the community as a whole as well, and offer solutions to problems that are rarely considered, and, still less, resolved, by individualistic, self-involved, short-run interests.[49] Moreover, there is a good chance that, in the environmental context, individual and private preferences will contradict the general good. Thus Jonathon Porritt writes:

> There may well have been a time, at the start of the Industrial Revolution, when Adam Smith's assertion that the sum of individual decisions in pursuit of self-interest added up to a pretty fair approximation of public welfare, with the "invisible hand" of the market ensuring that individualism and the general interest of society were one and the same thing. But in today's crowded, interdependent world, these same individualistic tendencies are beginning to destroy our *general* interest and thereby harm us all [emphasis added].[50]

Indeed, economic and self-interested individualistic preferences could easily lead to the continuing depletion of scarce resources, be it oil, clean air, or scenic landscape. As Ted Schrecker writes, the resistance of business to environmental regulations has been "bitter" and firms have fought "long and expensive court battles to avoid conviction," sometimes issuing threats to shut down firms.[51]

Garret Hardin's well-known "Tragedy of the Commons"[52] demonstrates this claim: according to him, the state of the environment resembles a pasture open to all. Each herdsman tries to keep as many cattle on the common as possible, but the carrying capacity of the land is insufficient. Each herdsman seeks to improve his own position. If he asks himself the utility of adding one more animal to his herd, he answers that the advantage is +1 (the herdsman receives all the proceeds from the sale of the additional animal), whereas the disadvantage is only a fraction of −1 (the effects of overgrazing being shared by all other herdsmen). The tragedy, of course, is that all herdsmen reach the same conclusion. Further, the question of how to reduce, say, pollution on the roads, illustrates the fact that environmental issues involve concepts of "public good," "collective action," and "free rider," and that the state is needed to provide the necessary solution: that is, environmental policies.

Thus, one must concede that "environmental imperatives are basically matters of principle that cannot be bargained away in an economic fashion," and that "not all of us think of ourselves primarily as consumers; many of us regard ourselves as citizens as well."[53] And as citizens we are concerned with the public interest, or the good of the community rather than with our own personal interests. As citizens, we have obligations that are not always compatible with our private preferences as individuals, and these obligations must receive priority.

> [The] cost-benefit analysis . . . prevents us from achieving a certain kind of self-determination. . . . It prevents us from deciding who we are, not just what we are. . . . There is a right and a wrong way to manage those national parks. . . . The wrong thing to do is to make a big drive-in for Winnebagos. This has nothing to do with what turns a social profit or maximizes wealth. . . .[54]

Many Greens claim that to live in rural areas, for instance, is "living more in harmony with nature" than living in an urban jungle of cars and industries.[55] In other terms, these Greens may be arguing that there is less alienation in village life, or none at all. So they actually claim that one sort of life is better than another, or, in other words, constitutes the good life. Is it? May they be kept poles apart, the Futurists and George Sorel thought that this type of harmony was merely a form of degeneration and degradation. Although I subscribe to the Greens' view here, this is not relevant to my purpose. The point to be established is that a debate on whether this sort of life is good is perfectly legitimate. One must realize that there *is* a debate here on the idea of the good. In the final analysis, this should be obvious. Any Green or counter-Green argument must make some assumption about the idea of the good, since the argument rests on a theory of value, that is, on the idea of an intrinsic, non-instrumental value.[56] And such a theory of value is simply a theory of the good.

Thus the state of the environment calls for politics of the common and a debate on the good. At this point the objection might be raised that, all the same, the Greens' environmental concern represents nothing but an individual's private preferences. The argument would be that the Greens' claim that the world will be destroyed if their suggestions are not implemented is similar to the warnings issued by an almost unknown candidate for the 1992 American presidential campaign, John Huglin, that if he were not elected and his proposals not taken seriously, there would be a worldwide holocaust, or, more seriously, any religious fanatic's prophecy, and his desire that we should all attend churches, synagogues, mosques, and so on. Moreover—the argument goes—a contractor's wish that a certain valley should be inhabited and developed (which is, for that matter, another private preference) is in no way inferior to the environmentalist demand that all work should stop and the beautiful valley should be preserved.

But this criticism is deceptive. With regard to the last point, the question is not a matter of which standpoint is inferior or superior; both developers and environmentalists express ideas of the good life, images of how this world should be and how humans should live. They even sometimes use the same arguments: for instance, developers put forward the psychological argument that if there are more roads and more jobs, then people will be less tense. And environmentalists argue that since tension is caused by noise, traffic, and the fast rhythm of our lives, if we wish to reduce tension, we must limit growth, build fewer roads, and so on. But the point is that these two programs are not preferences that can be bargained over until a compromise is reached. The two sides represent opposite conceptions of a good world, of what is and what is not desirable.

Now with regard to the fanatics, the challenge is easily answered: environmentalism is based on rational evaluations and scientific, empirical knowledge, whereas religious fanatics do not appreciate such evaluations. Their system is irrational in essence; the environmentalists, on the other hand, base their call for change on scientific grounds and empirical—though controversial—data. So environmentalists do not simply express private preferences, but put forward ideas of the good, based on scientific knowledge and phrased in moral terms.

The next question to ask, then, is the following: isn't there a price to pay for the liberals' insistence on regarding politics as a matter of individuals' autonomous decisions? There must be if it limits a consideration of the good of the community, welfare policies, and so on. For the ecologist, politics must provide the framework in which common and general interests are discussed and protected, if not promoted.

We are speaking, then, of state intervention.[57] Now many liberals would argue that one can remain neutral with regard to the idea of the good, but nonetheless advocate interventionism. You don't have to debate the nature of the good in order to justify state intervention. The Rawlsian theory of justice is neutral, it is argued, but is nevertheless in favor of state intervention. I subscribe to the view that in fact Rawls cannot put forward the idea of interventionism without being committed to some idea of the good.[58] This debate, however, is beyond the scope of this paper. For our purpose it is sufficient to claim that even if Rawls (or any other liberal), basing himself on the idea of neutrality, does justify a certain kind of interventionism, it cannot be the one that suits the case of the environment. As we have seen, where the latter is concerned, interventionism is based on and justified by the debate on the good. Any less weighty reason for interventionism would not justify the dramatic policies that are necessary to deal with the ecological disasters with which we are faced nowadays and the political difficulties that accompany them. Indeed, if such dramatic policies were implemented without being based on a genuine debate concerning the good, they would turn out to be nothing more than what Ophuls fears they would be: that is, regulations imposed on a large section of the population without this section understanding why they are needed.[59]

So although liberalism has been a fertile ground for environmental philosophy, it has a basic difficulty with regard to a public environmental policy and its justification: most liberals adhere to neutrality, and regard liberal-democratic politics primarily as a matter of concerning the wills of individuals, whereas environmental issues call for a politics of the common and consequently for interventionism.

Does this imply that liberal governments cannot tackle the environmental challenge? My argument is that if liberalism limits itself to a policy of neutrality and an aggregate of autonomous decisions, then it is likely to fail in this matter. Ecology implies state intervention, justified by a consideration of the common good, and hence abandoning neutrality as a justification for the liberal state and its policies. A sense of community is needed because in the environmental era social and environmental responsibilities should play a much more important role than self-interested profit-making motivation. If we do not wish to retreat to totalitarian regimes, we must take the opportunity that liberalism as a philosophy provided (as I argued in the first part of this article), and look for a liberalism that is more social: the politics of the aggregate of autonomous decisions and an economics of individuals' preferences are of little benefit. The politics of the common, however, that at the same time does not arbitrarily restrict liberties, can be found in the other, perhaps so far more neglected, tradition of liberalism accompanied by a strong welfare state. This conception of liberalism could, perhaps, allow for a justification of environmental policies in terms of liberal terminology, and is therefore much better suited to the environmental era.[60]

# NOTES

1. See Kristin Shrader-Frechette, "Science, Democracy, and Public Policy," *Critical Review* 6 (1993): 255–65.

2. Robert Goodin, "International Ethics and the Environmental Crisis," *Ethics and International Affairs* 4 (1990): 81–105, and "The High Road is Green," *Environmental Politics* 1 (1992): 1–8; Steven Yearley, *The Green Case* (London: Harper Collins Academic, 1991); A. de-Shalit, "Environmental Policies and Justice Between Generations," *European Journal of Political Research* 21 (1992): 307–16.

3. For the debate between individualistic liberalism and communitarianism see M. Sandel, ed., *Liberalism and its Critics* (Oxford: Blackwell, 1984); and S. Avineri and A. de-Shalit, eds., *Communitarianism and Individualism* (Oxford: Oxford University Press, 1992).

4. Throughout this essay I give a very broad and flexible interpretation of liberalism, both in a historical sense (I refer to the liberalisms of the eighteenth, nineteenth, and twentieth centuries) and in an analytical sense.

5. John Rawls, *A Theory of Justice* (Oxford: Oxford University Press, 1973), p. 512. See also M.S. Pritchard and W.L. Wade, "Justice and the Treatment of Animals: A Critique of Rawls," *Environmental Ethics* 3 (1981): 55–62; and Walter Achterberg, "Can Liberal Democracy Survive the Environmental Crisis?" in A. Dobson and P. Lucarde, eds., *The Politics of Nature* (London: Routledge, 1993), pp. 81–101.

6. Brendt Singer, "An Extension of Rawls' Theory of Justice to Environmental Ethics," *Environmental Ethics* 10 (1988): 217–32.

7. R. Taylor, "The Environmental Implications of Liberalism," *Critical Review* 6 (1993): 265–83.

8. The latter is Ronald Dworkin's formula. See his "Reverse Discrimination" in his *Taking Rights Seriously* (London: Duckworth, 1981), and his "Liberalism" in his *A Matter of Principle* (Oxford: Clarendon Press, 1986). But see also John Locke ("This equality of men by Nature . . . [is] so evident in itself, and beyond all question . . . ," in his *Second Treatise of Civil Government*, chap. II, 5), the French first declaration of the rights of man and of citizens ("Men are born, and always continue, free and equal in respect to their rights"), the American Declaration of Independence, Thomas Paine's *Rights of Man*, and Alexis de Tocqueville's *Democracy in America* (since everyone is equal, no one is entitled to be a despotic ruler: part II, chap. 10).

9. This is typical of ecofeminist philosophy. See A. Collard and J. Contrucci, *Rape of the Wild* (London: The Women's Press, 1988). But also of environmental philosophy in general: see R. Routely, "Against the Inevitability of Human Chauvinism," in K. Goodpaster, ed., *Ethics and the Problems of the 21st Century* (Notre Dame: Notre Dame University Press, 1979).

10. Aldo Leopold, *A Sand County Almanac* (Oxford: Oxford University Press, 1987 [1949]).

11. Christopher Stone, "Should Trees Have Standing?" *Southern California Law Review* 45 (1972), and *Earth and Other Ethics* (New York: Harper & Row, 1987).

12. Roderick Nash, *The Rights of Nature* (Madison: University of Wisconsin Press, 1989), p. 200. See also Robert Paehlke, *Environmentalism and the Future of Progressive Politics* (New Haven: Yale University Press, 1989), pp. 8–9.

13. Paul Taylor, "Frankena on Environmental Ethics," *Monist* 64 (1981): 217, and *Respect for Nature* (Princeton: Princeton University Press, 1986), pp. 56–57.

14. J. Horton and S. Mendus, *Aspects of Toleration* (London: Methuen, 1985).

15. For example, Alastair Gunn, "Traditional Ethics and the Moral Status of Animals," *Environmental Ethics* 5 (1983): 133–54.

16. Anna Brammwell traces the origins of environmentalism to romantic philosophy and right-wing political theories. But she fails to distinguish between anti-rational, antimodern ruralism, and modern, scientific-based and democratic Green environmentalism. See Anna Bramwell, *Ecology in the Twentieth Century* (New Haven: Yale University Press, 1991).

17. Michael Freeden, *The New Liberalism* (Oxford: Clarendon Press, 1978), and Ronald Dworkin, "Liberalism," in his *A Matter of Principle* (Oxford: Clarendon Press, 1986), pp. 187–88.

18. Three good examples of Green publications that warn of the dangers to individuals' rights are the books by Brian Price, *The Friends of the Earth Guide to Pollution* (London: Friends of the Earth, 1983); John May, *The Greenpeace Book of the Nuclear Age* (London: Victor Gollancz Ltd, 1989); and Ferencz and Keyes, *PlanetHood: The Keys to Your Survival and Prosperity* (Oregon: Vision Books, 1988). A famous green act was Greenpeace's attempt to stop French nuclear tests in the Pacific, which ended with the blowing up of the Greenpeace boat by members of French Intelligence in 1985.

19. Jonathon Porritt, *The Coming of the Greens* (London: Fontana, 1988), pp. 71–76.
20. Jonathon Porritt, *Seeing Green* (Oxford: Basil Blackwell, 1984), p. 115.
21. Consider, for instance, the damage being caused by all nations to the ozone layer, the problem of acid rain, or the contamination of the Mediterranean Sea. For a further discussion of the international aspects see G. Porter and J. Brown, *Global Environmental Change* (Boulder: Westview Press, 1991); R.E. Benedick, *Ozone Diplomacy* (Cambridge, Mass.: Harvard University Press, 1992); the Brundtland report, Brundtland Gro Harlem et al.; The World Commission on Environment and Development staff, *Our Common Future* (Oxford: Oxford University Press, 1987); and M. Grubb et al., *The Earth Summit Agreements* (London: Earthscan, 1993).
22. William Ophuls, *Ecology and the Politics of Scarcity* (San Francisco: W.H. Freeman, 1977), p. 145.
23. Robert Paehlke, "Democracy, Bureaucracy, and Environmentalism," *Environmental Ethics* 10 (1988): 293.
24. William Ophuls, op. cit., p. 227.
25. Ibid., p. 159. To be fair, Ophuls denied that he had wanted rule by elite: see his comment in William Ophuls, "On Hoffert and the Scarcity of Politics," *Environmental Ethics* 8 (1986): 287–88.
26. Carolyn Merchant, *Radical Ecology* (London: Routledge, 1992), pp. 159–63, describes such cases and such tendencies among the "big ten" environmental organizations in the U.S.A., and Andrew Dobson, *Green Political Thought* (London: Harper Collins Academic, 1990), discusses the differences between the public and private faces of green argumentation.
27. I discuss the manifestations in Europe of the latter in my article, in Bob Brecher, ed., *Liberalism and the New Europe* (London: Avebury Press, 1993), pp. 149–62.
28. Jeremy Seabrook, *The Myth of the Market* (London: Green Books, 1990), pp. 13–14 and chap. 7.
29. David Moberg, "Environment and Markets," *Dissent* 38 (1991): p. 511.
30. Robyn Eckersley, "Green versus Ecosocialist Economic Programmes: the Market Rules OK?" *Political Studies* 40 (1992): 319.
31. It is interesting to note that John Stuart Mill already thought this could be a solution to air pollution. See *Principles of Political Economy* (New York: The Coloral Press, 1990), p. 7.
32. Moberg, op. cit., p. 512.
33. For a more complicated distinction see Andrew Brennan, "Moral Pluralism and the Environment," *Environmental Values* 1 (1992): 15–33.
34. Robert Goodin, *Green Political Theory* (Oxford: Polity, 1992), p. 25.
35. See Robyn Eckersley, op. cit., p. 319. Some market advocates suggested that future generations' interests are, in fact, represented in any social arrangement that is decided upon now. See David Gauthier, *Morals By Agreement* (Oxford: Clarendon Press, 1986), p. 299. I argue elsewhere that bargaining with the not yet born is impossible, not only literally, but also theoretically. See my *Why Posterity Matters* (London: Routledge, 1994).
36. Robyn Eckersley, op. cit., p. 318.
37. Steidlmeier, for example, argues that pollution permits have a legitimacy as "a second-best solution." See "The Morality of Pollution Permits," *Environmental Ethics* 15 (1993): 133–50.
38. See the statement issued by the Centre for Science and Environment (New Delhi) on global environmental democracy, as a reaction to the "northern agenda," in *Alternatives* 17 (1992): 271–79. Also see J. Moberg, "Who Rules the Market," *Political Studies* 40 (1992): 337.
39. Robert Goodin, op. cit., p. 7, fn. 30.
40. See also Brian Barry, "The Continuing Relevance of Socialism," in Brian Barry, *Liberty and Justice* (Oxford: Clarendon Press, 1991); and Robyn Eckersley, "Free Market Environmentalism: Friend or Foe?" *Environmental Politics* 2 (1993): 1–20.
41. This is related to the question of whether only use value should count, or whether option value (that is, whether I can use and enjoy this environmental good in the future) counts as well. See Alan Randall, "Human Preferences, Economics, and the Preservation of Species," in B. Norton, ed., *The Preservation of Species* (Princeton: Princeton University Press, 1986).
42. David Gauthier, *Morals by Agreement*, p. 341. See also John Rawls, *Political Liberalism* (New York: Columbia University Press, 1993); Bruce Ackerman, *Social Justice in the Liberal State* (New Haven: Yale University Press, 1980); and Will Kymlicka, "Liberal Individualism and

Liberal Neutrality," *Ethics* 99 (1989): 883–905. But see Joseph Raz, "Liberalism, Autonomy and the Politics of Neutral Concern," *Midwest Studies in Philosophy* 7 (1980): 89–120.

43. This rationale is put forward in Ronald Dworkin, "Liberalism," op. cit., p. 202.

44. Compare R.M. Hare, "Ethical Theory and Utilitarianism," in A. Sen and B. Williams, eds., *Utilitarianism and Beyond* (Cambridge: Cambridge University Press, 1982).

45. Ronald Beiner, "Liberalism," in his *What's the Matter with Liberalism?* (Berkeley: University of California Press, 1992); and William Galston, *Liberal Purposes* (Cambridge: Cambridge University Press, 1991).

46. See, for example, Kenneth Arrow, *Social Choice and Individual Values* (New York: Wiley, 1962).

47. See also Charles Taylor, *Hegel* (Cambridge: Cambridge University Press, 1975), pp. 540–43.

48. On this see John Elster, "The Market and the Forum: Three Varieties of Political Theory," in J. Elster and A. Hylland, *The Foundations of Social Choice Theory* (Cambridge: Cambridge University Press, 1986).

49. See David Miller's account of energy policies to the two models of politics in his "Deliberative Democracy and Social Choice," *Political Studies* 40 (1992): 54–66.

50. Jonathon Porritt, *Seeing Green*, p. 116.

51. T. Schrecker, "Resisting Environmental Regulations," in R. Paehlke and D. Torgerson, eds., *Managing Leviathan* (London: Belhaven Press, 1991), pp. 165–99; and H. Feiveson, F. Sinden, and R. Socolow, eds., *Boundaries of Analysis* (Cambridge, Mass.: Ballinger, 1976).

52. Garret Hardin, "The Tragedy of the Commons," *Science* 162 (1968): 1243–48.

53. William Ophuls, *Ecology and the Politics of Scarcity*, p. 186; and Mark Sagoff, *The Economy of the Earth* (Cambridge: Cambridge University Press, 1988), p. 27.

54. Mark Sagoff, "Ethics and Economics in Environmental Law," in T. Regan, ed., *Earthbound* (Prospect Heights, Ill.: Waveland Press, 1984), pp. 172–73.

55. For example, Robert Goodin, *Green Political Theory*, p. 51.

56. Arne Naess, *Ecology, Community, and Lifestyle* (Cambridge: Cambridge University Press. 1989); Holmes Rolston III, *Philosophy Gone Wild* (Buffalo: Prometheus Books, 1989).

57. Indeed, it seems that the state "has generally been the only institution with the necessary resources to provide environmental policies." K. Walker, "The State in Environmental Management," *Political Studies* 37 (1980): 25–38.

58. I elaborate on this in "Community and the Rights of Future Generations," *Journal of Applied Philosophy* 9 (1992): 105–17. See also T. Nagel, "Rawls on Justice," in N. Daniels, *Reading Rawls* (Oxford: Basil Blackwell, 1975), pp. 1–16.

59. It is sometimes suggested by environmentalists that international environmental concern is also crucial for the much needed international cooperation in any valid environmental policy. See C. Spretnak and F. Capra, *Green Politics* (London: Paladin, 1985). pp. 157–81. But this forms another issue. See L.K. Caldwell, *International Environmental Policy* (Durham: Duke University Press, 1984).

60. I would like to thank David Miller and my students in the Environmental Ethics seminar for their comments.

# SOCIALISM AND ECOLOGY

*James O'Connor*

James O'Connor is professor of sociology and economics at the University of
California, Santa Cruz, and is Editor-in-Chief of *Capitalism, Nature, Socialism.*

It seems to me that today there are three general socioeconomic trends giving
rise to the possibility of a red green politics. The first is a global economy that
is undergoing a process of "accumulation through crisis" that is impoverishing tens of millions of people, destroying communities, degrading hundreds
of thousands of bioregions, and exacerbating a global ecological crisis. Crisis-
ridden and crisis-driven capitalist accumulation is wrecking the conditions of
production, and creating more poverty, unemployment, inequality, and economic insecurity and marginalization, on the one hand, and (often fatally)
harming human health, urban and rural communities, and ecological systems,
on the other. The second trend is the rise of environmental, urban, labor,
peasant, and other social movements to defend the conditions of production
and the conditions of life for workers and peasants, women, communities, and
the environment. These movements are divided in a thousand ways, running
ideologically from religious fundamentalism and reactionary nationalism to
old-style Marxist–Leninist–Maoist armed struggle to a broad range of "new social movements." The third premise is that solutions to the ecological crisis
presuppose solutions to the economic crisis (and the problem of global capital generally) and vice versa. Red green politics is premised on the belief that
both sets of solutions presuppose some kind of ecological socialism and socialist ecology.[1]

 Ecological socialism, in turn, presupposes the development of a specifically global class politics, first, because of growing economic oppression and
exploitation, and second, because ecological degradation is increasingly a
class issue (but rarely *only* a class issue). This is indicated, for example, by the

This essay appeared in *Natural Causes: Essays in Ecological Marxism* (New York and London: The
Guilford Press, 1997). Reprinted with permission.

growth of movements for environmental (and economic and social) justice in the North and the "environmentalism of the poor" in the South, where dominant groups owe an "ecological debt" to oppressed minorities and the third world as a whole, respectively (because the prosperity of dominant groups in the North is in some part based on the ecological damage done to minorities in the North and South). It is also indicated by the fact that present-day labor, community, and environmental struggles seek to make the workplace a healthier and safer place for both workers and communities, hence fight for more influence or control of technology, work relations, and the conditions of work generally. Labor, community, and environmental groups challenge in various ways (implicitly if not explicitly) criterea of production based on market values and profit. Also, human laborpower, community organization, and the environment are all "conditions of production," hence politicized and regulated in various ways by the state.

In the minds of most labor, community, and environmental leaders, however, socialism (of any type) and ecology remain contradictions in terms. Socialists are still seen as "productivist," Greens as "antiproductivist." Most socialists still believe that ecology is merely an ideology of austerity or is simply a system for ensuring amenities for the middle and upper middle classes. Most Greens think that socialism is an ideology promoting growth without limit or end. The effect: business and other groups use the false choices between "jobs versus environment," "the capitalization of land and economic growth versus community values," and "economic development versus sustainable society" as a handy scheme to divide and conquer.

Historically, Western socialists have sought two remedies for the condition of labor. The first is a more equitable distribution of wealth and income. The second is higher levels of productivity and production (which sometimes have been seen as a condition of more equality). Greater productivity is needed to create more free or leisure time; greater production is required to expand the economic pie to mute struggles over the share of the pie appropriated by different classes. These remedies roughly approximate the programs of the old socialist, social democratic, and labor parties as they functioned through the 1970s (and in some countries through the 1980s).

There are at least two major problems with this way of thinking. One is that in a capitalist society (no matter how "reformed") an equitable distribution of wealth and income is almost certain to harm economic incentives and also to promote political unrest from the right, thus impairing productivity and production. The second is that expanding productivity and production usually presuppose a higher (not a lower) level of exploitation of labor, which itself is premised on more (not less) economic inequality.

For their part, Greens, too, have two general remedies for the degraded condition of nature. The first is the same as that promoted by labor and old-style socialism: a more suitable distribution of wealth and income such that poverty no longer leads producers to degrade nature out of material necessity. Even in the North, environmentalists have shown increasing sensitivity to equity concerns because the impact of environmental reform typically has been regressive: workplace pollution and toxic waste contamination disproportionately affect minorities and lower income strata. The second remedy is the opposite of that of labor and socialists: slow growth, no growth, or sustainable growth (there are different versions). Slow or zero growth of production scales down the use of nature as tap and sink for human production, thus (it is thought) reducing both the depletion and the exhaustion of resources and pollution of all kinds.

Since a significantly more equal distribution of wealth and income would harm economic incentives, it would seem that increased equity would lower production and slow down the economic growth rate. Seen this way, the green position is fully coherent. The problem is that in a capitalist economy, a low- or no-growth policy would create an economic crisis, which, in turn, would lead to more ecological degradation as business scrambled to reduce costs in various ways. An alliance between labor (and socialists) and Greens around the redistribution of wealth and income might be possible. But in capitalist economy such a redistribution would harm productivity and production and generate economic crisis, which would adversely affect both labor (and socialists) and Greens.

Clearly, no way exists to make an alliance between labor (and socialists) and Green, *given the way the whole problem is usually framed.* (The main exceptions are labor-community alliances against workplace and community pollution.) For Greens, socialists are part of the problem, not the solution; for labor and socialists, Greens are part of the problem, not the solution. The former associate Greens with cutbacks and austerity; the latter identify labor and socialists with higher rates of economic growth, hence ecological unsustainability. The only way out of this trap is to redefine productivism: a society can achieve higher levels of productivity via more efficient reuse, recycling, and so on, of materials; via reducing energy use and the commute to work within reformed green cities; via preventing the "pesticide treadmill" by using organic agriculture; and so on, including and especially decommodifying labor and land. *Ecological* socialist productivism and ecological rationality are thus not mutually incompatible.

"Real socialism" in theory and practice has been declared by nonsocialists and many ex-socialists to be "dead on arrival." In theory, post-Marxist theorists of radical democracy are completing what they think is the final autopsy of socialism. In practice, in the North, socialism has been banalized into a species of welfare capitalism. In Eastern Europe, the moment for democratic socialism seems to have been missed almost 30 years ago and socialism has been overthrown. In the South, most socialist countries are introducing market incentives, reforming their tax structures, and taking other measures that they hope will enable them to find their niches in the world market. Everywhere market economy and liberal democratic ideas on the right, and radical democratic ideas on the left, seem to be defeating socialism and socialist ideas.

Meanwhile, a powerful new force in world politics has appeared, an ecology or green movement, that puts the earth first and makes the preservation of the ecological integrity of the planet the primary issue. The simultaneous rise of the free market and the Greens, together with the decline of socialism, suggests that capitalism has an ally in its war against socialism. This turns out to be the case, in fact. Most, if not all, Greens dismiss socialism as irrelevant. Some Greens attack socialism as dangerous. They are especially quick to condemn those whom they accuse of trying to appropriate ecology for Marxism.[2] The famous green slogan, "Neither left nor right, but out front," speaks for itself.[3]

But most Greens are not friends of capitalism, either, as the green slogan makes clear. The question then arises, Who or what are the Green allied with? The crude answer is "the small farmers and independent business," that is, those who used to be called the "peasantry" and "petty bourgeoisie"; "liveable cities" visionaries and planners; "small is beautiful" technocrats; and artisans, cooperatives, and others engaged in ecologically friendly production. In the South, Greens typically support decentralized production organized within village communal politics; in the North, Greens are identified with municipal and local politics of all types.

By way of contrast, mainstream environmentalists might be called "fictitious Greens."[4] These environmentalists support environmental regulations consistent with profitability and the expansion of global capitalism, for example, resource conservation for long-run profitability and profit-oriented regulation or abolition of pollution. They are typically allied with national and international interests. In the United States, they are environmental reformers, lobbyists, lawyers, and others associated with most of the organizations making up the famous "Group of Ten."

As for ecology, everywhere it is at least tinged with populism, a politics of resentment against not only big corporations and the national state and central planning but also against mainstream environmentalism.

Ecology (in the present usage) is thus associated with "localism," which typically has been opposed to the centralizing powers of capitalism. If we put two and two together, we can conclude that ecology and localism in all of their rich varieties have combined to oppose both capitalism and socialism. Localism uses the medium of ecology and ecology uses the vehicle of localism. They are both the content and context of one another. Decentralism is an expression of a certain type of social relationship of production historically associated with self-earned property and small-scale enterprise. Ecology is an expression of a certain type of relationship between human beings and nature—a relationship that stresses biodiversity, the integrity of local and regional ecosystems, and the like. Together, ecology and localism constitute the most visible political and economic critique of capitalism (and traditional state socialism) today.

Besides the fact that both ecology and localism oppose global capital and the national state, there are two main reasons why they appear to be

natural allies. First, ecology stresses the site-specificity of the interchange between human material activity and nature, hence opposes both the abstract
valuation of nature made by capital and the idea of central planning of production, as well as centralist approaches to global issues generally.[5] The concepts of site-specificity of ecology, local subsistence or semiautarkic economy,
communal self-help principles, and direct forms of democracy all seem to be
highly congruent.

Second, the socialist concept of the "masses" has been deconstructed
and replaced by a new "politics of identity" and "politics of place," in which
cultural and ecological factors, respectively, are given the place of honor. The
idea of the specificity of cultural identities seems to meld easily with the site-
specificity of ecology in the context of a concept of social labor defined in
ecogeographic terms. The most dramatic examples today are the struggles of
indigenous peoples to keep both their cultures and subsistence-type societies
intact. In this case, the struggle to save local cultures and local ecosystems
turns out to be two different sides of the same fight.

For their part (as noted above), most of the traditional Left, as well as
the unions, remain focused on enhanced productivity, growth, and international competitiveness, that is, on jobs and wages, or more wage labor—not to
abolish exploitation but (if anything) to be exploited less. This part of the
Left does not want to be caught any more defending policies that can be identified with "economic austerity" or policies that labor leaders and others think
would endanger past economic gains won by the working class. (Union and
worker struggles for healthy and safe conditions inside and outside of the
workplace obviously connect in positive ways with broader ecological struggles.) Most of those who oppose more growth and development are mainstream environmentalists from the urban middle class who have the consumer
goods that they want and also have the time and knowledge to oppose ecologically dangerous policies and practices. It would appear, therefore, that any
effort to find a place for the working class in this equation, that is, any attempt
to marry labor (and socialism) and ecology, is doomed from the start.

Yet, left green politics of different types has made an appearance in all
of the major countries of the world. One bold initiative in the "developed"
world is New Zealand's Alliance, organized in 1991, uniting the Greens, the
movement for Maori self-determination, the New Labour Party, and other
small parties. In the 1980s, Germany's Green Party was perhaps the most
influential left green grouping in the world. In general, Western European
countries have a wide variety of left green and green left tendencies. Hol-
land's Green Left Party and Norway's Green Socialist Party, for example, are
conscious attempts to fuse red green political tendencies via the parliamen-
tary route. France's Red Green Alternative and the Great Britain's Red-Green
Network are minuscule groupings which, however, have generated influential
theoretical and practical ideas. One might also mention Canada's New Democratic Party's green caucuses, and the movements in the United States to reduce and eliminate toxics and fight for environmental justice; these latter are

deeply influenced by the work of Barry Commoner, who calls for source reduction, the "social governance of technology," and economic planning based on a "deep scientific understanding of nature." In the North, there are also many left green/green left solidarity groups, as well as a greening of Labor, Socialist, and (ex-)Communist Parties, even if reluctantly and hesitatingly. In the South, there are thousands of organizations, electoral and otherwise, that have a green left perspective; both rural and urban movements (e.g., Brazil's Landless Rural Workers Movement and Mexico's Zapatistas) raise ecological along with socioeconomic and political issues. In the big, subimperialist countries of the South (e.g., Brazil, Mexico, India) where the contradictions of combined and uneven development are most acute, there are new ecological movements that engage many in the traditional working class and also new "peasant" movements concerned with ecological issues. And we should not forget the Nicaraguan and Cuban experiments, which combined policies aimed at deep environmental reforms with populism and traditional state socialism, respectively.[6]

There are good reasons to believe that these and other ecosocialist tendencies, however tentative and experimental, are no flash in the pan, and that they permit us to discuss ecology and socialism as if they are *not* a contradiction in terms (this is obviously especially true of radical *urban* ecology movements). Or, to put the point differently, there are good reasons to believe that the contradictions of world capitalism themselves have created the conditions for an ecological socialist tendency. These reasons can be collected under two general headings. The first pertains to the causes and effects of the world social and ecological crisis from the mid-1970s to the present. The second pertains to the nature of the key ecological issues, most of which are national and international, as well as local, in scope.

First, the vitality of Western capitalism since World War II has in large part been based on the massive externalization of social and ecological costs of production. Since the slowdown of world economic growth in the mid-1970s, the concerns of both socialism and ecology have become more pressing than ever before in history. "Accumulation of capital through crisis" during the past two decades of slow growth in the West has produced even more devastating effects, not only on wealth and income distribution, norms of social justice, treatment of minorities, and so on, but also on the integrity of community and the environment. An "accelerated imbalance of (humanized) nature" is a phrase that neatly sums this up. Socially, there has been more wrenching poverty and violence, and rising misery in all parts of the world, especially the South; and, environmentally, the toxication of whole regions, the production of drought, the thinning of the ozone layer, the greenhouse effect, the assault on biodiversity, rainforests, and wildlife. The issues of socioeconomic and ecological justice have surfaced as in no other period in history; in fact, it is increasingly clear that they are two sides of the same historical process.

Given the relatively slow rate of growth of worldwide market demand since the mid-1970s, capitalist enterprises have been less able to defend or restore profits by expanding their markets and selling more commodities in booming markets. Instead, big and small capitals alike have attempted to rescue themselves from a deepening crisis mainly by expanding exports and cutting costs, by raising the rate of exploitation of labor, by depleting and exhausting resources, and by subverting the integrity of local community.

This "socioeconomic restructuring" has a two-sided effect. Cost-cutting has led many, if not most, capitals to externalize more social and environmental costs, or to pay less attention to the global environment, pollution, depletion of resources, worker health and safety, and product safety (meanwhile, increasing efficiency in energy and raw material use in the factories). The modern ecological crisis is thus aggravated and deepened as a result of the way that capitalism has reorganized itself to get through its latest economic crisis.

In addition, new and deeper inequalities in the distribution of wealth and income are the result of a worldwide increase in the rate of exploitation of labor. In the United States during the 1980s and early 1990s, for example, property income increased three times as fast as average wage income, which has been stagnant for 20 years. Higher rates of exploitation have also depended upon the ability to abuse undocumented workers and set back labor unions, social democratic parties, and struggles for social justice generally, especially in the South. It is no accident that in those parts of the world where ecological degradation is greatest—Central America, for example—there is greater poverty and heightened class struggle. The feminization of poverty is also a crucial part of this trend of ecological destruction. The working class, oppressed minorities, women, and the rural and urban poor worldwide are the groups who suffer most from both economic and ecological exploitation. The burdens of "economic adjustments" and ecological destruction alike fall disproportionately on these groups.

Crisis-ridden and crisis-dependent capitalism has forced the traditional issues of socialism and the relatively new issues ("new" in terms of public awareness) of ecology to the top of the political agenda. Capitalism itself turns out to be a kind of marriage broker between socialism and ecology, or to be more cautious, if there is not yet a prospect for marriage, there are at least openings for an engagement.

The second point is that most ecological problems worldwide cannot be adequately addressed at the local (ecological/geographical) level. One reason pertains to the green concept of "site-specificity," which means that in any given area or region a wide diversity of conditions exists, hence that an ecologically rational unit of production is necessarily small in scale; that is, site-specificity is (wrongly) equated with the "local." But the former does not refer only or mainly to the scale of operations involved in productive activity, but also (or rather) to the necessary relationship between this activity and its necessary *conditions,* which in terms of scale may be regional, national, or even global in scope. The reproduction of fisheries, for example, presupposes that the fishing industry is able to deal with the consequences of its fishing activity for its own necessary conditions (e.g., a clean ocean, healthy fisheries elsewhere, etc.). These conditions can not be ignored, nor can the costs be externalized, without harming the reproductive capacity of the activity in question. Even (or especially) when the degradation of local ecological systems has local solutions, some planning mechanism is needed to integrate the local into the "general" or "total." Concerning agriculture, Richard Levins writes that "it may seem that large-scale production is itself inimical to ecological sensitivity to local conditions and to the imperative of diversity. But this is a misconception. The unit of planning (e.g., of pest control) must be large enough to allow precisely for the integration of diversity of conditions, while the unit of production will be much smaller and reflect the needs for the mosaic, alley, and polyculture patterns."[7]

Most ecological problems, as well as the socioeconomic problems that are both cause and effect of the ecological problems, cannot be solved at the local level *alone*. Regional, national, and international planning is *also* necessary. The heart of ecology, after all, is the *interdependence* of specific sites and problems and the need to situate local responses in regional, national, and international contexts, that is, to sublate the local and the central into new democratic socioeconomic and political forms.

National and international priorities are needed to deal with the problem of energy supplies and supplies of nonrenewal resources in general, not just for the present generation but especially for future generations. The availability of other natural resources, for example, water, is mainly a regional issue, but in many parts of the globe it is a national or an international issue. The same is true of many forests. Or take the problem of soil depletion, which seems to be local or site–specific. Insofar as there are problems of soil quantity and quality, or water quantity or quality, in big food exporting countries, for example, the United States, food importing countries are also affected. Further, industrial and agricultural pollution of all kinds spills over local, regional, and national boundaries. Ocean pollution, acid rain, ozone depletion, and global warming are obvious examples.

Localism also raises the danger that people will ground their resistance to neoliberalism and globalism in a sense of place alone—not also in the subjectivity of labor, women, peasant cultures, oppressed minorities, and so on.[8]

There is, finally, the problem of equity or distribution. Resource endowments vary widely from place to place, necessitating some central authority to redistribute wealth and income from rich to poor districts. Also, "a valid argument for channeling resources to certain segments of the population and to have a tight control over the resource flow is the high degree of inequality that usually exists in Third World countries [and between these countries and the North—J.O.'C.]."[9]

If we broaden the concept of ecology to include urban environments, problems of urban transport and congestion, high rents and housing, and drugs (seemingly local issues amenable to local solutions) turn out to be global issues pertaining to financial speculation, and the ways that mortgage markets work and that money capital is allocated worldwide; the loss of foreign markets for "legal" raw materials and foodstuffs in drug-producing countries; and the absence of regional, national, and international planning of infrastructures oriented to the direct needs of the people.

If we broaden the concept of ecology even more to include the relationship between human health and well-being and environmental factors, given the increased mobility of labor nationally and internationally, and greater emigration and immigration, and an explosion of foreign trade and investment, we are also talking about problems with only or mainly national and international solutions.

Finally, if we address the question of technology and its transfer, and the relationship between new technologies and local, regional, and global ecologies, given that the dominant technology and its transfer are more or less monopolized by international corporations and nation states, we have another national and international issue.

In sum, we have good reasons to believe that both the causes and the consequences of, and also the solutions to, most ecological problems are national and international (i.e., pertain to national economies and the global economy). Hence, that far from being incompatible, socialism and ecology might make a good fit. Socialism needs ecology because the latter stresses site-specificity and reciprocity, as well as the central importance of the material interchanges within nature and between society and nature. Ecology needs socialism because the latter stresses democratic planning and the key role of the social interchanges between human beings. By contrast, popular organizations or movements confined to the community, municipality, or village cannot by themselves deal effectively with most of both the economic and ecological aspects of the general destructiveness of global capitalism, and still less with the destructive dialectic between economic and ecological crisis.

If we assume that ecology and socialism presuppose one another, the logical question is, Why haven't they gotten together before now? Why is Marxism especially regarded as unfriendly to ecology and vice versa? To put the question another way, Where did socialism go wrong, ecologically speaking?

The standard and (in my opinion) correct view is that socialism defined itself as a movement that would complete the historical tasks of fulfilling the promises of capitalism. This meant two things: first, socialism would put real social and political content into the formal claims of capitalism concerning equality, liberty, and fraternity. Second, socialism would realize the promise of material abundance that crisis-ridden capitalism was incapable of doing. The first pertains to the ethical and political meanings of socialism, the second, to the economic meaning.

It has been clear for a long time to almost everyone that this construction of socialism failed on both counts. First, instead of an ethical political society, in which the state is subordinated to civil society, we have the party bureaucratic state—and thus one justification for the post-Marxist attempt to reconcile social justice demands with liberalism.

Second, and related to the first point, in place of material abundance, we have the economic crisis of socialism—thus the post-Marxist attempt to reconcile not only social justice demands and liberalism but also both of these with markets and market incentives.

However, putting the focus on these obvious failures obscures two other issues that have moved into the center of political debates in the past decade or two. The first is that the ethical and political construction of socialism borrowed from bourgeois society ruled out any ethical or political practice that is not more or less thoroughly human-centered, as well as downplayed or ignored reciprocity and "discursive truth." The second is that the economic concept of abundance borrowed (with some modifications, of course) from capitalism ruled out any material practice that did not advance the productive forces, even when these practices were blind to nature's economy. Stalin's plan to green Siberia, which fortunately was never implemented, is perhaps the most grotesque example.

These two issues, or failures, one pertaining to politics and ethics, the other to the relationship between human economy and nature's economy, are connected to the failure of historical materialism itself. Hence they need to be addressed in methodological as well as theoretical and practical terms (see Chapter 1 of *Natural Causes: Essays in Ecological Marxism*).

Historical materialism is flawed in two big ways. Marx tended to abstract his discussions of social labor, that is, the divisions of labor, from both culture and nature. A rich, developed concept of social labor that includes both society's culture and nature's economy cannot be found in Marx or traditional historical materialism.

The first flaw is that the traditional conception of the productive forces ignores or plays down the fact that these forces are *social* in nature, and include the mode of cooperation, which is deeply inscribed by particular cultural norms and values.

The second flaw is that the traditional conception of the productive forces also plays down or ignores the fact that these forces are *natural* as well as social in character.

It is worth recalling that Engels himself called Marxism the "materialist conception of history," where "history" is the noun and "materialist" is the modifier. Marxists know the expression "in material life social relations between people are produced and reproduced" by heart, but they know another important expression much less well: "in social life the material relations between people and nature are produced and reproduced." Marxists are very familiar with the "labor process" in which human beings are active agents, and much less familiar with the "waiting process" or "tending process" characteristic of agriculture, forestry, and other nature-based activities in which human beings are more passive partners and, more generally, where both parties are "active" in complex, interactive ways.

Marx constantly hammered away on the theme that the material activity of human beings is two-sided, that is, a social relationship as well as a material relationship; in other words, that capitalist production produced and reproduced a specific mode of exploitation and a particular class structure as well as the material basis of society. But in his determination to show that material life is also social life, Marx tended to play down the opposite and equally important fact that social life is also material life. To put the same point differently, in the formulation "material life determines consciousness," Marx stressed the idea that since material life is socially organized, the social relationships of production determine consciousness. He muted the equally true fact that since material life is also the interchange between human beings and nature, these material or natural relationships also determine consciousness. These points have been made in weak and strong ways by a number of people, although they have never been integrated and developed into a revised version of the materialist conception of history.

It has also been suggested *why* Marx played up history (albeit to the exclusion of culture) and played down nature. The reason is that the problem facing Marx in his time was to show that capitalist property relationships were historical, not natural. But so intent was Marx to criticize those who naturalized, hence reified, capitalist production relationships, competition, the world market, and the like that he failed to emphasize sufficiently the fact that the development of human-made forms of "second nature" does not make nature any less natural. This was the price he paid for inverting Feuerbach's passive materialism and Hegel's active idealism into his own brand of active materialism. As Kate Soper has written, "The fact is that in its zeal to escape the charge of biological reductionism, Marxism has tended to fall prey to an antiethical form of reductionism, which in arguing the dominance of social over natural factors literally spirits the biological out of existence altogether."[10] Soper then calls for a "social biology." We can equally call for a "social chemistry," "social hydrology," and so on, that is, a "social ecology," which for socialists means "socialist ecology."

Greens are forcing reds to pay close attention to the material interchanges between people and nature and to the general issue of biological exploitation, including the biological exploitation of labor, and also to adopt an ecological sensibility. Some reds have been trying to teach Greens to pay closer attention to capitalist production relationships, competition, the world market, and so on—to sensitize Greens to the exploitation of labor and the themes of economic crisis and social labor. And feminists have been teaching both Greens and reds to pay attention to the sphere of reproduction and women's labor generally.

What does a green socialism mean politically? Green consciousness would have us put "earth first," which can mean anything you want it to mean politically. As mentioned earlier, what most Greens mean in practice most of the time is the politics of localism. By contrast, pure red theory and practice historically have privileged the "central."

To sublate socialism and ecology does not mean in the first instance defining a new category that contains elements of both socialism and ecology but that is, in fact, neither. What needs to be sublated politically is localism (or decentralism) and centralism, that is, self-determination and the overall planning, coordination, and control of production. To circle back to the main theme, localism per se won't work politically and centralism has self-destructed. To abolish the state will not work; to rely on the liberal democratic state in which "democracy" has merely a procedural or formal meaning will not work, either. In my view, the only political form that might work, that might be eminently suited to both ecological problems of site-specificity and global issues, is a democratic state—a state in which the administration of the division of social labor is democratically organized.[11]

Finally, the only *ecological* form that might work is a sublation of two kinds of ecology, the "social biology" of the coastal plain, the plateau, the local hydrological cycle, and the like, and the energy economics, the regional and international "social climatology," and so on, of the globe—that is, in general, the sublation of nature's economy defined in local, regional, and international terms. To put the conclusion somewhat differently, we need "socialism" *at least* to make the social relations of production transparent; to end the rule of the market and commodity fetishism, and to end the exploitation of human beings by other human beings; we need "ecology" *at least* to make the social productive forces transparent, to end the degradation and destruction of the earth.

## NOTES

1. Ecological socialism means, generally, an ecologically rational and sensitive society based on democratic control of the means and objects of production, information, and so on, and characterized by a high degree of socioeconomic equality, and peace and social justice, where land and labor are decommodified and exchange value is subsumed under use value. "Socialist ecology" means (again roughly) a dialectical ecological science and sociopolitical practice that successfully sublates the local and the central, the spontaneous and the planned, and the like—in other words, the premises of traditional anarchism and traditional socialism.

2. This is a crude simplification of green thought and politics, which vary from country to country, and which are also undergoing internal changes. In the United States, for example, where Marxism historically has been hostile to ecology, "left green" is associated with anarchism or libertarian socialism.

3. This slogan was coined by a conservative cofounder of the German Greens and was popularized in the United States by the antisocialist "New Age" Greens, F. Capra and C. Spretnak. Needless to say, it was never accepted by left Greens of any variety.

4. "Mainstream environmentalists" is used to identify those who are trying to save capitalism from its ecologically self-destructive tendencies. Many individuals who call themselves "environmentalists" are alienated by, and hostile to, global capitalism, and also do not necessarily identify with the "local" (see below).

5. Martin O'Connor writes, "One of the striking ambivalencies of many writers on 'environmental' issues is their tendency to make recourse to authoritarian solutions, e.g., based on ethical elitism. An example is the uneasy posturings found in the collection by Herman Daly in 1973 on *Steady-State Economics.*"

6. "Social movements inscribed in the environmental perspective of development in Third World countries incorporate . . . a concept of environment that is much richer and more complex than that manifested by conservationist politics and ecological movements of the core countries. . . . The claims of environmental movements, even when incorporating the right to democratic access to resources and conditions for ecological equilibrium for a sustained development, are not guided by an ecological rationality. Environmentalism does not pretend to re-establish the 'natural' conditions of the human species' insertion in nature, but rather to incorporate ecological and natural conditions into the conjuncture of social conditions that determine human development, and that of each community, to satisfy culturally defined needs and demands" (Enrique Leff, "The Environmental Movement in Mexico and Latin America," *Ecologia: Politica/Cultura*, 2, 6, November 1988, translated by Margaret Villanueva).

7. Richard Levins, "The Struggle for Ecological Agriculture in Cuba," *Capitalism, Nature, Socialism*, 5, October 1990.

8. For example: "The only political vision that offers any hope of salvation is one based on an understanding of, a rootedness in, a deep commitment to, and a resacrilization of, *place*. Here is where any strategy of resistance to the industrial monolith and its merchants of death must begin; here is where any program of restoration and revitalization must be grounded" (Kirkpatrick Sale, "What Columbus Discovered," *The Nation*, 22 October 1990, p. 446).

9. Jan Lundquist, "Right Food, Right Way, and Right People," a revised version of a paper presented at a study group, "Famine Research and Food Production Systems," Freiburg University, 10–14 November, 1989.

10. Quoted by Ken Post, "In Defense of Materialistic History," *Socialism in the World*, 74–75, 1989, p. 67.

11. I realize that the idea of a "democratic state" seems to be a contradiction in terms, or at least immediately raises difficult questions about the desirability of the separation of powers, the problem of scale inherent in any coherent description of substantive democracy, and also the question of how to organize—much less plan—a nationally and internationally regulated division of social labor without a universal equivalent for measuring costs and productivity (however "costs" and "productivity" are defined) (courtesy of John Ely). On the other hand, we presently live under a bureaucratic democracy, so why cannot we have a democratic bureaucracy?

# WHAT IS SOCIAL ECOLOGY?

*Murray Bookchin*

Murray Bookchin has written on such topics as anarchist and utopian political theory, theory of technology, urbanism, and the philosophy of nature. He is the cofounder and director emeritus of the Institute for Social Ecology. His many books include *Toward an Ecological Society, The Ecology of Freedom, The Rise of Urbanization and the Decline of Citizenship, Remaking Society,* and *The Philosophy of Social Ecology.*

What literally defines social ecology as "social" is its recognition of the often overlooked fact that nearly all our present ecological problems arise from deep-seated social problems. Conversely, present ecological problems cannot be clearly understood, much less resolved, without resolutely dealing with problems within society. To make this point more concrete: economic, ethnic, cultural, and gender conflicts, among many others, lie at the core of the most serious ecological dislocations we face today—apart, to be sure, from those that are produced by natural catastrophes.

If this approach seems a bit too "sociological" for those environmentalists who identify ecological problems with the preservation of wildlife, wilderness, or more broadly, with "Gaia" and planetary "Oneness," it might be sobering to consider certain recent facts. The massive oil spill by an Exxon tanker at Prince William Sound, the extensive deforestation of redwood trees by the Maxxam Corporation, and the proposed James Bay hydroelectric project that would flood vast areas of northern Quebec's forests, to cite only a few problems, should remind us that the real battleground on which the ecological future of the planet will be decided is clearly a social one.

Indeed, to separate ecological problems from social problems—or even to play down or give token recognition to this crucial relationship—would be to grossly misconstrue the sources of the growing environmental crisis. The way human beings deal with each other as social beings is crucial to addressing the ecological crisis. Unless we clearly recognize this, we will surely fail to see that the hierarchical mentality and class relationships that so thoroughly permeate society give rise to the very idea of dominating the natural world.

Unless we realize that the present market society, structured around the brutally competitive imperative of "grow or die," is a thoroughly impersonal, self-operating mechanism, we will falsely tend to blame technology as such or population growth as such for environmental problems. We will ignore their root causes, such as trade for profit, industrial expansion, and the identification of "progress" with corporate self-interest. In short, we will tend to focus on the symptoms of a grim social pathology rather than on the pathology itself, and our efforts will be directed toward limited goals whose attainment is more cosmetic than curative.

While some have questioned whether social ecology has dealt adequately with issues of spirituality, it was, in fact, among the earliest of contemporary ecologies to call for a sweeping change in existing spiritual values. Such a change would mean a far-reaching transformation of our prevailing mentality of domination into one of complementarity, in which we would see our role in the natural world as creative, supportive, and deeply appreciative of the needs of nonhuman life. In social ecology, a truly *natural* spirituality centers on the ability of an awakened humanity to function as moral agents in diminishing needless suffering, engaging in ecological restoration, and fostering an aesthetic appreciation of natural evolution in all its fecundity and diversity.

Thus social ecology has never eschewed the need for a radically new spirituality or mentality in its call for a collective effort to change society. Indeed, as early as 1965, the first public statement to advance the ideas of social ecology concluded with the injunction: "The cast of mind that today organizes differences among human and other life-forms along hierarchical lines of 'supremacy' or 'inferiority' will give way to an outlook that deals with diversity in an ecological manner—that is, according to an ethics of complementarity."[1] In such an ethics, human beings would complement nonhuman beings with their own capacities to produce a richer, creative, and developmental whole—not as a "dominant" species but as a supportive one. Although this idea, expressed at times as an appeal for the "respiritization of the natural world," recurs throughout the literature of social ecology, it should not be mistaken for a theology that raises a deity above the natural world or that seeks to discover one within it. The spirituality advanced by social ecology is definitively naturalistic (as one would expect, given its relation to ecology itself, which stems from the biological sciences), rather than supernaturalistic or pantheistic.

To prioritize any form of spirituality over the social factors that actually erode all forms of spirituality, raises serious questions about one's ability to come to grips with reality. At a time when a blind social mechanism, the market, is turning soil into sand, covering fertile land with concrete, poisoning air and water, and producing sweeping climatic and atmospheric changes, we cannot ignore the impact that a hierarchical and class society has on the natural world. We must earnestly deal with the fact that economic growth, gender oppressions, and ethnic domination—not to speak of corporate, state, and bureaucratic interests—are much more capable of shaping the future of the natural world than are privatistic forms of spiritual self-regeneration. These forms of domination must be confronted by collective action and major social movements that challenge the social sources of the ecological crisis, not simply by personalistic forms of consumption and investment that often go under the rubric of "green capitalism." We live in a highly cooptative society that is only too eager to find new areas of commercial aggrandizement and to add ecological verbiage to its advertising and customer relations.

## NATURE AND SOCIETY

Let us begin, then, with basics—namely, by asking what we mean by nature and society. Among the many definitions of nature that have been formulated over time, one is rather elusive and often difficult to grasp because it requires a certain way of thinking—one that stands at odds with what we popularly call "linear thinking." This form of "nonlinear" or organic thinking is developmental rather than analytical, or, in more technical terms, dialectical rather than instrumental. Nature, conceived in terms of developmental thinking, is more than the beautiful vistas we see from a mountaintop or in the images that are fixed on the backs of picture postcards. Such vistas and images of nonhuman nature are basically static and immobile. Our attention, to be sure, may be arrested by the soaring flight of a hawk, or the bolting leap of a deer, or the low-slung shadowy loping of a coyote. But what we are really witnessing in such cases are the mere kinetics of physical motion, caught in the frame of an essentially static image of the scene before our eyes. It deceives us into believing in the "eternality" of a single moment in nature.

If we look with some care into nonhuman nature as more than a scenic view, we begin to sense that it is basically an evolving phenomenon, a richly fecund, even dramatic development that is forever changing. I mean to define nonhuman nature precisely as an evolving process, as the *totality*, in fact of its evolution. This encompasses the development from the inorganic into the organic, from the less differentiated and relatively limited world of unicellular organisms into that of multicellular ones equipped with simple, later complex, and presently fairly intelligent neural apparatuses that allow them to make innovative choices. Finally, the acquisition of warm-bloodedness gives to organisms the astonishing flexibility to exist in the most demanding climatic environments.

This vast drama of nonhuman nature is in every respect stunningly wondrous. It is marked by increasing subjectivity and flexibility and by increasing differentiation that makes an organism more adaptable to new environmental challenges and opportunities and renders a living being more equipped to alter its environment to meet its own needs. One may speculate that the potentiality of matter itself—the ceaseless interactivity of atoms in forming new chemical combinations to produce ever more complex molecules, amino acids, proteins, and, under suitable conditions, elementary life-forms—is inherent in inorganic nature. Or one may decide, quite matter-of-factly, that the "struggle for existence" or the "survival of the fittest" (to use popular Darwinian terms) explains why increasingly subjective and more flexible beings are capable of dealing with environmental changes more effectively than are less subjective and flexible beings. But the fact remains that the kind of evolutionary drama I have described did occur, and is carved in stone in the fossil record. That nature is this record, this history, this developmental or evolutionary process, is a very sobering fact.

Conceiving nonhuman nature as its own evolution rather than as a mere vista has profound implications—ethical as well as biological—for ecologically minded people. Human beings embody, at least potentially, attributes of nonhuman development that place them squarely within organic evolution. They are not "natural aliens," to use Neil Evernden's phrase, strange "exotics," phylogenetic "deformities" that, owing to their tool-making capacities, "cannot evolve *with* an ecosystem anywhere."[2] Nor are they "intelligent fleas," to use the language of Gaian theorists who believe that the earth ("Gaia") is one living organism. These untenable disjunctions between humanity and the evolutionary process are as superficial as they are potentially misanthropic. Humans are highly intelligent, indeed, very self-conscious primates, which is to say that they have emerged—not diverged—from a long evolution of vertebrate life-forms into mammalian, and finally, primate life-forms. They are a product of a significant evolutionary trend toward intellectuality, self-awareness, will, intentionality, and expressiveness, be it in oral or body language.

Human beings belong to a natural continuum, no less than their primate ancestors and mammals in general. To depict them as "aliens" that have no place or pedigree in natural evolution, or to see them essentially as an infestation that parasitizes a highly anthropomorphic version of the planet (Gaia) the way fleas parasitize dogs and cats, is bad thinking, not only bad ecology. Lacking any sense of process, this kind of thinking—regrettably so commonplace among ethicists—radically bifurcates the nonhuman from the human. Indeed, to the degree that nonhuman nature is romanticized as "wilderness," and seen presumably as more authentically "natural" than the works of humans, the natural world is frozen into a circumscribed domain in which human innovation, foresight, and creativity have no place and offer no possibilities.

The truth is that human beings not only belong in nature, they are products of a long, natural evolutionary process. Their seemingly "unnatural" activities—like the development of technology and science, the formation of mutable social institutions, of highly symbolic forms of communication, of aesthetic sensibilities, the creation of towns and cities—all would be impossible without the large array of physical attributes that have been eons in the making, be they large brains or the bipedal motion that frees their hands for

tool making and carrying food. In many respects, human traits are enlarge-
ments of nonhuman traits that have been evolving over the ages. Increasing
care for the young, cooperation, the substitution of mentally guided behavior
for largely instinctive behavior—all are present more keenly in human behavior. The difference between the development of these traits among nonhuman
beings is that among humans they reach a degree of elaboration and integration that yields cultures or, viewed institutionally in terms of families, bands,
tribes, hierarchies, economic classes, and the state, highly mutable *societies* for
which there is no precedent in the nonhuman world—unless the genetically
programmed behavior of insects is to be regarded as "social." In fact, the
emergence and development of human society is a shedding of instinctive behavioral traits, a continuing process of clearing a new terrain for potentially
rational behavior.

Human beings always remain rooted in their biological evolutionary
history, which we may call "first nature," but they produce a characteristically
human social nature of their own, which we may call "second nature." And
far from being "unnatural," human second nature is eminently a creation of
organic evolution's first nature. To write the second nature created by human
beings out of nature as a whole, or indeed, to minimize it, is to ignore the creativity of natural evolution itself and to view it onesidedly. If "true" evolution
embodies itself simply in creatures like grizzly bears, wolves, and whales—
generally, animals that *people* find aesthetically pleasing or relatively intelligent—then human beings are literally *de*-natured. In such views, whether
seen as "aliens" or as "fleas," humans are essentially placed outside the self-
organizing thrust of natural evolution toward increasing subjectivity and
flexibility. The more enthusiastic proponents of this de-naturing of humanity
may see human beings as existing apart from nonhuman evolution, thereby
dealing with people as a "freaking," as Paul Shepard puts it, of the evolutionary process. Others simply avoid the problem of humanity's unique place in
natural evolution by promiscuously putting human beings on a par with bee-
tles in terms of their "intrinsic worth." In this "either/or" propositional
thinking, the social is either separated from the organic, or flippantly reduced to the organic, resulting in an inexplicable dualism at one extreme
or a naive reductionism at the other. The dualistic approach, with its quasi-
theological premise that the world was "made" for human use is saddled with
the name of "anthropocentricity," while the reductionist approach, with its
almost meaningless notion of a "biocentric democracy," is saddled with the
name of "biocentricity."

The bifurcation of the human from the nonhuman reveals a failure to
think organically, and to approach evolutionary phenomena with an evolutionary way of thought. Needless to say, if we are content to regard nature as
no more than a scenic vista, mere metaphoric and poetic description of it
might suffice to replace systematic thinking about it. But if we regard nature
as the history of nature, as an evolutionary process that is going on to one degree or another under our very eyes, we dishonor this process by thinking of it

in anything but a processual way. That is to say, we require a way of thinking that recognizes that "what-is" as it seems to lie before our eyes is always developing into "what-it-is-not," that it is engaged in a continual self-organizing process in which past and present, seen as a richly differentiated but shared continuum, give rise to a new potentiality for a future, ever-richer degree of *wholeness.* Accordingly, the human and the nonhuman can be seen as aspects of an evolutionary continuum, and the emergence of the human can be located in the evolution of the nonhuman, without advancing naive claims that one is either "superior to" or "made for" the other.

By the same token, in a processual, organic, and dialectical way of thinking, we would have little difficulty in locating and explaining the emergence of the social out of the biological, of second nature out of first nature. It seems more fashionable these days to deal with ecologically significant social issues like a bookkeeper. One simply juxtaposes two columns—labeled "old paradigm" and "new paradigm"—as though one were dealing with debits and credits. Obviously distasteful terms like "centralization" are placed under "old paradigm," while more appealing ones like "decentralization" are regarded as "new paradigm." The result is an inventory of bumper-sticker slogans whose "bottom line" is patently a form of "absolute good versus absolute evil." All of this may be deliciously synoptic and easy for the eyes, but it is singularly lacking as food for the brain. To truly *know* and be able to give interpretative *meaning* to the social issues so arranged, we should want to know how each idea derived from others and is part of an overall development. What, in fact, do we mean by the notion of "decentralization," and how does it derive from or give rise in the history of human society to "centralization"? Again: processual thinking is needed to deal with processual realities so that we can gain some sense of *direction*—practical as well as theoretical—in dealing with our ecological problems.

Social ecology seems to stand alone, at present, in calling for the use of organic, developmental, and derivative ways of thinking out problems that are basically organic and developmental in character. The very definition of the natural world as a development indicates the need for an organic way of thinking, as does the derivation of human from nonhuman nature—a derivation that has the most far-reaching consequences for an ecological ethics that can offer serious guidelines for the solution of our ecological problems.

Social ecology calls upon us to see that nature and society are interlinked by evolution into one nature that consists of two differentiations: first or biotic nature, and second or human nature. Human nature and biotic nature share an evolutionary potential for greater subjectivity and flexibility. Second nature is the way in which human beings as flexible, highly intelligent primates *inhabit* the natural world. That is to say, people create an environment that is most suitable for their mode of existence. In this respect, second nature is no different from the environment that *every* animal, depending upon its abilities, creates as well as adapts to, the biophysical circumstances—or ecocommunity—in which it must live. On this very simple level, human beings are, in principle, doing nothing that differs from the survival activities of nonhuman beings—be it building beaver dams or gopher holes.

But the environmental changes that human beings produce are significantly different from those produced by nonhuman beings. Humans act upon their environments with considerable technical foresight, however lacking that foresight may be in ecological respects. Their cultures are rich in knowledge, experience, cooperation, and conceptual intellectuality; however, they may be sharply divided against themselves at certain points of their development, through conflicts between groups, classes, nation-states, and even city-states. Nonhuman beings generally live in ecological niches, their behavior guided primarily by instinctive drives and conditioned reflexes. Human societies are "bonded" together by institutions that change radically over centuries. Nonhuman communities are notable for their fixity in general terms or by clearly preset, often genetically imprinted, rhythms. Human communities are guided in part by ideological factors and are subject to changes conditioned by those factors.

Hence human beings, emerging from an organic evolutionary process, initiate, by the sheer force of their biology and survival needs, a social evolutionary development that profoundly involves their organic evolutionary process. Owing to their naturally endowed intelligence, powers of communication, capacity for institutional organization, and relative freedom from instinctive behavior, they refashion their environment—as do nonhuman beings—to the full extent of their biological equipment. This equipment now makes it possible for them to engage in social development. It is not so much that human beings, in principle, behave differently from animals or are inherently more problematical in a strictly ecological sense, but that the social development by which they grade out of their biological development often becomes more problematical for themselves and nonhuman life. How these problems emerge, the ideologies they produce, the extent to which they contribute to biotic evolution or abort it, and the damage they inflict on the planet as a whole lie at the very heart of the modern ecological crisis. Second nature, far from marking the fulfillment of human potentialities, is riddled by contradictions, antagonisms, and conflicting interests that have distorted humanity's unique capacities for development. It contains both the danger of tearing down the biosphere and, given a further development of humanity toward an ecological society, the capacity to provide an entirely new ecological dispensation.

## SOCIAL HIERARCHY AND DOMINATION

How, then, did the social—eventually structured around status groups, class formations, and cultural phenomena—emerge from the biological? We have reason to speculate that as biological facts such as lineage, gender distribution, and age differences were slowly institutionalized, their uniquely social dimension was initially quite egalitarian. Later it acquired an oppressive hierarchical and then an exploitative class form. The lineage or blood tie in early prehistory obviously formed the organic basis of the family. Indeed, it joined together groups of families into bands, clans, and tribes, through either intermarriage or fictive forms of descent, thereby forming the earliest social horizon of our ancestors. More than in other mammals, the simple biological facts of human reproduction and protracted maternal care of the infant tended to knit siblings together and produced a strong sense of solidarity and group inwardness. Men, women, and their children were brought into a condition of a fairly stable family life, based on mutual obligation and an expressed sense of affinity that was often sanctified by marital vows of one kind or another.

Outside the family and all its elaborations into bands, clans, tribes and the like, other human beings were regarded as "strangers," who could alternatively be welcomed hospitably or enslaved or put to death. What mores existed were based on an unreflected body of *customs* that seemed to have been inherited from time immemorial.What we call *morality* began as the commandments of a deity, in that they required some kind of supernatural or mystical reinforcement to be accepted by the community. Only later, beginning with the ancient Greeks, did *ethical* behavior emerge, based on rational discourse and reflection. The shift from blind custom to a commanding morality, and finally, to a rational ethics occurred with the rise of cities and urban cosmopolitanism. Humanity, gradually disengaging itself from the biological facts of blood ties, began to admit the "stranger" and increasingly recognize itself as a shared community of human beings rather than an ethnic folk—a community of citizens rather than of kinsmen.

In the primordial and socially formative world that we must still explore, other of humanity's biological traits were to be reworked from the strictly natural to the social. One of these was the fact of age and its distinctions. In the emerging social groups that developed among early humans, the absence of a written language helped to confer on the elderly a high degree of status, for it was they who possessed the traditional wisdom of the community, the kinship lines that prescribed marital ties in obedience to extensive incest taboos, and techniques for survival that had to be acquired by both the young and the mature members of the group. In addition, the biological fact of gender distinctions were to be slowly reworked along social lines into what were initially complementary sororal and fraternal groups. Women formed their own food-gathering and caretaking groups with their own customs, belief systems, and values, while men formed their own hunting and warrior groups with their own behavioral characteristics, mores, and ideologies.

From everything we know about the socialization of the biological facts of kinship, age, and gender groups—their elaboration into early institutions—there is no reason to doubt that people existed in a complementary relationship with one another. Each, in effect, was needed by the other to form a relatively stable whole. No one "dominated" the others or tried to privilege itself in the normal course of things. Yet with the passing of time, even as the biological facts that underpin every human group were further reworked into social institutions, so the social institutions were slowly reworked at various periods and in various degrees, into hierarchical structures based on command and obedience. I speak here of a historical trend, in no way predetermined by any mystical force or deity, a trend that often did not go beyond a very limited development among many preliterate or aboriginal cultures, and even in certain fairly elaborate civilizations. Nor can we foretell how human history might have developed had certain feminine values associated with care and nurture not been overshadowed by masculine values associated with combative and aggressive behavior.

Hierarchy in its earliest forms was probably not marked by the harsh qualities it has acquired over history. Elders, at the very beginning of gerontocracy, were not only respected for their wisdom but often beloved of the young, and their affection was often reciprocated in kind. We can probably account for the increasing stridency and harshness of later gerontocracies by supposing that the elderly, burdened by their failing powers and dependent upon the community's goodwill, were more vulnerable to abandonment in periods of material want than any other part of the population. In any case, that gerontocracies were the earliest forms of hierarchy is corroborated by their existence in communities as far removed from each other as the Australian Aborigines, tribal societies in East Africa, and Indian communities in the Americas. "Even in simple food-gathering cultures, individuals above fifty, let us say, apparently arrogated to themselves certain powers and privileges which benefitted themselves specifically," observes anthropologist Paul Radin, "and were not necessarily, if at all, dictated by considerations either of the rights of others or the welfare of the community."[3] Many tribal councils throughout the world were really councils of elders, an institution that never completely disappeared (as the word "alderman" suggests), even though they were overlaid by warrior societies, chiefdoms, and kingships.

Patricentricity, in which male values, institutions, and forms of behavior prevail over female ones, seems to have followed gerontocracy. Initially, this shift may have been fairly harmless, inasmuch as preliterate and early aboriginal societies were largely domestic communities in which the authentic center of material life was the home, not the "men's house" so widely present in tribal societies. Male rule, if such it can be strictly called, takes on its most severe and coercive form in patriarchy, an institution in which the eldest male of an extended family or clan has a life-and-death command over all members of the group. Women are by no means the exclusive or even the principal target of the patriarch's domination. The sons, like the daughters, may be ordered how to behave and whom to marry, and may be killed at the whim of the "old man." So far as patricentricity is concerned, however, the authority and prerogative of the male are the product of a slow, often subtly negotiated development in which the male fraternity tends to edge out the female sorority by virtue of the former's growing "civil" responsibilities. Increasing population, marauding bands of outsiders whose migrations may be induced by drought or other unfavorable conditions, and vendettas of one kind or an-other, to cite common causes of hostility or war, create a new "civil" sphere side by side with woman's domestic sphere, and the former gradually en-croaches upon the latter. With the appearance of cattle-drawn plow agricul-ture, the male begins to invade the horticultural sphere of woman, who had used the simple digging stick, and her earlier economic predominance in the community's life is thereby diluted. Warrior societies and chiefs carry the momentum of male dominance to the level of a new material and cultural constellation. Male dominance becomes extremely active and ultimately yields a world that is managed by male elites who dominate not only women but also other men.

"Why" hierarchy emerges is transparent enough: the infirmities of age, increasing population, natural disasters, certain technological changes that privilege male activities of hunting and caring for animals over the horticul-tural functions of females, the growth of civil society, the spread of warfare. All serve to enhance the male's responsibilities at the expense of the female's. Marxist theorists tend to single out technological advances and the presumed material surpluses they produce to explain the emergence of elite strata—in-deed, of exploiting ruling classes. However, this does not tell us why many so-cieties whose environments were abundantly rich in food never produced such strata. That surpluses are necessary to support elites and classes is obvious, as Aristotle pointed out more than two millennia ago. But too many communi-ties that had such resources at their disposal remained quite egalitarian and never "advanced" to hierarchical or class societies.

It is worth emphasizing that hierarchical domination, however coercive it may be, is not to be confused with class exploitation. Often the role of high-status individuals is very well-meaning, as in the case of commands given by caring parents to their children, of concerned husbands and wives to each other, or of elderly people to younger ones. In tribal societies, even where a considerable measure of authority accrues to a chief—and most chiefs are ad-visers rather than rulers—he usually must earn the esteem of the community by interacting with the people, and he can easily be ignored or removed from his position by them. Many chiefs earn their prestige, so essential to their au-thority, by disposing of gifts, and even by a considerable disaccumulation of their personal goods. The respect accorded to many chiefs is earned, not by hoarding surpluses as a means to power but by disposing of them as evidence of generosity.

Classes tend to operate along different lines. Power is usually gained by the acquisition of wealth, not by its disposal; rulership is guaranteed by out-right physical coercion, not simply by persuasion; and the state is the ultimate guarantor of authority. That hierarchy is more entrenched than class can per-haps be verified by the fact that women have been dominated for millennia, despite sweeping changes in class societies. By the same token, the abolition of class rule and economic exploitation offers no guarantee whatever that elabo-rate hierarchies and systems of domination will disappear.

In nonhierarchical and even some hierarchical societies, certain customs guide human behavior along basically decent lines. Of primary importance in early customs was the "law of the irreducible minimum" (to use Radin's expression), the shared notion that all members of a community are entitled to the means of life, irrespective of the amount of work they perform. To deny anyone food, shelter, and the basic means of life because of infirmities or even frivolous behavior would have been seen as a heinous denial of the very right to live. Nor were the resources and things needed to sustain the community ever completely privately owned: overriding individualistic control was the broader principle of usufruct—the notion that the means of life that were not being used by one group could be used, as need be, by another. Thus unused land, orchards, and even tools and weapons, if left idle, were at the disposition of anyone in the community who needed them. Lastly, custom fostered the practice of mutual aid, the rather sensible cooperative behavior of sharing things and labor, so that an individual or family in fairly good circumstances could expect to be helped by others if their fortunes should change for the worse. Taken as a whole, these customs became so sedimented into society that they persisted long after hierarchy became oppressive and class society became prodominant.

## THE IDEA OF DOMINATING NATURE

"Nature," in the broad sense of a biotic environment from which humans take the simple things they need for survival, often has no meaning to preliterate peoples. Immersed in nature as the very universe of their lives, it has no special meaning, even when they celebrate animistic rituals and view the world around them as a nexus of life, often imputing their own social institutions to the behavior of various species, as in the case of "beaver lodges" and humanlike spirits. Words that express our conventional notions of nature are not easy to find, if they exist at all, in the languages of aboriginal peoples.

With the rise of hierarchy and human domination, however, the seeds are planted for a belief that nature not only exists as a world apart, but that it is hierarchically organized and can be dominated. The study of magic reveals this shift clearly. Early forms of magic did not view nature as a world apart. Its worldview tended to be such that a practitioner essentially pleaded with the "chief spirit" of the game to coax an animal in the direction of an arrow or a spear. Later, magic becomes almost entirely instrumental; the game is coerced by magical techniques to become the hunter's prey. While the earliest forms of magic may be regarded as the practices of a generally nonhierarchical and egalitarian community, the later forms of animistic beliefs betray a more or less hierarchical view of the natural world and of latent human powers of domination.

We must emphasize, here, that the *idea* of dominating nature has its primary source in the domination of human by human and the structuring of the natural world into a hierarchical Chain of Being (a static conception, incidentally, that has no relationship to the evolution of life into increasingly advanced forms of subjectivity and flexibility). The biblical injunction that gave to Adam and Noah command of the living world was above all an expression of a *social* dispensation. Its idea of dominating nature can be overcome only through the creation of a society without those class and hierarchical structures that make for rule and obedience in private as well as public life. That this new dispensation involves changes in attitudes and values should go without saying. But these attitudes and values remain vaporous if they are not given substance through objective institutions, the ways in which humans concretely interact with each other, and in the realities of everyday life from childrearing to work and play. Until human beings cease to live in societies that are structured around hierarchies as well as economic classes, we shall never be free of domination, however much we try to dispel it with rituals, incantations, ecotheologies, and the adoption of seemingly "natural" ways of life.

The idea of dominating nature has a history that is almost as old as that of hierarchy itself. Already in the Gilgamesh Epic of Mesopotamia, a drama that dates back some 7,000 years, the hero defies the deities and cuts down their sacred trees in his quest for immortality. The *Odyssey* is a vast travelogue of the Greek warrior, albeit a more canny than a heroic one, who essentially dispatches the nature deities that the Hellenic world inherited from its less well-known precursors. That elitist societies devastated much of the Mediterranean basin as well as the hillsides of China provides ample evidence that hierarchical and class societies had begun a sweeping remaking and despoliation of the planet long before the emergence of modern science, "linear" rationality, and "industrial society," to cite causal factors that are invoked so freely in the modern ecology movement. Second nature, to be sure, did not create a Garden of Eden in steadily absorbing and inflicting harm on first nature. More often than not, it despoiled much that was beautiful, creative, and dynamic in the biotic world, just as it ravaged human life itself in murderous wars, genocide, and acts of heartless oppression. Social ecology refuses to ignore the fact that the harm elitist society inflicted on the natural world was more than matched by the harm it inflicted on humanity; nor does it overlook the fact that the destiny of human life goes hand-in-hand with the destiny of the nonhuman world.

But the customs of the irreducible minimum, usufruct, and mutual aid cannot be ignored, however troubling the ills produced by second nature may seem. These customs persisted well into history and surfaced almost explosively in massive popular uprisings, from early revolts in ancient Sumer to the present time. Many of those demanded the recovery of caring and communitarian values when these were under the onslaught of elitist and class oppression. Indeed, despite the armies that roamed the landscape of warring areas, the taxgatherers who plundered ordinary village peoples, and the daily abuses that were inflicted by overseers on workers, community life still persisted and retained many of the cherished values of a more egalitarian past. Neither ancient despots nor feudal lords could fully obliterate them in peasant villages and in the towns with independent craft guilds. In ancient Greece, religions based on austerity and, more significantly, a rational philosophy that rejected the encumbering of thought and political life by extravagant wants, tended to scale down needs and delimit human appetites for material goods. They served to slow the pace of technological innovation to a point where new means of production could be sensitively integrated into a balanced society. Medieval markets were modest, usually local affairs, in which guilds exercised strict control over prices, competition, and the quality of the goods produced by their members.

## "GROW OR DIE!"

But just as hierarchies and class structures tend to acquire a momentum of their own and permeate much of society, so too the market began to acquire a life of its own and extended its reach beyond limited regions into the depths of vast continents. Exchange ceased to be primarily a means to provide for modest needs, subverting the limits imposed upon it by guilds or by moral and religious restrictions. Not only did it place a high premium on techniques for increasing production; it also became the procreator of needs, many of which are simply useless, and gave an explosive impetus to consumption and technology. First in northern Italy and the European lowlands, later—and most effectively—in England during the seventeenth and eighteenth centuries, the production of goods exclusively for sale and profit (the capitalistic commodity) rapidly swept aside all cultural and social barriers to market growth.

By the late eighteenth and early nineteenth centuries, the new industrial capitalist class with its factory system and commitment to limitless expansion began to colonize the entire world, and finally, most aspects of personal life. Unlike the feudal nobility, which had its cherished lands and castles, the bourgeoisie had no home but the marketplace and its bank vaults. As a class, they turned more and more of the world into an ever-expanding domain of factories. Entrepreneurs of the ancient and medieval worlds had normally gathered their profits together to invest in land and live like country gentry—given the prejudices of their times against "ill-gotten" gains from trade. On the other hand, the industrial capitalists of the modern world spawned a bitterly competitive marketplace that placed a high premium on industrial expansion and the commercial power it conferred, and functioned as though growth were an end in itself.

It is crucially important, in social ecology, to recognize that industrial growth does not result from a change in a cultural outlook alone—and least of all, from the impact of scientific rationality on society. It stems above all from *harshly objective factors* churned up by the expansion of the market itself, *factors that are largely impervious to moral considerations and efforts at ethical persuasion.*

Indeed, despite the close association between capitalist development and technological innovation, the most driving imperative of the capitalist market, given the dehumanizing competition that defines it, is the need to grow, and to avoid dying at the hands of savage rivals. Important as greed or the power conferred by wealth may be, sheer survival requires that an entrepreneur must expand his or her productive apparatus to remain ahead of other entrepreneurs and try, in fact, to devour them. The key to this law of life—to survival—is expansion, and greater profit, to be invested in still further expansion. Indeed, the notion of progress, once identified by our ancestors as a faith in the evolution of greater human cooperation and care, is now identified with economic growth.

The effort by many well-intentioned ecology theorists and their admirers to reduce the ecological crisis to a cultural rather than a social problem can easily become obfuscatory. However ecologically concerned an entrepreneur may be, the harsh fact is that his or her very survival in the marketplace precludes a meaningful ecological orientation. To engage in ecologically sound practices places a morally concerned entrepreneur at a striking, and indeed, fatal disadvantage in a competitive relationship with a rival—notably one who lacks any ecological concerns and thus produces at lower costs and reaps higher profits for further capital expansion.

Indeed, to the extent that environmental movements and ideologies merely moralize about the "wickedness" of our anti-ecological society, and emphasize change in personal life and attitudes, they obscure the need for social action. Corporations are skilled at manipulating this desire to be present as an ecological image. Mercedes-Benz, for example, declaims in a two-page ad, decorated with a bison painting from a Paleolithic cave wall, that "we must work to make more environmentally sustainable progress by including the theme of the environment in the planning of new products."[4] Such deceptive messages are commonplace in Germany, one of western Europe's worst polluters. Advertising is equally self-serving in the United States, where leading polluters piously declare that for them, "Every day is Earth Day."

The point social ecology emphasizes is not that moral and spiritual change is meaningless or unnecessary, but that modern capitalism is *structurally* amoral and hence impervious to any moral appeals. The modern marketplace has imperatives of its own, irrespective of who sits in the driver's seat or grabs on to its handlebars. The direction it follows depends not upon ethical factors but rather on the mindless "laws" of supply and demand, grow or die, eat or be eaten. Maxims like "business is business" explicitly tell us that ethical, religious, psychological, and emotional factors have absolutely no place in the impersonal world of production, profit, and growth. It is grossly misleading to think that we can divest this brutally materialistic, indeed, mechanistic, world of its objective character, that we can vaporize its hard facts rather than transforming it.

A society based on "grow or die" as its all-pervasive imperative must necessarily have a devastating ecological impact. Given the growth imperative generated by market competition, it would mean little or nothing if the present-day population were reduced to a fraction of what it is today. Insofar as entrepreneurs must always expand if they are to survive, the media that have fostered mindless consumption would be mobilized to increase the purchase of goods, irrespective of the need for them. Hence it would become "indispensable" in the public mind to own two or three of every appliance, motor vehicle, electronic gadget, or the like, where one would more than suffice. In addition, the military would continue to demand new, more lethal instruments of death, of which new models would be required annually.

Nor would "softer" technologies produced by a grow-or-die market fail to be used for destructive capitalistic ends. Two centuries ago, the forests of England were hacked into fuel for iron forges with axes that had not changed appreciably since the Bronze Age, and ordinary sails guided ships laden with commodities to all parts of the world well into the nineteenth century. Indeed, much of the United States was "cleared" of its forests, wildlife, soil, and aboriginal inhabitants with tools and weapons that would have been easily recognized, however much they were modified, by Renaissance people who had yet to encounter the Industrial Revolution. What modern technics did was to accelerate a process that was well under way at the close of the Middle Ages. It did not devastate the planet on its own; it abetted a phenomenon, the ever-expanding market system that had its roots in one of history's most fundamental social transformations: the elaboration of hierarchy and class into a system of distribution based on exchange rather than complementarity and mutual aid.

## AN ECOLOGICAL SOCIETY

Social ecology is an appeal not only for moral regeneration but also, and above all, for social reconstruction along ecological lines. It emphasizes that an ethical appeal to the powers that be (that embody blind market forces and competitive relationships), taken by itself, is likely to be futile. Indeed, taken by itself, it often obscures the real power relationships that prevail today by making the attainment of an ecological society seem merely a matter of "attitude," of "spiritual change," or of quasi-religious redemption.

Although always mindful of the need for spiritual change, social ecology seeks to redress the ecological abuses that society has inflicted on the natural world by going to the structural as well as the subjective sources of notions like the "domination of nature." That is, it challenges the entire system of domination itself and seeks to eliminate the hierarchical and class edifice that has imposed itself on humanity and defined the relationship between nonhuman and human nature. It advances an ethics of complementarity in which human beings must play a supportive role in perpetuating the integrity of the biosphere, as potentially, at least, the most conscious products of natural evolution. Indeed humans are seen to have a moral responsibility to function creatively in the unfolding of that evolution. Social ecology thus stresses the need for embodying its ethics of complementarity in palpable social institutions that will give active meaning to its goal of wholeness, and of human involvement as conscious and moral agents in the interplay of species. It seeks the enrichment of the evolutionary process by diversification of life-forms. Notwithstanding romantic views, "Mother Nature" does not necessarily "know best." To oppose activities of the corporate world does not mean that one has to become naively romantic and "biocentric." By the same token, to applaud humanity's potential for foresight and rationality, and its technological achievements, does not mean that one is "anthropocentric." The loose usage of such buzzwords, so commonplace in the ecology movement, must be brought to an end by reflective discussion.

Social ecology, in effect, recognizes that—like it or not—the future of life on this planet pivots on the future of society. It contends that evolution, whether in first nature or in second, is not yet complete. Nor are the two realms so separated from each other that we must choose one or the other— either natural evolution with its "biocentric" halo, or social evolution, as we have known it up to now, with its "anthropocentric" halo—as the basis for a creative biosphere. We must go beyond both the natural and the social toward a new synthesis that contains the best of both. Such a synthesis will transcend them in the form of a creative, self-conscious, and therefore "free nature," in which human beings intervene in natural evolution with their best capacities—their moral sense, their unprecedented degree of conceptual thought, and their remarkable powers of communication.

But such a goal remains mere verbiage unless it can be given logistical and social tangibility. How are we to organize a "free nature" that goes beyond the rhetoric so plentiful in the ecology movement? Logistically, "free nature" is unattainable without the decentralization of cities into confederally united communities sensitively tailored to the natural areas in which they are located. It means the use of ecotechnologies, and of solar, wind, methane, and other sources of energy, the use of organic forms of agriculture, the design of humanly scaled, versatile industrial installations to meet regional needs of confederated municipalities. It means, too, an emphasis not only on recycling, but on the production of high-quality goods that can last for generations. It means the substitution of creative work for insensate labor and an emphasis on artful craftspersonship in preference to mechanized production. It means the leisure to be artful and engage in public affairs. One would hope that the sheer availability of goods and the freedom to choose one's material lifestyle would sooner or later influence people to adopt moderation in all aspects of life as a response to the "consumerism" that is promoted by the capitalist market.[5]

But no ethics or vision of an ecological society, however inspired, can be meaningful unless it is embodied in a living politics. By "politics" I do not mean the statecraft practiced by what we call "politicians"—namely, representatives elected or selected to formulate policies as guidelines for social life and to manage public affairs. To social ecology, politics means what it once meant in the democratic *polis* of Athens some two thousand years ago: the formation of policy by popular assemblies and their administration by mandated, carefully supervised boards of coordinators who could easily be recalled if they failed to abide by the decisions of the assembly's citizens. I am very mindful that Athenian politics, even in its most democratic periods, was marred by the existence of slavery, patriarchy, and the exclusion of the stranger from public life. In this respect, it differed very little from most of the Mediterranean civilizations—and Asian ones—of the time. What made Athenian politics unique, however, was that it produced institutions that were extraordinarily democratic—even directly so—by comparison with republican institutions in the so-called "democracies" of the Western world. Either directly or indirectly they inspired later, more all-encompassing democracies, such as certain medieval towns, the little-known "sections" of Paris (which were essentially forty-eight neighborhood assemblies) that propelled the French Revolution in a highly radical direction in 1793, New England town meetings, and more recent attempts at civic self-governance.[6]

Any community, however, risks the danger of becoming parochial, even racist, if it tries to live in isolation and develop a seeming self-sufficiency. Hence, the need to extend ecological politics into confederations of ecocommunities, and to foster a healthy interdependence, rather than an introverted, stultifying independence. Social ecology would embody its ethics in a politics of confederal municipalism, in which municipalities cojointly gain rights to self-governance through networks of confederal councils, to which towns and cities would send their mandated, recallable delegates to adjust differences. All decisions would have to be ratified by a majority of the popular assemblies of the confederated towns and cities. This institutional process could occur in the neighborhoods of giant cities as well as in networks of small towns. In fact, the formation of numerous "town halls" has already repeatedly been proposed in cities as large as New York and Paris, only to be defeated by well-organized elitist groups that sought to centralize power, rather than allow its decentralization.

Power will always belong to elite strata if it is not diffused, in face-to-face democracies, among the people, who are *empowered* as partly autonomous, partly social beings—that is to say, as free individuals, but as individuals responsible to popular institutions. Empowerment of the people in this sense will constitute a challenge to the nation-state—the principal source of nationalism, a regressive ideology, and of statism, the principal source of coercion. Diversity of cultures is obviously a desideratum, the source of cultural creativity, but never can it be celebrated in a nationalistic "apartness" from the general interests of humanity as a whole, without a regression into folkdom and tribalism.

The full reality of citizenship has begun to wane, and its disappearance would mark an irrevocable loss in human development. Citizenship, in the classical sense of the term, meant a lifelong, ethically oriented education to participation in public affairs, not the empty form of national legitimation that it so often indicates today. It meant the cultivation of an affiliation with the interests of the community, one in which the communal interest was placed above personal interest, or, more properly, in which the personal interest was congruent with and realized through the common.

Property, in this ethical constellation, would be shared and, in the best of circumstances, belong to the community as a whole, not to producers ("workers") or owners ("capitalists"). In an ecological society composed of a "Commune of communes," property would belong, ultimately, neither to private producers nor to a nation-state. The Soviet Union gave rise to an overbearing bureaucracy; the anarcho-syndicalist vision to competing "worker-controlled" factories that ultimately had to be knitted together by a labor bureaucracy. From the standpoint of social ecology, property "interests" would become generalized, not reconstituted in different conflicting or unmanageable forms. They would be *municipalized,* rather than nationalized or privatized. Workers, farmers, professionals, and the like would thus deal with municipalized property as citizens, not as members of a vocational or social group. Leaving aside any discussion of such visions as the rotation of work, the citizen who engages in both industrial and agricultural activity, and the professional who also does manual labor, the communal ideas advanced by social ecology would give rise to individuals for whom the collective interest is inseparable from the personal, the public interest from the private, the political interest from the social.

The step-by-step reorganization of municipalities, their confederation into ever-larger networks that form a dual power in opposition to the nation-state, the remaking of the constituents of republican representatives into citizens who participate in a direct democracy—all may take a considerable period of time to achieve. But in the end, they alone can potentially eliminate the domination of human by human and thereby deal with those ecological problems whose growing magnitude threatens the existence of a biosphere than can support advanced forms of life. To ignore the need for these sweeping but eminently practical changes would be to let our ecological problems fester and spread to a point where there would no longer be any opportunity to resolve them. Any attempt to ignore their impact on the biosphere or deal with them singly would be recipe for disaster, a guarantee that the anti-ecological society that prevails in most of the world today would blindly hurtle the biosphere as we know it to certain destruction.

## NOTES

1. Murray Bookchin, "Ecology and Revolutionary Thought," initially published in the eco-anarchist journal *New Directions in Libertarian Thought* (Sept. 1964), and collected, together with all my major essays of the 1960s in *Post-Scarcity Anarchism* (Berkeley: Ramparts Press, 1972; republished, Montreal: Black Rose Books, 1977). The expression "ethics of complementarity" is from *The Ecology of Freedom* (San Francisco: Cheshire Books, 1982; revised edition, Montreal: Black Rose Books, 1991).

2. Neil Evernden, *The Natural Alien* (Toronto: University of Toronto Press, 1986), p. 109.

3. Paul Radin, *The World of Primitive Man* (New York: Grove Press, 1960), p. 211.

4. See *Der Spiegel* (Sept. 16, 1991), pp. 144–45.

5. All of these views were spelled out in the essay "Ecology and Revolutionary Thought" by this writer in 1965, and were assimilated over time by subsequent ecology movements. Many of the technological views advanced a year later in "Toward a Liberatory Technology" were also assimilated and renamed "appropriate technology," a rather socially neutral expression in comparison with my original term "ecotechnology." Both of these essays can be found in *Post-Scarcity Anarchism*.

6. See the essay "The Forms of Freedom," in *Post-Scarcity Anarchism*, "The Legacy of Freedom," in *The Ecology of Freedom*, and "Patterns of Civic Freedom" in *The Rise of Urbanization and the Decline of Citizenship* (San Francisco: Sierra Club Books, 1987).

# THE MATTER OF FREEDOM: ECOFEMINIST LESSONS FOR SOCIAL ECOLOGY

*John Clark*

John Clark is professor of philosophy at Loyola University, New Orleans, and chairs the Environmental Studies Program. He has long been active in the green and bioregional movements. His books include *The Anarchist Moment: Reflections on Culture, Nature, and Power; Liberty, Ecology, Geography: The Social Thought of Elisée Reclus;* and a forthcoming reinterpretation of social ecology.

## THE PROMISE OF SOCIAL ECOLOGY

A social ecology is in the deepest sense a radical ecology. This is true not merely because social ecology—like deep ecology, ecofeminism, and ecosocialism—looks to social problems to discover the roots of ecological crisis.[1] The radicality of social ecology consists first in its theoretical orientation, which consists of dialectical inquiry into the mutual determination between the two inseparable realms of the social and the ecological. And, secondly, it lies in its practical dimension: its insistence on the gravity of the global ecological crisis and the need for radical social transformation in order to reverse the present ecocidal course of world history.

 The first area in which social ecology has made an essential contribution to radical ecology is in its dialectical approach. This contention may be met with general skepticism, for dialectical thought has become rather unfashionable today. Nevertheless, what is usually rejected as dialectic is but a caricature of itself (and an *undialectical* caricature at that) created, ironically, by its most celebrated exponents in support of those "grand narratives" of power, "mastery," and domination that are today so widely disdained. Yet even among these thinkers—Plato, Hegel, and Marx—the radical nature of dialectic was preserved. Indeed, it constitutes within their own thought an immanent critique of the very ideologies of domination of humanity and nature to which they fell prey. And there is also the example of the more radical, refractory dialectic of Nagarjuna, whose thought is a healthy corrective of the more compromising Western varieties.[2]

Dialectical thinking, in its most radical sense, means thinking process, motion, change, development, discontinuity, emergence, contradiction, transformation, negation, mutual determination, relativity, internal relatedness, and "dependent origination"—to mention a few of the key concepts in dialectical thought. A dialectical approach assumes the provisional nature of all concepts and theoretical frameworks, the importance of avoiding their use in a rigid, objectifying way, and the necessity of allowing all theoretical concepts to develop in the course of inquiry. It does *not* consist in the *attainment* or mastery of truth, but rather in an openness to the appearance of truth and a willingness to follow the path of truth, the way of the phenomena. (As we shall see later, this relates it to the concept of care.)

Dialectical thinking is therefore a practice of philosophical anarchism. It is the rejection of *archai* [from *archein,* to be first, to rule] or principles, in the sense of fixed, unquestioned presuppositions or ruling ideas. It rejects all forms of dogmatism, the transformation of moving, developing concepts into rigid, inflexible ideas. In following the path of truth, it rejects the sickness of attachment to ideas, and the egoistic illusion that any ideas are really "our" ideas. It is intimately related to anarchical politics in the sense of the radical critique of and engaged opposition to all forms of domination of humanity and nature. For there can be no effective challenge to domination by those whose thought and sensibility are themselves pervaded by a quest for power and control. In both its theoretical and practical dimensions, a dialectical approach means the affirmation of life, growth, transformation, openness, and temporality over the quest for control, certainty, domination, fixity, stability, and eternality.

The second area in which social ecology has been of enormous significance for radical ecology is in its recognition of the gravity of the global social and ecological crisis and of the fundamental changes that are necessary to reverse the present destructive course of world history.

We are in the midst of a world-historical and earth-historical crisis. The very future of life on earth is threatened, above all by massive species extinction and widespread ecosystem destruction, but also by a wide variety of perilous experiments, including the emission of thousands of untested organic chemicals into the biosphere, the stockpiling of highly dangerous nuclear materials, the production of significant changes in atmospheric makeup, and the creation of genetically engineered organisms.

At the same time, social crisis intensifies. The very survival of many of the world's cultures is threatened by the rapid expansion of the global economistic monoculture and economic neo-imperialism; the majority of the world's languages are doomed to extinction; and nearly a billion people live in absolute poverty, chronic malnutrition, permanent unemployment, and increasing marginalization. These and other crucial social and ecological developments have all occurred without public deliberation concerning what is at stake for human society or the biosphere. Nevertheless, they have all been the result of conscious, deliberate planning.

When we look back at the massive ecological destruction under the ancient empires that transformed the "fertile crescent" of ancient Mesopotamia into a desert, caused the collapse of successive societies, and imposed on human beings a life of toil, suffering, fear, and humiliating subordination, the basis for such conditions appears obvious. The imperial system itself, with its patriarchal, authoritarian, hierarchical institutions and values was inherently both a human and an ecological catastrophe.

If we undertake the more difficult task of looking at our own world, we find that there are similar systematic causes for the social and ecological devastation. Social ecologists contend that the roots are found in such (obviously interrelated) social conditions as economic oligarchy and concentrated corporate economic power; centralized, undemocratic political power; mass marketing and opinion control that increasingly shape values and personality; massive, unresponsive state and corporate bureaucracies; a culture of consumption that promotes a privatised, depoliticized world; patriarchal values and an egoic, power-seeking self; otherworldly, nature-denying spirituality; and a vast system of technology that appears as a self-moving megamachine.

Social ecologists contend that the social and ecological destructiveness of the global technological megamachine, the global corporate economic oligopoly, the global system of centralized nation-states, and the global monoculture of mass consumption are built into their structures, operating procedures, and decision-making processes. They therefore conclude that the social ecological crisis cannot be resolved without serious global catastrophe unless there are far-reaching, fundamental changes in the dominant institutions, cultural values, and ideologies. These changes must include a radical devolution of power through the democratization and decentralization of political, economic, technological, and informational systems. They must also encompass a radical transformation of values that replaces economistic values, consumer culture, and the egocentric self with ecological, communitarian, libertarian values, and a compassionate, nondominating, social self.

## TWO CONCEPTS OF SOCIAL ECOLOGY

From such an analysis the question obviously follows of what kind of social practice will be necessary in order to achieve such a transformation. On this, social ecologists are increasingly divided. One approach looks to the ways in which we can encourage the emergence of humane, mutualistic, ecologically responsible institutions in all areas of social life. It sees not only any narrowly defined "politics," but all areas of social interaction, including production and consumption, personal relationships, family life, child-care, education, the arts, modes of communication, spiritual life, ritual and celebration, recreation and play, and informal modes of cooperation to be *political* realms in the most profound sense. Each is seen as an essential sphere in which we can develop our social being and communal individuality, and in which a larger communitarian reality can find much of its basis. Such a conception of the political is not narrowly prescriptive concerning political forms, but implies that we must create, sustain, and defend practices and institutions that are humane in spirit and scale, life-affirming, creative, decentralized, nonhierarchical, rooted in the particularity of people and place, and based on grass-roots, participatory democracy to the greatest degree practically possible.

A second tendency within social ecology, Murray Bookchin and Janet Biehl's "libertarian municipalism," has a quite different conception of the political. Bookchin and Biehl hold that there are three very distinct social spheres, which they call the "statist," the "political," and the "social" realms. According to their analysis, the statist realm includes all the institutions and activities through which the state operates; the political realm encompasses activity in the public sphere, which is identified "with politics in the Hellenic sense of the term"; and the social realm includes everything else in society, including what we ordinarily think of the personal dimension or private life.[3]

Bookchin and Biehl's politics of social ecology is concerned primarily with the "political" in their sense, either as manifested in various "forms of freedom" that have emerged at certain points in history, in the proposed institutions of their libertarian municipalist system, or in their own efforts and those of their allies to create such a system. In practical terms, the political is identified with the program of creating libertarian municipalities in which a municipal assembly open to all citizens of the local community is to be the sovereign decision-making authority. The municipal assembly is to be the primary sphere in which the responsible, ethical person will be shaped through rational deliberation concerning policies in the interest of the community. It is noteworthy that according to Bookchin and Biehl's criteria, the realized political realm in the contemporary world (as distinguished from its mere "germs" and "potentialities" within existing municipalities) consists of the activities of the small group of social ecologists who are actively promoting the libertarian municipalist program.

One thesis of the present discussion is that Bookchin's and Biehl's politics succumbs to an abstract idealism or formalism. The idealist direction of Bookchin's thought is evident in one of his better-known early essays, which begins with the pronouncement: "Freedom has its forms."[4] The transcendental nature of these forms is made clear when he contemplates the form of all forms, that of the assembly. "Let us turn to the assembly," he says "for an insight into unmediated forms of social relations."[5] Bookchin and Biehl's libertarian municipalism continues to the present to identify the politics of social ecology with the quest for such unmediated forms.

But from a dialectical perspective, there are in this world no "unmediated" phenomena, much less any unmediated social forms. It is for this reason that the lessons of ecofeminism are so important for the social ecological conception of the political. For as we shall see, ecofeminism has important insights into the *materiality* of freedom that can greatly enrich social ecological analysis and help correct tendencies toward formalism. In view of the strengths of social ecology, creative dialogue between these two radical ecologies can make an important contribution to both.

## BIEHL'S REJECTION OF ECOFEMINISM

Bookchin and Biehl have not, however, recognized the value in such dialogue. Biehl has dismissed ecofeminism as a form of irrationalism that is unworthy of serious attention, concluding that "nearly all ecofeminists" simplistically "extol women as 'other' with nonhuman nature in a crude exaggeration" of what de Beauvoir developed in her more "subtle exposition" of the topic.[6] She contends that "[i]nstead of working to replace the virtues of the *polis* with those of an *oikos* that has historically oppressed them [as she thinks ecofeminists have done], women in ecological movements must become involved in the political world as part of a truly liberatory politics and claim citizenship for themselves. They must at long last break out of the *oikos*—whether that is the literal *oikos* of the household or the figurative *oikos* of 'women's values'— and work to expand the full range of their *human* capacities."[7]

Biehl is particularly hostile to the idea that the feminist care perspective (which will be discussed shortly) might illegitimately be extended from what she sees as its proper delimited sphere of intimate personal relationships into the larger arena of social ethics and politics. She and Bookchin have increasingly defended a sharp dualistic division between the public and private spheres (the "political" and "social" realms in their phraseology), and warned of the dangers of confusing the two realms. They perceive the feminist emphasis on care as a threat to their view of citizenship (and especially, deliberation in the municipal assembly) as the privileged form of political practice.

And rightly so. For Bookchin and Biehl have perpetuated in many ways a traditional masculinist conception of selfhood, with its autonomous ego and its rigidly defined ego boundaries. Accordingly, they have charged critics of this conception of selfhood, including ecofeminists, with "weakening" the self, reducing it to a "passive-receptive" and manipulable condition, or "dissolving" it into some vague and irrational "oneness." Their own masculinist citizen "forging" selfhood through active deliberation and debate in the assembly would be transformed considerably were care, with its diffuse, emotive, and highly personal implications, to become central to the idea of citizenship. From their standpoint, care must accordingly be banished from the realm of meaningful, coherent, rational political values.

In Biehl's own words, "the emotion of 'caring'" is not "something that one can authentically extend to 'all people.' . . . As an emotion, 'caring' cannot be universalized as the basis for social organization outside one's own small group, whether kinship-based or not."[8] For Biehl, the idea of care finding expression in the public or "political" sphere seems quite ludicrous. She quips sarcastically that "the kind of caring that a mother (or father) feels for a child" cannot be universalized "irrespective of whether one 'thinks like a mountain' or 'allows oneself to be a tree.'"[9] She concludes that "the very word *ecofeminism* has by now become so tainted by its various irrationalisms that I no longer consider this a promising project. . . . [I]n my view, it hardly makes sense to build a movement on metaphors that I oppose and on confused ideas that I cannot formulate in any coherent manner."[10]

Yet ecofeminist theorists themselves have managed to formulate their own ideas quite coherently. If we examine Biehl's contentions, we will find that theoretically sophisticated ecofeminist theorists not only avoid the irrationalisms with which she charges them, but they offer crucial insights in the very areas in which Bookchin and Biehl's version of social ecology is so weak.

## THE FEMINIST CARE PERSPECTIVE

To determine the extent to which the ecofeminist concept of care might have something to contribute to ecopolitics, it is useful first to clarify what feminist theory means in general by the concept of care. The feminist care perspective was classically discussed in Carol Gilligan's *In a Different Voice,* though writers such as Nell Noddings and Annette Baier, among others, have contributed to the development of the theory.[11] There is now a very large and quite sophisticated literature on this topic, in which its philosophical, psychological, sociological, educational, and other implications are explored.

Gilligan associates the ethics of care with "the moral injunction" that one should not "turn away from someone in need."[12] The rather legalistic term "injunction" might be misleading here unless one understands that the care perspective is fundamentally relational, rather than principle-based. Such an "injunction" is not an abstract, general moral rule to be applied to specific cases, but rather arises out of an underlying contextual basis: one's participation in a community, and a network of material, psychological, moral, symbolic, and imaginary relations. It "enjoins" in the etymological root sense of being an expression of all that "joins" us "to" the objects of care.

The care perspective reverses the ego-centered outlook (which is held not only by ethical egoists, but also by ethical universalists interested in placing constraints on the ego) with a more interpersonal, contextual, holistic, and communitarian viewpoint. While "from a justice perspective, the self as moral agent stands as the figure against a ground of social relationships," in the ethics of care, "the relationship becomes the figure, defining self and others."[13] The presuppositions of the care perspective are "that self and other are interdependent," that action is "responsive" and "aris[es] in relationship," and that it does not "emanat[e] from within the self" and is not "self-governed."[14]

Despite Biehl's claims, the very question of whether care, as conceived of by feminist ethical theorists, can be "extended" beyond the small family group is a pointless one. For the concept from the outset has referred to general feelings and dispositions that relate to other human beings in a variety of situations. Noddings, for example, explains that although there are many specific kinds and intensities of caring, the phenomenon can be described in general terms. "When we see the other's reality as a possibility for us, we must act to eliminate the intolerable, to reduce the pain, to fill the need, to actualize the dream. When I am in this sort of relationship with another, when the other's reality becomes a real possibility for me, I care."[15] This is not the language of narrowly circumscribed relationships. It is rather a very expansive conception of social selfhood that describes a distinctive sensibility and a certain disposition toward others (and, indeed, toward the other and otherness in general).

Neither does Gilligan limit the care perspective to close intimate relations in the manner that Biehl depicts it. Gilligan observes that "sensitivity to the needs of others and the assumption of responsibility for taking care lead women to voices other than their own and to include in their judgment other points of view."[16] Once again, the qualities of care in no way restrict it only to the most intimate relationships. Care consists of a distinctive way of perceiving reality, and a certain kind of openness to the other. Care involves "a mode of thinking that is contextual and narrative rather than formal and abstract," and which "centers moral development around the understanding of responsibility and relationships."[17] Such care is quite distinct from such acontextual perspectives an abstract benevolence, utilitarian disinterestedness, or Kantian good will. It is determinate rather than generalized, and focuses on relationships with specific others rather than categories. Yet within these parameters it may encompass a broad spectrum of relationships, and in a sense is the reconciliation of universality and particularity.

Although the care perspective is related to emotions or feelings, it also encompasses personality characteristics, sensibility, valuations, imagination, and ways of conceptualizing the self and others. Taken as a whole it constitutes a distinctive and comprehensive way of relating to the world and to other beings. In its classic statements by Gilligan and Noddings, we can already see its relevance not only to social ethics but also to environmental ethics and political ecology. As they describe it, it is a perspective that is open to the perspective of the other, it is relational and contextual, it focuses on interdependence, it is aimed at the reparation of injuries, and it is concerned with the needs and self-realization of the other. The profound ecological implications of such a perspective are made explicit in its ecofeminist versions.

## ECOFEMINIST THEORY AND
## THE POLITICS OF CARE

Ecofeminist theorists have pointed out that throughout the history of patriarchal civilization, its institutions and values have been pervaded by a hierarchical dualism. They note that it has traditionally delimited in a very rigid manner the boundaries between the masculine and the feminine and has placed the two spheres in a relationship of dominance and subordination.

Furthermore, they contend that no theory of the liberation of humanity and nature can succeed if it fails to come to terms with the dualism that is the legacy of patriarchal civilization.

A central tenet of patriarchal dualism has been the opposition between reason and intellect on the one hand and emotion and feeling on the other. As Val Plumwood states, this dualism depicts "'desire,' caring, and love as merely 'personal' and 'particular' as opposed to the universality and impartiality of understanding, and of 'feminine' emotions as essentially unreliable, untrustworthy, and morally irrelevant, an inferior domain to be dominated by a superior, disinterested (and of course masculine) reason."[18] It is important to investigate whether our conceptions of selfhood, of the processes of self-formation in various social realms, and of the nature of those social realms themselves perpetuate such a dualistic opposition. An examination of the ecofeminist care perspective can be helpful for social ecologists who might be interested in such an investigation.

The implications of this perspective for political ecology are demonstrated perhaps most clearly in the work of Ariel Salleh. Salleh's social analysis is notable for its defense of a nonessentialist ecofeminist position that dialectically and holistically recognizes the importance of the interplay between biological and psychological aspects of women, the particularities of woman's historical and cultural positions, and the social and political realities of a world in which the future of humanity and the earth are threatened by complex systems of power and domination. Salleh finds that given all the complex factors that shape the historical reality of women, this reality (in its concrete, particular expressions) offers a material basis for important social and ecological political struggle. In her view, "[t]he case for women as historical actors in a time of environmental crisis rests not on universal essences but on how the majority of women actually work and think now."[19] In other words, Salleh's ecofeminist politics looks for hope not in any abstract "forms of the feminine" but rather to the material realities of actually existing women around the world, to their life-conditions, their social practice, their values, and their modes of perception.

Salleh contends that women's "hands-on domestic and subsistence skills provide a means of resisting the irrational excess of a capitalist patriarchal system that they have little egoic need to preserve."[20] To the extent that women have been excluded from the exercise of power and from processes of conditioning to develop the power-driven, Oedipal ego of patriarchal men, this presents significant liberatory possibilities. One implication of such difference in the formation of the self is that Western radicals and reformers (especially men, but also many women) will have to undertake a process of deep self-examination to discover the ways in which they have been shaped by social psychological and social imaginary processes. In addition, they will have to admit that they may have something to learn from women and indigenous people of the traditional world, whose resistance is in many ways rooted more deeply in the concrete, specific conditions of life, and is not colored by the reactive Oedipal rebellion and machismo that characterizes so much Western leftism and "revolutionism."

Salleh suggests that the particular forms of labor and caring activities engaged in by women create modes of experiencing reality that are often at odds with the dominant system of values and are more in accord with an ecological perspective. Her discussion suggests that such experience creates what we might call a dissident ethos that challenges the dominant one. To call it an ethos implies that it is more than a set of concepts or an interpretation of reality. Rather, it involves deep levels of perception, feeling, and valuation.

For Salleh ecofeminism seeks "another conceptual space" that overcomes the dualistic, objectifying, atomizing propensities of the dominant modes of knowing. The epistemological issues cannot be discussed in any detail here. But in general terms, the goal is a way of knowing that accepts process, change, and development, that does not aim at control or domination of the object, that is sensitive to detail and to the particularity of beings and phenomena, and that accepts ambiguity, uncertainty, and mystery. In short, it is knowing based not on the *mastery* of objects, but on *careful attention to* and *attentive caring for* the beings and the world that are known.

Such knowing might be compared to the Taoist concept of *wu wei*, or nondominating activity that respects the integrity and unfolding of all beings. According to the *Tao te Ching*, to have such knowledge is to "play the role of the female," to "understand all and penetrate all without taking any [aggressive] action, [t]o produce things and to rear them, [t]o produce, but not take possession of them. . . ."[21]

Care involves an openness to its objects and to the web of relationships in which those objects exist and which constitute them. Thus, "[i]n careful labor, the unfoldment of internal relations is known."[22] Care is thus a challenge to the instrumental rationality, the atomistic and dualistic metaphysics, the methodological and practical individualism, and the egoistic ethics that have guided Western theory and practice. All of these are incompatible with a theory of internal relations, which implies a contextual or holistic conception of self, society, and nature.

## THE POLITICAL CULTURE OF CARE

Such a perspective could of course remain on a rather abstract or merely personal level, as some sort of beautiful ideal with few if any political implications. However, it quite clearly does not remain on this level in ecofeminist theory. This becomes evident if we look more carefully at what Salleh sees as the material basis for the care perspective in the life-activities of women and members of many indigenous and traditional cultures. In the case of women, she finds its basis in such phenomena as "the sensuality of birthing and suckling labors; historically assigned household chores; gardening or making goods; creating and implanting meanings in the next generation."[23] Similarly, the members of some indigenous and peasant communities are "organically and discursively implicated in the material rhythms of enduring time and, like domestic workers in the North, they develop practical expertise grounded in that materiality."[24] The politics that arises out of such situated practice is expressed in a deep and enduring commitment to practical social struggles in defense of families, communities, and the land.

Salleh contends that empirical evidence from community-based ecological and justice movements verifies the significance of these caring activities in forming committed activists. She observes that "in the North, it is grass-roots housewives, as opposed to so-called emancipated feminist women, who are generally the strongest fighters."[25] There is no reason to minimize the contribution of committed feminists who have joined grass-roots community struggles, but as Salleh points out, the energy, commitment, and eloquence are most striking in the case of women from local communities whose neighborhoods, homes, and children are threatened. In the United States, while official politics is still overwhelmingly male-dominated, it is typical in grass-roots environmental justice struggles that women will constitute a large proportion, if not a considerable majority, of the key organizers and leaders. Penny Newman, founder of Concerned Citizens in Action notes the qualities of these struggles that distinguish them sharply from mainstream liberal reform movements. She notes that "the women of the environmental justice movement have made it a movement known for its irreverence for the powerful, its willingness to take strong positions of principle, its unending persistence, and its impatience with token solutions."[26]

My own views concerning political ecology have been shaped significantly by a decade of work in support of the Papuan people in their struggle against cultural genocide and ecological destruction inflicted by Indonesian imperialism and corporate neocolonialism. This struggle exemplifies clearly many of the points made by ecofeminist thinkers such as Ariel Salleh and Vandana Shiva concerning the embodiment of the political in the lives and values of women and indigenous and traditional peoples.

In 1994, the Indonesian regime escalated its repression in West Papua. Dozens of Papuan tribal people were murdered and many more arrested and tortured in the pursuit of a policy of discouraging antigovernment and anticorporate activities through terror. One of the victims was Mama Yosepha Alomang, who is the most prominent female leader of the Amungme tribe, and a tireless human rights, ecological, and community development activist. She was accused of giving aid to antigovernment insurgents, and then tortured and imprisoned for over a month, suffering a week of confinement in a small, dark, flooded closet reeking of human feces. Mama Yosepha's account of her helping members of the Kwalik clan, to which she is related through her husband, is very instructive. Under interrogation by the military, she affirmed the fact that she had given food and supplies to people in need who had come to her asking for help. She explained to her captors: "Our custom teaches us that if you have more than enough, you have to share. So if I have it, I give it not to support them, but because if we live with other people, how can we not give if we have it, and people ask for it."[27]

Mama Yosepha Alomang acts out of a living tradition of care for others that goes far beyond the Western legalistic concept of "usufruct," and that is truly "second nature" to her and her people. It is certainly in large part because of her place in such a community that she can endure imprisonment, torture, persecution, and the death of children and other relatives, and still continue to speak out on behalf of her community and their land with eloquence, courage, and endurance. And it is in large part because of traditional practices of solidarity, mutual aid, and care that the Papuan people in general have been able to persevere through decades of resistance to oppression.

Tom Beanal, head of the Amungme tribal council, has explained how the struggle of the Amungme and other Papuan peoples against the social and ecological destruction wrought by the large Freeport mining corporation in partnership with the Indonesian regime is rooted in these peoples' traditional worldview and spirituality. Beanal points out that the Amungme reject the dualistic view of humanity and nature typical of Western cultures, and have instead a more holistic and ecological outlook. To the Amungme, he explains, "everything that has a use has a value greater than that ascribed to it by man."[28] The Amungme hold, to use the language of environmental ethics, a nonanthropocentric theory of value in which the natural world is attributed intrinsic and not merely instrumental value.

Beanal recounts an Amungme story of origins that begins with an original mother (the personification of the land of the island of Papua) who is the source of life. He notes that this narrative "tells us that if the mountains and nature are harmed, our mother is hurt as well."[29] Each particular tribal group has a specific place of origin that has a symbolic location in relation to the body of the mother. "The Amungme live on the land thought to reach from the mother's neck to her navel. This is the place closest to her."[30]

This mountainous area is the site of Freeport's mining operations, where the Amungme and other indigenous people have been brutally oppressed and the land has been ruthlessly exploited. While the Amungme see the mountains as sacred—as particular, culturally significant expressions of a benevolent, maternal nature—for Freeport it is no more than a stock of mineral resources to be extracted by the most economically profitable means possible. As Tom Beanal summarizes the plight of his people, "these companies have taken over and occupied our land. Even the sacred mountains we think of as our mother have been arbitrarily torn up by them, and they have not felt the least bit guilty."[31]

Tom Beanal expresses a view of the natural world that arises out of the Papuan traditions of foraging and horticulture that have been practiced for thirty thousand years. It is rooted in the traditional care for the land that is a response to the care that the Papuans have perceived as having been bestowed on them by nature. The relationship between humanity and nature is thus seen as one of reciprocity. Just as the generosity of Mama Yosepha is expressed as a free gift rather than an imposed moral obligation, the interaction between the people and the natural world is a form of gift exchange. This relationship to the land has helped sustain the Papuan people in over three decades of struggle against the destruction of the society and land.

One great strength of phenomena such as Mama Yosepha Alomang's caring sensibility, rooted in her practical relationship to her people, and the Amungme people's ecological spirituality, rooted in their practical relationship to their land, is that these phenomena are actually existing realities in the world today, and are powerful forces for the solidarity of human communities and for the defense of the land. In short, whatever their "emotional," "personal," "spiritual," or "social" dimensions may be, they are also powerful material and political realities.

## SOME LESSONS FOR SOCIAL ECOLOGY

It should now be clear that the ecofeminist conceptions of the relational self and the politics of care have extensive implications for social ecology. To begin with, they help correct a marked dualism in the some social ecological analyses of human nature and society. Despite its professed rejection of patriarchy, the libertarian municipalist version of social ecology perpetuates the dualistic split between reason and emotion that is the legacy of patriarchal society, in prioritizing the rational, public, and "political" realm of discussion, debate and policymaking, and subordinating the emotional, private, and merely "social" sphere of care.

In fact, Bookchin and Biehl's very project of dividing society into rigidly defined "spheres" is problematical from a dialectical perspective. A dialectical approach would, after delineating various "spheres" or "realms" of society, consider the ways in which each sphere might be conditioned by, dependent upon, and indeed constituted by those from which it is initially distinguished. It would recognize that as the political dimension emerges within society, it does not separate itself from the rest of the social world to embed itself in an exclusive sphere. It is the social whole that develops politically, and in the process there is a transformation and politicization of many aspects of what Bookchin and Biehl call "the social."

Thus, a critical and dialectical view of the *oikos*, will situate it within this social whole and examine both its limitations and the ways in which its liberatory potentialities can be realized. It will investigate how "women's values" have been distorted and utilized by the system of domination, but it will also analyze the essential contribution that such values can make to the achievement of a compassionate and just ecological society. It is not the ecofeminist project that is nondialectical, as Biehl contends, but rather the idea that the *oikos* and "women's values," in whatever form they might appear historically, contain *no* liberatory "directionality" that can be developed and *no* critical dimension.

Furthermore, a critical theory of democracy must recognize the possible threats inherent in any particular governmental form, including the assembly. The ecofeminist critique of the egocentric, power-seeking patriarchal self is highly relevant in this connection. Popular assemblies possess enormous potential to foster freedom, authentic democracy, communal solidarity, and civic virtue. But for assemblies and other organs of direct democracy to contribute effectively to an ecological community, they must be purged of the competitive, agonistic, masculinist aspects that have so often corrupted them, not merely in theory, but in actual practice, from ancient times through the present day.

It must be recognized that the exercise of far-ranging power (and especially of the sovereign power that Bookchin and Biehl propose) by municipal assemblies also creates a considerable potential for egoistic satisfactions and power-seeking behavior within those bodies. There are possibilities of domination of assemblies by participants who are drawn to public speaking, debate, political maneuvering, and competition. The ego gratifications that some derive from shaping decision-making, having influence over others, and distinguishing oneself before an audience are not insignificant threats to truly democratic and communitarian processes. Furthermore, there is a likelihood that persons with such inclinations might be disproportionately represented in assemblies in which, as Bookchin and Biehl concede, a considerable majority of the citizens might not regularly participate at all.

In a work that achieved some notoriety, an antifeminist writer once argued that patriarchal institutions are "inevitable" because of a "male advantage in aggression, competitiveness, and dominance."[32] According to this thesis, males as a group have innate biological and psychological characteristics that have allowed them in all societies to monopolize positions of power and authority. Male dominance has been greater in proportion to the degree that social structure has been competitive and hierarchical and has rewarded power-seeking behavior.

This analysis distorts social reality for ideological purposes but poses an important question for those interested in the creation of a just and compassionate ecological society. If male aggressiveness does indeed offer such "advantages" under certain social conditions, how can the socially destructive consequences of this phenomenon be avoided?

There are at least two general lines of response. The first is that social structure can be created that change forms of aggression that are harmful to the community into aggression *disadvantages*. Thus, positions of responsibility and social recognition could be allocated based on evidence of cooperative, compassionate, nonaggressive behavior, rather than on egoistic self-assertion (even when the latter is justified in the name of justice, freedom, progress, revolution, etc.). Secondly, and more importantly, the larger context of cultural institutions and practices can be transformed so that they nurture people's tendencies to be cooperative, compassionate, generous, and sociable.

A social ecology recognizes that any political forms, as important as they may be, are given meaning and realize whatever liberatory, communitarian, or ecological potential they may have within a larger political culture. Consequently, when contemplating any promising participatory democratic political forms (for example, citizens' assemblies, committees and councils, workers' assemblies, committees and councils, popular juries), a social ecology will consider the ways in which the political culture may liberate, limit, or negate the various possibilities contained in that form. It is certain that they can only fulfill their promise if they are an integral expression of a community that embodies in the personalities of its members feelings of solidarity and cooperation, compassion and care, deep respect for others, and freedom from ego-centered obsessions.

For this reason a political ecology is of necessity not only a politics of the public sphere, but also a politics of culture, of the personal, of care, and of particularity, as ecofeminism teaches us. Social ecologists have sometimes, in articulating the relationship between the social and the ecological, analyzed the relationship between a rather abstract humanity and a rather generalized nature. However, humanity consists of specific groups of human beings existing in quite particular historical and cultural contexts and having quite distinctive relationships with the highly particularized natural regions in which they live. Social ecology has much to learn from ecofeminism and other ecological viewpoints, such as bioregionalism, that have often had a deeper and more complex idea of the rich particularity of our relationships both with other human beings and human communities, and also with other beings, species, regions, and ecological communities. According to Plumwood, "care and responsibility for particular animals, trees, and rivers that are known well, loved, and appropriately connected to the self are an important basis for acquiring a wider, more generalized concern."[33] If our universal concerns are rooted in very particular ones, they will possess a richly concrete rather than a merely abstract universality.

A social ecology that fixes its gaze rigidly on the *forms* of freedom that might exist in an ideal world neglects the *material basis* for the actualization of freedom in a real world and in real history. It neglects the *material subjects* of freedom—real people with particular relationships to other human beings, to their communities and cultures, to specific places and natural regions, and with particular personal and collective histories, traditions, practices, and imaginations. The forms of freedom, abstracted from the rich social and natural context, attain the powerful aura of the unsullied ideal. But in the absence of a connection with the materiality of freedom, its embodiment in our most intimate personal relationships, in our values, perceptions and sensibilities, in the ethos of our communities, in our modes of imagining the world, in our interaction with other life-forms and with the natural regions in which we dwell, these forms become an ideological illusion and a source of disillusionment with the world.

Ecofeminists have given us reason to direct our hopes to the thick, dense, complex, and particular world of life and culture in which people live, rather than to the rarefied, abstract world of idealist political ideology. The ecofeminist politics of care helps us to keep our ideals in touch with this materiality of freedom—as embodied in the real interactions between living human beings, living communities, and the living earth.

## NOTES

1. These three ecophilosophies also trace ecological problems to certain social phenomena, which are variously identified as patriarchal institutions and values, anthropocentric practices and ideas, and economic class domination and ideology.
2. For Nagarjuna's most important work, see Jay L. Garfield's translation and commentary, *The Fundamental Wisdom of the Middle Way: Nagarjuna's Mulamadhyamakakarika* (New York: Oxford University Press, 1995). There has unfortunately been relatively little exploration of the connection between Madhyamika philosophy and ecological thinking. For an excellent analysis that is not explicitly on this topic but nevertheless highly suggestive concerning it, see David Michael Levin's "Liberating Experience from the Vice of Structuralism: The Methods of Merleau-Ponty and Nagarjuna" in *Philosophy Today* 41 (Spring 1997): 96–111.
3. Bookchin, "Comments on the International Social Ecology Gathering and the 'Deep Social Ecology' of John Clark," in *Democracy and Nature*, 9, 1997, p. 158.
4. Murray Bookchin, "The Forms of Freedom" in *Post-Scarcity Anarchism* (Berkeley, CA: Ramparts Press, 1971), p. 143.
5. Ibid., p. 155.
6. Janet Biehl, *Rethinking Ecofeminist Politics* (Boston: South End Press, 1991), p. 15.
7. Ibid., p. 154.
8. Ibid., p. 148.
9. Ibid.
10. Ibid., p. 5.
11. See Carol Gilligan, *In A Different Voice: Psychological Theory and Women's Development* (Cambridge, MA: Harvard University Press, 1982); Nel Noddings, *Caring: A Feminine Approach to Ethics and Moral Education* (Berkeley: University of California Press, 1984); and Annette Baier, "Caring About Caring: A Reply to Frankfurt," in *Postures of the Mind: Essays on Mind and Morals* (Minneapolis: University of Minnesota Press, 1985); "What Do Women Want in Moral Theory?" in *Nous* 19 (1985): 53–63; and "Trust and Antitrust" in *Ethics* 96 (1986): pp. 231–260.
12. Carol Gilligan, "Moral Orientation and Moral Development," in Eva Kittay and Diana Meyers, *Women and Moral Theory* (Rowman and Littlefield, 1987), reprinted in May and Serrat, eds. *Applied Ethics* (Englewood Cliffs, NJ: Prentice Hall, 1994), p. 262.
13. Ibid., p. 264.
14. Ibid., p. 266.
15. Noddings, *Caring*, p. 71.
16. Gilligan, *In a Different Voice*, p. 16.
17. Ibid., p. 19.
18. Val Plumwood, "Nature, Self, and Gender: Feminism, Environmental Philosophy, and the Critique of Rationalism," in *Environmental Philosophy*, 2d ed. (Upper Saddle River, NJ: Prentice Hall, 1998), p. 293.
19. Ariel Salleh, *Ecofeminism as Politics: Nature, Marx and the Postmodern* (London and New York: Zed Books, 1997), p. 6.
20. Ibid., p. 8.
21. Wing-Tsit Chan, "The Lao Tzu" in *A Source Book in Chinese Philosophy* (Princeton, NJ: Princeton University Press, 1963), p. 144. The insertion of the term "aggressive" is mine, to indicate that the doctrine of "nonaction" in ancient Taoist philosophy connotes non-dominating action rather than literal inactivity.
22. Salleh, *Ecofeminism as Politics*, p. 166.
23. Ibid., p. 141.
24. Ibid.
25. Ibid., p. 136.

26. Quoted in Mark Dowie, *Losing Ground: American Environmentalism at the Close of the Twentieth Century* (Cambridge, MA and London: The MIT Press, 1996), p. 130.

27. "Violations of Human Rights in the Timika Area of Irian Jaya, Indonesia: A Report by the Catholic Church of Jayapura" (Jayapura, West Papua: Catholic Church of Jayapura, August 1995).

28. "Amungme Leader Tom Beanal Speaks at Loyola," in *Freeport Watch Bulletin* (New Orleans, LA: Freeport Watch, Summer 1996), p. 1.

29. Ibid.

30. Ibid.

31. Ibid.

32. Steven Goldberg, *The Inevitability of Patriarchy* (New York: William Morris, 1973), p. 168.

33. Plumwood, "Nature, Self, and Gender," p. 288.

# THE PLACE, THE REGION, AND THE COMMONS

*Gary Snyder*

Pulitzer Prize–winning poet and essayist Gary Snyder teaches in the Department of English at the University of California, Davis.

> When you find your place where you are, practice occurs.
>
> *Dōgen*

## THE WORLD IS PLACES

We experience slums, prairies, and wetlands all equally as "places." Like a mirror, a place can hold anything, on any scale. I want to talk about place as an experience and propose a model of what it meant to "live in place" for most of human time, presenting it initially in terms of the steps that a child takes growing into a natural community. (We have the terms *enculturation* and *acculturation*, but nothing to describe the process of becoming placed or replaced.) In doing so we might get one more angle on what a "civilization of wildness" might require.

For most Americans, to reflect on "home place" would be an unfamiliar exercise. Few today can announce themselves as someone *from* somewhere. Almost nobody spends a lifetime in the same valley, working alongside the people they knew as children. Native people everywhere (the very term means "someone born there") and Old World farmers and city people share this experience of living in place. Still—and this is very important to remember—being inhabitory, being place-based, has never meant that one didn't travel from time to time, going on trading ventures or taking livestock to summer

This essay originally appeared in Gary Snyder, The *Practice of the Wild* (San Francisco: North Point Press, 1990). Reprinted with permission.

grazing. Such working wanderers have always known they had a home-base on earth, and could prove it at any campfire or party by singing their own songs.

The heart of a place is the home, and the heart of the home is the firepit, the hearth. All tentative explorations go outward from there, and it is back to the fireside that elders return. You grow up speaking a home language, a local vernacular. Your own household may have some specifics of phrase, of pronunciation, that are different from the *domus*, the *jia* or *ie* or *kum*, down the lane. You hear histories of the people who are your neighbors and tales involving rocks, streams, mountains, and trees that are all within your sight. The myths of world-creation tell you how *that mountain* was created and how *that peninsula* came to be there. As you grow bolder you explore your world outward from the firepit (which is the center of each universe) in little trips. The childhood landscape is learned on foot, and a map is inscribed in the mind—trails and pathways and groves—the mean dog, the cranky old man's house, the pasture with a bull in it—going out wider and farther. All of us carry within us a picture of the terrain that was learned roughly between the ages of six and nine. (It could as easily be an urban neighborhood as some rural scene.) You can almost totally recall the place you walked, played, biked, swam. Revisualizing that place with its smells and textures, walking through it again in your imagination, has a grounding and settling effect. As a contemporary thought we might also wonder how it is for those whose childhood landscape was being ripped up by bulldozers, or whose family moving about made it all a blur. I have a friend who still gets emotional when he recalls how the avocado orchards of his southern California youth landscape were transformed into hillside after hillside of suburbs.

Our place is part of what we are. Yet even a "place" has a kind of fluidity: it passes through space and time—"ceremonial time" in John Hanson Mitchell's phrase. A place will have been grasslands, then conifers, then beech and elm. It will have been half riverbed, it will have been scratched and plowed by ice. And then it will be cultivated, paved, sprayed, dammed, graded, built up. But each is only for a while, and that will be just another set of lines on the palimpsest. The whole earth is a great tablet holding the multiple overlaid new and ancient traces of the swirl of forces. Each place is its own place, forever (eventually) wild. A place on earth is a mosaic within larger mosaics—the land is all small places, all precise tiny realms replicating larger and smaller patterns. Children start out learning place by learning those little realms around the house, the settlement, and outward.

One's sense of the scale of a place expands as one learns the *region*. The young hear further stories and go for explorations which are also subsistence forays—firewood gathering, fishing, to fairs or to market. The outlines of the larger region become part of their awareness. (Thoreau says in "Walking" that an area twenty miles in diameter will be enough to occupy a lifetime of close exploration on foot—you will never exhaust its details.)

The total size of the region a group calls home depends on the land type. Every group is territorial, each moves within a given zone, even nomads stay within boundaries. A people living in a desert or grassland with great visible spaces that invite you to step forward and walk as far as you can see will range across tens of thousands of square miles. A deep old-growth forest may rarely be traveled at all. Foragers in gallery forests and grasslands will regularly move broadly, whereas people in a deep-soiled valley ideal for gardens might not go far beyond the top of the nearest ridge. The regional boundaries were roughly drawn by climate, which is what sets the plant-type zones—plus soil type and landforms. Desert wastes, mountain ridges, or big rivers set a broad edge to a region. We walk across or wade through the larger and smaller boundaries. Like children first learning our homeland we can stand at the edge of a big river, or on the crest of a major ridge, and observe that the other side is a different soil, a change of plants and animals, a new shape of barn roof, maybe less or more rain. The lines between natural regions are never simple or clear, but vary according to such criteria as biota, watersheds, landforms, elevation. (See Jim Dodge, 1981.) Still, we all know—at some point—that we are no longer in the Midwest, say, but in the West. Regions seen according to natural criteria are sometimes called bioregions.

(In pre-conquest America people covered great distances. It is said that the Mojave of the lower Colorado felt that everyone at least once in their lives should make foot journeys to the Hopi mesas to the east, the Gulf of California to the south, and to the Pacific.)

Every region has its wilderness. There is the fire in the kitchen, and there is the place less traveled. In most settled regions there used to be some combination of prime agricultural land, orchard and vine land, rough pasturage, woodlot, forest, and desert or mountain "waste." The de facto wilderness was the extreme backcountry part of all that. The parts less visited are "where the bears are." The wilderness is within walking distance—it may be three days or it may be ten. It is at the far high rough end, or the deep forest and swamp end, of the territory where most of you all live and work. People will go there for mountain herbs, for the trapline, or for solitude. They live between the poles of home and their own wild places.

Recollecting that we once lived in places is part of our contemporary self-rediscovery. It grounds what it means to be "human" (etymologically something like "earthling"). I have a friend who feels sometimes that the world is hostile to human life—he says it chills us and kills us. But how could we *be* were it not for this planet that provided our very shape? Two conditions—gravity and a livable temperature range between freezing and boiling—have given us fluids and flesh. The trees we climb and the ground we walk on have given us five fingers and toes. The "place" (from the root *plat*, broad, spreading, flat) gave us far-seeing eyes, the streams and breezes gave us versatile tongues and whorly ears. The land gave us a stride, and the lake a dive. The amazement gave us our kind of mind. We should be thankful for that, and take nature's stricter lessons with some grace.

## UNDERSTANDING THE COMMONS

I stood with my climbing partner on the summit of Glacier Peak looking all ways round, ridge after ridge and peak after peak, as far as we could see. To the west across Puget Sound were the farther peaks of the Olympic Mountains. He said: "You mean there's a senator for all this?" As in the Great Basin, crossing desert after desert, range after range, it is easy to think there are vast spaces on earth yet unadministered, perhaps forgotten, or unknown (the endless sweep of spruce forest in Alaska and Canada)—but it is all mapped and placed in some domain. In North America there is a lot that is in public domain, which has its problems, but at least they are problems we are all enfranchised to work on. David Foreman, founder of the Earth First! movement, recently stated his radical provenance. Not out of Social Justice, Left Politics, or Feminism did I come—says David—but from the Public Lands Conservation movement—the solid stodgy movement that goes back to the thirties and before. Yet these land and wildlife issues were what politicized John Muir, John Wesley Powell, and Aldo Leopold—the abuses of public land.

American public lands are the twentieth-century incarnation of a much older institution known across Eurasia—in English called the "commons"—which was the ancient mode of both protecting and managing the wilds of the self-governing regions. It worked well enough until the age of market economies, colonialism, and imperialism. Let me give you a kind of model of how the commons worked.

Between the extremes of deep wilderness and the private plots of the farmstead lies a territory which is not suitable for crops. In earlier times it was used jointly by the members of a given tribe or village. This area, embracing both the wild and the semi-wild, is of critical importance. It is necessary for the health of the wilderness because it adds big habitat, overflow territory, and room for wildlife to fly and run. It is essential even to an agricultural village economy because its natural diversity provides the many necessities and amenities that the privately held plots cannot. It enriches the agrarian diet with game and fish. The shared land supplies firewood, poles and stone for building, clay for the kiln, herbs, dye plants, and much else, just as in a foraging economy. It is especially important as seasonal or fulltime open range for cattle, horses, goats, pigs, and sheep.

In the abstract the sharing of a natural area might be thought of as a matter of access to "common pool resources" with no limits or controls on individual exploitation. The fact is that such sharing developed over millennia and always within territorial and social contexts. In the peasant societies of both Asia and Europe there were customary forms that gave direction to the joint use of land. They did not grant free access to outsiders, and there were controls over entry and use by member households. The commons has been defined as "the undivided land belonging to the members of a local community as a whole." This definition fails to make the point that the commons is both specific land *and* the traditional community institution that determines the carrying capacity for its various subunits and defines the rights and obligations of those who use it, with penalties for lapses. Because it is traditional and *local*, it is not identical with today's "public domain," which is land held and managed by a central government. Under a national state such management may be destructive (as it is becoming in Canada and the United States) or benign (I have no good examples)—but in no case is it locally managed. One of the ideas in the current debate on how to reform our public lands is that of returning them to regional control.

An example of traditional management: what would keep one household from bringing in more and more stock and tempting everyone toward overgrazing? In earlier England and in some contemporary Swiss villages (Netting, 1976), the commoner could only turn out to common range as many head of cattle as he could feed over the winter in his own corrals. This meant that no one was allowed to increase his herd from outside with a cattle drive just for summer grazing. (This was known in Norman legal language as the rule of *levancy and couchancy*: you could only run the stock that you actually had "standing and sleeping" within winter quarters.)

The commons is the contract a people make with their local natural system. The word has an instructive history: it is formed of *ko*, "together," with (Greek) *moin*, "held in common." But the Indo-European root *mei* means basically to "move, to go, to change." This had an archaic special meaning of "exchange of goods and services within a society as regulated by custom or law." I think it might well refer back to the principle of gift economies: "the gift must always move." The root comes into Latin as *munus*, "service performed for the community" and hence "municipality."

There is a well-documented history of the commons in relation to the village economies of Europe and England. In England from the time of the Norman Conquest the enfeoffed knights and overlords began to gain control over the many local commons. Legislation (the Statute of Merton, 1235) came to their support. From the fifteenth century on the landlord class, working with urban mercantile guilds and government offices, increasingly fenced off village-held land and turned it over to private interests. The enclosure movement was backed by the big wool corporations who found profit from sheep to be much greater than that from farming. The wool business, with its exports to the Continent, was an early agribusiness that had a destructive effect on the soils and dislodged peasants. The arguments for enclosure in England—efficiency, higher production—ignored social and ecological effects and served to cripple the sustainable agriculture of some districts. The enclosure movement was stepped up again in the eighteenth century: between 1709 and

1869 almost five million acres were transferred to private ownership, one acre in every seven. After 1869 there was a sudden reversal of sentiment called the "open space movement" which ultimately halted enclosures and managed to preserve, via a spectacular lawsuit against the lords of fourteen manors, the Epping Forest.

Karl Polanyi (1975) says that the enclosures of the eighteenth century created a population of rural homeless who were forced in their desperation to become the world's first industrial working class. The enclosures were tragic both for the human community and for natural ecosystems. The fact that England now has the least forest and wildlife of all the nations of Europe has much to do with the enclosures. The takeover of commons land on the European plain also began about five hundred years ago, but one-third of Europe is still not privatized. A survival of commons practices in Swedish law allows anyone to enter private farmland to pick berries or mushrooms, to cross on foot, and to camp out of sight of the house. Most of the former commons land is now under the administration of government land agencies.

A commons model can still be seen in Japan, where there are farm villages tucked in shoestring valleys, rice growing in the *tanbo* on the bottoms, and the vegetable plots and horticulture located on the slightly higher ground. The forested hills rising high above the valleys are the commons—in Japanese called *iriai*, "joint entry." The boundary between one village and the next is often the very crests of the ridges. On the slopes of Mt. Hiei in Kyoto prefecture, north of the remote Tendai Buddhist training temples of Yokkawa, I came on men and women of Ohara village bundling up slender brush-cuttings for firewood. They were within the village land. In the innermost mountains of Japan there are forests that are beyond the reach of the use of any village. In early feudal times they were still occupied by remnant hunting peoples, perhaps Japanese-Ainu mixed-blood survivors. Later some of these wildlands were appropriated by the government and declared "Imperial Forests." Bears became extinct in England by the thirteenth century, but they are still found throughout the more remote Japanese mountains, even occasionally just north of Kyoto.

In China the management of mountain lands was left largely to the village councils—all the central government wanted was taxes. Taxes were collected in kind, and local specialties were highly prized. The demands of the capital drew down Kingfisher feathers, Musk Deer glands, Rhinoceros hides, and other exotic products of the mountains and streams, as well as rice, timber, and silk. The village councils may have resisted overexploitation of their resources, but when the edge of spreading deforestation reached their zone (the fourteenth century seems to be a turning point for the forests of heartland China), village land management crumbled. Historically, the seizure of the commons—east or west—by either the central government or entrepreneurs from the central economy has resulted in degradation of wild lands and agricultural soils. There is sometimes good reason to kill the Golden Goose: the quick profits can be reinvested elsewhere at a higher return.

In the United States, as fast as the Euro-American invaders forcefully displaced the native inhabitants from their own sorts of traditional commons, the land was opened to the new settlers. In the arid West, however, much land was never even homesteaded, let alone patented. The native people who had known and loved the white deserts and blue mountains were now scattered or enclosed on reservations, and the new inhabitants (miners and a few ranchers) had neither the values nor the knowledge to take care of the land. An enormous area was de facto public domain, and the Forest Service, the Park Service, and the Bureau of Land Management were formed to manage it. (The same sorts of land in Canada and Australia are called "Crown Lands," a reflection of the history of English rulers trying to wrest the commons from the people.)

In the contemporary American West the people who talk about a "sagebrush rebellion" might sound as though they were working for a return of commons land to local control. The truth is the sagebrush rebels have a lot yet to learn about the place—they are still relative newcomers, and their motives are not stewardship but development. Some westerners are beginning to think in long-range terms, and these don't argue for privatization but for better range management and more wilderness preservation.

The environmental history of Europe and Asia seems to indicate that the best management of commons land was that which was locally based. The ancient severe and often irreversible deforestation of the Mediterranean Basin was an extreme case of the misuse of the commons by the forces that had taken its management away from regional villages (Thirgood, 1981). The situation in America in the nineteenth and early twentieth centuries was the reverse. The truly local people, the Native Americans, were decimated and demoralized, and the new population was composed of adventurers and entrepreneurs. Without some federal presence the poachers, cattle grazers, and timber barons would have had a field day. Since about 1960 the situation has turned again: the agencies that were once charged with conservation are increasingly perceived as accomplices of the extractive industries, and local people—who are beginning to be actually local—seek help from environmental organizations and join in defense of the public lands.

Destruction extends worldwide and "encloses" local commons, local peoples. The village and tribal people who live in the tropical forests are literally bulldozed out of their homes by international logging interests in league with national governments. A well-worn fiction used in dispossessing inhabitory people is the declaration that the commonly owned tribal forests are either (1) private property or (2) public domain. When the commons are closed and the villagers must buy energy, lumber, and medicine at the company store, they are pauperized. This is one effect of what Ivan Illich calls "the 500-year war against subsistence."

So what about the so-called tragedy of the commons? This theory, as now popularly understood, seems to state that when there are open access rights to a resource, say pasturage, everyone will seek to maximize his take, and over-grazing will inevitably ensue. What Garrett Hardin and his associates are talk-ing about should be called "the dilemma of common-pool resources." This is the problem of overexploitation of "unowned" resources by individuals or cor-porations that are caught in the bind of "If I don't do it the other guy will" (Hardin and Baden, 1977). Oceanic fisheries, global water cycles, the air, soil fertility—all fall into this class. When Hardin et al., try to apply their model to the historic commons it doesn't work, because they fail to note that the com-mons was a social institution which, historically, was never without rules and did not allow unlimited access (Cox, 1985).

In Asia and parts of Europe, villages that in some cases date back to ne-olithic times still oversee the commons with some sort of council. Each com-mons is an entity with limits, and the effects of overuse will be clear to those who depend on it. There are three possible contemporary fates for common pool resources. One is privatization, one is administration by government au-thority, and the third is that—when possible—they become part of a true com-mons, of reasonable size, managed by local inhabitory people. The third choice may no longer be possible as stated here. Locally based community or tribal (as in Alaska) landholding corporations or cooperatives seem to be sur-viving here and there. But operating as it seems they must in the world mar-ketplace, they are wrestling with how to balance tradition and sustainability against financial success. The Sealaska Corporation of the Tlingit people of southeast Alaska has been severely criticized (even from within) for some of the old-growth logging it let happen.

We need to make a world-scale "Natural Contract" with the oceans, the air, the birds in the sky. The challenge is to bring the whole victimized world of "com-mon pool resources" into the Mind of the Commons. As it stands now, any re-source on earth that is not nailed down will be seen as fair game to the timber buyers or petroleum geologists from Osaka, Rotterdam, or Boston. The pres-sures of growing populations and the powers of entrenched (but fragile, con-fused, and essentially leaderless) economic systems warp the likelihood of any of us seeing clearly. Our perception of how entrenched they are may also be something of a delusion.

Sometimes it seems unlikely that a society as a whole can make wise choices. Yet there is no choice but to call for the "recovery of the commons"— and this in a modern world which doesn't quite realize what it has lost. Take back, like the night, that which is shared by all of us, that which is our larger being. There will be no "tragedy of the commons" greater than this: if we do not recover the commons—regain personal, local, community, and peoples' direct involvement in sharing (in *being*) the web of the wild world—that world will keep slipping away. Eventually our complicated industrial capitalist/so-cialist mixes will bring down much of the living system that supports us. And, it is clear, the loss of a local commons heralds the end of self-sufficiency and signals the doom of the vernacular culture of the region. This is still happening in the far corners of the world.

The commons is a curious and elegant social institution within which human beings once lived free political lives while weaving through natural systems. The commons is a level of organization of human society that includes the nonhuman. The level above the local commons is the bioregion. Understanding the commons and its role within the larger regional culture is one more step toward integrating ecology with economy.

## BIOREGIONAL PERSPECTIVES

The Region is the elsewhere of civilization

*–Max Cafard*

The little nations of the past lived within territories that conformed to some set of natural criteria. The culture areas of the major native groups of North America overlapped, as one would expect, almost exactly with broadly defined major bioregions (Kroeber, 1947). That older human experience of a fluid, indistinct, but genuine home region was gradually replaced—across Eurasia—by the arbitrary and often violently imposed boundaries of emerging national states. These imposed borders sometimes cut across biotic areas and ethnic zones alike. Inhabitants lost ecological knowledge and community solidarity. In the old ways, the flora and fauna and landforms are *part of the culture.* The world of culture and nature, which is actual, is almost a shadow world now, and the insubstantial world of political jurisdictions and rarefied economies is what passes for reality. We live in a backwards time. We can regain some small sense of that old membership by discovering the original lineaments of our land and steering—at least in the home territory and in the mind—by those rather than the borders of arbitrary nations, states, and counties.

Regions are "interpenetrating bodies in semi-simultaneous spaces" (Cafard, 1989). Biota, watersheds, landforms, and elevations are just a few of the facets that define a region. Culture areas, in the same way, have subsets such as dialects, religions, sorts of arrow-release, types of tools, myth motifs, musical scales, art styles. One sort of regional outline would be floristic. The coastal Douglas Fir, as the definitive tree of the Pacific Northwest, is an example. (I knew it intimately as a boy growing up on a farm between Lake Washington and Puget Sound. The local people, the Snohomish, called it *lukta tciyats,* "wide needles.") Its northern limit is around the Skeena River in British Columbia. It is found west of the crest through Washington, Oregon, and northern California. The southern coastal limit of Douglas Fir is about the same as that of salmon, which do not run south of the Big Sur River. Inland it grows down the west slope of the Sierra as far south as the north fork of the San Joaquin River. That outline describes the boundary of a larger natural region that runs across three states and one international border.

The presence of this tree signifies a rainfall and a temperature range and will indicate what your agriculture might be, how steep the pitch of your roof, what raincoats you'd need. You don't have to know such details to get by in the modern cities of Portland or Bellingham. But if you do know what is taught by plants and weather, you are in on the gossip and can truly feel more at home. The sum of a field's forces becomes what we call very loosely the "spirit of the place." To know the spirit of a place is to realize that you are a part of a part and that the whole is made of parts, each of which is whole. You start with the part you are whole in.

As quixotic as these ideas may seem, they have a reservoir of strength and possibility behind them. The spring of 1984, a month after equinox. Gary Holthaus and I drove down from Anchorage to Haines, Alaska. We went around the upper edge of the basin of the Copper River, skirted some tributaries of the Yukon, and went over Haines Summit. It was White and Black Spruce taiga all the way, still frozen up. Dropping down from the pass to saltwater at Chilkat inlet we were immediately in forests of large Sitka Spruce, Skunk Cabbage poking out in the swamps, it was spring. That's a bioregional border leap. I was honored the next day by an invitation to Raven House to have coffee with Austin Hammond and a circle of other Tlingit elders and to hear some long and deeply entwined discourses on the responsibilities of people to their places. As we looked out his front window to hanging glaciers on the peaks beyond the saltwater, Hammond spoke of empires and civilizations in metaphors of glaciers. He described how great alien forces—industrial civilization in this case—advance and retreat, and how settled people can wait it out.

Sometime in the mid-seventies at a conference of Native American leaders and activists in Bozeman, Montana, I heard a Crow elder say something similar: "You know, I think if people stay somewhere long enough—even white people—the spirits will begin to speak to them. It's the power of the spirits coming up from the land. The spirits and the old powers aren't lost, they just need people to be around long enough and the spirits will begin to influence them."

Bioregional awareness teaches us in *specific* ways. It is not enough just to "love nature" or to want to "be in harmony with Gaia." Our relation to the natural world takes place in a *place*, and it must be grounded in information and experience. For example: "real people" have an easy familiarity with the local plants. This is so unexceptional a kind of knowledge that everyone in Europe, Asia, and Africa used to take it for granted. Many contemporary Americans don't even *know* that they don't "know the plants," which is indeed a measure of alienation. Knowing a bit about the flora we could enjoy questions like: where do Alaska and Mexico meet? It would be somewhere on the north coast of California, where Canada Jay and Sitka Spruce lace together with manzanita and Blue Oak.

But instead of "northern California" let's call it Shasta Bioregion. The present state of California (the old Alta California territory) falls into at least three natural divisions, and the northern third looks, as the Douglas Fir example shows, well to the north. The boundaries of this northern third would roughly run from the Klamath/Rogue River divide south to San Francisco Bay and up the delta where the Sacramento and San Joaquin rivers join. The line would then go east to the Sierra Crest and, taking that as a distinct border, follow it north to Susanville. The watershed divide then angles broadly northeastward along the edge of the Modoc Plateau to the Warner Range and Goose Lake.

East of the divide is the Great Basin, north of Shasta is the Cascadia/Columbia region, and then farther north is what we call Ish River country, the drainages of Puget Sound and the Straits of Georgia. Why should we do this kind of visualization? Again I will say: it prepares us to begin to be at home in this landscape. There are tens of millions of people in North America who were physically born here but who are not actually living here intellectually, imaginatively, or morally. Native Americans to be sure have a prior claim to the term native. But as they love this land they will welcome the conversion of the millions of immigrant psyches into fellow "Native Americans." For the non–Native American to become at home on this continent, he or she must be *born again* in this hemisphere, on this continent, properly called Turtle Island.

That is to say, we must consciously fully accept and recognize that this is where we live and grasp the fact that our descendants will be here for millennia to come. Then we must honor this land's great antiquity—its wildness—learn it—defend it—and work to hand it on to the children (of all beings) of the future with its biodiversity and health intact. Europe or Africa or Asia will then be seen as the place our ancestors came from, places we might want to know about and to visit, but not "home." Home—deeply, spiritually—must be here. Calling this place "America" is to name it after a stranger. "Turtle Island" is the name given this continent by Native Americans based on creation mythology (Snyder, 1974). The United States, Canada, Mexico, are passing political entities; they have their legitimacies, to be sure, but they will lose their mandate if they continue to abuse the land. "The State is destroyed, but the mountains and rivers remain."

But this work is not just for the newcomers of the Western Hemisphere, Australia, Africa, or Siberia. A worldwide purification of mind is called for: the exercise of seeing the surface of the planet for what it is—by nature. With this kind of consciousness people turn up at hearings and in front of trucks and bulldozers to defend the land or trees. Showing solidarity with a region! What an odd idea at first. Bioregionalism is the entry of place into the dialectic of history. Also we might say that there are "classes" which have so far been overlooked—the animals, rivers, rocks, and grasses—now entering history.

These ideas provoke predictable and usually uninformed reactions. People fear the small society and the critique of the State. It is difficult to see, when one has been raised under it, that it is the State itself which is inherently greedy, destabilizing, entropic, disorderly, and illegitimate. They cite parochialism, regional strife, "unacceptable" expressions of cultural diversity, and so forth. Our philosophies, world religions, and histories are biased toward uniformity, universality, and centralization—in a word, the ideology of monotheism. Certainly under specific conditions neighboring groups have wrangled for centuries—interminable memories and hostilities cooking away like radioactive waste. It's still at work in the Middle East. The ongoing ethnic and political miseries of parts of Europe and the Middle East sometimes go back as far as the Roman Empire. This is not something that can be attributed to the combativeness of "human nature" per se. Before the expansion of early empires the occasional strife of tribes and natural nations was almost familial. With the rise of the State, the scale of the destructiveness and malevolence of warfare makes a huge leap.

In the times when people did not have much accumulated surplus, there was no big temptation to move in on other regions. I'll give an example from my own part of the world. (I describe my location as: on the western slope of the northern Sierra Nevada, in the Yuba River watershed, north of the south fork at the three-thousand-foot elevation, in a community of Black Oak, Incense Cedar, Madrone, Douglas Fir, and Ponderosa Pine.) The western slope of the Sierra Nevada has winter rain and snowfall and a different set of plants from the dry eastern slope. In pre-white times, the native people living across the range had little temptation to venture over, because their skills were specific to their own area, and they could go hungry in an unfamiliar biome. It takes a long education to know the edible plants, where to find them, and how to prepare them. So the Washo of the Sierra east side traded their pine nuts and obsidian for the acorns, yew bows, and abalone shells of the Miwok and Maidu to the west. The two sides met and camped together for weeks in the summer Sierra meadows, their joint commons. (Dedicated raiding cultures, "barbarians," evolve as a response to nearby civilizations and their riches. Genghis Khan, at an audience in his yurt near Lake Baikal, was reported to have said: "Heaven is exasperated with the decadence and luxury of China.")

There are numerous examples of relatively peaceful small-culture coexistence all over the world. There have always been multilingual persons peacefully trading and traveling across large areas. Differences were often eased by shared spiritual perspectives or ceremonial institutions and by the multitude of myths and tales that cross language barriers. What about the deep divisions caused by religion? It must be said that most religious exclusiveness is the odd specialty of the Judeo/Christian/Islamic faith, which is a recent and (overall) minority development in the world. Asian religion, and the whole world of folk religion, animism, and shamanism, appreciates or at least tolerates diversity. (It seems that the really serious cultural disputes are caused by different tastes in food. When I was chokersetting in eastern Oregon, one of my crew was a Wasco man whose wife was a Chehalis woman from the west side. He told me that when they got in fights she would call him a "goddamn grasshopper eater" and he'd shout back "fish eater"!)

Cutural pluralism and multilingualism are the planetary norm. We seek the balance between cosmopolitan pluralism and deep local consciousness. We are asking how the whole human race can regain self-determination in place after centuries of having been disenfranchised by hierarchy and/or centralized power. Do not confuse this exercise with "nationalism," which is exactly the opposite, the impostor, the puppet of the State, the grinning ghost of the lost community.

So this is one sort of start. The bioregional movement is not just a rural program: it is as much for the restoration of urban neighborhood life and the greening of the cities. All of us are fluently moving in multiple realms that include irrigation districts, solid-waste management jurisdictions, long-distance area code zones, and such. Planet Drum Foundation, based in the San Francisco Bay Area, works with many other local groups for the regeneration of the city as a living place, with projects like the identification and restoration of urban creeks (Berg and others, 1989). There are groups worldwide working with Third and Fourth World people revisualizing territories and playfully finding appropriate names for their newly realized old regions (*Raise the Stakes*, 1987). Four bioregional congresses have been held on Turtle Island.

As sure as impermanence, the nations of the world will eventually be more sensitively defined and the lineaments of the blue earth will begin to reshape the politics. The requirements of sustainable economies, ecologically sensitive agriculture, strong and vivid community life, wild habitat—and the second law of thermodynamics—all lead this way. I also realize that right now this is a kind of theater as much as it is ecological politics. Not just street theater, but visionary mountain, field, and stream theater. As Jim Dodge says: "The chances of bioregionalism succeeding . . . are beside the point. If one person, or a few, or a community of people, live more fulfilling lives from bioregional practice, then it's successful." May it all speed the further deconstruction of the superpowers. As "The Surre(gion)alist Manifesto" says:

> Regional politics do not take place in Washington, Moscow, and other "seats of power." Regional power does not "sit"; it flows everywhere. Through watersheds and bloodstreams. Through nervous systems and food chains. The regions are everywhere & nowhere. We are all illegals. We are natives and we are restless. We have no country; we live in the country. We are off the Inter-State. The Region is against the Regime—any Regime. Regions are anarchic. (Cafard, 1989)

## FINDING "NISENAN COUNTY"

This year Burt Hybart retired from driving dump truck, backhoe, grader, and Cat after many years. Roads, ponds, and pads are his sculpture, shapes that will be left on the land long after the houses have vanished. (How long for a pond to silt up?) Burt still witches wells, though. Last time I saw him he was complaining about his lungs: "Dust boiling up behind the Cat you couldn't see from here to there, those days. When I worked on the Coast. And the diesel fumes."

Some of us went for a walk in the Warner Range. It's in the far northeast corner of California, the real watershed boundary between the headwaters of the Pit River and the *nors* of the Great Basin. From the nine-thousand-foot scarp's high points you can see into Oregon, Goose Lake, and up the west side of the Warners to the north end of Surprise Valley. Dry desert hills to the east.

Desert mountain range. A touch of Rocky Mountain flora here that leapfrogs over desert basins via the Steens Mountains of south-eastern Oregon, the Blue Mountains, and maybe the Wallowas. Cattle are brought up from Eagleville on the east side, a town out of the 1880s. The proprietor of the Eagleville Bar told how the sheepherders move their flocks from Lovelock, Nevada, in early March, heading toward the Warners, the ewes lambing as they go. In late June they arrive at the foot of the range and move the sheep up to the eight-thousand-foot meadows on the west side. In September the flocks go down to Madeline—the lambs right onto the meat trucks. Then the ewes' long truck ride back to Lovelock for the winter. We find the flock in the miles-long meadow heavens of Mule-ear flowers. The sheep business is Basque-run on all levels. Old aspen grove along the trail with sheepherder inscriptions and designs in the bark, some dated from the 1890s.

Patterson Lake is the gem of the Warners, filling an old cirque below the cliffs of the highest peak. The many little ledges of the cliffs are home to hawks. Young raptors sit solemnly by their nests. Mt. Shasta dominates the western view, a hub to these vast miles of Lodgepole and Jeffrey Pine, lava rock, hayfield ribbons, rivers that sink underground. Ha! This is the highest end of what we call "upriver"—and close to where it drains both ways, one side of the plateau tipping toward the Klamath River, the other to the Pit and the Sacramento. Mt. Shasta visible for so far—from the Coast Range, from Sierra Buttes down by Downieville—it gleams across the headwaters of all of northern California.

Old John Hold walks up a streambed talking to it: "So that's what you've been up to!" Reading the geology, the wash and lay of the heavy metal that sinks below the sand, never tarnishing or rusting—gold. The new-style miners are here, too, St. Joseph Minerals, exploring the "diggings," the tertiary gravels. The county supervisors finally approved the EIR and the exploratory drilling begins. This isn't full-scale mining yet, and they'll come back in eighteen months with their big proposal (if they do). The drilling's not noticeable: a little tower and a trailer lost in the gravel canyons and ridges that were left from the days of hydraulicking.

There were early strong rains this fall, so the springs started up. Then the rain quit and the springs stopped. A warm December. Real rains started in January, with heavy snows above six thousand feet and not much below that. This year more kids go skiing. Resistance to it (as a decadent urban entertainment) crumbles family by family. Most adults here never were mountain people, didn't climb, ski, or backpack. They moved up from the city and like to think they're in a wilderness. A few are mountain types who moved down to be here, and are glad to be living where there are some neighbors. The kids go to Donner Pass to be sliding on the white crystals of future Yuba River waters. I get back to downhill skiing myself; it feels wonderful again. Downhill must have provided one of the fastest speeds human beings ever experienced before modern times. Cross-country ski trips in Sierra Buttes too. On the full moon night of April (the last night of the month) Bill Schell and I did a tour till 2 A.M. around Yuba Pass, snow shining bright in the moonlight, skis clattering on the icy slabs. Old mountain people turned settlers manage to finally start going back into the mountains after the house is built, the garden fenced, the drip-systems in. February brought ten inches of rain in six days. The ponds and springs stream over, the ground's all silvery with surface glitter of a skin of water. Fifteen feet of snow at Sugarbowl near Donner Pass.

Two old gents in the Sacramento Greyhound station. I'm next to an elder who swings his cane back and forth, lightly, the tip pivoting on the ground—and he looks about the room, back and forth, without much focus. He has egg on his chin. A smell of old urine comes from him, blows my way, time to time. Another elder walks past and out. He's very neat: a plastic-wrapped waterproof blanket-roll slung on his shoulder, a felt hat, a white chin beard like an Amish. Red bandanna tied round his neck, bib overalls. Under the overall bottoms peep out more trousers, maybe suit pants. So that's how he keeps warm, and keeps some clothes clean! Back in my traveling days men said, "Yeah, spend the winter in Sac."

I caught the bus on down to Oakland. In Berkeley, on the wall of the Lucas Books building, is a mural that shows a cross section of Alta California from the Northwest Coast to the Mojave Desert. I walked backward through the parking lot to get a look at it whole, sea lions, coyote, redtail hawk, creosote bush. Then noticed a man at one corner of it, touching it up. Talked to him, he is Lou Silva, who did the painting. He was redoing a mouse, and he said he comes back from time to time to put in more tiny fauna.

Spring is good to the apples, much fruit sets. Five male deer with antler velvet nubs walk about the meadow in the morning. High-country skiing barely ends and it's time to go fishing. Planting and building. This area is still growing, though not as rapidly as several years ago. The strong spirit of community of the early seventies has abated somewhat, but I like to think that when the going gets rough this population will stick together.

San Juan Ridge lies between the middle and south forks of the Yuba River in a political entity called Nevada County. New settlers have been coming in here since the late sixties. The Sierra counties are a mess: a string of them lap over the mountain crest, and the roads between the two sides are often closed in winter. A sensible redrawing of lines here would put eastern Sierra, eastern Nevada, and eastern Placer counties together in a new "Truckee River County" and the seat could be in Truckee. Western Placer and western Nevada counties south of the south fork of the Yuba would make a good new county. Western Sierra County plus a bit of Yuba County and northern Nevada County put together would fit into the watershed of the three forks of the Yuba. I would call it "Nisenan County" after the native people who lived here. Most of them were killed or driven away by the gold rush miners.

People live on the ridges because the valleys are rocky or brushy and have no level bottoms. In the Sierra Nevada a good human habitat is not a valley bottom, but a wide gentle *ridge* between canyons.

## BIBLIOGRAPHY

BERG, PETER, and others. 1989. *A Green City Program for San Francisco Bay Area Cities and Towns.* San Francisco: Planet Drum.

CAFARD, MAX. 1989 (Autumn). "The Surre(gion)alist Manifesto." *Mesechabe.*

COX, SUSAN JANE BUCK. 1985 (Spring). "No Tragedy in the Commons." *Environmental Ethics.*

DODGE, JIM. 1981 (Winter). "Living by Life." *CoEvolution Quarterly.*

HARDIN, GARRETT, and JOHN BADEN. 1977. *Managing the Commons.* San Francisco: W. H. Freeman.

KROEBER, A. L. 1947. *Cultural and Natural Areas of Native North America.* Berkeley: University of California Press.

NETTING, R. 1976. What Alpine Peasants Have in Common: Observations on Communal Tenure in a Swiss Village." *Human Ecology.*

POLANYI, KARL. 1975. *The Great Transformation.* New York: Octagon Books.

*Raise the Stakes.* 1987. Journal of the Planet Drum Foundation. P.O. Box 31251, San Francisco, CA, 94131.

SNYDER, GARY. 1974. *Turtle Island.* New York: New Directions.

THIRGOOD, J. V. 1981. *Man and the Mediterranean Forest: A History of Resource Depletion.* New York: Academic Press.